This book is the first general study of politics and society in the Fourth Republic to be founded on extensive primary research. It approaches the period in terms of successful conservatism rather than thwarted reform, maintaining that conservatism in France was a more subtle and dynamic force than has previously been appreciated. Not the preserve of any single party, conservative ideas were often defended by institutions outside the realm of explicit politics altogether, such as business associations, civil service departments and the law courts. It is proposed that conservatives did not simply return to French politics in 1945 untouched by the events of the previous five years. The experiences of Vichy, the occupation and the purges produced new kinds of political synthesis, making conservatives more receptive to change than their 'progressive' opponents.

Bourgeois politics in France, 1945–1951

Bourgeois politics in France, 1945–1951

Richard Vinen

King's College, London

CAMBRIDGE
UNIVERSITY PRESS

Published by the Press Syndicate of the University of Cambridge
The Pitt Building, Trumpington Street, Cambridge CB2 1RP
40 West 20th Street, New York, NY 10011-4211, USA
10 Stamford Road, Oakleigh, Melbourne 3166, Australia

First published 1995

Printed in Great Britain at the University Press, Cambridge

A catalogue record for this book is available from the British Library

Library of Congress cataloguing in publication data

Vinen, Richard.
    Bourgeois politics in France, 1945–1951 / Richard Vinen.
       p.   cm.
    Includes bibliographical references and index.
    ISBN 0 521 47451 5
    1. France – Politics and government – 1945–   I. Title.
  DC404.V56 1995
  944.082–dc20 94-21349 CIP

ISBN 0 521 47451 5 hardback

SE

To Alison

Contents

Preface

I am grateful for the help that I received from a number of institutions and individuals in the preparation of this book. Permission to consult documents was given by the Archives Nationales, the Fondation Nationale des Sciences Politiques, Madame Bidault, Madame Lecompte-Boinet and Madame Demey. I particularly enjoyed my visit to the archives of Henri Queuille in Neuvic d'Ussel where everyone was more than helpful.

Richard Fisher, Peter Morris, Kevin Passmore and an anonymous publisher's reader all gave useful advice and encouragement. Hilary Scannell took great pains, and displayed heroic patience, while copy-editing the typescript. Grants to visit France were provided by Trinity College Cambridge, the British Academy, the Twenty Seven foundation and King's College London. Hospitality and companionship in France were provided by David Baker, Dagmar Braun, Joel Felix and Ella Felix-Braun. My parents and my sister have been an endless source of material and emotional support. Most importantly of all, Alison Henwood always reminded me that there is more to life than Fourth Republic politics and usually tolerated me when I failed to heed this wise reminder.

All translations from French language sources are by the author unless otherwise attributed.

Abbreviations and French political groups

AD	Alliance Démocratique
ADMP	Association pour Défendre la Mémoire du Maréchal Pétain
ARPTR	Association des Représentants du Peuple de la Troisième République
CEE	Centre d'Etudes Economiques
CFPC	Centre Français du Patronat Chrétien
CGA	Confédération Générale de l'Agriculture
CGPME	Confédération Générale des Petites et Moyennes Entreprises
CGT	Confédération Générale du Travail
CJP	Centre des Jeunes Patrons
CNC	Conseil National du Commerce
CNI	Centre National des Indépendants
CNIP	Centre National des Indépendants et Paysans
CNPF	Conseil National du Patronat Français
CRS	Compagnies républicaines de sécurité
ENA	Ecole nationale d'administration
FNSEA	Fédération Nationale des Syndicats d'Exploitants Agricoles
FFI	Forces françaises de l'intérieur
FR	Fédération Républicaine
GDC	Groupement de Défense des Contribuables et des Libertés Professionnelles
MDC	Mouvement de Défense des Contribuables
MRP	Mouvement Républicain Populaire
PCF	Parti Communiste Français
Peasant party	Parti Paysan
PRL	Parti Républicain de la Liberté
PRR	Parti de Rénovation Républicaine
PSD	Parti Socialiste Démocratique
PSF	Parti Social Français

Radical party	Parti Républicain Radical et Radical-Socialiste
RF	Réconciliation Française (or the Parti Républicain et Social de la Réconciliation Française)
RGR	Rassemblement des Gauches Républicaines
RGRIF	Rassemblement des Groupes Républicains et Indépendants Français
RI	Républicains Indépendants
RPF	Rassemblement du Peuple Français
RS	Républicains Socialistes
SFIO	Section Française de l'Internationale Ouvrière
UDFI	Union Démocratique des Français Indépendants
UDI	Union Démocratique des Indépendants
UDSR	Union Démocratique et Socialiste de la Résistance
UIE	Union des Intérêts Economiques
UNIR	Union des Nationaux et Indépendants Républicains
UPR	Union Patriotique Républicaine

1 Introduction

History is often seen from the winners' point of view, but writing on France between the Liberation and the early 1950s provides a conspicuous exception to this rule. Historical accounts of the Fourth Republic concentrate on the early hopes that are seen to have been incarnated by the French Resistance. Subsequent developments are then presented as a depressing and tedious slide into *immobilisme*, and the most serious consideration is reserved for the political left, which was defeated during this period, or for those bourgeois politicians – like Mendès-France or de Gaulle – who rebelled against the Fourth Republic system. Those politicians who succeeded during the 1940s have attracted few historians: Paul Reynaud is better known for his unsuccessful attempts to save France from defeat by Nazi Germany during the 1930s than for his part in a successful effort to contain Communism during the 1940s.

In 1944 the property-owning classes of France seemed under threat from increasing Communist power (many feared an outright Communist take over), from a general belief that in future the state would play a greater role in the administration of the economy, and from the measures that had been taken to exclude from public life those who had supported Marshal Pétain's Vichy government of 1940–44. By the early 1950s all these threats seemed to have passed: the Communist party had been forced out of government in 1947 and Communist supporters had been forced out of administrative jobs; *dirigiste* economics had come to be seen less as a threat to the rights of property than as a means of managing capitalism, and measures taken against Pétainists were beginning to be formally rescinded or discreetly forgotten. The new political climate was marked by three events: the 1951 election, which saw a large number of conservatives returned to parliament; the amnesty laws of 1951 and 1953; and the election in 1952 of Antoine Pinay (a businessman, former Pétainist and conservative) as prime minister.

The revival of bourgeois fortunes in France between 1944 and 1951 is significant for three reasons. Firstly, it marked a dramatic change: men moved from prison cells to boardrooms and from ineligibility to ministerial office in the space of a few years. Secondly, the means by which the French bourgeoisie preserved its interests were unusual. There have been many occasions in European history when property-owners have successfully reacted against threats to their interests. But most of these reactions involved violence and the suspension of democracy. Often the European bourgeoisie came to wonder whether the radical right cure to which it had turned might not be worse than the Bolshevik disease that it was designed to counter. By contrast the bourgeois leaders of Fourth Republic France achieved their aims without destroying democracy and without large-scale violence. There were no civil wars, no political murders, no private armies: the forces of order fired a total of eight live rounds during the strikes in 1948.[1] Thirdly, the bourgeois reconstruction of 1944 to 1951 is important because it left a legacy. Economic planning, European integration and a managed version of capitalism that pervaded both the public and private sectors survived the fall of the Fourth Republic to influence the whole of post-war French history, and indeed to establish models that many outside France sought to emulate.

This book will seek to describe and explain the triumph of bourgeois France in the early part of the Fourth Republic. It will pay particular attention to six political parties, or alliances of parties: the Mouvement Républicain Populaire (MRP); the Rassemblement des Gauches Républicaines (RGR); the Centre National des Indépendants et Paysans (CNIP); the Rassemblement du Peuple Français (RPF); the Parti Républicain de la Liberté (PRL); and the Groupement de Défense des Contribuables (GDC). It will also study business organizations, particularly the Conseil National du Patronat Français (CNPF), the civil service and the various agencies set up to defend the reputation of the Vichy government. The Fourth Republic will be examined from the perspective of those who operated it rather than those who rebelled against it. Three assumptions will be made. The first of these is that political parties cannot be studied in isolation from each other. Political commentators of this period often pointed out that the most important political divisions existed *within* rather than *between* political parties.[2] All but one of the Fourth Republic governments were coalitions, and bourgeois parties frequently merged or allied. Indeed, the capacity to form alliances was crucial to the survival of many loosely structured conservative parties after 1945. It was this capacity that helped them to survive the system of proportional representation, which would normally have benefited strong well-organized parties.[3] In 1951 the system of alliance

---

[1] Jules Moch, *Une si longue vie* (Paris, 1976), p. 281.

[2] This was a point made by the leading Fourth Republic politician Edgar Faure.

[3] Philip Williams, *Politics in post-war France: parties and the constitution in the Fourth Republic* (2nd edition, London, 1958), p. 316. See the appendix.

between parties was institutionalized by the *apparentement* law that allowed an alliance of national parties to pool their support in order to prevent 'wasted' votes. Furthermore, politicians and voters sometimes switched between one party and another, while the notables, businessmen and anti-Communist agencies that worked behind the scenes usually maintained relations with more than one political party simultaneously.

The second assumption on which this book is based is that political developments cannot be explained with reference to party politics alone. When the PRL proved an ineffective lobbying mechanism, businessmen worked through the CNPF. Local notables might seek to advance their standing through either the Radical party (Parti Républicain Radical et Radical-Socialiste) or the chamber of commerce or, more probably, they might use both bodies simultaneously. Many key political battles were fought in the supposedly 'apolitical' administration. The exclusion of the Communist sympathizers from the civil service, the dissolution of the *forces françaises de l'intérieur* and the purging of the *compagnies républicaines de sécurité* probably did more to alleviate the Communist threat than the exclusion of Parti Communiste Français (PCF) ministers from government in 1947. Similarly, the debate over economic policy was conducted as much within the ministry of finance or the *commissariat général du plan* (or between the two bodies) as it was in parliament. This book attempts to describe the institutions of the bourgeoisie both by devoting particular chapters to some of those institutions and by dealing with the links that individual political parties had to business associations, civil servants, church organizations and the press.

The third assumption on which this book is based is that attention should be devoted not just to the causes of the bourgeois triumph, but also to the reasons why that triumph took a particular form. It is necessary to explain why the large-scale disciplined parties, such as the MRP and the PRL, that emerged on the right of the political spectrum between 1944 and 1947 ultimately failed and why loose coalitions of small poorly organized parties, similar to those which had dominated the Third Republic, returned to prominence in the 1950s. It is also necessary to explain why Christian Democracy in France did not become the main representative of bourgeois interests as it did in Italy, Germany and, to a lesser extent, Belgium.

A number of objections could be advanced to the scheme outlined above. Firstly, it could be suggested that the very idea of 'bourgeois France' is flawed. It could be pointed out that the French bourgeoisie was never particularly united. Pierre Birnbaum has stressed that the 'bourgeoisie' represented by conservatives in parliament (a class with links to small-scale local business) differed sharply from the 'bourgeoisie' represented by upper level civil servants (a class linked to large-scale national and multinational industries).[4] Even within sub-sections of the French bourgeoisie it is possible to identify important conflicts and differences. Large-scale capitalism in France was riven by disputes between traditional and modernized industries or simply between firms that were competing with each other in the same sector. Similarly, the upper levels of French administration were the scene of intense rivalries over prestige. However, the conflicts and differences within sections of the bourgeoisie can be overstated. Internal squabbles within the bourgeois groups may have been frequent, and they seemed intense to those involved in them, but they concerned relatively minor issues and they rarely caused collaboration between the bourgeois agencies to break down.[5]

Many historians would argue that it is wrong to interpret French politics in primarily class terms at all. They would contend that divisions over the role of the catholic church and the constitution were as important, if not more important, than social struggles.[6] Such arguments clearly have some plausibility when applied to the Fourth Republic. Fourth Republic political parties that agreed on issues connected with the distribution of wealth might have violent disagreements about clericalism or the need to strengthen the executive. However, close examination makes it seem unlikely that either religious or constitutional differences cut as deeply as those of class. It is true that the clerical/anti-clerical division still mattered to large sections of the electorate in Fourth Republic France, but it mattered less to leaders of most political parties who laboured, with some success, to prevent the clerical issue from disrupting their projects.[7] Political alliances were often maintained across the clerical/anti-clerical divide. Furthermore, the clerical/anti-clerical division was less clear in the Fourth Republic than it had been before 1940. Broadly speaking, it is true to say that the MRP was perceived as being most closely linked to church interests and that the Radical party was perceived (among the parties representing property owners) as being the most anti-clerical. But distinctions were not absolute. Even the Radical party contained some defenders of the *école libre* and was sometimes viewed with favour by the religious authorities, and the Radicals were part of a larger alliance that associated them with pro-church parties (the Union Démocratique et Socialiste de la Résistance (UDSR) and Réconciliation Française (RF)). On the other side of the spectrum almost all the pro-clerical parties, including the MRP, periodically alleged that the church was acting against them.

[4] Pierre Birnbaum, *Les sommets de l'état. Essai sur l'élite du pouvoir en France* (Paris, 1977).
[5] Birnbaum stresses the gulf between the backgrounds of businessmen and parliamentarians, but he fails to describe the mechanisms (such as business funding of political parties) that linked the two groups.   [6] Williams, *Politics in post-war France*, p. 3.
[7] Politicians were less successful in preventing clericalism from creating divisions among them after 1951 than they had been before this date.

Defining right and left in constitutional terms also raises serious problems. The most important group in the Fourth Republic urging a more authoritarian constitution was the RPF, but the elements of the RPF that are normally regarded as right-wing were those elements that abandoned the party either before the 1951 election or in order to support the government of Antoine Pinay in 1952 – in other words those who were willing to sacrifice constitutional reform for more immediate goals. Furthermore, defining right and left in terms of constitutional position in the Fourth Republic would have the odd effect of placing the Vichy apologists in the Association des Représentants du Peuple de la Troisième République on the extreme left of the political spectrum.

This work will not seek to argue that disputes within the bourgeoisie were unimportant; such disputes are central to answering the question posed above about the particular form that bourgeois reconstruction took in France. However, it will be suggested that intra-class disputes were less important for the bourgeoisie than inter-class ones: neither the disputes inherited from the nineteenth century over clericalism and the constitution nor the social contradictions within the bourgeoisie ever prevented parties that represented property-owners from uniting against real threats to the interests of their class. A characteristic of the French bourgeoisie throughout the twentieth century has been its capacity to bury its differences at moments – 1920, 1936, 1944, 1968 – when left-wing governments or labour agitation seemed likely to undermine the rights of property. The sense that political disputes could be divided into 'primary' ones (concerning class interest) and 'secondary' ones (which took place within the bourgeoisie) was particularly strong during the late 1940s. One of the functions of the *apparentement* law of 1951 (the most important constitutional innovation of the Fourth Republic) was to ensure that division over 'secondary' issues did not threaten 'primary' interests by benefiting the Communists.

Other objections might be raised to the study of 'bourgeois France'. Bourgeois is a vague and subjective term: definitions of who was and was not bourgeois depended on lifestyle and self-image as much as objective economic status. The frontiers of 'bourgeois France' might even be said to run within households: workers sometimes referred to their wives as *la bourgeoise*[8] and public opinion surveys showed that the proportion of women who regarded themselves as bourgeois was higher than that of men who put themselves in this category. Furthermore, not all of the parties described in this book were exclusively bourgeois. The MRP had, or at least claimed to have, a substantial proletarian membership; the RPF attracted

[8] R. Magraw, *A history of the French working class*. I: *The age of artisan revolution 1815–1871* (London, 1992), p. 6.

votes from working class areas and the Peasant party appealed to voters who could hardly be described as bourgeois.

To some extent the use of the word bourgeois is justified by the absence of any other satisfactory term. In Fourth Republic France, 'right-wing' or 'conservative' were labels that almost all politicians would have rejected, while the description bourgeois would have been accepted by most of those whose career is described in this book. The term bourgeois was very widely used in the Fourth Republic. Charles Morazé wrote a book in 1946 entitled *La France bourgeoise*, while André Germain, grandson of the founder of the Crédit Lyonnais and cousin of the Pétainist Alfred Fabre-Luce, published his memoirs in 1951 under the title *La bourgeoisie qui brûle*.[9] Sociologists in the 1940s might debate the precise meaning of the word bourgeois but they had no doubt that it meant something.[10] Indeed, to some extent the debate over the limits of the bourgeoisie was a sign that the social group under discussion was a dynamic one that was constantly adjusting to circumstances – electrical devices were replacing domestic servants, and the 'cultural' capital provided by *lycées* and *grandes écoles* was becoming more important than the inheritance of property.[11]

In some respects the very subjectivity of the term is appropriate. Subjective notions sometimes played a key role in influencing electoral behaviour – women were not just more prone to describe themselves as bourgeois than their menfolk, they were also more prone to vote for parties such as the CNIP, the RPF and the MRP. Furthermore, political parties had a self-image just as individuals did: the *vins d'honneur*, the banquets and the soporific speeches identified the Radicals or the Independents as 'bourgeois parties' just as white table cloths and leather-bound editions of Montesquieu might identify an individual as bourgeois.

It is also possible to justify the use of the word bourgeois in more precise terms. The key groups who controlled most political parties and institutions described in this work were bourgeois by any definition. Most

[9] The works by Morazé and Germain, and a number of other books published in the 1940s and 1950s dealing with the French bourgeois, are cited in the opening pages of T. Zeldin, *France 1848–1945: ambition and love* (Oxford, 1979).

[10] M. Perrot's study of bourgeois living standards between 1873 and 1953 discussed three possible characteristics that might be used to identify the bourgeoisie: the possession of the *baccalauréat*, the employment of servants and the use of a room specifically to receive visitors. Perrot herself argued that all families who kept accounts were bourgeois (which was convenient since family accounts provided the source for her study). M. Perrot, *Le mode de vie des familles bourgeoises 1873–1953* (Paris, 1961).

[11] Some idea of changing bourgeois lifestyles is given in Perrot, *La mode de vie des familles bourgeoises* and in J. Morice, *La demande d'automobiles en France. Théorie, histoire, répartition géographique* (Paris, 1957). The memoirs of Philippe Ariès give a marvellous impression of how a family could retain its sense of being bourgeois even when its material circumstances changed. Philippe Ariès, *Un historien de dimanche* (Paris, 1980).

politicians were drawn from the liberal professions – the law, medicine, journalism – and much of the funding of political parties came from large-scale industry. Civil servants and the *éminences grises* who worked behind the political scenes were also bourgeois by education and background. A large proportion of industrialists and civil servants, and a smaller proportion of politicians, came from a very precisely defined section of the *haute bourgeoisie* that was united by education at the smart *lycées* and *grandes écoles*, service in the *corps d'état* and residence in the *beaux quartiers* of western Paris.[12]

It is not suggested that the bourgeois leadership exercised exclusive control of French politics during the period 1944 to 1951 or that class interest was the sole element in political struggles; indeed, it will be argued that the confusion of French politics in the period owes much to the complexity of forces and interests at work. However, it will be argued that the French bourgeoisie was the group that benefited most from developments in France between 1944 and 1951: they had most to lose from the nationalization, *dirigisme*, *épuration* and disorder of 1944, and they had most to win from the period of rapid growth in a neo-capitalist economy that began at the end of the 1940s. Furthermore, it will be argued that, to some extent at least, the conscious defence of class interests by bourgeois leaders laid the foundations for the benefits that their class was to enjoy.

A second objection that might be raised to the structure of this book concerns the choice of political parties studied. It might be argued that the decision to include the UDSR and to exclude the main socialist party (the Section Française de l'Internationale Ouvrière or SFIO) is arbitrary. It is true that there was frequent discussion of alliances between the SFIO and the MRP or the UDSR immediately after the war, and that some in all three parties aspired to form a broader *travailliste* grouping, which would provide a French equivalent of the British Labour party. However, this book will argue that *travaillisme* was always something of a mirage and that those in the MRP and UDSR who espoused it were either hopelessly isolated from their own colleagues or had failed to realize how radical the social policies necessary to sustain such a union would be.

After attempts to form a *travailliste* union were abandoned, the SFIO retained close links with the bourgeois parties with which it frequently entered into electoral alliances or coalition governments. However, the long-term aims of the SFIO remained radically different from those of its

---

[12] A large number of works deal with the social origins of the ruling class during the Fourth Republic. See particularly Alain Girard, Henri Laugier, D. Weinburg, Charretier (sic) and Claude Lévy-Leboyer, *La réussite sociale en France. Ses caractères, ses lois, ses effets* (Paris, 1961); E.N. Suleiman, *Elites in French society: the politics of survival* (Princeton, 1978); Pierre Birnbaum, *La classe dirigeante française* (Paris, 1978).

allies: no Socialist leader would have said that he wished to defend capitalism, though the practical impact of the party's action was often precisely that. Perhaps more importantly, the SFIO's internal structure differed from that of the bourgeois parties: it was made up of well-disciplined militants, not powerful notables, and, although its electorate sometimes overlapped with that of bourgeois parties (particularly the Radicals), the SFIO retained a larger number of proletarian voters, members and, most importantly, leaders than any other party except the Communists. Business relations with the SFIO reveal its curious position poised between the Communist ghetto and the anti-Communist alliance. Though businessmen funded the SFIO, their relations with the party were conducted at arm's length. SFIO leaders were much more discreet about their links with capitalism than the leaders of any other party were, and no prominent business leader ever joined the SFIO (though businessmen joined all the parties of the bourgeois grouping). For these reasons the SFIO will not be the subject of a detailed investigation in itself, but it will be mentioned when it formed part of larger strategies conceived by bourgeois leaders.

Another objection that might be raised to the party content of this book concerns the degree of attention given to various groupings. It might be argued that it is perverse to devote as much space to the UDSR, which gained only 9 seats in the 1951 election, as to the RPF, which gained 120 seats in 1951 making it the largest group in the National Assembly. To some extent the degree of attention given to various parties is justified by previous work done on the subject. Considerable space has been devoted to explaining parties that have been neglected by previous historians (especially where there are substantial archive sources available relating to those parties). The RPF has already been the subject of several excellent studies on which this book draws.

The weight of attention given to 'minor' parties in this book can also be justified with a more radical critique of traditional ways in which the Fourth Republic has been understood. Previous historians have been attracted to the RPF by its spectacular electoral success and by the exciting novelty of its programme. Philip Williams justified the space that he devoted to the RPF in his *Politics in post-war France* on the grounds that 'A volcano remains interesting even when the eruption is over'.[13] Previous accounts of the Fourth Republic have been based on the, at least implicit, assumption that the Fourth Republic was a 'failure'. In this context those parties that came nearest to overthrowing the whole regime are most worthy of interest. However, such an emphasis on the parties that attacked the Fourth

---

[13] Williams, *Politics in post-war France*, p. v.

Republic neglects those forces that entered governments and ran France between 1947 and 1951.

An alternative point of view, and one adopted in this book, is that there was no single criterion of success in Fourth Republic politics. The point can be underlined through a comparison with English politics. In England, politics could be likened to a game of draughts: there were only two players each of whom had a simple aim which could only be achieved in one way. Success in terms of the number of votes obtained translated, more or less, into success in terms of the number of seats in parliament gained, which translated into the right to form a government, implement policy and distribute portfolios. Politics in Fourth Republic France was more like some fiendishly complicated variation on the game of poker involving a number of skilled, and not always honest, players. Definitions of success varied according to whether votes, seats in parliament, ministerial offices or policies implemented were counted, and the leaders of political parties did not always subscribe to the same kind of goal.

The MRP was mainly concerned to affect policy, and particularly policy relating to the integration of Europe – hence the tenacious grip that the party kept on the ministry of foreign affairs. For this reason the MRP leaders were willing to remain in government even at times when it seemed likely that their presence would damage their own electoral fortunes.[14] Indeed, MRP leaders might well have argued that their losses in the election of 1951 were justified in view of the role that MRP foreign ministers had played in the early stages of European integration.

The Radicals and the Socialist SFIO presented a sharp contrast to the MRP. Both parties were more concerned with the fortunes of their party than with the implementation of any particular policy. This accounted for the store that the SFIO and the Radicals set by control of the ministry of the interior, which exercised considerable power at election times. However, the means by which the SFIO and the Radicals tried to advance their party interests were very different. The SFIO tried to keep its austere militants happy by frequently leaving governments to take the proverbial *cure d'opposition*, while the Radicals tried to keep their worldly notables happy by remaining in government at almost any cost in order to distribute favours. Some political parties changed their aims over the course of the Fourth Republic. Thus the PRL and the UDSR began life with grand ideas about forming large-scale new parties *à l'anglaise* that might even be able to form single party governments. However, both parties renounced these early ambitions and emulated the Radicals – participating in government

---

[14] Archives Nationales (AN), 350 AP 76, Francisque Gay to Félix Gouin, 28 February 1946. Gay pointed out to Gouin (a member of the SFIO) that the MRP had probably damaged its electoral chances by remaining in the government after the resignation of de Gaulle.

whenever possible in order to secure whatever advantages might be derived from the distribution of patronage.

Most other bourgeois groupings never had any illusions about the possibility of forming single party governments. Some party leaders claimed that they did not wish to have more than a handful of parliamentarians in their groupings;[15] others, such as the leaders of the CNIP or the RGR, explicitly announced that they did not wish to exercise discipline over the parties or individuals who joined their groups. Sometimes candidates in elections did not even wish to win. Many of the candidates in the 1951 election who obtained half a dozen votes, or sometimes no votes at all, had been put up merely in order to allow the parties that they represented to claim the thirty candidatures necessary to benefit from the *apparentement* laws.[16] Sometimes presenting candidates was a form of blackmail: parties or candidates would be forced to buy off potential rivals.[17] In 1951, the Groupement de Défense des Contribuables institutionalized this system by seeking to exercise influence over the electoral lists presented all over France, and by threatening to put up its own candidates in areas where the existing parties refused to allow it to exercise such influence.

Parties that were seeking to secure influence rather than the prestige of electoral success often thought of their results in terms quite different from those that spring to the mind of Anglo-Saxon historians. The Groupement de Défense des Contribuables was a 'success' in the 1951 election because it had exercised influence over the selection of over three hundred successful candidates, even though it gained only one seat itself. The Radicals were a 'success' because they managed to gain seats and ministries consistently in spite of a continuously declining vote. The UDSR was a 'success' because it managed to hold ministerial office in spite of losing both votes and seats in parliament. Seen in the same light, the RPF was a failure because, in spite of

[15] Antier, leader of the Peasant party, told a representative of the Fédération Républicaine that he wished his grouping in parliament to remain small; undated report in AN, 317 AP 84.

[16] The two most commonly used sources used to study electoral politics in France, i.e. the electoral results printed in *le Monde* and the electoral declarations of successful candidates printed in the *Recueil des textes authentiques des programmes et engagements électoraux des députés proclamés élus à la suite des élections générales du 17 juin 1951* (commonly known as *Barodet*), both ignore those candidatures that attracted very few votes. The nearest thing to a comprehensive set of electoral results was produced by the ministry of the interior and published by Documentation Française. This list showed that the Groupement de Défense des Contribuables obtained no votes at all in the second constituency of the Bouches du Rhône.

[17] J.-L. Anteriou reported that his fellow Radical, Bastid, had faced the threat of electoral competition in his constituency from a shadowy organization called the URIAS (which was headed by a professional stamp-dealer). Bastid had been obliged to buy off his potential rival for 200,000 francs. AN, 373 AP 73, Anteriou to Bollaert, 19 May 1947.

the huge number of votes that it obtained, its inspiring mass rallies and the grandeur of its rhetoric, it did not obtain a single ministerial position or exercise any direct power over the action of government.

This book aims to understand the political parties and bourgeois institutions of Fourth Republic France in their own terms. It will argue that there were broad class interests at work behind the complicated factions, alliances and coalitions of Fourth Republic politics and attempt to show that the period from the Liberation to the early 1950s can be understood as much in terms of successful conservatism as of failed reform.

2   A historiographic overview

The historiography of the Fourth Republic has a curiously backward feel. Many of the best works on the subject were written almost contemporaneously. Two institutions helped to raise the standard of political analysis to new levels. The first of these was a new newspaper, le Monde, which allowed its journalists to digress at great length on their particular interests. Many of those who wrote for le Monde, such as Jean Planchais, Jean Lacouture and Jacques Fauvet, were later to become recognized authorities on their subject.[1] The second institution was the Fondation Nationale des Sciences Politiques which launched two new publications during the period: the Cahiers de la Fondation Nationale des Sciences Politiques and the Revue Française de Science Politique. Political science was a prestigious discipline in post-war France which attracted a succession of brilliant students such as Stanley Hoffmann, Jean Touchard and Georges Vedel. The subject was stimulated by new approaches and ideas that were coming from the other side of the Atlantic and by a mass of empirical data that was made available by the beginning of large-scale opinion polling in France. Political scientists accumulated information on subjects ranging from the consumption of toiletries among the Parisian bourgeois to the statistical correlation between possession of motor cars and divorce rates.[2]

Work on Fourth Republic France was also produced by scholars from overseas. Some of this work was journalistic and superficial,[3] and most of it

[1] On the history of le Monde see J.-N. Jeanneney and J. Julliard, 'Le Monde' de Beuve-Méry ou le métier d'Alceste (Paris, 1979). Jean Planchais went on to write Une histoire politique de l'armée. II: 1940–1967 de de Gaulle à de Gaulle (Paris, 1967); Jean Lacouture's studies of de Gaulle led to his biography published in the 1980s, De Gaulle, 3 vols (Paris, 1984) and Jacques Fauvet's study of political parties was encapsulated in his La IVème république (Paris, 1959).

[2] M. Perrot, Le mode de vie des familles bourgeoises 1873–1953 (Paris, 1961), and J. Morice, La demande d'automobiles en France. Théorie, histoire, répartition géographique (Paris, 1957).

[3] Two foreign journalists, Alexander Werth and Herbert Luthy, produced accounts of the Fourth Republic that continue to be influential. Alexander Werth, France, 1940–1955 (London, 1956) and Herbert Luthy, The state of France (London, 1955). For the continued influence of these authors see M. Larkin, France since the Popular Front: government and people 1936–86 (Oxford, 1988), p. viii.

suffered from the absence of good sources.[4] However, some work did produce an immediate and lasting impact. Georgette Elgey's political histories of the Fourth Republic are still useful,[5] while the books by Francis de Tarr,[6] on the French Radical party, and Henry Ehrmann,[7] on organized business, remain the most authoritative treatments of their subjects. The most striking example of such work was Philip Williams' *Politics in post-war France*[8] which has been widely praised in France. the *Revue Française de Science Politique* described it in glowing terms and, thirty years after its publication, Jean-Pierre Rioux recognized that it was 'still the best synthesis on the subject'.[9] Williams brought great erudition to bear on his subject, and produced a careful, balanced account.

For all its virtues, the work produced by contemporary analysts should not have been the last word on the subject. All of these works depended either on information that was already in the public domain or, occasionally, on private, and often anonymous, interviews.[10] Sometimes such an approach made it hard for scholars to remain detached about the subjects of their study: the introduction to de Tarr's book on the Radical party was written by Mendès-France;[11] Ehrmann's links with French political figures became so intimate that some of his 'sources' began to quote him.[12] The scarcity of written sources encouraged political scientists to draw many of their conclusions about Fourth Republic parties from what was already known about the Third Republic, and hence to overstate the continuity of French political life.[13] Absence of precise information, and the understandable enthusiasm to draw broad conclusions, sometimes made students of the Fourth Republic neglect tiresome and messy detail. This was especially

---

[4] D. Thompson, *Democracy in France: the Third and Fourth Republics* (Oxford, 1952); G. Wright, *The reshaping of French democracy* (New York, 1948).

[5] Georgette Elgey, *La république des illusions 1945–1951 ou la vie secrète de la IVème république* (Paris, 1965).

[6] Francis de Tarr, *The French Radical party from Herriot to Mendès-France* (Oxford, 1961).

[7] Henry W. Ehrmann, *Organized business in France* (Princeton, 1957).

[8] Philip Williams, *Politics in post-war France: parties and the constitution in the Fourth Republic* (2nd edition, London, 1958).

[9] J.-P. Rioux, *The Fourth Republic 1944–1958* (Cambridge, 1987), p. 507.

[10] Georgette Elgey kept transcripts of the interviews on which she based her works on the Fourth Republic. These transcripts have been made available to some historians. See G. Bossuat, *La France, l'aide américaine et la construction européenne 1944–1954* (2 vols, Paris, 1992), II, p. 915.

[11] De Tarr, *The French Radical party*.

[12] E. Beau de Loménie, *L'Algérie trahie par l'argent. Réponse à M. Raymond Aron* (Paris, 1957), pp. 52–53. Beau de Loménie describes how he discovered the 'internationalism' of French big business: 'It was revealed to me for the first time a few years ago, during a conversation with a young American entrusted by his university with a research project on the French business community.'

[13] Philip Williams' analysis of the Radical party is particularly dependent on information from the pre-1940 period: Williams, *Politics in post-war France*, p. 91.

serious because tiresome and messy details sometimes held the key to real understanding of Fourth Republic politics.

There is another more general problem with the approach of political scientists to Fourth Republic politics. Men formed in a tradition that owed much to Anglo-Saxon (especially American) influence implicitly, and sometimes explicitly, assumed that 'normal', 'healthy' or 'mature' political systems were characterized by stable governments, large well-organized parties and effective 'transmission belts' between society and politics. The complexity of the Fourth Republic was often treated as a freak show and the most sympathetic and extensive attention was given not to those who played the political game well but to those, like Mendès-France or de Gaulle, who sat sulkily on the sidelines.

Not only were Fourth Republic politics often judged against Anglo-Saxon political values, they were often judged against a particular kind of Anglo-Saxon value: that of the non-marxist left.[14] This tendency led students of French politics to give excessive weight to the fumbling attempts at *travaillisme* that had been made after the Liberation. It also had the paradoxical effect that parties like the Mouvement Républican Populaire (MRP) and the Union Démocratique et Socialiste de la Résistance (UDSR) were prone to be dismissed as failures because political scientists took their claims to be 'progressive parties' more seriously than some members of those parties took those claims themselves.

The gaps left by the analysts of the 1940s and 1950s might have been filled by later scholars able to benefit both from the added perspectives conferred by time and from the increasing availability of sources. However, in practice this did not happen. The problem was that the dramatic fall of the Fourth Republic and the introduction of a new constitution shaped by General de Gaulle provided political scientists and journalists with more exciting subjects for study. De Gaulle's France was conspicuously not *immobiliste*. The relative simplicity of politics under de Gaulle lent itself to neat conceptual analysis and did not require painstaking examination of party factions or local notables. The complicated, and now apparently irrelevant, Fourth Republic, fell into the gap that opened up between history and political science. For example, the suggestion that it might be possible to study the varieties of 'apoliticism' in French public life was first raised by Jean Touchard in an essay published in 1956 on Poujadism.[15] But, by the time that such a study was completed, the Fourth Republic was dead

---

[14] Ibid., p. v: 'The reader is ... entitled to know my political standpoint, which is that of a supporter of the moderate wing of the Labour party.' Williams also wrote a hagiographic biography of Gaitskell.

[15] Jean Touchard, 'Bibliographie et chronologie du Poujadisme', *Revue Française de Science Politique* (1956), 18–42.

and the articles collected in it hardly mentioned the period between the Liberation and 1958.[16]

The students and associates of Stanley Hoffmann, who had begun his career with research on the Fourth Republic, epitomized the way in which the recent history of France was forgotten. Hoffmann encouraged historians, such as Robert Paxton,[17] to study Vichy France, and political scientists, such as George Ross and Sylvia Malzacher, to study the Fifth Republic.[18] Charles Maier, an associate of Hoffmann's, has worked both as a historian studying Third Republic[19] and as a political scientist studying the Fifth Republic, but has never published primary work on the Fourth Republic.

Recent work on the Fourth Republic has also been restrained by the unevenness of sources. There are some exceptionally good sources for Fourth Republic politics (notably the archives of political parties that have been gathered and catalogued by the FNSP). But many of these sources have been opened too recently to have been much used by historians. Furthermore, sources remain inconsistent. The archives of private bodies are more accessible than those of government agencies and there are gaps in the information available. For example, it is possible, with a little ingenuity, to obtain a large number of documents relating to the Rassemblement des Gauches Républicaines (RGR), but there are very few documents relevant to the Centre National des Indépendants et Paysans (CNIP).[20]

The unevenness of sources has posed particular problems for French historians who have needed to produce the exhaustive *thèses* required by the juries that award the *doctorat d'état*. This has encouraged many young scholars to adopt a biographical approach to the Fourth Republic, concentrating on a single individual whose papers are available. Such works can be valuable sources of information, but they also suffer from a warped perspective: they tend to be reticent about certain aspects of their subjects' careers and they focus on individuals to an extent that obscures the workings of the broader political system.[21]

[16] Georges Vedel (ed.), *La dépolitisation. Mythe ou réalité?* (Paris, 1962).
[17] Robert Paxton, *Vichy France: old guard and new order, 1940–1944* (New York, 1972).
[18] G. Ross, S. Hoffmann and S. Malzacher, *The Mitterrand experience* (Oxford, 1987).
[19] C. S. Maier, *Recasting bourgeois Europe: stabilization in France, Germany, and Italy in the decade after World War 1* (Princeton, 1975).
[20] The archives of Henri Queuille, Pierre Etienne Flandin, Jean-Louis Anteriou, René Mayer, and the UDSR are all available to historians and all cast light on the RGR. So far as I am aware, the only archives that contain detailed information on the CNIP are those of Paul Reynaud.
[21] Sylvie Guillaume is characteristic of the biographical tendency among French historians. She has written two works that concentrated on the careers of particular individuals: *Antoine Pinay ou la confiance en politique* (Paris, 1984) and *La Confédération Générale des Petites et Moyennes Entreprises. Son histoire, son combat, un autre syndicalisme patronal 1944–1978* (Paris, 1987). The latter work is effectively a biography of Léon Gingembre;

Studies of the Fourth Republic right, both those produced contemporaneously and those that came later, suffer from a particular problem. Apart from the sinister glamour of fascism, there is little about the French right to attract historians. The right lacked the coherent ideology of the left (indeed, part of the right's ideology consisted in denying that it was ideological); its party organization was obscure, and most historians find the right personally unsympathetic. Tony Judt sums up the feelings of many historians when he writes: 'there is not a culture of the right or centre in the same way that there is one of the left'.[22]

Three historians – Jean-Luc Pinol, Malcolm Anderson and, most famously, René Rémond[23] – have written about the Fourth Republic right. However, all three face important problems of definition. It is widely recognized that there was more than one right in France. Rémond talked of legitimist, bonapartist and orleanist rights. Others have talked of a right defined by attitudes to the church, the constitution or class. All of these analyses are rooted in the assumption that the dominant feature of the right was continuity and that the politics of the mid-twentieth century can be explained in terms of conflicts that had begun in the eighteenth or nineteenth century.

The tendency to emphasize continuity in political life was increased by the importance that electoral geography assumed in French political science. The publication of André Siegfried's *Tableau politique de la France de l'ouest sous la IIIème république* in 1912 founded a whole tradition of electoral geography in France,[24] and this tradition flowered after the Second World War under the aegis of François Goguel. Electoral geography was particularly influential among students, and perhaps even leaders,[25] of the French right. René Rémond wrote that Goguel and le Bras

both say very little of the Vichy careers of their subject. Sometimes the biographical approach leads historians to produce a photonegative of the conventional picture of the Fourth Republic. Thus some of the studies in the collection devoted to Henri Queuille present him as an altruistic and far-sighted statesmen – a view only marginally less misguided than that of Queuille as the incarnation of hopeless *immobilisme*.

22 Tony Judt, *Marxism and the French left: studies in labour and politics in France* (Oxford, 1986), p. 2.
23 Jean-Luc Pinol, manuscript in press; Malcolm Anderson, *Conservative politics in France* (London, 1974); René Rémond, *Les droites en France* (Paris, 1982).
24 For an idea of the impact that electoral geography had in France see François Goguel and Georges Dupeux, *Sociologie électorale. Esquisse d'un bilan. Guide des recherches* (Paris, 1951).
25 In the absence of proper party organization, conservative leaders often had little idea about their potential support other than that provided by the assumption that certain regions were 'naturally right-wing'. Most politically interested bourgeois Frenchmen would have been aware of Siegfried's ideas, which were expressed in articles for the *Figaro* as well as more academic works.

had shown him the importance of 'differences between places and continuity over time'.[26]

It is easy to see why the works of electoral geographers appealed to those concerned with the right. They tended to focus on rural areas, where conservatism was strongest, and the emphasis on tradition and continuity seemed well suited to explain defenders of the *ordre établi*. Unfortunately, electoral geography sometimes became a substitute for political analysis rather than a means of enhancing it. Electoral geographers worked with a broad brush: sometimes politics was reduced to a simple left/right dichotomy (or rather a conflict between *ordre établi* and *mouvement*, as Goguel put it) and the full range of differences that existed among the fragmented and confusing parties of the right were never explored. An alarming illustration of the influence of electoral geography is provided in the recent work of Emmanuel Todd: 'Between 1900 and 1987, the inland West, Brittany, Vendée, the Basque country, Alsace and Lorraine, parts of Savoie and of the Jura Mountains, and the southern part of the Massif Central between Ardèche and Aveyron voted for the right with remarkable constancy. In fact over a long period, all these regions *had no political history* at all.'[27]

Electoral geographers proved better at mapping voting patterns than in explaining those patterns. Those who looked to levels of religious practice or land tenure systems to explain the persistence of certain political traditions in particular areas were then faced with the problem of explaining how similar arrangments in different areas produced a different kind of politics.[28] The post-war period presents particular problems for the electoral geographer. Siegfried's seminal work dealt with a highly stable population. Voters in late nineteenth-century France rarely moved outside their native area except to perform military service, usually in a regiment made up of men from the region. By 1945 this had changed. Many people from northern France had been obliged to flee their homes in 1940; many inhabitants of Alsace had been exiled or forced to serve in the German army (some of the latter group had finished up as prisoners of war in the Soviet

---

[26] René Rémond, 'Le contemporain du contemporain', in P. Nora (ed.), *Essais d'ego-histoire* (Paris, 1987), pp. 293–350.

[27] E. Todd, *The making of modern France: politics, ideology and culture* (Oxford, 1991), p. 89 (my italics).

[28] François Goguel argued that there were four possible explanations of regional politics: land tenure patterns, religious practice, the activities of political parties and the experience of rapid economic change. He added that electoral geographers had concentrated on the first two of these explanations. Goguel and Dupeux, *Sociologie électorale*; Alain de Vulpain, 'Physionomie agraire et orientation politique dans le département des Côtes du Nord 1928–1946', *Revue Française de Science Politique*, 1 and 11, January and July (1957), 110–132.

Union); many young men had been sent to perform *service du travail obligatoire* in Germany or fled to the Maquis in a bid to avoid such an obligation. Most importantly, the enfranchisement of women in 1945 meant that over half the French electorate was made up of people who had never voted before 1940 and whose votes could not necessarily be explained in terms of the categories that had been used for the Third Republic.

There was also, by the standards of earlier times, a very high degree of internal migration in France. A sociological study of Auxerre carried out in 1950 made the astonishing discovery that less than one-eighth of the town's inhabitants had been born there. This statistic was made all the more surprising by the fact that Auxerre was, and is, so often presented as a pillar of social and political stability.[29] Lucien Febvre pointed out that trying to explain how certain traditions survived in such a town was like trying to explain how a certain 'spirit' survived in First World War regiments even after all their initial members had been killed.[30]

The movement to towns was not one way. The Nièvre, for example, contained so many people who had retired to the countryside after making their careers in towns that only 30 per cent of inhabitants of the area earned their living from agriculture though 69 per cent lived in rural areas. Pataut described the dramatic effects that such a pattern had on the area: 'These sons of peasants who have become city people are now so numerous that they often transform the countryside into a sort of large suburb. [One finds] the coexistence in the same village of a world that lives from the land and quite another group, remaining partly urbanized by its habits, pastimes, preoccupations, "perspectives", and prejudices, which comes to seek refuge and peace far from the town.'[31]

The interpretations of conservatism that hinge around ideological tradition and electoral geography produce a strange view of the Fourth Republic. They emphasize continuity at a time of rapid change: it is faintly absurd to examine the politicians who presided over the programme to develop France's first atomic bomb in terms of 'orleanism' and 'bonapartism'. The interest in continuity also leads historians to place an undue emphasis on the insignificant vestiges of distinguished traditions and to place too little emphasis on parties founded after 1945. Most importantly,

[29] Lucien Febvre, preface to Charles Bettelheim and Suzanne Frère, *Une ville française moyenne. Auxerre en 1950. Etude de structure sociale et urbaine* (Paris, 1950), p. ix.
[30] Ibid. In another medium sized town (Vienne) the proportion of the population born outside the area (52.6 per cent) was smaller than in Auxerre, but still sufficiently striking to make sociologists surprised that a sense of community was so strongly maintained. Pierre Clément and Nelly Xydias, *Vienne sur le Rhône. La ville et les habitants situations et attitudes. Sociologie d'une cité française* (Paris, 1955), p. 35.
[31] J. Pataut, *Sociologie électorale de la Nièvre au XXème siècle (1902–1951)* (Paris, 1956), p. 171.

the emphasis on political issues inherited from a pre-industrial age under-plays the role of social class in the Fourth Republic.

The most thought provoking recent work on the Fourth Republic has been produced by economic rather than political historians. Economic historians tend to describe a success story that begins in 1945 and lasts until the present day, where political historians describe a failure that started in the Third Republic and ended in 1958. This means that the economic history of the Fourth Republic is continuously rethought in the light of more recent events. The slowdown in industrial concentration that occurred during the 1970s or the turbulence of the 1980s both caused re-evaluations of recent French economic performance.

Writing on the recent economic history of France has been characterized by its broad perspective. Explanations have not collapsed into dry econo-metric details. There has been an emphasis on the links between social, political and economic events. The school of historians influenced by Jean Bouvier has stressed that the decisions taken by the makers of economic policy concerned the exercise of power and the distribution of wealth as well as the best means of securing economic growth.[32] American historians have been struck by the role of the state in France and laid great emphasis on the political influences that govern the state's action.[33] In many respects it is economic historians who have offered the best general overview of French politics between 1945 and 1958.

However, the absence of work on French politics as detailed as that carried out by economic historians has cramped the style of the latter. Economic historians can draw broad conclusions about how social pres-sures affected economic decisions, but they often have a limited under-standing of the mechanisms by which those pressures were applied. Economic historians are better informed about civil service departments and the *commissariat général du plan* than they are about political parties or private pressure groups.[34] The limitation is particularly important for the early years of the Fourth Republic because relations between social groups and political power were so complicated and often produced such paradox-ical results.

[32] Bouvier's views are set out most fully in F. Bloch-Lainé and Jean Bouvier, *La France restaurée. Dialogue sur le choix d'une modernisation* (Paris, 1986).

[33] R. F. Kuisel, *Capitalism and the state in modern France: renovation and economic management in the twentieth century* (Cambridge, 1983); P. A. Hall, *Governing the economy: the politics of state intervention in Britain and France* (Cambridge, 1986).

[34] There is a strong tradition of works on the French administration that was shown in works like P. Lalumière, *L'inspection des finances* (Paris, 1959). In recent years the focus on the administration rather than party politics has been increased partly by the collaboration between the historian Bouvier and the civil servant Bloch-Lainé and partly by the establishment of the *comité pour l'histoire économique et financière de la France* (a body that exists under the aegis of the ministry of finance).

The problems of economic analysis divorced from its political context are illustrated by Michel Margairaz's recent book *L'état, les finances et l'économie. Histoire d'une conversion 1932–1952*. Margairaz takes his cue from Bouvier and presents his analysis in a broad social context, but he constantly misses opportunities to make specific links between economic policies and political developments. For example, Margairaz remarks that the levy operated by René Mayer in 1948 fell hard on non-salaried workers, especially 'les classes moyennes, de l'agriculture et du commerce'. However, Margairaz does not see any particular significance in the fact that these very classes made up the electoral bedrock of Mayer's own party (the Radicals), nor does he mention the changes within the Radical party and the RGR that were stimulated by the Mayer plan.[35] What is still missing from the historiography of the Fourth Republic is an attempt to link up the economic/political history of writers like Margairaz with a detailed party political analysis. Such an analysis might help explain why a period that is almost universally regarded as a political 'failure' should have been, for some groups at least, such an economic 'success'.[36]

The aim of this overview of the historiography of the Fourth Republic has been to demonstrate the gaps that this book seeks to fill. But a recognition of earlier work is also necessary to understand aspects of this book that may otherwise seem idiosyncratic. Considerable time has been spent examining relatively obscure political parties that have previously been neglected. Similarly, examination of some important parties and institutions (such as the ministry of finance) has been based on the extensive primary research of other historians. Most importantly, an attempt has been made to tie together both primary and secondary sources to produce an overall interpretation of the Fourth Republic. This approach has been adopted partly on the assumption that an area of history that has been neglected in recent years needs broad interpretations in order to rekindle interest. In short this book is meant to be a contribution to a debate: the author is keenly aware of his debt to previous research and hopes that other historians will be stimulated, or provoked, into study of some of the matters discussed below.

[35] Michel Margairaz, *L'état, les finances et l'économie. Histoire d'une conversion 1932–1952* (2 vols, Paris, 1991), p. 1009.
[36] One recent historian has attempted to explain the apparently paradoxical relationship between economic 'success' and political 'failure' in the Fourth Republic. Irwin Wall, *The United States and the making of post-war France 1945–1954* (Cambridge, 1991), p. 291.

3   International comparisons

The history of the Fourth Republic is often compared with what went before and came after in France. However, this period can equally well be compared with what happened simultaneously in other European countries. Such a comparison throws up many similarities. Almost all the countries of Europe were involved in physical and economic reconstruction after the war. Almost all countries were also involved in social reconstruction to rebuild the order that been shaken by the war. In all countries, there was an expectation of social reform: the occupation of France and Belgium, and the fascist regimes of Italy and Germany, seemed to have discredited part of the ruling class. This expectation was disappointed and a variety of conservative forces triumphed in general elections of 1948 (Italy), 1949 (Belgium and Austria) and 1951 (France and the United Kingdom). Furthermore, all European countries were affected by the Cold War, and by the increasing influence of the United States. This triumph of bourgeois Europe was also marked at an international level by the North Atlantic Treaty of 1949 that brought together most west European nations under American aegis. This chapter will attempt a brief general survey to show how France fitted in with, and diverged from, a general European model.

The most obvious common denominator linking France with Germany, Belgium and Italy after the war was the fact that all four countries had endured a period of authoritarian government. However, the post-war impact of this period was not the same in all four countries. In West Germany, the pre-war ruling class was damaged by foreign intervention. Political elites who had been too closely tied to the Nazis were put on trial, German industry was restructured by the Americans and the homelands of the *Junkers* were occupied by the Russians. However, those members of the German ruling class who survived these measures did not have to face a challenge from an internal resistance movement, and association with the regime of 1933 to 1945 seems often to have been an advantage rather than a disadvantage in post-war careers.[1] In Belgium, the ruling class also

---

[1] V. Berghahn, *The Americanization of West German industry, 1945–1973* (Leamington Spa, 1986), p. 53.

survived well in the post-war period. The government and most of the political class had gone into exile after the defeat of 1940, but those that had remained in the country were seen as part of a wide-ranging consensus, developed in advance, about how the occupation should be managed. In particular the 'collaboration' of Belgian industry was generally accepted as having been a necessary means of preserving national interests.[2] France presented a sharp contrast to Germany and Belgium. Contemporaries were particularly aware of the contrast between Belgium and France (two countries that resembled each other in so many ways): it was widely felt that post-war purges in France, and particularly measures taken against large-scale business, were more severe than those in Belgium.[3] The reasons for this were rooted in the fact that no consensus existed about actions taken in France during the occupation. The internal Resistance and the London based Gaullists disputed the legitimacy of the Vichy government and those who had supported it – a group that was seen to include most members of the Third Republic parliament, and much of French large-scale industry.

The impact of the Cold War was also felt differently in various parts of Europe. The bourgeoisie of every European country were increasingly preoccupied by the Communist threat, but the particular kind of threat to which they responded varied from country to country. The United Kingdom, Belgium, West Germany and Austria had small internal Communist parties: they were mainly concerned by the military threat posed by the Soviet Union, a threat that was particularly acute for the last two of these countries, rather than by the threat of internal revolution. France and Italy, on the other hand, had large internal Communist parties that attracted the support of more than a quarter of the electorate during the two decades after the war. The threat felt by the French bourgeoisie was especially great because the French Communist party was more obedient to Moscow than that of any other west European nation, and because the French Communists were seen to have derived such strength from their participation in the Resistance. This had an obvious impact on former Pétainists, but it also influenced bourgeois Resistance leaders who felt that they had been victims

[2] On the tactics of Belgian industry during the occupation see J. Gillingham, *Belgian business in the Nazi new order* (Brussels, 1977). As late as 1974, the doyen of Belgian economic history, F. Baudhuin, felt it necessary to defend Belgian industrialists against what he saw as Gillingham's attack on their motives. F. Baudhuin, 'L'article de John Gillingham Phd sur la politique de production de l'industrie belge durant l'occupation nazie. Une réplique', *Revue Belge d'Histoire Contemporaine*, 5, 1–2 (1974), 265–267.

[3] The leaders of the Belgian coal industry were shocked by what they saw as the punitive nationalization of the French coal industry: see N. Caulier-Mathy, 'Les dirigeants de l'industrie houillère belge 1935 à 1955. Essai d'étude des comportements', in *Revue Belge d'Histoire Contemporaine*, 19, 1–2 (1988), 35–54.

of Communist ruthlessness during the war. In this context many French-men saw the Cold War as a national conflict that had begun in 1941, rather than an international conflict that began in 1947.

Another important difference between France and its neighbours con-cerned its relations with the wider international community, and particu-larly with America. Belgium, West Germany and Italy were all locked into a system of international co-operation after 1945. Belgium always played a key role in international politics and the country's political journals contained almost as much information on events outside its borders as those occurring within them.[4] In part this interest sprang from the simple fact that Belgium was so small that its most ambitious leaders were naturally inclined to seek an influence beyond the country.[5] It also sprang from the fact that Belgium was too vulnerable to hope to defend itself with its own resources. After 1945 Belgian rulers sought to circumvent this problem through membership of an international defence community working under American aegis. West Germany was even more obviously locked into the international system by the allied occupation, and even after this ended, by the continued presence of allied troops on its soil. Austria was similarly subject to international influence, though the terms on which it finally obtained freedom from foreign occupation prevented it from taking the explicitly atlanticist position assumed by other west European states. Italy had also been occupied, rather than liberated, by allied troops, and American intervention in Italian affairs remained striking. Ginsborg writes: 'American intervention [in the Italian election of April 1948] was breath-taking in its size, its ingenuity and its flagrant contempt for any principle of non-intervention in the internal affairs of another country.'[6] France was more able to detach itself from international events than its eastern neighbours. American influence in France was considerable, but it was less direct than that which America exercised in Germany or Italy.[7]

The response of the French elites to American aid was also different from that of elites elsewhere. In most European countries the elites disliked the results of American influence within their countries. West German right-wingers objected to the denazification and decartelization that the Ameri-cans had imposed,[8] while Belgian royalists objected to what they saw as the

---

[4] See the numerous reports on French politics in the *Revue Belge*.

[5] For the importance that international events could assume in the mind of Belgian politicians see Paul-Henri Spaak, *Combats inachevés. De l'espoir aux déceptions* (Paris, 1969).

[6] Paul Ginsborg, *A history of contemporary Italy: society and politics 1943–1988* (London, 1990), p. 115.

[7] I. Wall, *The United States and the making of post-war France 1945–1954* (Cambridge, 1991).

[8] Berghahn, *The Americanization of West German industry.*

American humiliation of the king and his family.[9] In both Belgium and Germany, the ruling classes saw American intervention in their domestic affairs as something that had to be endured in return for American support in international affairs. In France, by contrast, much of the political right positively welcomed American interference in domestic affairs because they believed that the Americans would be favourable to free market economics and to supporters of the Pétain government, which the USA had recognized until the end of the 1942. The French willingness to throw itself so whole-heartedly into the American camp, which seems so bizarre to historians of international relations,[10] is much less mysterious when viewed in the light of France's internal politics.

Constitutional debate in France also occurred in a very different context from that in which it occurred elsewhere. French historians, especially historians of the right, have been much concerned with constitutional arrangements. However, when placed in an international context, the French debate about the constitution seems less important. No one in post-war France seriously imagined that there was any chance of restoring the monarchy (indeed, the remoteness of such a possibility was illustrated by the decision to allow the pretender to the throne to return from exile). Furthermore, the defence of the Vichy regime led many leaders of the extreme right to adopt the language of republican legality. The consti-tutional debate was no longer between legitimists, bonapartists and republicans, but between those who supported a democratic republic with a weak president and a strong parliament and those who wanted a democra-tic republic with a strong president and a weaker parliament. Yet at the same time three others countries – Belgium, Italy and Spain – were divided by constitutional disputes of a kind that France had not seen since the 1870s. Spanish leaders contemplated the long-term possibility of a restored monarchy (with or without democracy). Italy saw the monarchy that had governed it since unification deposed in 1945. Belgium was gripped by a debate over whether or not the monarchy should be restored and, more particularly, whether the king who had apparently submitted to German demands could be allowed to return. The debate over the Belgian monarchy was sufficiently serious to cause riots and strikes; it also accounted for an important difference between Belgium and France. In Belgium the blame

---

[9] On the resentments of Belgian royalists see two articles by J. E. Helmreich: 'United States policy and the Belgian royal question (March-Oct 1945)', *Revue Belge d'Histoire Contem-poraine*, 9, 1–2 (1978), 1–15; and 'American strategic services planning for Belgium, 1943', *Revue Belge d'Histoire Contemporaine*, 21, 1–2 (1990) 211–224; Robert Capelle, *Dix-huit ans auprès du roi Leopold* (Paris, 1970); J. Pirenne, *Mémoires et notes politiques* (Verviers, 1973), p. 280. Pirenne claims that at one point an American GI guarding the royal family removed a piece of chewing gum from his mouth and handed it to one of the king's sons.

[10] J. Young, *France, the Cold War and the western alliance 1944–1949* (Leicester, 1990), p. 231.

for submission to the Germans was placed on the king alone and, though many people resented such attacks, no one, except a few loyal courtiers, felt that their own fate was tied up with this individual. In France, by contrast, blame for the Vichy government was placed on the whole political class and in particular on those parliamentarians who had voted full powers to Marshal Pétain.

The nature of the French party system was another sign of the peculiarity of France's post-war history. In every other democratic country of western Europe, the reconstruction of bourgeois politics was mainly brought about by single large parties. In the UK this role was played by the Conservative party, membership of which peaked at several hundred thousand during the early 1950s. In Italy, Austria, West Germany, and to a lesser extent Belgium, the role was played by Christian Democrats. In France, it seemed possible for much of the 1940s that a single strong bourgeois party would emerge. The Christian Democrat Mouvement Républicain Populaire (MRP) was the most obvious contender for such a position though the Gaullist Rassemblement du Peuple Français (RPF) and the Parti Républi-cain de la Liberté (PRL) were also seen in such a light by some of their supporters. However, ultimately all these parties failed to live up to the expectations that had been vested in them. Furthermore, small parties and loosely structured alliances such as the Rassemblement des Gauches Républicaines (RGR) and the Centre National des Indépendants (CNIP) became more powerful in the late 1940s and early 1950s. The reasons for the failure of individual parties, and particularly the reasons why Christian Democracy was less successful in France than elsewhere, will be discussed in detail below. There was also a more general reason why the French political system was more fragmented than that of other European countries. In England and Belgium the political parties of the post-war period had all existed before 1940: the war was not seen to have discredited them. In Germany and Italy, by contrast, the war, and the regimes that had taken these countries into war, had discredited most of the old parties so badly that they were replaced by new formations after 1945. France fitted into neither of these categories. New parties did emerge out of the Resistance, but these parties coexisted with groups – such as the Radicals and the Alliance Démocratique (AD) – that had survived from the Third Republic. The result of this was that the war and occupation complicated and fragmented politics in France where it simplified politics everywhere else.

Comparisons between France and other European countries need to take account of the world of interest group representation as well as party politics. Olson has suggested that the most important economic problem of modern times is the fact that certain interests are particularly prone to organize themselves in an effective way. He suggests that such groups obtain benefits for their members at the expense of society as a whole and that appeasement of such groups impedes economic efficiency, except in cases, such as Sweden, where membership of such groups is so widespread that they effectively represent the whole of society. Olson argues that the economic success of post-war continental Europe, relative to that of America or the UK, can be explained by the fact that war, fascism and occupation had destroyed so many interest groups.[11] Olson's arguments are conspicuously inapplicable to France where interest groups remained very powerful in the post-war period. Indeed, in some respects interest groups were strengthened by the events of 1939 to 1945. Workers' unions benefited from the prestige of association with Resistance, while employers' federations benefited from the habits of industrial organization that had grown up during the war, and from the recognition that organizations were needed to respond to Marshall aid and the Monnet plan. It should also be stressed that interest group representation in post-war France was not necessarily associated with low economic growth. Some bodies such as the Association des Bouilleurs de Cru were seen to resist change but others, such as the Conseil National du Patronat Français (CNPF), were sometimes agents of change.

Some political scientists have argued against Olson and suggested that 'centralized' or 'cogent' interest groups are associated, both as a cause and effect, with economic modernization. These arguments have been developed most fully by Maier, who writes: 'What began to evolve was a political economy that I have chosen to call corporatist. This involved the displacement of power from elected representatives or a career bureaucracy to the major forces of European society and economy, sometimes bargaining directly among themselves, sometimes exerting influence through a weakened parliament, and occasionally seeking advantages through new executive authority. In each case corporatism meant the growth of private power and the twilight of sovereignty.' [12] At first glance, Maier's analysis looks plausible with regard to post-war France. Groups like the CNPF certainly exercised a much greater degree of power over their own members than their pre-war equivalents had possessed, while the legislature and governments of the Fourth Republic seemed weak. However, there are important respects in which Maier's model fails to fit the Fourth Republic.

[11] M. Olson, *The rise and decline of nations: economic growth, stagflation and social rigidities* (New Haven and London, 1982); *The logic of collective action: public goods and the theory of groups* (Cambridge, Mass., 1971).

[12] C. S. Maier, *Recasting bourgeois Europe: stabilization in France, Germany and Italy in the decade after World War 1* (Princeton, 1975), p. 9. Maier's arguments are applied to the period after 1945 in 'The two post-war eras and conditions for stability in twentieth century Western Europe', *American Historical Review*, 81, 1 (1981), 327–352.

Maier suggests that corporatism was accompanied by a change in the nature of the state as power shifted from legislature to bureaucracy,[13] and also by an expansion in the activities of the state as it became increasingly involved in economic and social arrangements. However, this increase in the *activity* of the state was accompanied by a decrease in the *power* of the state. Civil servants were reduced to mere rubber stamps as they implemented decisions that had been taken by private interest groups. In France, by contrast, the state remained powerful. Business leaders may not have had much respect for parliamentary politicians, but they were highly aware of the capacity of those politicians to damage their interests. Even more importantly, businessmen remained very obviously subordinate to a powerful administration. There was a 'convergence' between the values of certain business leaders and senior civil servants in the Fourth Republic, but this convergence took place on the civil service's terms and often resulted in a gulf between the leaders of business organizations and the businessmen that they purported to represent. It might be argued that, just as an expanded state in some countries proved a means by which business imposed its will, so expanded, and better disciplined, business organizations in France proved a mechanism by which the state imposed its will.

The reasons why Maier's model fails to work for France are to be found in the French labour movement. Corporatism worked well in West Germany, Belgium, Scandinavia and the UK because all these countries had a high degree of political consensus and moderate labour organizations that were willing to work within the political system. In such countries business leaders found it relatively easy to maintain direct contact with their opposite numbers in the trade unions. When unions and business organizations negotiated, the state had little role to play except to implement or oversee arrangements that had been agreed by the two sides of industry and to provide the proverbial beer and sandwiches. In France such corporatist arrangements were briefly possible between 1943 (when the Comintern was dissolved) and 1947 (when Communist ministers left the government). Corporatism was made possible by the Communist party's willingness to work within a capitalist system, and by the fact that some labour leaders and industrialists had shared a hostility to certain measures of the Vichy government. During this period some business leaders did try to initiate direct contact with the labour movement,[14] and one senior civil servant believed that the CGT/CNPF accords of 1946 were a corporatist attempt to create links between industry and labour that would circumvent the state.[15]

[13] Maier, *Recasting bourgeois Europe*, p. 580, 'The need for brokerage switched the fulcrum of decision making from the legislature as such to ministries or new bureacracies.'

[14] R. Vinen, *The politics of French business 1936–1945* (Cambridge, 1991), p. 134.

[15] L. Franck, *697 ministres. Souvenirs d'un directeur général des prix 1947–1962* (Paris, 1990), p. 14.

In part such corporatist arrangements were undermined by the changes in the labour movement that followed the dismissal of Communist ministers in 1947. However, even if Communist ministers had remained in government or if France had developed a reformist labour leadership, corporatist arrangements would have been undermined by the nature of French labour protest. As Gerard Noiriel has pointed out, the French working class had a particular propensity for spontaneous violent strikes that ran out of the control of union leaders.[16] Under these circumstances French business leaders would never have been able to trust their counterparts in the labour movement to deliver on agreements.[17] Employers' leaders were dependent on the state to protect them in the event of labour disturbance. In labour disputes employers' leaders rarely made contact with their trade union counterparts, but relied on politicians or civil servants to act as intermediaries. In such circumstances the increasing role of interest group organizations was accompanied by an ever increasing power exercised by the state.

The last element that requires consideration when comparing France with the rest of Europe is economic management. French economic planning in the post-war period has often been seen as an unqualified success and is presented as a model that other countries would do well to imitate.[18] In this context it is well to remember that in the first few years after the war France seemed one of the least successful economies in Europe and that the policies adopted during these years were often the products of weakness rather than strength.[19] The first weakness of the French economy, relative to that of Belgium, Germany and the UK, was a small banking sector, and it could be argued that the leading role assumed by the French state sprang partly from the fact that private banks were unable to co-ordinate and stimulate economic growth as they did elsewhere. France was less industrialized than Britain, Germany or Belgium and it also suffered from the fact that economically backward sectors were politically powerful and therefore well placed to resist measures that damaged their interests. It was in large measure this fact that ruled out the kind of vigorous

---

[16] Gerard Noiriel, *Workers in French society in the 19th and 20th centuries* (New York, 1990).

[17] A good example of the way in which corporatist arrangments were undermined by the spontaneous nature of French labour protest is provided by Henri Weber. In 1968 François Ceyrac, the president of the CNPF, wished to have a minor operation. At a meeting with union leaders in February 1968, he asked whether the spring would be an appropriate time to go into hospital. His interlocutors assured him that 'May will be calm'. Three months later France was gripped by the most serious strikes to affect it for more than twenty years. H. Weber, *Le parti des patrons. Le CNPF (1946–1986)* (Paris, 1986), p. 161.

[18] D. Marquand, *The unprincipled society* (London, 1988), p. 106.

[19] The French business commentator Auguste Detoeuf had written during the 1930s that 'France is statist a little by weakness and much by necessity': cited in Henry W. Ehrmann, *Organized business in France* (Princeton, 1957), p. 284.

monetary policies that were pursued in Belgium in 1944 or in Germany in 1948.[20] France appeased its shopkeepers and peasants at the price of continuous inflation that was far worse than that which the appeasement of unionized workers in Britain was alleged to have produced; efforts to resist inflationary pressures (such as those of Mayer in 1948 or Pinay in 1952) had limited success and provoked vigorous protests.

The kind of state economic intervention that occurred in France was also different from that which occurred in other countries. The country whose economic problems most resembled those of France was Italy. However, there was a difference between the solutions that the rulers of these two countries adopted. In Italy the distribution of state investment was kept in the hands of a political party (i.e. the Christian Democrats). This meant that large sums were spent on projects in the Italian South that were of political rather than economic value. In France, by contrast, the distribution of aid remained largely in the hands of the civil service elite, and some close allies of this elite in business organizations. This meant that no French conservative party gained the chance to buy itself a basis of mass support, but it also meant that money was directed at more clearly economically useful projects.[21] English state intervention was also subject to political pressures (though of a different kind from those that existed in Italy). The Labour government was widely expected to increase living standards, and such expectations undermined attempts of 'supply side socialists' to increase the productivity of British industry.[22] Even the Conservative government that came to power in 1951 was constrained from reducing welfare spending, whether by the conversion of its leadership to consensus politics or by simple inability to dismantle a structure that had been established.[23] By contrast with Britain, French state spending was concentrated on economic rather than social objectives and on heavy *industries de base* rather than the satisfaction of consumer needs. It was not until the

[20] On Belgian monetary policies see Léon Dupriez, *Monetary restoration in Belgium* (New York, 1947). For an interesting examination of the reasons why such policies would have been inappropriate in France see R. Courtin, 'L'expérience monétaire belge', *Les Cahiers Politiques*, 7 (1945), 47–58.

[21] On the difference between the distribution of state money in Italy and France see S. Tarrow, *Between centre and periphery: grassroot politicians in France and Italy* (New Haven, 1977).

[22] The most vigorous statement of the case that the Labour government of 1945 sacrificed economic reconstruction to social aims is made by C. Barnett in *The audit of war* (London, 1986). J. Tomlinson states the opposite case in 'Mr Attlee's supply side socialism' *Economic History Review*, 46, 1 (1993), 1–22. For a sceptical look at the extent to which the Conservative party changed between 1945 and 1951 see J. Ramsden, 'A party for owners or a party for earners? How far did the British Conservative party really change after 1945?', *Transactions of the Royal Historical Society*, 37 (1987), 49–63.

[23] H. Jones, 'New tricks for an old dog? The Conservatives and social policy 1951–5', in A. Gorst, L. Johnman and W. Scott Lucas (eds.), *Contemporary British history 1931–61: politics and the limits of policy* (London, 1991), pp. 33–43.

1960s that the *commissariat général du plan* would concern itself with mainly social objectives.

The comparisons made in the preceding pages illustrate two points. The politics of Fourth Republic France cannot be considered in isolation. French leaders were confronting problems that arose elsewhere in Europe and they were aware that they worked in an international context. However, this does not mean that French politics can simply be explained as the product of broad international trends. External pressures interacted with domestic French constraints and preoccupations in a complicated manner; anti-Communism and atlanticism often took a peculiarly French form and even the most apparently internationalist French politicians sometimes had motives that would have seemed strange to the foreign politicians with whom they co-operated. The only way to understand these peculiarities is to embark on a detailed study of French political institutions.

4   Notables

Its [the right's] characteristic representatives are local personalities. They convey the general view of their village or their neighbourhood. They are granted their mandates much more by virtue of their reputation than by virtue of their membership of a party ... They are the archetypes of notables, great and small, who can become mayors, members of the *conseil général*, deputies or senators on the strength of their prestigious ancestors. When they arrive at the Palais Bourbon or the Palais Luxembourg, they are suspicious of those who recruit to party groups – the title that fits them best is that of Independents.[1]

The MRP has only a few ... of those 'notables': large landowners, veterinary surgeons, doctors, artisans and shopkeepers, in contact with the country who, until recently, formed almost the only structure of local politics. It is they who still hold the majority of electoral mandates, whence the strength of the Radicals in the *conseil de la république*.[2]

Visiting the village notable to ask him to stand for the *conseil général* in a few months under our colours [one was told]: 'here you know extreme positions are not liked'. The notable had just retired as a colonel or inspector of education and he wanted something to do; or he had quarrelled with the incumbent councillor over some local matter and suddenly become interested in politics; or again he had always been 'for the General' and he supported our action, but in standing for election did he not risk losing the credit that his family had built up over such a long time and which he was allowing us to benefit from?[3]

Politicians themselves often explained the political history of the Fourth Republic in terms of notables The ideal notable was someone who drew power from his own resources – wealth, reputation, professional contacts and family – rather than from the official position that he occupied in the state or a political party. Notable influence was seen to account for the diminishing success of disciplined parties like the Mouvement Républicain

[1] Georges Riond, *Chroniques d'un autre monde* (Paris, 1979), p. 225.
[2] R. Plantade, 'Le MRP', in J. Fauvet and H. Mendras (eds.), *Les paysans et la politique dans la France contemporaine* (Paris, 1958), pp. 119–130.
[3] O. Guichard, *Mon général* (Paris, 1980), p. 254.

Populaire (MRP) and the Rassemblement du Peuple Français (RPF) and for the increasing prominence assumed by loose groups like the Independents and the Rassemblement des Gauches Républicaines (RGR). But the fact that notability was seen to be of considerable, and increasing, importance in the mid-twentieth century raises some important questions. Max Weber, writing in the early part of the century, had argued that notability was an archaic form of politics and that it would be eroded by the growth of organized parties and the state bureaucracy. Halévy entitled his history of late nineteenth-century France *La fin des notables*.[4] The particular mechanisms by which notable power had been exercised in the nineteenth century had largely ceased to exist by 1945. Urbanization and industrialization had broken down many of the constraints that had tied men to employers and landlords, the ballot was recognized to be genuinely secret, and large multi-member constituencies made it impossible for any individual to have personal contact with the majority of voters in an area. Most importantly, Fourth Republic France did see an increase in the state bureaucracy and, for a time at least, an increase in party organizations. This chapter will argue that notability was important in Fourth Republic politics, but that this notability was not the same as that of the nineteenth century. Beneath their carefully cultivated image as powerful and independent men, most Fourth Republic notables drew their power not from their own resources but from their ability to act as intermediaries between institutions, including those institutions (the state and party organizations) that they often disparaged.

Sources for the examination of notability pose a problem. Influence that was exercised in an informal or irregular way is hard to trace.[5] Many studies, especially those that adopt an ethnological approach, often depend on the evidence provided by the testimony of notables themselves.[6] There are dangers in this approach. Nathaniel Leites' work on parliamentary politics has shown how often the Palais Bourbon became 'a house without windows' in which political deals and manoeuvres had little impact on anyone other than the parliamentarians themselves.[7] Similar reservations

[4] D. Halévy, *La fin des notables* (Paris, 1930).

[5] Some of the problems involved in studying notability are outlined in S. Silverman, 'Patronage as myth', in E. Gellner and J. Waterbury (eds.), *Patrons and clients in Mediterranean societies* (London, 1977), pp. 7–19.

[6] The tendency of works on notable politics to reproduce the notables' own self-image is particularly marked in the study of the ethnologist Abélès: the use of informal research techniques (largely based on private converations) inevitably ends up laying a heavy emphasis on 'informal politics' (in which power is exercised largely through private conversations). Abélès himself writes, 'the anthropologist works on the principle of accepting everything that he is told'. M. Abélès, *Quiet days in Burgundy* (Cambridge, 1991), p. 73.

[7] N. Leites and C. Melnik, *The house without windows: France selects a president* (White Plains, 1958).

can be expressed about local politics. Village king-makers may have been motivated by vanity or self-interest to present themselves as more powerful than they really were. Those who portray themselves as hard-headed fixers may be as dishonest, or self-deluding, as those who present themselves as civically minded altruists.[8]

However, there are two good sources for the study of notable influence (or at least for the study of its intersections with national politics and the state). The first of these is provided by the archives of Paris politicians who kept lists of people in the provinces likely to be of use to them or their party.[9] A particularly useful list for historians of the Fourth Republic is that drawn up in 1945 by the leaders of the Fédération Républicaine (FR) when they were trying to reconstruct their party. The list contains a total of 104 names with connections in seventy-four departments of mainland France and Algeria.[10] The FR followed this up by sending a representative to important regions (Marseilles, Lyons and the Loire) to talk to particular individuals.[11]

A second source for the study of notability is provided by elected office. It was widely recognized that notability was associated with the holding of such office (whether as a reflection of informal powers or as a means of enhancing power). Particularly important in this context were the departmental *conseils généraux*. Representatives to these bodies were elected by each canton. Since cantonal elections involved single individuals running for office in their immediate locality, it was widely assumed that notables would do especially well in such elections. Mayors, especially mayors of small towns or communes, were also seen as notables. National elections provide another source for the study of notability. Party managers knew that usually only the top one or two people on each electoral list stood any serious chance of being elected. They therefore often filled the bottom three or four places on the list with notables who, it was hoped, would attract the support of voters from a particular area or group.

Several characteristics emerge from the study of local officials and *co-listiers*. The first of these characteristics related to family origins. Notables liked to emphasize that they were the product of dynasties that had been prominent in their area for generations.[12] Electoral declarations made

---

[8] An example of self-delusion on the part of notables was the widespread expectation that the MRP would lose large numbers of seats in the 1946 elections.

[9] Flandin, for example, kept a notebook containing the names of innkeepers, mayors, etc., in his native Yonne. Abélès, *Quiet days in Burgundy*, p. 54.

[10] Archives Nationales (AN), 317 AP 73, report cited at meeting of 25 October 1945.

[11] AN, 317 AP 73, undated report.

[12] In his conversations with Abélès, Devoir (the former mayor of a small town in the Yonne) laid great emphasis on the fact that his family had been prominent in the area since the eighteenth century: Abélès, *Quiet days in Burgundy*. On the perceived importance of notable 'dynasties' see S. Maresca, *Les dirigeants paysans* (Paris, 1983).

much of family associations. It was reported that Paul Reydellet, third on the list of the RGR in the Ain in the legislative elections of 1951, came from: 'An old family of ... the Gex area because his uncles include senator Eugène Chanel and the former *conseiller général* of Gex: M. Montbarbon.'[13] One of the Radical candidates in the Allier was described as 'the great nephew of senator Gacon',[14] and the second place on *chanoine* Kir's *liste de concentration républicaine* in the Côte d'Or was held by Colette Tainturier, daughter of a senator and daughter-in-law of a long-standing member of the *conseil général*.[15]

However, the role of family in establishing notability deserves to be regarded with a certain amount of scepticism. Those with family connections were keen to advertise the fact, while outsiders or recent arrivals who built up local power bases kept quiet about their origins.[16] Objective evidence suggests that the second category may have been more numerous than the first. Almost three-quarters of mayors who responded to a survey of 1954 were not related to previous mayors of their towns.[17]

A better verified characteristic of notables was age. It took time to build up a reputation and range of contacts: the average age of *conseillers généraux* in 1945 was 50 years and 11 months.[18] The age of Radical *conseillers généraux* (54) and of *modérés* (53) was substantially higher than that of *conseillers* from the new and left-wing parties.[19] The average age of mayors who responded to a survey in 1954 was 54 years and 7 months.[20] Stability of office holding was another characteristic of local power brokers: 25 per cent of *conseillers généraux* elected in 1945 (i.e. 734 men in total) had previously held the same office in the Third Republic,[21] and the average *conseiller général* in the Côte d'Or held office for thirteen years.[22]

Personality was an important aspect of notability: charm and wit were needed. Paul Seguin, a power broker behind Edgar Faure in the Jura, was a travelling salesman who had toyed with the idea of becoming a music hall

[13] *Recueil des textes authentiques des programmes et engagements électoraux des députés proclamés élus à la suite des élections générales du 17 juin 1951* (generally known as *Barodet*), entry for Ain, p. 2.   [14] Ibid., Allier, p. 29.   [15] Ibid., Côte d'Or, p. 172.

[16] Abélès, *Quiet days in Burgundy*, p. 83 reveals that Daniel Dolfuss became a power-broker in the Yonne although he had only recently moved to the area. Dolfuss, however, emphasized his non-local origins far less than men like Devoir emphasized their family's implantation in the area.

[17] M. Agulhon, L. Girard, J. L. Robert and W. Serman (eds.), *Les maires en France du consulat à nos jours* (Paris, 1986), p. 64; 19 per cent of mayors were not related to any previous incumbent, 6 per cent were related to one, 1 per cent were related to two or more previous mayors and 74 per cent failed to reply.

[18] Marie-Hélène Marchand, *Les conseillers généraux en France depuis 1945* (Paris, 1970), p. 45.   [19] Ibid., p. 51.

[20] Agulhon et al., *Les maires en France*, p. 39.   [21] Ibid., p. 51

[22] R. Long, *Les élections législatives en Côte d'Or depuis 1870* (Paris, 1958), p. 265.

artist; Faure gave the following description of him: 'He had a taste for social life, a sense of collective interests, a talent for being interested in others.'[23] Local heroes could always be politically useful and the Resistance had given many notables a chance to enhance their reputations in the area.[24] The occupation also sometimes destroyed the reputation of notables: the Farjon dynasty in Boulogne never recovered its power after one of its members betrayed a Resistance network to the Gestapo.[25]

Personal wealth underwrote the influence of some notables. Candidates in parliamentary elections often raised funds at local level and were interested in individuals who might be capable of providing such funds. Five of the notables listed by the FR in 1945 were described as industrialists, financiers or large landowners. The detailed report submitted by an FR representative sent on a tour of the provinces was more explicit about the need for electoral funds: 'Rastouin stays on the political sidelines, but he is one of the financial figures whose support is indispensable.'[26] One form of business of special relevance to local politics was newspaper proprietorship. Local dynasties often controlled newspapers: in the Yonne the Flandin family maintained the *Revue d'Yonne* while the Ribière clan owned *la Constitution*. An FR report on politics in the Eure et Loir suggested that the party leaders should 'come to terms with the people who control *la Dépêche de Chartres*, the editor [of which is] M. Berthelin'.[27]

Notability was also linked to professions. Certain sorts of work provided the opportunity to make contact with local people, do favours and earn respect. Medicine provided the most obvious example of such a profession: 382 out of 3,067 *conseillers généraux* elected in 1945 were doctors (almost two-thirds of whom were Radicals or *modérés*). Doctors had the special advantage of familiarity with social security regulations which put them in an excellent position to protect the interests of their clientele.[28] Pharmacists also had the chance to build up a range of contacts and often featured on the electoral lists of successful candidates. In rural areas, agricultural experts frequently featured on electoral lists. Veterinary surgeons were another

---

[23] E. Faure. *Mémoires*. I: *Avoir toujours raison ... c'est un grand tort* (Paris, 1984), p. 160.

[24] Ibid. Seguin had sung the Marseillaise outside the local *Wehrmacht* on 14 July 1943, and one of Faure's other backers had earned a reputation by rescuing a drowning girl; ibid., p. 176.

[25] Olivier Chovaux, 'La dynastie des Farjon à Boulogne-sur-Mer. De la politique des affaires aux affaires politiques (1850–1979)', *Revue du Nord*, 72, 228 (1990), 875–890.

[26] Undated report in AN, 317 AP 73.

[27] AN, 317 AP 73, 25 October 1945.

[28] Marchand, *Les conseillers généraux*, p. 63, on the link between the practice of medicine and the ability to help the protégés negotiate the social security system. See also Marion Démosier, *Rapport de recherche pour le musée du vin de Bourgogne à Beaune*. 'Les saints protecteurs de la vigne en Côte d'Or. Analyse anthropologique d'un culte. Nouvelles fonctions, nouvelles formes' (1991), no pagination.

important profession in certain areas,[29] and Henri Queuille, an arch political fixer of the Third and Fourth Republic and himself a doctor, took such trouble to cultivate this group that he earned himself a long obituary in the *Bulletin de l'Académie Vétérinaire de France*.[30]

Certain professions seemed to enjoy special power in particular areas. Doctors were particularly likely to become *conseillers généraux* in the south of France, for example.[31] Sometimes particular professions enjoyed such a concentration of power in particular areas that personal contacts seem likely to be the explanation: for example all four of the men contacted by the FR in the Dordogne were doctors[32] and three out five of the candidates on the electoral list of the RGR in the Aisne were connected to the legal profession (as notary, clerk of the court and bailiff).[33]

Professional organizations provided another mechanism by which notability operated. Electoral declarations made much of candidates' roles in such associations. The second candidate on the list of the RGR in the Ain was the president of the national veterinary association; the third on the same list was described thus: 'His activity in his profession has earned him the confidence of his colleagues whose votes carried him to the vice presidency of the national union of confectioners', while the fourth was president of a livestock association.[34]

Office holding in professional bodies was not just a sign of power; it was also a means by which power could be created or reinforced. Associations often controlled access to mutual aid funds designed to tide members over bad times; sometimes the very facilities that were needed for the practice of certain professions – such as communal wine cellars – were controlled by associations. For this reason the presidency of a local association could give its holder substantial powers to grant or withhold favours and to create a clientele.

Notables had a horror of controversy. They disliked disagreement and division: they stressed that their power came from a universally acknowledged prestige in the community and not from any sordid political campaigning. The reality was far from this picture of serene and unquestioned authority. An illusion of consensus could be maintained only because vigorous efforts were made behind the scenes to settle or quell

[29] As late as 1980, the proprietor of a food processing company recognized the importance of maintaining good relations with the local vet, who was also mayor of the town. P. Calixte, interviewed in L. Duroy and S. Moles, *Paroles de patrons* (Paris, 1980), p. 156.

[30] R. Fleckinger, 'Henri Queuille et les vétérinaires', *Bulletin de l'Academie Vétérinaire de France*, 1985. Coste-Floret told Edgar Faure that the Radical Party was 'bon pour les vétérinaires': Faure, *Avoir toujours raison*, p. 152. When Faure stood as a Radical candidate the third candidate on his list was indeed a vet.

[31] Marchand, *Les conseillers généraux*, p. 65.

[32] AN, 317 AP 73, report cited at meeting of 25 October 1945.   [33] *Barodet*, p. 14.

[34] *Barodet*, p. 2.

conflicts before they became public. The mayor of Vienne sometimes adjourned meetings of the town council when controversial matters were discussed so that a deal could be fixed up *dans la coulisse*.[35]

Olivier d'Harcourt provides an interesting example of the way in which 'notable' status was founded on careful deals to avoid controversy. D'Harcourt looked like an archetypal notable; he belonged to a noble family that had been prominent in the area since the eighteenth century, he became mayor of his village in 1929 and in 1951 was elected to the departmental *conseil général*. In fact d'Harcourt's family or personal prestige had not been enough to earn him uncontested authority: his position had been challenged by a popular local ironmonger who had looked set to be elected mayor in 1929. D'Harcourt had only saved his position by coming to terms with the ironmonger, who was appointed his adjoint in return for withdrawing his candidacy.[36]

Notables set much store by the fact that the professional bodies from which they derived much of their power were 'non-controversial'. Elections took place in chambers and tribunals of commerce, but they were usually uncontested. This air of consensus was easily maintained because participation levels in professional bodies were so low that matters could be settled by a small clique. In moments of controversy, such as the aftermath of the Popular Front or the Poujadist campaign of the 1950s, *listes de contestation* were put forward which were able to mobilize greater participation in professional elections than was normal. The striking successes of these rebels exposed the vulnerability of notable power when its 'uncontested prestige' was challenged. The notables expressed outrage at the assault on the 'impartiality' of their associations, but they often accompanied expressions of outrage with discreet efforts to come to terms with their challengers. Once again 'apoliticism' was shown to be the product of backstairs deals.

One of the most important claims made by notables was that they were independent of any party organization. Whereas party militants worked within a single party and drew whatever power and prestige they possessed from that party, notables felt free to maintain relations with several parties and stressed that it was the political parties who were dependent on them not vice versa. The organizational weakness of conservative parties and the rivalry between those parties did allow notables to indulge in some

[35] Pierre Clément and Nelly Xydias, *Vienne sur le Rhône. La ville et les habitants, situations et attitudes. Sociologie d'une cité française* (Paris, 1955), p. 133.
[36] Alain Corbin, 'Les aristocrates et la communauté villageoise. Les maires d'Essay (1791–1986)', in Agulhon et al., *Les maires en France*, p. 361. Abélès mentions that Jean Devoir, one of the Yonne notables that he studied, had been involved in a similar local dispute with the mayor of his village, which had caused him to withdraw from local politics for ten years. Abélès, *Quiet days in Burgundy*, p. 3.

remarkably cavalier behaviour. Powerful individuals often exercised their local influence in favour of parties other than those to which they themselves belonged: André Baud (a member of the FR) supported the Radicals in the Jura;[37] Flandin supported the Independents in the Yonne though his own Alliance Démocratique (AD) was part of the RGR.

The independence of many notables from any particular party loyalty was important because it allowed them to serve as intermediaries who could fix up the inter-party deals on which conservatism so often depended. J. Demarescaux, the editor of the *Indicateur des Flandres*, wrote to Paul Reynaud during the 1951 elections in the following terms: 'From the beginning of discussions over the composition of electoral lists, friends approached me to ask me, in view of my non-political nature [*en ma qualité d'apolitique*], to bring about the union of all the national lists.'[38]

However, it is easy to overstate the extent to which notables exercised power over political parties. The truth was that political parties could play notables off against each other more easily than notables could play political parties off against each other. *Chanoine* Kir, mayor of Dijon, was one of the best-known local power brokers in France, but in 1951 he overplayed his hand and found himself excluded from the lists of all the major parties. Furthermore, the Independents and the RPF used another local notable (Thénard) to fix up an *apparentement* deal that would leave Kir isolated. Kir managed to scrape into parliament on a list made up of his own supporters, but it was a close run thing and by 1956 he had made his peace with the CNIP again. In most areas where there was no outstanding figure like Kir the position of party managers was even stronger. They could pick and choose the men with whom they would be associated from among a large pool of potential 'notables': when Edgar Faure wanted a representative of clerical conservatism to strengthen his list, he simply picked a likely looking individual from the departmental gazette.[39]

The institutions that were most important of all to notable power were those connected to the state. This was a fact that many notables preferred to ignore. The parties with which notables were most associated (i.e. the Radicals and the Independents) proclaimed themselves hostile to state power, and notables liked to emphasize that their authority was attached to themselves personally and not to any institution with which they were associated. They saw the holding of official office as a reflection rather than a source of their power. However, in reality the state was essential to notable power. Many of the bodies with which notables were associated,

[37] Faure, *Avoir toujours raison*, p. 171.
[38] AN, 74 AP 32, Demarescaux to Reynaud, dated 12 June 1951.
[39] Faure, *Avoir toujours raison*, p. 177.

such as army recruiting boards, were mechanisms of the state.[40] The chambers of commerce, agriculture and the artisans were state regulated bodies.

Access to means of lobbying or manipulating the state became particularly important during the Fourth Republic because post-war reconstruction, Marshall aid and new social security arrangements meant that there were much larger sums of government money available than ever before. Effective notables had to show their clients that they were capable of persuading state authorities to build roads or create jobs in the area: 'The notable, in this perspective, is a man who disposes of a certain power to act on the apparatus of the state at privileged levels and, in return, sees his power increased by these contacts when they produce results.'[41]

Notables' relations with national politics were as ambiguous as their relations with the state. In spite of the language of local interests with which notables described and justified their action, local and national politics were intimately linked. A high proportion of national politicians (at least those in conservative parties) were also local notables; the proportion of local notables who also played a role at national level was, of course, much smaller, but all local notables sought to maintain contact with national politicians. Twenty-five of the notables contacted by the FR in 1945 were also deputies.[42] Thirty- five of the men elected as *conseillers généraux* in 1945 (and twenty-five of those representing bourgeois parties) were also deputies; a further six of them were senators.[43] By 1946, 28 per cent of deputies were also *conseillers généraux*, and by 1951 the figure had risen to 31 per cent; among senators the proportion of *conseillers généraux* was 44 per cent in 1946, rising to 44.5 per cent in 1948, and falling again to 40 per cent in 1952.[44]

The relations between local notability and national office holding were complicated. Sometimes an ambitious individual might use local institutions as a springboard and support for a national political career. Michel Debré wrote in 1955: 'It is an almost intolerable handicap for a parliamentarian not to have a local mandate at the same time.'[45] The *cursus honorum* leading to national politics explains why some men obtained local office at

---

[40] Jean Devoir attributed part of his power in the Yonne to his role in the army recruiting board: Abélès, *Quiet days in Burgundy*, p. 8.

[41] Pierre Grémion, *Le pouvoir périphérique. Bureaucrates et notables dans le système politique français* (Paris, 1976), p. 166.

[42] AN, 317 AP 73, report cited at meeting of 25 October 1945.

[43] *Le Monde*, 2 October 1945.   [44] Marchand, *Les conseillers généraux*, p. 161.

[45] M. Debré, 'Trois caractéristiques du système parlementaire français', *Revue Française de Science Politique*, January–March (1955), 22, cited in Marchand, *Les conseillers généraux*, p. 161.

such a young age – Roger Duchet (secretary of the Independents) had been mayor of Beaune at 26. However, such people were exceptional. Most local office holders could not hope to make a career at national level. They were restrained by three things. The first of these was age: the average *conseiller général* was eleven years older than the average deputy in 1945. The second restraint was provided by professional background: professions that gave the wide range of contacts valued at local level did not give the liberal culture or rhetorical abilities that were valued at national level. Generally speaking veterinary surgeons, pharmacists and tradesmen had to accept that the Palais Bourbon was reserved for lawyers and journalists (only doctors were able to operate effectively at both political levels and even they were much more heavily represented in local institutions than in parliament).[46]

A third category of notables who could not hope to enter national politics was created by the special circumstances of the post-war period. This category was composed of men who had previously held political office, but who had been declared ineligible because of their support for the Vichy government. In some departments, such as the Côte d'Or, all deputies who had been in place in the 1940 period fell into this category. Many ineligibles subsequently regained their right to stand for election but some were condemned to confine their political action to the informal sphere for several years and their own locality often provided a prime forum for such behind the scenes manipulation (as the manoeuvres of the former prime minister Pierre Etienne Flandin in the Yonne demonstrated).[47]

Just as there were many notables who had no national dimension to their power, so there were a few national politicians who had no local influence. The RPF deputy, General Billotte, fell into this category. He was a distinguished soldier, but he lacked local contacts. The RPF organizers recognized that he was a '*parachuté*, albeit one with a glorious past'.[48] In 1951 Billotte was swept to power by the RPF success of that year. However, even then, some local notables took care to remind him of the primacy of local considerations: one mayor said that he would support the RPF not because of Billotte or even de Gaulle, but because he had been at primary school with one of Billotte's *co-listiers*.[49] Once elected Billotte neglected the

---

[46] The exception that proved this rule was the Poujadist campaign of the mid-1950s. A large number of vets, dispensing chemists and similar people were swept into the National Assembly by Poujadist success in the 1956 election, but they proved very unsuccessful as deputies. See Annie Collovald, 'Les Poujadistes, ou l'échec en politique', *Revue d'Histoire Moderne et Contemporaine*, 36 (1989), 113–133.

[47] Flandin's post-war career is discussed by Abélès in *Quiet days in Burgundy*.

[48] Guichard, *Mon général*, p. 265.

[49] P. Billotte, *Le passé au futur* (Paris, 1979), p. 78. On Billotte's career see, Long, *Les élections législatives*, p. 271.

significance of this episode. He became absorbed in his new role as minister of defence and neglected his constituency until it was too late. The secretary of the CNIP, to which Billotte had transferred his loyalties, tried to persuade the general to visit the Côte d'Or and obtain notable support for his list, but this advice came too late and Billotte was defeated in 1956.[50] Léon Noel was another RPF deputy who suffered from a neglect of local considerations. Noel did begin with good local contacts in his constituency, the Yonne; he was a member of the Flandin family that had dominated the area before the war. However, Noel's professional life, as a diplomat, had focused his attention on national and international matters at the expense of local ones and in 1956 he too was defeated.

Abélès concludes, from Léon Noel's fate, that real power lay with local notables rather than national politicians.[51] However, in reality there was an interaction between power at the local and national level. Just as some politicians could use the support of notables to propel themselves into parliament, so a skilful man could use office holding in Paris to build up a local power base. The most striking example of success in this field was provided by the early career of François Mitterrand. Few men can have had a less promising introduction to an area than Mitterrand had to his constituency in the Nièvre. He was not a local man (he had been born in the Charente); at 28 he was too young to have acquired a range of contacts and he had never practised any profession other than politics or journalism. Mitterrand was only placed on the electoral list of the RGR as a result of deals stitched up among Paris based politicians two days before the deadline for the registering of candidatures, and, when he arrived in Nevers, the prefect was initially reluctant to authorize the candidature of an outsider.[52]

When Mitterrand had secured election to parliament, he used his position to earn himself favour with the very professional and agricultural groups who were the key to local notable politics. The Société Syndicale des Pharmaciens de la Nièvre recognized the sympathy that Mitterrand had shown to their cause,[53] and institutions such as the *comices agricoles* or the *comité d'étude et d'aménagement du Morvan* could all count on Mitterrand's active interest, even when he was minister of the interior.[54] Mitterrand remained a representative for the Nièvre, with only one brief interlude, until 1981. Indeed, when Mitterrand was removed from national office during

---

[50] He only went to his constituency late in the campaign by which stage many notables refused to support his list. Roger Duchet, *La république épinglée* (Paris, 1975), p. 188.

[51] On Noel in the Yonne see Abélès, *Quiet days in Burgundy*, p. 65.

[52] F.-O. Giesbert, *François Mitterrand ou la tentation de l'histoire* (Paris, 1977), p. 91.

[53] AN, 412 AP 65, circular of the Société Syndicale des Pharmaciens de la Nièvre, dated January 1955.

[54] For documents relating to Mitterrand's various local activities see AN, 412 AP 65.

the Fifth Republic he was able to find consolation in a second career as a Nièvre notable, becoming president of the departmental *conseil général* and mayor of Château-Chinon.[55]

Edger Faure also used his success in national politics to build up a local position. Like Mitterrand, he was given the chance to try for a seat (the Jura) as a result of deals struck in Paris. He too began as an outsider but, once he had been elected as a deputy, he cultivated local people and mannerisms and was elected as mayor of Port-Lesney in 1947 and as a member of the *conseil général* in 1949.[56] Faure made such great efforts to steep himself in local culture that he came to acquire a stock of anecdotes about local events that had occurred years before he set foot in the Jura;[57] he was later to write of the 'second identity' that his 'belated implantation in the provinces' had brought about.[58] Not only did Faure turn himself into a notable, he also showed how power emanating from Paris could benefit other local power brokers. A Jura notable, Charles Laurent-Thouverey, had provided Faure with local support (he served as his *co-listier* and instructed him in local history). After Faure's election, Laurent-Thouvery benefited from the support of the rising young minister to help him become a mayor and eventually a senator.[59]

Jacques Chaban-Delmas managed the early stages of his career in a somewhat similar manner to Mitterrand and Faure. Like them he was a young man who had first come to prominence in the Resistance. After the war he was elected as a deputy for a town (Bordeaux) in which he did not have an established reputation or range of contacts. However, Chaban, unlike many of his RPF colleagues, took care to cultivate his local power as much as his national career. He was elected mayor of the town and launched a campaign for modernization, which involved spending a large amount of tax-payers' money. Eventually Chaban was so successful that he became the archetypal example of notability: a political scientist studying Bordeaux was told that 'nothing can threaten the hegemony of the deputy/mayor'.[60]

Mitterrand, Chaban-Delmas and Faure were all exceptional men, as their later careers showed. But they were not unique in their capacity to build up local support from unpromising beginnings. René Mayer became deputy for Constantine in 1946 as a last minute expedient after he had failed to find a mainland constituency, but he developed such good contacts there

---

[55] For Mitterrand's career see D. S. Bell and B. Criddle, *The French Socialist party: the emergence of a party of government* (2nd edition, Oxford, 1988), p. 300.

[56] Faure, *Avoir toujours raison*, p. 307.   [57] Ibid., p. 165

[58] After his election, Faure joked that 'I have just become a Franc-Comtois by birth': ibid., p. 181.   [59] Ibid., p. 177.

[60] Jacques Lagroye, *Société et politique. J. Chaban-Delmas à Bordeaux* (Paris, 1973), p. 52.

that he was regarded as the 'manager' of the department by 1951. Similarly when Robert Buron became deputy for Mayenne in 1945 his only local contact was provided by the uncle of his wife. Yet he became so integrated into the area that he entitled his political memoirs *La Mayenne et moi*.[61]

The interaction between local and national politics was made especially important in Fourth Republic France by the role of the department. The department was important to national politicians because it served as the constituency for parliamentary elections. However, the department was equally important to local politicians because the *conseil général* and other essential agencies operated at departmental level. The problem for local politicians was that an average department had a population of almost half a million; it was clearly impossible for any individual to dominate such a large area through personal reputation or professional contacts. Local politicians had to conquer the departmental level from below as much as national politicians had to conquer it from above.[62]

The result of this was that alliances were formed between local notables and would-be parliamentarians, alliances that were often cemented by the inclusion of the notables on the candidates' electoral list. The parliamentary candidate gained from whatever prestige his backers were able to command within their own communes, cantons or professions. A wise candidate took care to ensure that his notable backers appealed to different areas of the department or different sections of its population so that he accumulated as much support as possible. In return the notable backers acquired prestige at departmental level, which would help them make bids for the presidency of the *conseil général* or *comité d'étude départemental*. At best they might achieve such prestige from their contacts with a powerful Paris politician who was well placed to grant favours to his friends. Even an unsuccessful candidacy might bring advantages to notable supporters: the posters, speeches and official electoral declarations of the campaign would have brought their names to the attention of voters throughout the department in a way that years of personal contact could never have done.

The Weberian interpretation of notability hinges on sharp distinctions: between the world of notables (archaic, localized and personal) and the world of bureaucracy and party politics (modern, statist, organized and centralized). The evidence of this chapter suggests that this sharp distinction cannot be applied to the Fourth Republic. Notables may have presented themselves as pragmatic and independent men who opposed the ideologies of party politicians, but this presentation took place in a political

---

[61] Robert Buron, *La Mayenne et moi ou la démocratie chrétienne au socialisme* (Paris, 1978), p. 9.
[62] For example Faure's *co-listier* Seguin was mayor of Lors-le-Saunier but, by his own admission, little known in the department as a whole. Faure, *Avoir toujours raison*, p. 161.

system where pragmatic 'apoliticism' was widely regarded as a form of ideology, and in which at least one political party existed to group 'non-party' men. Divisions between the state and civil society were similarly blurred: some bodies, such as chambers of commerce, functioned as both private societies and agencies of government.[63] Even a supremely modernizing venture such as the Monnet plan (which involved investing large amounts of state money in certain key sectors) might help to reinforce archaic notable power as central government money was distributed by agricultural associations or local government agencies.[64]

The ambiguity and contradictions outlined above illustrate the nature of notable power in the Fourth Republic. The key to notable influence did not lie in any single discrete sphere. Rather it lay in interaction between different levels of power: between the formal and informal, the private and the state, the centre and the localities. Notable power often seemed considerable because the mythology of conservatism placed such heavy emphasis on localism and because it often suited national politicians to present their local associates as big fish. However, the reality was that the foundations of notable power were fragile. As professional intermediaries they were constantly dependent on other bodies and institutions for their power. Some notables had enough informal power to survive at local level without access to the state (this was why conservatism at local level survived in 1945 when it seemed at a low ebb nationally) but this power was limited and most of all it was short lived: a notable who exercised no power other than that of his own personal reputation would soon find that even that was gone.

A reassessment of notable influence can lead to a reassessment of Fourth Republic politics. It is tempting to present 'notables' as the 'real' power in French politics and to argue that the reassertion of their influence after their temporary eclipse by centralized parties after the Liberation made the course of post-war politics inevitable. The reality was more complicated. National politicians, parties and local notables were all mutually interdependent and their relationship might be likened to that of a market economy in which each participant needs to trade his particular commodities in order to survive. However, the terms of trade in relations between

[63] Gellner's discussion of patronage networks sheds some light on the apparently odd links between notables, ideology, parties and the state. His remark that 'the essence of a patronage system ... belongs to some *pays réel* which is ambivalently conscious of not being the *pays légal*' is particularly interesting in view of the fact that the phrase *pays légal* was coined to describe the very *république des camarades* which was built on notable influence. E. Gellner, 'Patrons and clients', in E. Gellner and J. Waterbury (eds.), *Patrons and clients in Mediterranean societies* (London, 1977), pp. 1–6.

[64] On the channelling of some of the money from Monnet plan investment to agriculture see Plantade, 'Le MRP'.

notables and national politicians underwent a shift in favour of the latter group after the Liberation.

This shift was produced by two things. Firstly, the more *dirigiste* climate meant that the resources that the state had to buy or threaten local supporters were much greater than they had been before 1940. Secondly, the impact of the Resistance/Pétainist split increased the power of national politicians over local notables. Notables depended on their ability to play off one politician against another, but after the war most pre-war politicians (especially those from the right and centre of the spectrum) were declared ineligible for having supported the Vichy government in 1940. Furthermore, Resistance records were useful to obtain election at national level and in getting access to state favours. Under these circumstances notables had greatly reduced room for manoeuvre as they were forced to work through a comparatively small group of bourgeois politicians who had good war records.

National politicians could have exploited the monopoly of links with the state that they acquired in the 1940s in several ways. They could have used their power to break existing notables by insisting that the ineligibility laws remain in force. This would have excluded all former Pétainists and maintained the monopoly of power enjoyed by those politicians powerful at the Liberation. They could have used state resources, as the Italian Christian Democrats did, to create new networks of clientelism centred around political parties rather than individuals. They could have used their power to appease notables and establish good relations with the existing power-brokers: Faure, Mitterrand and Chaban-Delmas showed how this could be done.

However, most politicians and parties that emerged from the Resistance failed to exploit the potential strength that they had at the Liberation. They alienated notables by seeking to impose party discipline and by priggish *résistantialisme*. But at the same time they repealed the ineligibility laws and allowed the resources of the state to fall into the hands of semi-private local bodies, thus paving the way for notables to rebuild their power. In short, the politicians of the Liberation fell into the trap Machiavelli had warned about several centuries earlier: they were sufficiently ruthless to make enemies without being sufficiently ruthless to destroy them. The haughty manners of the new parties annoyed the notables, while their actual policies ensured that the notables would eventually be restored to their former influence.

5 Bourgeois parties and the female electorate

One of the most important, and frequently ignored, facts of political life in the Fourth Republic was that well over half the electorate voted for the first time in 1945: French women had been granted the vote by an ordinance of the provisional government in 1943.[1] Furthermore, the success of conservatism in post-war France cannot be understood without reference to women's suffrage. The three major conservative parties had predominantly female electorates. Women provided around 53 per cent of the support for the Rassemblement du Peuple Français (RPF) and Centre National des Indépendants et Paysans (CNIP), and they made up between 58 and 62 per cent of the Mouvement Républicain Populaire (MRP) electorate.[2] Without female suffrage, the Communists and Socialists would have secured an absolute majority of seats in parliament at the November 1946 election.

The reasons why women voted for conservative parties in the Fourth Republic have received very little attention. At the time, many political scientists regarded gender as a trivial issue and suggested that women merely voted as their husbands directed. Maurice Duverger had trouble persuading his colleagues to take his 1955 survey of women's voting habits seriously.[3] In recent years, historical studies of the role of women have become fashionable, but this has not led to any renewal of interest in the female electorate of the Fourth Republic. Even the limited attention that has been given in recent years to the electoral conservatism of women in Switzerland and the UK has not been replicated with reference to post-war France. There are three reasons for this neglect: firstly, the complexity of Fourth Republic politics is simply impenetrable to non-specialists;

[1] Women made up a majority of the total potential electorate, though the number of men and women who actually voted seems to have been about equal. The calculation of abstentions among women voters is a difficult matter. Duverger estimates that women were 5–10 per cent more likely to abstain than men – though in some areas, particularly those with high clerical influence, abstention rates among women were lower than those among men. M. Duverger, *The political role of women* (Paris, 1955), pp. 16 and 18.

[2] M. Dogan and J. Narbonne, *Les françaises face à la politique. Comportement politique et condition sociale* (Paris, 1955), p. 88.   [3] Duverger, *The political role of women*, p. 8.

secondly, the conservative parties for which most French women voted do not engage the sympathy or the interest of the self-consciously progressive people who study women's history;[4] thirdly, the explosion of interest in women's history coincided, and became connected, with an explosion of interest in the social and cultural history of France, which distracted historians from what were seen as mundane political questions. More has been written about the philosophy of Simone de Beauvoir or about the changing role of midwives than about the millions of women who voted for the CNIP.

Huguette Bouchardeau's seminal work *Pas d'histoire, les femmes* exemplifies the limitations of recent work on the political role of women.[5] She attacks the exclusion of women from the conventional narratives of political historians, but her own narrative concentrates on a minority of urban, educated and often male activists. Bouchardeau's work also illustrates the widespread equation of women's history with the history of progressive causes. She suggests that women's history can be summed up under three headings: birth control, peace and suffrage. However, no evidence is provided that these issues ever preoccupied a majority of French women.

The absence of attention given to the female electorate of the Fourth Republic is unfortunate because the sources for this subject are exceptionally good. The beginning of large-scale opinion polling coincided with the beginning of women's suffrage. The Institut Français d'Opinion Publique and the ministry of the interior conducted surveys of voting habits at regular intervals during the Fourth Republic. Though these surveys need to be used with some caution,[6] they provide a degree of detail about how women cast their votes, immediately after their enfranchisement, that is not available to the historian of any other major country. Furthermore, three constituencies in France (Belfort, Grenoble and Vienne) had, for at least

---

4 See Jane Jenson, 'The liberation and new rights for French women', in M. Randolph Higonnet, Jane Jenson, S. Michel and M. Collins Weitz (eds.), *Behind the lines: gender and the two world wars* (New Haven, 1987), pp. 272–284.

5 Huguette Bouchardeau, *Pas d'histoire, les femmes* (Paris, 1977).

6 Public opinion polls never provide an entirely satisfactory account of people's behaviour in the polling booth. Furthermore, the most detailed public opinion survey into voting habits (conducted in 1952) obtained its sample by using criteria that were slightly different from those that defined the electorate (for example respondents were chosen from among people aged over 18 rather than over 20). For the results of the 1952 survey see M. Larkin, *France since the Popular Front: government and people 1936–1986* (Oxford, 1988), p. 169. For an explanation of its limits see R. Aron, 'Electeurs, partis et élus', *Revue Française de Science Politique*, April–June (1955), 256.The most detailed survey relating to women's voting habits was that conducted by the ministry of the interior in Privas (a town in the Ardèche) in 1952 and 1953; but Privas seems to have been an exceptional area for a variety of reasons: see Duverger, *The political role of women*, p. 18.

part of the Fourth Republic, different polling stations for men and women and counted the votes of the sexes separately.

This chapter will draw most of its evidence from the works of Dogan and Narbonne, Duverger, and Barral. It will argue firstly that there were significant differences between the political behaviour of men and women, and that the former were more conservative than the latter. Secondly, it will be argued that Dogan and Narbonne are right to assume that these differences can be explained in terms of the different age structures and social situations of the two sexes. However, it will also be argued that Dogan and Narbonne's study is flawed by their assumption that there is one pattern of 'rational' political behaviour and that this pattern is exhibited by men. In reality the differences between male and female voting can be explained as much in terms of the peculiar influences acting on French male voters as those acting on female voters.

In view of the importance that the female electorate had for the success of conservatism it is worth investigating the possible roots of female voting patterns at some length. The first point to emerge from the opinion poll evidence about women's voting was that they were less politically committed than men, or at least that they were less prone to express certainty about political matters. In October 1946 a poll taken one week before the constitutional referendum showed that 30 per cent of women (as opposed to 21 per cent of men) had yet to make up their mind how they would vote.[7] Polls showed that women were less likely than men to express strong opinions on political issues of the day,[8] to describe themselves as interested in politics, or to discuss politics.[9] Abstention rates were higher among women than men.

Women's relative lack of interest in politics (or at least in what male politicians defined as politics) proved an advantage for political conservatism. This was because left-wing parties, and particularly the Communist party, presented themselves as intensely ideological formations with an aggressive programme for the transformation of France. On the other side of the political spectrum things were much less clear; indeed, in some respects there was no other side of the political spectrum since no political party presented itself as explicitly right-wing. Conservative politicians claimed to be 'apolitical', and the reassuring consensus that a man like Antoine Pinay appeared to represent may well have appealed to voters who thought of themselves as undecided.

If women were less influenced than men by 'politics', they seem to have been more interested than men in personalities. Pollsters found that 39 per

[7] Ibid., p. 14.
[8] Dogan and Narbonne, *Les françaises face à la politique*, pp. 74 and 75.
[9] Ibid., pp. 75 and 76.

cent of women (as opposed to 31 per cent of men)[10] said that they were influenced by the personality of candidates in elections. In constituencies where voters were separated by gender, prominent personalities seem to have attracted a disproportionate number of women's votes. In Belfort the local Radical deputy was in this position and a large number of women changed their votes when this individual moved to a new electoral list.[11] Similarly in Vienne the charismatic Socialist mayor attracted votes from women who did not normally vote Socialist in national elections.[12] Women were also more likely than men to exploit the possibilities offered by *panachage* (a complicated process by which voters could give a portion of their vote to a particular individual from a party list other than the one for which they reserved the greatest part of their support).[13]

Women displayed enthusiasm for one politician in particular: Charles de Gaulle. Opinion polls consistently showed that women were more Gaullist, or less anti-Gaullist, than men. In November 1946 more women than men admitted that de Gaulle's advice would influence their vote in the forthcoming referendum, and in May 1947 33 per cent of women (against 25 per cent of men) expressed a wish to see de Gaulle return to power.[14] Furthermore, two of the parties with predominantly female electorates (the MRP and the RPF) had special associations with de Gaulle.

The third area relevant to sexual differences in political behaviour is religion. The parties with predominantly female electorate were all associated with the defence of the church and many assumed that the supposed piety of women was one of the main reasons for their tendency to vote for such parties. Dogan and Narbonne disagreed with this assumption. They argued that religion played a relatively small part in the political behaviour of women. They accepted that women were more likely to be practising catholics than men, but stressed the difference between private devotion (i.e. attendance at mass) and public clericalism (i.e. the willingness to accept church influence in political matters). They pointed out that only around 20 per cent of women admitted that religion played a part in deciding their vote, and that only a relatively small proportion of women voted for the party preferred by the church (the MRP).[15]

However, all these points are open to question. Firstly, the distinction between clericalism and devotion is one that could equally well be made for men. There were many areas of Third Republic France where church attendance had been high but religious influence in politics low; but no one

---

[10] Duverger, *The political role of women*, p. 70.   [11] Ibid., p. 71.

[12] P. Barral, 'Pour qui votent les femmes à Vienne?', in François Goguel (ed.), *Nouvelles études de sociologie électorale* (Paris, 1954), pp. 185–193.

[13] Dogan and Narbonne, *Les françaises face à la politique*, p. 111. In Vienne a total of 452 men and 490 women used *panachage* votes.

[14] Duverger, *The political role of women*, p. 70.   [15] Ibid., pp. 57–60.

would suggest that the church was not an important force in Third Republic politics.

Secondly, the statistics of Dogan and Narbonne are by no means conclusive. The 20 per cent of women who admitted to being influenced by the church in political matters may well include that highly significant group of women whose votes were cast differently from those of men of equivalent social position. Furthermore, there is no reason to assume, as Dogan and Narbonne seem to do, that only women who voted for the MRP could have been affected by religious considerations. In fact the hierarchy only expressed a preference for the MRP from 1951, and even then it expressed this preference in a highly discreet and subtle manner,[16] which must have escaped the attention of many women. The church made it clear to women that it was perfectly acceptable for practising Christians to vote for non-marxist parties other than the MRP,[17] and many individual priests and bishops made their preference for such parties over the MRP obvious.

How are the differences between male and female voting patterns to be explained? Politicians and journalists often explained them in terms of the different characters of men and women. Women were simply less rational than men and more prone to be influenced by superstitious regard for the church or a trivial regard for the personality of candidates.[18] Dogan and Narbonne reacted sharply against the explanation of female behaviour in terms of innate characteristics. They argued that the differences between male and female voting patterns were just a reflection of other differences between the experiences of men and women: 'Explanation in terms of sex thus seems to be an explanation, in terms of age, socio-professional category and religious sentiments, which explains the unequal divisions of male and female voters among the various political parties.'[19]

Age was certainly one cause of the differences in the political behaviour of the sexes. The average life expectancy of women was greater than that of men. The result of this was that there were 6,339,000 French women over the age of 50 compared with only 4,548,000 French men in the same age group. Since the old were particularly prone to vote for conservative parties, it might be expected that the conservative electorate would contain

[16] The hierarchy's support for the MRP was expressed in a nuanced article in *L'Osservatore Romano*. Since Dogan and Narbonne point out that few women in France read the *presse d'information* with any attention (*Les françaises face à la politique*, p. 63), they can hardly believe that many women scanned the pages of the French language edition of obscure Vatican publications.

[17] Dogan and Narbonne actually cite evidence of such advice, given by the Ligue Féminine d'Action Catholique, in ibid., p. 127.

[18] Herriot advanced the more diplomatic argument that women had 'cold' political reason as opposed to the 'hot' political reason of men. Francis de Tarr, *The French Radical party from Herriot to Mendès-France* (Oxford, 1961), p. 5.

[19] Dogan and Narbonne, *Les françaises face à la politique*, p. 92.

a disproportionately high number of women. Widows were especially important in this context. Women living from pensions or savings were partially separated from the economic world in which their neighbours belonged.[20] Furthermore, the high male casualties of the First World War meant that there was a large number of elderly widows living in France during the 1940s; it is easy to imagine that these women would have been especially vulnerable to the right-wing exploitation of the *poilu* myth that had been operating for the previous two decades.

Differences of age also tied in closely with other differences between the sexes that were seen to have political implications: the old were more likely to be practising catholics[21] than the young, and less likely to work for their living. Dogan, Narbonne and Duverger believed that the disproportionate number of old women was the main reason for the difference between male and female voting patterns.[22] It should, however, be stressed that this explanation only works for certain conservative parties. The political group with the largest proportion of old voters (the Rassemblement des Gauches Républicaines (RGR)) was also the one with the lowest proportion of female voters, while the party most attractive to women (the MRP) had a comparatively youthful electorate.[23]

The second element underlying differences between male and female political preferences was the sexual division in the labour force. Only 45 per cent of female voters (as opposed to 88 per cent of male voters) worked outside the home.[24] Consequently, left-wing parties, whose appeal was

[20] It is important to note that widows of working-class origin were particularly likely to live alone, whereas bourgeois widows frequently lived with their children and therefore retained economic interests and political sympathies in common with their sons or sons-in-law. Pierre Clément and Nelly Xydias in *Vienne sur le Rhône. La ville et les habitants, situations et attitudes. Sociologie d'une cité française* (Paris, 1955), p. 25 report that 88 per cent of workers' families contained only one or two generations; the comparable figure for bourgeois households was only 64 per cent.

[21] Dogan and Narbonne, *Les françaises face à la politique*, p. 99; 52 per cent of women over the age of 65 and 48 per cent of those between 50 and 65 were classed as 'devout'. The figures for men were substantially smaller: indeed, 34 per cent of men over the age of 65 (as against only 9 per cent of women over 65) said that they 'never' went to church. It should also be noted that militant anti-clericalism was more common among the old than the young.

[22] Ibid.

[23] Of the RGR's electorate 65 per cent were over 50; only 36 per cent of its electorate was female. The MRP by contrast had a predominantly female electorate of which only 34 per cent were over 50. Dogan and Narbonne suggest that 'If the party recommended by the church (the MRP), and in general the parties favourable to the christian tradition, attract more female votes than the party of secularized left, these [votes] come, in large measure, from old widows' (ibid., p. 100). In fact the suggestion that the MRP electorate was particularly old is one that Dogan and Narbonne are only able to sustain by comparing the MRP with the Communist party (which had an exceptionally youthful electorate). In every political party, other than the Communists, the proportion of voters over 50 was higher than in the MRP. It should also be noted that only 6 per cent of MRP voters fell into the category of '*rentiers* and pensioners' (only the Communist party was less attractive to these groups). For the statistics on electorates see Larkin, *France since the Popular Front*, p. 169.

[24] Dogan and Narbonne, *Les françaises face à la politique*, p. 19

based on class and labour relations, meant little to many women. Further-more, the kind of employment that women found was different from that of men. Only 4 per cent of workers in heavy industry were women, while the textile industry employed 237,000 women and only 105,000 men.[25] Gener-ally women worked in smaller enterprises than men and were less likely to be unionized. Most working women were employed outside industry altogether in commercial and office jobs. The wives and daughters of industrial workers were more likely to wear white collars and keep clean hands than their menfolk. Women displayed many characteristics that are usually associated with the lower middle class: they prized respectability, identified with their superiors and sought salvation in individual rather than collective action. Certain political characteristics associated with women, such as a propensity for abstention, were also associated with male clerical workers,[26] and a survey in Vienne showed that women were more prone than men to identify themselves as members of the *classes moyennes* or bourgeoisie rather than members of the proletariat.[27]

Marriage had important implications for women's perception of their social position. Widows seem to have continued to identify with the economic standing that they had enjoyed when their husbands were alive long after the financial basis of that standing had disappeared. Similarly, many young women of humble origin seem to have hoped to rise through marriage. Dogan and Narbonne describe the view of the world put forward by the popular women's magazines as follows: 'the boss is usually generous and energetic; the worker is usually a drunkard. The heroine in these stories does not work. She waits to meet the ... masculine marvel whom she will end up marrying ... This press falsifies the meaning of life. It turns young readers away from social problems and nurtures the hope of an individual success due to luck and patronage.'[28]

Dogan and Narbonne's interpretation of the female electorate is much more subtle than that advanced by previous commentators. However, it did not mark a total break with the prejudices of the Third Republic. Dogan and Narbonne still assumed that women's political behaviour was irratio-nal; they differed from misogynistic Radicals only in their belief that this 'irrationality' could be explained by external influences rather than the

[25] Ibid., pp. 26 and 27.
[26] Duverger, *The political role of women*. See M. Crozier, *Petits fonctionnaires au travail* (Paris, 1956) and *Le monde des employés du bureau* (Paris, 1965).
[27] Clément and Xydias, *Vienne sur le Rhône*, p. 93. The proportion of women identifying themselves as belonging the *classes moyennes* was 50 per cent (as opposed to 43 per cent of men); the proportion of women claiming to be proletarian was 45 per cent (as opposed to 53 per cent of men); the proportion of women who regarded themselves as bourgeois was 5 per cent (as opposed to 4 per cent of men).
[28] Dogan and Narbonne, *Les françaises face à la politique*, p. 69.

innate characteristics of women. Furthermore, Dogan and Narbonne assumed that specifically female voting patterns belonged to the past, and that they were associated with the old or with the non-integration of women into the workforce.

It is possible to criticize this assumption of female irrationality on several grounds. Firstly women did not define their class interests differently from men purely because of false consciousness. Women's rejection of working-class organization and strikes can be explained in entirely rational terms. Much labour militancy revolved around aims formulated within the factory gates. Men were concerned to assert their dignity, to control their own time and to weaken the authority of foremen. Struggles over such issues, which might well deprive households of income during strikes while not holding out much prospect of increase in living standards through wage rises, may have been rational to the worker, but were not rational for his wife. Similarly the large number of widows who lived off *rentes*, savings or pensions had economically rational reasons to vote for right-wing candidates. Pensioners and *rentiers* were particularly vulnerable to the inflation that afflicted France during the post-war period, and it was the political right (especially the CNIP) who were perceived to be the most committed and effective opponents of inflation.

Women's apparent apoliticism and tendency to personalize politics need not necessarily be taken as a sign of irrationality. Differences between political parties within the bourgeois bloc were often rooted in issues that dated back to the nineteenth century. Furthermore, the factional and personal divisions within Fourth Republic political parties were often more important than the apparent differences between them. Under these circumstances it might be argued that it was entirely rational to focus loyalty around an individual. Indeed, it might be suggested that the women who followed a candidate from one party to another were being more rational than the men who remained loyal to a single party because of some half-forgotten position that the party had taken in 1901 or in 1920.

The fact that women appeared more 'Gaullist' than men may also be explained in terms other than women's irrational attachment to strong personalities. After 1945 de Gaulle was identified with a savage attack on the Third Republic, which he blamed for both the defeat and for the granting of full powers to Marshal Pétain. De Gaulle wanted to see the constitution of the Third Republic replaced, and his government denied political rights to those pre-1940 parliamentarians who had voted for the granting of full powers to Pétain. It might be expected that a proportion of Third Republic voters would resent the ineligibility of those politicians that they had supported before 1940, and would consequently be hostile to de Gaulle. There is indeed evidence that some men whose political and social vision matched that put forward by the RPF refused to support the party because of its leader. Women who had not voted in the Third Republic and who had not, for that matter, held positions of authority under Vichy, had less reason than men to resent de Gaulle.

Finally, and most importantly, there is no reason to assume that the role of religion in affecting the gender biases of voting can be reduced to the influence of the church on women. It could be argued that male anti-clericalism underlay the difference more than female clericalism. Women were overrepresented in the electorates of the main conservative parties because men (whose social and economic views might have been expected to make them conservative) aligned themselves on the 'left' over the religious issue.[29] It should also be noted that anti-clericalism, as measured by refusal ever to attend church and by electoral support for the Radical party, seems to have been particularly associated with the old and with economically backward areas. The modernization of France that Dogan and Narbonne expected to erase specifically female political behaviour, was actually erasing specifically male political behaviour.

The female electorate was not a homogeneous bloc. Those parties that attracted female votes did not do so for the same reasons. The MRP's electorate, composed of youthful women (often voting in opposition to their husbands), was quite different from the elderly widows who seem to have made up a significant part of the CNIP or RPF electorate.[30] Qualities that attracted women were not evenly distributed among conservative parties: the CNIP was more 'apolitical' than the MRP; the MRP was more clearly identified with the defence of the church than its conservative rivals. Some attractions were specific to particular parties. It is easy to imagine that many women, who had not undergone military service and who were less likely to have travelled outside their native area than men, would have been attracted by the homely localism of the CNIP; but this can hardly explain their attraction to the MRP or the RPF, both of which laid great emphasis on foreign and defence policy.

In spite of all these variations, it is possible to make certain broad points about the female electorate in the Fourth Republic. The first of these is that contemporary analysis almost invariably took male voting patterns for granted. It was assumed that the study of gender differences among voters would mean the study of special conditions affecting women,[31] and it was

[29] There is, of course, something rather artificial about discussion of 'right' and 'left' in the context of the clerical issue since the 'clerical issue' itself often provided the only point of disagreement between the 'left-wing' Radicals and their conservative rivals.

[30] Only 3 per cent of married women over 50 voted independently of their husbands; the comparable figure for women under 50 was 20 per cent. Ibid., p. 51.

[31] On the tendency of political scientists to assume that male political behaviour is 'natural' and female behaviour an aberration see S. L. Bourque and J. Grosshultz, 'Politics an

also assumed that these special conditions were rooted in the past status of women and that they would disappear with time.[32] In fact there was nothing necessarily 'rational' about male politics in the Fourth Republic. The striking Communists who burnt effigies of Trotsky or the Radical notable who ate *tête de veau* on 14 July were as much influenced by tradition, superstition and ritual as they were by any cool-headed calculation of economic benefit or class interest. Many gender differences make more sense when studied in terms of special conditions (such as anti-Gaullism or anti-clericalism) that mainly affected men. To a large extent it was male politics not female politics that were rooted in the outdated issues of the Third Republic or the debates about the legitimacy of Vichy. This fact underlies the most straightforward characteristic of the parties that attracted disproportionately large numbers of women voters: they were all new. Every party that drew more than half its support from women had been founded after 1945; every major party that drew less than half its support from women had originated in the Third Republic.

unnatural practice: political science looks at female participation', *Politics and Society*, 4, 2 (1974), 225–266. See especially p. 229: 'Rational political behaviour is defined as the male pattern ... and irrationality is by definition the expression of female roles.'

[32] Dogan and Narbonne, *Les françaises face à la politique*, p. 191.

6   Organized business and politics

Historians have made much of the power that organized business exercised in the Fourth Republic. Georgette Elgey entitled a section of a chapter on the 1951 election 'L'église et le patronat interviennent',[1] and numerous commentators repeated the allegation that every successful candidate in that election had received 50,000 francs of business subsidy. This perception of business power is increased by the anti-capitalist perspective of many Fourth Republic writers, and by the magnifying power of repeated gossip.

Hard information about the political influence of the *patronat* is hard to come by, but it is worth beginning by making three general points. Firstly, in spite of the alleged power of big business in France, there was not a single political party that was willing to present itself as a defender of big business. In post-war Britain, the Conservative party openly claimed to be the spokesman of business. Subsidies to the party were declared in company accounts and substantial donors were rewarded with honours. In America, the assumption that business interests, and particularly big business interests, ran parallel to those of the rest of the nation was even more widespread: both major political parties expressed this point of view and individual companies often chose the recipients for their largesse on the basis of specific advantages offered to certain kinds of activity.[2] In France, by contrast, all parties expressed some degree of hostility to large-scale business. At each end of the political spectrum, catholics and marxists had their own reasons for being opposed to the unrestricted operations of capitalism while, in the political centre, the Radicals devoted their efforts, or at least their rhetoric, to the defence of small producers and traders.

Secondly, business opinion itself was not homogeneous or coherent. Business organizations were dogged by conflicts of interest between, and

[1] Georgette Elgey, *La république des illusions 1945–1951 ou la vie secrète de la IVème république* (Paris, 1965), p. 555.
[2] E. Handler and J. Mulkern, *Business in politics: the campaign strategies of corporate political action committees* (Lexington, Mass., 1982) and G. K. Wilson, *Business and politics* (London, 1985).

within, sectors, by institutional rivalry and by personal animosity. Business leaders had to persuade their supporters to agree on common policies and, more awkwardly, to provide funds to support those policies before they could seek to influence politicians. Furthermore, the ill-disciplined and individualistic behaviour of particular companies and businessmen meant that it was rarely possible to enforce boycotts of those politicians who defied the wishes of business leaders.

Thirdly, most historians have tended to approach the question of business influence over politics by starting from the political side. The sources used for such studies are the memoirs of politicians or the papers of political parties. But this approach has a number of drawbacks. Firstly, it leads to the neglect of those businessmen (the great majority) who had no consistent political interest. Often a small group of eccentric individuals who were in regular contact with political circles are taken as representative of 'business interests'. Furthermore, historians who approach the business/politics relationship from the political side are generally unaware of the negotiations and struggles within the business community that preceded, and sometimes undermined, each intervention. Under these circumstances historians tend either to assume that business was an all powerful *deus ex machina* manipulating politics from behind the scenes or to assume that each individual intervention in politics by capitalists was an isolated episode without any general significance at all. This chapter will seek to reverse the traditional approach by providing an account of business and politics that begins from the business side. It will seek to show that the business world was riven by conflicts and contradictions that in many respects mirrored those that divided the political world; it will be argued that business leaders expended at least as much energy trying to control and discipline their fellow businessmen as they did trying to influence politicians.

The structure of French business

The average French enterprise was smaller than its counterpart across the Rhine or the Channel and many firms remained under the control of families. This affected styles of industrial management. French businessmen were sometimes more concerned with pride, status and tradition than with the rational calculation of profit and loss. Even large-scale industries were imbued with an ethos that made Schneider or de Wendel treat their firms much as an aristocrat might treat his lands.

The nature of French business had important implications for business organization. It was harder to get the myriad of small companies that characterized the French economy to come together in associations than it was to get the giants of German industry to do so. The tradition of *auto-financement* and suspicion of any expenditure that did not tie in with the immediate interests of the firm made it hard for business organizations to raise funds from their members. Most importantly, the 'family values' of French business made organization difficult. Collaboration between businessmen was made difficult by pride, fierce defence of independence, jealous rivalries and the widespread inability to separate professional and personal life. Indeed, often it seemed that it was impossible to get managers within a single firm, let alone all the employers in an industrial sector, to bury their differences in pursuit of a common policy. One business leader wearily described the difficulties that he faced to a colleague: 'it is still common for little questions of private interests to obstruct unity on decisions of general importance.'[3]

Business organizations

The oldest business organizations in France were the chambers of commerce; first established under Napoleon, their existence had been set on a legal footing during the late nineteenth century. The activities of the chambers of commerce are fairly easy to trace because each chamber was legally obliged to make records of its proceedings available to the public. However, the chambers' status as public bodies also made them reluctant to engage in explicit political discussion. The result of this was that chambers often seemed like technical discussion groups in which the details of local public works were discussed in interminable detail; at other times the chambers functioned as social groups and their published proceedings recounted recent births, deaths, marriages and, most importantly, promotions to the *légion d'honneur*.[4] Furthermore, chambers of commerce tended to be dominated by comparatively old men who had already made their careers and who were left free to enjoy semi-retirement as notables.[5] Only when faced with serious political threats such as that posed by the Popular Front in 1936 or the Poujadist movement in 1954–55 did the chambers of commerce adopt clear stands on political issues. In normal times discussion of controversial matters seems to have taken place in the corridors of the chambers rather than in their *salles de réunion*, and formal meetings of

---

[3] Archives Nationales (AN), 56 AS 2, president of Syndicat Professionnel des Fabricants de Matières Plastiques et des Résines Synthétiques to president of Union des Syndicats de la Transformation des Matières Plastiques, dated 11 February 1954.

[4] See for example the proceedings of the chamber of commerce of Toulon and the Var for 12 September 1951.

[5] In the 1950s only 35 per cent of voters in chamber of commerce elections were less than 50 years old. Paris chamber of commerce archives, 4 AJ 29, transcript of meeting of 22 December 1954.

chambers provided opportunities for the display of a prestige that had already been acquired in other arenas rather than the acquisition or exercise of power.[6]

Private business associations offered more scope for open discussion and for the exercise of influence. Some associations of this kind had existed in France since the mid-nineteenth century (though, technically, they only became legal in 1884). There were two kinds of business association. The first of these represented single industries; the second were inter-professional groups that tried to bring together a variety of industries. Generally speaking the former of these two groups dealt with matters like pricing, tariffs, safety regulations, while the latter dealt with more general matters relating to politics and labour relations. Inter-professional bodies came to the fore at moments of crisis when the whole capitalist economy seemed in jeopardy and when representatives were needed to deal with the government and unions. However, such moments were rare and brief. Inter-professional organizations found it difficult to hold their members together when there was no external threat against which to unite. In normal times consensus was easier to achieve among leaders of a single industrial sector than it was among those representing a whole range of industries whose interests conflicted.

After 1945, large-scale business organizations became more prominent in French public life. This was partly because of the increased economic role of the state. Some industries had acquired the habit of professional discipline when subjected to the authority of the *comités d'organisations* (COs) established by the Vichy government during the war. After the Liberation, professional organization was still needed to allocate scarce resources during French participation in the remainder of the war and during the 'battle for production' after hostilities had ended. The COs (renamed *offices professionnels*) remained in existence until April 1946; even after this, allocation of resources was often devolved to private business syndicates.[7]

The institution of the Marshall and Monnet plans also created a role for business associations as links between private industry and the state. A senior civil servant wrote to the presidents of the associations representing the chemical industries in 1948 asking them to liaise with him about the

---

[6] For example Yves Glotin, an industrialist from Bordeaux, had already been leader of the main private employers' association in the city for almost a decade before he became president of the chamber of commerce; see Jacques Lagroye, *Société et politique. J. Chaban-Delmas à Bordeaux* (Paris, 1973), p. 110. It should, however, be stressed that Glotin was an exception to the general rule since he remained dynamic even after his election to the presidency of the chamber of commerce.

[7] For example the authority exercised by the CO for the steel industry was transferred to a private industrial syndicate. R. Martin, *Patron de droit divin* (Paris, 1984), p. 46.

allocation of Marshall aid: 'The government wants a close collaboration to be established between technical departments [of the civil service] and industrialists . . . I therefore have the honour of asking you to let me know as soon as possible . . . the spokesman for the profession with regard to the direction of chemical industries.'[8] Business associations nominated individuals to serve on *missions de la productivité* sent to America as well as missions sent with French troops to inspect plants in occupied Germany.[9] This new prominence made it much easier for business leaders to impose discipline on their members.

The horizontal or inter-professional level of business organizations had been badly damaged by the war and Vichy. The Confédération Générale du Patronat Français (CGPF) had lost much of its influence by 1939 and had been formally dissolved in 1940. After the war, some businessmen recognized that they needed a general representative body to handle relations with the government and trade unions. Pierre Fournier, a grain merchant and Resistance leader, headed a committee of businessmen who were summoned to advise de Gaulle, but the members of this group were seen as marginal by their colleagues.[10] Pierre Ricard, leader of the foundry association and a former head of two COs, began to create an organization for the *patronat* as a whole. He was aided in this task by Henri Davezac, a metallurgist who had also been active in Vichy's COs and who had been connected to Auguste Detoeuf's iconoclastic *Nouveaux Cahiers* before the war.[11] A *comité de liaison et d'études* brought together members of the pre-war Centre des Jeunes Patrons (CJP) and the newly created Confédération Générale des Petites et Moyennes Entreprises (CGPME). On 21 December 1945 a 'constituent assembly' of the French *patronat* was held, and on 12 June 1946 the first meeting of the Conseil National du Patronat Français (CNPF) took place.[12]

The first president of the CNPF was Georges Villiers. Villiers was a metallurgist from Lyon were he ran a family firm employing 700 men (a large enterprise when compared to the average French firm, but small by comparison with the companies that had traditionally dominated the

---

[8]   AN, 56 AS 50, Direction des industries chimiques to presidents of syndicates representing the chemical industry, 22 June 1948.
[9]   AN, 56 AS 47, contains a number of documents about the arrangement of industrial missions to Germany and America.
[10] J.-N. Jeanneney, 'Un patronat au piquet, septembre 1944–janvier 1946', *L'argent caché. Milieux d'affaires et pouvoirs politiques dans la France du XXème siècle* (Paris, 1984), pp. 242–264.
[11] R. F. Kuisel, 'Auguste Detoeuf, conscience of French industry, 1926–47', *International Review of Social History*, 20, 2 (1975), 149–174.
[12] This brief history of the CNPF is taken from two sources. The first of these is the booklet produced by the CNPF itself, *CNPF. Structure et mission* (Paris, 1989); the second is Henry W. Ehrmann, *Organized business in France* (Princeton, 1957).

employers' movement). Previous leaders of inter-professional organizations, especially those who had been appointed in moments of crisis, had been in a precarious position. Industrialists were prone to discard representatives who seemed to have outlived their usefulness: Claude Gignoux, the pre-war leader of the CGPF, had lasted only three years in the job. However, Villiers enjoyed considerable prestige and power; he even had his own private 'cabinet' of aides. In 1957 Ehrmann pointed out that Villiers enjoyed a respect comparable to that accorded to the prime minister and was considerably more secure in his position than any Fourth Republic minister[13] (as it turned out, Villiers' tenure as president of the CNPF was to last longer than the entire Fourth Republic).

It was clear that Ehrmann, and many of the businessmen who provided him with information, were rather confused by Villiers' position: 'If charismatic leadership has come to denote authority which cannot be explained rationally then M. Villiers is a charismatic leader.'[14] It seemed strange that someone from a comparatively humble background should exercise such authority; the fact that Ricard (who had been placed first in his year at the *école polytechnique*) deferred to Villiers (who had graduated from a middle ranking provincial technical school) was especially perplexing to the status obsessed *bêtes de concours* who composed much of the French managerial class. Many assumed that Villiers was a mere cipher controlled by Ricard. In fact the archives of the CNPF show Villiers rather than Ricard as the dominant figure, and in April 1948 a confidential note circulated among business leaders suggested that Ricard was to be forced to resign after a conflict with Villiers.[15] Ricard did not resign, but he certainly remained subordinate to Villiers who continued to be president of the CNPF long after Ricard's death.

Villiers' hegemony over the French *patronat* in general, and Ricard in particular, which surprised so many business observers, is more explicable if the broad political context in which the CNPF operated is examined. At

---

[13] Ibid., p. 132.   [14] Ibid., p. 134.
[15] AN, 57 AS 22, 'La crise Ricard', dated 8 April 1948. This unsigned note (marked 'very confidential'), seems to have been circulated among members of the Centre des Jeunes Patrons. The note suggested that Ricard and Villiers had quarrelled after Ricard had asked to be made head of a special committee to be set up to administer Marshall aid. Villiers had refused Ricard's request and also blamed Ricard for being excessively aggressive in his relations with the government and excessively prone to defend the interests of the iron and steel industry. It was suggested that Ricard would leave the CNPF as soon as some appropriate post in a semi-public body could be found to which he could move with dignity. The CJP, which was closely linked to the CNPF, ought to have been well informed, but the details given in the note are not entirely convincing because of the suggestion that Ricard was too aggressive and on bad terms with the government. In fact Ricard seems to have been very tactful in his relations with ministers and civil servants and sometimes restrained his colleagues from making attacks on them (see below).

the Liberation the *patronat* was widely believed to have behaved badly during the war. Some employers were specifically punished for their actions by committees set up to purge particular sectors, but more frequently informal pressure was applied to drive compromised industrialists out of their positions or simply to limit their power. Frequently trade unionists or the representatives of the state made it clear that they did not wish to deal with business representatives who were seen as compromised by Pétainism or collaboration.[16] All this obviously strengthened the hand of the state *vis-à-vis* private enterprise, but it also strengthened the hand of a section of business leaders *vis-à-vis* their colleagues. The very rarity of businessmen with Resistance credentials gave them power. Resistance businessmen became intermediaries with whom their colleagues were obliged to deal when they wished to approach the state.

Villiers' Resistance credentials were impeccable. The Vichy government had chosen him to replace Edouard Herriot as mayor of Lyon, but he had used this position to protect Resistance fighters and Jews. Subsequently he had joined a Resistance network, been arrested by the Gestapo and eventually deported to Dachau where his conduct aroused admiration from many of his fellow prisoners. All his potential rivals, on the other hand, were constrained from challenging Villiers by their wartime pasts. Claude Gignoux and Aymé Bernard (pre-war leaders of the *patronat* who had been appointed to Marshal Pétain's *conseil national*) never held office in the employers' movement again (though both retained an unofficial role); other business leaders who had held office under Vichy such as André Boutemy, Jean Fabre, Pierre Ricard[17] and Léon Gingembre all did gain office in the CNPF, or in organizations closely linked to the CNPF, but their pasts would have made it impossible, at least in the years immediately after the Liberation, to occupy a position of too much public prominence. All of these individuals grumbled about Villiers' leadership, but none of them could hope to displace him. It may be significant that the only real attack on Villiers came in 1951, the year of the first amnesty law for offences committed during the war, when many Pétainists returned to public life.

The CNPF made much of its claim to represent the whole *patronat*. Traditionally, French business organizations had been dominated by large-

---

[16] On the business *épuration* see A. Lacroix-Riz, 'Les grandes banques françaises de la collaboration à l'épuration, 1940–1950, I: La collaboration bancaire', *Revue de l'histoire de la deuxième guerre mondiale*, 141 (1986), 3–44 and 'Les grandes banques françaises de la collaboration à l'épuration, II: La non épuration bancaire 1944–1950', *Revue de l'histoire de la deuxième guerre mondiale*, 142 (1986), 81–101; and R. Vinen, *The politics of French business 1936–1945* (Cambridge, 1991), 193–204.

[17] Ricard had headed a *comité d'organisation* though his friend Louis Franck insisted that 'during the occupation his behaviour was perfect'. L. Franck, *697 ministres. Souvenirs d'un directeur général des prix 1947–1962* (Paris, 1990).

scale well organized industries, particularly those with Parisian *sièges sociales* which were well placed to attend meetings. The CNPF stressed that it gave greater representation to commerce, to small enterprises and to firms based in the provinces. The new basis on which the organization purported to be founded was reflected in the allocation of representatives who attended the general assembly of the CNPF: 275 of these came from ordinary industrial associations, 75 came from commerce, 75 from the Fédération des Associations Régionales (representing provincial business) and 75 from the CGPME. However, the outward deference shown to small and provincial business deserves to be viewed with scepticism – the previous restructuring of the employers' movement, in 1936, had been accompanied by similar rhetoric. Large-scale business was well represented in the board and bureau of the CNPF and, most importantly, the large-scale industries of steel, metallurgy, chemicals and oil were estimated to provide around 80 per cent of the movement's funds.[18] Indeed, probably the greatest change in the employers' movement came not from any attempt to give power to new groups but rather from by-products of nationalization.[19] The French coal industry, which had been second only to the iron and steel industry in the influence that it exercised in the pre-war CGPF, was nationalized after the war.

Not all organizations of businessmen regarded themselves as lobbying groups for business interests. In particular two business associations took their cue from the catholic church. The CJP (founded by the Jean Mersch in 1938) and the Centre Français du Patronat Chrétien (CFPC) (founded in 1926) thought of their function in terms of altruism that might have seemed alien to more conventional economic associations. The president of the CJP described his organization's role thus: 'We are a group of employers, but we do not defend employers' interests. We have raised ourselves above [concern for] our own interests to a level where we seek the general interest.'[20]

Henri Weber suggests that four things distinguished the thinking of the reforming *patronat*: firstly, a belief in a *bien commun* that united the interests of workers and employers; secondly, a belief that employers should give attention to their responsibilities as well as their rights; thirdly, a belief that economic and social affairs could not be separated; fourthly, a belief that decisions should be devolved to a level close to those who were affected by them.[21] It was widely believed that the catholic employers'

---

[18] Ehrmann, *Organized business in France*, p. 152.
[19] One conservative leader believed that nationalization had been explicitly intended to gain control of the most generous providers of political funds. Geroges Riond, *Chroniques d'un autre monde* (Paris, 1979), p. 197.
[20] AN, 57 AS 22, Jacques Warnier speaking to *assemblée générale* on 19 June 1947.
[21] H. Weber, *Le parti des patrons. Le CNPF (1946–1986)* (Paris, 1986), pp. 113–115.

organizations were more dynamic and forward looking than conventional business associations.[22] They were seen to look favourably on ideas such as industrial modernization, economic planning and European integration.

However, close examination of the reality of catholic organizations and particularly of the CJP (for which good archival sources are available) suggests that the role of the catholic *patronat* in 'modernization' was ambiguous. Firstly, for all their rhetoric of modernization, most members of the CJP actually came from small family firms in backward sectors of the economy.[23] The movement had its roots in the textile and leather industries and was led between 1947 to 1951 by Jacques Warnier (a Rheims textile manufacturer). Secondly, activism in the CJP often seems to have been an alternative to, rather than an extension of, business activity. Many leading members of the movement had inherited companies, but felt that their real interests were political, social and religious rather than entrepreneurial. This was the case of Jacques Warnier who was said, by his wife, to have been unhappy in business until he discovered escape from the daily chores of running his factory in being a CJP militant.[24] Another CJP member gave an even more bizarre and self-pitying account. He explained that he had wanted to be a priest but that filial loyalty had obliged him to take over the family foundry.[25]

Thirdly, it is hard to classify the ideas that motivated the CJP as being either modern or 'anti-modern'. It is true that an opposition to the unrestricted operations of liberal capitalism sometimes caused the *patronat* to align themselves with aspects of 'modernity' such as economic planning and *comités d'entreprise*. However, the same ideas were also linked to corporatist and authoritarian notions. The CJP was certainly not a collaborationist or fascist organization (the German authorities had banned the publication of the movement's bulletin in 1942), but it had supported the Vichy government and the majority of the CJP's members had joined between 1940 and 1944.[26] Henri Weber suggests that after 1945 the catholic business organizations turned away from corporatist authoritarianism and invested their faith in the *économie concertée*. In fact, the process was much slower. Jacques Warnier, who became president of the CJP in 1947, had been interested in corporatist, authoritarian and even

---

[22] The conventional view of the CJP was expressed by Henri Descamps, *La démocratie chrétienne et le MRP de 1944 à 1959* (Paris, 1981), p. 188. See also F. Bourricaud, 'Sociologie du chef d'entreprise: le "Jeune Patron"', *Revue Economique*, 6 (1958), 896–911.

[23] Ehrmann suggests that the CJP appealed to much the same clientele as the CGPME. Ehrmann, *Organized business in France*, p. 118.

[24] AN, 57 AS 28, 'Renseignements sur la personnalité de Jacques Warnier'.

[25] AN, 57 AS 22, undated, 'Témoignage Jeune Patron'.

[26] P. Bernoux, *Les nouveaux patrons. Le centre des jeunes dirigeants d'entreprise* (Paris, 1974), p. 27. Bernoux reports that the CJP's membership increased from 900 in 1941 to 2,195 in 1944.

royalist solutions to French problems during the 1930s. After 1940 he had enthusiastically embraced the policies of the Vichy government and particularly the *charte du travail*. Even if he had undergone a road to Damascus conversion to democracy (and there is no evidence that he did), Warnier would have found it hard to leave his Pétainist past behind: he was, after all, a well-known supporter of the Vichy government and he remained in close contact with like-minded people.

Fourthly, there were some notable contradictions in the CJP rhetoric. Modernization was often seen to be associated with a shift of power away from owners to managers.[27] However, the members of the CJP were almost invariably members of the *patronat de possession* rather than the *patronat de compétence*. The only people who could be sure that they were going to exercise senior managerial responsibility before the age of 40 (which was initially the maximum age for membership of the movement) were those who were due to inherit the family firm. Managers generally reached a position of responsibility later in life than owners. Jacquin's study of the cadres during the 1950s showed that managers tended to reach senior positions at a particularly late age immediately after the Second World War,[28] and also found that cadres who were in mid-career very rarely had time for membership of clubs or discussion circles.[29]

Fifthly, the audience of the christian *patronat* was limited. The CFPC represented about 6,000 employers in 1950s, but this figure was only half the membership that the movement had mobilized during the 1930s, and many members were believed to be of lukewarm enthusiasm. The CJP had around 2,500 members (who employed a total of 200,000 people) immediately after the war. Its membership was seen as more enthusiastic than that of the CFPC, but it had difficulty in fulfilling its aim of influencing more mainstream employers' organizations. It had been hoped that members of the CJP would graduate to holding positions of responsibility in the CNPF. However, this rarely happened (at least during the Fourth Republic), and by the 1950s the most active *jeunes patrons* were often men of over 45.[30]

The fact that many self-conscious reformers in the catholic *patronat* do not seem to have particularly modernizing in their own business careers did not mean that their ideas had no effect. There were areas where the CJP had

---

[27] Bernoux entitled a chapter in his book on the CJP 'Du patron au manager'. Ibid., chapter 2.
[28] F. Jacquin, *Les cadres de l'industrie et du commerce en France* (Paris, 1955), p. 88. Jacquin suggests that managers had a high average age during the immediate aftermath of the Second World War because the *années creuses* caused by low birth rates during the First World War meant that there had been little recruitment of young men during the 1930s.
[29] Ibid., p 161.
[30] After the war, the maximum age for membership of the CJP was raised from 40 to 45. Bernoux suggests that this was to allow for the fact that some *patrons* had spent time in prisoner of war camps. Bernoux, *Les nouveaux patrons*, p. 37.

considerable success; the movement seems to have been especially influential in Bordeaux in spite of, or perhaps because of, the fact that christian *patrons* were not very numerous in the city. A group of dynamic catholic employers such Henri Nazat and Yves Glottin both modernized their enterprises and came to control much of the local business organization.[31] Furthermore, certain ideas of the catholic reformers were influential in more mainstream employers' organizations even when the individuals who had formulated those ideas were not. Georges Villiers, who had been linked to christian employers' organizations before the war, attended some CJP meetings and listened to their ideas with sympathy. Most importantly, the CJP served an indirect purpose by providing an opportunity for those who attended their meetings and read their publications to reflect on and discuss their experience. Such reflection produced some abstract and self-indulgent hot air, but it could also produce consideration of long-term problems that were rarely raised in more conventional business groups. One leader of the movement pointed out that: 'Employers tend, through lack of foresight or intellectual laziness, to neglect the obvious fact that all their efforts to keep their enterprises going will be in vain, if the political regime or the general economic situation condemn them to extinction.'[32]

The policies of organized business

Three broad issues dominated discussions that were held in business organizations during the early Fourth Republic. The first of these was wages and labour relations. Business organizations were almost obsessively concerned to keep wages down. The CNPF bombarded individual businessmen and other business organizations with circulars urging them to restrain pay increases.[33] This was an issue that produced frequent conflicts between business leaders, who feared escalating costs, and individual *patrons*, who were continuously tempted to settle particular disputes with wage rises to obtain an immediate resumption of production. At a meeting of October 1946 the following remarks were recorded: 'M. Paul Levy deplores the fact that the Print Federation of Paris has agreed with the [workers'] union to pay for days off [*jours fériés*]'; the president added 'every concession at the moment will provoke a fatal generalization'.[34] The CNPF was often obliged to remind its members that other less fortunate employers might be unable to match the rates agreed by prosperous firms: 'The heads

---

[31] Lagroye, *Chaban-Delmas à Bordeaux*, p. 80.
[32] Circular from Coret (undated) in 57 AS 22.
[33] See for example the circular signed by Villiers and dated 8 November 1947, in AN, 58 AS 1.
[34] AN, 72 AS 74, 18 October 1946.

of firms must never forget that, if they can raise salaries, some of their colleagues will not be in a position to do so.'[35]

In 1955, the issue of wage control produced the most savage conflict recorded in the CNPF archives. In this year the Saint-Nazaire shipyards agreed to a wage rise after a particularly frightening strike and works occupation. The discussion produced among business leaders by this decision was so animated that the normally restrained Villiers had to apologize for the vigour with which he had expressed himself: 'We are caught in an unbelievable brawl, and one ends up a little annoyed.'[36] The discussion concerning Saint-Nazaire brought forward a number of themes that frequently emerged when particular employers had made concessions to their workers that seemed unacceptable to other businessmen. The shipbuilders were accused of being in a privileged position because they received 'state subsidies',[37] and special mention was made of the difficulties in which small businessmen would be put by high wage costs. The feeling that concessions on wages represented a betrayal of the business community as a whole was summed up by Villiers: 'If we do not manage to stop the slogan that the 22 per cent [pay rise] accepted in one place can be accepted elsewhere, the economy of the country is finished'. Pisson put the same point in more direct terms: 'Unless there are some bosses who say "no", we are buggered.'[38]

Desire to control wage costs often led the leaders of the *patronat* into a working alliance with the state. Government could impose wage control on individual employers much more easily than could the heads of business organizations; in 1949 the CNPF's director of social affairs talked of the need to 'depoliticize' matters of labour relations by avoiding all discussion of matters that were regulated by the government.[39] Business leaders also recognized that keeping down wages depended on the capacity to break strikes, which in turn depended on deployment of force that could only come from the state.[40]

Links between employers' leaders and the state over matters of wage restraint were strongest during the two periods when the government imposed a general *baisse* on prices and wages. During the first of these, which took place in 1946, the employers' leaders' enthusiasm was somewhat muted, no doubt partly because the government behind the policy was a Socialist one. During the second *baisse* undertaken in 1952 by Antoine

---

[35] AN, 72 AS 74, Meunier addressing *comité directeur* on 7 January 1947.
[36] AN, 72 AS 74, Villiers addressing *comité directeur* on 6 September 1955.
[37] AN, 72 AS 74, Humbert to *comité directeur*, 6 September 1955.
[38] AN, 72 AS 74, Pisson to *comité directeur*, 6 September 1955.
[39] AN, 72 AS 74, Meunier speaking to CNPF *comité directeur* meeting of 5 October 1949.
[40] See the debate on 6 September 1955 in AN, 72 AS 74.

Pinay, a conservative with close business links, enthusiasm was more evident. However, both attempts to bring down prices and wages exposed divisions within the ranks of the *patronat* and posed problems for employers' leaders. Lowering of prices was widely seen to be harmful to distributors, traders and those who were obliged to maintain large stocks of goods that could only be sold at a depreciating prices. The association of breweries decided that it would support the *baisse* for reasons of general economic principle, while drawing attention to the damage that its members were suffering.[41] Other leaders of the retail sector made their dissatisfaction obvious at CNPF meetings.[42] One business leader expressed concern that 'misunderstandings' along the chain of distribution would undermine the policy.[43]

The second broad issue to confront business organizations during this period was that of *dirigisme*. After 1945 the French state played a much larger role in the economy than it had ever done before. The Monnet plan and the distribution of Marshall aid gave the state new powers. French industrialists with a tradition of fierce independence and 'Malthusianism' often resented interference in their affairs. However, the attitude of business organizations was more nuanced. A report for the plastic manufacturers' association weighed up the advantages and disadvantages of creating a *comité de modernisation* within the framework of the Monnet plan to oversee the chemical industry: 'If this commission is created, the needs of the chemical industry will be especially expressed and it will be easier to satisfy them, but it is to be feared then that industrialists will be obliged to carry out the plans that they have drawn up. Furthermore, if they are slow to do so, it is possible that new companies will take advantage of the projected plan to obtain authorization to start operating.'[44]

There was frequent conflict between leaders of business associations, and individual businessmen who felt that their representatives should take a more aggressive attitude towards government intervention in the economy. In 1948 Ricard had to use all his diplomatic skills to restore calm after an industrialist told a government minister that he 'got up every morning and wondered what new measures the government would devise to make life difficult for businessmen'.[45] It was widely recognized that many individual businessmen would have liked the CNPF to be more aggressive in its

---

[41] AN, 58 AS 1, letter to *M. le directeur des prix* dated 6 June 1947.
[42] AN, 72 AS 74, Benaerts speaking to *comité directeur* of CNPF on 17 January 1947.
[43] Boisdé speaking to *comité directeur* on same occasion.
[44] AN, 56 AS 2, M. Plane speaking at meeting of 10 February 1947.
[45] Antoine Pinay, *Un français comme les autres. Entretiens avec Antoine Veil* (Paris, 1984), pp. 40 and 41. The industrialist concerned was Raty the steel manufacturer.

dealings with the government.[46] Three things restrained the leaders of employers' associations. The first of these was simply the realism that came from daily dealings with government representatives: 'The President asked whether one could best stop the excesses of *dirigisme* by taking an intransigent doctrinal position or by trying to take account of the times. The principle of total freedom stands no chance of being accepted in official circles.'[47]

Leaders of business associations were influenced by the fact that they themselves depended on the state in many respects. Not only did they look to the government to impose discipline on workers over wages, they also knew that state action, or the threat of it, was the only means to impose discipline on employers over the question of professional organization. The links between state interference in the economy and the attempts of the *patronat*'s own leaders to impose greater discipline emerged most clearly in 1947 when the Gaullist deputy Palewski proposed a law imposing professional regulation. The CNPF leaders responded to this by drawing up their own plans for self-imposed professional discipline. They presented these plans as means of resisting *étatisme*,[48] but they also stressed that their members might find themselves faced with something worse if they did not accept the measures proposed by the CNPF leadership: 'M. Ricard believes that one cannot neglect the mood of the political parties of which the recent congresses have brought new evidence. A minimum of concessions will be inevitable.'[49]

The common interests that sometimes existed between business organizations and the state were underwritten by the similar backgrounds of business leaders and civil servants. Both groups were largely insulated from the day to day pressures of running a business, and both groups felt that their own view of the economy was more detached and long term than that of private sector employers. Many officials of business organizations had trained alongside civil servants in the *grandes écoles*, and had sometimes spent a period working in the civil service. Many of these men maintained the style of the public sector even when they had entered the employ of business associations. The president of the pre-war *comité des houillères* had said 'we are all civil servants now'. Ricard, the vice president of the CNPF, was an extreme example of this mentality. After graduating first in his year from the *école polytechnique*, he had spent fifteen years working for the

---

[46] As late as 1980, one employer complained that the CNPF was 'not violent enough.' P. Calixte quoted in L. Duroy and S. Moles, *Paroles de patrons* (Paris, 1980), p. 142.

[47] AN, 72 AS 74, 21 March 1947.

[48] AN, 72 AS 74, transcript of *comité directeur* meeting of 21 March 1947: Boisdé remarked that 'the whole text is driven by a concern to build barriers against statism'.

[49] Ibid.

corps des mines and the ministry of industrial production. It was widely recognized that his long-term ambitions lay in the public sector,[50] and Ehrmann wrote of him: 'In his self-image ... M. Ricard remained a technician rather than an employer, an administrator at least as much as the defender of a patrimony.'[51] The verdict of a senior civil servant on Ricard is even more revealing: 'I liked his warmth, his often witty cynicism, and his freedom of language and thought which had not been hampered by his ... daily contact with the *maîtres des forges* ... this ex civil servant of the *corps des mines* and industrial production felt at home in ministerial cabinets.'[52] Relations such as these made it easier for the leaders of the CNPF to find common ground with the representatives of the state, but they also encouraged many employers to regard their own representatives with suspicion.

The third issue to be discussed extensively in employers' meetings was that of European integration. The Schuman plan that gave birth to the European Coal and Steel Community (ECSC) had obvious implications for French industry. Reactions to questions of European integration illustrated the complexity of the influences that bore on decisions made by business organizations. Discussion of European matters among the *patronat* took place on three different levels. The first of these levels concerned the business interests at stake. Iron and steel manufacturers feared exposure to fresh competition, and resisted the plan vigorously. Other industries, such as those manufacturing electrical goods, had traditions of international co-operation and regarded the plan favourably.

However, reactions to the Schuman plan were not just a simple function of business interest. The reaction of the mechanical industry reflected the difficulty of identifying particular sectors with pro- or anti-European interests. The secretary general of the association of mechanical industries, Jean Constant, was one of the first employers' leaders to welcome the Schuman plan, but immediately after this welcome the presidency of the association passed to Métral who turned the association's position around, purged pro-Europeans from its leadership and argued against the Schuman plan.[53] Both sides of the debate advanced arguments based on the business interests of the mechanical industry. Supporters of the plan suggested that the industry would benefit from cheaper raw materials. Opponents of the

---

[50] It was rumoured that Ricard wished to become the head of revived ministry of industrial production. The note of 8 April 1948 on 'La crise Ricard' in AN, 57 AS 22, see above, stated that Ricard would only be willing to leave the CNPF if he went to a post in the public service – it was suggested that he might be placed in overall charge of the distribution of Marshall aid in France.   [51] Ehrmann, *Organized business in France*, p. 137.

[52] Franck, *697 ministres*, p. 15.

[53] Ehrmann, *Organized business in France*, p. 412.

plan suggested that the powers granted to the ECSC commission to order the conversion of steel plants might create new competitors for existing firms in the industry, and it was suggested that measures applied to coal and steel might subsequently be applied to other sectors.[54] The truth was that neither side could be completely sure what effect the Schuman plan would have on their industry. It is significant that Métral wrote an article entitled 'The Schuman plan is a leap into the unknown'.[55]

Business leaders were not just concerned with the fate of their members in the new system envisaged by the Schuman plan – they were also worried about their own role. Such men had spent years building up contacts and positions in France; now they risked being brushed aside by the creation of new organs. Georges Villiers went to some trouble to have himself elected as president of Conseil des Fédérations Industrielles d'Europe (a post that he kept until the mid-1960s), and one of the aspects of the Schuman plan that worried the CNPF most was the fact that the *patronat* had been so little consulted about the details of its implementation: 'The composition of the plan, confided to the *commissariat général du plan* [the planning body for France's internal economy], has been carried out in odd circumstances because the French employers' representatives, the CNPF and the steel syndicate, have been kept out of things and little informed about the elaboration of the plan, while the foreign delegations have discussed the project for five months; in particular the German delegation was made up of representatives of the administration, industry, and even finance.'[56]

The third level on which business reacted to the Schuman plan was political. There were a variety of broad political motives, unrelated to immediate business concerns, that encouraged businessmen to support European integration. Members of catholic business associations were especially enthusiastic about the ECSC, which had been devised largely by Christian Democrat politicians. One industrialist, Edmond Giscard d'Estaing, seems to have devoted almost all his time to the promotion of European union. He wrote regular articles on the subject in the *Revue de Paris*. He was president of the international chamber of commerce, he was also French representative of the Ligue Européenne de Coopération Economique, a body that claimed to represent business but was in reality

[54] Ricard encapsulated both sides of the argument in the speech that he made to the CNPF bureau on 19 December 1950. On the one hand he talked of the 'hopes of the mechanical industry'; on the other hand he warned that 'the possibility of closing a steel factory and converting it, constitutes a threat to the large scale mechanical industry' and asked 'will action be limited to coal and steel?' AN, 72 AS 74.

[55] Article in the *Nouvelle Revue de l'Economie Contemporaine* cited in Ehrmann, *Organized business in France*, p. 413.

[56] AN, 72 AS 74, Ricard to *comité directeur*, 19 December 1950.

subordinated to the Mouvement Européen lead by the Belgian Socialist Spaak and supported by French parties such as the MRP.[57]

The enthusiasm of men like Giscard d'Estaing for the ECSC was not shared by the majority of business leaders. However, even the most hard-headed employer could not afford to reject the Community entirely. It was widely recognized that European integration was part of a broad strategy co-ordinated by the Americans that was designed to strengthen Europe against the Communist threat. Giscard d'Estaing reminded his colleagues that they must not let the defence of particular interests or argument about details undermine this broad strategy: 'One must stress the distinction between the position of bodies interested in the technical application of the Schuman plan, the reactions of which are known, and the political interest of European unity in the face of the Communist threat, a unity that the slightest false move could break.'[58]

The CNPF's public stance on the Schuman plan sprang from trying to strike a balance between the objections of some businessmen and business leaders to particular aspects of the plan and the general political interest that the *patronat* understood to be attached to European integration. Business leaders also knew that outright confrontation with the government over the Schuman plan, as over *dirigisme*, would do no good: 'adopting an intransigent position will get nothing'.[59] The CNPF responded to these competing pressures with a prudent strategy that involved delay and the search for concessions rather than opposition: 'It is vital to add to the delays ... to reduce the powers and the financial resources of the High Authority, to look for an appeal against arbitrary measures that will be available to governments and concerned industrialists.'[60]

Business and politics

Business leaders found it difficult enough to persuade their own members to reach a consensus, but trying to exercise influence in the wider world was harder still. The large-scale industrialists who controlled the main business associations were unpopular in France. In 1951, even after an election that was seen to have strengthened the position of business, Georges Villiers bluntly told a CNPF meeting that: 'No proposition concerning questions such as taxation or social security ... stands any chance of achieving anything if it comes from big business.'[61]

[57] See F. Bonafé, *Edmond Giscard d'Estaing. Un humaniste, homme d'action* (Paris, 1982).
[58] AN, 72 AS 74, 22 May 1951.
[59] AN, 72 AS 74, Villiers addressing *comité directeur* on 22 May 1951.
[60] AN, Ricard to *comité directeur*, 19 May 1951.
[61] AN, 72 AS 74, 19 June 1951.

Under these circumstances big business tried to exercise influence through a kind of social ventriloquism. The CNPF sought to present its demands as part of a broader coalition of the bourgeoisie, tax-payers and, especially, small business. During the late 1940s, big business took a particular interest in the Mouvement de Défense des Contribuables (MDC). The MDC was, as its name suggests, set up to call for a reduction in levels of taxation. The MDC was not set up by big business and never presented itself as a representative of industrial interests. The movement's early leaders were members of the liberal professions and were seen to have masonic links; this was very much the social milieu on which radicalism had been founded – though many of the movement's leaders became members of the Rassemblement du Peuple Français (RPF). The business associations soon recognized the potential value of the movement and sent agents to investigate its meetings.

The reports of business agents presented the MDC, in somewhat condescending terms, as one with which organized business might collaborate. Vimar of the Société pour la Défense du Commerce et de l'Industrie de Marseille wrote that the leader of the MDC 'is, on the whole, considered reasonable' and added: 'The speeches were not very exalted and that of M. Clouard in particular, was measured, we could have taken the words of the orators for our own ... All in all ... the Movement, whose creation we have facilitated in the locality, seems promising for the presentation ... of our claims – depending, of course, on the direction given to it by its current leaders, who you know better than us.'[62] The CNPF provided subsidies for the MDC (it had given 1,500,000 francs by October 1951),[63] but the movement proved a disappointment. Even favourably disposed commentators had to admit that the MDC's meetings were sparsely attended (the meeting in Marseilles attracted only 300 people). The leader of the Rouen *patronat* wrote 'obviously such a limited audience does not suggest that the Rouennais network was really affected by this conference',[64] while the Association des Producteurs des Alpes Françaises wrote, 'It is not felt that this new movement is particularly useful.'[65] In 1952 the CNPF seems to have suspended subsidies to the MDC.[66]

---

[62] AN, 72 AS 118, Vimar of the Société pour la Défense du Commerce et de l'Industrie de Marseille to Lagarde of the Fédération des Associations Régionales, undated.

[63] AN, 72 AS 128, Note for the attention of Mayolle, dated 15 October 1951.

[64] AN, 72 AS 128, Jeanniot to Lagarde, 27 February 1950.

[65] AN, 72 AS 128, unsigned letter to Lagarde, 18 March 1950.

[66] AN, 72 AS 128. Fabre to Boulenger 4 April 1952. 'Apart from the material problems that this plan raises in terms of obtaining sufficient co-operation to allow the revival of the movement in the provinces, I found President Villiers more preoccupied by questions of saving and subscription to future loans than by the question of tax-payer defence ... personally I regret this suspension.'

The CNPF also had relations with better established organizations representing the *classes moyennes* rather than big business. The Conseil National du Commerce (CNC) was led by Georges Maus and affiliated to the CNPF. It represented, or claimed to represent, small businessmen. How real the foundations of the CNC's support ever were is hard to say. During the 1930s one business leader had dismissed it as a 'ghost organization',[67] and it always had links with, and presumably subsidies from, big business. However, the length of Maus's career (which lasted from before the First World War until his death in 1950) suggests that he did enjoy some genuine support.[68]

The other small business organization with which the CNPF was linked was the CGPME. The leader of the CGPME, Léon Gingembre, had been active in business organizations since 1936, and had been an official concerned with small business interests under the Vichy government. Before 1944 his career was marked by the series of checks and rebuffs that frequently befell those who depended on big business subsidy while claiming to represent small business interests. After the war Gingembre founded the CGPME, though because of his links with the Vichy government he was not able to assume the new movement's presidency straight away. The CGPME acquired a much more solid basis than any previous small business association; it had a network of local officials, contacts with ministers and a high public profile. Gingembre's position was so strong that he remained at the head of the movement, and a man of widely recognized importance, until 1984.[69]

The CGPME and the CNC were affiliated to the CNPF but relations between the organizations were far from placid. Léon Gingembre frequently complained about the policies of his colleagues and, in 1948, he ceased attending CNPF meetings. The CGPME was seen to have almost broken contact with the CNPF, and the position of the CNC was increasingly uncomfortable.[70] Conflict sprang from three things. Firstly, there were certain issues on which the interests of small and large business were incompatible. Fiscal issues mattered more to small shopkeepers than to large industrialists (the state collected much of its money through sales tax), and the price *baisses*, which were supported so enthusiastically by George Villiers, hit *commerçants* who were holding large stocks of goods.

Secondly, there was a difference of approach between large- and small-scale business. As has been stressed, the unpopularity of large-scale

---

[67] Vinen, *The politics of French business*, p. 48.

[68] On the pre-1945 career of Georges Maus see ibid., and Philip Nord, *Paris shopkeepers and the politics of resentment* (Princeton, 1986).

[69] On Gingembre's career see S. Guillaume, 'Léon Gingembre défenseur des PME', *Vingtième siècle. Revue d'histoire*, 15 (1987), 69–81.

[70] AN, 57 AS 22, unsigned note, dated July 1947.

business meant that it had to be subtle and discreet when approaching government to ask for concessions. Small business leaders, by contrast, represented an electorally important and popular group: they could afford to be much more open in their demands and their members were filled with high-minded indignation when these demands were not met. It was of course precisely this capacity for open mobilization that made small business allies useful for the CNPF, but it also led to differences of approach. Gingembre berated the CNPF for not taking on the government in outright confrontation.[71]

Thirdly, there was a clash of personalities. In spite of, or perhaps because of, the fact that they came from similar backgrounds, Léon Gingembre and Georges Villiers disliked each other. Their dislike made relations between the CNPF and CGPME difficult even when it was recognized that there were sound reasons for the two movements to co-operate. After Gingembre's abrupt departure from the CNPF in 1948, his movement's treasurer continued to attend CNPF meetings and keep communication lines between the two organizations open; the secretary general of the CNPF seems to have played a similar role in trying to smooth relations between the representatives of big and small business.[72]

Some historians have suggested that small business and the *petite bourgeoisie* generally were an 'object class', who were doomed to be manipulated and led from outside by their social superiors.[73] The history of the CNPF's relations with small business organizations certainly suggests that big business sought to manipulate small representatives in its own interests. However, it also shows that the possibilities of succeeding in such manipulation were limited. It was true that small business associations were reliant on big business subsidy; but big business associations were reliant on the political credibility conferred by links with small business. Some organizations, such as the MDC, were indeed entirely dependent on big business subsidy and condemned to fade away if that subsidy was withdrawn. But this dependence also meant that the MDC was of little use to its paymasters because it was not capable of mobilizing large numbers or putting pressure on the government. Established petit-bourgeois leaders like Gingembre and Maus, on the other hand, were able to deploy real power. But established small business leaders had an agenda of their own and they knew that they needed to maintain the support of the rank and file within their own organizations as well as their big business paymasters.

---

[71] See Gingembre's speech to the *comité directeur* of the CNPF on 21 February 1947 in AN, 72 AS 74.

[72] On the role of personal hostility in relations between the CNPF and the CGPME see, S. Guillaume, *La Confédération Générale des Petites et Moyennes Entreprises. Son histoire, son combat, un autre syndicalisme patronal 1944–1978* (Paris, 1987), pp. 27–28.

[73] L. Boltanski, *The making of a class: cadres in French society* (Cambridge, 1987), p. 42.

Maintaining rank and file support was perceived to be particularly difficult during the late 1940s because of the efforts that the Communist party was making to take over petit-bourgeois organizations. Gingembre and Maus knew that their members might turn to more radical representatives if their interests were not represented aggressively. An anonymous report made to Georges Bidault in January 1948 pointed out that 'the Confédération Générale des Petites et Moyennes Entreprises runs a great risk of being outflanked by the Confédération du Commerce et de l'Artisanat, which is known to have Communist leanings'.[74] Maus warned the CNPF in January 1947 that his association was the subject of 'the sly attacks of paracommunist organizations'.[75] Big business leaders were faced with the dilemma that those movements that were powerful enough to be useful were also too powerful to be controlled; small business leaders were faced with the need to balance the interests of those who provided them with money against the interests of those who provided them with mass support. Under these circumstances, relations between the organizations of large and small business were characterized neither by goodwill nor by unlimited manipulation but rather by an ill-tempered interdependence.

Big business leaders did not just act under small business covers. They also maintained direct, though discreet, relations with national politicians. Once again the main asset of business in these relationships was its capacity to provide money. The political parties of the Fourth Republic were chronically short of funds.[76] Business provided funding for politicians through a variety of mechanisms. The best known of these was the Centre d'Etudes Economiques (CEE) based in the rue de Penthièvre in Paris. The CEE was established in 1946. The driving force behind it was Maurice Brulfer, a manager of Etablissements Progilel. Brulfer was assisted by Périlhon of Kuhlman, and subsequently enlisted the aid of André Boutemy. Boutemy was a former civil servant (he had become prefect of the Lyons region under the Vichy regime); he also had political connections and ambitions. However, association with the Vichy government had made it impossible for Boutemy to return to politics or public service immediately after the war. Like Jean Jardin (Laval's former *chef du cabinet*) and Georges Albertini (wartime aide of the collaborationist Marcel Déat), Boutemy was compelled to carve out a new career in the twilight world of informal influence brokerage. The aim of the CEE was to transmit money from

---

[74] AN, 457 AP 135, report made on night of 6–7 January 1948.
[75] AN, 72 AS 118, Maus to meeting of CNPF *conseil* on 7 January 1947.
[76] Roger Duchet, secretary of the CNIP, wrote as follows: 'The political parties of the Fourth Republic had no ... legal resources. They all received subsidies from the coffers of interest groups and especially from the *patronat* (I was always told that the only exception to this was the Communist Party).' Roger Duchet, *La république épinglée* (Paris, 1975), p. 267.

business circles to selected politicians. It worked in close association with the CNPF; relations were facilitated by the fact that Boutemy's intervention had saved the life of Georges Villiers when he had been arrested by the Gestapo in Lyons. Villiers' desire to prevent the CNPF from being compromised by direct intervention in politics made him refuse to attend the meetings organized in the rue de Penthièvre, but he was kept informed about such meetings by Brulfer and Boutemy.[77]

Though André Boutemy had not founded the CEE he soon became its most prominent and best known leader. Georgette Elgey ascribed the 'stupefying' role of business in the 1951 elections to Boutemy.[78] Boutemy was never simply the obedient representative of business interests; he had interests and ambitions that did not always fit in with those who provided him with money. Boutemy's flamboyance stood in sharp contrast to the discretion that business normally sought to impose on its political dealings. Furthermore, Boutemy eventually embarked on a political career himself; he became a Peasant senator and served briefly as minister of health in René Mayer's government of 1952, before Communist attacks on his notorious role in the 1951 election forced him to resign. It is significant that Boutemy's colleagues in the parliament believed that his actions could be explained in terms of personal ambition as much as business interests. De Gaulle had refused to allow Boutemy to contest the 1948 senatorial elections on a Gaullist ticket, and Michel Debré believed that pique at this refusal, rather than fear of Gaullist economic policy, underlay Boutemy's hostility to the RPF.[79] Similarly, Isorni believed that Boutemy's support for decolonization during the 1950s sprang from a desire to regain a ministerial career (by earning the support of the left) as much as it did from the drain that the Algerian war imposed on the French economy.[80]

The attention given to Boutemy often obscured the fact that he was not the only channel of communication between business and politics. One political organizer stressed the complexity of the mechanisms by which capitalists subsidized political parties: 'There is no one sort of money [*Il n'y a pas d'argent avec un grand A*]. There are different reservoirs which do not necessarily flow out in the same direction.'[81] Alongside the CEE were older institutions: the Union des Intérêts Economiques, which had been established by Ernest Billiet in the 1920s, and the Comité Républicain du Commerce et de l'Industrie, which had been established during the early twentieth century, were both still active in the early years of the Fourth

---

[77] An account of the foundation of the CEE and its relations with the CNPF is given in Georges Villiers, *Témoignages* (Paris, 1978), p. 121.

[78] Elgey, *La république des illusions*, p. 515.

[79] M. Debré, *Trois républiques pour une France. Mémoires. II: 1946–1958. Agir* (Paris, 1988), p. 147.   [80] Jacques Isorni, *Mémoires. II: 1946–1958* (Paris, 1986), p. 10.

[81] Riond, *Chroniques d'un autre monde*, p. 199.

Republic.[82] In addition to these institutionalized arrangements, many businessmen maintained individual relations with particular politicians and provided subsidies from their own resources or from those of their companies.

How much power did business acquire as a result of the political subsidies that it dispensed? Some commentators argued that the *patronat* was an all powerful influence pulling the strings of French politics.[83] Politicians were understandably reluctant to admit that business called the political tune; they insisted that those who gave subsidy gained little in return. A leader of the Parti Républicain de la Liberté (PRL) wrote: 'This support called for nothing in return ... He [Boutemy] dispensed his envelopes with the pride of a nabob in splendid surroundings, but he was poorly rewarded for his generosity.'[84] Jacques Isorni, founder of the Union des Nationaux Indépendants et Républicains, supported this interpretation: 'Nothing was asked. No one lost their freedom.'[85] Roger Duchet, secretary general of the CNIP, claimed that he had driven Boutemy to fund his organization by sheer willpower: 'André Boutemy, distributor of business funds, called me to the rue de Penthièvre to ask me to "leave the Independents in peace". The coldness of André Boutemy, solemn and aggressive behind his desk with the guilded sphinxes, did not impress me. I dug my heels in, and finished up getting some meagre financial support.'[86]

It would be easy to dismiss the quotations cited above as self-serving distortions of the truth: clearly politicians did not want to admit the extent to which their independence was circumscribed by the orders of their business backers. However, there are three arguments to support the claim that the influence of business paymasters over politicians was limited. Firstly, the amount of money at the disposal of business leaders for political purposes was always relatively small. It was notoriously difficult to get French businessmen to spend money even on the equipment in their own factories; raising money for business organizations to spend on the remote world of politics was all the more awkward. Roger Duchet frequently attended meetings at which businessmen discussed their political projects: 'But when it was a question of fixing contributions, the meetings broke up

---

[82] Ernest Billiet had died by 1945. J.-N. Jeanneney reports that Louis Billiet (Ernest's brother) was unsuccessful in his attempt to relaunch the UIE in 1945; however business organizers still spoke of the UIE as a potential source of funds as late as 1951. AN, 72 AS 118, *Assises de l'économie privée*, 10 May 1951, 'Rapport de la commission de voies et moyens'.

[83] For similar interpretations, coming from opposite ends of the political spectrum, see H. Claude, *Gaullisme et grand capital* (Paris, 1960) and E. Beau de Loménie, *Les responsabilités des dynasties bourgeoises* (5 vols, Paris, 1977).

[84] Riond, *Chroniques d'un autre monde*, pp. 196–197.

[85] Jacques Isorni, *Ainsi passent les républiques* (Paris, 1959), p. 10.

[86] Duchet, *La république épinglée*, p. 12.

like feathers in the wind.'[87] Furthermore, the increasing electoral success of conservative deputies, the fragmentation of conservative parties, and the unwillingness, or inability, of business leaders to concentrate their largesse on any single group meant that such money as was available had to be spread ever more widely.

Facts and figures about business subsidy of politicians are hard to come by. It was said that slightly more than 160 candidates in the 1951 election had received business support, and that each Radical deputy had received a subsidy of half a million francs. But there is no archival evidence to support this. A more authoritative source suggested that the CEE provided the RGR with a total subsidy of 360,000 francs per month (the same source pointed out that this sum would barely cover the administrative expenses of running the RGR's central office).[88] It is possible to put business funding of politics into perspective by remembering that the MRP obtained thirteen million francs per year from the profits made by its weekly newspaper,[89] and that the RPF obtained one hundred million francs from the stamps sent by supporters to de Gaulle's home in Colombey-les-deux-Eglises. Even the small conservative parties of the Fourth Republic could find funds from other sources, notably discreet government subsidies, if business money was withheld.[90]

The second limitation on the power of business in the Fourth Republic sprang from the fact that politics had many dimensions other than the financial. Money was important to politicians, but reputation among voters and contacts with colleagues were essential. Business leaders who had grown up outside the political milieu often failed to understand such considerations. When de Nervo (the gas and automobile industrialist) tried to pressure the Alliance Démocratique to join a broader right-wing grouping in Paris, one of the party's leaders reminded his colleagues of how little money counted alongside established political loyalties: 'M. de Nervo does not exist, what exists in Paris are the old representatives of Parisian politics.'[91] Business leaders were often brusque and insensitive; they sometimes annoyed their political contacts so much that their interventions backfired. One conservative leader wrote that 'Bouchayer is a an ill-

[87] Ibid., p. 239.
[88] AN, 373 AP 73, Anteriou to Bollaert, 21 May 1948. 'I have just learnt from an indiscretion that the Rassemblement des Gauches gets 350,000 francs per month from the rue de Penthièvre.'
[89] R. Bichet, *La démocratie chrétienne en France. Le Mouvement Républicain Populaire* (Besançon, 1980), p. 221.
[90] For example the minister of the interior returned part of the electoral deposit to the Républicain Socialiste candidates in Paris after the party's severe defeat of 1945. E. Faure, *Mémoires.* I: *Avoir toujours raison ... c'est un grand tort* (Paris, 1982), p. 156.
[91] Bibliothèque Nationale (BN), Archives of Alliance Démocratique (AD) 4, M. Montigny addressing meeting of 28 May 1952.

mannered princeling. Once when he demanded that I bring him a dossier, I almost threw it in his face.'[92] Business paymasters sometimes became victims of their own success, as their protégés became too powerful to need their original backers. One industrialist who funded Chaban-Delmas' bid to become a deputy and mayor in Bordeaux made the mistake of assuming that Chaban could be discarded in the future: 'if he does not fit we will break him'.[93] However, by the 1950s Chaban's prestige and contacts were so well established that business had no choice but to try to work through him.[94]

The third limitation on the power of business over politicians was the extent of division and ill-discipline within business itself. The difficulty of persuading businessmen to arrive at any consensus even about those issues that touched their interests most directly has already been outlined. Persuading them to agree about broader political issues was even more difficult. If men like Boutemy were to be effective they had not only to persuade businessmen to give money to chosen politicians, but also to persuade businessmen to stop giving money to the rivals of chosen politicians. The multiplicity of mechanisms linking business with politics and the wide variety of particular political commitments on the part of business leaders made such an achievement almost impossible. Some businessmen insisted on funding several parties on the assumption that the aim of such subsidy was to buy favour with whoever won rather than to ensure the victory of a particular candidate: 'The interested parties never put all their resources on one side. Whoever wins, it is necessary to have him in hand.'[95] Those business leaders who did have clear commitments to particular candidates or parties often disagreed with each other, and found that their disagreements did much to blunt the impact of their action. In the 1951 election, matters were made especially awkward by the appearance of the RPF (a party that aroused particular divisions among capitalists). The divisions on this occasion extended to the offices of the CEE itself: when Boutemy arranged for posters showing de Gaulle shaking hands with Thorez to be circulated, he had to conceal his actions from his own colleagues.[96]

Not only were there contradictions within the business movement at any one time, there were also contradictions between the strategies adopted by sections of business from one time to another. In 1946 Brulfer and Boutemy sought to persuade conservative politicians to unite behind a single strong party (which became the PRL). However, within a few years the PRL was conscious that business support was slipping away and in the 1951 election, business strategy seemed to be opposed to the creation of strong party

[92] Riond, *Chroniques d'un autre monde*, p. 194.
[93] Lagroye, *Chaban-Delmas à Bordeaux*, p. 57.   [94] Ibid.
[95] Riond, *Chroniques d'un autre monde*, p. 199.   [96] Isorni, *1946–1958*, p. 215.

apparatuses. Similarly, Boutemy initially sought to discourage the creation of the Centre National des Indépendants in 1949,[97] but by 1952 de Nervo was pressing the Alliance Démocratique to break out of its alliance with the Radicals and join the CNIP.[98]

The fact that almost all bourgeois politicians had some contact with large-scale business made the numerous anti-capitalist observers of both left and right conclude that big business leaders were omnipotent puppet masters who controlled Fourth Republic politics according to some carefully worked out master plan. This chapter has suggested that such an interpretation is wrong. Business subsidy undoubtedly strengthened certain general trends in the Fourth Republic: it made anti-Communist unity easier, and encouraged the defence of private property. However, when it came to the implementation of specific policies within these general lines, the ubiquity of large-scale business subsidy and intervention was a symptom of weakness rather than a source of strength. Business was obliged to act through associations of small businessmen or through large numbers of political parties because it was unable to intervene more directly. Furthermore, the complexity of big business interventions in politics made them inefficient. Each small business ally or political contact that big business sought to activate had an agenda of his own that he tried to impose. At each turn big business had to compromise, to offer concessions to its associates and to dilute its own aims. Furthermore, business paymasters knew that politicians or parties who became too powerful would also become too independent of business subsidy. For this reason business leaders were nervous of strong and aggressive parties like the PRL or the RPF. In the 1951 election subsidy was spread over a range of small parties to produce a political balance of power. The aim of business intervention was not to produce strong parties that would pursue business interests, but to produce weak parties that would not be in a position to damage business interests.

[97] Duchet, *La république épinglée*, p. 12.
[98] BN, AD 4, Mme Gilbert Privat addressing meeting of 28 May 1952.

7 Administration

Vichy's finance minister Yves Bouthillier described the regime that he had served as 'the triumph of administration over politics'. An attentive reader of recent research on modern France might well conclude that this judgement could be extended to the whole of the twentieth century. Historians have devoted great attention to the workings of the French civil service, and especially its upper levels. In part this is due to the conscious efforts of civil service departments to encourage the study of their own role.[1] In part it also springs from a certain affinity between French academics and civil servants: the professor who has been formed by the *école normale supérieure*, the *agrégation* and the *doctorat d'état* is not so different from the functionary who has been formed by the *institut d'études politiques*, the *école nationale d'administration* and a *grand corps*. Most importantly of all, it is easier to study the Fourth Republic civil service than it is to study Fourth Republic politics. Documents for the administration are centralized and catalogued while those of politicians are scattered, lost or inaccessible.

Historians who study the civil service emphasize the degree of power that it exercised, particularly with reference to economic matters. Civil servants led more stable lives than politicians. Francis Bloch-Lainé remained in place as *directeur du crédit* while nine ministers of finance came and went.[2] Louis Franck smugly entitled his autobiography *697 ministres. Souvenirs d'un directeur général des prix*.[3] Furthermore, civil servants had the experience of economic management that most politicians lacked. Politicians who were preoccupied by the short-term threat posed by the latest

---

[1] After a conference in 1971, it was decided to produce histories of the various *corps d'état*. An Association pour l'Histoire de l'Administration Française was set up under the aegis of R. Brouilleet (an *inspecteur des finances*). Long, beautifully produced and excruciatingly tedious volumes were then published by the CNRS. For a brief history of this venture see p. xiii of the volume devoted to the *cour des comptes*. In more recent years the ministry of finance has established a *comité pour l'histoire économique et financière de la France*.

[2] F. Bloch-Lainé, *Profession fonctionnaire. Entretiens avec Françoise Carrière* (Paris, 1976), p. 96.

[3] L. Franck, *697 ministres. Souvenirs d'un directeur général des prix 1947–1962* (Paris, 1990).

cabinet crisis and the medium-term threat of Communism and Gaullism could not spare much energy for the long-term possibilities that were opened up by economic growth.

Two interpretations are presented of the autonomy that civil servants enjoyed with relation to politicians. Some view civil servants as the real heroes of the Fourth Republic: as an *aristocratie de la fonction publique* who used their independence in a disinterested manner to promote the public good.[4] The second interpretation is advanced, or at least hinted at, by Pierre Birnbaum. He suggests that the distance between upper level administrators and politicians was accompanied by intimate relations between administrators and large-scale business, and that these relations weakened democracy.[5]

The chapter will be divided into four parts. The first part will describe the nature of recruitment to the *corps d'état*. The second section will seek to explain the fact that the upper civil service preserved its prestige and power after 1945: it will be suggested that an extended comparison between the civilian administration and the armed forces (which lost both prestige and power in the Fourth Republic) highlights the peculiarity of the success of civilian administrators, and provides some clues about the reasons for their success. The third part will examine relations between politics and administration in the Fourth Republic. It will be argued that, alongside the widely discussed differences between the world of politics and the administration, were some equally important similarities. The fourth part will examine relations between business and the civil service. The quantitative evidence of links between the two will be described, but it will also be suggested that qualitative evidence about how links between business and administration were perceived suggests that the administration was not just a tool of large-scale capitalism. Indeed, it will be argued that the administration's value as a protector of the capitalist system in general lay partly in its detachment from the interests of any particular part of that system.

Upper level civil servants in post-war France were seen, and saw themselves, as set apart from the rest of society. Indeed, Napoleon had stated his intention to make the *corps d'état* into a closed order: 'I want to create a corporation, not of Jesuits who have their sovereign in Rome, but of Jesuits who have no other ambition than that of being useful, and no other interest but the public interest.'[6] The sense of group identity was particularly developed in the so-called *grands corps*. There were two sorts of

---

4   G. Bossuat, *La France, l'aide américaine et la construction européenne 1944–1954* (2 vols, Paris, 1992).
5   Pierre Birnbaum, *Les sommets de l'état. Essai sur l'élite du pouvoir en France* (Paris, 1977).
6   Quoted in E. N. Suleiman, *Elites in French society: the politics of survival* (Princeton, 1978), p. 19.

grands corps. The first category was made up of departments concerned with general administration, of which the most important were those concerned with public expenditure (i.e. the *inspection des finances* and the *cour des comptes*); the *conseil d'état* (a sort of constitutional think-tank); the diplomatic service and the prefectoral corps (which provided administrators for each department of France). The second category was made up of technical corps of which the most important were the *corps des mines* and the *ponts et chaussées*.

Entry into each of these corps was difficult; it was also largely controlled by existing members of the corps. Until 1945, the most important corps controlled their own recruitment. Candidates for the *inspection des finances* were trained by serving *inspecteurs* in 'stables', and the more technical corps (*mines, ponts et chaussés*) had their own schools which in turn took the best graduates from the *école polytechnique*. The *polytechnique* was a competitive engineering school (originally established to train artillery officers). Entry to the school was restricted to around 200 people per year and had remained remarkably stable for almost a century.[7] Graduates displayed a high degree of loyalty to their school and to each other. There was no official school for recruits to the non-technical corps before 1945, but in practice the great majority of these had came from the *école libre des sciences politiques*: a brochure produced by this school in 1935 claimed that among its graduates were to be found 228 of 332 *inspecteurs des finances*, 119 of 122 members of the *conseil d'état*, 88 of 101 members of the *cours des comptes* and 250 of 285 members of the diplomatic service.[8]

After 1945, the *corps d'état* lost their right to recruit their own members and a new school – the *école nationale d'administration* (ENA) – was established to prepare candidates for certain corps. ENA recruited around seventy-five candidates per year among graduates or serving members of the civil service. It was intended to democratize the civil service, but in practice it recruited the same kind of people who had previously entered the *corps d'état*.[9] Training in all the *grandes écoles* that prepared entry into the upper ranks of the civil service was largely undertaken by young men who were serving members of the *corps d'état* and who inculcated their charges with the values, as well as the technical skills, of their chosen profession. Careers in the civil service were mapped out from an early age. One *polytechnique* graduate recalled that an entire life might be affected by the

---

[7] In 1860, 143 men had entered the *polytechnique*; in 1950 the figure was 181. Ibid., p. 70.
[8] P. Lalumière, *L'inspection des finances* (Paris, 1959), p. 28.
[9] For explicit information about the intentions of ENA and implicit information about its failure to achieve those aims see ENA, *Rapport du directeur à son conseil d'administration 1945–1952* (Paris, 1952).

result of a single oral examination.[10] Students were subjected to unceasing competition. A man who decided that he wanted to become an *inspecteur de finances* via the *école polytechnique* (admittedly an unusual career route) would have first to pass the *polytechnique* entrance exam, then to pass out in the top third of his class at the *école polytechnique* in order to gain a place at ENA and then to be placed among the top eight graduates of ENA in order to be eligible for the inspectorate of finances.[11]

Competition persisted within the *corps d'état*. There was a recognized hierarchy of civil service departments. Graduates of ENA sought to go into the *inspection des finances*, the *conseil d'état*, the *cour des comptes*, the *administration civile*, the diplomatic corps and the prefectoral corps (in that order). The *corps des mines* was the most prestigious destination for graduates of the *école polytechnique* followed by *ponts et chaussés*.[12] Even within individual departments there was an established *cursus honorum*, and ambitious men knew that failure to occupy certain positions by the age of 40 would almost certainly mean failure to reach the very highest posts later in life.

Entry to, and success in, the civil service was linked to social background as well as academic ability. Membership of the *grands corps* was over-whelmingly bourgeois and Parisian; senior civil servants often came from particular dynasties of *noblesse de robe*. Wealth gave access to the kind of education that was required for entry into the *grandes écoles*, and the selection process for the *grands corps* emphasized social polish (the 1945 essay test for the inspectorate of finance on 'Le snobbisme comme stimulant de l'activité humaine' must have given particular advantages to those candidates who had grown up in the sixteenth *arrondissement*).[13] A study of the family backgrounds of *inspecteurs des finances* in the 1950s showed that 11.5 per cent came from the upper bourgeoisie and aristocracy, 19.5 per cent from commercial and banking backgrounds, 15.6 per cent from the liberal professions and 29.1 per cent from the higher reaches of the administration.[14] Of those recruited to ENA between 1945 and 1952, 39.2 per cent came from the Parisian region, and 41.5 per cent were the children of people who worked in the administration (only 3.9 per cent were the children of artisans and shopkeepers).[15]

The fact that the *grands corps* survived into the post-war period with their privileges intact seems all the more remarkable when their fate is compared to that of the officer corps of the French armed services. Before 1940 the

[10] Roger Martin, *Patron de droit divin* (Paris, 1984), p. 17.
[11] Lalumière, *L'inspection des finances*, p. 27.
[12] Suleiman, *Elites in French society*, p. 98.
[13] Lalumière, *L'inspection des finances*, p. 22.
[14] Ibid., p. 39.   [15] ENA, *Rapport du directeur*, p. 609.

French officer corps had occupied a social position similar to that of the civilian civil servants. Officers also came from upper class backgrounds, also trained at *grandes écoles* (the *école polytechnique* was still, in theory, a military school), and also had an acute sense of their own special position.

After 1945, the officer corps changed dramatically. Officers were less likely to come from haut-bourgeois backgrounds and *grandes écoles*; they were more likely to be promoted non-commissioned officers or the sons of NCOs. St Cyr (the traditional school for infantry officers) found it difficult to attract the right number of candidates, and the number of graduates of the *école polytechnique* who chose to make their career in the army dropped.[16] The contrast between civilian *corps d'état* and army officers is revealed in the attempts that both bodies made to recruit men from lower ranks to the highest level. On the civilian side, attempts were made to recruit lower civil servants to ENA, but these failed because the competition from students with conventional *grande école* backgrounds was so fierce.[17] In the army, on the other hand, young men from conventional backgrounds were so unenthusiastic about a career as an officer that a special *école de troupe* was established to train NCOs for promotion.[18]

The sense that the army occupied a special place in national life also changed. The fact that soldiers were given the right to vote was seen to reflect the descent into sordid party politics by an institution that had formerly exercised power through unspoken influence. Most importantly, the army was no longer seen as a representative of the nation. Traditionally, republican rhetoric had presented the army as the 'the nation in arms', and, between the wars, the *poilu* veterans of the Marne and Verdun had been seen as an important group.[19] After 1945 the army came to be seen as a more marginal part of national life; commentary on the military focused not on the army as a whole but on certain exceptional sections of it. Right-wing militarists lauded the heroism of the paras; *gauchiste* critics of French imperial policy condemned the atrocities of a largely German, and by implication Nazi, foreign legion.

There were three reasons why the military lost prestige and power after 1945. Firstly, it suffered from the overexpansion that afflicts most armies after a war. Large numbers of soldiers had been granted commissions on the strength of their achievements on the battlefield or in the *forces françaises de l'interieur*, and the army consequently had a bloated base of relatively old lieutenants, which made promotion prospects seem bad. The

[16] R. Girardet with M. Boujou and J. P. Thomas, *La crise militaire française 1945–1962. Aspects sociologiques et idéologiques* (Paris, 1964), pp. 30–31.
[17] ENA, *Rapport du directeur.*
[18] Girardet et al., *La crise militaire française*, p. 55.
[19] A. Prost, *Les anciens combattants et la société française 1914–1939* (Paris, 1977).

army also fell victim to financial retrenchment after the war; 50,000 army cars were removed and army pay dropped in comparison with that of other state employees.[20]

Secondly, the army suffered from association with defeat and collaboration and from the divisions of the years that followed the Liberation. All officers who had remained in mainland France were obliged to apply for reintegration into their services. The total number who were forced to resign or punished in some more explicit way is unclear;[21] what is certain is that many officers believed that large numbers of their comrades had been harshly punished (one authority claimed that there were 20,000 victims of the military purge)[22] and that doubts had been cast on their own loyalty. The large intake of new men from Free France and the Resistance who were socially and politically very different from traditional officers made the atmosphere in many messes tense, and the subsequent purging of unreliable (i.e. Communist) officers only added to the confusion of the army.

Thirdly, the army was damaged by broad economic, technological and diplomatic changes. Economic growth and the increasing importance of engineers provided an alternative career for *polytechnique* graduates who might otherwise have entered the army. Furthermore, the fact that these technically proficient potential recruits were reluctant to enter the armed forces coincided with the fact that warfare was becoming increasingly technological and that the qualities of leadership and courage that were valued in the non-technological parts of the armed forces seemed less and less relevant. The result of this was a spirit that sociologists labelled 'military Poujadism'[23] as soldiers grumbled about the 'push button army'.

The military was also damaged by the sense that it lacked a role. Between 1870 and 1940, the French army had gained respect as France's defender and avenger against Germany. In the Cold War, it became obvious that France's security was to be guaranteed, if at all, by international forces acting under American control and using nuclear weapons. A survey of French industrialists showed that many of them believed Supreme Headquarters Allied Powers in Europe (SHAPE) to be merely the forward headquarters of the United States army.[24] The growing power of international military organizations also affected the position of the French army within France. One element of the military's prestige had been the feeling that the army might step into power in a moment of national crisis,

---

[20] Jean Planchais, *Une histoire politique de l'armée*. II: *1940–1967, de de Gaulle à de Gaulle* (Paris, 1967), pp. 115–126.
[21] Girardet et al. estimate that only 658 officers were formally purged though many thousands more resigned or were demobilized. Girardet et al., *La crise militaire française*, p. 21.
[22] Edmond Ruby, 'L'épuration dans l'armée', *Défense de l'occident*, 39 (1957), 99–105.
[23] Girardet et al., *La crise militaire française*, p. 60.
[24] Planchais, *De de Gaulle à de Gaulle*, p. 237.

as it had done in 1940. But after 1945, the most vehement nationalist was obliged to admit that France's allies would probably never permit a coup d'état.[25] Even the army's role as keeper of public order on the streets was usurped by the *compagnies républicaines de sécurité* which had been created in 1945 and purged of Communists in 1947.[26]

The humiliation of the army was exhibited in a series of symbolic ways: military cemeteries were not maintained properly,[27] and soldiers were used to empty Paris rubbish bins in 1948.[28] The *Figaro* printed an article entitled 'poverty in battle dress' and arguing that the army had 'neither the force nor the cohesion that would make it a means of applying political pressure'.[29] The army was made an object of public ridicule when it attempted to issue khaki underwear for the use of women soldiers.[30] The result of this was that the army became bitter and increasingly attached to France's overseas possessions as the only area in which the dignity, traditional infantry skills and living standards of officers could be maintained.

The divergence between soldiers and the civil service elites was reflected in the declining number of sons of civil servants who made their career in the army: the proportion of officers who were the sons of civil servants fell from 21 per cent in 1945–48 to 14 per cent in 1954–58. It was also reflected in Birnbaum's study of the French ruling class, which found that the military members of the elite (as measured by entries in *Who's Who*) were being squeezed out by men with backgrounds in economic management.[31] The early years of the Fifth Republic were to show how absolute the divergence between the officer corps and the civilian administration had become. On the one hand these years saw the apotheosis of civilian administrators as de Gaulle filled important posts with *énarques*; on the other hand this period also saw the final humiliation of the 'lost soldiers' who made one last effort to defend their position through rebellion.[32]

The civil service was not immune to the kind of changes that afflicted the officer corps after the Liberation. The prefectoral corps was the most affected of all the *corps d'état*. Involvement in the maintenance of order and the suppression of Resistance activity had made many prefects participants in the French civil war of 1943 and 1944. As a result of this certain prefects such as René Bousquet and André Boutemy were forced to leave the corps

[25] C. Mauriac, *The other de Gaulle: diaries 1944–1954* (London, 1973), p. 290.
[26] On the CRS, see M. Agulhon and F. Barrat, *CRS à Marseille. 'La police au service du peuple' 1944–47* (Paris, 1971), and Jules Moch, *Une si longue vie* (Paris, 1976), p. 281.
[27] P. Ariès, *Un historien du dimanche* (Paris, 1980).
[28] Planchais, *De de Gaulle à de Gaulle*, p. 176.   [29] Ibid., p. 234.   [30] Ibid., p. 115.
[31] Pierre Birnbaum, *La classe dirigeante française* (Paris, 1978), p. 130.
[32] The phrase 'lost soldiers' was first used by de Gaulle. See G. Kelly, *Lost soldiers: the French army and empire in crisis 1947–62* (Boston, 1965).

after 1945,[33] and new *commissaires de la république* were brought in to administer regions on behalf of the Free French forces. However, unlike the army, the prefectoral corps maintained an important role in post-war France. Indeed, in two respects the power of the prefects increased after 1945. Firstly, the maintenance of order became recognized as a government priority after the departure of the Communists from government. For this reason the IGAMEs[34] or 'super prefects' were created to administer certain key areas in the wake of the strikes of 1948. Secondly, local government began to play an increasing role in the economy after 1945 and prefectoral officials became more and more involved with decisions about investment and public works.[35]

The prefectoral corps had always been regarded as the most politicized, and least prestigious, of the *corps d'état*. The turbulence in this corps after the Liberation did not, therefore, cause much concern for the other members of the civil service elite. The most important part of that elite (i.e. those connected with finance) escaped more easily than the prefects. Finance officials had not been involved in direct military conflict. In this area of the civil service, relations between men of different political loyalties had often remained cordial throughout the war, and most officials had maintained an overriding loyalty to their own corps.[36] Members of the corps on good terms with Vichy had protected their *résistant* colleagues during the occupation and the favour was often returned at the Liberation. Mendès-France was depressed, but not surprised, when the Resistance leader and civil servant Bloch-Lainé refused to provide information about Vichy sympathizers in the ministry of finance.[37]

The complexity of much economic work allowed civil servants to explain away relations that they may have had with the Germans as part of a 'double game'. Furthermore, many civil servants had anticipated allied victory at an early stage, and taken steps to distance themselves from the Vichy regime or to acquire links with the Resistance. Such efforts had been particularly strenuous in the ministry of finance: in 1943, the *inspecteur des finances* and future Gaullist prime minister Couve de Murville had defected

---

[33] Boutemy and Bousquet were both protected from serious punishment after the Liberation by the fact that they had assisted members of the Resistance. It is also interesting to note that both Boutemy and Bousquet subsequently acquired posts connected with large-scale business (although the prefectoral corps had traditionally been the corps that provided least opportunity for *pantouflage*).

[34] Inspecteur générale de l'administration en mission extraordinaire.

[35] On the increased economic role of prefects see the memoirs of the prefect for Alsace; René Paira, *Affaires d'Alsace* (Paris, 1990).

[36] Bloch-Lainé, *Profession fonctionnaire*, p. 55.   [37] Ibid., p. 57.

to the Free French and the Germans had subsequently arrested forty-three civil servants whom they believed to be undermining Vichy policy.[38]

There were, of course, certain upper level civil servants who were purged after the Liberation, and there were some Resistance leaders whose records gave them particular advantages in public service. However, those civil servants who enjoyed the benefits of a good war record had similar backgrounds and training to their colleagues. The self-confidence and authority that Resistance leaders had acquired often simply added to the autonomy that civil service departments were able to display towards politicians.

American influence, which did so much to damage the prestige and power of the army, might have been expected to have similar effects on the civil service. The Marshall plan and the aid provided under the Blum/ Byrnes agreement certainly gave America considerable leverage in the French economy. This leverage might have been used to overrule French civil servants; some French conservatives and business leaders hoped that American influence would be used to restrain the French administration and veto nationalization and *dirigisme*. An editorial in a right-wing journal asked: 'Why do you expect a liberal America to allow you to pursue a policy hostile to its interests with its subsidies?'[39] However, far from restraining the influence of French administrators, American subsidy increased it. This was because Marshall aid was channelled through the French state and its distribution was controlled by French civil servants.

Furthermore, certain civil servants came to be perceived as representatives of the Americans. The arch example of this achievement was Jean Monnet. Monnet had worked in Washington during the war. After the war his links with the USA were perceived to be so close that Debré, a colleague who helped negotiate the Blum/Byrnes agreement, wrote: 'the suggestions and the behaviour of Jean Monnet are ambiguous. Is he the skilful advocate of French positions to the Americans. Is he the interpreter of American policy for the French?'[40] Louis Franck described Monnet as being 'strong because of his American contacts'.[41] A few years later the author of a note on European integration in the Flandin archives presented Monnet as an American spokesman: 'American finance finds it convenient to have its idea defined by Monnet who was, in the inter-war period, one of its most distinguished advisers'.[42] The perceived links between Monnet and the

[38] R. Vinen, *The politics of French business 1936–1945* (Cambridge, 1991), p. 146.
[39] Marcel Geiswiller, 'Sauver le franc', *Ecrits de Paris*, March (1947).
[40] M. Debré, *Trois républiques pour une France. Mémoires.* II: *1946–1958. Agir* (Paris, 1988), p. 33.   [41] Franck, *697 ministres*.
[42] Bibliothèque Nationale, Flandin papers, 77, unsigned, undated note on European steel industry.

Americans accounted, in large measure, for his success in building up the *commissariat général du plan* (CGP) into such an influential body while having so few formally defined powers.

In the short term, the newly created state agencies that burgeoned after the Liberation weakened the traditional *corps d'état* by creating new centres of power. This was particularly true of Jean Monnet's CGP, which was specifically designed to circumvent existing civil service structures. The CGP had a small staff and deliberately avoided the formality and precise regulation of the traditional civil service; it was also placed under the direct authority of the prime minister's office in order to emphasize its autonomy. However, in the long term, the *corps d'état* retained their hegemony over the public sector and even seem to have strengthened their position as a result of the expansion of the economic role of the state. The very fact that the CGP's powers were informal meant that it was difficult to defend them in the long term, especially after the departure of Jean Monnet.

The increase of the power of the *corps d'état* was marked by the fact that the CGP became increasingly subordinate to the ministry of finance. Indeed, since the inspectorate of finance controlled the purse strings, any increase in public spending was bound to enhance its power. The nationalized industries proved particularly important for the *corps d'état*, and large numbers of former civil servants became directors of nationalized industries.[43] Participation in nationalized industries was financially advantageous for former civil servants (average salaries were around 40 per cent higher than for those directly employed by the state and maximum salaries could be two or three times those of upper level civil servants).[44] Most importantly, the passage of some civil servants to nationalized industries gave useful contacts and added prestige to those who remained in the *grands corps*.

The capacity of the *grands corps* to survive, and even exploit, the changes that occurred in post-war France was very much linked to their new found willingness to accept a more *dirigiste* view of the economy. This marked a sharp change. Before the war, French civil servants, especially those in the ministry of finance, had defended a conventional liberalism that emphasized the importance of low government spending and government restraint from interfering in the economy. This orthodoxy was expressed in the work of the *inspecteur des finances* and economist Jacques Rueff. After the war, ministry of finance officials accepted certain elements of *dirigisme* and were even willing to defend it against liberal politicians such as Antoine Pinay.

[43] By 1973, 60.8 per cent of *directeurs d'établissements d'état* were former members of *grands corps*. Suleiman, *Elites in French society*, p. 110.
[44] Lalumière, *L'inspection des finances*, p. 82.

Many historians have seen the adoption of *dirigisme* by the French civil service as part of an intellectual revolution that was rooted in the adoption of a new intellectual approach (i.e. Keynesianism).[45] Pierre Rosanvallon entitles the chapter dealing with the post-war period in his history of the French state 'The modernizing Keynesian state', and talks of a 'real intellectual revolution'.[46] It is certainly true that Keynes did become more respected after the Second World War and that his works were available in French for the first time. However, civil servants like Louis Franck and Bloch-Lainé made little reference to academic economics in their memoirs and those who did describe themselves as Keynesian often used the word rather loosely.[47] It seems likely that Jacques Rueff was much more familiar with the *General Theory* (a work that he devoted much energy to refuting) than any of the supposedly 'Keynesian' young turks who rose to prominence in the ministry of finance after 1945. What characterized the *grands corps* was their intensely pragmatic approach to policy making. This pragmatism was enhanced by a training that emphasized practical problems rather than theoretical discussion. Whereas students in French universities would listen to lectures by aged professors expounding the venerable orthodoxies of a previous generation, students at ENA were taught through class discussion with serving civil servants who were only a few years older than themselves.[48]

Under these circumstances, new approaches could gain quick and wide acceptance. Furthermore, as Thoenig has argued, what mattered to members of the French administrative elite was not the intellectual coherence of any particular approach, but its practical utility, and in particular its utility to the members of the corps themselves.[49] The ministry of finance was particularly willing to adopt strategies that might allow it to increase its influence because it was locked in rivalry with the ministry of

[45] Antoine Veil talked of Pinay having been surrounded by 'brilliant civil servants who had read Keynes'. A. Pinay, *Un français comme les autres. Entretiens avec Antoine Veil* (Paris, 1984), p. 83.

[46] P. Rosanvallon, *L'état en France de 1789 à nos jours* (Paris, 1990), p. 250.

[47] Georges Boris expressed admiration for Keynes, but it is hard to accept Margairaz's claim that vague statements by Boris about the inseparability of finances and economics represent an 'explicitly Keynesian approach'. M. Margairaz, *L'état, les finances et l'économie. Histoire d'une conversion 1932–1952* (2 vols, Paris, 1991), p. 10,071. It is useful to read the standard histories of French economic history in the light of the more rigorous English examinations of what precisely Keynesianism meant. See S. Newton, 'The Keynesian revolution debate: time for a new approach?', in A. Gorst, L. Johnman and W. Lewis (eds.), *Contemporary British history 1931–1961: politics and the limits of policy* (London, 1991), pp. 75–79.

[48] The interpretation of the French bureaucracy's capacity to adapt advanced here runs counter to M. Crozier's argument that the administration was characterized by its inflexible attachment to general principles and inability to respond to events. M. Crozier, *The bureaucratic phenomenon* (London, 1964).

[49] J.-C. Thoenig, *L'ère des technocrates. Le cas des ponts et chaussées* (Paris, 1973), p. 214.

national economics. Michel Margairaz has pointed out that this conflict was not so much one of theoretical approaches as 'one of corps, services and even individuals'.[50] It was desire to enhance their own influence and power that made members of the *ponts et chaussées* accept *urbanisme* during the 1960s. Similarly it was desire to enhance their influence that made members of the inspectorate of finance accept economic *dirigisme* during the late 1940s: civil servants soon realized that decisions about state spending, price control and public investment would involve increases in their own power. When the *directeur des prix* was told that Antoine Pinay had become minister of finance, his first thought was that: 'Such a liberal minister means the death of the directorate of prices'.[51]

Members of the *corps d'état* liked to present themselves as separate from, and superior to, politicians. Parliamentarians seemed to be everything that upper level civil servants were not. Parliament was mainly composed of lawyers, doctors, and teachers; it contained few former civil servants. The image of civil servants and politicians was as different as could be. The archetypal civil servant in France was seen to be a cold Parisian who lived in a highly formal world of precise rules, written examinations and clearly defined ranks; the archetypal politician was a fat and sweaty southerner who spent his days pressing flesh in the Café du Commerce and whose importance was derived from informal influence and personal reputation: Gambetta had said that 'in politics one must be someone and in administration one must be something'.[52]

Most important, in the eyes of many scholars, was the difference between the varieties of capitalism with which civil servants and politicians were associated. Few politicians had personal links with large-scale business. Few of them came from industrial families and few ex-deputies attained posts with national companies. Those politicians who did become businessmen generally did so in small locally based enterprises.

Members of the *grands corps*, on the other hand, had intimate connections with large-scale business. The backgrounds of civil servants and large-scale industrialists tended to be similar. The same families often produced sons who went into both the *corps d'état* and large firms. Pierre Lalumière wrote: 'An attentive study shows that the names of the great bourgeois families are found as frequently in the almanacs of private companies as in those of the administration.'[53] Both businessmen and civil servants passed

---

[50] Margairaz, *L'état, les finances et l'économie*, p. 10,088.
[51] C. Rimbaud, *Pinay* (Paris, 1990), p. 65. The enthusiasm of state officials for *plannisme* snowballed as increasing numbers of them came to see that their own influence was dependent on the existence of planning institutions. See P. Hall, *Governing the economy: the politics of state intervention in Britain and France* (Cambridge, 1986), p. 278.
[52] Cited in A. Siegfried, *De la IIIème à la IVème république* (Paris, 1957), p. 242.
[53] Lalumière, *L'inspection des finances*, p. 46.

through *grandes écoles*. Many ex-civil servants became industrialists. The chances that a high level administrator would obtain employment with a national company were far higher than those that an ex-minister would do so. Elite civil servants could acquire links with private industry by undertaking an industrial stage while students at ENA. Serving administrators might take prolonged leave to try their chances in private enterprise, and resignation from the civil service to join private firms was so institutionalized that it had a special name: *pantouflage*.

Members of the French bourgeoisie claimed to regard politics as a vulgar and undignified occupation when compared to administration. Deputies were badly paid and civil servants who presented themselves for election had to endure a fall in living standards.[54] Many post-war politicians from haut-bourgeois backgrounds claimed that they only entered politics because they were unable to pursue administrative careers. Olivier Guichard became a Gaullist politician after failing the entrance examination for ENA;[55] Jacques Chaban-Delmas presented his entry into politics as a last resort after his further career in the *inspection des finances* was blocked: 'Since I did not want to take anything in business, and since I had cut myself off from public service, there only remained one way ahead: politics.'[56]

Jacques Lecompte-Boinet, a leader of Ceux de la Résistance, did have a choice between politics and administration and did not hesitate to choose the latter. Even before the Liberation, he wrote: 'The administration is the only authority in the country, and the extent to which the Resistance becomes accepted by it will determine whether or not it [i.e. the Resistance] survives.'[57] Lecompte-Boinet turned down the chance to become a deputy or a leader of the Union Démocratique et Socialiste de la Résistance (UDSR) and toyed with the idea of becoming a director of RATP, a treasury official, *commissaire de la république* in Lyons or Montpellier or a diplomatic envoy to Finland.[58] He finally decided to enter the diplomatic service and was sent as an ambassador to Bogotá before enjoying a moderately successful career as French representative in Oslo and at the European council of ministers.

The apparent gulf between politicians and members of the *grands corps* and the apparent intimacy between members of the *grands corps* and large-scale industry underlies Pierre Birnbaum's interpretation of the Fourth Republic. According to Birnbaum, there were two separate elites in the

---

[54] Barthélemy Ott's salary dropped when he changed from being a French adminstrator in Germany to being a deputy. See Barthélemy Ott, *Il était une fois le conseil de la république 1946–1948* (Annonay, 1976), p. 26.

[55] Olivier Guichard, *Un chemin tranquille* (Paris, 1976), p. 57.

[56] Jacques Chaban-Delmas, *L'ardeur* (Paris, 1975), p. 132.

[57] Unpublished diary of Lecompte-Boinet, kindly lent to the author by Madame Lecompte-Boinet, entry for 4 January 1945.   [58] Ibid., entries for 24–27 August 1945.

Fourth Republic. The first was that of politicians and their allies in small-scale industries of local importance, represented by Léon Gingembre's Confédération Générale des Petites et Moyennes Entreprises (CGPME); the second was that of civil servants and their allies in large-scale national firms, represented by the Conseil National du Patronat Français (CNPF). It is implied that the second of these elites possessed a kind of *pouvoir réel* as opposed to the mere *pouvoir légal* possessed by parliamentarians. In this context, the success of large-scale business and the entry of high level administrators into political office during the Fifth Republic can be seen as the inevitable dénouement of realities that had existed before 1958.

Birnbaum's conclusions are supported by a detailed statistical analysis of the careers of members of the French elites. They are also supported by the mythologies that both civil servants and politicians found useful to maintain. Civil servants wished to present themselves as detached from the squabbles and deals of politics; politicians wished to appear as representatives of the 'little man' against the faceless 'technocrats' of the *grands corps*. However, his interpretation is flawed in a number of ways. Firstly, both the political and administrative elites contained important divisions within their ranks. The most important of these divisions was that in the political elite between the Communist party and the bourgeois parties. The single greatest aim of the bourgeois parties was to exclude the Communist party from power and to protect the existence of private property. This aim was one that united bourgeois politicians with civil servants whatever their differences about the means of achieving it.

There were other similarities between bourgeois politicians and civil servants. The two groups may have come from different ends of the bourgeois spectrum but, judged from the perspective of the working class or peasantry, this was a fairly narrow spectrum. Both politicians and civil servants depended on private property and both were particularly dependent on the 'cultural capital' that was provided by an expensive education. Both tended to accumulate wealth and power across the generations. The concern of members of the *ponts et chaussées* to defend their own power, described by Thoenig,[59] is similar to the concern of parliamentarians with political 'fiefdoms', described by Leites.[60] Similarly, the administrative 'dynasties' described by Lalumière[61] are similar to the political dynasties described by Abélès.[62]

Even the 'apoliticism' (or anti-politicism) of civil servants might be

[59] Thoenig, *L'ère des technocrates*, p. 121.
[60] N. Leites, *On the game of politics in France* (Stanford, 1959).
[61] Lalumière, *L'inspection des finances*, p. 44. Lalumière stressed that the *corps d'état* dynasties were becoming less frequent after 1945.
[62] M. Abélès, *Quiet days in Burgundy* (Cambridge, 1991)

interpreted as evidence of the parallels between the administrative and political worlds. Apoliticism was, as Vedel pointed out, ubiquitous in the Fourth Republic, and anti-political statements were often made by people who participated in politics themselves.[63] The very terms in which members of the *corps d'état* attacked the political system were similar to those used by the local notables and bourgeois deputies on whom that political system was founded. Both groups disdained controversy and 'ideology'; both groups presented their own motives as disinterested and argued that their legitimacy was built on widespread recognition of their particular expertise rather than the electoral machine of organized parties.

Furthermore, alongside their ostentatious expressions of contempt for the political system, some civil servants made discreet but vigorous efforts to enter that system. Michel Debré turned down the opportunity to rejoin the *conseil d'état* in order to wait for a parliamentary seat to become vacant.[64] In this context it might be argued that the comparative scarcity of upper level civil servants in Fourth Republic politics was not a sign that they were too powerful to bother with politics, but rather a sign that they were too weak to force themselves into political positions of a level that they believed to be their due. The political world, unlike that of large-scale business, felt no need to defer to men from prestigious *corps d'état*, and the civil service elite had no power to compel the members of the *conseil général* of the Yonne or the voters of Neuvic d'Ussel to support a parliamentary candidate simply because he had passed first in his year at ENA.

The hypothesis that civil servants were kept out of Fourth Republic politics by forces outside their own control is lent some substance by the fact that they entered politics in such large numbers when they were given the chance to do so. De Gaulle, who had an almost mystical faith in the abilities of the *corps d'état*, was willing to allow civil servants straight into ministerial office during the provisional government and many members of *corps d'état* flocked to support the RPF. Upper level civil servants also showed themselves enthusiastic when they were given the opportunity to participate in ministerial cabinets, and such cabinets contained significant numbers of *énarques* from 1950 onwards.[65] Both these developments paved the way for the large-scale entry of administrators into political office when de Gaulle returned to power in 1958, and members of the *grands corps* were very active in politics from then on.[66]

The most awkward problem of all in Birnbaum's interpretation is his

[63] Georges Vedel (ed.), *La dépolitisation. Mythe ou réalité?* (Paris, 1962).
[64] Margherita Rendel, *The administrative functions of the French conseil d'état* (London, 1970), p. 41.　　[65] Suleiman, *Elites in French society*, p. 103.
[66] Ibid., p. 101.

reliance on studies of the careers and backgrounds of members of the elite. There is no necessary reason to assume that people from similar backgrounds would share common interests or aims. F. Bloch-Lainé enjoyed easy relations with Paul Reynaud, an archetypal Third/Fourth Republic politician. However, Bloch-Lainé got on badly with Valéry Giscard d'Estaing, a politician who had himself begun in the inspectorate of finance. Bloch-Lainé argued that those 'ex-future senior civil servants' who gained political power in the Fifth Republic were suspicious of their former colleagues from the *grands corps* and excessively prone to surround themselves with political cabinets who restricted the access that civil servants had to ministers.[67]

Birnbaum's emphasis on common educational backgrounds and career patterns obscures other relations that existed between sections of the French elite. Birnbaum assumes that civil servants were 'close' to big business because many of them went on to take jobs in this sector of the economy. However, in reality, the big and small business sectors were not as mutually distinct or as internally coherent as they first appeared. Small business associations were often funded by, and to some extent influenced by, large-scale business. Furthermore, many bourgeois politicians whose background and rhetoric appeared to link them to small-scale business were funded, and advised, by large-scale business.

The limitations of studying the Fourth Republic elite in Birnbaum's terms can be exposed by examining the most notorious confrontation between a politician and the civil service in the Fourth Republic: that between Antoine Pinay and the officials of the finance ministry when the former became finance minister in 1948. Feelings ran so high on this occasion that Pinay suggested that his civil servants might have to resign if they did not wish to implement his policies.[68] At the first glance this episode fits neatly into Birnbaum's analysis. The finance ministry was the home of the most elite section of the French civil service; Antoine Pinay, on the other hand, epitomized the Fourth Republic provincial politician. He was a provincial, and the proprietor of a medium-sized business. However, in reality Pinay's confrontation with the civil service did not pit the political/CGPME elite against the civil service/CNPF elite. For, in spite of Pinay's background and the rhetorical emphasis that he placed on his links with Gingembre's CGPME, he was also regarded favourably by an important group within the CNPF. Furthermore, Pinay's confrontation with the civil service concerned his desire to dismantle *dirigiste* measures that had been

[67] Bloch-Lainé, *Profession fonctionnaire*, pp. 9 and 96–97.
[68] Pinay, *Un français comme les autres*, p. 60.

applied after the war: a desire that was vigorously supported by some representatives of large-scale business.[69]

Birnbaum's ideas about the relationship between large-scale business and the civil service are also open to question. Birnbaum argues that there was a 'convergence' between large-scale business and the administrative elite. This interpretation is based on two pieces of evidence. The first of these is the similarity between the careers of those in large-scale business and those in the upper civil service. The second is the fact that the post-war French state became intimately involved in promoting certain measures – such as industrial concentration, large-scale investment and European integration – that turned out to be of long-term benefit to French capitalism. However, the fact that measures taken by the French state turned out to be of benefit to French capitalism did not mean that relations between capitalists and the state were good. On the contrary, these relations were characterized by coercion rather than co-operation. The role of the public bodies in buying services, the provision of raw materials and energy through nationalized industries, and, most importantly, government control of credit gave the state enormous powers to enforce its will on industry.[70] Many observers commented on the haughty manner in which civil servants treated businessmen.[71]

Upper level civil servants were quick to use their powers. They made their disapproval of the backwardness of French industry clear, while capitalists railed against the interventions of the French state. Furthermore, some of the most indignant protests came from those business leaders or conservative politicians such as Jacques Rueff and Edmond Giscard d'Estaing whose backgrounds closely resembled those of the civil service elite. Indeed, in many ways the usefulness of the *corps d'état* to French capitalism lay precisely in their relative detachment from the interests of any particular part of the capitalist system. French businessmen were notoriously divided by commercial rivalries, conflicting interests and personal animosity. They were also notoriously cautious and short-sighted in their outlook; they were

[69] On Pinay's image as a man linked to small business, and on his links to large business see chapter 13. Pinay's relations with both large and small business were complicated. Ehrmann suggests that large-scale business became disillusioned with Pinay's 'mild trust busting' activities, and that Pinay's policies were opposed by both modernizing civil servants and the most dynamic section of large-scale business. Henry W. Ehrmann, *Organized business in France* (Princeton, 1957), p. 265. However, the split between Pinay and part of big business did not occur until after Pinay became prime minister in 1952. Furthermore S. Guillaume notes that the CGPME also became disillusioned with Pinay's activities as prime minister. S. Guillaume, *La Confédération Générale des Petites et Moyennes Entreprises. Son histoire, son combat, un autre syndicalisme patronal 1944–1978* (Paris, 1987), p. 51.   [70] Hall, *Governing the economy*, p. 152.
[71] Guichard, *Un chemin tranquille*, p. 98. See also the views of a businessmen himself, Henri Pollet, on his need for contact with *énarques* in L. Duroy and S. Moles, *Paroles de patrons* (Paris, 1977), p. 77.

reluctant to take the risk involved in large-scale investment or in seeking new markets. Under these circumstances observers like Michel Crozier suggested that the function of the state in France was to push entrepreneurs into innovations that, left to themselves,[72] they would resist, or to provide what marxists would describe as a 'relatively autonomous state' that could rise above the short-term and conflicting interests of individual capitalists to impose long-term strategies that were in the interests of the capitalist system as a whole.[73]

Evidence provided by autobiographies suggests that the presence of numerous civil servants in the private sector can be interpreted as a sign of the state's power over private industry rather than vice versa. This impression is confirmed by several things. Firstly, civil servants did not regard entry into the private sector as a particularly attractive option. In 1952, one observer wrote that 'the seduction of great *corps d'état* turns the best of our young people away from taking on industrial employment'.[74] Most preferred the power that came with working for the state to the wealth that came with working for the private sector, and those who left the civil service were often willing to do so because it had already become obvious that they would not reach the top in their own departments.[75] This suggests that the most successful, and powerful, civil servants were those whose judgement was least likely to be affected by considerations of a future career in business.

Secondly, even those civil servants who did join private firms seem to have done so because they were approached not because they actively sought positions: 'It was not me who ran after the *pantoufle*, but the *pantoufle* that came looking for me.'[76] Most importantly, the civil servants who took jobs as managers seem to have taken the values of the public sector with them rather than absorbing the values of their new employers. As has often been pointed out, large-scale business in France had never developed its own set of values, and French industrialists had little sense of

---

[72] Crozier, *The bureaucratic phenomenon*, p. 284.
[73] See F. Block, 'The ruling class does not rule: notes on the Marxist theory of the state', *Socialist Revolution*, 33 (1977), 6–28; C. Offe, 'Structural problems of the capitalist state: class rule and the political system. On the selectivity of political institutions', *German Political Studies*, 1 (1974), 33–57. For a critical analysis of ideas about the autonomous state see J. Zeitlin, 'Shop floor bargaining and the state: a contradictory relationship', in S. Tolliday and J. Zeitlin (eds.), *Shop floor bargaining and the state* (Cambridge, 1985). For an attempt to apply some of these ideas to France see Vinen, *The politics of French business*, pp. 216–221.
[74] J. E. Sawyer quoted in F. Bourricaud, 'Sociologie du chef d'entreprise: le "Jeune patron"', *Revue Economique*, 6 (1958), 896–911.
[75] Lalumière points out that the average age of resignation from the *inspection des finances* was 40 (by which age a man would know whether or not he stood any chance of reaching the heights of public service).
[76] Martin, *Patron de droit divin*, p. 58.

their own legitimacy.[77] Civil servants by contrast had an enormously strong sense of their own worth and purpose in life. Members of the *corps d'état* took it for granted that that they had a right to enjoy the best positions in industry, and they were often rather cavalier in their attitudes towards their new employers. Roger Martin, a member of the *corps des mines* who joined Pont-à-Mousson, entitled his autobiography *Patron de droit divin*; one of his friends arrived for his first day of work at Schneider wearing a pair of cycling shorts. Civil servants who went into private industry often turned the firms of their new employers into self-sustaining oligarchies that employed further members of the *grands corps*; the habit of managers ensuring that their successors were chosen from their own corps of origin came to be known as 'sending down the lift'.[78]

Civil service habits of thought often remained with industrial managers who had left public service and they sometimes influenced even those former functionaries who seemed most intimately linked to private industry. Léon Daum was a civil servant from a family of Lorraine industrialists. He began his career with a training at the *école polytechnique* and service in the *corps des mines*, but he left public service to join a steel company, Marine et Homécourt, where he worked for many years and was groomed as the successor for the managing director of the firm, Théodore Laurent. In 1952 Daum despaired of ever obtaining the succession when Laurent was reappointed for a further six years at the age of 90.[79] For this reason Daum resigned and was made a member of the High Authority of the European Coal and Steel Community. Industrialists welcomed Daum's appointment and assumed that he would act as an effective representative of industrial interests. But in fact he proved notably detached from the day to day interests of the industry in which he had worked, and soon French steel associations were complaining about his lack of concern for them.[80]

Civil servants joined large national firms, and often firms that belonged to the *secteur abrité* (i.e. those firms that depended on contracts from the state). The atmosphere in such firms was not so different from that of the civil service. Some civil servants also went to work for business associations. Such associations were concerned with the long-term interests of a sector, or even the whole business community, rather than the short-term interests of a single company, and they were often intimately linked to the state.

Relations between private and public sectors in France were not immune to the changes that affected the rest of French society. Studies conducted in

[77] F. Bourricaud, 'Malaise patronal', *Sociologie du Travail*, 111 (1961), 221–225.
[78] Suleiman, *Elites in French society*, p. 182.
[79] Martin, *Patron de droit divin*, pp. 37 and 142. Martin recorded that Laurent complained that Daum had left 'just when I had finished training him'. Laurent himself died the year after Daum's resignation.   [80] Ehrmann, *Organized business in France*, p. 414.

the 1970s showed that civil servants viewed administration in public and private sectors as much the same activity, and, where their predecessors had regarded *pantouflage* as something to be undertaken only by those who could not reach the summits of a state career, those who entered the *grands corps* during the Fifth Republic often stated explicitly that their ultimate aim was to work in a private corporation. Suleiman and Birnbaum suggest that this process illustrated the triumph of business values in France.[81]

In fact greater willingness of civil servants to enter private business might better be explained in terms of subordination of private business to the state. The private sector had changed between 1950 and 1970: it had been transformed by industrial concentration, large-scale investment, development of new capital intensive sectors (often ones that were dependent on the state) and increasing industrial organization. All these changes tied in with the vision of a 'modern economy' that civil servants had presented to private industry during the Fourth Republic, but they also ensured that in many respects private industrial management came to resemble the upper reaches of the civil service. The growing numbers of large firms, *secteur abrité* firms, business organizations and the replacement of owners by salaried managers all meant that those who ran business were increasingly detached and long term in their view of business life; these developments also meant that the number of firms or organizations that were willing to employ former members of the *grands corps* increased.

The nature of relations between industry and the state in France can be illustrated by comparing Fifth Republic France with Britain in the 1980s. In Britain there was a convergence between private enterprise and the state that took place on business terms. Public institutions were sold off or 'commercialized', business consultants were brought in to advise the civil service and 'think-tanks' were filled with young men from merchant banks. All these processes were explained and defended in a language of 'market testing', 'unit costs' and 'total quality management' that came from the private sector. In France, by contrast, the movement from public to private sector was entirely one way. Few businessmen were taken on to advise government,[82] and it was the public sector language and techniques of ENA and the *corps d'état* that seeped into the private sector rather than the private sector that influenced the public sector.[83] In short, French civil servants may have been responsible for the survival and prosperity of capitalism, but they ensured that it survived in a form that was acceptable to them.

---

[81] Suleiman, *Elites in French society*, p. 234.

[82] Ministerial cabinets in the Fifth Republic drew 90 per cent of their members from the private sector, and this proportion had increased slightly during the post-war period. Réné Rémond, 'Conclusion', in René Rémond, A. Coutrot and I. Broussard (eds.), *Quarante ans de cabinets ministériels. De Léon Blum à G. Pompidou* (Paris, 1982), pp. 232–242.

[83] Hall, *Governing the economy*, p. 279.

8   *Opposition nationale*

The leaders of the extreme right in post-war France often referred to themselves as the *opposition nationale*. However, there is something rather odd about the behaviour of this group during the Fourth Republic. Its leaders presented themselves as intransigent opponents of everything that the regime stood for; their attitude was summed up by Jean Mazé's scathing and wide-ranging denunciation of what he called *le système*.[1] However, in reality, the Fourth Republic *opposition nationale* often had links with the very parties, politicians and governments that they claimed to despise. Mazé's own career illustrates this paradox: in 1951 he became secretary of Isorni's party, the Union des Nationaux et Indépendants Républicains (UNIR). UNIR set out to defend the reputation of Pétain and the interests of those who had supported him. However, UNIR also sought to enter the Centre National des Indépendants et Paysans (CNIP), a mainstream conservative group, and received discreet support not only from conservatives like Duchet and Mutter but from the Socialist president of the republic.[2] This chapter will seek to show that the Fourth Republic was not confronted by an isolated and marginal *opposition nationale*, but rather that several partially overlapping sets of belief – Pétainism, anti-Gaullism and anti-Communism – bound together a wide range of men.

At one extreme of this range, were the small minority of unrepentant defenders of everything that the Vichy government had done. Maurice Bardèche, who nurtured the post-war cult of his executed brother-in-law, the fascist poet Brasillach, was the most prominent representative of this group. Bardèche wrote: 'We ... maintain that everything done under the orders of a legitimate authority ... was legal'.[3] However, another larger and less extreme group did not seek to defend everything that the Vichy regime had done, or to attack 'honest Resistance fighters', but did argue that the penalties applied to former Pétainists were unfairly harsh. This group was represented by *chanoine* Desgranges, and by Alfred Fabre-Luce, a wealthy

---

[1] Jean Mazé, *Le système* (Paris, 1951).
[2] J. Isorni, *Mémoires*. II: *1946–1958* (Paris, 1986), pp. 209–211.
[3] M. Bardèche, *Lettre à François Mauriac* (Paris, 1947), pp. 25–26.

and eccentric intellectual who had been imprisoned both under Vichy and at the Liberation.[4] Desgranges wrote a book attacking what he called *résistantialisme* – the political exploitation of the Resistance[5] – while Fabre-Luce addressed his work to the 'silent men' who had been punished for their loyalty to Marshal Pétain.[6]

After 1945, the Pétainist legacy was less apparent than that of the Resistance. Almost every political party made some claim to being *a* party, if not *the* party, of the Resistance. Pétainism, on the other hand, was widely seen as an electoral liability; men who had voted full powers to Pétain in 1940 or held office under the Vichy government were barred from standing for office, and many of the most prominent figures from Vichy were imprisoned or exiled after 1945. No political party dedicated itself to the defence of the Marshal's memory until Jacques Isorni, Pétain's defence counsel, set up the UNIR to contest the 1951 election. However, several agencies did defend the reputation of Pétain or the rights of those who had supported him.

The first of these was the *comité d'honneur* for the liberation of Marshal Pétain that was established in 1948 by Isorni, and presided over by the historian Louis Madelin.[7] In spite of the fact that it defined its functions very narrowly, and sought to avoid provocative political stands, the committee was soon banned. Three years later an Association pour Défendre la Mémoire du Maréchal Pétain (ADMP) was founded under the presidency of General Weygand; the ADMP had a broader appeal that its predecessor and survives today.[8] The second body concerned with the defence of Pétainists was the Association des Représentants du Peuple de la Troisième République (ARPTR) founded by *abbé* Desgranges, which will be described below. The third body was the Association de Notre Dame de la Merci, also established by Desgranges – its aim was to defend the rights of prisoners, and particularly those of political prisoners.[9]

---

[4] Fabre-Luce wrote numerous autobiographical works, notably *Vingt-cinq années de la liberté*. II: *L'épreuve 1939–1946* (Paris, 1963). There were also frequent articles on Fabre-Luce in the right-wing press: see H. Saint-Charnot, 'Alfred Fabre-Luce, pyschoanalyste de la résistance', *Questions Actuelles*, December 1946. Fabre-Luce was a grandson of the banker Henri Germain; see the autobiography of Fabre-Luce's cousin, André Germain, *La bourgeoisie qui brûle. Propos d'un témoin 1890–1940* (Paris, 1951).

[5] J. Desgranges, *Les crimes masqués du résistantialisme* (Paris, 1949). On *résistantialisme*, see Michel Dacier, 'Le résistantialisme', *Ecrits de Paris*, 1 January 1947.

[6] A. Fabre-Luce, *Au nom des silencieux* (Bruges, 1945).

[7] On the *comité d'honneur*'s brief history see the Madelin papers in Archives Nationales (AN), 455 AP 4. See particularly the letter from Isorni to the prefect of police, dated 8 May 1948, denying that the committee had ever proposed to organize public demonstrations.

[8] On the history of the ADMP see Henry Rousso, *Le syndrome de Vichy (1944–198 ...)* (Paris, 1987), pp. 54–61.

[9] On the Association de Notre Dame de la Merci see, in addition to the works cited above, Jean Popot, *J'étais aumônier à Fresnes* (Paris, 1962).

The press and publishing houses were also important in the presentation of the Pétainist case. Maintaining publications was not easy because of censorship, the seizure or suppression of newspapers that had supported Vichy and the inability of journalists who lacked good contacts to obtain scarce newsprint. Some works had to be published clandestinely,[10] and journalists often mockingly took the names of Resistance publications that had been produced in similar circumstances a few months earlier.[11] Other works were published abroad. The Cheval Ailé press established by Constant Bourquin in Switzerland was heavily influenced by the former Vichy official Jean Jardin,[12] and published works by his Pétainist associates;[13] the Belgian journal *Europe/Amérique* played an important in French right-wing thought until it was banned in 1946.[14] Eventually an openly Pétainist press emerged in France (often as papers that had initially claimed to be supporters of the Resistance revealed their true colours). The Grub Street of journalists who wrote for these papers often seemed rather ludicrous. They lived irregular lives characterized by constant battles with the courts and struggles to make ends meet (one supported himself by writing books about the English royal family under the pseudonym Caroline Jones).[15] However, Pétainist publications reached tens of thousands of readers, including the wealthy and influential. Three journals proved particularly important. The first of these was *Paroles Françaises*, which started as a right-wing Resistance paper but became increasingly associated with Pétainism after a boardroom battle; its circulation was estimated to have peaked at between 100,000 and 200,000 copies. *Ecrits de Paris* was another paper that emerged from a journal that claimed links with the Resistance; it was initially entitled *Bulletin Intérieur*, and then became increasingly explicit in its Pétainism. *Ecrits de Paris* was estimated to have a circulation of around 30,000,[16] and, judging from the pages devoted to economic analysis and advertisements directed at businessmen,

---

[10] See the bound volume of 'clandestine journals' in the Bibliothèque Nationale.

[11] Fabre-Luce arranged for some his early work to be published by Editions du Midi.

[12] P. Assouline, *Jean Jardin 1904–1976. Une éminence grise* (Paris, 1986), pp. 197–198.

[13] Works published under this imprint included G. Bonnet, *De Washington au Quai d'Orsay* (Geneva, 1945); H. du Moulin de Labarthète, *Le temps des illusions. Souvenirs juillet 1940– avril 1942* (Geneva, 1946); L. Rougier, *Mission secrète à Londres* (Geneva, 1946); A. Fabre-Luce, *Le mystère du maréchal. Le procès Pétain* (Geneva, 1945); A. Fabre-Luce, *Journal de la France (1939–1944)* (Geneva, 1945).

[14] On the banning of this journal in France see *Europe/Amérique*, 65, 12 September 1946. The leading writer on *Europe/Amérique* (Ossian Mattheiu) was subsequently enlisted by Jean Pleyber and François Brigneau to work in the French right-wing press. F. Brigneau, *Mon après guerre* (Paris, 1985), p. 140.

[15] Brigneau, *Mon après guerre*, p. 189. The work that 'Caroline Jones' published was entitled, *Dans le secret d'une reine*.

[16] Estimate by Henry Coston, cited in J. Algazy, *La tentation néofasciste en France 1944–1965* (Paris, 1984), p. 66.

much of this readership seems to have been affluent. *Ecrits de Paris* was edited by 'Michel Dacier' (René Malliavin); it carried articles by prominent Vichy apologists such as Fabre-Luce and Isorni as well as former Vichy officials such as Flandin and Gignoux. The third journal to take up the defence of the Vichy government after the war was *Rivarol*. Founded in 1951, this was the most extreme of the major post-war right-wing journals. It eventually attracted 45,000 readers and appealed to monarchists and fascists as well as Pétainists. Its readers seem to have been more engaged in political struggle than those of other journals; one-third of those who answered a survey in 1957 had been imprisoned at the Liberation.[17]

Pétainist apologia changed the right's thinking in an important way. This concerned legality. The extreme right had traditionally despised the *pays légal*, and it had often placed its hopes in violent action to overthrow the Third Republic. However, after the war, many right-wingers found themselves defending the Vichy regime, which had sprung not from a putsch but from a vote of the Third Republic parliament. Furthermore, at the Liberation judges were more sympathetic than politicians to former Pétainists.[18] A strict interpretation of the law was often the only thing between right-wingers and political banishment, prison or the firing squad: it was no coincidence that two of the most prominent leaders of the post-war extreme right – Jacques Isorni and Jean Louis Tixier-Vignancour – were defence lawyers. It was even argued that legal proceedings had become the only means of expression for right-wingers: 'speech has taken refuge in the law court'.[19]

The right's new concern for legality was linked to an increasing enthusiasm for the Republic on which that legality was founded. The retroactive legislation with which de Gaulle's government punished those who had supported the Vichy government was attacked as a betrayal of the traditions of 1875 or even those of 1789. Some of these attacks were simply attempts to embarrass the government by attacking it in the language that was normally used by the left: 'Since the government invokes republican principles, while practising dictatorship, I wanted to take it at its word and give it the choice of hearing the truth or publicly renouncing its principles.'[20] But other attacks on the *épuration* came from those with a genuine horror of legislation that punished men for having a obeyed a legally constituted government. Louis Rougier, who had acted as an informal envoy for Pétain and who became a leading figure on the extreme right after

---

[17] Ibid., p. 132.

[18] On the role of law courts in defending newspapers that had appeared under Vichy see J. Mottin, *Histoire politique de la presse* (Paris, 1949).

[19] J. Tixier-Vignancour, *J'ai choisi la défense* (Paris, 1964).

[20] Fabre-Luce, *Au nom des silencieux*, p. 22.

1945, lamented 'the destruction of republican constitutional legality'.[21] Jacques Isorni was most explicit about the change that had been brought about in the language of the right. 'From then on it was impossible to resort to the opposition imagined by Maurras between the *pays réel* and the *pays légal*.'[22]

The ineligibility laws of the Liberation gave particular offence to those who proclaimed themselves to be defenders of Republican legality. These laws forbad deputies who had voted full powers to Pétain and all those who held office under the Vichy government from presenting themselves for election. Such measures were contrary to several constitutional principles: they were retroactive, they were not applied by properly constituted courts, and they involved the punishment of deputies for their votes. The campaign against ineligibility was led by the *abbé* Jean Desgranges. Desgranges had been a Christian Democrat deputy before the war, and he had voted full powers to Pétain. After the war, he was excused from the provisions of the ineligibility laws on account of his Resistance activity. He chose not to resume a parliamentary career but to devote his energies to defending those whom he regarded as the victims of the *épuration*. Desgranges was a man of great enthusiasm, and his commitment to his cause seems eventually to have become counterproductively intense. However, for a time he was highly effective. He recruited support from both French politicians and even from foreign leaders such as Salazar in Portugal and Van Zeeland in Belgium.[23] In 1946 he founded the ARPTR. The association published a journal, *Résistance à l'Oppression*, and organized a petition to the United Nations. Most importantly, it staged a banquet in 1948 for 'one thousand ineligibles' to mark the centenary of the 1848 revolution. The banquet was important for two reasons. Firstly, it attracted considerable attention and was widely seen as as a sign of how influential former Pétainists could be. Secondly, it showed the extent to which Pétainist apologia had become integrated into the republican tradition. It was particularly significant that the *banquet des mille* occurred in the same year that the *cagoulards* were tried for having sought to overthrow the Third Republic by violence.

Defence of the Vichy government often tied in with violent opposition to General de Gaulle. However, Pétainism and anti-Gaullism were never synonymous. There were some defenders of Pétain who were not anti-Gaullist. Rémy, the Gaullist Resistance leader who became a member of the

---

[21] Rougier, *Mission secrète*, p. 132.

[22] Jacques Isorni, *Ainsi passent les républiques* (Paris, 1959), p. 53.

[23] On Desgranges' relations with Van Zeeland see J. D. M. Dutroncy, *L'abbé Desgranges. Conférencier et député 1874–1958* (Paris, 1962), p. 227. On Desgranges' relations with Salazar see Rémy (pseudonym for Gilbert Renaud), *Mes grands hommes et quelques autres* (Paris, 1982), p. 337.

Association pour Défendre la Mémoire du Maréchal Pétain (ADMP), argued that France had needed both the General and the Marshal.[24] Emmanuel Berl, who had written one of Pétain's first speeches, recognized, somewhat grudgingly, that de Gaulle had served a useful purpose: '[I am] convinced that the troubles, pillages and murders of 1945 would have been worse without de Gaulle, as the fascist excesses would have been without Pétain'.[25] On the other side of the spectrum were men who had opposed Vichy but also disliked de Gaulle. Many leaders of the Resistance within France had had frosty relations with the General, and many Fourth Republic politicians resented and feared what they perceived as the undemocratic tendencies of the Rassemblement du Peuple Français (RPF). Even among those who had worked with the Free French, there was a strain of anti-Gaullism. Two right-wing supporters of the Free French, de Kérillis[26] and Mengin,[27] wrote books after the war in which they denounced de Gaulle's arrogance and authoritarianism. Furthermore, the two men who had clashed most violently with de Gaulle during his leadership of the Free French both enjoyed brief political careers in the Fourth Republic. General Giraud, who had been displaced by de Gaulle as leader of Fighting France in Algeria, became a deputy with the support of the Parti Républicain de la Liberté (PRL). Admiral Muselier, who had been imprisoned by de Gaulle in London, wrote a book entitled *De Gaulle contre le gaullisme*,[28] joined the Rassemblement des Gauches Républicaines (RGR) for a short time,[29] contested the election of November 1946 on his own ticket,[30] and eventually helped to form one of the first organizations devoted exclusively to opposing de Gaulle.[31]

A wide range of, sometimes contradictory, accusations, were levelled at the General by his opponents. Many argued that the General's wartime alliance with the Communist party and subsequent introduction of Communist ministers into the government were his principal offences. Condemnations of de Gaulle often involved 'turning points' in his career when

[24] On Rémy's career see Rousso, *Le syndrome de Vichy* and Rémy's own numerous autobiographical writings, notably *Mes grands hommes et quelques autres*.

[25] Emmanuel Berl, *La fin de la IIIème république. 10 juillet 1940* (Paris, 1968), p. 15

[26] Henri de Kérillis, *De Gaulle dictateur. Une grande mystification de l'histoire* (Montreal, 1945).

[27] R. Mengin, *No laurels for de Gaulle* (London, 1967).

[28] E. Muselier, *De Gaulle contre le Gaullisme* (Paris, 1946).

[29] On Muselier's career in the RGR see the microfilm of his pamphlet, *Ma position devant le Parti Radical et le Rassemblement des Gauches Républicaines et l'Union des Gauches*, in the Bibliothèque Nationale.

[30] *Le Monde*, 12 November 1946. Muselier received 3,826 votes as candidate for the Union pour la Défense de la République.

[31] A confidential report to Bidault made on the night of 7–8 January 1948 suggested that the RPF had warned its suppporters against Muselier's Ligue des Droits et Devoirs du Résistant Républicain. AN, 457 AP 135.

he had deserted the 'real France'. Some writers placed this turning point in 1940 when de Gaulle had become an *émigré* at a time of national emergency. Louis Rougier developed a whole interpretation that revolved around a distinction between the politicized *gaullisme des militants* of London and the patriotic *gaullisme des militaires* of Resistance fighters: 'In occupied France ... Gaullism meant complete collaboration with England and America, outside France it is clear that de Gaulle was explicitly anti-English and anti-American; inside France, Gaullism meant Resistance to Germany, outside France, Gaullism meant death to Vichy and everything that was presumed to be ... the successor of Vichy: Darlanism and Giraudism.'[32] But the period most focused on by anti-Gaullists was that following the liberation of Algeria when Darlan had been assassinated – an act for which de Gaulle was often blamed – Giraud evicted from power, the Communist alliance sealed and Pucheu executed.

Just as Pétainism encouraged some right-wingers to move away from their anti-republicanism, so anti-Gaullism encouraged some of them to reconsider their aggressive nationalism. This change had roots that can be traced back to the 1930s when a small group of non-conformist intellectuals – Simone Weil, Emanuel Berl and Auguste Detoeuf – had argued that France was not suited to be a major power. After the defeat of 1940 similar arguments gained a wider currency as the Vichy government's propagandists sought to justify its submission to German power.[33] After 1945 apologists for the Vichy government, who wished to explain the armistice of 1940, argued more fervently than ever that France was too weak and impoverished to undertake an ambitious foreign policy, and they were very hostile to de Gaulle's post-war initiatives in this domain. The editor of *Documents Nationaux*, a clandestine journal with royalist tendencies, feared that 'General de Gaulle ... will choose the romantic formula ... he will abandon himself to sensational displays that do not correspond to our real state of weakness.'[34] The following year, the same journal argued: 'It was a lie to let the French believe that they had the means to launch a policy of *grandeur*, before any reconstruction.'[35] Such writers regarded de

---

[32] Rougier, *Mission secrète*, p. 139.

[33] For examples of the critique of nationalism during the late 1930s see Weil's article in *Nouveaux Cahiers*, 2 (April 1937) or Auguste Detoeuf's in ibid., 14, 15 November 1937, which positively celebrated France's 'happy mediocrity' and suggested that Belgium and Sweden would be more appropriate national models than Germany or the USA. It would, of course, be hard to prove that a group of largely pacifist intellectuals exercised much direct influence on the military regime that governed France after 1940. Weil and Berl both fled abroad to escape from anti-semitic legislation – though Berl stayed long enough to write Pétain's speech of 25 June 1940. Weil was connected with the Gaullists in London though her memory inspired vigorous opponents of de Gaulle like Robert Mengin and Philippe Ariès. Certain *Nouveaux Cahiers* contributors, notably Detoeuf, did hold office under Vichy.   [34] *Documents Nationaux*, 1 (2 November 1945).   [35] Ibid., 6 and 7.

Gaulle's attempts to maintain French prestige with gestures like the occupation of the Val d'Aosta as 'a policy of prestige ... carried out by a state that is still feeble'.[36] If the key word in Gaullist foreign policy was *grandeur* the key word for néo-Pétainists was *réelisme*.

Defenders of the Vichy government were prone to explain the differences between Pétain and de Gaulle in terms of the former's greater concern for the interests of the French people: 'The voice that came from France saved and protected. The voice that came from London maintained the hope of revenge.'[37] After the war, similar arguments were deployed: it was suggested that de Gaulle was willing to sacrifice France's chances of foreign aid, economic recovery and perhaps even the life of its citizens in order to obtain the entirely abstract benefits of international prestige. Bardèche contrasted the Pétainist view that 'the fatherland is a matter of flesh and blood' and that 'the life of France is the life and safety of the people of France' with de Gaulle's willingness to 'turn the country into a desert so that it will eventually be in the image of the promised land'.[38] Emphasis on the inhuman abstraction of Gaullist *grandeur* was to be a lasting element in the right's critique of Gaullism. In 1964 Fabre-Luce wrote: 'That sensibility that consists of identifying with human beings who suffer, is hardly found in Charles de Gaulle. His emotions are more aroused by abstract themes: France, victory.'[39]

The right also attacked de Gaulle for making France unpopular. Robert Mengin, who had opposed both Vichy and de Gaulle, hoped for: 'A France which will behave fraternally to other peoples and not with suspicion and mistrust, which will strive for moderation rather than grandeur'.[40] The Pétainist Fabre-Luce complained: 'At the head of a ruined nation ... General de Gaulle has succeeded in irritating the world.'[41] Right-wingers wished to see France adopt a more conciliatory approach to its allies and especially towards America. The favour with which America was viewed on the French right was linked to France's internal politics as well as its external interests. The right could hardly believe that America, which had recognized the Vichy government until the end of 1942, would welcome the exclusion from political life of all those who had supported that government. Nor could they believe that America was sympathetic to the collectivist economic policies of the provisional government.[42] Furthermore, the American government was known to have had bad relations with

[36] Fabre-Luce, *Au nom des silencieux*, p. 67.
[37] Alain Darlan, 'L'amiral Darlan et la "Résistance"', *Ecrits de Paris*, January 1953.
[38] Bardèche, *Lettre à François Mauriac*, p. 182.
[39] Alfred Fabre-Luce, *Le couronnement du prince* (Paris, 1964), p. 104.
[40] Mengin, *No laurels for de Gaulle*, p. 9.
[41] Fabre-Luce, *Au nom des silencieux*, p. 21.
[42] M. Dacier, 'Choisir', *Bulletin Intérieur*, March 1946.

de Gaulle during the war – a fact revealed by the memoirs of Kenneth Pendar, which were gleefully reviewed by right-wingers.[43] Between 1944 and 1946 the right continually expected some intervention by the Americans to replace the de Gaulle government with some more acceptable grouping, and when de Gaulle left the government in 1946 many believed that just such an intervention had taken place: 'This precipitate resignation was provoked by an intervention of the US ambassador in Paris, M. Jefferson Caffrey who had told the French government that it was useless to ask for further American aid, as long as French politics remained so chaotic.'[44]

The history of the post-war *opposition nationale* is often presented as a continuous bloc in which the resentment caused by the abandonment of Algeria merely exacerbated that already caused by the *épuration*. In reality the *opposition nationale* of the Fourth Republic was very different from that which emerged in the Fifth. The defence of Algérie Française during the Fifth Republic was to make the leaders of the *opposition nationale* ever more marginal: they found themselves pitted against a strong and popular ruler in a system of increasingly disciplined parties. Some started the period as ministers or members of established parties and finished either bitter and isolated, like Duchet, or exiled and criminalized, like Bidault and Soustelle. The defence of Vichy during the Fourth Republic, on the other hand, allowed the *opposition nationale* to enjoy increasingly close relations with the parties and the men in power. *Chanoine* Desgranges even attracted the solicitous interest of two presidents of the Republic: Auriol regretted that he would not return to parliament,[45] and Coty put him forward for the legion of honour.[46]

Three things facilitated relations between the *opposition nationale* and the parties of government. The first of these was anti-Communism. Pétainism was closely linked to anti-Communism and former Pétainists seemed useful allies to bourgeois politicians after the exclusion of the Communist party from government in May 1947. However, it should not be assumed this alliance marked a complete rupture with what had gone before. Even those politicians who had been allied with Communists in the Resistance and in the tripartite governments were often vigorously anti-Communist and sometimes willing to contemplate alliances with former Pétainists. There were three reasons for this anti-Communism. Firstly, many early Resistance leaders came from bourgeois backgrounds and nationalistic tra-

---

[43] Rougier, *Mission secrète*, p. 206 and Catherine de Bar, 'Sur une témoignage Américaine', in *Questions Actuelles*, 10 (February 1946).
[44] M. Dacier, 'Les leçons de la Roche Tarpéienne', *Questions Actuelles*, 10 (February 1946).
[45] Rémy, *Mes grands hommes et quelques autres*, p. 137.
[46] Dutroncy, *L'abbé Desgranges*, p. 226.

ditions that had always made them suspicious of the Communist party. Secondly, the fact that the Communist party did not enter the Resistance until the invasion of the Soviet Union was deeply resented by those who had begun Resistance networks in 1940. Talk of the Communists' inactivity at the start of the Occupation and allegations about Communist attempts to fraternize with the Germans was common among bourgeois politicians in the early years of the Fourth Republic. Jacques Lecompte-Boinet (a founder of the Union Démocratique et Socialiste de la Résistance (UDSR)) wrote in his diary: 'In 1940 the Communists were collaborators after having been deserters in 1939. In 1941, there was almost only the bourgeoisie in the Resistance'.[47] Resistance leaders who joined the Mouvement Républicain Populaire (MRP) had equally bitter memories. One MRP member blamed the defeat of 1940 on 'Communist infiltration in the army', while another kept a private archive of Communist publications that had appeared between September 1939 and June 1941.[48]

The Communist party's entry into the Resistance in the summer of 1941 attracted further resentment because it was often seen as an attempt to take over established organizations. Lecompte-Boinet remarked in 1945 that Ceux de la Libération was 'a movement founded by conservatives which is now exploited by men of the extreme left'.[49] This suspicion was exacerbated by the fact that the Communists, who had the discipline and experience of clandestine life that the non-Communist movements so conspicuously lacked, were highly successful in the internal struggles of the Resistance leadership.[50] The conflict for control of the Resistance became so fierce that Frenay (leader of Défense de la France) recalled that Communist attacks on him resembled those that Gringoire had made on Salengro.[51] As late as 1969, François Mitterrand recalled, in a characteristically double-edged remark: 'It was in the Resistance that I learned to work with Communists. From that period date friendships that have not been weakened by time. Among other benefits that I owe them ... they did me the favour of teaching me never to close my eyes if I wanted to avoid being crushed by their formidable machine.'[52]

After the Liberation, the Communist party continued to co-operate with

---

[47] Diary of Jacques Lecompte-Boinet (LBD), entry for 9 July 1945.
[48] Bruno Béthouart, *Le MRP dans le Nord–Pas-de-Calais 1944–1967* (Paris, 1984), p. 25.
[49] LBD, 1 March 1945.
[50] The tendency of the Communist party to win struggles within the bureaucracy continued to cause bitterness after the Liberation. Lecompte-Boinet commented on the speed with which the administrative 'robots' of the Communist party handled matters in committee meetings. LBD, 16 February 1945.
[51] H. Frenay, *La nuit finira* (Paris, 1973), p. 315.
[52] C. Manceron and B. Pingaud, *Mitterrand l'homme, les idées, le programme* (Paris, 1982), p. 24.

bourgeois and democratic forces. Communist ministers sat in de Gaulle's provisional government and in the tripartite governments of 1946 and 1947. Most historians have argued that Stalin's strategy during this period ruled out revolution in Western Europe. However, things seemed far less clear to those who had to deal with the Communists at the time. Even the most unsophisticated observer knew that France was in chaos and that Communist forces in the Resistance had carried out numerous requisitions and reprisals whether or not their leaders approved of their action. Sophisticated observers knew that the intentions of leaders did not always determine whether or not Communists took power – a point that had been reinforced by the fate of republican Spain.

Even if they been perceived to pose no revolutionary threat, the Communists would still have aroused considerable antagonism between 1944 and 1947. The Communists used the prestige acquired in the Resistance and the power of ministerial office to fill the administration with their own supporters and to eject their opponents. Henri Frenay found that Communist influence in his own ministry was so great that civil servants prevented him from entering the building,[53] and the minister of the interior was unable to depend on the *compagnies républicaines de securité* because he knew them to be heavily infiltrated by Communists.[54] The irritation caused by these events was exacerbated the fact that the Communist party was still nominally the ally of many of its victims. Criticism of the party generally had to be confided to private diaries to await publication many years later, and published attacks on the Communists could only appear in near *samizdat* form.[55]

Even before the exclusion of Communists from government, anti-Communism often led former Resistance members and Pétainists to collaborate. In particular, Pétainists often found employment and influence in the shadowy agencies and publications that were funded by business or American money to co-ordinate and inform anti-Communist activity. The *Bulletin d'Etudes et d'Information Politiques et Internationales* was presided over by Georges Albertini, as was the review *Est/Ouest*. Albertini was a former associate of the fascist leader Marcel Déat; he had been imprisoned at the Liberation and had been lucky to escape execution, but his role as an anti-Communist agitator allowed him to become a political *éminence grise*.[56] Furthermore, Albertini's activities brought him into contact with men who had emerged from the Resistance. His agency

---

[53] Frenay, *La nuit finira*, p. 315. It was sign of the paranoia that was often associated with anti-Communists that Frenay believed that even Mitterrand had joined the Communist demonstrations against him.   [54] Jules Moch, *Une si longue vie* (Paris, 1976).

[55] H. Frenay's *Méthodes d'un parti alerte aux démocrates*, appears to have been published in this manner: there is no copy of the work in the Bibliothèque Nationale.

[56] On Alberti's career, see Laurent Lemire, *Georges Albertini 1911–1983* (Paris, 1990).

was funded partly by Etienne Villey, a Paris industrialist and Resistance leader,[57] and the archives of Georges Bidault contain numerous editions of *Est/Ouest*.

Pétainists and Fourth Republic politicians were also sometimes brought together by common views on issues other than anti-Communism. Many Fourth Republic politicians felt uneasy about the severity with which all aspects of Vichy had been condemned; there was particular concern about the ineligibility laws. Some, such as Laniel and Robert Schuman, had themselves voted full powers to Pétain in 1940, and were only able to return to politics in the Fourth Republic because they had been granted special dispensation from ineligibility laws on account of their Resistance activity. Not surprisingly, these men were unhappy to see others condemned for having supported Pétain. Even some Resistance leaders felt that the legislation of the Liberation was an affront to republican principles: Lecompte-Boinet described it as 'a swindle'.[58]

The loosely structured political parties of the Fourth Republic facilitated the maintenance of relations between the *opposition nationale* and mainstream politicians. Groups like the RGR and the CNIP did not seek to impose tight discipline on their members, and they found it relatively easy to tolerate extreme figures such as Louis Rougier or Jean Dides. The *opposition nationale* were also kept in the political mainstream during the Fourth Republic by the choices that their own leaders made. In part these choices were tactical ones: many of them disliked the potential replacements for the regime – Gaullism or Communism – even more than they disliked the regime.

However, there were also some respects in which the defence of Vichy and opposition to de Gaulle brought about changes in the attitude of the extreme right that dovetailed with those happening in the rest of French political life. Before 1940 the writings of Maurras had expressed an *idée conquérante* that exercised great influence on the French right even over men who were not members, or even active supporters, of Action Française.[59] After 1945, this changed. The two central ideas of the Action Française had been aggressive nationalism and contempt for republican legality, but defence of the Vichy government and hostility to de Gaulle led much of the Fourth Republic right to favour the republican legacy and condemn aggressive nationalism. The change was brought about partly because men who had always been republican, who often thought of

---

[57] It is also worth noting that the only copy of H. Frenay's, *Méthodes d'un parti alerte aux démocrates* that I have been able to locate is in the Institut d'histoire sociale (an institution closely linked with Albertini).   [58] LBD, 26 September 1944.

[59] See Steven Wilson, 'The *Action Française* in French intellectual life', *Historical Journal*, 12 (1969), 328–359.

themselves as left-wingers, became associated with the right as a result of their Pétainism. However, there was also a change within the group that had previously regarded itself as Maurrasian. *Aspects de la France*, the Maurrasian journal founded by Pierre Boutang, never achieved the kind of audience that *Action Française* had enjoyed in the Third Republic. Furthermore, many prominent Pétainists actively sought to avoid implication in Maurrasianism.[60]

The new emphasis on legality, and particularly on the legacy of the Third Republic, meant that the extreme right was able to get on with groups like the Radicals who were also nostalgic for the period before 1940. Similarly, the internationalism of the extreme right and particularly its enthusiasm for America meant that it fitted into a political system that was increasingly influenced by the Marshall plan and the Cold War. In short, Pétainism and anti-Gaullism provided a bridge from the old Maurrasian right to the new atlanticist right, and the defence of its recent past helped the *opposition nationale* to adjust to its future.

[60] Louis Madelin had been linked to *Action Française* in the Third Republic, but the committee that he established to campaign for the release of Pétain denied that it was concerned with the case of Maurras (who was also imprisoned). See letter from Isorni to the prefect of police dated 8 May 1948 in AN, 455 AP 4. It is not, of course, necessary to believe that Maurrasians underwent a complete and sincere conversion to republican values. As Quentin Skinner has pointed out, even when agents use rhetoric purely in order to 'legitimize' their action, there are still important reasons why they choose one form of rhetoric over another. Furthermore, the adoption of a particular kind of rhetoric may subsequently circumscribe the actions of the agent. Q. Skinner, 'Some problems in the analysis of political thought and action', in J. Tully (ed.), *Meaning and content: Quentin Skinner and his critics*, Cambridge, 1988, p. 110.

9   The Parti Républicain de la Liberté

Conservatism in the early Fourth Republic was rarely explicit. In his history of the extreme right, François Duprat described the post-war period as that of 'the right that dare not speak its name'. The Parti Républicain de la Liberté (PRL) was an exception to this general rule. On its foundation in December 1945, the PRL was the only significant party to describe itself as right-wing. Yet the attitudes that it represented were not so unusual. The political make up of France before 1944, and after 1951, showed that conservatism had considerable support. Furthermore, the policies advocated by the PRL – namely the exclusion of the Communist party from power, close relations with America and amnesty for former Pétainists – were all to be enacted between 1947 and 1953. Under these circumstances it seems reasonable to assume that the PRL was the dorsal fin of French conservatism, revealing tendencies that remained discreetly submerged in other parties.

The PRL was unusual in the means by which it sought to attain its ends as well as the frankness with which it admitted those ends. The party's formation was an attempt to break from the loose coalitions grouped around prominent individuals that had usually characterized the French right. The founders of the PRL wanted to create a single, disciplined and well-organized movement that would match the English Conservative party and challenge the 'big three' of post-war French politics. The PRL was not insignificant: it obtained forty seats in the National Assembly, provided a focus of loyalty for another twenty or so right-wingers[1] and preserved some degree of influence even after its formal dissolution in 1951.[2] But judged against the high hopes of its founders it failed. Examining why the PRL failed, and especially why its failure as an organization

---

[1] When the leader of the PRL was a candidate for the presidency, he obtained around sixty votes.
[2] The PRL merged with the Centre National des Indépendants, but the negotiators of the Alliance Démocratique who discussed relations with conservatives in Lyons and Paris in 1952 continued to describe their interlocutors as representatives of the PRL: BN, Flandin Archives, AD 4. Meeting of AD 28 May 1952.

coincided with the success of many of the ideas that it represented, may shed some light both on the early history of the Fourth Republic and on the nature of French conservatism.

The origins of the PRL

The PRL made much of its Resistance credentials: its leader, Michel Clemenceau, had been deported. General Giraud, who had briefly shared the leadership of the Free French with General de Gaulle, was elected to the Constituent Assembly with PRL support. More importantly, two of the party's most prominent leaders, Mutter and Laniel, had been members of the Conseil National de la Résistance. The PRL's own notes for orators provided detailed accounts of the Resistance activities of thirty-one out of thirty-five of party's representatives in the National Assembly, almost a third of whom had been imprisoned or deported by the Germans.[3] Historians have recognized that the Resistance contained some men with right-wing backgrounds, but they have usually assumed that they were isolated individuals who eventually assimilated the generally left-wing culture of the Resistance.[4] Examination of the origins of the PRL suggests that there was in fact a coherent and self-conscious group of *modérés* in the Resistance, and that certain aspects of right-wing ideology, notably anti-Communism, not only survived the Resistance, but were strengthened by it.

André Mutter was the Resistance leader who did most to lay the foundations of a new political party. He was a former member of Colonel de la Rocque's Parti Social Français (PSF) and a leader of the Ceux de la Libération network. Mutter's eyes were fixed on the prospect of a post-war political career.[5] Before and immediately after the Liberation, when most Resistance movements found their ranks swelled by an ever increasing number of left-wing members, Mutter set out to turn Ceux de la Libération into a right-wing organization. Lecompte-Boinet (a leader of Ceux de la Résistance) recorded Mutter's success in grouping the 'résistance bourgeoise'[6] with some envy. In December 1944 he wrote: 'Mutter chose the right solution in grouping around "Ceux de la Libération" former elements of the PSF and conservative members of the Resistance'.[7] He also commented, 'Mutter only keeps reactionaries, and a few with fascist

---

[3] The Resistance records of PRL members of parliament were discussed in the party's *Notes d'orientation à l'intention des orateurs du parti*, 2 (5 February 1946). Clearly such a source should not be accepted without question. However, it should be noted that accounts of Resistance activity given included details of specific decorations awarded, ranks held and punishments inflicted.

[4] H. R. Kedward, *Resistance in Vichy France: a study of ideas and motivation* (Oxford, 1978).

[5] Unpublished diaries of of Lecompte-Boinet (LBD), 5 August 1944. Mutter advised Lecompte-Boinet to secure his own future by seeking election as a deputy after the war.

[6] Ibid.; 7 April 1945.   [7] Ibid., 29 December 1944.

tendencies, in his movement, thus eliminating the radicals who want to join the MLN.'[8]

After the war a variety of new political groupings emerged to represent the right. Veterans of the PSF formed the Parti de Réconciliation Française (RF). Former members of the PSF such as Barrachin and Vallin, who felt that their associations with the Resistance had distanced them from the party, founded a new grouping, the Union pour la République (UPR), in February 1945.[9] André Mutter founded the Parti de Rénovation Républicaine (PRR). Antier formed an agrarian or peasant party.[10] In addition to these groupings certain pre-war parties such as the Fédération Républicaine (FR) and the Alliance Démocratique (AD) continued to operate, and some Resistance movements had political functions that transcended parties. Efforts were soon made to unite these disparate groups. A report written by a delegate of the FR described these efforts: 'this group takes in the electorate of the Fédération Républicaine, the Alliance Démocratique, the Union Nationale, the Jeunesses de France, and Femmes Françaises Libres. In short it extends from the extreme right to the left of the right, including the Independent Radicals.'[11]

On 1 March 1945 Lecompte-Boinet attended a meeting of the Camiran committee, which brought together representatives of the Reynaud faction in the AD, the FR and the new party represented by Barrachin.[12] The parties of the right eventually came together in a loose formation, Unité Républicaine, that grouped around forty members of the constituent assembly. In November 1945 a series of meetings were held between representatives of the PRR, the UPR and the AD; a variety of other individuals also attended these meetings, either as observers or in a personal capacity. On 22 December 1945 the constitutive meeting of the PRL was held at the Palais de Glace. The meeting was addressed by Laniel, Jules Ramarony, Frédéric Dupont and André Mutter.

[8] Ibid., 23 March 1945.
[9] The party led by Barrachin and Vallin was variously described as the Union Patriotique Républicaine and the CRR.
[10] The *Année politique* (AP) gives details of most political formations. Pimenta, a member of the Fédération Républicaine (FR), questioned a number of politicains about their intentions. The results of his enquiries can be found in Archives Nationales (AN), 317 AP 84.
[11] AN, 317 AP 84, undated report with illegible signature. The writer stated that the grouping's current provisional committee was to be transformed into a more formal body in March; presumably this is a reference to the convocation of the Camiran committee described below.
[12] LBD, 1 March 1945. A footnote to this entry says that this meeting laid the foundation of the PRL. The Camiran committee was still in existence in September 1945, when its activities were described by Jean Guiter in a letter to Marin, dated 17 September 1945 in AN, 317 AP 81. The author has not been able to identify Camiran, though an undated, unsigned note on the position of the FR in AN, 317 AP 73 described him as an employee of Ramarony.

The efforts to unite the right that were made in 1945 and 1946 took place in circumstances of considerable confusion and acrimony.[13] There were three reasons for this. Firstly, ordinary political organization had been made impossible by the circumstances of the occupation, so that links between party militants and leaders had been eroded. This made it unclear what mandate politicians possessed: de Fels, the vice president of the AD was repeatedly accused of representing no one but himself.[14] Secondly, many prominent right-wing politicians had been discredited by their support for the Vichy regime and were confined to the political touchline. Only a small group of right-wingers who had been active in the Resistance were in a position to organize new political parties after the war. Such men had been formed in a milieu where leaders selected themselves, or were nominated from above, and were often insensitive to the views of their followers. Typically, Mutter assumed the chairmanship of the constitutive meeting of the PRL without a debate or a vote.[15] Thirdly, trouble was caused by disputes over which groups and individuals had joined the PRL. New members of the party often claimed, or implied, that they had brought the official support of their party with them.[16] Sometimes the PRL claimed the support of public figures who then wrote indignant letters denying that they had ever expressed such support.[17]

One particular source of dispute during the formative stages of the PRL was the role to be played by politicians with pre-war reputations, such as Marin and Reynaud. Naturally enough, such men assumed that they would be important in the new formation. However, this view was sharply disputed by PRL leaders like Mutter, Vallin and Ramarony.[18] Ultimately,

[13]   Both the confusion and the acrimony are reflected in the transcript of a meeting held on 21 November 1945. Sollar, an FR representative, wanted to know 'what the Parti Démocrate Socialiste represents'. Levêque, who had been described as the delegate of this party, was forced to admit 'that he still [had] no mandate to represent this party which [was] not formed'. AN, 317 AP 84.

[14]   AN, 317 AP 84, account of meeting dated 23 November 1945, Ramarony claimed that de Fels had no support even in his home area; at a meeting of 29 November 1945 Mutter remarked that he had been contacted by 'M. de Fels who . . . claims the proprietorship of the Alliance Démocratique'.

[15]   AN, 317 AP 73, account of meeting dated 15 November 1945: 'Without being invited, M. Mutter assumed the presidency the meeting.'

[16]   An extract of the *Nouvelle République* for 11 February 1946 (contained in AN, 317 AP 84) acussed M. Moynet of having pretended that other members of the Radical party had joined the PRL with him: 'Not content with having betrayed and abandoned his Party, M. Moynet is now inciting others.' A letter from M. Becquart of the FR to M. Grousseaud urged him to resign from the FR after having joined the PRL: AN, 317 AP 84, dated 20 February 1946.

[17]   AN, 317 AP 82, letter from editor of PRL paper *la République*, dated 3 August 1946, apologizing to Marin for having falsely suggested that Marin had signed a circular letter organized by the party.

[18]   AN, 317 AP 84. The hostility to former politicians of the Third Republic came out in the interviews that Pimenta conducted with Mutter and Vallin.

Reynaud and Marin did not join the PRL and the exclusion of the latter was the main reason for the refusal of the FR to support the new party.[19] These exclusions are interesting because they highlight the peculiar position of the PRL's leadership. No one pretended that there were important ideological differences between the PRL and the pre-war politicians,[20] and ordinary PRL members, as opposed to leaders, had no hostility to established politicians.[21] Furthermore, right-wingers, even right-wingers in the Resistance, were generally favourable, or at least reconciled, to the return of pre-war politicians in order to counter-balance the influence of the Resistance, which was predominantly left-wing.[22] However, the leaders of the PRL were generally young, with an average age of just over 42,[23] and ambitious to launch political careers of their own; they did not want to be overshadowed by an older, more experienced generation.[24]

A similar logic affected Mutter's attitude to the question of when elections should be held. After the Liberation, France was ruled largely by unelected bodies that had issued from the Resistance. Such bodies gave considerable importance to left-wingers. It was widely believed that the country was more conservative than the Resistance organizations and that early elections would therefore benefit the right.[25] But Mutter, whose Resistance credentials were his strongest card, wished to see the *comités départementaux de la libération* kept in place.[26]

The PRL's relations with other new political formations that emerged

---

[19] AN, 317 AP 84, letter 'Pour nos militants' unsigned, undated. 'Far from following up these advances, two of these parties took the initiative by holding meetings where they immediately sought to exclude the leaders of the old parties and particularly ... Louis Marin.'

[20] AN, 317 AP 84, letter from PRL delegate general to Becquart, secretary-general of the FR, dated 26 January 1946. The letter underlined the agreement of the two parties about final goals. It is also worth noting that the constitutional proposals of the PRL submitted by Ramarony on 11 April 1946 amounted to a restoration of the arrangements of 1875: AP 1946, p. 78.

[21] AN, 317 AP 84. It was reported that the majority of those attending the meeting of 23 November 1945 believed that 'there is no reason not to accept M. Marin and M. Reynaud'.

[22] LBD, 30 September 1944.

[23] The average age of the sixteen PRL leaders, whose biographies are given in Henry Coston's *Dictionnaire de la politique française* (Paris, 1967), was just over 42 when the PRL was founded.

[24] AN, 317 AP 84, undated note. Mutter told Pimenta that he was in favour of a party led by new men: 'because he believed that the newcomers would not wish to place themselves under the authority of the senior men'. The PRL director of publicity recognized that the youth and inexperience of the party leadership had caused problems: 'Haste pushed them to accept novices who were hungry for an electoral mandate and whose main qualifications were social connections.' Georges Riond, *Chroniques d'un autre monde* (Paris, 1979), p. 203.

[25] LBD, 4 March 1944. Lecompte-Boinet told Bidault 'I am for legality and quick elections.' Asked whether he did not fear the action of Pétainists, he replied 'I fear the action of Communists much more.'   [26] AP 1945, p. 7.

after the Liberation are revealing. The most important of these was the Mouvement Républicain Populaire (MRP). The leadership of the PRL was deeply hostile to the leadership of the MRP; much of the constitutive meeting of the PRL was taken up by a denunciation of the Christian Democrats. The MRP was especially disliked for its alliance with the Communist party.[27] But it was well known that many voters who supported the MRP were *modérés* who were well to the right of the national leadership.[28] The PRL therefore combined its attacks on the MRP leaders with messages addressed to its supporters stressing that the difference between the two parties was one of means rather than ends. This point was made explicitly by Rollat. He described the MRP and the PRL as 'two brother parties which are concerned, whatever is said, with identical aims: the happiness of the people, the greatness of France and the destruction of anti-Christian Communist materialism.' In his view the differences between the two parties were just a 'matter of tactics'.[29]

However, the PRL's attempts to win over the MRP electorate were notably unsuccessful. The MRP obtained almost four times as many seats as its rival, and when conservative voters finally defected it was to the RPF or the Independents that they turned. Explaining this fully would require a locally based study of the MRP, rather than a national study of the PRL. However, there are two plausible, and not mutually exclusive, theories that can be advanced to explain the greater attraction of the MRP. Firstly, right-wingers were often confronted with immediate and dangerous problems during this period: they had relatives in prison, their newspapers were sequestered, their business interests were threatened by the power of *comités d'entreprises.* Under these circumstances, many must have preferred to vote for a deputy who would be closely linked to the government, and who could therefore lobby for immediate, if limited, concessions from within, rather than an intransigent right-winger who would demand large-scale concessions without hope of immediate satisfaction.[30] The PRL's own leaders recognized that the *apparentes subtilités* of the MRP might seem reassuring to those 'numerous conservatives' who wished to place 'a brake on the tripartite machine'.[31]

---

[27] AP 1945, p. 384: 'A vigorous mistrust was shown towards the MRP.'

[28] François de Beaumont, 'Pitcuse défense', *la République*, 24 February 1946: 'I always drew a clear distinction between the rank and file of the MRP and its leaders.'

[29] *La République*, 3 March 1946, 'A propos d'une lettre'; and 12 October 1946, 'Question de tactique'.

[30] Georges Riond's remark about one of his colleagues, Legendre, could equally well apply to the whole party's preference for oppositional extremism over office holding: 'slights were revenged when it came to the formation of ministries'. Riond, *Chroniques d'un autre monde*, p. 203.

[31] PRL, *Notes d'orientation à l'intention des orateurs du parti*, 1 (15 January 1946); 3 (20 March 1946).

Secondly, and perhaps more importantly, the PRL's attempts to present itself as a defender of the church were never very convincing.[32] None of the party's leaders had been associated with political catholicism before the war; the party never obtained the official endorsement from the catholic hierarchy that the MRP received in 1951, or even the local unofficial endorsement that was sometimes given to right-wingers such as Antoine Pinay.[33] The PRL leaders did not understand the potential force of religion, and believed that catholic voters would be won over by a mixture of anti-Communism and a defence of liberal economics; they even tried to persuade French bishops to denounce nationalization.[34] They were willing to support church schools not because they believed in them, but because they wished to end the lay–clerical divide in right-wing politics. Experienced conservatives were sceptical about their chances. Louis Marin remarked: 'There is little chance now that catholics would vote for masons and vice versa'.[35] An unsigned note in the archives of the FR argued that the religious blind spot of the PRL would cripple the party: 'The group offers the antithesis of what is offered by the MRP both from the social and the spiritual point of view. The laicism comes from business, while the rank and file are devoutly catholic and conservatives of the simplest sort.'[36]

The way in which the religious issue could be used against the PRL was shown in the electoral campaigns of 1946 when a catholic newpaper said that the PRL represented the 'libéralisme condamné par le Pape'.[37] The PRL's director of publicity estimated that the attacks of religious leaders cost the party eight seats in the west of France alone.[38] Religion surfaced again in the 1951 election when a candidate in Haute Savoie was accused by the MRP of association with a notorious blasphemer.[39] In the Vendée, the MRP manifesto drew attention to the fact that the PRL candidate had failed to attend the parliamentary commission on education, a key forum for the defence of church interests, on twenty-three out of twenty-six occasions.[40]

The other new political formation of the post-Liberation period was the

---

[32] Marin said at a meeting of the FR on 25 January 1946: 'We do not find the firmness with regard to religious freedom that we would like in the new party'. AN, 317 AP 73.

[33] AN, 317 AP 73, undated, unsigned report on politics in the provinces: 'The Bishop vigorously encouraged Pinay to stand for election; he told him that he was disappointed in the MRP.'   [34] *La République*, 3 August 1946.

[35] AN, 317 AP 73, transcript of the meeting of the *comité directeur* of the FR dated 25 January 1946.

[36] AN, 317 AP 73, note headed 'la position de la fédération', undated and unsigned (though obviously by Marin or one his close associates).

[37] Riond, *Chroniques d'un autre monde*, p. 189.   [38] Ibid.   [39] Ibid.

[40] *Recueil des textes authentiques des programmes et engagements électoraux des députés proclamés élus à la suite des élections générales du 17 juin 1951* (commonly known as *Barodet*) (1952), p. 880.

Rassemblement des Gauches Républicaines (RGR), formed in 1945 in order to group several political parties together. In spite of its nominal attachment to the left, this group was closely related to the PRL. One promising member of the RGR, François Mitterrand, fought the 1946 election in alliance with the PRL;[41] another member of the RGR admitted that he felt more at home in the Camiran committee, which was to give birth to the PRL, than in his own party.[42] Several political parties provided members for both the RGR and the PRL and during the confused years of 1945–46 the PRL often worked in alliance with groups that ultimately joined the RGR, such as the Parti Socialiste Démocratique (PSD) and the Radicals.[43]

What, then, was the dividing line between the two political formations? Contemporary observers had little doubt that the RGR lay to the left of the PRL, and the members of the AD who joined the RGR justified their rejection of the PRL on this basis: 'There were . . . elements in it that were a little too far to the right and which were not in the line that we had always followed.'[44] But the political position of the two formations bore a curious relation to the pasts of their members; the ostensibly left-wing RGR attracted Pétainists while the right-wing PRL did not. Most leaders of the RGR had been supporters of Vichy.[45] On the other hand, all the leaders of the PRL, and all but four of its parliamentary representatives, had been Resistance activists.[46] When old Third Republic parties divided between the PRL and the RGR, they did so on the basis of the Vichy–Resistance split. It was the pro-Resistance faction of the PSF, the URR, that joined the PRL while the pro-Pétain section of the party, RF, joined the RGR; it was the pro-Resistance faction of the AD who joined the PRL while the Pétainists, under Flandin, joined the RGR.

The attractiveness of the RGR, and the unattractiveness of the PRL, to Pétainists was rooted in the ineligibility laws that barred most politicians who had supported Vichy from public life during the early years of the Fourth Republic. Such men kept clear of the PRL partly because its ambition to create a new party of the right was accompanied by a desire to

---

[41] Indeed according to Riond, it was a PRL leader (Barrachin) who arranged for Mitterrand to become a candidate in the Nièvre. Riond, *Chroniques d'un autre monde*, p. 204.

[42] LBD, 1 March 1945.

[43] At a meeting of the bureau of the FR on 25 January 1946, M. Vernes reported that he had attended 'a meeting between representatives of the PRL, radicals, and socialists of the Paul Faure faction'. AN, 317 AP 73.

[44] Bibliothèque Nationale (BN), papers of the Alliance Démocratique (AD), 4, M. Ventenat addressing meeting of AD on 12 May 1950.

[45] The only element of the RGR that had not been associated with Pétainism was the UDSR. Perhaps it is significant that the RGR member who maintained the closest relations with the PRL, François Mitterrrand, was a member of this party.

[46] *Notes d'orientation à l'intention des orateurs du parti*, 2 (5 February 1946).

bring to the fore a new generation of young leaders. This was a dangerous prospect for all politicians with established pre-war reputations, but it was especially so for those whose exclusion from political life prevented them from defending their interests effectively. The RGR, by contrast, was a loose grouping of parties with little central control, in which ineligible politicians such as Paul Faure and Flandin found it far easier to exercise power from the wings. The RGR's comparatively moderate stance and its acceptability as a provider of government ministers after May 1947 also meant that it could take practical steps to bring about the repeal of the ineligibility laws,[47] while the PRL's extremism confined it to crying in the wilderness. Explicitly right-wing talk was a luxury that only those with impeccable Resistance records could afford.

The PRL and the press

Newspapers were one of the PRL's greatest obsessions. After the Liberation all papers that had continued to publish in occupied France were banned. This deprived the right of much of its press support.[48] Furthermore, the rationing of newsprint supplies made it difficult for organizations that lacked good relations with the government to publish. The PRL railed against these restrictions repeatedly; in January 1947 half of the points that the PRL drew to the attention of the incoming government were concerned with press freedom.[49] The PRL had close links with several papers. *La République*, a Lyonnais weekly, was an official organ of the party, which could also usually count on the support of two other newspapers: *l'Epoque* and *le Courrier de Paris*.[50]

The most important publication connected with the PRL was *Paroles Françaises*. The paper was founded by André Mutter in 1945. Between March 1946 and January 1949 the journal described itself as the official organ of the PRL. However, the editorial policy of the paper was highly independent. The first editor was Pierre Boutang. The paper's journalists, who wrote under a variety of pseudonyms, were mostly Maurrasians.[51]

---

[47] For evidence of the RGR's concern with the lifting of the ineligibility laws see the transcript of the AD general assembly of 12–14 May 1950 in BN, AD 4.

[48] In 1939, 29 per cent of newspapers in France had supported the right; in 1944, this figure was 7.3 per cent. Peter Novick, *The Resistance versus Vichy* (London, 1968), p. 117.

[49] AP 1947, p 6. The PRL asked about nationalization, foreign policy, the need of prior authorization for publication, and the dispossession of newspaper owners.

[50] AP 1946, p. 144. In September 1948, Vincent Auriol described *l'Epoque* as the 'paper of Laniel and Paul Reynaud'. *Journal du septennat (1947–53)* (7 vols, Paris) II, 1974, p. 433, entry for 9 Septembr 1948. M. André Bougenot, the co-editor of *l'Epoque* was to be Laniel's under secretary; ibid., p. 677.

[51] Two of the men behind *Paroles Françaises* discuss the paper in their autobiographies. Philippe Ariès, *Un historien du dimanche* (Paris, 1980), and F. Brigneau, *Mon après guerre* (Paris, 1985).

The extreme muck-raking style of the journal, which anticipated the large circulation *Minute* of the Fifth Republic,[52] brought frequent complaints from the political authorities[53] and also helped the journal to build a circulation that was variously estimated at between 100,000 and 200,000.[54]

The editorial team of *Paroles Françaises* eventually went too far for Mutter and was sacked, although the most outspoken of them, François Brigneau, was soon rehired.[55] In 1949, Mutter himself was ejected from the paper after a boardroom coup which placed a Pétainist group in control.[56] *Paroles Françaises* now moved on from calling for amnesty and national reconciliation to launching outright attacks on the legacy of de Gaulle and the Resistance. Such attacks made the paper an object of loathing in most political circles: members of the SFIO and MRP refused to sit on a committee chaired by the editor of *Paroles Françaises*,[57] and even the secretary of the Independents regarded association with the paper as a liability.[58] *Paroles Françaises* ceased to describe itself as the official organ of the PRL in 1949, but its editor, Paul Estèbe, was a member of the party committee,[59] so the PRL, and the hapless Mutter, continued to be blamed for the newspaper's excesses.

The PRL and business

French business played a considerable role in the establishment of the PRL. The policies of the party, its opposition to Communism and *étatisme*, its

[52] François Brigneau (who had started journalistic life on *Paroles Françaises*) later became one of the moving spirits behind *Minute*.

[53] Auriol complained to Mutter about the attacks that *Paroles Françaises* had made on his family in 1949; Auriol, *Journal du septennat*, III, 1977, p. 554.

[54] J. Algazy, *La tentation néofasciste en France 1944–1965* (Paris, 1984), p. 67, gives the lower of these two figures. Philippe Ariès claims that he and his colleagues built the paper's circulation from 20,000 to 200,000. Ariès, *Un historien du dimanche*, p. 104.

[55] Brigneau, *Mon après guerre*, p. 49. Brigneau claims that the editorial team of *Paroles Françaises* was sacked because of an article by him on the role that the Communist party had played in the administration of concentration camps. Philippe Ariès believed that the dismissal resulted from an admiring profile of Daudet. Ariès, *Un historien du dimanche*, p. 105.

[56] *Le Monde* (2 September 1949) reported that Mutter had been deposed, several months previously, by a group of shareholders led by M. René Château (a former socialist deputy who had been declared ineligible for having voted full powers to Pétain in 1940).

[57] AN, 350 AP 76. Note dated 15 January 1952 referring to the *commission d'information* of the Assembly of the French Union.

[58] Roger Duchet, *La république épinglée* (Paris, 1975), p. 218. Duchet complained that *Paroles Françaises* had wrongly claimed that it had been granted an exclusive interview with him in 1951. Duchet was under the incorrect impression that Mutter was then still editor of *Paroles Françaises*.

[59] Estèbe's roles in both the PRL and *Paroles Françaises* were described in his manifesto when he was a candidate in the Gironde in the 1951 election. *Barodet* (1952), p. 292. Estèbe was an unusual PRL leader in that he had relatively close links with Pétainism.

favourable attitude to America and its interest in economic affairs, mirrored the wishes of most industrialists. A wide range of industrialists, who do not seem to have come from any single sector of the economy, were linked with the party. The FR delegate sent to investigate the early efforts to group the right at the beginning of 1945 reported: 'As non-parliamentary members, I was given the name of several industrials: Schaffler?, Binoche.'[60] François de Nervo, of the gas and automobile industries, and Robert Bouchayer, an industrialist from Grenoble, attended the meetings that led to the formation of the PRL.[61] François de Wendel, former president of the *comité des forges*, pressed the FR to join the new party.[62] Pierre André, the PRL deputy for the Meurthe and Moselle, was well known as a spokesman for the interests of the steel industry.[63] Laniel, PRL deputy for Normandy, was a textile manufacturer.

French business was grouped in 1945 and 1946 into the Conseil National du Patronat Français (CNPF) which was led by Georges Villiers. Villiers' political position, in particular his role as a Resistance hero who refused to condemn Pétainism entirely, was very close to that of many PRL members. Villiers took an interest in politics immediately after the war and was rumoured to finance the PRL in Lyons, his home town. There is no direct evidence of Villiers' involvement with the PRL in either his own memoirs or in the archives of the CNPF, but, given the discretion with which the CNPF pursued its political manoeuvres, this is not surprising. A more direct role was played by the Centre d'Etudes Economiques (CEE) based in the rue de Penthièvre. This body was specifically set up to convey funds from industry to political parties. It was headed by André Boutemy, the former prefect for the Rhône, and Maurice Brulfer, who had worked for the Gillet textile firm. In October 1945, immediately before the foundation of the PRL, Brulfer and Boutemy tried to pressure Marin to accept a united right-wing party, and the rue de Penthièvre continued to provide funding for the PRL.[64]

However, business association with the PRL was a mixed blessing. The party's reputation for being the tool of business lowered its standing even

---

[60] AN, 317 AP 84, undated report with illegible signature. The name which the writer recorded as 'Schaffler?' was probably Schauffler, who became the PRL deputy for the third constituency of Paris.

[61] See, for example, AN, 317 AP 84, account of meeting of November 1945. On the business backgrounds of de Nervo and Bouchayer see J. N. Jeanneney, *L'argent caché. Milieux d'affaires et pouvoirs politiques dans la France du XXème siècle* (Paris, 1984), p. 254.

[62] AN, 317 AP 73, note dated 13 June 1946 by Marin.

[63] H. Weber, *Le parti des patrons. Le CNPF (1946–1986)* (Paris, 1986), p. 105. Weber mistakenly describes André as an Independent deputy.

[64] Jeanneny, *L'argent caché*, p. 254. It is worth noting that, though Marin resisted the pressure applied by Boutemy and Brulfer to submit himself to the leaders of the PRL, it was de Nervo and Bouchayer who persuaded him to send an FR representative to the constitutive meeting of the PRL. AN, 317 AP 84, account of meeting of 15 November 1945.

among right-wing politicians: 'This party was formed under the aegis of money and it is obvious that it is run in an autocratic manner by financial powers. This is known, in detail, by our political opponents'.[65] Furthermore, two of the party's contacts with the business world – Boutemy[66] and de Nervo[67] – were celebrated for their lack of tact and discretion. Established conservative politicians did not like being told what to do by such men. It was widely believed that the PRL's business backers were responsible for the party's insensitivity to non-economic issues, especially religion, and the excessive haste with which the party sought to assimilate other right-wing parties: 'The whole party was started exclusively by the financial powers. In fact, they are inexperienced and prone to cause trouble by their haste to settle things'.[68]

If the PRL had all the disadvantages that came from being seen as a tool of business, it did not have the advantages that might have come from being the sole recipient of business funding. Business paymasters believed in covering their bets. Sometimes one business leader undermined the actions of his colleagues by funding a politican of whom they did not approve,[69] but more often single business leaders spread their support over several parties. Thus Georges Villiers, while supporting the foundation of the PRL, was also funding a paper controlled by the remnants of the FR,[70] and was even pencilled in as a potential member of the *comité directeur* of the RGR.[71]

Things were made worse for the PRL by the very success of conservatism, which provided business with a wide range of organizations and parties willing to represent its interests. Boutemy spread his subsidies over all the non-Communist parties;[72] in the 1951 election it was believed that over 160

---

[65] AN, 317 AP 73, Marin addressing *comité directeur* of FR on 25 January 1946.
[66] Boutemy was said to treat his clients 'as an ill-tempered master would not dare to treat his servants': Georgette Elgey, *La république des illusions 1945–1951 ou la vie secrète de la IVème république*, Paris, 1965.
[67] De Nervo's lack of sensitivity was to irritate politicians again during the 1950s, when he tried to bully the leaders of the AD into joining the Independents. BN, AD 4, transcript of meeting of bureau of 28 May 1952.
[68] AN, 317 AP 73, undated, unsigned note headed 'La position de la fédération'.
[69] Thus, for example, de Peyerimhoff, a representative of the coal industry, handed Marin a cheque for 100,000 francs at the end of the very meeting during which Boutemy and Bouchayer had threatened to withdraw funds from the FR if it refused to merge into the PRL: Jeanneney, *L'argent caché*, p. 255.
[70] AN, 317 AP 73, undated, unsigned note on the political situation in the provinces reported that Villiers 'controls everything from behind the scenes'. In Lyons, it was reported that Xavier Brun, a supporter of the FR 'has relaunched the the newspaper *l'Echo du Soir* with the financial help of the same group that supports the RPF (Villiers). However, he conducts a policy that is hostile to the PRL and in favour of the radicals, but cannot, and does not wish to, take an initiative that would displease his paymasters.'
[71] Undated list in AN, 317 AP 73, which included 'Debruiter (Pechiney) and Villiers (Patronat)'.
[72] Jacques Isorni, *Ainsi passent les républiques* (Paris, 1959), p. 9.

candidates had received business funding.[73] Georges Villiers was said to have helped draw up an RPF shadow cabinet,[74] and Boutemy himself eventually became a deputy for the Peasant party. Organized business even discreetly established a new party – the Groupement de Défénse des Libertés Professionnelles et des Contribuables – to contest the 1951 elections.[75]

All this meant, firstly, that as the general political climate became less threatening business felt less compelled to spend money on political action, and, secondly, that an ever larger number of bodies were competing for such funds as were available. The PRL found that far from being the 'business party' it was just one rather unimportant supplicant for subsidy. The PRL deputy for les Deux Sèvres wrote a plaintive letter to Boutemy in 1948 complaining that he would be obliged to abandon politics if the rue de Penthièvre continued to deny him the funds that it provided for other politicians.[76] La République carried a leader complaining that local industrialists were more interested in their immediate business concerns than political action.[77]

The success of the CNPF also undercut all right-wing parties. For in 1945 political representation had seemed necessary to parry government assaults on business. However, as the CNPF itself became recognized as a worthy interlocutor by the government, it found that discreet lobbying could often achieve more than direct political confrontation.[78] Indeed, CNPF leaders sometimes felt obliged to apologize for the heavy-handed assaults on the government made by politicians who claimed to represent business. Perhaps fear of being undercut in this way underlay the request, in 1948, by two PRL deputies that the government should avoid direct negotiations with the CNPF.[79]

The ideology of the PRL

The ideology of the PRL was dominated by one issue: anti-Communism. A report of one of the meetings that led to the party's formation described an orator's attitude thus: 'He speaks of the Communist danger, and [says] "There is our policy."'[80] La République carried a regular column exclusi-

---

[73] Henry W. Ehrmann, *Organized business in France* (Princeton, 1957), p. 224.
[74] Ibid.
[75] See chapter 14.
[76] Weber, *Le parti des patrons*, p. 102.
[77] F. Lestier, 'Pas de politique', *la République*, 24 February 1946.
[78] AN, 72 AS 74, transcript of *conseil* of CNPF, 7 January 1947: 'M. Ricard stressed how much the position of employers has improved. The CNPF is treated by the Government on an equal footing with other organizations.'
[79] Auriol, *Journal du septennat*, II, p. 395, entry for 28 August 1948.
[80] AN, 317 AP 73, meeting of FR de la Seine, 12 February 1946.

vely devoted to attacking the Communist party. Felix Rollat interpreted the results of the the the referendum of 1945: 'From this consultation, one great idea emerges: those who voted, voted against Communism more than anything else.'[81] In November of the same year he advised his readers 'First of all vote anti-Communist.'[82] Ideological hostility sometimes spilled over into physical violence. PRL meetings were attacked by Communist militants. More significantly, anti-Communism influenced almost every aspect of PRL policy. It was anti-Communism above all that made the party implacably hostile to the tripartite governments that ruled France until May 1947.

The PRL leaders justified their attitude in terms of republican virtue and a defence of liberty. It would be naive to accept such rhetoric at its face value. The PRL's anti-Communism was linked to the class interest of the business and bourgeois constituency that the party represented, or sought to represent. However, it would be equally naive to reduce the anti-Communism of the PRL exclusively to class interests. There are three reasons for this. Firstly, anti-Communism was not always associated with a straight defence of property against collectivism. Many believed in 1945 and 1946 that the best way to combat Communism was to make alliances with left-wing leaders. It was argued that the left had the public credibility which the right lacked and also that left-wing leaders had developed a particularly sophisticated set of anti-Communist arguments. Léon Blum, who had denounced the Communists as 'foreign nationalists', was especially important in this context. Some PRL leaders seem to have shared this view. Clemenceau appealed to the Socialists to join a coalition of anti-Communist forces;[83] the majority of PRL deputies voted in favour of the Blum government at the end of 1946 and even Mutter, who voted against the Blum government, quoted Blum's remarks about Communism with approval.[84]

Secondly, in 1945 and 1946 the Communists remained a party of government concerned to maintain production levels and rebuild French industry. As a result of this, the Communists did not, at first, take an especially radical line in social matters and Communist controlled trade unions sometimes sought to restrain pay demands. In 1946 André Mutter voted in favour of pay increases for civil servants which were opposed by the Communists.[85] Finally, the PRL's claim that it resented threats to

[81] *La République*, 14 (11 May 1946), 'Après le référendum'.
[82] *La République*, 36 (26 October 1945), 'Changer la majorité'.
[83] *La République*, 23 November 1946.
[84] *Paroles Françaises*, 2 (24 November 1946). An article in *la République* (3 March 1946) by Felix Rollat 'A propos d'une lettre' attacked the choice of Blum as special ambassador to negotiate for American aid – though the article also expressed the hope that he would succeed.   [85] AP 1946, p. 234.

liberty from both right and left should not be entirely dismissed. Some party leaders did denounce de Gaulle's RPF, though such denunciations were much less vociferous and unanimous than their anti-Communism. More importantly, many party leaders had been members of the Resistance; it was not class interest that had taken men like Richet to German concentration camps.[86] Indeed, some of the most virulent anti-Communists in the PRL were those Resistance veterans who had seen Communist tactics at first hand.[87]

Closely linked to the anti-Communism of the PRL was its vigorous enthusiasm for the USA. The party's intention to 'collaborate completely with the great American republic'[88] was stated early on. On 3 March 1946 Pierre Montel wrote: 'Who until now, if not the United States, has supplied us with arms, equipment, and credits ... Who has struggled with us and for us? No doubt our ideas sometimes differ ... None the less, America understands freedom as we do, and she has the most reliable and modern means to ensure that it is respected.'[89] The origins of the PRL's atlanticism can be traced back to before the Liberation of France. The PRL leaders were hostile to punishments imposed on those who had supported Pétain in 1940. These men expected the USA, which had maintained diplomatic relations with Vichy until the end of 1942, to be sympathetic to such a point of view. Furthermore, many PRL members had been associated with America during the war. General Giraud, the deputy elected with PRL support for the Meurthe and Moselle, had been the Americans' choice for leader of the Free French.

After the Liberation, right-wing enthusiasm for America was increased by the credits that the USA granted to France, especially those given under the terms of the Blum–Byrnes agreement of January 1946. These credits were welcomed partly because they were believed to assist an economic reconstruction that would make it easier to resist the spread of Communism in France. However, there was another dimension to the PRL's attitude. For it was widely, and often wrongly, believed, that American aid was linked to an attempt to control France's internal political life.[90] It is well known that such beliefs were important on the left of the politcal spectrum, where American influence was regarded with hostility. What is less well known is that many on the right also believed that there were conditions attached to American aid. But, far from regarding these conditions with

---

[86] Richet, who presided over a PRL meeting in February 1946 had been deported to Buchenwald. *La République* (10 February 1946).
[87] On Mutter's resentment of Communist tactics in the Resistance see LBD, 20 June 1944.
[88] *Paris Matin*, 8 March 1946, 'La droite nous annonce le succès de la droite aux élections'.
[89] *La République* 4 (3 March 1946), Pierre Montel, 'Propos sur la liberté'.
[90] I. Wall, *L'influence américaine sur la politique française, 1945–1954* (Paris, 1989).

disfavour, the right positively welcomed them. In particular many in the PRL believed that the Americans disapproved of France's economic policy: 'Are they happy to see us tie ourseves up in Communist *dirigisme*?'[91] 'The American newspapers stress . . . that, if in Germany the desire to reconstruct is seen in every individual, no such thing is found in France.'[92] It was believed that America was especially hostile to France's nationalization programme and was willing to use its financial muscle to stop this programme. Laniel hinted in parliament that nationalizations had been discussed during the Blum–Byrnes negotiations of 1946.[93] Joseph Denais even suggested that American financial pressure was behind de Gaulle's resignation of 1946: 'the departure took place after an official ultimatum that was given to him by the ambassador of the United States'.[94]

The third main theme underlying PRL rhetoric was the demand for amnesty for those who had supported the Vichy government. André Mutter first suggested an amnesty law in 1946.[95] Calls such as these were accompanied by more discreet expressions of concern for Pétainists. Louis Rollin signed the petition in protest at the ineligibility laws presented to the United Nations, *la République* carried out an investigation into prison conditions,[96] not an issue that had been of great concern to right-wingers before 1944, and a PRL militant, Richet, was one of the three doctors who testified in 1951 that Pétain was not well enough to remain in prison.[97] Many observers did not know what to make of a party that combined a leadership of Resistance veterans with a willingness to defend Pétainists. Vincent Auriol made the following entry in his diary on 21 February 1947:[98]

The minister of the interior told the cabinet of a meeting organized by the PRL at the salle Wagram; . . . where a defence of Pétain was made, further meetings are being organized and counter-demonstrations are anticipated. He said that in the circumstances it would be best to ban them all. A lively discussion [took place] . . . certain ministers claimed that a man like Clemenceau, who had been deported, could not be lumped with Pétainists and fascists and asked that the demonstrations and counter-demonstrations be tolerated. Others advised that they be banned.

But the PRL's desire for amnesty was less strange than it first appeared. The ineligibility laws that were enacted in France after the Liberation were

---

[91] *La République*, 4 (3 March 1946), 'Erreur de direction' by PA.
[92] *La République*, 3 (24 February 1946), 'Le redressement nécessaire' by François Gagnaire.
[93] AP 1946, p. 140.
[94] Denais speaking to the *comité directeur* of the FR for the Seine in February 1946, AN, 317 AP 73. At this stage Denais, and many of his colleagues, appear to have been members of both the FR and the PRL before opting for the latter party.
[95] A. Mutter, 'Réconciliation par l'amnestie', *Paroles Françaises*, 56 (6 December 1946).
[96] *La République*, 18 May 1946, 'Que passe-t-il dans nos prisons?', unsigned.
[97] Auriol, *Journal du septennat*, V, 1975, p. 238, entry for 26 June 1951.
[98] *Journal du septennat*, I, p. 93, entry for 21 Feb 1947.

harsh. In theory every deputy who had voted full powers to Marshal Pétain in 1940, that is over 80 per cent of deputies in parliament, and everyone who had accepted office from the Vichy government, was to be banned from public life. Many right-wingers in the Resistance regarded this arrangement as both unfair and, in that it would weaken the electoral forces of conservatism, imprudent. Furthermore, there was not always a clear distinction between Pétainism and the Resistance. Some had voted for Pétain in 1940 and then gone on to join the Resistance. PRL leaders such as Laniel and Vallin were themselves in this position. Special arrangements had been made to lift the ineligibility of those who had subsequently distinguished themselves in the Resistance, but such men could hardly be expected to support the punishment of others for something that they had done themselves.

However, the leaders of the PRL soon found that the divisions that had emerged from the occupation, like the divisions over the church, could not just be wished away. The PRL's position made it vulnerable to attack from both sides. Resistance supporters suspected that the party was just a cover for Pétainists: 'It [the PRL] is already more and more infested by Pétainists, Vichyists, anti-Resistants and anti-Gaullists. They have accepted the head of the office of M. Cathala, men from inter France etc.'[99] On the other hand, former Vichy supporters believed that the PRL was simply trying to gain political advantage from the issue of amnesty. François Brigneau wrote that 'Mutter played the amnesty card in a calculating manner as others played the purge card.'[100] When Pétainists were able to express their opinion openly, they were soon directing their fire at the leaders of the PRL.[101]

Previous right-wing groups in France had been concerned with clerical, cultural or nationalistic matters. The PRL was novel in that its interests were largely economic. The majority of PRL interventions in parliamentary debates were concerned with economic matters. Opposition to nationalization, and subsequent efforts to limit the effects of nationalizations, played an especially large part in the party's programme during its early days.[102] Thereafter the party was a resolute defender of the financial orthodoxy practised by Paul Reynaud.[103] PRL leaders claimed that they had an

[99] AN, 317 AP 73, transcript of meeting of *comité directeur* of FR for 25 January 1946.
[100] Brigneau, *Mon après guerre*, p. 48
[101] In particular the industrialist Christian Wolf, who frequently funded extreme right-wing organizations, insisted that one of his papers publish a virulent attack on Clemenceau in 1951. Details of this episode can be found in the letter from Roger de Saivre to Robert Giron of the *Figaro*, dated 15 May 1951 in AN, 74 AP 33.
[102] The PRL seems to have seen nationalization as a question of almost religious gravity. The party organized a letter to bishops on the subject: *la République*, 3 August 1946.
[103] AP 1948, p. 154, Félix Rollat expressed the party's anger in September 1948 that special powers initially given to Reynaud were to be exercised by a Socialist finance minister.

innovative social policy: the party sometimes even described itself as socialist.[104] However, very little attention was given to the content of social policy and it was always made clear that any measure which threatened the rights of property would be ruled out. In general terms, the PRL believed that social policy should be subordinated to economic policy and that economic policy was fundamentally monetary policy.[105]

The PRL's focus on economic issues was widely recognized as a source of weakness. Economic issues often seemed abstract to ordinary voters: few peasants could have shared the solemn view of one party spokesman that the recently nationalized deposit banks had been 'real property as sacred as the properties of peasants'.[106] Concentration on economic issues also led party leaders to underestimate the complexity of the motives that underlay conservativism in France. One leader of the FR wrote in a critique of the PRL's policy: 'At the moment there are three possible right-wing formations depending on whether one looks at the religious question, the economic question or the political question.'[107] In truth the PRL sought to appeal to social groups who could only be united in terms of economic interest. Discussion of other issues would either divide the party or divide it from its potential supporters. This was shown by the success of the MRP in raising the religious question and the success of the RPF in raising the 'political' (that is constitutional) question.

So far attention has been given to those aspects of the PRL that divided it from other parties. However, there was one issue that created divisions within the PRL, which mirrored those of other parties. This issue was Gaullism. The PRL's leaders, like those of other parties, made much of their attachment to General de Gaulle. Mutter voted in the referendum of 1945 in accordance with the General's wishes and lamented de Gaulle's departure from government.[108] Twelve of the forty PRL deputies elected in November 1946 had stood on tickets that included the word Gaullist.[109] However, there was always some ambiguity about the party's attachment to Gaullism. In part this was a product of de Gaulle's alliance with the

---

[104] Rollat, la République, 23 November 1946, 'Pour un socialisme libéral et humain'.

[105] Auriol, Journal du septennat, II, p. 423, entry for 4 September 1948. 'I saw Laniel ... who was still in favour of the Reynaud plan. He told me that Marie could have 17 votes from among the PRL. He added that the monetary point was more important than any other. I told him that it would be overridden by social crisis, but he replied "it is monetary instability that provokes social troubles".'

[106] François Gagnaire in la République, 20 April 1946.

[107] AN 317 AP 73, transcript of meeting of the comité directeur of FR on 25 January 1946. Significantly, the speaker who was describing the weakness of the PRL, Pierre Lebon, was a banker.

[108] A. Mutter, 'Raisons d'un vote', Paroles Françaises, 3 (1 December 1945).

[109] This figure is calculated from the (sometimes rather confusing) list of party tickets given in le Monde, 12 November 1946.

Communist party and his support for social and economic reforms. The PRL's doubts about some aspects of Gaullism were summed up by Laniel at the party's constitutive meeting: 'Our position is perfectly clear. We were yesterday, and we will be tomorrow, admirers of the General, at whose sides André Mutter and I had the honour to walk down the Champs Elysées on the day of liberation. But we are against the second Popular Front.'[110]

There was another aspect to the PRL's attitude to de Gaulle. Behind public protestations of loyalty, it was clear that some party leaders had a personal hostility to the General that went beyond opposition to his policies and allies.[111] This anti-Gaullism, like the PRL's anti-Communism, must, in part, be traced back to the Resistance. Many Resistance leaders had resented the General's rudeness, his extremism, his demands for exclusive control of the Resistance movement, and his capacity for annoying allies, especially the Americans. The annoyance felt at the pretensions of Gaullism must have been made all the more sharp by the fact that so many PRL members had belonged to American-linked and Giraudist parts of the Resistance.

In 1947, divisions over attitudes to de Gaulle within the PRL were brought to light by the formation of the RPF. The RPF seemed to offer much of what the PRL had promised. It was violently anti-Communist, and it favoured some degree of rehabilitation for Pétainists. But there were also important differences between the two formations. The anti-Communism of the RPF, or at least of its leader, was rooted in nationalist resentment of 'separatists', not in social conservatism; the RPF's position on relations with America remained far less enthusiastic than that of the PRL leaders; it may even be that some members of the PRL took their rhetoric about republicanism and liberty seriously enough to be repelled by the authoritarian style of the RPF.[112] The divisions that existed within the PRL as a whole were reflected among the party's deputies, but were complicated by purely electoral considerations. On the one hand, it suited many PRL deputies to earn prestige in the eyes of part of the electorate by associating with the RPF;[113] on the other hand sitting deputies saw very little to be gained from the RPF's anti-parliamentarianism or from risking their own seats by supporting its call for an early dissolution.[114] Consequently many

---

[110] AP 1945, p. 384.

[111] AN, 317 AP 84, report on meeting of 29 November 1945: 'Note the resentment of M. Ramarony at seeing the name of General de Gaulle cited.'

[112] At the party congress of 1948, PRL delegates expressed their reluctance to join the RPF in attacking parliament AP 1948, p. 76.

[113] Auriol, *Journal du septennat*, II, p. 201, entry for 28 April 1948. Laniel told Auriol that more than half of PRL deputies who supported the RPF did so 'for exclusively electoral reasons'.

[114] AP 1948, p. 92. Much to de Gaulle's annoyance the PRL abstained rather than voting against the government.

PRL deputies were half members of the RPF, supporting it on all questions except those that mattered.

The exclusion of the Communists from the Ramadier government in May 1947 followed closely on the creation of the RPF. The two events combined to affect a transformation in the behaviour of the PRL. When the government had contained Communists, the PRL had had a clear sense of purpose: it had been a disciplined party of opposition.[115] After May 1947, things were much less clear. Where anti-Communism had united the party, anti-Gaullism divided it. Certain leaders of the PRL now sought not to attack every government but to defend them against the external threat posed by the Communist party and the RPF. Two PRL deputies, Betolaud and Bruyneel, became ministers in the Queuille government of 1948,[116] and PRL leaders who had been noted for intransigence now turned up to offer their support for any threatened government with a regularity that the president of the republic sometimes found positively irritating.[117] But it was too late for the PRL to become a party of government; its reputation for extremism was too well established and its participation was likely to cause more damage than good.[118]

Conclusion

The PRL failed. Its founders had hoped to gain over a hundred seats in Parliament and to create a single united party of the right that would be as solid and long lasting as the British Conservative party.[119] But the PRL only won about forty parliamentary seats and it never gained much support outside urban and industrialized areas: half the party's deputies came from the twenty-six most economically advanced departments,[120] one-fifth of them came from Paris alone. At the party conference of May 1948 it was

---

[115] AN, 317 AP 84, the FR's letter 'pour nos militants', undated, attacked the PRL for its 'totalitarian conception of discipline'.

[116] Elgey, *La IVème république*, p. 393. Betolaud was minister for *anciens combattants*, Bruyneel was under-secretary of state to the *président du conseil*.

[117] Auriol, *Journal du septennat*, II, p. 395, entry for 28 August 1948. Laniel persuaded Auriol, somewhat against his wishes, to see a PRL delegation who wished to discuss how the latest governmental crisis might be resolved. On 21 July 1949 Auriol wrote: 'It is almost a tradition that Ramarony comes to the Elysée during each ministerial crisis.' Ibid., p. 326.

[118] Ibid., II, p. 153, entry for 16 March 1948. Auriol was told that a section of MRP deputies would be alienated if the PRL, which they regarded as too right-wing, joined the government.

[119] On the PRL's hopes for over one hundred seats in parliament, *Paris Matin*, 8 March 1946, 'La droite nous annonce le succès de la droite aux élections'; on the comparison between the PRL and the British Conservative party see the 'Le point de vue anglais', in *la République*, 3 March 1946.

[120] The twenty-six most 'dynamic departments' were so described by a survey of the Institut national de la statistique et des études économiques in 1951: F. Goguel, *Géographie des élections françaises sous la troisième et la quatrième république* (Paris, 1970).

recognized that the PRL had not achieved its initial objectives.[121] On the eve of the 1951 elections, Laniel conceded that his party would be unable to draw up the thirty departmental lists without which it would not obtain the advantages that came from legal recognition as a national party. He therefore asked Roger Duchet, secretary of the CNIP, for an electoral alliance. Duchet agreed, but insisted that in return the PRL should agree to merge with the CNIP after the elections.[122] This was duly done and the PRL disappeared as an independent organization.

Accounting for the relative failure of the PRL seems simple. The party was founded on the idea of class politics. It was designed to defend the interests of the bourgeoisie from state intervention in the economy and, most of all, from the threat of Communism. Its leaders sought to exclude non-class issues from the political debate: they supported subsidies for church schools and amnesty for Vichy supporters, not because they were devout catholics or Pétainists but because they wanted to stop such issues from dividing the right. However, politics in France was not so straightforward; debates about the church and the legitimacy of Vichy continued to divide the right, and debate about the constitution eventually divided the PRL leadership itself.

The explanation given above is partly true, but it is not the whole story. The founders of the PRL were not entirely wrong to argue that class issues would be the key to Fourth Republic politics. Anti-Communism did dominate almost all the bourgeois political parties, and other issues, while continuing to count, were always subordinated to it. However, this tendency did not benefit the PRL for two reasons. Firstly, many felt, especially in the first few years after the Liberation, that explicitly right-wing politics would confine the representatives of the French bourgeoisie to sterile opposition at a time when dangerous policies were being enacted. They preferred the tacit conservatism of parties such as the MRP or the RGR, or even the ostensibly non-political action of civil servants, which could quietly impede reform from within. A good illustration of this tacit conservatism is the reconstruction of the right-wing press in France. The press had been one the PRL's greatest obsessions and they had repeatedly demanded the repeal of legislation that made it difficult for a right-wing press to flourish. But the PRL was so powerless in this area that it was unable to guarantee even the supplies of newsprint that it needed to keep its own journals in business. In contrast, ministers from the MRP and the RGR, by working within government, and even working alongside Communist ministers, were able discreetly to undermine the press laws and prevent the transfer of newspapers away from right-wing owners.[123]

---

[121] AP 1948, p. 76.   [122] Duchet, *La république épinglée*, p. 14.
[123] Novick, *The Resistance versus Vichy*, p. 122.

Eventually the success of tacit conservatism undermined the very organizations that had played host to it. The exclusion of the Communist party from government and the increasing tolerance of former Pétainists in public life meant that openly conservative parties could be re-established. However, once again the PRL did not benefit from this change. For the problem now was that, while anti-Communism remained the most important basis of conservatism, other issues were often superimposed. The 1951 electoral law, which allowed rival parties to attack each other over many issues such as religion while forming *apparentements* against the Communist party, was the product of this situation.[124] In these circumstances a disciplined party such as the PRL, which claimed to command the absolute loyalty of its members, stood no chance. The future belonged to loose groupings with blurred edges, such as the CNIP, that could tolerate a wide range of difference, and even bitter disputes, within their ranks. Yet, though the party stucture of the CNIP was the antithesis of the PRL, the policies that it supported when in government – the consolidation of the Atlantic alliance, the end of *dirigiste* economics and amnesty for those who had supported Vichy – were those that the PRL had advocated in 1945.[125] The founders of the PRL had been right about the ends of Fourth Republic conservatism, but wrong about the means by which those ends could be achieved.

[124] The headline in *le Monde* on 14 June 1951 described the way in which the electoral campaign was approached; 'L'anticommunisme domine mais est bien divisé'.

[125] In September of 1949, the PRL published a pamphlet defiantly entitled 'Le PRL a eu raison' (Paris, 1949), in which it claimed the credit for having 'defended ideas that seemed daring in 1945, but which now many wished to claim as their own'. It listed numerous propositions of PRL deputies that had subsequently been taken up by other parties.

10 *Machine à ramasser les Pétainistes*? The Mouvement Républicain Populaire and the conservative electorate

Introduction

One of the most spectacular novelties of the Fourth Republic was the new Christian Democrat party: the Mouvement Républicain Populaire. The party gained 26 per cent of votes cast in the November 1946 election, which made it the second largest group in parliament after the Communist party, but this level of support proved impossible to maintain. Support for the party, as reflected in municipal elections, dropped in 1947 and in the general election of 1951 the MRP obtained only 12.5 per cent of votes cast. The nature of the electorate that propelled the MRP to such great, and short-lived, success has received little attention. Historians sympathetic to the MRP gloss over the subject while others simply take it for granted that the party was supported by 'Millions of French conservatives, bewildered by the discrediting of their former leaders, were seeking a powerful bulwark against Communism and believed that they had found it in the MRP.'[1]

This chapter will argue that the MRP's electorate was indeed a conservative one (or at least that it came from areas and social groups that had voted conservative before 1944 and did so again after 1951). However, it will also argue that the supporters of the MRP were characterized by a particular *kind* of conservatism as well as by attitudes that did not fit into any neat left/right model. It will further be suggested that these conservatives did not vote for the MRP simply because there was no alternative, but because they positively approved of the party in certain key respects. In this context the conventional contrasts drawn between 'left-wing' leaders and 'right-wing' followers of the MRP are misguided. Finally, it will be argued that historians have been wrong to ask why the MRP did not develop into a clerical version of the Gaitskellite Labour party; the real question is rather

---

[1] Philip Williams, *Politics in post-war France: parties and the constitution in the Fourth Republic* (2nd edition, London, 1958), p. 79. The most extensive discussion of the MRP electorate occurs in Henri Descamps, *La démocratie chrétienne et le MRP de 1944 à 1959* (Paris, 1981), pp. 139, 172.

why the MRP did not develop into a new kind of mass Christian/ conservative party along the lines of the Italian Christian Democrats.

Contemporary views of the MRP

Many contemporary commentators believed that the MRP owed its success to the support of right-wingers. Communist manifestos coined the jibe 'MRP = *machine à ramasser les Pétainistes*';[2] similar arguments were advanced by the Radicals: 'the MRP is constantly sliding towards a sort of Pétainism'.[3] The right-wing leader Tixier-Vignancour wrote: 'Decapitated, suspected, rejected, the great nationalist bloc broke up, turned in on itself or took refuge in a lesser evil: the MRP.'[4]

The public statements of the MRP's rivals might be dismissed as propaganda, but the private reports of civil servants and MRP supporters themselves have to be taken more seriously. François Closon, the *commissaire de la république* in the North, wrote 'There are right-wing voters in the Nord and Pas-de-Calais, and in the absence of sufficiently authoritative candidates, it is possible that, making the best of a bad job, the MRP will benefit from this situation.'[5] When the MRP did make gains in the North, a sympathetic observer analysed the success in these terms: 'The socially minded catholics should be under no illusion about their real strength: too many conservatives voted for them without really supporting their programme.'[6]

The reports of right-wing party bosses also suggested that a 'naturally conservative' electorate was lending its support to the MRP:[7] a confidential newsletter circulated among Pétainist businessmen analysed the MRP in precisely the terms used by the Communists; 'The MRP was little more than a machine for collecting Pétainists.'[8] Most strikingly of all, many MRP

[2] The MRP was always unfortunate in its choice of acronyms; originally the party was to be called the Mouvement Républicain Démocratique, but it was realized that the initials MRD might produce the wrong impression when pronounced rapidly. Claude Michelet, *Mon père Edmond Michelet d'après ses notes intimes* (Paris, 1971), p. 141.

[3] Archives Nationales (AN), 350 AP 76, 'consignes données au parti radical', circular dated 6 September 1946.

[4] J. L. Tixier-Vignancour, *La France trahie. Plaidoirie de Me Tixier-Vignancour dans l'affaire des fuites* (Paris, 1956), p. 18.

[5] Françis Closon, *Commissaire de la république du général de Gaulle. Lille septembre 1944– mars 1946* (Paris, 1980), p. 163.

[6] Derôme (a professor at London University) speaking to an MRP meeting on 3 January 1946, cited in Brunon Béthouart, *Le MRP dans le Nord–Pas-de-Calais 1944–1967* (Paris, 1984), p. 42.

[7] See the numerous undated reports made to Louis Marin about the position of the right in various areas (AN, 317 AP 73).

[8] AN, 57 AS 12, 'Note sur la propagande anti-communiste en France' (dated 14 January 1947) found among the papers of Jacques Warnier, a business leader and later president of the Centre des Jeunes Patrons.

leaders themselves believed that their success came from a conservative electorate.[9]

The MRP and right-wing competition

It was widely suggested that conservative voters supported the MRP because they had no alternative: they saw the new party as a 'lesser evil' which only succeeded 'in the absence of sufficiently authoritative candidates'. According to this interpretation, taken up by most historians of the Fourth Republic, there were few candidates of the 'real right' in 1945 and 1946 because right-wing politicians had been eliminated from political life as a result of their conduct before 1940. This interpretation was expressed most fully by Robert Buron (a leader of the MRP). He attributed his party's success to 'the elimination of a large number of former members of parliament who, having granted full powers to Marshal Pétain, did not then take a stand against collaboration'.[10]

There is, however, an obvious flaw in these arguments. The right was badly hit by public opprobrium and legal sanctions after the Liberation, but these problems did not afflict all conservatives. Some right-wingers had been untainted by associations with Vichy, and these men were able to reform their parties, or found new groups, after the war. Louis Marin's Fédération Républicaine (FR) was re-formed and the Parti Républicain de la Liberté (PRL) was founded in December 1945. In the elections of 21 October 1946 the MRP faced a challenge from its right in seventy-one out of ninety-four constituencies.[11] The parties of the right believed that the MRP electorate was naturally conservative and not properly represented by the MRP leadership, and they assumed that this electorate would naturally pass from the MRP to them in the 1946 elections: 'It is believed that the MRP will lose votes, so the the conservative list will have at least one seat.'[12] This conspicuously failed to happen.[13] In October 1946 the MRP gained several times as many seats as the largest explicitly right-wing parties, and the right failed to insert itself into the catholic areas of the West, Haute Savoie and Alsace-Lorraine.

---

[9] Robert Buron, *Le plus beau des métiers* (Paris, 1963) p. 12. See also Barthélemy Ott, *Vie et mort du MRP. La démocratie chrétienne est-elle possible en France?* (Annonay, 1978), p. 48: 'In May 1945 the MRP was a refuge for the bourgeois who ... had accepted the regime of Marshal Pétain and who could no longer vote for the old discredited parties or the ineligible deputies.' [10] Buron, *Le plus beau des métiers*.
[11] J.-P. Rioux, *The Fourth Republic 1944–1958* (Cambridge, 1987), p. 60.
[12] AN, 317 AP 73, undated report on political situation in Marseilles.
[13] According to D. MacRae, the MRP had lost about 16 per cent of its electorate to the PRL between November 1945 (immediately before the PRL's establishment) and April 1946. D. MacRae, *Parliament, parties and society in France 1946–1958* (New York, 1967), p. 234.

If the MRP's success in areas traditionally seen as conservative cannot be explained by the absence of competition, can it be explained by the positive attraction of MRP policies to a certain kind of conservative voter? Such an interpretation sounds strange. The MRP leaders certainly presented themselves as men of the left. Most observers accepted this estimation and believed that the links between the MRP leadership and the conservative voters were unnatural and temporary. François Mauriac wrote: 'Their rise to power, due to unforeseen circumstances, was the result of a misunderstanding.'[14] Jean Mazé argued that the MRP 'collected votes that did not belong to it'.[15] Nathaniel Leites suggested that the desire of the MRP leadership to be classified on the left (when its electorate lay on the right) made it 'a tortured, unstable party'.[16]

However, there is no reason why the desire of the MRP's leaders to be classified on the left should be regarded as the last word in defining their, or their party's, stance. Almost all political parties in the Fourth Republic denied being on the right (though with varying degrees of enthusiasm); Pétainists and former members of the Parti Social Français (PSF) joined the Rassemblement des Gauches Républicaines (RGR), and even the ferociously reactionary Parti Républicain de la Liberté (PRL) sometimes claimed to be 'socialist'. In this context it is clearly worth examining the MRP's claims to be on the left.

The socialist alliance

The claims of the MRP leadership to be classified on the left were most plausible during its early alliance with the Socialist party. The MRP supported the Blum government after the resignation of General de Gaulle and some MRP leaders continued to talk of *travailliste* alliances that would include both themselves and the Section Française de l'Internationale Ouvrière (SFIO) during the 1950s. Béthouart interpreted this as a sign of distance between the MRP's progressive leaders and its conservative electorate: 'there is a marked paradox for the MRP, which wants to be a *travailliste* party, and therefore seeks an alliance with the Socialists, and is making progress thanks to voters who, far from sharing this view, hope to get as far away as possible from them [i.e. the Socialists]. Whether to remain faithful to its beliefs or its voters: the problem will soon arise.'[17]

There is an element of truth in this analysis, but it is not the whole story. The MRP/Socialist alliance reflected splits in the SFIO as well as in the

---

[14] *Le Figaro*, 22 October 1946.   [15] Jean Mazé, *Le système* (Paris, 1951), p. 240.
[16] N. Leites and C. Melnik, *The house without windows: France selects a president* (White Plains, 1958), p. 311.   [17] Béthouart, *Le MRP dans le Nord–Pas-de-Calais*, p. 49.

MRP. The Resistance leader Lecompte-Boinet wrote in his diary: 'the separation between Socialists and Communists is more apparent to the leaders than to the rank and file, while that between Socialists and the MRP is more apparent to the rank and file than to the leaders, that it is to say that the rank and file are more worried about laicism than about the notion of liberty itself. As for the MRP, its supporters are on the right while its leaders are on the left.'[18] MRP leaders were able to countenance an alliance with the SFIO and especially with Blum partly because of the latter's desire to end the clerical issue in French politics. Relations between the leaders of the SFIO and the MRP were also facilitated by anti-Communism.[19] Léon Blum was noted in the immediate aftermath of the Second World War as the man who had denounced the Parti Communiste Français (PCF) as 'a nationalist party of foreign allegiance' and during this period he attracted admiration even from some leaders of the extreme right. *Travaillisme*, as defined by the leaders of the MRP, always involved an element of anti-Communism as well as social reform.[20] Furthermore, Guy Mollet, who had led the SFIO opposition to alliance with the MRP during the 1940s, became an acceptable interlocutor for the MRP during the 1950s not because he had abandoned anti-clericalism but because he had taken up anti-Communism. Of course, the anti-Communism that united the MRP leadership with certain factions of the SFIO was a particular kind of anti-Communism – one that sprang from having worked with the Communists in the Resistance and that was compatible with continuing to work with them in government during *tripartisme*. The subtlety of such a position may well have escaped many conservative voters.[21]

MRP membership

Many observers argued that the the membership of the MRP identified it as a left-wing party. The MRP was a party of mass membership, like the SFIO and PCF, rather than a loose grouping of notables, like the Radicals or the conservative parties. In 1946 the MRP had 200,000 members; this rose to

---

[18] Diaries of Lecompte-Boinet (LBD), 23 November 1945.

[19] On SFIO/MRP relations as seen from the SFIO side see B. D. Graham, *French socialists and tripartisme* (London, 1965), p. 90.

[20] In July 1953 the MRP issued an appeal to a variety of bodies including the SFIO: 'The MRP calls on the elites of all social classes ... to nurture together the great *travailliste* alliance which, against communism and conservatism, will constuct with enthusiasm and resolution the future of France and Europe.' AN, 350 AP 76, Teitgen to Mollet dated 18 July 1953.

[21] Of course, many conservative voters did come to see the SFIO as an effective anti-Communist force and 7,000 of them gave *panachage* votes to Jules Moch (the strongly anti-Communist SFIO minister of interior) in 1951, but this was after the expulsion of Communists from government. Williams, *Politics in post-war France*, pp. 66, 347 and 450.

450,000 in the following year before declining to 100,000 in 1950.[22] Furthermore, the rank and file membership of the MRP was more radical in its social outlook than the party leadership. It was also widely believed that rank and file members were more likely to be of working class origin than either the party leaders or its electorate. Information provided by the MRP leadership itself suggested that around 20 per cent of MRP members were of working class origin during the early 1950s, a period when only 15 per cent of the party electorate came from the working class.[23] The representation of the working class seems to have been even higher among those who were active militants rather than just members of the MRP.[24]

This recruitment drive cannot be explained in terms of electoral advantage. On the contrary, an emphasis on industrial rather than agricultural areas, and workplaces rather than homes, alienated the MRP from two of the most important parts of its electorate: peasants and women. Furthermore, there was no large group of potential MRP voters among the French working classes. This was partly because the working class itself was a relatively small part of the French population, partly because the proportion of workers who were at all liable to vote for any party other than the PCF or the SFIO was small and partly because even workers who were devout catholics were often repelled by the intensity and zeal of catholic militants – only about 20 per cent of practising catholic workers joined Action Catholique Ouvrière.[25] One MRP leader wrote ruefully that his party had represented 'travaillisme sans travailleurs'.[26]

Should we assume that the nature of MRP membership made it a 'left-wing' party? To some extent the answer to this question is yes. The image that parties projected in the Fourth Republic was important and the fact that the MRP proclaimed itself to be an '*ouvriériste* party' meant that many

[22] E. F. Callot, *Le Mouvement Républicain Populaire. Un parti politique de la démocratie chrétienne en France. Origine, structure, doctrine, programme et action politique* (Paris, 1978), p. 225. Bichet suggests that party membership peaked at 235,000 in late 1945. Robert Bichet, *La démocratie chrétienne en France. Le Mouvement Républicain Populaire* (Besançon, 1980), p. 219.

[23] Jean Fontenau, assistant secretary of the party, stated in 1951 that 20 per cent of members were working class. Williams, *Politics in post-war France*, p. 84. The major survey was carried out by D. Pépy, 'Note sur le Mouvement Républicain Populaire', in M. Duverger (ed.), *Partis politiques et classes sociales* (Paris, 1955), pp. 209–218. Pépy suggests, on the basis of an examination of 5,000 membership cards, that around 20 per cent of the MRP's members were working class in 1950 and around 14.8 per cent were working class in 1954. It should be noted that the undated survey and the survey of 6 April 1955 in AN, 350 AP 55 of 12,837 and 4,327 party members respectively both suggest that the proportion of workers was much smaller (8.43 per cent and 8.85 per cent).

[24] Descamps, *La démocratie chrétienne*, p. 204.

[25] R. Bosworth, *Catholicism and crisis in modern France: French catholic groups at the threshold of the Fifth Republic* (Princeton, 1962), p. 115.

[26] L. Biton, *La démocratie chrétienne dans la politique française. Sa grandeur, ses servitudes* (Angers, 1955), p. 128.

regarded it as being on the left. Indeed, *ouvriériste* rhetoric clearly annoyed some right-wing members of the MRP. Terrenoire complained about the 'conformisme ouvriériste' of his colleagues;[27] Michelet made the following note in November 1947: 'Always among our friends, this same disruptive tendency. "The masses! The working people!" An undeniable trickle of marxist vocabulary.'[28] Both Michelet and Terrenoire were soon to leave the MRP for the RPF.

However, the MRP's interest in the working class cannot entirely be fitted into a left/right dichotomy. The enthusiasm that the MRP leadership displayed for the recruitment of working class members was rooted in a more general preoccupation of the French church. This preoccupation dated back to the nineteenth century, but in the aftermath of the Second World War churchmen became fascinated by industrial areas. L'abbé Godin wrote an influential book in 1950 in which he remarked: 'Our missionary lands are made up of proletarians.'[29] Catholic organizations of all kinds neglected other sections of society in their enthusiasm to recruit working class members. This enthusiasm was reflected in the worker priest experiment,[30] and in the establishment of Action Catholique Ouvrière.[31] William Bosworth talks of the catholic hierarchy having a 'workers can do no wrong' attitude during this period.[32]

The MRP leaders were heavily influenced by these currents of thought and also by the fact that social catholicism, which exercised an influence over the early MRP, had begun in the northern industrial areas where it was assumed that the 'social problem' loomed especially large. At the root of all these tendencies was a belief that recruitment had more to do with missionary activity than electoral politics: MRP organizers seem to have believed that there was more rejoicing in heaven over the conversion of a single Anzin coal miner than the continued loyalty of a hundred Breton peasants.

It should also be stressed that, though the left-wing and working class membership of the MRP may have had a considerable influence on public perception of the party, it had very little influence on the policies pursued by its leadership. The leadership of the MRP was almost exclusively bourgeois

---

[27] L. Terrenoire, *De Gaulle 1947–1954. Pourquoi l'échec. Du RPF à la traversée du désert* (Paris, 1981), p. 41.

[28] Claude Michelet, *Mon père Edmond Michelet d'après ses notes intimes* (Paris, 1971), p. 180.

[29] H. Godin and Y. Daniel, *La France pays de mission* (Paris, 1950), p. 26. Anyone wishing to capture the full awfulness of this brand of missionary catholicism should read Maisie Ward, *France pagan? The mission of abbé Godin* (London, 1949).

[30] Oscar Arnal, *Priests in working class blue: the history of the worker priests (1943–1954)*, (Mahwah, N.J.), 1986.

[31] J. Debès, *Naissance de l'Action Catholique Ouvrière* (Paris, 1982).

[32] Bosworth, *Catholicism and crisis*, p. 113.

(no MRP minister came from the working class).[33] Furthermore, like most parties that laid some claim to the Resistance heritage, the MRP was built from the top down. The discipline and centralization of the MRP prevented its working class membership from exercising much influence over party policy.[34] The party's national council and executive council contained a large number of *ex officio* members chosen from among party officials, ministers, ex-ministers and deputies. In 1951 all but one of the members of the bureau of the party executive were deputies and most were former ministers.[35] Modifications to the statutes that protected the position of party deputies were difficult. The effect of the MRP's top heavy structure was that there was a *décalage* between what was said at party congresses and what was adopted as party policy. The party secretary admitted that the leadership toned down or ignored radical propositions.[36]

The MRP and the Resistance legacy

Another respect in which the MRP is often placed on the left of the political spectrum relates to Resistance activity. Historians usually assume that the MRP leadership was almost exclusively made up of Resistance veterans: 'All the leaders of the MRP, without exception, belonged to the Resistance, some played a prominent role in it.'[37] Charlot suggests that 80 per cent of MRP deputies had participated in Resistance activity.[38] The Resistance credentials of the MRP were not, in fact, quite as impeccable as its admirers liked to think. Some party leaders (Robert Schuman and Reille Soult) had voted for Pétain in 1940; one (Johanes Dupraz) had held office at Vichy, and many had 'resisted' in extremely prudent ways: one MRP deputy listed 'reading anti-German books' as her 'Resistance activity'.[39]

---

[33] On the social origins of MRP deputies and ministers see Callot, *Le Mouvement Républicain Populaire*, p. 243.

[34] There was a sliding scale of representation at party congresses: each federation was granted one delegate for every 50 members up to 200 members, one delegate for every 100 members between 200 and 5,000 members and one delegate for every 200 members thereafter. The sliding scale ensured that it was difficult for a few powerful federations to dominate the party; it also ensured that disproportionate influence was given to rural areas that contained few MRP members, as opposed to voters. Williams, *Politics in post-war France*, p. 84.

[35] On MRP structure and discipline see ibid., p. 83. See also Bichet, *La démocratie chrétienne*, pp. 48–50. Bichet recognized in retrospect that the MRP's structures were 'too frequently dominated by the representatives of central bodies'.

[36] Bichet, *La démocratie chrétienne*, p. 212. Of course, MRP ministers had even greater freedom from militant pressure than party officials, and they could always blame right-wing measures on the need to keep on good terms with their coalition partners.

[37] Ibid., p. 54.

[38] J. Charlot, 'Les élites politiques en France de la IIIème à la Vème république', *Archives Européennes de Sociologie*, 14 (1973), 78–92.

[39] See the list of biographies of deputies in AN, 350 AP 73.

Even those MRP leaders who had genuine Resistance credentials cannot be classed simply as left-wing. In particular, many Resistance veterans had acquired a vigorous distaste for the Communist party which they associated with the Hitler/Stalin pact and the manoeuvres through which the PCF had sought to gain power over clandestine movements. In the Nord-Pas-de-Calais, one MRP leader blamed the defeat of 1940 on 'Communist infiltration of the army' while another kept a private archive of Communist party publications between September 1939 and June 1941.[40] In his history of the MRP, Robert Bichet (the party's former secretary general) recalled the PCF's efforts to get permission to publish *Humanité* during the occupation at some length.[41] For men like this, anti-Communism was present in the MRP from its creation, and not something that developed after the break up of Resistance alliances and *tripartisme*.

The Resistance credentials of the MRP also deserve to be seen in the light of the party's treatment of former Pétainists. The MRP supported *épuration* of Pétainists in theory, but in practice was often moderate. Edgar Faure wrote of de Menthon, the Christian Democrat minister of justice: '[he] was exhausted by the task, because he stood up to the extreme supporters of purges and repression'.[42] Pétainists, or those concerned for their welfare, could sometimes obtain concessions by making direct appeals to MRP ministers: for example the chaplain of Fresnes prison met the MRP minister of justice (Teitgen) and persuaded him to improve conditions for political prisoners.[43] For those concerned to save relatives or friends the MRP, which could grant special favours from within the government, was far more useful than explicitly right-wing parties which could only rail against government action from the sidelines.

Anti-capitalism

The MRP's economic policy was rooted in 'personalism': its leaders believed that men were not just the sum of their material interests. MRP propaganda emphasized the importance of communal feeling, family loyalty and collective bodies.[44] Most historians accept that the party's opposition to the unrestricted operations of the free market associated it with the left, and the MRP leaders themselves seem to have thought of their economic ideas as progressive. The party supported nationalization,

[40] Béthouart, *Le MRP dans le Nord–Pas-de-Calais*, p. 25.
[41] Bichet, *La démocratie chrétienne*, p. 35.
[42] E. Faure, *Mémoires*. I: *Avoir toujours raison ... c'est un grand tort* (Paris, 1982), p. 157.
[43] Jean Popot, *J'étais aumônier à Fresnes* (Paris, 1962), p. 92.
[44] Biton, *La démocratie chrétienne en France*, p. 104.

though with some reservations.[45] Some party members advocated an enhanced role for professional organizations that was close to corporatism,[46] as was the bill put forward by Paul Bacon in 1946 to establish *sociétés de travail et d'épargne* or the MRP proposal that the Berliet company be run under a complicated system of joint ownership.[47]

However, anti-capitalism was not an unambiguously left-wing ideology. Andrew Shennan highlights the paradox of the MRP as a party that 'at the same time as proposing to carry through a socio-economic 1789 ... wanted to undo the loi Le Chapelier and reintegrate the individual into natural communities'.[48] Paxton points out that anti-capitalists had been attracted to Pétain's corporatism in 1940 for much the same reasons that they were attracted to the MRP economic policies in 1946.[49] Furthermore, the public statements of the MRP were often distinguished not so much by opposition to capitalism as by opposition to that section of capitalism connected to large-scale financial operations. MRP denunciations of big business could sometimes seem close to the attacks on *capitalisme apatride* made by extreme right-wingers such as Beau de Loménie. An account of political events in January 1948 reported:

Some parliamentarians ... vigorously criticized M. René Mayer who they reproached for having deformed the idea ... of the plan and making himself ... the docile servant of industrial and banking interests. In their criticisms of M. Mayer, the parliamentarians recalled that the minister was a director, and remains a friend, of the Rothschild bank, which is only waiting for the chance to invest money in troubled companies which it will thus be able to take over at a good price.[50]

The divide over free market economics did not always coincide with the left/right divide on other issues. Mendès-France, generally seen as a hero of the left, was highly liberal on economic matters and this partly explains the MRP's refusal to support him,[51] a refusal usually dismissed as a futile and

---

[45] One MRP leader suggested that the real function of his party had been to use its position in government to control and restrict nationalization: 'The role of the MRP, faced with its Socialist and Communist associates, was often to prevent the extension of nationalizations beyond the limits laid out in the protocol and, above all, to see that the it took place without *étatisation* or confiscation.' Francisque Gay, *Les démocrates d'inspiration chrétienne à l'épreuve du pouvoir. Mémoire confidentiel* (Paris, 1951), p. 75.

[46] Andrew Shennan, *Rethinking France: plans for renewal 1940–1946* (Oxford, 1989), p. 275.

[47] Mario Einaudi and François Goguel, *Christian democracy in France and Italy* (Notre Dame, 1952), p. 141.   [48] Shennan, *Rethinking France*, p. 83.

[49] 'The catholic left, marginal in the 1930s, found that the same anti-capitalism and rejection of the atheist radical republic that had made it Pétainiste in 1940 put it in harmony with the Resistance in 1944.' Robert Paxton, *Vichy France: old guard and new order 1940–1944* (New York, 1982), p. 349.

[50] AN, 457 AP 135, report of political activity dated 10 January 1948.

[51] AN, 350 AP 74. In a meeting of the bureau of the MRP group at the *assemblée nationale* on 14 June 1954, Demey refused to support Mendès on the grounds that 'Mendès has no more social concern than Pinay'. The similarity with Mendès-France was recognized, retrospectively, by Pinay. See A. Pinay, *Un français comme les autres. Entretiens avec Antoine Veil* (Paris, 1984), pp. 36 and 37.

spiteful revenge for the shelving of the European Defence Community. Similarly many of those who supported restrictions on the free market were in fact right-wingers, and particularly catholic right-wingers.[52] For example the Centre des Jeunes Patrons (CJP) was associated with the MRP and with assaults on unrestricted capitalism.[53] Most observers assumed that this reflected the progressive nature of the CJP,[54] but an early president of the Centre, Jacques Warnier, was an extreme right-winger whose opposition to capitalism was rooted in Pétainist and right-wing corporatism.

Conservative anti-capitalism was especially influential in those areas of MRP strength that had agricultural economies: many inhabitants of such areas may well have supported the 'new left' anti-capitalism of the MRP leadership because it resembled the 'old right' anti-capitalism of Pétain and Dorgères. One leader of the PRL recognized that the *chouan* voters of Brittany preferred the MRP to his own party which they saw as representing: 'the liberalism condemned by the Pope'.[55]

Clericalism and the church

The MRP, was less explicitly clerical than its counterparts in Germany and Italy and most party leaders presented it in fairly secular terms.[56] Levels of support for the MRP from the church varied from one area to another: Henri Descamps suggested that 90 per cent of the clergy supported the MRP in areas under the influence of liberal prelates (such as Cardinal Lienart in the Nord), whereas only around 40 per cent of priests supported the MRP in the centre and south-west of France.[57] The party's relations with Rome were always better than those with the Catholic hierarchy in France,[58] and even Rome was measured in the support that it gave to the new party. Open expression of support was confined to an article of 1951 in *l'Osservatore Romano* in which Catholics were urged, in moderate terms, not to desert the MRP for the RPF.[59]

[52] Emile Poulat, *Eglise contre bourgeoisie* (Paris, 1977), p. 155.
[53] See the letter from the president of the CJP, Raclet, to Teitgen dated 30 July 1953 in AN, 350 AP 76.
[54] E.F. Callot, *L'action et l'œuvre politique du Mouvement Républicain Populaire* (Paris, 1986), p. 312, describes the CJP as 'more open to social ideas'. See also Descamps, *La démocratie chrétienne*, p. 188.
[55] Georges Riond, *Chroniques d'un autre monde* (Paris, 1979), p. 189.
[56] Faure, *Avoir toujours raison*, p. 152. Robert Schuman was the notable exception among MRP leaders. He solemnly weighed up the religious credentials of potential ministers before appointing cabinets and was particularly upset when Jules Moch insisted that he appoint Fily Dabo-Sissoko (a fetishist). Jules Moch, *Une si longue vie* (Paris, 1976), p. 324.
[57] Descamps, *La démocratie chrétienne*, p. 185. It should be noted that Descamps was writing in the early 1960s after currents of progressive thought had begun to sweep the church: he may therefore have underestimated the support that the clergy had given to the conventional right in earlier years.
[58] Bichet, *La démocratie chrétienne*, p. 228: 'the links with Rome were, perhaps, more sure than those with the French episcopate'.   [59] Ibid., p. 230.

Relations between the church and politics in the Fourth Republic were further complicated by the fact that so many parties presented themselves as defenders of church interests. In the early Third Republic, when the clerical/anti-clerical divide had been clear cut and important, no one had been in any doubt about the way in which the political influence of the church was exerted: the Radical deputy of the Nièvre had been able to say with confidence in 1909 that the local bishop was the real leader of the opposition.[60] However, after 1945 several parties believed that they had reason to expect church support; the fact that church influence was exercised in a private and discreet manner (or was seen to be), made it difficult for particular candidates to know how the priests in an area would encourage their parishoners to vote. A seasoned political observer wrote the following remarks after talking to conservative candidates in 1946: 'Everyone expects a collapse of the MRP. The bishop vigorously encouraged Pinay to stand for election. But I think that Pinay and his friends have received some holy water and mistaken their wishes for realities.'[61]

Men who had expected support from the church were bitter when that support was not forthcoming or when they believed that church influence was being exercised against them. Whereas the anti-clericalism of the Third Republic had been the preserve of those who despised the church and took it for granted that clerical influence would work against them, the anti-clericalism of the Fourth Republic was often expressed by those who believed themselves to be favourable to the church and were disappointed when this favour was not reciprocated. Church influence could seem enormous when the electorate were being asked to choose between conservative parties that were indistinguishable on most issues. The politician who expressed the anti-clerical paranoia of Fourth Republic conservatism most vigorously was Edmond Michelet whose *Sur la fidélité en politique. Lettres à l'abbé G* alleged that the church had encouraged Michelet's supporters to desert him after he left the MRP for the RPF.[62]

Not surprisingly, the Radical party was the one that found it most difficult to compete with the MRP in religious areas. Though some Radicals regarded the religious question as no longer relevant and though the policies of the Radical party on other issues were often similar to those of the MRP, they could not shake off the burden of the past. When Edgar Faure stood as a Radical candidate in the Jura, he was horrified to find that the abbé Thurel was urging his flock, through the pages of the *Croix du Jura*, to vote MRP and attacking the Radical party: 'He stressed that the Radical party, in spite of the goodwill of some who wanted to rejuvenate it,

[60] J. Pataut, *Sociologie électorale de la Nièvre au XXème siècle (1902–1951)* (2 vols, Paris, 1956), I, p. 62.   [61] AN, 317 AP 73, undated report on politics in the Loire.
[62] Michelet, *Mon père Edmond Michelet*, p. 149.

remained the party of the inventories, of the separation of Church and State, of Combes, etc.' Faure was particularly astonished by the attack because he himself had no strong views on the religious question (he soon took steps to ensure that a peasant well known for piety was inserted on his electoral list) and he had been pressed to join the MRP: 'I had underestimated this kind of objection which no longer existed in in the South and was unknown in Paris.'[63]

The other main parties of the right, such as the Alliance Démocratique (AD), the PRL and the FR, did not have the Radicals' associations with explicit anti-clericalism. They did not have to live down their Third Republic past and the concrete policies that they advocated (such as the continuation of state subsidies to church schools) were exactly the same as those advocated by the MRP. However, it is clear that all the conservative rivals to the MRP had an image problem: no one believed that they were enthusiastic or convinced defenders of the church. In part this sprang from the fact that right-wing parties were so clearly preoccupied with economic issues and so clearly linked to industrial interests, which were not noted for their religious concerns.

The perception among conservative voters that the parties of the conventional right were dominated by secular interests may have been increased by the fact that these parties all worked in alliance with the Radicals at some point during the post-war period. Of course, the MRP also had links with the Radicals: it attempted to obtain the support of certain prominent Radicals (such as Faure and Raoul Dautry) and it seems to have taken some Radical votes. As late as 1955, a would-be senator hesitated about whether to present his candidacy as a member of the MRP or a Radical.[64] However, the MRP, unlike its conservative competitors, was careful to keep its relations with Radicals on an informal and individual basis. In public the MRP continued to present the Radical party as its greatest enemy. Orators at MRP congresses could always earn themselves a round of applause with some choice abuse of the Radicals. At the party congress of 1946 Max André said: 'I say that the Radical party is ... the most right-wing party in France [applause]'; Teitgen added: 'I want to be fair to the radicals ... that will be difficult for me ... they are social conservatives, they are the worst conservatives',[65] and innumerable speakers repeated the old chestnut that 'the Radicals sleep with everyone but do not reproduce'.

The MRP seems to have drawn especially large benefits from church influence and religious voters during the period immediately after the war. There were two reasons for this. Firstly, the memories of the Third

[63] Faure, *Avoir toujours raison*, p. 172.
[64] AN, 350 AP 74, letter with illegible signature to Le Brun Keris dated 18 June 1955.
[65] AN, 350 AP 56, speeches to party congress, 20 August 1946.

Republic were still fresh and continued to discredit many of the MRP's older rivals. Secondly, the French church itself had been heavily compromised by Pétainism during the occupation. This meant that some prominent priests who might normally have encouraged their flock to vote for explicit right-wingers had been muzzled by their superiors or even by the state.[66] It also meant that the church hierarchy needed what one MRP senator called 'a party of provisional refuge'.[67] What they wanted was a party that could work within the government to head off possible retribution.[68]

During the 1950s, church influence in favour of the MRP seemed to be exercised less frequently. Barthélemy Ott wrote of 'a lack of support from the church'.[69] Indeed, it was sometimes alleged that priests were working against MRP candidates. Even the despised Radical party was sometimes seen to be gaining church support. As early as 1947, it was believed that most of the catholic vote in Bordeaux was going to the Radicals.[70] Edgar Faure believed that he had benefited from church support more than the MRP candidate in the 1956 election.[71] In 1956 one MRP candidate noted: 'In the course of the last two days, in spite of the pledges of the hierarchy, some priests, many of them members of the committees for educational freedom, encouraged votes for ANTHONIOZ'[72] (Anthonioz was the radical candidate). An unsigned 'Note on the electoral situation in the Vendée' alleged that Baudry d'Asson (the Independent candidate) had 'energetic friends among the public and in an important section of the

[66] For example the report made in 1945 to Louis Marin on conservative notables in France stated that in the Gironde 'L'abbé BERGEY is under house arrest; you should start by seeing him. He is anti-MRP.' AN , 317 AP 73, cited at meeting of 25 October 1945. For more details on Bergey's trial and removal from Gironde politics see J. Lagroye, Société et politique. J. Chaban-Delmas à Bordeaux (Paris, 1973).

[67] Ott, Vie et mort du MRP, p. 57.

[68] R. Buron claimed that he had been in contact with senior clerics who had recognized the need for links with Resistance parties, which would defend them after the Liberation, since 1943. R. Buron, La Mayenne et moi ou la démocratie chrétienne au socialisme (Paris, 1978), p. 43. Bichet (La démocratie chrétienne, p. 228) claims that Bidault's interventions ensured that only three individuals in the French church were dismissed as a result of their attitude during the occupation. Noel claimed that far from protecting priests Bidault had actually forced the removal of several prominent churchmen, but this claim was expressed in a work published long after the events and when Bidault and the Gaullists were violently opposed to each other. L. Noel, La traversée du désert (Paris, 1973), p. 33. Contemporary sources suggest that the MRP was concerned to protect the church: in a meeting of the MRP executive commission of 20 January 1946, Teitgen expressed the fear that 'The priests will be terrorized if we are not in the government'. J. Charlot, Le gaullisme d'opposition 1946–1958 (Paris, 1983), p. 47.

[69] Ott, Vie et mort du MRP, p. 57.

[70] Lagroye, Société et politique, p. 135.

[71] Faure, Mémoires. II: Si tel doit être mon destin ce soir (Paris, 1984), p. 172. 'The great concern of the catholics at elections was to balance their votes enough to secure the simultaneous election of Charles Viatte and myself.'

[72] AN, 350 AP 94, note dated 16 January 1956 by A. Billimaz.

clergy'.[73] On 12 January 1956 thirty leaders of Action Catholique wrote to Monseigneur Deffreix of the Dordogne blaming him for the recent political return of Georges Bonnet 'on the advice of, and sometimes under pressure from, the spiritual authorities, he was supported by you and several members of Dordogne clergy'.[74]

Remarks such as those quoted above may reflect the end of the especially propitious circumstances that had existed for MRP/church relations during the early years of the MRP's existence. The MRP began to lose its monopoly of clerical support during the late 1940s and early 1950s as all non-marxist political parties made vigorous efforts to distance themselves from anti-clericalism. The Radical André Marie used Laniel as an intermediary to approach the church.[75] The Association Parlementaire pour la Liberté de l'Enseignement, formed after the 1951 election, contained all the MRP deputies, but it also contained almost all the members of the CNIP and the RPF, and even eleven Radicals.[76]

The growing rift between the MRP and some churchmen was an effect as well as a cause of MRP decline. MRP leaders, like other politicians, were prone to blame the church when they lost support.[77] Furthermore, once the MRP began to decline, the church had far less reason to support it. Politically minded priests were more worldly than religiously minded politicians; they approached elections much like other local notables and they knew that it was not worth doing favours for a party too weak, or too naive, to reciprocate.

Foreign policy

Foreign policy was the area in which the MRP exercised the greatest power. France had only two foreign ministers during the whole period 1944–1954 and both of them (Robert Schuman and Georges Bidault) were members of the MRP. The MRP leaders, particularly Schuman, were closely associated with the early moves towards European integration. This fact has had a considerable influence on historical interpretations of the MRP; many historians see European integration as a 'progressive' and 'modern' development that marked the MRP's distance from the old right. There is not much evidence that the voters thought of European integration in these terms. In fact, there is little evidence that voters thought of the issue much at

[73] AN, 350 AP 95, dated 12 December 1955.
[74] AN, 350 AP 94, note 'addressed by thirty leaders and militants of Action Catholique to Mgr Deffeix', dated 12 January 1956.
[75] Joseph Laniel, *Jours de gloire et jours cruels 1908–1958* (Paris, 1971), p. 145.
[76] Ibid., p. 158.
[77] The allegation that priests had supported the Radical candidate Anthonioz in the Ain was vigorously denied by other figures in the Ain. AN, 350 AP 94, 18 February 1957, letter from Dubois.

all: the technical and apparently abstract nature of the European Coal and Steel Community was not likely to stir a nation that still faced material deprivation and the aftermath of civil war.

It is worth stressing, however, that the opinions of conservative catholics do seem to have been more favourable towards international bodies after 1945 than they had been before 1940. In the inter-war period catholicism had been closely linked to nationalism and the League of Nations had been presented as being a dangerous centre of masonic power. After 1945, this changed. Catholic organizations were enthusiastic proponents of international harmony, within the western bloc at least,[78] and Christian Democrat parties in all European countries were so intimately linked to European integration that some began to feel that Europe was being built under the aegis of the 'catholic international'. The reasons for this new-born enthusiasm are not hard to discern: a united Europe was seen (especially by Bidault who took an obsessive interest in the Communist threat) as a bastion against Soviet power.[79]

There was one apparently minor aspect of Fourth Republic diplomacy that may have been important in building a conservative image for the MRP; this was the conduct of Franco–Spanish relations. Reference to Spain evoked important memories for catholic conservatives. Much publicity had been given to allegations about republican atrocities against the church during the civil war and Franco's Spain was probably the closest political relative to Vichy France (Pétain had served briefly as ambassador to Franco in 1939).

The MRP leadership were remarkably successful in preventing discussion of the stance that they had adopted during the Spanish Civil War: even a normally sceptical observer accepted that Christian Democrats had opposed 'Franco's rising in Spain and capitulation to Hitler with equal determination'.[80] At the funeral of Francisque Gay (an MRP deputy and editor of the party paper) no mention was made of the vigorous denunciation that he had made of the Spanish republican government in 1936.[81] However, many conservative voters must have read Gay's book in which he wrote 'government success everywhere is accompanied by terrible acts of terrorism, and horrible attacks mainly perpetrated against priests, monks, nuns, churches and monasteries'.[82] Even more significantly, many must

---

[78] On the shift in French catholic attitudes from nationalism to internationalism see René Rémond, 'Droite et gauche dans le catholicisme français contemporain', *Revue Française de Science Politique*, 3 (September 1958), 529–542.

[79] On the role of anti-Communism in the MRP's enthusiasm for Europe see the comment of Bichet (the former party secretary) in Bichet, *La démocratie chrétienne*, p. 299.

[80] Williams, *Politics in post-war France*, p. 78. Of course, some MRP leaders had opposed neither Franco nor Munich so perhaps Williams' remark is intended to be double edged.

[81] Georges Bidault, *Resistance: the political autobiography of Georges Bidault* (London, 1967), p. 133.

[82] Francisque Gay, *Dans les flammes et dans le sang. Les crimes contre les églises et les prêtres en Espagne* (Paris, 1936), p. 6.

have remembered that Robert Schuman had resigned from the Parti Démocrate Populaire in 1938 to mark his disapproval of the party's support for the Spanish Republicans.

Deciphering the extent to which such memories influenced the MRP leadership is hard. France did not have diplomatic relations with Spain during the late 1940s and early 1950s.[83] However, as foreign minister, Bidault presided over a resumption of commercial relations with Spain in September 1946. Bidault, who had been much less compromised than many of his colleagues by support for Franco during the Civil War,[84] was later to write that he regarded Spain as a necessary part of an alliance of western nations against communism: 'In 1946, I was not sure that I ought to complicate our existence, and even that of our neighbours, by arguing with Spain.'[85] The widespread perception that the MRP were well disposed towards, or at least tolerant of, Franco's Spain caused rifts between Socialist and MRP ministers;[86] it seems likely that it also attracted some conservative voters.

Gaullism

The MRP's close links with de Gaulle were another part of its appeal to conservatives. Michelet, an MRP deputy who later joined the RPF, wrote of the MRP 'they passed for the Gaullist party'.[87] The MRP liked to present itself as the *parti de fidélité*; membership cards had 'Avec de Gaulle' printed on them,[88] and a number of close associates (or even relatives) of the General's were associated with the MRP. Jacques Vendroux (de Gaulle's son-in-law) claimed that Schuman, who asked him to join the MRP, 'did not hide from me the fact that the MRP would be happy to display its attachment to the General through me'.[89]

The MRP was particularly successful in Alsace-Lorraine (a Gaullist stronghold since the defence of Strasbourg), and among women, who seem

[83] On Franco–Spanish relations in this period see A. Dulphy, 'La politique de la France à l'égard de l'Espagne Franquiste 1945–49', *Revue d'Histoire Moderne et Contemporaine*, 35 (1988), 123–140.

[84] Bidault's leaders in *l'Aube* had condemned Franco's rising – though he had also condemned Republican atrocities in an article that was quoted in Francisque Gay's book.

[85] Bidault, *Resistance*, p. 134. Bidault cited attitudes to Franco as one issue on which European Christian Democratic parties did not agree. AN, 457 AP 166, meeting of European Christian Democrats on 10 June 1949: 'Some accept, or tolerate, Franco, others want nothing of it.' However, Bidault did not specify where the MRP stood on the issue.

[86] On conflict with the Socialists over relations with Franco see Francisque Gay to Félix Gouin dated 28 February 1946 in AN, 350 AP 76.

[87] E. Michelet, *Le gaullisme, passionnante aventure* (Paris, 1962), p. 89.

[88] Béthouart, *Le MRP dans le Nord–Pas-de-Calais*, p. 38.

[89] J. Vendroux, *Souvenirs de famille et journal politique*. I: *Cette grand chance que j'ai eue: 1920–1957* (Paris, 1974), p. 133.

to have been especially prone to Gaullism (see chapter 5 and below). The loss of support for the MRP after the foundation of the RPF also suggests that Gaullism had been a feature of the MRP's appeal. It is easy to see why this appeal should have been especially potent among conservative voters.[90] De Gaulle was a soldier, a practising catholic, a member of a legitimist family and, perhaps most importantly, a representative of order who was expected to bring the *forces françaises de l'intérieur* (FFI) under control.

Age and sex of the MRP electorate

The conservative appeal of the MRP is not something that can be explained with exclusive reference to the party leadership. Some attention also needs to be paid to those who supported the MRP. It is worth starting by making an obvious, but often neglected, point: the majority of the electorate in 1945 were voting for the first time. This majority included all women and all men under 31, i.e. those who had been too young to vote in 1936. The MRP seems, during its early stages at least, to have been a youthful party. The first detailed survey, conducted in 1952, showed that only the Communist party and the RPF attracted a higher proportion of voters under the age of 34. It seems reasonable to assume that in 1945, when there was no competition from the RPF, the MRP had attracted an even higher proportion of youthful voters: certainly the MRP deputies elected in 1945 were younger than those of any other group.

The MRP was also especially attractive to female voters. Bichet, the party secretary, estimated that 58 per cent of MRP supporters were women at the movement's peak.[91] It is important to stress that while other conservative parties (the RPF and the Independents) attracted a high proportion of female voters, their success with the female electorate was partly explained by their special appeal for the old and the consequent benefits that they drew from the fact that women's life expectancy was greater than that of men. Only the MRP had an electorate that was both predominantly youthful and predominantly female.

Because so many voters were political virgins in 1945, conservative party organizers were quite wrong to assume that the MRP's electorate was simply 'the former clientele of the conservatives'. The nature of the

---

[90] For a good example of how de Gaulle did appeal to a young man from a conservative background see B. Marin, *De Gaulle de ma jeunesse 1944–1970* (Paris, 1984) Note how Marin's family refused to make a clear choice between Pétain and de Gaulle.

[91] Bichet, *La démocratie chrétienne*, p. 220. A public opinion survey of 1951 found that the proportion of women among MRP voters was only 53 per cent (cited in Williams, *Politics in post-war France*, p. 452) but this poll was taken after the MRP electorate had shrunk by around 50 per cent.

electorate in 1946 favoured the MRP in important ways. Firstly, it meant that much of the electorate had no particular links with the old Third Republic parties and no reason to prefer those parties to a newly formed movement. Most of all the notables who usually marshalled support for conservative politicians, and whose support the MRP conspicuously lacked,[92] had no established links with the new electorate. It is easy to see how the local influence brokers contacted by the FR in 1946 failed to anticipate the scale of the MRP success:[93] the places where party agents normally sought out their electorates – cafés, agricultural markets, workplaces – were all male dominated.

Pétainism

It might be argued that previous electoral experience of MRP voters was irrelevant in 1946 because the real formative experience of this group had been their support for Pétain during the period 1940–44. Certainly there is some evidence that voters were attracted to the MRP because they disapproved of the savagery with which some leaders of the traditional right had attacked Pétain. One organizer of the Fédération Républicaine wrote to Louis Marin:

Many of our friends were distressed by the position that you felt obliged to take during the trial of P. Everyone saw this as a very regrettable political trial, and the attitude of the Communist party seemed to show that it was the French army and thus eternal France itself that was under attack. I have to say that since this many of our friends have joined the MRP.[94]

However, there was a difference between sentimental concern about the treatment of Pétain and unqualified support for what the Vichy government had done. The widespread assumption that MRP voters were 'Pétainistes' is one that begs important questions. There certainly were some Frenchmen (Isorni, Rougier, Fabre-Luce) who argued after 1944 that the Vichy government had been a legitimate one, and these men believed that their, largely clandestine, writings were being read by a much larger group of secret sympathizers.[95] However, the advice given in such publications would not have led many people to vote for the MRP for two reasons.

---

[92] Bichet, *La démocratie chrétienne*, p. 62.

[93] See especially the four page list of notables attached to the account of the meeting of the bureau of the FR of 25 October 1945 (AN, 317 AP 73). The conservative notables whose opinions are expounded in these documents either assumed that the MRP vote would collapse or were simply unable to give an opinion about the MRP. The long report on political life in various regions (undated in AN, 317 AP 73) concluded lamely: 'There is great uncertainty about the future of the MRP.'

[94] AN, 317 AP 81, R. Toutain to Marin dated 8 September 1945.

[95] Alfred Fabre-Luce addressed his first book after the war to the *silencieux* Pétainists. A. Fabre-Luce, *Au nom des silencieux* (Bruges, 1946).

Firstly, the most plausible defence of Pétainism after the Liberation was one that hinged around 'republican legality': the basis of this defence was that Pétain had been granted full powers by a vote of parliament and that the *état français* was therefore the lawful extension of the Third Republic. Those who used this argument resented the abolition of the Third Republic constitution and the exclusion of those who had voted full powers to Marshal Pétain from political life. The key forum for this group was the Association des Représentants du Peuple de la Troisième République (ARPTR) which was joined by almost a thousand Third Republic politicians who had been declared ineligible after the Liberation. Significantly the leader of this group, *chanoine* Desgranges, was one of the few men associated with the pre-war Parti Démocrate Populaire who did not go on to join the MRP.[96] If the Third Republic/Vichy lobby supported any political party in the mid-1940s it was the old Third Republic parties that were eventually grouped in the RGR. Men whose formative political experiences had taken place before 1940 certainly felt no sympathy for 'the party of the Fourth Republic' whose leaders proclaimed 'we Christian Democrats have a personal revenge to take on the old parties of the Third Republic'.[97]

The second issue that was unlikely to endear the MRP to those who still thought of themselves as Pétainists was Gaullism. It has been suggested that its associations with de Gaulle helped the MRP to win over conservative voters. However, the open defenders of Vichy did not approve of de Gaulle during the 1940s: they denounced him as a usurper and the enemy of Pétain.[98] Furthermore, they believed that the Americans, who played a key role in Pétainist thinking because they had recognized Vichy until the end of 1942, would translate their well-known personal hostility to de Gaulle into political action and evict him from government.[99]

If MRP supporters were not Pétainists, what were they? Certainly they were not all Resistance activists. The answer probably lies in the fact that most Frenchmen never believed that there was a stark choice between Vichy and the Resistance. It was certainly true that most French people, and presumably most supporters of the MRP, had supported Pétain in 1940 and continued to feel some affection and respect for him even after the

[96] J. D. M. Dutroncy, *L'abbé Desgranges. Conférencier et député 1874–1958* (Paris, 1962), p. 194. It was rumoured that objections by some MRP leaders had kept Desgranges out of the *conseil de la république* in 1946. Desgranges preserved good relations with some MRP leaders – notably Robert Schuman, who had voted full powers to Pétain in 1940 – in spite of his hostility to the party.

[97] Michelet, *Le gaullisme*, p. 90.

[98] The literature of right-wing anti-Gaullism is immense. The most important expressions of anti-Gaullism during the late 1940s were probably Alfred Fabre-Luce's *Au nom des silencieux*, and Louis Rougier's *Mission secrète à Londres* (Bruges, 1948).

[99] On the links between atlanticism and anti-Gaullism see Rougier, *Mission secrète*, p. 209.

Liberation, but they did not approve of everything that the Vichy government had done. Attitudes to the Resistance were equally ambiguous. Most people approved of anti-German activity in principle while having reservations about the requisitions, assassinations and reprisals that Resistance activity was likely to bring in their own areas. Feelings were especially mixed in the MRP strongholds of Brittany and Haute Savoie which, because of their terrain, had played host to much of the Resistance movement.

Women, who made up such a large proportion of the MRP electorate, had particularly complicated feelings about the Vichy/Resistance divide. This was because the world of politics even under Vichy was still a largely male one. Pétain's councillors were as exclusively male as the parliamentarians of the Third Republic had been. Women were not much better represented among the Resistance elites: they often took great risks and many Resistance networks could not have functioned without their support, but the Conseil National de la Résistance was exclusively male and most heads of *réseaux* were men. Many women must have regarded the whole civil war between Vichy and the Resistance as an exceptionally dangerous form of boys' game. After the war the rhetoric of most political parties, other than the MRP, can only have served to increase women's sense of exclusion. The right often seemed to be agitating for a restoration of the Third Republic constitution (hardly an issue that can have filled women with enthusiasm) while the Resistance parties took a boy-scoutish pleasure in stressing their military origins (many candidates gave their Resistance code names in their electoral manifestos).

The MRP was attractive to people who had been neither Resistance activists nor committed Pétainists. Such people may have seen voting for a party with such ostentatious Resistance credentials as a means of disguising the ambiguity of their previous stance, if only from themselves. On the other hand the 'Resistance' with which the MRP was identified was the distant Resistance leadership of the London based Free French or the Paris based Conseil National de la Résistance. MRP leaders had generally 'resisted' by making radio broadcasts (Maurice Schumann),[100] chairing committees (Bidault) or drawing up constitutional documents (Teitgen). It was possible to combine support for the MRP with dislike for the ill-disciplined teenage *réfractaires* from *service du travail obligatoire* who had made up the active Resistance fighters in most areas. The MRP leadership laid great emphasis on the need to bring Resistance activists under proper regulation: one of their slogans was 'revolution *dans la loi*' and the party's constitutive meeting passed a motion advocating the integration of the FFI

---

[100] Astoux reports meeting a man who joined the MRP 'because they had Schuman and Schuman was London'. A. Astoux, *L'oubli de Gaulle 1946–1958* (Paris, 1974), p. 104.

into the regular army. In short, MRP supporters were distinguished from explicit Pétainists by the definition that they gave to the word 'legality'. The latter group used this word to mean constitutional legality (i.e. the repeal of ineligibility laws); the former simply meant the restoration of order (i.e. an end to requisitions and summary executions).

The decline of the MRP

The theory that the MRP was seen, in many respects, as a conservative party, explains how it overcame right-wing rivals, but it also raises an important new question: if the MRP was such a satisfactory party for conservatives why did they stop voting for it and transfer their support to first the RPF and then the CNIP? It was the foundation of the RPF in April 1947 that first tempted conservative voters away from the MRP. Some believed that this was unfortunate and that competition between the two parties was unnecessary; the MRP had made much of its allegiance to de Gaulle, and the General clearly hoped that the MRP would come to terms with his movement. However, the MRP leadership soon denounced the RPF.[101] Furthermore, the leaders of the MRP evoked article 7 of their rules that forbad members from belonging to any other party. This move effectively forced certain Gaullists in the MRP to leave the party.

Why did the MRP, which had made so much of its allegiance to de Gaulle, and which shared some of the concerns of the RPF, take such a firm stance against the new party? Why did the leaders of the MRP not rally to de Gaulle or why, at least, did they not discreetly tolerate *double apparte-nance* as the Radicals did? Two answers have been suggested to this question. The MRP senator, Barthélemy Ott believed that the key reason for the split was to be found in the personal quarrel between de Gaulle and Georges Bidault.[102] Henri Descamps suggested on the contrary that: 'the gulf opened between de Gaulle and the MRP. Not between him and the great leaders like R. Schuman and G. Bidault. But between him and the bloc of deputies and militants.'[103] Descamps argued that it was the desire of MRP deputies such as Simonnet to maintain their own positions in parliament that accounted for the MRP's hostile reaction to de Gaulle.

The first of these interpretations deserves to be viewed with scepticism. Ott and Bidault were to become fanatically anti-Gaullist during the Algerian war, but many contemporary observers did not see the split between Bidault and de Gaulle as final in the late 1940s.[104] Descamps'

[101] Bidault sent a telegram to Teitgen on 25 April 1947 in the following terms: 'In spite of the absence of a clear reply on the exact nature of his enterprise, I see no other interpretation of his conception other than the creation of a new party.' AN, 457 AP 167.
[102] Ott, *Vie et mort du MRP*, p. 37.   [103] Descamps, *La démocratie chrétienne*, p. 141.
[104] For the negotations between Bidault and de Gaulle see Charlot, *Le gaullisme d'opposition*.

interpretation is more plausible, though perhaps it should be added that what really distinguished MRP deputies from those of other parties was not a cynical desire to keep their own positions, but a naive belief that opposing the RPF would be an effective way to do this.

However, it would be wrong to suggest the MRP's actions can be explained entirely in terms of self-interest. Some MRP leaders simply disapproved of what they saw as a 'Boulangist' emphasis on personal leadership and executive power.[105] The fact that catholicism in France had often been associated with opposition to the Republic seems to have made the MRP leaders all the more keen to prove their republicanism.[106] Furthermore, and perhaps even more importantly, the RPF was seen to threaten the constitution of the MRP as well as the constitution of France. MRP leaders were characterized by a scrupulous concern for their own rules, for party discipline, and for loyalty.[107] The whole basis of the MRP's self-image lay in the belief that it was not just another one of the interchangeable bourgeois parties. Under these circumstances, it was inconceivable that the MRP would tolerate the deliberate ambiguity and blurring of distinctions that allowed other parties to maintain relations with the RPF. The fact that some of those who flocked to join the RPF during the first few years of its existence came from the Radical party, which personified the unprincipled opportunism that Christian Democrats depised, only served to confirm the belief of the MRP leadership that they were right to shun the RPF.[108]

Once it became clear that most of the leadership and membership of the MRP would not pass over to the RPF, then it was inevitable that a large part of the electorate of the MRP would do so. The RPF in 1947 had many of the strengths that the MRP had possessed in 1946: it was opposed to the unrestricted operation of capitalism, it supported subsidy for church schools and it combined Resistance prestige with a functional tolerance of former Pétainists. The RPF had the support of de Gaulle which the MRP

---

[105] Ott attributed the hostility that MRP leaders felt towards the RPF in terms of their 'tripe républicaine'. Ott, *Vie et mort du MRP*, p. 48

[106] This point was made by both Léon Blum and by the gaullist Olivier Guichard. O. Guichard, *Mon général* (Paris, 1980), p. 199.

[107] The importance that MRP members attached to party loyalty was illustrated when Bidault formed a semi-independent party, Démocratie Chrétienne, during the late 1950s. Although many party members supported the intentions of Bidault's new group and had great personal respect for Bidault, they found his defiance of party discipline very hard to accept. See for example the letter dated 27 November 1958 to Bidault from his loyal *co-listier* Barthélemy Ott in AN, 457 AP 167.

[108] For the belief of the MRP leadership that the RPF was composed of unprincipled Radicals see AN, 457 AP 175, 'Rapport sur les élections générales', dated 21 June 1951. This report speaks of the *maçonniques* tendencies of the RPF. See also 457 AP 166, Bidault reported to an international meeting of Christian Democrats on 22 December 1948 that the RPF was 'a bonapartist movement supported by Radicals'.

had been seen to enjoy in 1946. Most of all the RPF benefited from being untainted by the recent past. The MRP was compromised by the fact that the party's ministers had served in government with Communists and presided over the trial and imprisonment of Pétainists.[109] People who had voted MRP in 1946 in order to turn their back on the Third Republic and the Occupation, voted RPF in 1947 in order to turn their back on the *épuration* and *tripartisme*.

MRP leaders bitterly resented the fact that they suffered from their association with the *épuration* and *tripartisme*. They pointed out that their presence in government alongside the Communists had been necessary to contain Communist power: 'The MRP has been reproached for its participation in tripartism with the Communists. What would have happened if the MRP had not been there? The Communists and Socialists, for the only time in French history, then had a majority in the assembly ... Would we not have seen the brutal establishment of the first popular republic in western Europe?'[110] It has been suggested above that at least some conservatives had recognized that the MRP's participation in government as a restraining influence during the tripartite period was necessary. However, the MRP rarely won credit for the restraints that it had imposed on Communist power. Jean Mazé argued that the MRP's participation in government had played a key role in the construction of what he called the *système*, and he dismissed the suggestion that the MRP had worked privately to prevent something worse from happening: 'history takes account of facts not intentions'.

Even those who had recognized the value of the MRP's participation in government were not always grateful to the MRP after the event. General Billotte had privately advised Schuman that the MRP should remain in government to control Communism after the departure of de Gaulle in January 1946,[111] but by 1947 he himself had become a leader of the RPF which savagely denounced tripartism. Conservatives did not care to be reminded of the recent past when they had been so vulnerable that they required MRP protection. The MRP's ceaseless claims about the valuable role that it had played between the Liberation and May 1947 began to annoy right-wingers.[112]

The question why the MRP, unlike the Radical party, failed to rebuild its electoral fortunes once the RPF declined is harder to answer. The CNIP

---

[109] The MRP leadership were aware that the question of prisoners in Fresnes (i.e. Pétainists) was being used against Bidault and Teitgen. See account of meeting of executive commission of MRP on 27 February 1947 in AN 457 AP 167.

[110] Bichet, *La démocratie chrétienne*, p. 384.

[111] Jean Planchais, *Une histoire politique de l'armée*. II: *1940–1967, de de Gaulle à de Gaulle* (Paris, 1967), p. 135.   [112] Mazé, *Le système*.

was a less obvious successor to the MRP than the RPF had been; indeed, the CNIP included many of the Third Republic politicians that the MRP had defeated in 1946. In part, it was again the high principles of the MRP that stood in the way of reconstruction. The fact that members of the MRP put such a high value on loyalty made it difficult for them to welcome those who had defected to the RPF back into the fold.[113] Many would explain the success of the CNIP in the 1951 elections and thereafter as part of a general rightward movement of European politics that occurred thoughout Europe as a result of the fading of the youthful idealism of the post-war electorates and the influence of the Cold War. But this general explanation fails to allow for the possibility that a conservative revival might have been contained within the MRP.

The possiblity that the French right might have been rallied behind the Christian Democrats can be illustrated by an examination of the international context. All the other major continental west European democracies (Belgium, Holland, West Germany, Austria and Italy) had Christian Democrat parties. Two things distinguished these parties from the MRP. Firstly, they were more successful. In Belgium and Germany the Christian Democrats were strong enough to form single party governments during the 1950s; in Austria they won an absolute majority in the elections of 1947 and ruled in a 'red/black' coalition with the Socialists until 1965, in Italy the Christian Democrats were the dominant political force from 1947 until almost the present day. Secondly, the Christian Democrat parties of Italy, Austria, West Germany, Holland and Belgium were all much more closely associated with the conservative electorate than was the post-1951 MRP.[114] This characteristic was particularly marked in Italy. One French student of Italy pointed out: 'The clientele of the DC is the same as that of the MRP and French conservatives added together'.[115] An MRP internal report admitted that the German CDU was closer to Antoine Pinay's independent grouping than to the MRP.[116]

---

[113] Edmond Michelet made the following entry in his diary on 24 October 1947: 'A stormy session of the political committee of the MRP. Friendship plays such an important role among us that separations . . . will not be without conflict.' Michelet, *Mon père Edmond Michelet*, p. 181.

[114] The most general overall survey of Christian democracy in western Europe is Michael P. Fogarty, *Christian democracy in Western Europe 1820–1953* (London, 1957).

[115] Jean-Paul Chassériaud, *Le Parti Démocrate Chrétien en Italie* (Paris, 1965), p. 354. There has been strangely little effort to make systematic comparisions between the Italian and French Christian Democrats, although a Frenchman has written about the DC, an Italian about the MRP, and a Frenchman and an Italian wrote essays about Christian Democracy in their respective countries for a single volume. See Chassériaud, *Le Parti Démocrate Chrétien en Italie*; Maria Grovia Mariani, *Il Mouvement Républicain Populaire. Partito della IV Repubblica* (Rome, 1983); and François Goguel and Mario Einaudi, *Christian democracy in France and Italy* (Notre Dame, 1952).

[116] AN, 458 AP 167, undated, unsigned report.

MRP leaders had regular meetings with their colleagues in other European countries,[117] and they were aware of the possibility that a more conservative Christian Democrat grouping might be formed in France. Indeed, there were attempts to launch such a grouping. In 1948 a number of ex-MRP leaders who had joined the RPF (notably Louis Terrenoire and Edmond Michelet) formed an 'independent Christian' group;[118] in October 1953 the bureau of the parliamentary party of the MRP heard of an initiative by some elements in the CNIP and the ARS (the Gaullists who had broken away from the RPF to support Antoine Pinay) to create a *groupe catholique de droite*.[119]

The MRP leaders might have sought to create a party of christian conservatism themselves.[120] In 1958, Georges Bidault did form an explicitly right-wing group, Démocratie Chrétienne, with the participation of Tixier-Vignancour and the tacit support of other conservatives like Duchet and Morice.[121] Démocratie Chrétienne frightened sections of the MRP, particularly the working class and left-wing militants,[122] and it sometimes ran candidates against the MRP,[123] but the leaders of the MRP never expelled Bidault and they sometimes tried to make contact with other right-wing leaders via him.[124]

Bidault's initiative seems to have been welcomed by many leaders of Christian Democracy outside France,[125] and by some conservative catholics within France. However, it was widely recognized that the initiative had come too late. A deputy from the Rhône wrote: 'Many christians would certainly have remained loyal to a party that had had the courage not to hide its origin under a "social concern" that fooled no one, without really dissipating ambiguities.'[126]

The MRP's failure to become a party of clerical conservatism was partly a question of personalities. One MRP member who left to join the RPF wrote: 'The main cause of the terrible failure of the Mouvement Républicain Populaire lay in the personality and the ambitions of its main leaders,

---

[117] See the accounts of informal meetings of Christian Democrat leaders contained in AN, 457 AP 166.

[118] J. Charbonnel, *Edmond Michelet* (Paris, 1987), p. 78.

[119] AN, 350 AP 74, account of meeting of bureau of parliamentary MRP, 6 October 1953.

[120] Williams, *Politics in post-war France*, p. 87.

[121] AN, 350 AP 76, Bidault to Pointillart, dated 14 November 1958. For further information on the origins of Démocratie Chrétienne see Bidault's correspondence in AN, 457 AP 167.

[122] AN, 350 AP 76, unsigned note, dated 8 July 1958.

[123] AN, 350 AP 76, note dated 27 November 1958, from Barthélemy Ott, refering to Robert Lecourt's candidacy in the Hautes Alpes.

[124] AN, 350 AP 76, Pflimlin letter to Fontenau, dated 3 November 1958, asking him to ask Bidault to prevent Tixier-Vignancour from attacking the MRP.

[125] AN, 457 AP 167, undated and unsigned note.

[126] J. Villard, deputy for the Rhône to Bidault dated 8 August 1958 in AN, 457 AP 168.

but especially those of Georges Bidault. This small man – small in height, but also in character ... was spoiled by his rapid rise.'[127] Georges Bidault was the obvious leader of the right-wing faction of the MRP and he ultimately formed the break away Démocratie Chrétienne. But Bidault's manners and behaviour put off many who might have supported him: his low tolerance of drink, his untidiness,[128] his domineering wife,[129] and his taste for bizarre turns of phrase repelled many colleagues.

More importantly, Bidault was compromised by his campaign against Munich, his opposition to Franco and his role in the Resistance. The man who sought a right-wing future for the MRP was one of the few party leaders with a genuinely left-wing past. Even when Georges Bidault was an exiled anti-Gaullist in the aftermath of the Algerian war, conservatives found it hard to forgive his Resistance activities.[130]

There were also structural reasons that accounted for the differences between the MRP and its European sister parties. The Christian Democrats in Germany, Austria and Belgium all existed in simpler political systems than that of Fourth Republic France,[131] and all of them faced more limited competition on the right of the spectrum. By contrast the Christian Democrats in Italy did face competition from the right. Indeed, the competition for clerical conservative votes was more intense in Italy than in France. In France the right-wing parties of 1945 and 1946 were considered

---

[127] Noel, *La traversée du désert*, p. 27.

[128] Michelet claimed that when Bidault had been a teacher, a pupil had sarcastically offered to sew on one of his buttons. Ibid., p. 30. Attention to sartorial detail might sound a ludicrously trivial matter to discuss alongside serious political issues, but French right-wingers (whose formative experiences had been in strict Jesuit schools and smart regiments) took such matters seriously. Bidault's dress sense let him down again during the 1960s: General Massu justified his refusal to join the clandestine anti-Gaullist forces on the grounds that 'Bidault wore a coat with a fur lining'.

[129] Attacks on Suzanne Bidault are an almost standard part of the memoirs of Fourth Republic politicians. Roger Peyrefitte had particularly savage feelings; see his *roman à clef, Les ambassades* (Paris, 1951) and *Propos secrets* (Paris, 1977), p. 96. Suzanne Bidault was also a bar room brawler. In her own memoirs she recounts that even the notoriously truculent Jean Nocher was frightened enough of her to apologize during a brawl at a political meeting in the Loire; she adds that she was sorry not to have had a bottle to hand to break over Nocher's head. Suzanne Bidault, *Souvenirs* (Paris, 1987), p. 59.

[130] *Rivarol* welcomed Bidault into the right-wing fold with a somewhat sarcastic article entitled 'Travail, famille, patrie. Ce n'était pas mal non plus', *Rivarol*, 563 (25 January 1962). Pierre Fontaine supported Bidault while stressing that he had not forgotten Bidault's role in the purges of 1944. 'Sur une pétition en faveur de Georges Bidault', *le Soleil*, 8 (September 1966).

[131] Peter Mair, 'The electoral universe of small parties in post-war western Europe', in G. Pridham and F. Muller-Rommel (eds.), *Small parties in western Europe* (London, 1991), pp. 41–70. Mair classifies Germany and Austria as large party systems, he classifies Italy as an 'intermediate' party system and France and Belgium as small party systems. The classification of France and Belgium in the same category is rather deceptive since the Belgian political system became much fragmented during the 1950s and 1960s as a result of linguistic divisions.

too secular and too compromised by the Third Republic to attract many voters. This made the MRP all the more vulnerable when it was faced by the more clerical conservatism of the RPF and the CNIP. The Italian DC, on the other hand, faced competition from a wide variety of right-wing parties from the very beginning. In 1945 it had to meet the challenge posed by both the neo-fascist MSI and the 'small man's party', L'Uomo Qualunque, as well as the conventional right. In doing so, the DC made specific efforts to win a conservative electorate early on. Italian Christian Democrats even had to face the threat of the conservative leader of Catholic Action, Luigi Gedda, that he would put forward candidates in the 1948 election if the DC did not proclaim its anti-Communism with sufficient vigour.[132]

Another peculiarity of the MRP was that there had been no major Christian Democrat party in France before 1945, whereas the Belgian Catholic party, the German Centre party and the Italian Popular party had all been major political forces which held ministerial offices and ran national organizations by the 1920s. The advantage that non-French Christian Democratic parties derived from having been established for a long time lay partly in having built up an electoral base; it is significant that the electorate of the MRP was much younger than that of any comparable party.

However, Christian Democrat parties did more than simply reconstruct their pre-war electoral base. In Germany, a genuinely inter-confessional party was constructed for the first time after 1945 and in Italy the DC acquired support in the south to an extent that no previous Christian Democrat party had managed. The key to post-war Christian Democrat success was not so much the fact that they had an established electorate as the fact that they had an established leadership. The fact that the Christian Democrats had been weaker before the Second World War than after it meant that the movements' leaders in most countries had acquired the vital experience of compromise and negotiation that came from being important enough to matter without being strong enough to form a single party government.

The German Centre party, the very name of which suggests its hinge position, exemplified this pragmatism: indeed in many respects the Centre party was the German equivalent of the French Radical party. In France Christian Democracy had the misfortune to proceed directly from being an insignificant group to being the largest party in the national assembly, and party leaders recognized, in retrospect, that 'this inexperience, this political naivety was a serious handicap for the MRP'.[133] It also emerged at a time when left-wing rhetoric was fashionable, and though, as has been suggested

---

[132] Paul Ginsborg, *A history of contemporary Italy: society and politics 1943–1988* (London, 1990), p. 99.   [133] Ott, *Vie et mort du MRP*, p. 31.

above, this climate did not affect the policies that the MRP sought to enact, it certainly did affect the image that the party acquired.

The specific characteristics of French Christian Democracy can be highlighted by looking at the exception that proves the rule: Alsace. Alsace was an MRP stronghold, but the context in which the party operated was quite different from that in which it operated in the rest of France. Christian Democracy in Alsace had much older roots than it did in the rest of France, roots that had been planted by the German Centre party before 1914 and cultivated by the Union Populaire Républicaine between the wars.[134] A local prefect explained matters thus: 'It was the MRP that held power, but an MRP very influenced by old echoes ... L'UPR gave the new party a particular imprint.'[135] MRP leaders in Alsace were much less likely to sacrifice electoral advantage to high principle than their counterparts. The party arranged, for example, for an awkward political trial to be moved from Colmar so that a prefect, who was also an MRP candidate in the forthcoming elections, would not have to preside over it.[136] The MRP in Alsace may also have been helped to maintain its support among conservatives by the pre-war activities of some of its militants: Alsatians had not forgotten that the local MRP deputy, Pierre Pflimlin, had been a leading light of the Jeunesses Patriotes.[137]

The fact that the MRP was a newer creation than its European counterparts manifested itself in several ways. Christian Democracy in most European countries had grown up over a long period and had become intertwined with a whole variety of other institutions such as charitable associations, social clubs and professional organizations. Christian Democracy was part of a 'sub-culture' as well as being the incarnation of a particular ideology.[138] The result of this was that Christian Democracy became associated with the distribution of favours and patronage and with the creation of a network of clients; some commentators have gone so far as

[134] On local politics in interwar Alsace see P. C. F. Bankwitz, *Alsatian autonomist leaders 1919–1947* (Kansas, 1978); Francis Arzalier, *Les perdants. La dérive fasciste des mouvements autonomistes et indépendantistes au XXème siècle* (Paris, 1990); Samuel H. Goodfellow, *Fascism in Alsace, 1918–1945* (PhD, Indiana University, 1992); C. Baechler, *Le Parti Catholique Alsacien 1890–1939* (Paris, 1983), F.-G. Dreyfus, *La vie politique en Alsace 1919–1936* (Paris, 1969).

[135] René Paira, *Affaires d'Alsace* (Paris, 1990), p. 201.

[136] Ibid., p. 187. Teitgen, the MRP minister of justice, was persuaded to move the trial of Roussé in order to help Fonlupt, who was Teitgen's father-in-law as well as being an MRP candidate. It is interesting to note that Teitgen's behaviour in Alsace was much more worldly than his behaviour in his own Gironde constituency (see below). The Gironde was, of course, an area where there was no tradition of Christian Democracy and consequently no fund of political savvy on which Teitgen could draw.

[137] Dreyfus, *La vie politique en Alsace*, p. 239.

[138] See D. Blackbourn, *Class, religion and local politics in Willhelmine Germany* (New Haven and London, 1980).

to suggest that clientelist politics are particularly associated with catholicism.[139]

The construction of clientelist networks can be seen most clearly in post-war Italy, where Christian Democratic politics has become almost a byword for the manipulation of clientelist networks. Initially, the Italian DC drew most of its support from the northern Italian working class. The south of Italy was dominated by the Liberal party and various groupings of the extreme right. However, the DC succeeded in winning over the notables on whom these parties were based and established itself as the dominant force in the area.

The MRP conspicuously failed to emulate the success of the DC in building a notable base. Even when the MRP was attracting large numbers of votes from conservative areas, it failed to win over many of these power brokers. Out of 106 conservative notables contacted by Louis Marin's FR in 1946, only one supported the MRP.[140] The role of notable support, or its absence, in the fortunes of the MRP was reflected in the departmental *conseils généraux*. The MRP never succeeded in these local bodies to the same extent that it did at national level. The party secretary later wrote: 'cantonal elections favoured groups with an important network of notables. This was still not the case for the MRP.'[141] The MRP came fourth in the 1946 cantonal elections (behind the Communists, Socialists and Radicals).

In particular the MRP failed to capture the *conseils généraux* in the right's traditional homeland of western France. Right-wingers were able to use such local bodies as springboards to reclaim the area from the MRP in the national elections of 1951.[142] In some areas the MRP won parliamentary seats in 1946 without being able to muster the much smaller number of votes necessary to win departmental representation: this was the case in Calvados, the Hérault, the Pas-de-Calais and the Vosges. In Maine et Loire the MRP won half the seats at stake in parliamentary elections but only 12 per cent of places in the *conseil général*; in Moselle the MRP took four out of seven parliamentary seats but only 19 per cent of the places on the *conseil général* and in victory in Morbihan it took five out seven parliamentary seats but only 18 per cent of the places on the *conseil général*. In all these

---

[139] J. Chubb, *Patronage and poverty in southern Italy: a tale of two cities* (Cambridge, 1982), p. 8.

[140] Undated report in AN, 317 AP 73; see also the memoirs of Robert Buron in which he reveals that 'Our friends were not sufficiently strong to intervene in complicated local situations'. Buron, *La Mayenne et moi*, p. 50.

[141] Bichet, *La démocratie chrétienne*, p. 62.

[142] Marie-Hélène Marchand, *Les conseillers généraux en France depuis 1945* (Paris, 1970), p. 81.

areas the MRP suffered serious reverses in 1951. Correspondingly, in those, rare, areas where the MRP did penetrate the *conseils généraux* successfully (such as Haute Savoie or the Aveyron) it actually increased its representation in 1951.[143]

As has been suggested, this absence had little effect in 1945 and 1946 when traditional links between politicians and the electorate had been broken by the war and by the arrival of a new voters. However, by 1951 traditional networks were re-established and frameworks of local interest brokering that excluded the MRP had been rebuilt. It became clear that many MRP deputies lacked local foundations of support: Noel Barrot, for example, lost his place as mayor of Yssingeaux to a coalition of Radicals and Independents in 1947.[144] By 1951 the MRP was so badly excluded from networks of local power that it was unable to obtain jobs for its own defeated MPs.[145]

The absence of notable support was partly explicable in terms of the MRP's image as 'the party of the Fourth Republic'; over 25 per cent of *conseillers généraux* had been first elected before 1940 and many of them owed their power to institutions or traditions established before 1940; it is not surprising that such men should have been hostile to a party that condemned France's recent past with such vigour. However, this explanation is not entirely sufficient. The power of notables was not absolute or immutable and national politicians were not merely the passive objects of such power; central government authority could be used to change local power structures and determined national politicians could create their own notables.

In theory the MRP was well placed to build its own structures of local influence. The party believed in emphasizing the role of intermediate institutions.[146] It professed a desire to strengthen local bodies and sought to develop close relations with professional organizations. But the MRP's relations with notables were full of missed opportunities. The catholic leader of the Association des Classes Moyennes, Roger Millot, could have been exploited and greater efforts might have been made to prevent the peasant leader Abel Bessac from leaving the MRP. Both Bessac and Millot

[143] Ibid., p. 105.
[144] J.-A. Rivet, 'Les maires d'Yssingeaux: 1814–1983. Une histoire de familles', in M. Agulhon, L. Giraud, J. L. Robert and W. Serman (eds.), *Les maires en France du consulat à nos jours* (Paris, 1985)
[145] Béthouart, *Le MRP dans le Nord–Pas-de-Calais*, p. 75. The party was unable to obtain employment for Robert Prigent after his defeat as deputy for the Nord.
[146] Some MRP leaders seem to have become more wary of local institutions after their experience in the Fourth Republic. In 1977, Robert Bichet wrote a book entitled *La décentralisation, commune, région, département? Faut-il supprimer le conseil général?* (Paris, 1977).

ended up fighting the 1951 election on the lists of a small conservative party sponsored by big business.[147]

Why did the MRP leaders not cultivate notables and build up local networks of influence more effectively? The answer to this question lies in the style of the party rather than its policies. The MRP leaders were not separated from their conservative rivals by what they believed governments should do, but their ideas about how political parties should be run were very different. They had an almost monastic disdain for the wheeling and dealing of French politics.[148] The internal rules of the MRP forbad members of parliament from making special approaches to ministers or civil servants on behalf of their constituents[149] (a rule which, if observed, would have rendered most French deputies very idle indeed). Jacques Lagroye's study of politics in Bordeaux describes the failure of the local MRP deputy Teitgen to enter into the backscratching of notable based politics:

M. Teitgen is a generous man of principle . . . an outsider, foreign to local problems and ignorant of the Bordeaux scene. 'He was unable to put down roots in Bordeaux', said one of his former associates, 'he did not know the municipal councillors, or the notables, he talked about the vocation of the army to trade unionists from the defence industry who had come to discuss their salaries'.[150]

Not surprisingly, the MRP failed to maintain its support in Bordeaux and, by the 1960s, the party had only a few militants, and, significantly, most of these were newcomers to the area.

The informal contacts on which conservative politics were founded required an easy-going smoothness: electoral deals were fixed up over a drink and every major political development was marked with a banquet. The MRP did not fit into this world. Its members placed great emphasis on asceticism. MRP heroes, like Robert Schuman and Franisque Gay, were presented as men of almost saintly denial (Schuman publicly claimed to be a virgin at the age of 62), while Bidault's party never forgave him his partiality to the occasional glass of white wine. Disapproval of drink was an especially serious handicap for any political party:[151] much political

---

[147] On Bessac's departure from the MRP see AN, 457 AP 175, report of MRP meeting in Durand to Bidault, dated 3 July 1951. Piere Boudent remarked that Bessac's departure had effected 'A sort of purge – the conservatives having voted for Bessac.'

[148] AN, 350 AP 56, Poimbeuf, addressing the meeting of the *conseil national* on 25 and 26 August 1946, said electoral deals, which reduced the electorate to 'merchandise or cattle', should be avoided.   [149] Bichet, *La démocratie chrétienne*, p. 79.

[150] Lagroye, *Société et politique*.

[151] On the MRP's campaign against the abuse of alcohol see the undated electoral circular (relating to the 1951 election) in AN, 350 AP 93. The same circular noted that the leader of the campaign against stricter regulation in this matter was one of the MRP's right-wing opponents: Robert Betolaud.

business was conducted in bars and restaurants, and the willingness to be seen drinking was a vital symbol of communal solidarity. Furthermore, important economic interests were at stake in the wine trade and *vignerons'* assocations often played a key role in local politics.[152] MRP activists often seemed priggish and awkward. They were associated with embarrassing and intrusive customs such as the *revision de vie* (a public confession that was encouraged by Action Catholique).[153] Etienne Borne wrote about the shortcomings of the average MRP member in these terms: 'If young, he is too nice, even if he is in his forties, and has all the sickly traits of a prolonged adolescence, well protected by private schooling and "scouting."'[154]

The way in which MRP's moralistic tone affected its relations with notables is best exemplified by the way in which party leaders treated their *co-listiers.* The men who stood on the same list as nationally prominent politicians were often locally influential figures: this combination allowed the national politician to benefit from local contacts while allowing the notables with whom he was associated to improve their standing and ultimately increase their influence. Radical leaders, like Edgar Faure, were proud of the fact that their *co-listiers* obtained ample rewards for their support,[155] but the MRP regarded such attractions as dishonest. Barthélemy Ott was second on the electoral list of Georges Bidault at a time when Bidault was one of the most prominent politicians in France. Yet Ott derived no advantage from his association. He recalled, in the sanctimonious tones typical of the MRP, that his relations with Bidault 'earned me neither a ministry ... nor honours, nor stipends, nor decorations, nor

---

[152] Marion Démosier reports that the Christian Democrat mayor of Beaune failed, unlike most local politicians, to build up informal power in the local *vignerons'* association. She quotes a local's comment on the mayor: 'he did not have the style of a notable'. Marion Démosier, *Rapport de recherche pour le musée du vin de Bourgogne à Beaune.* 'Les saints protecteurs de la vigne en Côte d'Or. Analyse anthropologique d'un culte. Nouvelles formes, nouvelles fonctions', 1991, no pagination.

[153] Bosworth, *Catholicism and crisis*, p. 101.

[154] Etienne Borne, 'Emmanuel Mounier. Juge de la démocratie chrétienne', *Terre Humaine*, February 1951, 66–67, cited in Goguel and Einaudi, *Christian Democracy in France and Italy*, p. 81. The reference to 'boyishness' is interesting. Christian organizations in France do seem to have been based largely on the young: the average age of members of the *jeunesse ouvrière chrétienne* was only 18 and the MRP admitted people from the age of 18 (i.e. two years before they could vote in national elections). Military service, which generally occurred at the age of 21, was seen as a rite of passage into adulthood and it also exposed young men to customs and values that permanently alienated them from Christian organizations. On the damage done to *jeunesse ouvrière chrétienne* by the extension of military service during the Algerian war see Bosworth, *Catholicism and crisis*, p. 117.

[155] Faure boasted that his *co-listier* (Thouvery) had subsequently become a mayor and senator, and regretted that Thouvery had never become a minister. Faure, *Avour toujours raison*, p. 177.

distinction of any sort'.[156] When Ott was defeated in a senatorial election he simply returned to life as a teacher of German in a provincial *lycée*.[157]

However, inability to handle relations with notables was not the only explanation for the failure of the MRP to build effective networks of patronage. In most European countries, as time went on, the clientelist politics of Christian Democrat parties changed in nature. Distribution of private largesse by individuals gave way to distribution of state largesse by party organizations. The process could be seen in Belgium as early as 1890. It was said that Christian Democrat ministers in Belgium were 'the instruments . . . of catholic clubs. Carefully, methodically, the cabinet used its formidable and mysterious "fourth power", that of the administration, to people the public service with its creatures.'[157] Similar pressures could be seen in the career of Konrad Adenauer, often regarded as the incarnation of political rectitude. Adenauer began his career as a notoriously high-spending mayor of Cologne, and one whose first act was to put his own brother-in-law on the payroll.[158]

Once again it was the Italian DC that deployed patronage most effectively. During the 1950s the DC freed itself from dependence on powerful individuals and drew its power increasingly from the exploitation of semi-autonomous state agencies which could provide jobs and lucrative contracts for DC supporters. The results of this process could be seen in Calabria and Sicily. In Palermo Salvo Lima, a young leader of the DC, used the position of assessor of public works, which he acquired in 1956, to build up a power base that allowed him to become mayor of the city only two years later.[159] In the southern town of Catania, the hospital Vittorio Emanuele was used not only as a means of providing jobs, or the hope of jobs, for DC supporters, but also as a convenient residence for voters who needed to be shipped into a key constituency at election time.[160]

Post-war France provided propitious circumstances for the creation of a state-based system of clientelism. State spending was increasing and the weakening of traditional notables, through the ineligibility laws, might have provided a new mass party with an opportunity to establish new patronage networks. Why did the MRP fail to exploit such opportunities? The answer to this question lies in attitudes to office holding at central government level. The key to the construction of local patronage networks was access to the largesse that was provided by central government funds. Central government funding was particuarly important in comparatively underdeveloped areas such as the Italian *mezzogiorno* or the south-west of

---

[156] Barthélemy Ott, *Georges Bidault. L'indomptable* (Annonay, 1975), p. 67.
[157] Van Kalken, *La Belgique contemporaine*, p. 154, cited in Fogarty, *Christian Democracy in western Europe*, p. 315.
[158] Harold James, *The German slump: politics and economics 1924–1936* (Oxford, 1987), pp. 21, 88 and 92.   [159] Chubb, *Patronage and poverty*, p. 61.
[160] Ginsborg, *A history of contemporary Italy*, p. 179.

France. It was in order to get access to such funding that the Italian Christian Democrats attached such importance to office holding, and particularly to the control of certain key ministries.

Like the DC, the MRP attached great importance to participation in ministries. But their attitude to such participation was quite different from that of the DC. For French Christian Democrats office holding was a painful duty which brought electoral disadvantages rather than opportunity to gain votes: 'there is no doubt that in the present grave circumstances we would have derived greater advantage from being in opposition'.[161] Parts of the conservative electorate had been willing to tolerate their deputies' involvement in government during the first few years after the Liberation, when the threats of the *épuration* had to be headed off, but after this they preferred parties that took a more intransigent attitude (such as the RPF). In the eyes of many erstwhile MRP supporters, an enthusiasm for office was characteristic of old parties of the Third Republic. Léon Noel argued that the MRP had 'constantly sacrificed its mystique to a mediocre conception of politics and entered into the habits of the old hacks of ... parliamentarianism'.[162]

The MRP rarely obtained the kind of benefits that the Italian DC, or other French parties, derived from office holding In part this was a general problem of all large parties because small parliamentary groupings had a leverage disproportionate to their size when it came to bargaining with would-be prime ministers trying to form a coalition. Even more important than the number of MRP ministers were the kind of posts that they obtained. Italian Christian Democrats attached great importance to those ministries that carried large powers of patronage: the post office, which was almost continuously held by Christian Democrats, was especially important in this context.[163] However, in France it was the Radical party that monopolized such ministries. The area in which the MRP exercised greatest power – foreign affairs – was that which counted for least in building up a domestic power base. Most strikingly of all, no MRP member ever held the ministry of the interior and consequently the MRP had little access to the important electoral machine of the French state: in 1951 not a single prefect or sub-prefect in France was a member of the MRP.[164]

---

[161] AN, 350 AP 76, Francisque Gay to Félix Gouin, 28 February 1946.

[162] Noel, *La traversée du désert*, p. 26.

[163] J. Walston, *The Mafia and clientelism: roads to Rome in post-war Calabria* (London, 1988), p. 77.

[164] Williams, *Politics in post-war France*, p. 385. Francisque Gay recognized that the MRP had failed to exploit the possibility of building up a clientele of grateful state employees: 'Among many other failings, we often had to let the important administrative offices – prefectures, colonial services, the diplomatic service, finances, public works and justice, be re established without being able to propose, if not impose, appropriate candidates of our own.' Francisque Gay, *Les démocrates d'inspiration chrétienne*, p. 12.

Conclusion

This chapter has sought to revise the conventional picture of the MRP as a 'progressive party' with conservative supporters. It has been stressed that the Fourth Republic did not revolve around any single left/right political spectrum, but was rather a kaleidoscope in which there were several different rights and lefts, and in which certain ideas might be defined as either right or left depending on the context. The MRP's supporters were generally conservative, but they espoused a particular *kind* of conservatism: a kind that was often anti-capitalist and violently hostile to anything that resembled the Third Republic. In the peculiar circumstances of 1945 and 1946 this 'old conservatism' could no longer be represented by established conservative politicians. This was not because conventional conservative politicians did not contest elections, but rather because such people were seen as too secular and too compromised by the legacy of the Third Republic. The MRP succeeded in this climate because only new men were perceived as fit to represent old ideas.

Previous historians have often seemed to suggest that the MRP had a historic mission to represent non-marxist progressivism in France, and that the party was seduced away from the fulfilment of this mission by an unnatural alliance with a conservative electorate. This chapter has argued that the relations between conservative voters and the MRP leadership were underwritten by a wide range of genuine agreement. What led this alliance to collapse at the 1951 election was disagreement over how a political party should be run rather than disagreement over how France should be run. The MRP failed in electoral terms because of its refusal to build up a basis of notable support or to leave office rather than implement unpopular policies. However, the aim of this chapter is not to suggest that the reasons for the MRP's eventual decline were trivial or that the party might have easily prevented that decline. The MRP's refusal to play a certain kind of political game was as much a part of the party's nature as its views on the economy or European integration. In this context it might be argued that the eventual split between MRP voters and leaders was inevitable from the beginning in spite of, or perhaps because of, their agreement about so many issues. Nothing characterized conservative politicians more than a contempt for the electorate and nothing characterized conservative voters more than a contempt for politicians.

11   The Rassemblement des Gauches
        Républicaines

Allow me to remind you of some analogies with a situation that you know well. After the elections of October 1945, following the terrible defeat of the Radical party, it seemed necessary to create a great movement capable of succeeding the Radical party ... It was a question of changing name, it was a question of seeming strong. It was then that a number of small parties grouped together, some of these parties only existed on paper, others were invented for the occasion. The aim of the operation was two fold: firstly to influence the Radical party, and then to increase its importance in the eyes of the public. In spite of some problems, these two aims were achieved. The Radical party entered the Rassemblement des Gauches and the RGR obtained a very clear electoral success.[1]

The above quotation occurs in a letter from Jean-Louis Anteriou, a young official of the Radical party to Emile Bollaert, high commissioner in Indo-China and an important figure in the same party. It reflects many beliefs about the Rassemblement des Gauches Républicaines (RGR), a loose grouping of half a dozen parties that was formed in November 1946. In particular Anteriou's remarks suggest that the RGR was just a cynical electoral ploy by the Radical party. Anteriou was not the only Radical to hold such jaundiced views: an internal party circular dismissed the new formation thus: 'we accepted the word *Rassemblement* because it seems to be fashionable'.[2] If this was the attitude taken by men within the Radical party who had played a part in bringing the RGR into existence then the attitude of outside commentators, who regarded the Radical party itself with some disdain, was even more dismissive. The RGR's resistance to collectivist economics, and its loose organization seemed to belong to an earlier age. Furthermore, all but one of the constituent parties in the RGR dated back to the Third Republic and most of these parties were seen to have been compromised by the defeat and the Vichy regime.

[1] Paris, Archives Nationales (AN) 373 AP 7, Anteriou to Bollaert, 23 May 1947. Anteriou's interpretation was supported by an article in a conservative newspaper published in 1949 which described the RGR as 'an assembly of little parties around a leading party, the Radical Party, that is trying to acquire a new skin'. Bos, 'Notre enquête sur le regroupement des Indépendants', in *l'Indépendant Français*, 8 October 1949.
[2] Article in *Action* in AN, 465 AP 7.

However, the RGR was the most characteristic political formation of the Fourth Republic. Like the PRL, the RGR was right about the policies that were to be enacted between 1946 and 1958 – the return to economic liberalism, amnesty for Pétainists, the exclusion of the Communist party from government. But unlike every other party, the RGR was also right about the mechanisms by which those policies were to be enacted. The loose structure of the RGR anticipated the groupings that were to be most successful in the 1951 election. Most important was the RGR's role in government. The RGR provided more prime ministers than any other formation and its members held office in all but one of the Fourth Republic cabinets. This chapter will argue that the RGR leaders need to be understood in terms of the internal dynamics of their group rather than dismissed as remnants of the Third Republic.

The origins of the RGR can be traced to the aftermath of the elections of October 1945. Bourgeois parties of the Third Republic had done badly in these elections and certain members of such parties, mainly Radicals, began to meet to discuss the possibility of alliances that might improve their fortunes. A variety of bodies sprang up in 1946 notably the Ligue de la République (made up of members of the Radical party), Jeune Republique and the Union Démocratique et Socialiste de la Résistance (UDSR). In March 1946, Jean Paul David (a young Radical) formed a *comité d'initiative en vue d'un rassemblement républicain* which encompassed members of several parties.[3] On 28 March 1946, a meeting was held between the Rassemblement Républicain and the Ligue de la République which drew up a *comité directeur* of a new joint body and asked for support from the Radical party.[4] These initiatives led to a formal alliance that was known first as the Front de la République and then as the Rassemblement des Gauches Républicaines. The RGR contained six political parties in all. Two of these, the Radical party and the UDSR, were major groupings with representatives in parliament. The other four groups, the Parti Républicain Socialiste (RS), the Parti Socialiste Démocratique (PSD) and Parti Répub-

---

[3] AN, 465 AP 7. On 8 March 1946, David wrote to Herriot telling him of a *comité d'initiative* comprising six Radicals (Varenne, Bastid, Astier, Giaccobi, Verger and Anxionnaz), four members of the UDSR (Malbrunt, Soustelle, Kreiger and Saulnier), one Independent Radical (Guadet), one member of the *parti démocrate* (Alphone), one Independent (Billotte) and ten representatives of professional associations (Arthuys, Boisdé, Chaussonière, Cousteix, Ducrox, Fournier, Lafay, Marius, Mayolle, Meunier). The list of representatives was a peculiar one; it included several people who had no further dealing with the RGR but subsequently became prominent in the RPF (Boisdé and Billotte). For the negotiations leading to the formation of the RGR see also E. Bonnefous, *Avant l'oubli*. II: *La vie de 1940 à 1970* (Paris, 1987), p. 84.

[4] Ibid. The meeting of 28 March 1946 comprised three groups: Kayser, Martinaud Deplat, Maroselli and Dreyfus Schmidt represented the Radical party; Astier, Varenne, Chevalier, Avinin, Soustelle and David represented the Rassemblement Républicain; Rarge, Valabrègue, Gruber, Lacroix and Monnerville represented the Ligue de la République.

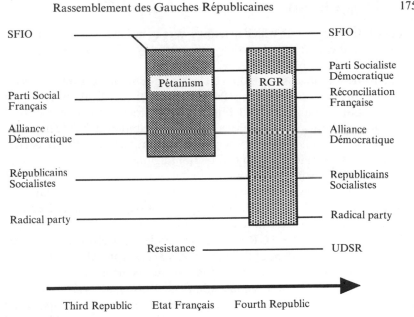

Figure 1 The origins of the Rassemblement des Gauches Républicaines

licain et Social de la Réconciliation Française, had few or no representatives in parliament (their most prominent members were usually ineligible) and their representation on the bureau of the RGR was small. The RGR also maintained close relations with various conservative groupings. Attempts had been made to persuade the Fédération Républicaine (FR) to join the RGR in 1946 and the RGR bureau always contained representatives of Independents and Independent Radicals. Furthermore, an RGR circular of 1949 suggested that some seventeen Independent parliamentarians were 'administratively attached' to the RGR.[5]

The first president of the RGR was the Radical senator Cudenet. After Cudenet's death in 1948, the RGR's secretary general (J. P. David) served as acting president until 1950 when Daladier was elected as president. The RGR's *comité exécutif* contained between twenty and thirty people including the holders of eleven specific offices and representatives of all the affiliated parties. In 1951 this body contained sixteen Radicals, and seven members of the UDSR; the Alliance Démocratique (AD), Réconciliation Française (RF), the Independent Radicals, the Independents, and the PSD each sent a single representative to the *comité exécutif*. The details of the *comité exécutif*'s organization were vague: there were contradictory rules

[5] RGR, *Que veut le RGR?* (Paris, 1949).

about the frequency with which meetings were to be held, and, although the *comité* was theoretically elected by an assembly of the RGR, no such assembly ever took place.

The RGR was always more than a clearing house for electoral alliances. It had a high degree of autonomy. Parties such as the Radicals, which had a weak central organization and blurred boundaries with other political formations, were in a poor position to impose discipline on their 'delegates'. Furthermore the divisions between (and within) the constituent parties allowed the RGR leaders to play off factions against each other. The RGR secretariat also benefited from the fact that a certain number of members of the *comité exécutif* were effectively selected by the RGR secretariat itself (this was particularly true of the two representatives of Femmes Républicaines and the two representatives of youth).

The men who ran the RGR used it to provide themselves with a power base that was independent of the particular parties from which they came. People could join the RGR as individuals as well as through its constituent parties and in 1951 it was claimed that the RGR had 17,547 members distributed across thirty federations in mainland France and six in the French Union. The RGR's monthly paper, *Unité Française*, sold around 30,000 copies. In 1949 the RGR *comité exécutif* altered its own statutes in a number of ways that made it appear more like a political party: henceforth the *comité exécutif* was to be known as the bureau, the *assemblée générale* was to known as the congress, and all members of the bureau were to be known as *membres fondateurs*. In 1950 there were rumours that the RGR was on the verge of declaring itself to be an independent political party and, after the splits in the Radical party of 1955, this was effectively what happened.[6]

The minor parties of the RGR

The four minor parties of the RGR were all composed of splinters of parties that had existed under the Third Republic. The Parti Républicain et Social de la Réconciliation Française (usually known as Réconciliation Française or RF) was made up of people who had been members of Colonel de la Rocque's Parti Social Français (PSF) before 1940, though party leaders were initially reticent about their links with de la Rocque. After the war former members of the PSF divided: those who had been members of the Resistance usually joined the Parti Républicain de la Liberté (PRL) while those who had been Pétainist joined RF. The leaders of RF claimed that their meetings attracted around 6,000 people, that the party had around

[6] Philip Williams, *Politics in post-war France. Parties and the constitution in the Fourth Republic* (2nd edition, London, 1958), pp. 147–149.

10,000 members and that they had an active organization in a number of regions.[7] Party members were generally wealthy, even by the standards of French conservatism.[8]

The broad lines of RF doctrine were revealed in the party journal, *le Flambeau de la Réconciliation Française*. As its name suggests, the RF was much concerned to end the division between Pétainists and *résistants*. The party's leaders denounced purges and called for an end to what they regarded as the political exploitation of the Resistance. The party was also vigorously anti-Communist – desire to combat Communism underlay the party's increasing enthusiasm for unity among bourgeois parties. Economic matters were the other main interest of the RF leadership. The party called for a balanced budget and criticized high taxation and *dirigisme*.[9] RF leaders were also much concerned to demonstrate that they were not a conventional right-wing party (a concern that was characteristic of conventional right-wing parties). They attacked other conservative parties, especially the PRL, and denounced the operations of large-scale capitalism.[10]

The RF's relations with other political parties were obscure and ambiguous. Conventional accounts present the RF as one of the constituent parties of the RGR. In fact RGR propaganda was very discreet about the participation of a party that was widely associated with fascism. *Le Flambeau de la Réconciliation Française* was equally discreet about its associations with the RGR. It reported the results of the 1946 elections without making any reference to links between RF and other political parties and it was not until March 1948 that a party leader sought to justify what he called 'une politique de présence' in the RGR.[11] Even after this date RF candidates were not confined to RGR electoral lists. Of thirteen candidates in the 1951 election, five fought on RGR lists, three fought on Independent and Peasant lists, one fought on a combined Independent/

---

[7] *Le Flambeau de la Réconciliation Française*, 30 November 1945.
[8] I am grateful for this information to Dr Kevin Passmore whose researches on the social profile of *Réconciliation Française* are based on the de la Rocque archives in the Archives Nationales. Passmore's research shows that the proportion of industrialists among members of RF was almost seven times the proportion of industrialists in the population as a whole, the proportion of people from the liberal professions in RF was almost five times that in the population as a whole. Workers and farmers were under represented in RF: so too were students and the retired, which suggests that membership was linked to a very specific generation, presumably that which had reached political maturity at the apogee of the PSF's success.
[9] The first article that *le Flambeau de la Réconciliation Française* published on 30 November 1945 was entitled 'Equilbre budgétaire et équilibre économique'. Characteristic of the journal's attitude to taxation was the article, by Passerieux, published on 19 January 1946 entitled 'Le système fiscal actuel est à jeter à bas'.
[10] *Le Flambeau de la Réconciliation Française* published a series of articles in 1946 entitled 'Un danger réel les trusts'.   [11] Ibid., 8 March 1948.

RGR list and four fought on *listes d'union*.[12] After the election an RF 'inter-group' was formed in the National Assembly: it contained eight men who sat in the RGR, Independent and Peasant groupings.

The Parti Républicain Socialiste (RS) was the most obscure of the groupings that made up the RGR. Before the war, the RS had consisted mainly of politicians who had left the Section Française de l'Internationale Ouvrière (SFIO). It had contained some distinguished figures: notably Briand and Painlevé. After 1945 the party had a small number of loyal members, but it was an artificial body controlled by officials of the Radical party or the RGR. When Edgar Faure sought to become a Radical candidate in 1945, he was told by a Radical party official 'Since you are not officially a member of any party, you will run on a Républicain Socialiste ticket. You make the speeches, and we will pay the bills.'[13] Faure accepted the offer and fought, unsuccessfully, on behalf of the Républicains Socialistes in Paris. Faure himself described his party as 'a phantom group'.[14] Even his close friends believed that Faure was fighting on a Radical ticket in 1945,[15] and in the following year he did become an open Radical.

At local level the leaders of the RGR simply drafted supporters into the Républicains Socialistes for electoral purposes. In the first *arrondissement* of Nevers, Jean Locquin was listed as the Républicain Socialiste representative although his background (as a former member of the SFIO who had been expelled for Pétainism)[16] would normally have been associated with membership of the PSD.[17] However, in 1948 the Républicains Socialistes seem to have become more independent of their RGR partners. They condemned the RGR in increasingly bitter terms (see below) and they established their own newspaper *Liberté Républicaine*.

The PSD was led by men who had been purged from the SFIO in 1945 for having supported Pétain. Paul Faure was leader of the party. In 1946 it claimed to have thirty federations in existence and a further twenty in the

---

[12] Ibid., 10 June 1951, 'Nos candidats'. See also 'PSF et RGR' in *l'Evénement* for 23 June 1951, which claimed that 'Réconciliation Française which continues the work of the Parti Social Français' had presented fourteen candidates.

[13] Edgar Faure, *Mémoires*. I: *Avoir toujours raison ... c'est un grand tort* (Paris, 1982), p. 153.

[14] Ibid.

[15] Jacques Dumaine, *Quai d'Orsay, 1945–1951* (Paris, 1956), entry for 27 October 1945, pp. 27–28. Dumaine reported, after lunching with Faure, that Faure had decided to fight on a Radical ticket, rather than an MRP one, because he believed that the former stood a better chance of winning. Dumaine's mistake is repeated by the semi-official historian of the Radical Party, Francis de Tarr, *The French Radical party from Herriot to Mendès-France* (Oxford, 1961), p. 155.

[16] See AN, 310 AP 18 for details of Locquin's post-war electoral career.

[17] Locquin did maintain some relations with the Parti Socialiste Démocratique and his archives contain a letter from Paul Faure addressed to readers of *la République Libre* (the PSD paper) dated 16 January 1950 in AN, 310 AP 93.

process of formation.[18] Williams estimated that by the mid-1950s the PSD had forty federations and around 30,000 members (mainly in the south-west). From November 1948, the party published a journal: *la République Libre*. In spite of its socialist origins, the PSD's policies were those of conventional conservative groups. It opposed economic *dirigisme*, 'suffo-cating fiscality' and the purges.[19] Indeed, an article in the party paper even seemed to flirt with royalism.[20] Though the PSD remained, nominally at least, part of the RGR until the mid-1950s, Paul Faure fought the 1951 election on the list of the conservative Rassemblement des Groupes Républicains et Indépendants Français (RGRIF).

The AD was the most important of the minor parties in the RGR. It was a continuation of the pre-war grouping and was led by Paul Etienne Flandin (who had been prime minister in the Vichy government). However, most prominent members of the AD who had supported the Resistance left in 1945 and 1946 to join the PRL. The post-war AD was dominated by two issues. The first of these was anti-Communism: there were frequent calls at party congresses for the outright banning of the Communist party. The second issue to exercise the AD was the defence of those who had supported Pétain and particularly the AD's own leader who made a number of unsuccessful attempts to return to parliamentary politics.[21]

The minor parties of the RGR had an awkward relationship with their senior partners in the RGR. Radical leaders often dismissed their associates as insignificant vestiges of the political past. Jacques Kayser said that many parties described as members of the RGR were not even listed in the Paris telephone directory.[22] Marc Rucard (who was to become a Radical senator for the Ivory Coast) said that the minor parties were to politics what the Haitian army was to war.[23] Most striking of all was the judgement of Jean-Louis Anteriou that the minor parties of the RGR only existed on paper or had been invented for the occasion (see above). The past of some leaders of the minor parties also caused tension with the leaders of the Radicals and the UDSR. There was a storm of protest when *le Flambeau de la Réconciliation Française* published an article eulogizing de la Rocque. Personal animosity rooted in the Vichy period could inflame comparatively trivial disputes about policy.

[18] AN, 310 AP 71, account of meeting of *conseil national* of Parti Socialiste Démocratique on 3 and 4 May 1946.   [19] 'Salut au lecteur', *la République Libre*, 19 November 1948.

[20] L. Hudelle, 'Faut-il rester Républicain?', *la République Libre*, 10 December 1948.

[21] Report on policy since liberation made by Ventenat to party conference of 12 May 1950 contained in Bibliothèque Nationale, Alliance Démocratique papers (AD), 4.

[22] De Tarr, *The French Radical party*, p. 90. Kayser's position on the RGR was odd. He wrote to Herriot on 28 February 1946 expressing concern about rumours that a '*bloc républicain* was being formed', but on 7 March he presided over one of the meetings that led to the formation of the RGR (documents relating to Kayser's relations with the RGR can be found in AN, 465 AP 7).   [23] De Tarr, *The French Radical party*, p. 93.

The leaders of the minor parties felt excluded from the important decisions made by the RGR. The president of RF wrote in 1951: 'Having belonged to the RGR since 1946, we still have no precise idea about its intentions.'[24] Candidacies in the 1951 elections exposed the strained relations within the RGR. Those leaders of the minor parties who were eligible were consistently refused places on RGR election lists. Often the reasons given for such refusals were ludicrous. When de Léotard of RF sought a place on an electoral list, the RGR leaders wrote 'an aristocratic name [would be] too difficult here, especially with an appearance that is very different to that of our Burgundians'.[25] One of the leaders of RF wrote to the president of the RGR in 1951 that the meeting to allocate electoral lists had seen 'a series of con tricks'.[26]

The leaders of the minor parties were equally cavalier in their attitude to the RGR. They often gave their support to Independent candidates in preference to members of the RGR. Flandin did his best to help the Independent Jean Moreau in the Yonne;[27] Pinay (a former member of AD) stood for parliament as an Independent; Ventenat, the secretary of the AD, headed an (unsuccessful) Independent list in the Dordogne and Guy Petit (of RF) sat in parliament with the Peasant group. Both RF and the AD flirted with the Independents and, in 1954, both were formally to join the CNIP group.[28] The leaders of the Républicains Socialistes were even more prone to support parties outside the RGR: Henri Torrès, the most prominent orator of the party, was also a Gaullist senator.[29]

Conflict between the minor parties of the RGR and their partners became particularly acute between 1948 and 1951. The entry of Radical and UDSR ministers into government after January 1947 created a gulf in the RGR. On the one hand were the leaders of the major parties who were enjoying the fruits of ministerial office; on the other hand were the leaders of

[24] AN, 412 AP 45, Portier to Daladier dated 4 May 1951.
[25] AN, 412 AP 45, 'Enquête en Côte d'Or sur les possibilités de prendre un candidat venu de l'extérieur', dated 30 April 1950.
[26] AN, 496 AP 51, Portier to Daladier, dated 18 May 1951. Portier's complaint was made all the more remarkable by the fact that Daladier owed his position as president of the RGR partly to the support of Réconciliation Française.
[27] See M. Abélès, *Quiet days in Burgundy* (Cambridge, 1991), p. 64.
[28] On the negotiations that were to lead both RF and the AD to join the Independents; see various documents in the AD papers carton 4, and in particular 'Histoire des rapports entre l'Alliance Démocratique et le Centre des Indépendants', dated 5 May 1959.
[29] For the roles of René Gounin and Torrès in the Seine federation of the Républicains Socialistes see *Liberté Républicaine*, June 1948. The political manoeuvres of Torrès, an ex-Communist, were of particularly fiendish complexity. In his capacity as a member of the RS he condemned the Third Force, though the RS was part of the RGR which officially supported the Third Force; in his capacity as a member of the RPF he supported the Third Force, though the RPF was opposed to it.

the minor parties who were excluded not just from office but even from parliament.[30] In March 1948 a meeting of the RS called for an immediate summoning of an RGR *conseil* and a withdrawal of its members from participation in government.[31]

Tension was exacerbated by the death of Cudenet, who had been seen as a defender of the interests of the minor parties, and by the formation of the RPF. The RPF aroused particularly complicated feelings among the leaders of the minor parties. Its vigorous anti-Communism and its opposition to the governments of the Third Force appealed to men like Faure and Flandin, but the RPF's discipline, and the personality of its founder, did not bode well for former Pétainists or men associated with minor parties. Some members of the minor groups in the RGR did join the RPF, but many others simply encouraged their own group to take a more intransigent anti-governmental position.[32]

Leaders of the minor parties of the RGR also became involved with the splits that occurred within the Radical party in 1950. They supported Daladier's candidacy as president of the RGR, and they supported the Lyonnais Radical Chambaretaud who clashed with Herriot over the latter's condemnation of the RPF. A number of members of minor parties of the RGR became involved with the RGRIF that Chambaretaud set up to contest the 1951 elections.[33]

In spite of continuous quarrels and occasional defections, the various component parties of the RGR remained together for almost ten years. The fact that they did so reflects some important common interests that united them in spite of their well-aired public differences. Firstly, the minor parties, or at least their leaders, were almost obsessively concerned with revoking the ineligibility laws, and membership of the RGR fitted in with this aim. A comparatively large group, which had representatives in almost all cabinets after 1947, provided former Pétainists with a better platform for lobbying than they would have possessed as leaders of isolated and ostracized parties that were perceived as belonging to the extreme right. In spite of frequent grumbling about the ministerial participation of Radicals,

---

[30] For denunciations of Radical participation in government see P. Faure, 'Régime pourri', in *la République Libre*, 26 November 1948; 'Contre les incurables' (an unsigned article supporting Cudenet's opposition to Radical participation in government) in ibid.; and 'Le Parti Républicain Socialiste proteste contre la stérilité du RGR', unsigned article in *l'Indépendant Français*, 22 October 1949.   [31] *Liberté Républicaine*, March 1948.

[32] The minor parties of the RGR also wanted closer relations with the RPF; Léotard, of Réconciliation Française, rallied his supporters with the slogan 'Avec le RPF et avec la Troisième Force contre le Communisme', *le Flambeau de la Réconciliation Française*, 22 March 1948.

[33] Paul Faure, leader of the Parti Socialiste Democratique, fought the 1951 election as an RGRIF candidate.

some former Pétainists in the minor parties of the RGR seem to have recognized that such participation was in their interest.[34]

Furthermore, the rhetoric that the leaders of the minor parties used to justify the repeal of the ineligibility laws laid great emphasis on the Third Republic origins of Vichy. It was stressed that Pétain had come to power as a result of a vote of the last Third Republic parliament and both Faure and Flandin were prominent members of the Association des Représentants du Peuple de la Troisième République (ARPTR). This emphasis on the Third Republic obviously fitted in well with an alliance with the Radicals (the archetypal part of the Third Republic).

The Radical party and the UDSR had equally strong reasons for desiring the survival of the RGR. Firstly, right-wingers in the Radical party were able to use the minor parties as allies against the left-wing factions in their own party who might otherwise had gained control of the bureau of the RGR.[35] Secondly, the fact that leaders of the minor parties so often had close relations with conservative parties may have been a source of benefit as well as irritation to the leaders of the RGR. The RGR leaders themselves often raised the possibility of some broader alliance of bourgeois parties and they were keen to keep lines of communication to the Independents and Peasants open.[36]

Finally, and most importantly, the Radicals and the UDSR wished to maintain the alliance with the minor parties because they believed that the very qualities which made professional politicians deride those parties would attract a certain proportion of the electorate to them. Anteriou, the man who had mocked the minor parties of the RGR in 1946, anticipated the political *rentrée* of Flandin and certain Pétainists in 1948: 'the return of FLANDIN to the presidency of the Alliance Démocratique and the speech that he made on this occasion, marked the first attack of the Vichyssoises. On 14 March a great banquet of the association of former representatives of the Third Republic presided over by M. Paul Faure will bring together 2,000 people at the Parc des Expositions.' Anteriou added an estimate of the public support that such individuals might enjoy: 'It is reckoned that a million families have seen one of their members touched by the purge in various ways, both administrative and judicial.'[37] Men like Flandin and

---

[34] For example, Flandin made a sudden and unexpected announcement that he supported Queuille's government and opposed dissolution of parliament in February 1949. *L'Indépendant Français*, 5 February 1949.

[35] AN, 373 AP 9, Anteriou to Colin, dated 27 March 1951: 'The right of the Radical Party ... which has been eliminated from the executive committee, will attempt a new manoeuvre, supported by the RGR.'   [36] *Le Monde*, 14/15 May 1950.

[37] AN, 373 AP 7, Anteriou to Bollaert dated 10 March 1948. The return of Flandin was recorded in *Résistance à l'Oppression* (a Pétainist journal) for February 1948. It is also worth noting that the archives of Georges Bidault contain a complete text of Flandin's speech of 8 February 1948, AN, 457 AP 135.

Faure made ideal political allies in that they were seen to have a reservoir of electoral support while their own ineligibility obliged them to mobilize that support on behalf of someone else.

The UDSR

During and immediately after the occupation many people had hoped that the Resistance would give birth to a new type of political party that would be more far sighted, noble and disinterested than the squabbling interest groups that had dominated the Third Republic. Sometimes such hopes had been linked with *travaillisme*, a vague notion that a broad party of the left comparable to the British Labour party might be created in France. These hopes were dented in 1945. Firstly in January 1945 the Mouvement National de la Libération (an umbrella group of Resistance organizations) was divided between those who advocated fusion with the Communist dominated Front National and those who opposed it. Those who were against unity (rallied by André Malraux) obtained 250 votes against 119 who voted for fusion. In June a second division over the question of forming a *union travailliste* drove the remaining Communist sympathizers to form a new movement of their own: the Mouvement Unifié de la Renaissance Française.

This event dissipated the illusion that the idealistic unity of the left that some had perceived in the Resistance could be maintained in peace time. Other problems arose for those who wanted to see a large *travailliste* party: the Socialist SFIO refused to commit itself to such a party and maintained contact with the Communist party, while the Mouvement Républicain Populaire (MRP) had already absorbed a large number of non-Communist Resistance leaders who wanted to make a career in politics.

In June 1945 a group of Resistance leaders who had not been absorbed by one of the parties already in existence decided to found a new organization: the UDSR. Ceux de la Résistance, the Organisation Civile et Militaire, Combat, Défense de la France, Franc-Tireur, Gallia and the Mouvement National des Prisonniers de Guerre were all represented in the movement. It remained a somewhat hazy federation and did not declare itself to be a formal party until October 1946. Some of the most distinguished Resistance leaders in France were members of the UDSR: they included Philippe Viannay, Claude Bourdet, Henri Frenay, Maxime Blocque-Mascart, Eugène (Claudius) Petit, Antoine Avinin, Pierre Bourdan, René Capitant and François Mitterrand.

The UDSR was widely seen as a disappointing organization, which failed to live up to the high hopes that had been placed in it. Forty years on one of its founders dismissed it as 'fifteen or so buddies who wanted to take some political action'.[38] The UDSR's willingness to join with former Pétainists and Third Republic politicians in the RGR and its participation in the governments of the late 1940s and 1950s was widely seen as a betrayal of the Resistance heritage. Now historians generally remember the UDSR, if they remember it at all, only because it provided the first political vehicle for François Mitterrand. However, the judgements passed on the UDSR were unfair: they reflected the naive expectations of the Liberation not the realities of the Fourth Republic. It will be argued here that the UDSR's entry into the RGR and its willingness to participate in the game of ministry formation was the logical outcome of the position that many of its leaders had adopted before the Liberation.

The ideology of the UDSR

Placing the UDSR on the political spectrum of the Fourth Republic is a difficult, and perhaps rather pointless, exercise. Its leaders would probably have described their party as a left-wing formation, but so would the leaders of almost every other Fourth Republic party. Certainly, the UDSR was not left-wing in the same sense of the Parti Communiste Français (PCF) or the SFIO. Roger Duchet described the UDSR as a centre-left formation, which implies that it was not so far removed from his own 'centrist' Independent group.[39] A member of the UDSR also defined his party's appeal in centrist terms: 'It is obvious that the UDSR is a party of the centre left which addresses itself above all to the middle classes [*classes moyennes*].'[40]

Perhaps the most revealing clue about the UDSR's political position came from the very vagueness with which its ideology was defined. This vagueness worried some of its leaders, especially those idealistic young men who had risen to prominence through the Resistance. Philippe Viannay wrote that the UDSR was: 'A sort of residue of movements ... to which all sorts of personalities and ambitions without political homeland became attached.'[41] However, the absence of ideological coherence that seemed so confusing to those, like Viannay, who assumed that the UDSR was a party of the left, is easier to understand if we assume that the UDSR was a party of bourgeois conservatism. It is notable that Edouard Bonnefous, a member of a dynasty of Third Republic politicians who joined the UDSR, was attracted to the group by the very absence of clear definition that repelled men like Viannay. Furthermore, Bonnefous described the qualities

---

[38] Jacques Piette, cited in Roger Faligot and Rémi Kauffer, *Les résistants. De la guerre de l'ombre aux allées de pouvoir 1944–1989* (Paris, 1989), p. 51.

[39] Roger Duchet, *La république épinglée* (Paris, 1975), p. 164. Duchet expressed approval for most of the leaders of the UDSR.

[40] AN, 412 AP 4, Gauthier Walter speaking to party congress on 24 May 1947.

[41] P. Viannay, *Du bon usage de la France* (Paris, 1988), p. 177.

of the UDSR that appealed to him in terms of approval that could equally well have been used by any member of the Independent or AD groups: 'a spiritual family rather than a party, a community of thought rather than a coterie . . . and, above all, a determined rejection of all brutal discipline.'[42]

Three things associated the UDSR with conservatism: the careers of its leaders, the policies that it advocated, and the alliances that it formed. The UDSR leaders did not all have backgrounds on the right. Men like Leenhardt were genuine socialists, but they were always in a minority and most of them defected to the SFIO when the UDSR broke off its electoral alliance with that party in April 1946. Furthermore, the UDSR also attracted a number of men who had undergone some youthful flirtation with the extreme right or with Vichy: Mitterrand came from a family linked to Action Française and had been attracted by the Parti Populaire Français (PPF);[43] Frenay[44] and Viannay[45] had both expressed admiration for Pétain in the early years of the Vichy regime. Jacques Lecompte-Boinet had been a reader of *Action Française* before the war.[46]

After the war, some of these men turned away from their youthful conservatism. Viannay and Frenay came to regard themselves as leaders of the independent left, but they also felt obliged to leave the UDSR in order to expound their ideas with freedom. Those who remained in the party often had associations with conservative politics. Jacques Lecompte-Boinet wrote in his diary, after attending a meeting of an explicitly right-wing organization: 'at last in this committee one dares to describe oneself as right-wing'.[47] Roger Duveau, who became a UDSR deputy, was seen by his friend Jacques Isorni as 'A man of the left by his label, but a man of the right by many of his tendencies'.[48] Alfred Dolfuss, who became party treasurer, was an associate of Antoine Pinay and the Independent deputy Jean Moreau. He said that he had joined the UDSR because he liked its 'level-headed social and economic doctrine'.[49]

The UDSR deputy whose political beliefs and associations have been most scrutinized was François Mitterrand. Some placed Mitterrand on the left of the UDSR. Bonnefous believed that Mitterrand belonged with

---

[42] Bonnefous, *La vie de 1940 à 1970*, p. 95.

[43] D. S. Bell and B. Criddle, *The French Socialist party: the emergence of a party of government* (2nd edition, Oxford, 1988), p. 231.

[44] Daniel Cordier, *Jean Moulin. L'inconnu du Panthéon. II: Le choix d'un destin. Juin 1936–Novembre 1940* (Paris, 1989), pp. 464–465.

[45] AN, 2 AJ 50, testimony collected on Resistance organizations, interview with Salmon: 'At the beginning Viannay and Lebon remained very Pétainist . . . a number [of the movement's publication] which cannot be found today defended the Marshal after Montoire'.

[46] The diary of Jacques Lecompte-Boinet (LBD) was kindly lent to the author by Madame Lecompte-Boinet.   [47] LBD entry for 28 February 1945.

[48] Jacques Isorni, *Mémoires. II: 1946–1958* (Paris, 1986), p. 268.

[49] Abélès, *Quiet days in Burgundy*, p. 83.

Frenay in the Socialist (as opposed to Gaullist or centrist) section of the party.[50] Mitterrand certainly frequented Frenay and Viannay's discussion circle even after his two colleagues had left the UDSR. However, Mitterrand was also linked with Duveau and Dolfuss, and the later believed that Mitterrand was 'a man of the centre supported by the votes of the right', who had only turned to the left during his presidential bid of 1965.[51]

Mitterrand was elected in the Nièvre on a manifesto that expressed conventional conservatism: 'No to bankruptcy, no to high prices, no to administrative chaos, no to nationalizations, no to the installation of the Communist party in power.' Mitterrand's most respected biographer accepts that Mitterrand was elected on a conservative programme but also accepts Mitterrand's own claim (made in 1972) that his *légende d'homme de droite* sprang from the views of his voters not from his own preferences. Giesbert concludes that Mitterrand 'disguised himself as a *modéré* to win an election'.[52]

However, Giesbert ignores the fact that Mitterrand also maintained more discreet contacts with eminent conservatives. He had been an employee of Eugène Schueller, the founder of l'Oréal and a well-known supplier of funds for politicians.[53] He was liked and admired by Jacques Isorni[54] and Roger Duchet.[55] Twice conservatives intervened to help Mitterrand at election time. In 1946 the PRL leader, Barrachin, who had defeated Mitterrand in the fifth sector of the Seine, helped him to gain acceptance as a candidate in the Nièvre.[56] In 1951, the secretary of the Centre National des Indépendants granted Mitterrand's request that no conservative candidate should be run against him in the Nièvre.[57] Given Mitterrand's studied inscrutability it is doubtful whether it will ever be possible to say for sure whether he is a right-winger who hid his real views in the Fifth Republic, a left-winger who hid his real views in the Fourth Republic, or a cynical opportunist who has hidden his real views for most of his life. For the study of the UDSR, all that it is necessary to know is that many, both inside and outside the party, saw Mitterrand as a man of conservative sympathies and associations.

Alongside the ambiguities and contradictions of the UDSR, one doctrine stood out as being crucially important to the party: anti-Communism. Most non-Communist leaders of the Resistance loathed the Communist

[50] Bonnefous, *Avant l'oubli*, p. 84.   [51] Ibid.
[52] F.-O. Giesbert, *François Mitterrand ou la tentation de l'histoire* (Paris, 1977), p. 93.
[53] Duchet believed that Schueller had facilitated Mitterrand's election to parliament in 1946; Duchet, *La république épinglée*, p. 239.   [54] Isorni, *1946–1958*, pp. 15–16.
[55] Duchet, *La république épinglée*, p. 165.
[56] Georges Riond, *Chroniques d'un autre monde* (Paris, 1979), p. 204.
[57] Duchet, *La république épinglée*, pp. 51 and 164.

party. Men like Frenay, Lecompte-Boinet and Mitterrand remembered the PCF's neutrality during the period of the Hitler/Stalin pact and its subsequent ruthlessness in taking over Resistance organizations. Avinin started a brawl in the National Assembly by shouting 'get on your knees allies of Hitler' at the Communist benches.[58] Anti-Communism was always a linchpin of the UDSR and the party leadership became closely connected to the anti-Communist organization Paix et Liberté.

The right-wing origins of many UDSR leaders may have had little influence on the party's rhetoric, but they did have an influence on the policies that the party supported. This was particularly apparent in the field of economics. René Pleven, who became president of the UDSR, had opposed Mendès-France's radical and austere financial policies in 1944. Subsequently the UDSR proved a vigorous supporter of a strong franc, and denounced *dirigisme* as 'pure folly'.[59]

The political alliances of the UDSR also tended to associate the party with the right. It is true that the party worked in partial alliance with the SFIO until April 1946. However, this alliance was closest at a time when certain elements of the SFIO seemed strongly associated with anti-Communism, and when Léon Blum's denunciation of 'un parti nationaliste d'obédience étrangère' had made him a hero even on the extreme right. The UDSR leaders (and the MRP leaders who sought a similar alliance) had every reason to assume that a *travailliste* front involving the SFIO would be an effective anti-Communist weapon. Jacques Lecompte-Boinet believed that anti-Communism was the only virtue of the SFIO alliance: 'The problem for me is that I am not a socialist and that neither of the two blocks that are proposed, UDSR/Socialist or MURF/Front National, suits me, and it is only through anti-Communism that I am a member of the UDSR.'[60] When the SFIO's relations with the Communist party improved, its alliance with the UDSR collapsed.

Furthermore, the SFIO alliance was an exception in the history of the UDSR. Generally the party sought its allies on the right. The most famous of the alliances that the UDSR concluded with conservative parties was the RGR (discussed below), but it also frequently made local deals with members of the other conservative groupings. Edouard Bonnefous headed a list that brought together Independents and the RGR in Seine et Oise.[61] In the Ile et Vilaine, the UDSR leaders recognized that they lacked the organization to launch a candidature on behalf of their own party, but they decided instead to throw their support behind la Chambre, a member of the

---

[58] AN, 373 AP 7, Anteriou to Bollaert, dated 12 March 1948.
[59] See the declarations contained in AN, 412 AP 4.
[60] LBD, entry for 9 July 1945.   [61] Bonnefous, *Avant l'oubli*, p. 114.

CNIP.[62] Local studies, such as those conducted by Pataut in Nevers[63] or by Clément and Xydias in Vienne,[64] invariably classified the UDSR as part of the conservative bloc.

Organization

The most awkward problems that the UDSR faced related to organization. Once again these problems had their roots in the nature of clandestine Resistance activity. Resistance organizations had been built from the top downwards. Founders of movements went out and looked for members and, even when they began to acquire a large following, Resistance movements were never democratic: there were no party congresses or elections during the occupation. After the war those who had been 'dictators of clandestine empires'[65] were ill equipped for party politics in a democracy. Lanet told the party congress of 1947: 'If the UDSR was born politically before being born administratively, it is because the UDSR was a parliamentary group before being a reality in the country.'[66] The UDSR lacked roots in many regions. Resistance leaders had tended to concentrate in Paris during the months preceding the Liberation and the UDSR's membership was concentrated overwhelmingly in Paris and a few other areas. The Seine region contained 1,502 of the UDSR's 5,532 members, the Côtes du Nord (the next largest departmental federation) had 797 members while Loir et Cher and Moselle were reported to have only one member each.[67]

Resistance leaders had been formed in a culture where information was

---

[62] AN, 412 AP 13, Report to the *comité exécutif* of 15 February 1950. It was noted that la Chambre 'will certainly stand as an independent' but that he 'will subsequently be a sympathizer'.

[63] J. Pataut, *Sociologie électorale de la Nièvre au XXème siècle (1902–1951)* (2 vols, Paris, 1956), p. 92.

[64] Pierre Clément and Nelly Xydias, *Vienne sur le Rhône. La ville et les habitants, situations et attitudes. Sociologie d'une cité française* (Paris, 1955), pp. 122–123.

[65] J.F. Sweets, *The politics of Resistance in France 1940–1944: a history of the Mouvements Unis de la Résistance* (Dekalb, Ill., 1976) p. 47.

[66] AN, 412 AP 4, Lanet to party congress, 24 May 1947.

[67] Undated list of federations in AN, 412 AP 1. The full figures are as follows: Alpes Maritimes 240; Bouches du Rhône 500; Corse 51; Côtes du Nord 797; Creuse 9; Deux Sèvres 15; Gironde 101; Hérault 86; Ile et Vilaine 35; Indre et Loire 10; Isère 208; Loire 195; Loire Inférieure 82; Loiret 69; Loir et Cher 1; Meurthe et Moselle 66; Meuse 11; Moselle 1; Nièvre 400; Orne 52; 'outre mer' 20; Puy de Dôme 37; Pyrénées Basses 0; Rhin Bas 0; Haut Rhin 19; Rhône 144; Savoie 5; Seine 1502; Seine et Oise 281; Seine Inférieure 28; Var 18; Vienne 1; Vendée 10; Vosges 0; Alger 163; Oran 223; Maroc 22; Tunisie 11; Madagascar 16. The leaders of the UDSR themselves expressed scepticism about the reliability of departmental membership lists. Membership lists of the UDSR were sometimes distorted in order to provide strong positions for negotiations with other parties in the RGR. See the discussion at the *comité exécutif* on 15 February 1950.

conveyed by word of mouth and where meetings were held at short notice and in secret. Such an apprenticeship proved disastrous when the UDSR had to confront the committee meetings and paper work of post-war politics. Initiatives sometimes failed just because people summoned to meetings failed to turn up at the right time. Lanet complained of the 'complete lack of political organization in the movement'.[68] Tixier commented of his UDSR colleagues, 'clandestine life has not given them a taste for sustained work'.[69]

The Resistance origins of the UDSR also created an atmosphere of mutual suspicion and hostility among the leaders of the party. During the occupation, there had been frequent conflicts between rival Resistance groups, between *résistants de la première heure* and latecomers, and between groups based in the northern and southern zones. Resistance leaders, or at least those that survived, were haunted by the fear of betrayal or simply by the fear that their associates might be indiscreet or careless. All of these animosities carried over into post-war life. At the 1947 party congress Avinin complained about the 'small squabbles' that dogged the UDSR.[70]

The UDSR and the RGR

The UDSR entered the RGR in June 1946. The alliance was regarded with mystification and hostility by some members of the UDSR. In their view, the Resistance had stood against everything that was represented by the Third Republic parties assembled in the RGR. They blamed such parties for the squalid failure of France during the 1930s, the defeat and the installation of Marshal Pétain (who had been voted full powers by a majority of the Third Republic parliament that included many parties that were now part of the RGR). Frenay and Bourdet both left the UDSR, and party politics, in protest: 'Have our comrades made so many sacrifices so that the Radical party, which lacks principles and courage, should see its name attached to that of the Resistance! It is folly. Worse it is shameful.'[71]

However, the alliance between the UDSR and the RGR (particularly the Radicals) was by no means as irrational as it seemed to some. Not all Resistance leaders felt as hostile to the Third Republic parties as Frenay and Bourdet. Jacques Lecompte-Boinet's diary shows that he had progressed from feeling violent hostility to pre-war politicians in 1940 to feeling grudging respect for them by the Liberation. Lecompte-Boinet had been

---

[68] AN, 412 AP 4, 'Réflections sur l'UDSR' dated 8 July 1946.
[69] LBD, 23 February 1945.
[70] Reported in *Combat Républicain* for June 1947 in AN, 412 AP 4.
[71] Faligot and Kauffer, *Les résistants*, pp. 52 and 53.

influenced partly by personal contact with politicians whose courage and charm had impressed him, and who had sometimes seemed models of far sighted and disinterested statesmanship when compared to the squabbling Resistance groups. More importantly, Lecompte-Boinet had come to feel that a return of Third Republic politicians, including those who had voted full powers to Pétain,[72] would be necessary to counterbalance Communist power: 'I have come after four years of experience ... in the Resistance to prefer the republican order of the Third Republic to the adventure and the probable dictatorship of the Fourth Republic.'[73]

In terms of electoral advantage, the difference between the Radicals and the UDSR only increased the case for an alliance of the two parties. The leaders of the UDSR had a large amount of prestige without real political contacts or experience; the Radicals had an enormous fund of experience and contacts but lacked prestige. The UDSR was unable to match its national status with local support. It was particularly weak at cantonal level (i.e. the level at which departmental *conseils généraux* were elected) where unknown outsiders from Paris found it impossible to dislodge established village figures. The Radical party, by contrast, was particularly strong at cantonal level, and was able to cover the UDSR's local weakness.

The structure of the Radical party facilitated its alliance with the UDSR. A party built on a mass membership, like the SFIO, would simply have swallowed a party which had as few members as the UDSR. However, the Radical party was based on personal contacts and the support of local notables and this made the arrangement of bargaining and electoral deals easier. The relationship with the Radicals was not without friction. UDSR members complained when, for example, the Radicals put a man fined for economic collaboration at the top of an RGR electoral list.[74] But generally the UDSR seems to have done remarkably well from the local support that the Radicals gave it. At the party congress of May 1947, Avinin admitted that the RGR had allowed UDSR candidates to be elected even in areas where the party 'had no real existence'.[75]

The RGR proved particularly beneficial to the UDSR because of the opportunities that it offered for playing off allies against each other: 'It is why I say that the interests of our party lie in an unswerving loyalty to the Rassemblement des Gauches, because, with these latest events that Lanet has just explained to us, it will be us who will in reality be the strongest ... because facing us we have do not have one Radical party, but really two opposed parties between which we will be the sovereign arbitrators.'[76] The

---

[72] LBD, 26 September 1944. Lecompte-Boinet described the exclusion of those who had voted full powers to Pétain as 'a swindle'.   [73] LBD, 30 September 1944.
[74] AN, 412 AP 4, Davaine speaking to party congress on 24 May 1947.
[75] AN, 412 AP 4, Avinin speaking to party congress on 24 May 1947.
[76] AN, 412 AP 13, Avinin speaking to *comité directeur*, 15 February 1950.

Radical Jean-Louis Anteriou reported on 8 April 1948 that 'the president of the UDSR wishes to prove the predominance of his party in the Rassemblement des Gauches Républicaines'.[77] The manner in which the UDSR was able to exploit divisions in the Radical party to its advantage was shown in Seine et Oise. Here the local UDSR deputy, Edouard Bonnefous, used RGR machinery in a conflict with the local Radical party. Not only did Bonnefous win his struggle, but he persuaded the prime minister, a Radical, to boycott the Radicals of Seine et Oise during the conflict.[78]

Thirdly, alliance with the Radicals was seen to be advantageous by leaders of the UDSR because they believed that the Radicals represented a permanent element in the French electorate. UDSR leaders knew that the Radical leaders were old and they hoped that this would leave a gap for them to fill. Avinin remarked: 'It is the legacy of the republican party in the country that we want. It is our party which in a few months or years will the heir of that great republican party between collectivism and confessionalism which our country cannot do without.'[79] On the same occasion, another speaker suggested that the UDSR would gain the support of 'the sons of Radicals'.[80]

The idea of the UDSR that the electorate of the Fourth Republic would need a centre party to fill the kind of gap that the Radicals had filled in the Third Republic was well founded as was their idea that the Radicals were old and that there was scope for some younger movement to take up the baton. However, the UDSR was conspicuously unsuccessful in filling this role. Though the RGR allowed the UDSR to gain great successes in the politics of government formation, the UDSR declined in electoral terms, at least in mainland France.

The electoral failure of the UDSR

A comparison between the UDSR and the MRP sheds light on the electoral failure of the former. UDSR leaders frequently blamed their poor performance on the competition provided by the MRP. Lanet explained the early history of his party thus: 'the operation was much more difficult than it would have been after the Liberation because of the place that the MRP has assumed in country'.[81] The UDSR leaders were not alone in their fear of MRP competition; almost all conservative parties believed that 'their

---

[77] AN, 373 AP 7, Anteriou to Bollaert, 8 April 1948.
[78] De Tarr, *The French Radical party*, p. 93. Bonnefous himself does not mention this unedifying conflict in his memoires. Bonnefous, *La vie de 1940 à 1970*.
[79] AN, 412 AP 4, Avinin speaking to party congress on 24 May 1947.
[80] Ibid. Combradet speaking.
[81] AN, 412 AP 4, 'Réflections sur l'UDSR' by J. Lanet, dated 8 July 1946.

voters' were being poached by the Christian Democrats. However, there were similarities between the UDSR and the MRP that made it particularly likely that the two parties would appeal to the same electorate. Both were new formations led by young men; both were unencumbered by the legacies of the Third Republic; both were able to claim the prestige associated with the Resistance; both might have been expected to appeal to those who were voting for the first time in 1945 (i.e. the majority of the electorate).

Furthermore, it was not just the UDSR leaders who believed that they and the Christian Democrats were competing for the same electorate. A speaker at the MRP *conseil national* of 26 August 1946 explained relations between the two parties in these terms: 'In this context I mention the situation in my Paris constituency where the UDSR, which will probably ally with the Socialist party, has roughly the same number of votes as us. I am convinced that these votes are more or less interchangeable and that the people who vote for the UDSR could just as well have voted for us. They are voting for a new formation.'[82]

There were two reasons for the failure of the UDSR to match the MRP in electoral terms. Firstly, the UDSR failed to exploit the single greatest change in French political life after the Liberation: the enfranchisement of women. The UDSR's obsessive desire to obtain the support of the 'sons of Radicals' led it to neglect their wives and daughters. In theory the UDSR should have been well placed to obtain the votes of women. Public opinion surveys and local studies showed that women were more influenced by the personality of candidates than by 'ideological considerations'. This should have benefited the UDSR, which contained a number of prominent individuals but lacked a coherent doctrine. The UDSR might also have been expected to gain female votes because it was a new formation that was not associated with the all-male political world of the Third Republic; because it was not anti-clerical and because it was associated with General de Gaulle (or perhaps more importantly not associated with anti-Gaullism).

On its own, the UDSR was attractive to women voters. In the 1951 legislative election in Vienne (the only occasion on which an exclusively UDSR list was presented in a constituency where male and female votes were counted separately) over half of the UDSR's supporters were women.[83] However, the UDSR rarely presented independent lists. Usually its candidates stood on joint RGR lists and this condemned it to association with the Radicals (the party that was least attractive to women voters).

[82] AN, 350 AP 56, Max André speaking to *conseil national* of MRP on 26 August 1946.
[83] P. Barral, 'Pour qui votent les femmes à Vienne?', in François Goguel (ed.), *Nouvelles études de sociologie électorale* (Paris, 1954), pp. 185–193.

Furthermore, the UDSR never seems to have appreciated the potential benefits that it might have derived from female suffrage. The party leaders seem to have shared the Radical party's mixture of suspicion and condescension towards women voters. Madame Corinne of the Rassemblement des Femmes Républicaines told the party conference that MRP success could be attributed to: 'the effect of the confessional on women who are perhaps not at all interested in politics, but who receive the order to go to vote'. Madame Corinne's only solution to this problem was to urge 'You should never accept the membership of man unless it is accompanied by the membership of his wife. It is necessary to get the two at the same time.'[84] The extent of the UDSR's failure to attract female votes was reflected in 1951 when the party put up a female candidate in Lozère – who voted against herself.[85]

The second reason for the electoral failure of the UDSR was to be found in its relations with the Resistance. The UDSR was not the only Resistance party but it was the party that was most explicitly and exclusively associated with the Resistance. This association created a gulf between the party leaders and the electorate. The UDSR leaders had joined the Resistance as young men and they took it for granted that they were an elite: they often regarded those Frenchmen who had not joined Resistance organizations, and indeed those Frenchmen who had joined Resistance organizations late in the war, with contempt, and expected their compatriots to regard them with fear. Jacques Lecompte-Boinet wrote in his diary in September 1944: 'The whole nation is made up of 10 per cent of *résistants* and 90 per cent of the spineless.'[86]

The UDSR obsession with its Resistance past induced bemusement in most voters. Claude Bourdet wrote: 'At that time one needed a Resistance title to be involved in politics, but the voter was not interested in subtleties, and it was not important to him whether such and such a candidate had played a really fundamental role in clandestine work.'[87] Furthermore, emphatic association with the Resistance came to mean, in the minds of many conservative voters, association with measures taken against Pétainists – purges, newspaper seizures and the ineligibility laws. The UDSR was unfortunate in being blamed for such measures. In practical terms the

[84] AN, 412 AP 4, Madame Corinne speaking to Party Congress on 24 March 1947. This speech was greeted by a shout of 'what about freedom?' from a member of the audience, but it is not clear whether the heckler was defending the freedom of women or that of men who wished to leave their wives at home. For the assumptions of the UDSR leaders about female voters see also C. Bourdet, *L'aventure incertaine de la résistance à la restauration* (Paris, 1975), p. 395.

[85] Williams, *Politics in post-war France*, p. 322: 'In Lozère the two UDSR candidates, a husband and wife, had only one vote between them – the husband's it was alleged.'

[86] LBD, 23 September 1944.   [87] Bourdet, *L'aventure incertaine*, p. 405.

UDSR did everything to help former Pétainists: it voted for amnesty laws, it allied with the parties led by ineligibles in the RGR, it supported the candidacy of Antoine Pinay (a member of Pétain's *conseil national*) for the premiership. The problem was that the UDSR did not claim credit for such achievements. On the contrary UDSR propagandists painted a misleading picture of their party as a representative of Robespierran justice.

The trial of Marshal Pétain showed how vulnerable the UDSR could be to the unpopularity of the *épuration*. Baumel, who was general secretary of propaganda in the UDSR, remarked that the Pétain trial had had more of an effect on the political reputation of the Resistance than 'all the Resistance's activity and propaganda since the Liberation'.[88] These words were true, but not in the sense that Baumel meant them. For Pétain had been regarded with almost religious adoration only a few years previously, and even if intervening events had destroyed the belief that the Marshal was an omniscient saint, it is hard to believe that a majority of Frenchmen regarded him as a traitor who deserved to be shot. The diaries of Lecompte-Boinet, who was both a founder of the UDSR and a juror in the Pétain trial, show an awareness of the political damage that the trial did. Lecompte-Boinet himself had doubts about the legality of the trial, but he knew that it would be impossible to distance himself from the verdict. He also knew that henceforth he would be labelled a 'Pétainicide'[89] and that this would wreck his political career: 'From an electoral point of view, my presence at this trial completely ruins my position.'[90]

The UDSR and the RPF

The formation of the RPF brought problems to all the bourgeois political formations, but it caused particular difficulty for the UDSR. A number of the UDSR leaders were loyal Gaullists: two of them, Soustelle and Baumel, were also leaders of the RPF. Many of the UDSR deputies had been elected on tickets that included the word Gaullist. Some took it for granted that the UDSR would join with the new movement. Baumel told the UDSR congress of 1947: 'For most people, the UDSR was the preliminary to the Rassemblement du Peuple Français.'[91]

However, views such as this were not universal in the UDSR. Alongside the loud declarations of Gaullism, there was a more discreet current of anti-Gaullism in the party. De Gaulle's relations with the internal Resistance in France had often been strained; UDSR leaders like Jacques Lecompte-

---

[88] AN 412 AP 1, undated circular.
[89] LBD, 4 August 1945.   [90] LBD, 21 July 1945.
[91] AN, 412 AP 4, Baumel speaking to party congress of 24 May 1947.

Boinet[92] and François Mitterrand[93] had had memorably frigid meetings with the General in Algiers. Furthermore, the ruthlessness of de Gaulle's entourage, particularly Colonel Passy of the Gaullist intelligence service, had impressed many Resistance activists. In 1959, a UDSR militant recalled: 'General de Gaulle may not be a fascist ... but ... from 1940 he had some unpleasant characters in his entourage.'[94]

There was a third group of UDSR leaders who were motivated by neither Gaullism nor anti-Gaullism, but by a desire to hold their own group together. The dilemma of this group was particularly awkward. Not only did they have to balance between Gaullists and anti-Gaullists in their own party, they also had to balance the advantages and disadvantages of collaborating with the RPF from a purely tactical point of view. On the one hand the UDSR had ceased to be a party of systematic opposition in January 1946; two of its members, François Mitterrand and Pierre Bourdan, sat in the Ramadier cabinet and the departure of the Communist ministers from the government in April 1947 opened up the possibility of further ministerial participation with all its attendant benefits. On the other hand the RPF seemed to be riding the wave of an enormous popularity. Outright opposition to the new movement might well be fatal to the UDSR. Davaine told the party congress of 1947: 'hostility by the UDSR to the RPF would have been dangerous for the UDSR itself (much more than for the RPF). I think that in practice it would have killed the UDSR.'[95] On the other hand, collaboration with the RPF might allow the UDSR to establish some of the political roots that it so conspicuously lacked.

The aim of those Third Force leaders who were neither Gaullist nor anti-Gaullist was to avoid making a final decision between the RPF and the Third Force for as long as possible: 'The UDSR must not commit itself completely, but avoid taking a hostile position.'[96] Avinin made heroic efforts to prevent the issue of the RPF from being discussed at all at the party congress of 1947. *Double appartenance*, i.e. the toleration of UDSR members who belonged to another political formation, also helped to prevent the relations with the RPF from breaking up the UDSR.

Certain UDSR leaders maintained positions of studied ambiguity on the question of the RPF. Avinin hesitated about whether or not to join the Gaullist parliamentary inter-group for so long that eventually his name was printed on the list of members without his permission and had to be withdrawn.[97] Pleven carried out a delicate balancing act during this period.

[92] LBD, 14 November 1943. [93] Giesbert, *François Mitterrand*, p. 64.
[94] AN, 412 AP 13, M. Maseux speaking to 12th Congress of UDSR on 31 January 1959.
[95] AN, 412 AP 4, Davaine speaking to party congress of 24 May 1947.
[96] Secretary general of Loire Inférieure section speaking to a meeting of party cadres on 19 April 1947, cited in J. Charlot, *Le gaullisme d'opposition 1946–1958* (Paris, 1983), p. 97.
[97] Ibid., p. 99.

In order to maintain the support of Gaullists within his own party, he had to pretend to be a Gaullist acting through the UDSR. He arranged meetings with de Gaulle and made public statements that implied that he was seeking to act as a bridge between the parties in government and the RPF, and even that he was willing to bring down the government if it failed to respond to his overtures.

Pleven's double game was made difficult by de Gaulle's growing distrust,[98] and some shrewd observers saw through the act – Jacques Fauvet pointed out that Pleven only risked bringing about a ministerial crisis when he was quite certain that solutions to that crisis had already been prepared.[99] However, other well placed observers were taken in by Pleven's act. Vincent Auriol described him as 'not only a distinguished Gaullist, but a dangerous Gaullist and a perfect Jesuit'.[100] Jean-Louis Anteriou, a colleague of Pleven's in the RGR, considered the possibility that Pleven was trying to break up his political formation on de Gaulle's instruction: 'I do not know how far General de Gaulle, whose views are often echoed by monsieur Pleven, wishes to break up the RGR.'[101]

Pleven was fortunate in that one of the first issues on which politicians were obliged to choose between the RPF and its opponents related to the cantonal elections that were due to be held in 1948. The opponents of the RPF wished to defer these elections until 1951 so that they would not provide the Gaullists with a further victory of the kind that they had already obtained in the municipal elections of 1947. For a time the UDSR made themselves the principal opponents of this move; indeed, their minister threatened to resign from the government if it was implemented.[102] This tactic ensured that the Gaullists in the party were kept happy, but it was also acceptable to other sections of the party because the UDSR had done so badly in the cantonal elections of 1946 that they had nothing to lose through the holding of new elections as soon as possible.

The efforts of men like Avinin and Pleven to avoid presenting their members with a clear cut choice between the UDSR and the RPF could only last for a limited period. As the RPF threatened the system, and the parties behind that system refused to come to terms with the Gaullists, it became clear there was no possibility of compromise between the two forces. On 9 December 1948, the Gaullists finally departed from the UDSR leaving the party with only thirteen of its original twenty-seven parliamentary representatives.

---

[98] Ibid., p. 121.   [99] Cited in ibid., p. 123.   [100] Cited in ibid., p. 120.
[101] AN, 373 AP 7, Anteriou to Bollaert dated 6 April 1948.
[102] Charlot, *Le gaullisme d'opposition*, p. 127.

The UDSR as a party of government

At first glance, the history of the UDSR is one of unrelieved failure. The party that had begun by claiming to be the incarnation of the spirit of the Resistance obtained only a small number of seats in the 1946 election, it saw this representation halved by defections to the RPF and, in the 1951 election, it lost support again to make it one of the least significant groups in the National Assembly. However, the party's history can be looked at from another perspective. As the UDSR's electoral significance diminished, its ministerial importance increased. UDSR members held ministerial office six times between 1947 and 1951, and four times in the 1951–56 legislature. Furthermore, they held important offices: Pleven held the premiership twice; Mitterrand was minister of the interior in 1954.

The ministries that the UDSR gained were not only prestigious. They were also important because many of them provided their holders with considerable opportunities for building up a clientele. The ministry of reconstruction, held by Pleven, and the ministry of *anciens combattants*, held by Mitterrand in 1946, both involved spending public money in ways that could bring great benefit to favoured individuals. The ministry of the interior, held by Mitterrand in 1954, was able to exercise influence at election time through its control of departmental prefects. Mitterrand proved particularly adept at using access to government favours to establish networks of patronage. In 1950 Mitterrand proposed that the definition of *anciens déportés* should be widened to include those who had performed *service travail obligatoire* in Germany. Such a move would have widened Mitterrand's own pool of support (he was closely linked to the *anciens déportés* movement) but, as his indignant colleagues pointed out, it would also have ensured that all reference to the Resistance was removed from the concept of deportation.[103]

The electoral advantage in mainland France that could be extracted from office holding was real, but limited. Mitterrand could ensure that his own position in the Nièvre was secure, but he could not do much to increase the total number of UDSR deputies in parliament. However, in the overseas constituencies things were very different. Powers of patronage in the overseas departments were much greater and the minister of colonies could exercise a greater influence. As a stalwart of many governments, the UDSR could usually count on the support of the administration in elections. Furthermore, UDSR members made great efforts to capture the unglamorous but vital post of minister for colonial affairs. Edouard Bonnefous

[103] AN, 412 AP 13, *comité directeur* of party, 15 February 1950.

refused the ministry of justice in the Schuman cabinet, but he let it be known that would have accepted the ministry of colonies.[104] When Pleven became prime minister he appointed Mitterrand as minister for colonies.

Those who left the UDSR in 1946 and 1947 heaped bitter criticism on their former party. They suggested that its association with the RGR and its membership of numerous conservative cabinets had compromised the ideals of the Resistance, and they ridiculed the status of a party that could only muster a dozen or so supporters in parliament. However, these critics had led sheltered lives. Those, like Henri Frenay and Claude Bourdet, whose political activity was conducted through an informal study group, or those, like Baumel and Soustelle, who joined the RPF, never faced the problem of trying to put their fine words into practice. Safe in opposition or outside party politics altogether, they could afford to make impossible demands, and they could ignore the divisions that existed within their own political formations.

The UDSR did not enjoy the luxury of opposition. It leaders had to live with the compromises of politics and to take responsibility for the actions of governments which they supported. The change of spirit that is evident when reading UDSR documents over the period 1946 to 1951 can be presented as a sign of maturity rather than decadence. The naive young men of 1945 had become worldly and realistic. The party no longer worried about its lack of ideological coherence. This was not because the UDSR had acquired an ideology but because its leaders had come to realize that parties could be help together by pragmatic self-interest more effectively than by doctrine. The change can be illustrated by two quotations. In 1946 a speaker at the party congress had remarked that the UDSR needed 'a new Karl Marx'; in 1949 the UDSR deputy for Seine et Oise gave a speech at the banquet of his local party in which he suggested that the party should look to a model of realism and moderation: 'If we had to bring someone back to this earth, it would not be Karl Marx or Proudhon that we would call, but that good and intelligent M. de Palice who represents the French spirit so well.'[105]

Judged against the realities of history rather than the hopes of the Liberation the UDSR looks rather a successful party. A group with no roots in the country, no tradition or reputation, succeeded making itself a regular part of government formation. The inexperienced young men who had emerged from the Resistance turned themselves into seasoned Tammany Hall politicians in a few years. François Mitterrand's construction of an electoral clientele for himself and Pleven's bluffing of the Gaullists were brilliant examples of political gamesmanship. As an attempt to challenge

[104] Bonnefous, *Avant l'oubli*, p. 93.
[105] A. Marès, *Un siècle à travers trois républiques. Georges et Edouard Bonnefous 1880–1980* (Paris, 1980), p. 209.

the political system of the Fourth Republic, the UDSR was a failure; but when it took to operating that system it was a dazzling success.

The Radical party

The Parti Républicain Radical et Radical-Socialiste (Radical party) was the oldest political party in France. It had been founded in 1901, but in 1945 it looked as if it was not likely to last much longer. The party did badly in the legislative elections of 1945 and 1946, when important party leaders like Henri Queuille were defeated. Members of rival parties could always earn an easy round of applause at meetings by denouncing the Radical party.

The unpopularity of the Radical party sprang partly from its recent past. The Radicals were compromised by the disdain in which the Third Republic was held: they were blamed for being the linchpin of a system that had overseen French decline and led France to defeat in 1940. They were also discredited by the occupation. Radical leaders indignantly pointed to the Resistance record of their group,[106] but their claims cut little ice at the Liberation. The kind of Resistance in which the Radicals had indulged was a political and legal Resistance; it did not have the glamour of the military action that had been taken against the German forces. Radical politicians did not have exciting code names left over from their wartime careers; they did not look like men who had brandished sten guns or clambered into Lysander aircraft in the small hours of the morning. Henry Frenay, leader of Combat, had written during the occupation: 'It would be absurd to claim ... that men died for the Radical party or the Alliance Démocratique.'[107] When a Radical party pamphlet described Edouard Herriot – the aged and portly mayor of Lyons – as the 'the most prestigious *résistant* of mainland France',[108] it showed how widely the Radical conception of Resistance differed from that of most of the party's political rivals.[109]

Most importantly the Radicals did not suit the spirit of the times in 1944. The Liberation was a period of idealism and youthful optimism; the Radical party was led by old men and marked by worldly cynicism. Many believed that the future would belong to organized parties with coherent doctrines and large numbers of well-disciplined militants; the Radicals' organization was notoriously lax and most of their members denied that

---

[106] *Patrie et liberté. Le Parti Radical Socialiste pendant la Résistance* (Paris, no date).
[107] Article published on 21 August 1943, republished in *Voilà la Résistance* (Paris, 1945), p. 67.   [108] *Patrie et liberté*, p. 6.
[109] On the unsuitability of the Radical party for clandestine organization see *Esprit*, 80 (May 1939) cited in Williams, *Politics in post-war France*, p. 105. On legal resistance and the tendency of post-war commentators to disparage such activity see C. Andrieu, 'Paul Ramadier, un exemple de résistance légale 1940–1944', in S. Bernstein (ed.), *Paul Ramadier, la république et le socialisme* (Paris, 1992), pp. 185–221.

they had a doctrine at all. Furthermore, it seemed likely that France would move towards the two party system of Anglo-Saxon states and this was bound to reduce the influence of the Radicals who had always benefited from their ability to swing behind either right or left.

To some extent all the perceived problems listed above were short-term ones linked to the circumstances of the Liberation and to misconceptions about the pattern that politics would assume in the Fourth Republic. However, the Radical party also faced a more serious long-term problem: the erosion of its electorate. The Radicals had a predominantly male electorate: the party's anti-clericalism and periodic anti-Gaullism,[110] its roots in the period before women had been enfranchised and its social life of banquets, cafés and rough camaraderie excluded women. The party also had the oldest electorate in France; it drew its support from the non-industrial areas of the south-west where the birth rate was low and departures from the land were frequent. The average age of shopkeepers (a group traditionally associated with Radicalism) was high, and the new-comers who entered this profession after the war were young men in a hurry who did not fit into the culture of Radicalism: they were easily seduced by more aggressive groups like the RPF in the 1940s or Poujadism in the 1950s.

Most importantly, the political issue that had held Radicalism together – anti-clericalism – condemned the party to a declining electorate. The problem was not, as Williams suggests, that the anti-clerical issue had been settled by the separation of church and state.[111] The church question continued to haunt Fourth Republic politics because of the debate over state subsidies to church schools; indeed, church–state relations came up rather more frequently than some Radical leaders would have liked. The problem that the Radicals faced was the growing secularization of French society: religious practice was giving way to what Georges le Bras called 'seasonal conformity'.[112] People regarded the church as a social institution rather than a focus of belief and attended on certain public occasions: marriages, baptisms, funerals. This development worried many priests for obvious reasons. But 'seasonal conformity' also had dangerous implications for the Radical party. Alongside the decline in religious devotion was a decline in active distaste for religion. The proportion of people who attended church regularly was dropping but the proportion of people who made it a point of honour never to set foot in church was also falling. Local surveys reflected the change. In Vienne increasing proportions of people were married in church, had their children baptized in church and were

[110] On the basis of sexual differences in voting patterns see chapter 5.
[111] Williams, *Politics in post-war France*, p. 91.
[112] G. le Bras, 'Géographie électorale et géographie religieuse', in C. Morazé (ed.), *Etudes de sociologie électorale* (Paris, 1947).

buried in church. In 1921 the proportions of people baptized, married and buried according to religious rites were 74.1 per cent, 73.2 per cent and 68.6 per cent respectively; by 1949 the comparable figures were 90.3 per cent, 77.9 per cent and 75.1 per cent.[113] Furthermore, the fact that marriage and baptism (events that involved the young) were more likely to take place in church than funerals (events that generally involved the old) suggested that the natural constituency of Radicalism was dying out.

Sociologists in Auxerre (which had been notorious for anti-clericalism) found similar trends: 'now, militant anti-clericalism has not only lost its virulence, but seems to have few supporters in the town'.[114] The proportion of burials conducted according to religious rites in Auxerre was, as in Vienne, smaller than the proportion of marriages that took place in church.[115] Philippe Bernard's study of Seine et Marne observed similar tendencies: the *opposants de principe* who participated in no religious act were less and less frequent, and attitudes to religion were characterized by 'indifference rather than opposition'.[116] Non-believers were more likely to regard their local church as an aesthetic curiosity than as a centre of superstition and reaction; by 1950 town councils in the traditionally anti-clerical area of Provins often gave money for church restoration funds.[117]

Despite its short-term political problems and its long-term electoral problems, the Radical party survived and prospered in the early Fourth Republic. Although the party vote declined slightly between 1945 and 1951 (from 8.5 per cent to 8 per cent), the number of deputies that it managed to get elected with that vote increased: in October 1945 the Radicals had won twenty-four seats in mainland France; in 1951 they won sixty-eight seats on the mainland and, eventually, both houses of parliament were presided over by Radicals. Radical leaders regained their position at the centre of the political stage, they became an indispensable part in the negotiations

---

[113] Clément and Xydias, *Vienne sur le Rhône*, pp. 171–173.

[114] Charles Bettelheim and Suzanne Frère, *Une ville française moyenne. Auxerre en 1950. Etude de structure sociale et urbaine* (Paris, 1950), p. 240.

[115] Ibid., p. 245. Bettelheim and Frère argue that more people were married in church than buried in church because of the fact that a proportion of married couples deferred to the religious sensibilities of their future spouse. For the purposes of our argument it should be pointed out that a willingness to defer to the wishes of a future spouse is itself evidence of the absence of militant anti-clericalism. It should also be stressed that Bettelheim, Clément and Xydias all ignore two things that would normally have inflated the number of religious funerals: firstly, women (especially old women) were generally considered more devout than men and since most women outlived their husbands most funerals must have been arranged by women; secondly, the demographic shadow of the First World War would normally have meant that an exceptionally high proportion of those left to die of natural causes during the late 1940s and early 1950s would have been women.

[116] Philippe Bernard, *Economie et sociologie de la Seine-et-Marne 1850–1950* (Paris, 1953), p. 196.   [117] Ibid., p. 199.

leading to the formation of any government, and they frequently headed the governments that resulted from such negotiations. How did the Radicals achieve this recovery?

The first advantage that the Radical party possessed in 1945 lay in the support that it traditionally enjoyed from local notables. Notables could alleviate the effects of a shrinking electorate by arranging alliances that made the most efficient use of whatever support the Radicals had. A key forum for the exercise of notable power was the departmental *conseil général* (a body that was elected at cantonal level where personal reputation and influence counted for much). The Radicals lost ground at cantonal level after the Liberation (they presided over two *conseils généraux* in 1945 compared to forty-five in 1939),[118] but the damage was less severe than that which the party suffered at national level. Seven hundred and thirty-four *conseillers généraux* (i.e. around 25 per cent of the total) elected after the Liberation were veterans of the Third Republic and 39.5 per cent of these men were Radicals.[119]

It was not just good fortune and traditional links that maintained notable help for the Radical party. Support was cultivated and earned. While the leaders of other parties were pontificating about grand schemes for national and international renewal, Radicals like Edgar Faure made active efforts to establish contacts in their constituencies and to win the support of local notables, including those who had formerly supported other parties.[120] In some respects the very qualities that seemed to make the Radical party weak in the immediate aftermath of the Liberation proved to be sources of strength in the long term. Firstly, the weak organization of the Radical party meant that it did not bruise sensitivities by trying to impose national discipline on important men. Indeed, local party sections were able to form whatever alliances suited local circumstances while the national leadership disclaimed all responsibility for such manoeuvres. Thus when Paul-Boncour, a right-wing socialist who had strong links with the RGR,[121] complained that Radicals in the Loir et Cher were campaigning for the PRL in opposition to himself,[122] the national leadership of the Radical party were able to disclaim all responsibility for the actions of their local

---

[118] Marie-Hélène Marchand, *Les conseillers généraux en France depuis 1945* (Paris, 1970), p. 80.   [119] Ibid., p. 52.

[120] For example André Baud, an eminent conservative in the Jura, was won over to the Radical party after many hours of persuasion by Edgar Faure.

[121] Paul-Boncour claimed in a declaration dated 4 December 1946 that he had actually been asked by the RGR to head their electoral list (AN, 424 AP 40).

[122] Letter by Paul-Boncour to *Nouvelle République* and the *République du Centre* dated 9 December 1946.

membership.[123] Secondly, the fact that the Radicals were not seen as a Resistance party meant that they did not usually suffer as a result of the resentment aroused by measures taken to punish former Pétainists.

Henri Queuille provides an example of the effort that Radical leaders made to maintain local support. Queuille was a well established figure in the Corrèze, where he had first held office as a member of the *conseil général* in 1912. He was also a national politician who became prime minister three times between 1948 and 1951. However, Queuille's national activities never led him to neglect his local power base. He spent a good deal of time in his constituency: during the 1951 election he excused himself from important business in Paris to address 186 meetings in his own area.[124] The results of Queuille's activities were seen at elections. Immediately after the war, Queuille had lost his own seat in the general rout of the Radical party, but by 1951 his position in the Corrèze had been so successfuly rebuilt that the leaders of the MRP (not a party noted for pragmatism) sought to conclude an *apparentement* with Queuille and even asked his advice about their own choice of candidate.[125] Queuille's tact could also be seen at national level. Edouard Bonnefous gave the following description of his colleague: 'He is ... subtlety itself ... always affable and courteous, he knows how to reconcile opposites, avoid wounding and, by a smile, prevent a discussion from becoming bitter. He always seems resolved to follow you. But do not be deceived, this polite colleague ... has firm views and it is his great political intelligence that makes him want to convince you rather than contradict you.'[126]

One aspect of Queuille's post-war career is particularly striking. He had a distinguished career in the Resistance. However, after the war he rarely referred to this career in his political campaigns. He politely excused himself

---

[123] AN, 424 AP 40, Bollaert to Paul-Boncour dated 3 December 1947, and unsigned letter to Paul-Boncour of 5 February 1948 (424 AP 41) in which reference is made to Queuille having talked of problems in Loir et Cher. In fact the claim by the national leadership of the Radical party that their local section was out of control was disingenuous. Hermann, the RGR candidate in Loir et Cher, had been sent into the area from Paris: indeed he made a most unusual declaration in which he stressed that he was an outsider and that his candidature was 'political' (declaration made by Hermann on 8 December 1946 in AN, 424 AP 40). For all their protestations of sympathy, Radical leaders did nothing to discipline the Radicals who opposed Paul-Boncour and it seems likely that they welcomed the confusion in Loir et Cher because it provided them with a chance to gain allies on both left and right while disclaiming reponsibility for both.

[124] Archives of Henri Queuille, Neuvic d'Ussel, D5 , letter from Queuille to Petsche dated 20 May 1951.

[125] AN, 457 AP 175, Fontenau to Bidault dated 8 May 1951. Fontenau wished to know whether Queuille would find Victor Faure acceptable as a candidate and also whether, in the event of Faure being elected, Queuille would permit the MRP to replace Faure in his position as mayor of a local town.   [126] Bonnefous, *Avant l'oubli*, p. 100.

from acting as a juror in the Pétain trial,[127] avoided sitting on the *comité départemental de libération*,[128] and did his best to help a number of people who had been hurt by post-war measures against Pétainists.[129] Queuille conducted a friendly correspondence with *abbé* Desgranges, the campaigner for the rights of Pétainists,[130] and he lent discreet support to Jacques Isorni's Union des Nationaux et Indépendants Républicains that defended the record of the Vichy government in the 1951 elections.[131] The result of this forbearance was that Queuille, unlike so many other Resistance politicians, never aroused the resentment of power-brokers who had been damaged by the purges or by post-war ineligibility laws; the former Vichy supporters in the AD asked Queuille to succeed Cudenet as president of the RGR.[132]

Administrative pressure on elections

The second advantage that the Radical party had in the Fourth Republic was their tradition and experience as a party of government. The Radicals had learned in the Third Republic of the advantages that support from the administrative apparatus of the state could confer during election times. Furthermore, even though the Radicals were out of power during the first few years of the Fourth Republic, many important civil servants in the ministry of the interior had begun their career during the Third Republic under Radical party aegis, and such men continued to dominate local prefectures.[133] As the break up of tripartism made the Radicals a 'hinge party' once again, party leaders regained their power to secure advantageous positions in government. The ministry of the interior, a traditional Radical fiefdom during the Third Republic, was dominated by the Socialists for several years, but in October 1949 a Radical, Queuille, returned to the ministry of the interior and thereafter the Radicals did not allow this

---

[127] Queuille archives, D5, 12 June 1945, Queuille to Paul-Boncour.

[128] Queuille archives, C 19, president of CDL to Queuille dated 15 January 1946 and Queuille to president of CDL (Caulet) dated 20 January 1945. The precise reasons why Queuille never sat on the CDL are somewhat unclear. Queuille himself claimed that he had not been told that he was eligible, though his correspondence also makes it clear that he was not on good terms with the leaders of the CDL.

[129] Ibid. Note by Queuille dated 30 November 1945 expressing hope that a former aide of his would not be suspended from his functions in the town hall after having been removed from the ministry of the interior.

[130] Queuille archives, D5, Desgranges to Queuille, dated 20 July 1951.

[131] Isorni, *Mémoires*. II: *1946–1958*, p. 208.

[132] BN, AD 4, Ventenat report on policy since the Liberation to party congress of 12 May 1950.

[133] AN, 457 AP 135, a note in the Bidault archives on the political situation on 11/12 January 1948 reveals that, even after a recent reshuffle of prefects by the Socialist minister of the interior Jules Moch, the vast majority of prefects were still men of Radical temperament.

vital post to come under the control of anyone except themselves or their RGR allies for the next seven years.[134]

Emile Bollaert, who became a prefect in Alsace in 1945, was an example of the role that Radical prefects could play in the promotion of their party's interests. His colleague René Paira wrote with some irritation in his memoirs that 'Bollaert was always courteous but . . . very much a Radical of the Third Republic. He always had a finger raised to take the direction of the wind.' Paira recounted how Bollaert had tried to persuade him to declare the candidature of a local MRP politician invalid.[135] Michel Debré, a Radical who had defected to the RPF, found out how useful the control of the ministry of the interior could be when he attempted to have himself elected in a cantonal by-election of 1950: pressure from the Radical minister of the interior forced his local backers to withdraw their support and Debré was obliged to give up.[136]

The Radicals devoted particular effort to the management of elections in overseas France. They did not control the colonial ministry for most of the Fourth Republic, but they did manage to ensure that Radical supporters were frequently appointed to administrative positions in the colonies. The loyal Bollaert was made high commissioner to Indo-China in 1946. He wrote to Henri Queuille in terms that left no doubt about his willingness to use his position for political ends: 'In the light of the information Robert Schuman gives you, let me know, in the name of the Radical party, what I should do.'[137] He was kept in touch with domestic politics, and particularly with the life of the Radical party, by his contact in Paris, Jean-Louis Anteriou. In March 1948 Anteriou asked his superior to arrange the appointment of Poussard (a former sub-prefect who had had 'quelques difficultés avec l'épuration') as secretary general for Indo-China. Poussard had been recommended by the Radical leader Emile Roche.[138] Anteriou's correspondence also makes it clear why the Radicals cared so much about who exercised influence in Indo-China. Considerable attention was devoted to the organization of the Radical party in the colony,[139] and on 9 April 1948 Anteriou reported that he had been asked to direct delegates from Indo-China to the RGR.[140]

---

[134] Jacques Isorni wrote of his decision to stand in the 1951 elections: 'I was more and more linked to Henri Queuille. He was minister of the interior and prime minister at the time of the elections. One could not wish for more.' Isorni, *Mémoires*. II: *1946–1958*, p. 163.

[135] René Paira, *Affaires d'Alsace* (Paris, 1990), p. 184.

[136] M. Debré, *Trois républiques pour une France. Mémoires*. II: *1946–1958. Agir*, Paris, 1988, p. 111.   [137] Queuille archives, D1, Bollaert to Queuille, 10 February 1948.

[138] AN, 373 AP 7, Anteriou to Bollaert, dated 13 March 1948.

[139] AN, 373 AP 7, 'Transmission d'une lettre de M. Dubourg chargé de la réorganisation du Parti Radical en Cochinchine', dated 6 April 1948.

[140] AN, 373 AP 7, Anteriou to Bollaert dated 9 April 1948.

Support from the administration was also important to the Radicals in Algeria. This was the political base of René Mayer, who benefited from the support of local administrators such as the prefect Papon. Mayer was careful to cultivate a local clientele in Constantine, his constituency, and he became so powerful there that an MRP candidate wrote to his party's leaders in Paris that he would have to adjust the MRP electoral list to fit in with Mayer's wishes.[141] Politics, administration and business were intimately connected in Algeria, and the Radicals used their leverage to attract the support of powerful local magnates, such as Borgeaud, who could provide funds and swing newspapers behind the party.[142] This kind of support allowed the Radicals to acquire strength in the most unexpected of areas. An article in a party newspaper even claimed that a branch of the RGR had been formed in a south Saharan oasis: the article was accompanied by an improbable photograph of Radical leaders drinking Dubonnet with bemused Bedouin elders.[143]

The second strength of the Radical party lay in its capacity for making alliances. During the first five years of the Fourth Republic, the Radicals were allied with the Communist party, on the extreme left of the spectrum, the PRL, on the extreme right of the spectrum, and the variety of centre parties that made up the RGR. The Radicals were never too proud or too ideologically strict to seek help from other forces. The fact that the party was founded on notables rather than a mass organization of militants facilitated such alliances. Earnest party members in the MRP or the SFIO often protested against and undermined the deals done by their leaders in Paris, but the Radical notables were themselves masters of the electoral deal. Indeed, the high degree of autonomy exercised by local power barons in the Radical party often proved an electoral advantage because it allowed arrangements to be concluded according to local circumstance.

The first alliance that the Radicals entered after the war was with the Communist party. On the face of it this seemed the most bizarre of all alliances given that the Communist party were soon to become the pariahs of the Fourth Republic and that the Radical party was to provide some of the most vehement leaders of anti-Communism. The Radical/Communist alliance was rooted partly in their dissimilarity. On the whole, the small property owners who supported the Radical party were not prone to vote Communist and the workers who provided the backbone of the Communist electorate were not likely to vote for the Radicals: the absence of electoral competition facilitated co-operation. The alliance was also based on certain shared rhetoric. In very general terms both parties made much of

---

[141] AN, 457 AP 175, Agarde to Bidault, dated May 1951.
[142] Daniel Leconte, *Les pieds noirs. Histoire et portrait d'une communauté* (Paris, 1980), p. 165.   [143] 'Un cercle RGR dans le sud algérien', *l'Unité Française*, May 1949.

the Jacobin heritage, and such rhetoric could seem important at a time when neither party was in much of a position to enact policy on a more day to day basis. However, what united the two parties most effectively was not their beliefs, but their lack of beliefs. The Radicals and the Communists were the only two parties to have remained immune to the illusions about a new *travailliste* politics emerging from the Resistance. Throughout the post-Liberation period the Radicals kept their eyes fixed firmly on the Third Republic past, and the Communists kept their eyes on the revolutionary future. This left both parties free to pursue their short-term tactical interests. In 1945, it suited the Radicals to ally with a stronger party that was seen to possess impeccable Resistance credentials, and it suited the Communist party to give the impression of being part of a broad Popular Front alliance

The Communist alliance broke up when the Radicals entered the RGR in 1946, but it had already served its purpose by helping to tide the Radicals over their most difficult period. In the process of the break up the Radicals also lost a certain number of their members. Cot, Meunier and Dreyfus-Schmidt all subsequently operated as part of 'progressive' alliances with the Communist party. But even the loss of parliamentary supporters may not have unduly distressed the Radical leadership, who must have known that high principles would be dangerous in the political manoeuvres that lay ahead.

The Radicals and the RPF

The Radicals derived considerable benefits from their relations with the RPF. At first glance the fact that such relations existed at all seems strange. It is hard to imagine two doctrines more different than Radicalism and Gaullism. The Radicals looked back to the constitution of 1875 while de Gaulle looked forward to the constitution of 1958. The Radicals believed in parliament; de Gaulle believed in a strong presidency. The Radicals believed in the liberal economy; de Gaulle put forward a variety of plans controlling or transcending capitalism. The Radicals (or their traditional supporters) were anti-clerical; de Gaulle supported state subsidies to church schools. The Radicals seemed to incarnate the short-term opportunistic *politique à la petite semaine* that de Gaulle despised.

In spite of all this there were Radical Gaullists. Some of these men were motivated by genuine conviction. Michel Debré and Jacques Chaban-Delmas were the most prominent representatives of this group. Both were young (born in 1912 and 1914 respectively) and both men had begun their careers in de Gaulle's Free French movement. Debré and Chaban had joined the Radical party simply because it seemed a useful vehicle for their careers (Chaban-Delmas described his relations with the party as 'un mariage de raison'),[144] and their Radicalism had always lacked conviction. Perhaps lack of conviction would not have caused much trouble with their Radical colleagues, if it were not for the fact that Chaban-Delmas and Debré did preserve strong loyalties to de Gaulle (Debré had said in 1947 that he was a 'microphone for the General').[145] It was inevitable that the convinced Gaullists would leave the Radical party when their political master founded the RPF, and there was probably nothing (short of dissolving their own party) that the Radical leaders could have done to keep them.

Alongside the convinced Gaullists was a much more important group of men who found it useful to play along with Gaullism for electoral or tactical reasons. The most prominent member of this group was Giacobbi. Giacobbi came from Corsica (which had a strong bonapartist/Gaullist tradition) so there was an electoral advantage for him to gain from association with de Gaulle. In addition to this, Giacobbi was the only Radical represented in de Gaulle's first government, and his willingness to co-operate with de Gaulle therefore fitted in with a long Radical tradition of governmentalism (even though his presence in the government was condemned by jealous party colleagues and almost led to his expulsion from the party). Giacobbi played an important part in the formation of the RPF and he joined several colleagues in abstaining when a government led by André Marie was formed in July 1948, and when the Queuille government was formed in September 1948.

Not surprisingly, the refusal of Gaullists to support governments led by Radicals caused some ill-feeling in the Radical party. However, the Radicals tolerated *double appartenance* or 'political bigamy', as some party leaders described it. They gained two advantages from such a stance. Firstly, they avoided driving their own Gaullist members of parliament out of their party. Secondly, they gained certain electoral advantages from association with the Gaullists.

In electoral terms the Gaullists were especially important to the Radicals in 1947 and 1948 because the refusal of the government to call a general legislative election forced the RPF to present their case through a series of local elections: first the municipal elections of 1947, then the cantonal elections (to the departmental *conseils généraux*) that were scheduled for 1948, then the senatorial elections of 1948. Local institutions and particularly the *conseils généraux* were the political strongholds of the Radical party and, for a time, the astonishing success of the RPF seemed to present

---

[144] Jacques Chaban-Delmas, *L'ardeur* (Paris, 1975), p. 135.
[145] Cited in de Tarr, *The French Radical party*, p. 136.

a threat to this stronghold. In particular it seemed likely that the local notables on whom Radical influence was built would be forced to defect to the RPF.

However, though the Radicals could only lose in an outright confrontation with the Gaullists, they could win by means of an alliance with the RPF. The Radicals were experts at playing local politics and striking deals with notables. The RPF, by contrast, was led by naive men who had often only recently emerged from the Resistance, army or administration. They had little experience of national politics and almost no experience of local politics; furthermore, they often despised the glad-handing and back-scratching that was necessary to keep local notables happy. Not surprisingly when Radicals and the RPF collaborated in drawing up electoral lists, the former usually arranged things to give themselves the better part of the deal. In the municipal elections 25 per cent of Radical lists were formed in alliance with RPF candidates and the Radicals obtained 20.5 per cent of the votes (compared to the 8 per cent of the vote that they had gained in the legislative election of 1946).

The cantonal elections that were scheduled for 1948 posed a more awkward problem for the Radical leadership. They had a great deal to lose at cantonal level, yet if they supported the call of some Third Force parties (such as the MRP) for the elections to be deferred they would suffer from RPF hostility and also annoy their own allies in the UDSR. The problem was made even more acute by the fact that the economic policies of René Mayer had antagonized the *classes moyennes* who made up the electoral basis of the Radicals and encouraged many Radical supporters to turn to Gaullism. Jean-Louis Anteriou wrote on 8 April 1948 that 'The RPF takes a terrible toll among the Radicals, its demands grow with our concessions. The RPF federation in Nantes has just told the anti-marxist *conseillers généraux* that they must resign from their party and join the RPF or else face electoral competition from the Gaullists.'[146]

Fortunately for the Radicals, Queuille was eventually able to defer the cantonal elections until 1949 without driving his UDSR colleagues out of the government. This meant that the senatorial elections of 1948 were fought in *conseils généraux* which were dominated by loyal Radical supporters. The power balance with the RPF was now reversed; instead of laying down terms, the RPF had to fight on ground that the Radicals controlled. Not surprisingly, the Radicals got the better of the electoral deals that were struck with the RPF in 1948. The RGR gained thirty-five senate seats, giving it seventy-nine seats in total and making it the largest

[146] AN, 373 AP 7, Anteriou to Bollaert, dated 8 April 1948.

party in the senate (twenty-six of its successful candidates were also members of the Gaullist inter-group).[147]

The tolerance that the Radicals extended to those of their members who flirted with Gaullism paid rich dividends. Whereas other parties drove their Gaullist members out with condemnations and harsh disciplinary measures that made future reconciliation impossible, the Radicals kept every possible door open for those who wished to return. Three things gradually drew Radicals back from the RPF. Firstly, the RPF's electoral star began to wane as it became obvious that legislative elections would be deferred (and eventually that they would be fought on terms that disadvantaged the RPF). Secondly, the advantages of belonging to the Radical party became ever more apparent as that party played an increasing part in the formation of governments and the consequent division of political spoils. Thirdly, the RPF itself began to impose discipline on its members – discipline that those used to the easy-going Radical party found intolerable. The RPF's disciplinary measures began to drive out Gaullist/Radicals in January 1949 when Jean Masson, a Radical deputy, resigned from the Gaullist inter-group in protest at the constraints imposed on him. In July of the same year another Radical deputy, Bégouin, was expelled from the RPF after a dispute over a candidacy in a cantonal election. This incident led Giacobbi, the most important Gaullist Radical, to resign from the RPF inter-group.

The Radicals were careful to give their returning prodigal sons a warm welcome. They knew that office holding was the most important bait that could be offered to Gaullists and they insisted that Giaccobbi be given a post in the Queuille government of July 1950. Even when the Radical party finally did force their members to make a final choice between the Radical party and the RPF in March 1951 they allowed the potential rebels three weeks to make up their mind, and they stressed that local electoral alliances with the RPF would still be permitted. The success of the delicate handling of Radical Gaullists was revealed in the statistics. The Radicals lost only one deputy, Chaban-Delmas, and only one senator, Debré.[148]

Neo-Radicalism

The survival of Radicalism was mainly the result of a successful defensive strategy: party leaders succeeded in holding on to existing votes, preventing deputies from defecting, and manipulating electoral alliances to the best

[147] For the details of the Radicals' performance in the elections of 1947 and 1948 see de Tarr, *The French Radical party*, p. 142.

[148] On the ways in which the Radicals wooed back their members who had been tempted by Gaullism, see de Tarr, *The French Radical party*, pp. 144–152.

possible effect. However, the Radical party also managed to conquer some new ground after 1946. This conquest was seen at two levels. Firstly, the Radical party acquired the allegiance of some promising politicians. In spite of its ageing clientele and leadership, the Radical party offered certain advantages to ambitious young men: it was possible to rise rapidly in the party without having to waste time building up a reputation among party militants. The Radical party was business-like in its attitude to new recruits; it recognized that young men who could offer ability, energy or the prestige of the Resistance were tradeable commodities and it was willing to woo them into the party with safe seats and privileged treatment. The result of all this was that though the Radical party parliamentary group was the oldest in the National Assembly, it also contained more deputies under the age of 35 than the Socialist or Conservative groups.[149]

The Radical party also conquered new ground at the electoral level. After 1945, a number of seats outside the traditional Radical strongholds were won. Edgar Faure in the Jura, André Morice in Nantes, Léon Martinaud-Déplat in Marseilles, Edouard Ramonet in Indre and Emile Hugues in the Alpes Maritimes were all based in areas that had not previously been associated with Radicalism. Most importantly seats were won in the Paris region: Dr Laffay won a constituency in right-bank bourgeois Paris in 1951 and Jean-Paul David was deputy for Seine et Oise from 1946.

The fact that all these men were based in new areas meant that they had to espouse a new kind of radicalism (what de Tarr called 'neo-Radicalism'). They had to win over electorates that were more conservative (or at least more prone to think of themselves as conservative) than the electorates of south-western France. Anti-clericalism had little appeal in these areas. Indeed, in the Jura and Brittany anti-clericalism was a positive disadvantage and Edgar Faure took the precaution of having a devout conservative peasant as one of his *co-listiers*. The so-called neo-Radicals were often among those members of the party who refused to vote down pro-church measures (such as the Ponsio-Chapius law) and some of them even joined the *comité d'action pour la liberté scolaire*.[150]

The neo-Radicals filled the gap left by the abandonment of anti-clericalism with an increased emphasis on economic matters. They proclaimed themselves to be liberals and attacked nationalization, *dirigisme* and excessive economic controls. In theory there was nothing new about this liberalism, except perhaps the need to proclaim it: the Radicals had always supported the unimpeded operation of capitalism. In practice, however, the liberalism that the neo-Radicals expounded after 1945

---

[149] Williams, *Politics in post-war France*, p. 100.
[150] Ibid., p. 330. The *comité d'action pour la liberté scolaire* contained a dozen members of the RGR.

involved measures to remove the special privileges and subsidies that had favoured small producers, especially farmers, and thus risked alienating the very groups that made up the bedrock of the party's support.

The emphasis on economics was seen to be connected to the close relations that some neo-Radicals had with the leaders of the *patronat* who financed the Radical party. Edgar Faure said of Dr Mazé: 'It was allowed to be understood in the corridors that he was better placed than anyone to refill the coffers of the place de Valois [the Radical party headquarters].'[151] René Mayer also had close relations with the *patronat* (he was himself a former employee of Rothschilds), and a good personal relationship with the main business paymaster of French politics – André Boutemy. Mayer later appointed Boutemy to a post in the cabinet and, among all the numerous Fourth Republic politicians who accepted money from Boutemy, Mayer seems to have been the only one who had the grace to say thank you. How close the relationships between the neo-Radicals and the *patronat* really were is harder to say. It was, after all, in the interests of many to denounce Radical leaders as having sold out to big business and it was occasionally in the interests of Radical leaders themselves to increase their authority within the party by hinting that they had access to secret resources. It is worth remembering that for all the talk of business links, the subsidy provided to the RGR by the Centre d'Etudes Economiques was relatively modest and that even Mayer, the Radical with the best documented business links, expressed the private belief that business was conspiring against him.[152]

The neo-Radicals won over new areas to their party and provided it with many of its most vigorous leaders. However, neo-Radicalism also generated new problems. There was a growing gulf between the Radical party's leaders and its traditional electorate. This was seen over the clerical question. As has been suggested, the secularization of post-war France meant that the clerical question was only of concern to a minority of the population, largely composed of old men from the backward areas of the south-west. The problem for the Radical party was that this group still made up a large proportion of their electorate. The attempts of the neo-Radicals to win new voters risked antagonizing the party's old supporters. This tension led Radical leaders to spend much of the 1940s trying to prevent the clerical question from being raised. Jean-Louis Anteriou wrote in 1948 of the dilemma that the Ponsio-Chapius law posed for a Radical colleague: 'On the one hand he cannot denounce laicism, but, on the other

[151] Faure, *Avoir toujours raison*, p. 152.
[152] Mayer believed that employers had refused to support him after the 1951 election; see note of 19 April 1952 in Denise Mayer (ed.), *René Mayer. Etudes, témoignages, documents* (Paris, 1983), p. 171.

hand, if he takes a clear position, he will have to abandon the nuanced policy that he has pursued since the Liberation.'[153]

Neo-Radicalism also alienated many Radicals for reasons connected with economic policy. Increasing numbers of the party leaders had constituencies in Paris or in industrial cities. Contacts with men like Boutemy made the Radical party ever more mindful of the interests of large-scale capitalism. However, industrialists and cadres were comparatively scarce in the Radical electorate. Most Radicals came from economically backward areas; 60 per cent of Radical voters were from towns with fewer than 5,000 inhabitants; 31 per cent of them were farmers. The Radical voters were suspicious of talk of modernization and they hated taxation or assaults on their own property. The financial plan introduced by René Mayer in 1947 and 1948 brought the two parts of the Radical party into conflict. Mayer's plan involved a bracing dose of economic liberalism, an attempt to bring back economic stability and a loosening of currency regulation. It was supported by most of Mayer's allies in large-scale business. But the Mayer plan horrified the traditional Radical electorate. Its aim to reduce agricultural prices relative to industrial ones and to cut down small-scale retailing caused alarm. Most strikingly of all Mayer's removal of 5,000-franc notes from circulation caused panic among social groups who were prone to keep their life savings safe from *le fisc* under the mattress.

The Mayer plan sparked hostility among the Radical party's electoral base.[154] Anteriou reported:

The committee of the Radical party was an undoubted victory for the government. However, the militants seem very unhappy about the financial projects of René Mayer. The aggravation of taxation, the levy and the withdrawal of 5,000-franc notes provoked violent protests in the ranks. The majority of militants who came to our conference had important sums in 5,000-franc notes. Poor Meguey, for example, had fifteen.[155]

It was reported to Bidault that: 'The growing disfavour of M. René Mayer in the Assembly is due in part to the express reservations of professional groups who put more and more pressure on deputies. They [the deputies] make no secret of the fact that they do not wish to arouse popular disfavour, especially as the plan is far from certain to succeed.'[156] Queuille and Cudenet were so worried by the anger of Radical voters that they tried to persuade Mayer to abandon his project.[157]

---

[153] AN, 373 AP 7, Anteriou to Bollaert, dated 2 June 1948.
[154] For reports made to Mayer himself about the protests aroused by his measures see AN, 363 AP 8.   [155] AN, 373 AP 7, Anteriou to Bollaert, dated 5 February 1948.
[156] AN, 457 AP 135, unsigned report dated 7/8 January 1948.
[157] AN, 373 AP 7, Anteriou to Bollaert, 10 March 1948.

Conclusion

It is unfair that the RGR, and particularly, the Radical party, was so often described as *immobiliste*. The leaders of the RGR were frantically active and mobile during the early years of the Fourth Republic. They sought to overcome their declining popularity by forming complicated alliances, using government resources to reward supporters and seeking to build new foundations of power outside the traditional heartlands of Radicalism.

The problem with this approach was that the parties of the RGR became hopelessly contorted as they sought to exploit every possible advantage in every event. Attitudes to Gaullism reveal how great these contortions could be. Every bourgeois party was divided by the advent of the RPF, but the RGR managed to encompass every possible reaction to the new force. Some of its leaders (such as Chaban-Delmas or Debré) were committed Gaullists who ultimately left the RGR for the RPF; some (like Torrès or Jean Marin) remained as members of the RGR while simultaneously becoming prominent in the RPF; some (like Giacobbi) joined the RPF, perhaps for tactical reasons, and then later resigned; some (like Pleven) feigned sympathy for the RPF while seeking to protect the government that it opposed; some (like Daladier) refused either to join the RPF or to oppose it; some (like Rougier) combined violent hostility to de Gaulle as an individual with sympathy for the anti-Communism of the RPF. Finally, some leaders of the RGR (like Mitterrand or Herriot) were unqualified opponents of the RPF.

The effort to win new supporters for the RGR also produced divisions in its ranks. The alienation of the neo-Radicals from the economically backward anti-clerical electorate of south-western France has been described. The RGR was able to survive the divisions that this alienation produced in its ranks during the late 1940s, but during the 1950s many traditional Radical supporters were to turn away from the party towards the more dramatic defence of their interests offered by Poujadism. Even more serious were the divisions introduced by the RGR's relations with France overseas. The RGR gained greatly from the support that it obtained in the French empire, but it did so at a price. It became associated with an area where politics were notoriously unstable and faction ridden. Further divisions were introduced by the fact that some neo-Radicals began to desert Algérie Française because they believed it to be an impediment to modernization, while other Radicals became almost obsessively committed to the defence of an area that they believed to be an indivisible part of the Third Republic legacy, as well as a useful source of votes. Finally, as some Radicals were dragged to the right by their links with Algeria, the UDSR was dragged to the left by its links with Black Africa. It was the Algerian issue that finally split the Radical party and the RGR in the mid-1950s.

However, the ultimate break up of the RGR does not mean that it should be dismissed as a failure. Internal contradictions affected all other bourgeois parties and indeed the whole regime. Furthermore, the frenetic dealmaking and alliance formation of the Radical leaders allowed them survive for far longer than had seemed probable in 1945. In this context the apparent stability of the Radical party needs to be seen not as the product of passivity but rather as a vigorous and skilfully conducted defensive battle against impossible odds.

12   The Rassemblement du Peuple Français

> Comme tous les mal aimés, ce RPF dont je devenais le fonctionnaire semble voué à l'oubli de ceux qui l'ont vécu. De rares thèses de spécialistes, bien peu de souvenirs.[1]

Edmond Michelet's remark on the attention given to the Rassemblement du Peuple Français (RPF) is only partly true. The two most important leaders of the RPF were de Gaulle, who founded the movement in April 1947, and Jacques Soustelle, who became its secretary. Neither of these men devoted more than a few pages of their memoirs to the description of the movement's activities. However, the RPF has been the subject of three distinguished academic books since its dissolution,[2] and has attracted extensive discussion in more general works on the Fourth Republic. There are several reasons for this interest. Firstly, the sources for the RPF are exceptionally good, and access to the movement's archives has been granted to a number of historians. Secondly, the RPF contained a number of eminent political analysts, notably Raymond Aron, and other writers, such as René Rémond, felt sympathetic to Gaullism. Thirdly, de Gaulle's importance during the Second World War and later during the Fifth Republic encouraged analysts to see the RPF as part of a continuing tradition long after the other parties of the Fourth Republic had been consigned to the dustbin of history. Fourthly, the RPF's ambitions to win an absolute majority in parliament and its attempt to establish a direct relation with the electorate, as opposed to one mediated by notables or party organization, made it seem familiar to those who assumed that an 'Anglo-Saxon' party system was the 'natural' pattern of politics.[3]

---

[1] Edmond Michelet, *La querelle de la fidélité. Peut-on être gaulliste aujourd'hui?* (Paris, 1981), p. 231.
[2] J. Charlot, *Le gaullisme d'opposition 1946–1958* (Paris, 1983); P. Guiol, *L'impasse sociale du gaullisme. Le RPF et l'Action Ouvrière* (Paris, 1985); C. Purtschet, *Le Rassemblement du Peuple Français 1947–1953* (Paris, 1965).
[3] On the presumed similarities between the appeal of the RPF and that of General Eisenhower see D. MacRae, *Parliament, parties and society in France 1946–1958* (London and New York, 1967), p. 269.

216

The result of the scholarly attention given to the RPF is that the details of the movement's history are better known than those of any Fourth Republic party. A Union Gaulliste was set up by Capitant and Closterman as early as 1946. However, this initiative took place without any direct sign of de Gaulle's own approval and it obtained only around 300,000 votes in the election of November 1946.[4] It was not until April 1947 that de Gaulle announced his political *rentrée* with a speech at Strasbourg calling for a coming together of Frenchmen and a reform of the constitution to produce strong presidential government. The RPF obtained 40 per cent of the vote in the municipal elections of November 1947. It was hoped that this success would encourage the leaders of other formations, such as the MRP and the UDSR, to rally behind Gaullism. Such hopes were disappointed. The Gaullist inter-group that was formed in the National Assembly acquired the support of only about 80 deputies. The RPF obtained 120 seats in the 1951 elections, but 27 of its members broke off in 1952 to support the government of Antoine Pinay; this event marked the effective end of the RPF's chances of obtaining power. At a meeting in St Maur in July 1952 the RPF enacted more rigorous rules of party discipline that made reconciliation with its own rebels unlikely, in January 1953 the parliamentary RPF group defied the extra parliamentary leadership to join the government, and in May 1953 de Gaulle himself withdrew from active politics and announced the dissolution of the RPF.

Most accounts of the RPF present the movement as a failure. At first glance there is something rather strange about such interpretations. The RPF gained 4,266,000 votes in the 1951 general election. This level of support was second only to that accorded to the Communist party, and the 120 RPF deputies who were returned, even after the operation of a disadvantageous electoral law, made the party the largest in the national assembly. However, the RPF's success cannot be judged by the standards applied to other Fourth Republic political parties. De Gaulle's ambitions were so extraordinary that his supporters had to resign themselves to the fact that anything less than triumph would be viewed as disaster.[5] Furthermore, de Gaulle and most of his associates were so inflexible that, unlike some other parties that had emerged from the Resistance, they could not adapt to take advantage of success that was less great than expected. Having failed to overthrow the Fourth Republic, the RPF also failed to exercise any influence in it.

Explaining the failure of the RPF has proved more contentious and difficult than describing that failure. De Gaulle was to come to power with

[4] Philip Williams, *Politics in post-war France: parties and the constitution in the Fourth Republic* (2nd edition, London, 1958), p. 120.
[5] O. Guichard, *Mon général* (Paris, 1980), p. 264.

comparative ease in 1958, and most commentators who are sympathetic to Gaullism naturally believe that France needed the General in 1948 as much as it did ten years later. Consequently, most accounts tend to emphasize short-term, almost accidental, obstacles that prevented the RPF's success. If only, it is implied, de Gaulle had been a little more flexible, or de Gaulle's opponents a little less resourceful, then the RPF would have come to power. Memoirs of RPF leaders are full of moments when circumstances seemed 'almost' to work in the movement's favour. This chapter will describe the obstacles that blocked the RPF's path. However, it will argue that these obstacles were not just the products of bad luck: they were deep rooted and the very advantages that allowed the RPF to achieve such apparent success – ideological ambiguity, business and notable support, authoritarian leadership – also ensured that it would ultimately fail.

Timing is obviously an important element in explaining the RPF's failure. The movement gained 40 per cent of the vote in the municipal elections of 1947; had such a success been reproduced in a legislative general election, it would almost certainly have swept the RPF to power and the Fourth Republic out of existence. However, legislative elections did not come until 1951 and by this time the RPF was less strong. Pierre Lefranc believed that the RPF had been created 'four years too early'.[6] Olivier Guichard wrote 'In 1947 to be a Gaullist was a sin or a hope; in 1951 it was a mistake.'[7] During the four years between municipal and legislative elections, the RPF lost support for two reasons. Firstly, the circumstances that had made so many voters disenchanted with French politics in 1947 had changed by 1951. The Communist threat seemed less intense in 1951 than it had in 1947 when Communist ministers had just left the French government, CGT strikes were rife and war with the Communist bloc seemed possible. Perhaps more importantly, the French economy was beginning to improve in 1951 and this improvement was translated into rising living standards. De Gaulle commented bitterly on the benefits that his electoral rivals derived from these improvements: 'To hear them, you would think that it was to the credit of the men of the so-called majority if, in spite of it all, wheat grows, machines run and children are born.'[8]

Secondly, the RPF was a 'surge movement'; it was built on an enthusiasm that blotted out many conflicts of interest and ideological differences among its supporters. As time went on, such divisions became increasingly apparent. Furthermore, the RPF demanded a much higher level of commitment from members than conventional bourgeois parties: the organization of rallies, the drive for recruitment and the production of

---

[6] Pierre Lefranc, *Avec qui vous savez. Vingt-cinq ans avec de Gaulle* (Paris, 1979), p. 68.
[7] O. Guichard, *Un chemin tranquille* (Paris, 1975), p. 5.
[8] Guichard, *Mon général*, p. 278.

publications all took time and money. Such commitment was difficult to sustain, and it was made all the more so by the fact that the RPF was a party of opposition that could not offer its supporters access to jobs, contracts or power. Lefranc summed up the difficulty : 'For a rapid operation, it is relatively easy to obtain disinterested help. But to finish a long haul, the problem becomes more complicated.'[9] Finance became a particular problem. Guichard wrote, 'The RPF spent a great deal of money, until 1951 it never had enough. It had become, after the elections of 1947, an enormous and costly machine.'[10]

The problems that the RPF experienced in sustaining its support exposed deeper seated problems. The first of these was the extent of ideological division in the party. Many of the divisions in the RPF – such as that between *laïques* and clericals or between Resistance supporters and Pétainists – also existed in other parties. However, the divisions of the RPF were exacerbated by the fact that the movement's leadership, and particularly de Gaulle himself, were less tolerant of indiscipline than the leaders of, say, the Radicals or the Independents. The insistence on imposing central discipline was seen in de Gaulle's refusal to accede to Soustelle's request that the question of state subsidies to church schools should be recognized as a matter of private conscience.[11] The divisions in the RPF were particularly severe because the party did not appeal to any clearly established tradition. Michelet wrote that his colleagues 'only had in common their feeling of allegiance to the General, often some activity in the Free French or the Resistance, and sometimes memories of shared adventures'.[12] In the short term the vagueness about what the RPF stood for helped to avoid conflict. One enthusiastic young recruit gushed: 'we were influenced by sentiment rather than doctrine'.[13] However, attempts to define RPF doctrine were bound to produce conflict. Furthermore, the definition of RPF doctrine became more urgent as the party seemed to approach power, and it would have been impossible to maintain the ambiguity, on which the RPF so often depended, had it actually been in a position to put its doctrines into practice. It might be argued that the RPF would not have been saved by early elections but destroyed by them.

Several areas of RPF doctrine were particularly open to conflicting interpretations. The first of these was anti-Communism, which was such an important part of the movement's appeal. Many regarded RPF anti-Communism as being an attack on Communists within France and a bid to

[9] Lefranc, *Avec qui vous savez*, p. 75.   [10] Guichard, *Mon général*, p. 244.
[11] L. Terrenoire, *De Gaulle 1947–1954. Pourquoi l'échec. Du RPF à la traversée du désert* (Paris, 1981), p. 141.
[12] Michelet, *La querelle de la fidélité*, p. 233.
[13] Bernard Marin, *De Gaulle de ma jeunesse 1944–1970* (Paris, 1984), p. 51.

preserve the social order. The activities of the RPF *service d'ordre* gave considerable support to this interpretation and encouraged many traditional conservatives and businessmen to associate with the RPF. However, other supporters of the RPF were 'anti-Soviet' rather than anti-Communist. They focused not on the internal threat that the Communist party posed to the social order in France, but on the external threat that the USSR posed to the independence of France. In this context de Gaulle's anti-Communism was a version of pre-war nationalism in which the USSR had replaced Germany as the object of France's hostility. Gaullist hostility to Communists within France was seen as being rooted in the belief that the *séparatistes* had placed loyalty to a foreign power above loyalty to France and submitted themselves to Stalinist discipline. The appeal of anti-Soviet rhetoric was particularly strong in the traditionally nationalist east of the country, an area that was, in de Gaulle's striking phrase, separated from the advance divisions of the Red Army by less than the distance of two stages in the Tour de France. Alsace-Lorraine was also receptive to the anti-Soviet version of anti-Communism, because a large number of its inhabitants had been prisoners of war in the USSR after being conscripted into the German army.[14]

Anti-Soviet rhetoric attracted some former Communists who had rebelled against the slavish obedience of the Parti Communiste Français (PCF) to the party line defined in Moscow. Henri Torrès, Louis Vallon and Manuel Bridier all fell into this category. The problem was that such men's abandonment of the PCF obedience to Moscow did not mean that they had abandoned demands for radical social transformation within France.[15] The coexistence of socially radical ex-Communists with conventional conservatives in the RPF was a recipe for continuous dispute. This could be seen in the battle between Torrès, the ex-Communist secretary of the RPF in Paris, and the former Parti Républicain de la Liberté (PRL) leaders who ran the RPF in the Loir et Cher,[16] or by the conflicts between ex-Communists and conservatives in the Gaullist Action Ouvrière.[17]

The RPF's economic and social policies were also open to more than one interpretation. De Gaulle did not subscribe to the conventional *laissez-faire* economics that was supported by most of the parliamentary right in the

[14] Archives Nationales (AN), 350 AP 76, 23 April 1947, 'Note sur le RPF'. The report by the MRP on the RPF's appeal in eastern France suggested 'Anti-Communist feeling is very strong among our population. It is inspired, not so much by social conservatism, as by the horror provoked by the oppression of the Soviets and in all of eastern Europe, a regime about which repatriated Alsatians have brought some horrifying details.'

[15] Marin, *De Gaulle de ma jeunesse*, p. 51.

[16] AN, 424 AP 41, Boncour to Torrès, dated 1 November 1948. See also the report made to Bidault on 12 January 1948 which alluded to the conflict between Torrès and the 'cagoulard' elements in the RPF.

[17] On conflicts in the Action Ouvrière see Guiol, *L'impasse sociale du gaullisme*.

Fourth Republic. De Gaulle supported some nationalization and *dirigisme*; he also supported a somewhat vague policy in labour relations that would involve 'association' between workers and employers. Gaullist ideas on economic and social matters remained ill defined. This was partly because de Gaulle himself was less interested such matters than in foreign policy, the army and constitutional reform; Malraux suggested that de Gaulle's economic and social policy was simply a by-product of his desire to promote French grandeur: 'In his eyes nationalizations were a means of resurrecting France.'[18] It was also partly because supporters of the RPF disagreed so violently about how the vague principles enunciated by de Gaulle might be implemented.

Gaullist social and economic policy was open to three different interpretations. The first was that of those left-wing, largely ex-Communist, members of the RPF who wished to see a real assault on economic privilege. These men welcomed state intervention in the economy and support for social security measures, but they felt nervous about measures that might seem to recall Vichy corporatism.[19] An exactly contrary interpretation of Gaullism was upheld by some who had been involved with Vichy's *charte du travail*. Such people were socially conservative in that they did not support the redistribution of wealth, but they did support some degree of corporatist restriction on the freedom of businessmen and workers. De Gaulle's associationism bore certain resemblances to the measures that had been proposed by the *charte du travail*, and this encouraged some ex-*chartistes*, such as the textile employer, Jacques Warnier, to look on it with favour.[20] The third interpretation of RPF social and economic policy was that held by conventional economic liberals. Such men were hostile to the RPF's policy, which they saw as threatening the free market economy. Doubts about the RPF's *étatisme* were expressed in *Ecrits de Paris* (a right-wing paper with links to business leaders),[21] and at the annual congress of the Alliance Démocratique (AD).[22] However, even those liberals who disapproved of Gaullism's economic policies were often willing to go along with the RPF, at least for a time, because the movement's stance on other issues, such as anti-Communism, appealed to them, and perhaps because they did not believe that the RPF would ever implement its economic policies.

---

[18] André Malraux, *Les chênes qu'on abat* (Paris, 1971), p. 29.
[19] This nervousness was reflected in the fact that Vallon's book, *Le dilemme français* (Paris, 1951), contained an appendix comparing the RPF's proposal with Vichy's *charte du travail*.
[20] AN, 57 AS 24, observations on association, undated.
[21] *Ecrits de Paris*, editorial 24 April 1947.
[22] Ventenat speaking to congress of Alliance Démocratique on 12 May 1950: 'We have still not heard the RPF make unambiguously liberal statements and there are many people among the leaders of the RPF who remain faithful to *dirigisme*'. Bibliothèque Nationale, Alliance Démocratique Archives, 4.

Regional differences were another source of conflict in the RPF. Alsace was the area most associated with Gaullism; it was here that the Union Gaulliste had achieved its greatest success, and it was here that de Gaulle launched the RPF. However, the very terms in which de Gaulle described his reasons for making this choice hinted at the difficulty that the RPF would encounter elsewhere: 'The General chose Strasbourg because the Alsaciens had suffered much during the war and because, not having undergone the the ordeal of Vichy, there was no systematic and visceral anti-Gaullism there.'[23] The problem for de Gaulle was that support could not be taken for granted in the rest of France, and particularly in the southern part of France where the Vichy government had exercised the highest degree of influence.

The RPF had special problems in France's overseas possessions. These areas had never been occupied by the German troops and they had never experienced the loss of confidence in Marshal Pétain that was felt in the mainland. This did not necessarily mean that they were anti-Gaullist, but it did mean that they had a special view of Gaullism. Gaullism was valued in overseas France partly because it was seen as the political party most likely to protect the status of France's overseas possessions and that of French settlers in them. This clearly posed potential problems for the RPF since the movement contained settlers' leaders, such as Léon Delbecque and Jean-Jacques Susini, who were to prove the most intransigent defenders of Algérie Française alongside proponents of a liberal but integrationist solution, such as Soustelle, and others, like de Gaulle himself, who would ultimately decide that France's overseas possessions could be sacrificed for the greater glory of metropolitan France.

The most dangerous division in the RPF was that engendered by reactions to de Gaulle himself. Loyalty to the General was supposed to be the cornerstone of the RPF, but not all those who joined the movement shared this loyalty. Many notables, politicians and voters found it useful to support the RPF as a means of combating Communism and securing their own position without feeling admiration for its founder. In the Loir et Cher, it was believed that the RPF was simply 'the camouflage for the PRL'.[24] Some who joined the RPF felt positive hostility to de Gaulle. Rémy's memoirs recount a conversation overheard between an RPF deputy and a friend: 'What is this that I hear, you are going to stand under the colours of de Gaulle, that miserable bastard, who deserved to be shot twenty times. I agree with you, replied the recent recipient of the Gaullist endorsement, but one must be patient.'[25] Rémy's account may owe something the vivid

[23] A. de Boisseau, *Pour servir le général 1946–1970* (Paris, 1982), p. 59.
[24] AN, 424 AP 41, Boncour to Torrès, dated 1 November 1948.
[25] Rémy, *Mes grands hommes et quelques autres* (Paris, 1982), p. 131.

imagination of a former film director, but there is other evidence of anti-Gaullism in the RPF. Louis Rougier, an apologist for Pétain who hated de Gaulle, believed that the majority of members of the RPF shared his views: 'I do not want to harm a movement of which 80 per cent of the voters and sympathizers profess anti-Gaullism.'[26] Some RPF deputies were seen as more loyal to the conservative anti-Gaullist Bruyneel than to their own group.[27] Jean-Louis Anteriou, the Radical organizer, believed that a majority of 'Gaullist' deputies in parliament were really opponents of the RPF: 'The majority of members of the National Assembly who have declared themselves to be RPF belong to the right; they were elected campaigning against Gaullism. If they are given the chance to enter into a cabinet of national union, there is every reason to suppose that they would be ready to struggle against de Gaulle and his friends.'[28] Not surprisingly, men who had joined the RPF for electoral reasons left the party when it seemed advantageous to do so: 'They enter the RPF to get votes, they leave it to get posts.'[29]

Business and the RPF

The RPF had intimate links with big business. Many RPF leaders came from Parisian, or northern haut-bourgeois families. Their personal links with French big business were closer than those of other parties which recruited much of their leadership from 'le sud qui gouverne'. Former deputies from the RPF were more likely to obtain jobs in national companies than those of any other group. The RPF sought to obtain huge sums of money from businessmen. Bridier claimed that one RPF leader wrote to 1,000 industrialists asking them to contribute to a special fund devoted to 'the very special anti-Communist project of the General'.[30] A number of businessmen were members of the RPF. Alain Bozel, president of the Bozel-Maletra chemicals combine and son of Richemond (the vice president of the Confédération Générale du Patronat Français (CGPF)), was treasurer of the RPF. Pierre Lebon of the Union des Banques, Jonas of Crédit Lyonnais, Diethelm of Urbain, Léon Noel of Rhône Poulenc, Pigozzi of Simca and Dassault, the aircraft manufacturer, were all prominent in the party.[31]

These links attacted much attention. Marxist writers suggested that

---

[26] L. Rougier, *De Gaulle contre de Gaulle* (Paris, 1948), p. 1.
[27] AN, 424 AP 41, Buhler to Dupont, dated 5 August 1948.
[28] AN, 373 AP 7, Anteriou to Bollaert, 18 March 1948.
[29] Guichard, *Mon général*, p. 267.   [30] Guiol, *L'impasse sociale du gaullisme*, p. 253.
[31] The most exhaustive study of the links between RPF members and business is contained in H. Claude, *Gaullisme et grand capital* (Paris, 1960).

Gaullism was the instrument of 'grand capital'; an extreme right-winger solemnly plotted the family links between Gaullists and the 'bourgeois dynasties',[32] while a Socialist deputy recalled the 'synarchic' conspiracy that had been discussed under Vichy and suggested that the Worms bank was behind the RPF.[33] The links between Georges Villiers, the head of the CNPF, and de Gaulle were scrutinized with particular intensity. An English writer argued that the links between the RPF and the CNPF were so close that Georges Villiers had drawn up a provisional RPF cabinet to be headed by Paul Reynaud.[34] Even Gaullists believed that Villiers was potentially sympathetic to their movement; indeed, de Gaulle expressed the fear that Villiers would exercise too much influence. He told Bidault that without the MRP's support 'we will all come under the sway of M. Villiers'.[35]

However, in the long run, the RPF's relations with the *patronat* proved too weak rather than too strong. This was reflected in the financial problems of the movement. The initial promises of business subsidy were not converted into cash, and money became increasingly scarce as the activities of the RPF became more expensive. Far from receiving huge cheques in plain envelopes from captains of industry, RPF militants were soon reduced to scrabbling for money wherever it could be found. Bernard Marin funded local election campaigns by asking the mother of a friend for money;[36] André Astoux searched for buried treasure.[37]

There were several reasons why business support for the RPF proved disappointing. Firstly, the impression of unanimous support for the RPF among industrialists was an illusion. Those businessmen most associated with the movement were often unrepresentative individuals who were motivated by personal commitment that was unconnected with, or even contrary to, their business interests.[38] Furthermore, alongside those businessmen who supported the movement were at least an equal number who opposed it. The perceived *étatisme* of the RPF and the role of its founders in punishing those who had supported Vichy alienated many businessmen. André Boutemy, the dispenser of business funds who was credited with

---

[32] E. Beau de Loménie, *Les responsabilités des dynasties bourgeoises* (5 vols, Paris, 1977).
[33] Paul Rassimier, *Le parlement aux mains des banques* (Paris, 1956).
[34] R. Matthews, *The death of the Fourth Republic* (London, 1954). Matthews' claim is reproduced by Henry W. Erhmann, *Organized business in France* (Princeton, 1957); Purtschet, *Le Rassemblement du Peuple Français*, p. 108; Guiol, *L'impasse sociale du gaullisme*, p. 151. However, neither the memoirs of Georges Villiers, the archives of the CNPF nor the private papers of Paul Reynaud provide any evidence to support this claim.
[35] Terrenoire, *De Gaulle 1947–1954*, p. 67.   [36] Marin, *De Gaulle de ma jeunesse*, p. 65.
[37] A. Astoux, *L'oubli de Gaulle 1946–1958* (Paris, 1974), p. 166.
[38] On Bozel's willingness to sacrifice his own interests for those of the movement see ibid., p.104, and Guichard, *Mon général*, p. 238. Pierre Lebon's committment to Gaullism can be seen in his perceptive book, *Le gaullisme au pouvoir* (Paris, no date).

dissuading Villiers from joining the RPF,[39] and who co-ordinated anti-Gaullist propaganda in the 1951 election, was the most prominent and active member of this group. Some switched from Gaullism in 1947 to anti-Gaullism in 1951 as they switched subsidies from the RPF to the CNIP.[40] This switch fitted in with the broad strategy adopted by business paymasters. Business power was at its greatest when a large number of anti-Communist parties were competing for subsidy. It therefore made sense to provide initial help for the RPF to become a viable party, but it did not make sense to fund a large disciplined party that might turn itself into a monopoly supplier of political representation.

Secondly, those businessmen who did subsidize the RPF did not necessarily share all the aims of the movement's founder. De Gaulle wished to overthrow the whole regime; many businessmen conceived of the RPF merely as a means of working within the regime. They wanted the RPF to function as an anti-Communist strong-arm squad that would break strikes, and take the Communists on in street fights. The RPF's Action Ouvrière was largely subordinated to these aims: 'It was the muscular and right-wing side that won out, that it is to say preventing strikes and favouring workers' groups in the service of employers'.[41] An RPF deputy for Vaucluse was quite explicit about the RPF's function as an employment agency for street-fighters: 'I am sure of being able to provide the right sorts, this is another means of fighting the reds and terrorists.'[42] In the Ardennes, the *patronat* seem to have treated the RPF as a centre for organizing anti-strike action.[43]

Thirdly, there were divisions of interest among the businessmen who supported the RPF. French industry contained concentrated sectors that contrasted with backward *petites et moyennes entreprises* and new industries that did not always share the interests of established ones. These conflicts of interest were to become fully obvious after 1958 when de Gaulle's decision to abandon Algeria was supported by dynamic sectors of the economy, but vigorously opposed by previously Gaullist industrialists whose firms worked in backward sectors such as textiles.[44]

The extent of contradiction in the social base of the RPF was revealed by one issue: taxation. High taxes were a feature of the late 1940s and René Mayer's attempt to impose a heavier fiscal burden on small peasants and traders accounted for much of the general discontent from which the RPF

[39] M. Debré, *Trois républiques pour une France*. II: *1946–1958. Agir* (Paris, 1988), p. 147.
[40] Guiol, *L'impasse sociale du Gaullisme*, p. 253.   [41] Bridier quoted in ibid., p. 224.
[42] Ibid., p. 229.   [43] Ibid., p. 229.
[44] Jacques Marseille, *Empire colonial et capitalisme français. Histoire d'un divorce* (Paris, 1984). It is an indication of the confusion in the minds of those who assumed French capitalists to be unanimous in their support for de Gaulle that Claude, writing in 1960, argued that Gaullism would serve business interests by maintaining the empire.

benefited. RPF activists like Jean Nocher railed against *le fisc*,[45] and two Gaullist deputies, Vendroux and Godin, published a pamplet entitled 'Pas d'impôts nouveaux'.[46] One of the main grievances of those members of the Rassemblement des Gauches Républicaines (RGR) – such as Léon Chambaretaud – who turned to the RPF was Mayer's plan to increase certain kinds of taxation.[47] The RPF had close links with the numerous tax-payers' associations of the Fourth Republic; Benazet's Ligue des Contribuables was reported to be favourable to the RPF;[48] the leader of the Mouvement de Défense des Contribuables, Boisdé, became an RPF deputy, and the Groupement de Défense des Contribuables had sponsored many RPF deputies in the 1951 election.[49] Much of the demagogic fiscal rhetoric of the RPF presaged that of Poujadism, and Poujade himself was elected to the municipal council of St Céré on an RPF ticket. But in spite of this anti-fiscal rhetoric from the *petit bourgeois* electorate of the RPF, and those who sought to appeal to them, it is hard to believe that Gaullism would have cut taxes. De Gaulle's most cherished aims – a foreign policy of *grandeur*, an economic policy of modernization and a social policy designed to produce consensus – would all have cost money.

There is some evidence that the leaders of small business who cared most about high taxes may have come to realize that they had been mistaken in backing the RPF. They imposed pressure on RPF deputies with whom they had contact to support Pinay, who was more interested in the fiscal issue. Léon Noel gave the following account of the meeting of RPF deputies convoked by Léon Gingembre (leader of the Confédération Générale des Petites et Moyennes Entreprises) in January 1952: 'Recalling that the majority of us had signed a declaration of the Front Economique (which I had flatly refused to do), Gingembre, unaware of his shocking presumption, did not hesitate to give us political advice. He advised us to develop links with the Independents, on the condition that we deserted de Gaulle.'[50]

Alongside the conflicts of ideas and interests in the RPF were conflicts of personality. RPF militants tended to make a great deal of the impact of personality on their movement and to imply that things might have been very different if a few key men had been less awkward. Soustelle attracted criticism for being unworldly and clumsy – Lefranc described him as an

[45] Jean Nocher, *Le pamphlet atomique*, 1 (Paris, 1947).
[46] J. Vendroux, *Souvenirs de famille et journal politique*. I: *Cette grande chance que j'ai eue 1920–1957* (Paris, 1974), p. 277. It is interesting to note that Vendroux himself recognized that his pamphlet was 'demagogic'.
[47] On Chambaretaud see Williams, *Politics in post-war France*, pp. 147–148.
[48] Report made to Bidault on 12 January 1948 in AN, 457 AP 135.
[49] R. Vinen, 'Business intervention in the 1951 general election: the Groupement de Défense des Contribuables', *Modern and Contemporary France*, 1 (1993), 3–16. See also chapter 14.
[50] L. Noel, *La traversée du désert* (Paris, 1973), p. 97. The Front Economique had participated in the 1951 election under the name Groupement de Défense des Contribuables.

'intellectual thrown into action, feeling ill at ease, he always did too much or too little'.[51] De Gaulle himself was celebrated for brusqueness and for unwillingness to compromise. One diplomat remarked that 'the General knew nothing of the subtle art of not forcing his interlocutor to lose face'.[52] De Gaulle also made no secret of his contempt for parliamentary and party politics and this made life difficult for a political party that could only succeed through parliamentary elections. It was characteristic of both de Gaulle's detachment from politics and his treatment of subordinates that he should say to a loyal supporter in the mid-1950s, 'when will you stop boring me with *your* RPF?'[53]

However, it was not accidental that the RPF attracted awkward personalities, and they were not only to be found at the top of the movement. The violent hostility of the RPF to the existing order of things tended to attract rebellious and contentious men, and this tendency was exacerbated by the fact that many who joined the RPF had previously broken with other parties. The RPF was full of difficult and eccentric personalities. René Serre was such a person. His autobiography is as much a subject for a psychologist as a historian. Serre was raised in an orphanage, where he was badly treated, and did not learn to read until his twenties. Since he was both anti-semitic and filled with resentment against his father, who had abandoned his mother, Serre was somewhat disconcerted to find that his father was a Jew who had not returned from deportation. Membership of the RPF, where he became a bodyguard for de Gaulle and a protector of the movement's meetings, seems to have given him some outlet for his anger, and his autobiography was entitled *Fisticuffs Crusade*.[54]

Jean Nocher was a more high ranking member of the RPF whose bloody-mindedness also caused problems. Nocher was a Resistance leader in the Loire where he became a member of the Union Démocratique et Socialiste de la Résistance (UDSR) after the war. As early as 1946, a representative of the Fédération Republicaine suggested that Nocher's attitude would damage the Union Gaulliste, with which he was associated: 'He is tactless [*il est gaffeur*], he lacks antennae, which led him to make unwise remarks that upset several members of the audience.'[55] Nocher's career in the UDSR reflects his considerable talent for causing trouble: most of the UDSR's archive on contentious matters was taken up by the 'conflict Nocher'; his swansong in the party occurred at a meeting in March 1948 when he accussed Lanet and Bourdan of black market activities, called a local Resistance hero 'a dirty Pétainist' and finally told his assembled colleagues:

---

[51] Lefranc, *Avec qui vous savez*, p. 75.
[52] Dumaine cited in Guichard, *Mon général*, p. 298.
[53] Lefranc, *Avec qui vous savez*, p. 91.
[54] René Serre, *Croisade à coups de poing* (Givors, 1954).　　　[55] AN, 317 AP 82.

'I'll smash your faces in.'[56] In 1948, Nocher left the UDSR for the RPF, where he continued to cause trouble. His paper *l'Etincelle* clashed with the official Gaullist paper *l'Espoir*.[57] He published a series of 'atomic pamphlets' with titles such as 'Messieurs les grands, un petit vous dit merde', 'Trafiquants et profiteurs de la résistance' and 'Le temps des cocus'.[58] He aroused protests from his RPF colleagues by printing extracts from the writings of Georges Bidault that had been taken out of context in order to suggest that Bidault had supported the Munich settlement.[59] RPF organizers came to dread having to deal with Nocher's antics.[60] Men like Nocher made it very difficult for the RPF to enjoy the kind of relations with other political formations that might have helped it to come to power,[61] and as time went on they made it increasingly difficult to hold the RPF itself together.

Conflicts within the RPF were exacerbated by the contempt that many of its leaders, and particularly de Gaulle himself, had for conventional politics. This contempt was evident in the RPF's attitude to *apparentement* deals in the 1951 election. The *apparentement* system was a complicated variety of electoral alliance designed to allow bourgeois parties to pool their votes when it was advantageous to do so. It was designed to reduce the electoral success of both the Communist party and the RPF. Some Gaullists supporters believed that the RPF might have benefited from the tactic being used against them by agreeing to join *apparentements* themselves.[62] However, de Gaulle refused to allow the RPF to become involved in *apparentement* agreements in all but a dozen constituencies. He took this decision against the advice of most of the RPF's leaders and against the pleas of other interest groups: in Alsace even the bishops urged the RPF to join *apparentements*.[63] In retrospect many came to feel that *apparentements* were the greatest single reason for the disappointing performance of the RPF: General Billotte entitled an entire chapter of his memoirs 'Les apparentements terribles, 1951'.[64] Some Gaullists believed that their leader had misjudged events, either because he refused to believe that parliament would change the electoral law until it was too late to act or because he

---

[56] AN, 412 AP 16, account of meeting of 13 March 1948.

[57] Marin, *De Gaulle de ma jeunesse*, p. 59.

[58] The first two of these works were published in 1947, the third in 1948.

[59] Terrenoire, *De Gaulle 1947–1954*, p. 79.

[60] Ibid. p. 62. See also C. Mauriac, *The other de Gaulle: diaries, 1944–1954* (London, 1973), pp. 267 and 290.

[61] Even de Gaulle himself was obliged to concede that Nocher would make it impossible to enforce an electoral alliance with the MRP in the Loire (since the Loire was the constituency of Georges Bidault this was a serious problem). Ibid., p. 63.

[62] Debré, *Agir*, p. 152.   [63] Astoux, *L'oubli de Gaulle*, p. 255.

[64] P. Billotte, *Le passé au futur* (Paris, 1979).

believed that the RPF would attain an absolute majority without recourse to *apparentements*.[65]

There may be some truth in both these interpretations, but de Gaulle may also have had more sophisticated reasons for his refusal to permit *apparentements*. RPF participation in *apparentements* would have reduced the number of Communists in parliament and thus given the parties that supported the regime more room for manoeuvre. Furthermore, experience of the elections held to the Council of the Republic in 1948 suggested that when the RPF tried to draw up electoral lists in collaboration with other political parties, those parties benefited more than the RPF.[66] There is no reason to suppose that those elected as a result of *apparentements* with the RPF would have shown any disposition to be loyal to de Gaulle; given the rapid defection of many RPF deputies, it may be that a larger parliamentary group would simply have given the movement's leaders more problems in imposing discipline on their followers. Calculations of this kind may have been responsible for the curious sense of relief that de Gaulle seems to have displayed at the electoral debacle of 1951: 'deep down, careerists cannot be loyal to us'.[67]

De Gaulle's intransigence could also be seen in his attitude to local notables who played such a large role in Fourth Republic politics. Guichard wrote of his leader: 'He had a collective mistrust of that category of men that he called notables. He felt privileged men lacked backbone.'[68] Guichard pointed out the conflict between the realities of local politics that he had to deal with as a regional delegate and the attitude of his leader: 'Really it was absurd: as the personal representative of the General I fell into a world that he distrusted, that of parochialism and notables.'[69] The RPF showed its contempt for local politics when it set up its own Union Nationale des Maires de France to rival the venerable Association des Maires de France.[70]

The RPF's emphasis on centralized discipline and command from above annoyed local notables who were used to having their sensibilities respected. Many RPF candidates were distinguished at an international or national level but they rarely had the local reputation and experience of their rivals. The RPF representative in the Bas Rhin was the only one of forty-five candidates there in the 1951 election who was unable to speak

---

[65] Billotte claimed in retropect that de Gaulle had refused to believe Barrachin, a member of the electoral commission of the national assembly, who told him of the impending electoral law. Ibid., p. 72. Olivier Guichard flatly contradicts this and claims that de Gaulle always believed that the *apparentement* law would be passed by parliament. *Mon général*, p. 269.
[66] Williams, *Politics in post-war France*, p. 122. Williams is one of the few commentators who believes that de Gaulle was wise not to enter into *apparentement* agreements.
[67] Astoux, *L'oubli de Gaulle*.   [68] Guichard, *Un chemin tranquille*, p. 15.
[69] Ibid., p. 16.   [70] Terrenoire, *De Gaulle 1947–1954*, p. 103.

Alsatian.[71] Alongside its generals and ambassadors, the RPF did have a mass base of dedicated supporters, but these men were militants rather than notables. Their position was based on loyalty to de Gaulle and work within his movement rather than years of building up influence in the *conseil général* or the *chambre de commerce*. Most importantly, many RPF militants were very young men who lacked contacts and experience. Guichard was less than 30 years old when de Gaulle made him regional delegate for the South-West, and when another regional delegate, Pierre Lefranc, sought a man to lead the RPF in the Creuse he found a young lawyer whom he had just met and who was so far from being established that he still lived with his parents.[72]

Debré and Chaban-Delmas were the exceptions that proved the rule about the RPF's approach to local politics. They originated in the Radical party and they did know how to build up notable support at local level, as their support in their own areas showed. Both men were also utterly loyal Gaullists: they left the Radicals, stayed in the RPF until its disssolution, and supported de Gaulle throughout the Fifth Republic (a support that was particularly painful for Debré). Both men also attempted to persuade their leader to take more account of local sensitivities. Debré even wrote to de Gaulle: 'I long to see the RPF *propagandistes* among the peasants in clogs and *béret basque*.'[73] However, they received few thanks for their trouble. Debré felt mistrusted by the RPF leaders,[74] while de Gaulle said of Chaban-Delmas: 'I like him, but do not forget he is a Radical.'

One of the problems with the young and inexperienced militants who exercised so much power in the RPF is that they succeeded in annoying the notables without displacing them. This was partly a matter of conscious choice. Many RPF militants followed the example of their leader and avoided contesting elections. Guichard wrote: 'Over the years a certain snobbish disdain for elected men developed in the Rassemblement.'[75] Furthermore, the RPF itself decided that regional delegates would not put themselves up for election in 1951 (a decision that in retrospect some came to see as a mistake).[76] RPF militants also suffered from the fact that they lacked the contacts and the political skill of more established figures. When it came to drawing up electoral lists, it was usually the old guard who came out best: 'Wherever a notable and a militant were in competition, it was the notable who was chosen.'[77] The infiltration of RPF lists by local notables was especially bad in North Africa, where politics was notoriously corrupt. The fact that delegates from the mainland were unfamiliar with the complexities of Algerian politics meant that they were vulnerable to

[71] Williams, *Politics in post-war France*, p. 350.   [72] Lefranc, *Avec qui vous savez*, p. 70.
[73] Debré, *Agir*, pp. 133–134.   [74] Ibid., p. 153.   [75] Guichard, *Mon général*, p. 263.
[76] Ibid., p. 262.   [77] Lefranc, *Avec qui vous savez*, p. 87.

manipulation by local wirepullers. The organization of municipal elections in Algeria was so improper that even the thuggish ex-boxer René Serre was shocked.[78] When it came to the legislative elections of 1951, the RPF list was simply swallowed up by that produced by Alain de Serigny, editor of the *Echo d'Alger* and political fixer, who arranged for Blanchette, a local millionaire, to be placed on the list.[79] The result of all this was that a large number of RPF parliamentarians returned in 1951 owed their places to notable influence: it is not surprising that such men despised the intransigence of RPF militants and rebelled against the centralized discipline of their own grouping. When Barrachin broke away from the RPF parliamentary group to vote for Pinay, he assured the earnest young Bernard Marin: 'of the 80 orthodox RPF supporters, at least 70 share my view. Only ill informed militants are unaware of this fact.'[80]

Conclusion

The glamour and historical significance of Gaullism usually encourages historians to treat the RPF as a party apart that is to be contrasted, but not compared, with the other parties of the Fourth Republic. However, in many respects the problems that afflicted the RPF were the same as those that affected other parties. The naivety and intransigence of the RPF that showed itself in poor relations with notables was characteristic of new parties and particularly those that emerged out of the Resistance. Similar traits were displayed by the UDSR, the PRL and the Mouvement Républicain Populaire (MRP), though the first two of these parties learned to be more flexible as time went on. The RPF's awkward and ambiguous relations with many of the businessmen who funded it were also typical of some Fourth Republic parties. Finally, the RPF's rapid rise on the crest of a wave of enthusiasm that declined as rapidly as it had arisen was typical of Fourth Republic surge movements such as Poujadism and Mendésisme.

Olivier Guichard suggested that there was a *parallélisme* not just between the RPF and other political parties but between the RPF and the whole Fourth Republic regime. At first, this remark seems odd: the RPF attacked the Fourth Republic and sought its overthrow. However, as far as the

---

[78] René Serre, *Croisade à coups de poings*, p. 166. 'The elections in Oran could not have been more of a farce if they had been organized by the Marx brothers.'

[79] Lefranc, *Avec qui vous savez*, p. 88.

[80] Marin, *De Gaulle de ma jeunesse*, p. 61. The fact that the RPF parliamentary group subsequently defied the extra parliamentary leadership in order to join the government suggests that Barrachin was right. It should also be noted that some RPF deputies, such as Boisdé, had supported the Pinay government privately even though they did not vote for it. L. Franck, *697 ministres. Souvenirs d'un directeur général des prix 1947–1962* (Paris, 1990), p. 73.

notables, businessmen and, to some extent voters, of the Fourth Republic were concerned, the RPF and the Third Force were not polar opposites but alternative means to the same end – that end being countering the Communist threat.

Even the techniques that the RPF and the Third Force adopted were similar, and it became increasingly obvious that the Third Force were much more skilled at using these techniques than their RPF opponents. The RPF called for a *rassemblement* of all anti-Communist forces that would bring together the various political parties under the aegis of de Gaulle. The men of the Third Force called for a *rassemblement* of anti-Communist forces, though one that was also directed against de Gaulle. The Third Force's *rassemblement* was facilitated by the *apparentement* law that allowed electoral alliances to be arranged on advantageous terms; it was also facilitated by the negotiating skills and political realism of the Third Force's experienced leaders. Michelet summed up his defeat as an RPF candidate in Corrèze (at the hands of Queuille) in these terms: 'everyone was in league against me in the name of anti-Communism'.[81] By contrast, the RPF leaders were too unworldly and tactless to form effective alliances and their quarrels made them appear as the men who were splitting the anti-Communist vote.

The RPF had also called for strong government to counter the Communist threat. Yet the forces that opposed the RPF contained the three strongest men to hold office in the Fourth Republic: Auriol, Queuille and Moch. Auriol used his presidential powers to intervene heavily in politics and to encourage resistance to the RPF. Queuille survived as the longest serving prime minister of the Fourth Republic, and masterminded effective, if unscrupulous, tactics such as the *apparentement* law. Moch used his powers as minister of the interior to suppress public disorder with unprecedented firmness. Moch attracted the particular dislike of RPF leaders. This was partly because the ministry of the interior prevented the RPF itself from indulging in some of its more colourful forms of public agitation. More importantly, it was because Moch's success in controlling the Communist party robbed the RPF of the hope that public opinion, or even the authorities themselves, would turn to the RPF as the only means of restoring public order. A report made to Georges Bidault in January 1948 described in detail how Moch's success weakened the RPF:

It seems that the precautions taken by Jules Moch are not to the taste of the RPF for whom everything that tends to assert the government's authority obviously casts a

[81] Michelet, *La querelle de la fidélité*, p. 227. See also Debré, *Agir*, p. 154. Debré spoke on Michelet's behalf in the Corrèze but was confronted by the Radical Lafay who asked why the RPF had split the anti-Communist vote.

shadow. Not, for sure, that it itself wishes to create any kind of agitation – this hypothesis is certainly out of the question – but rather because it would like the authorities to be obliged to resort to it to restore order which has been damaged by others. In view of this, a circular sent by the central organism of the RPF to its departmental committees is very instructive: it authorizes its members to lend their support to the local authorities on the express condition . . . that a formal request has been made to the departmental leader of the RPF by the proper administrative authorities.[82]

The similarities between the RPF and the Third Force can also be traced beyond 1951. After this date the threat from Communism was no longer great enough to persuade parties to unite effectively or to persuade individual politicians to yield to the discipline exercised by strong leaders. Both the RPF and its opponents broke down into squabbling factions.[83]

[82] AN, 457 AP 135, report made on the night of 7/8 March 1948.
[83] Guichard, *Mon général*, p. 300.

13   Independents and Peasants

The Centre National des Indépendants et Paysans (CNIP) was set up at the beginning of 1951 to preside over an electoral alliance between two parliamentary groups: the Centre National des Indépendants (CNI) and the Centre Républicain d'Action Paysanne et Sociale.[1] It was a loose grouping that only really functioned at election time. Candidates presented by the CNIP decided which of its constituent groups in parliament they would join after their election.

Roger Duchet, who initiated the Centre and became its secretary general, was a self-consciously machiavellian senator from Burgundy. Like many Independents he had been a Radical before the war,[2] and he had become mayor of Beaune at the unusually early age of 26. The functions of the CNIP were ill defined. Duchet was not a politician of great national prominence and he presented a modest view of his role. He suggested that the CNIP was merely a clearing house for electoral alliances. However, this apparently humble position provided Duchet with considerable power. This was reflected in the allegation that leaders of the CNIP were a hidden and self-selecting oligarchy.[3] It was also reflected in the resentment that more established politicians, notably Paul Reynaud, came to feel towards him: in March 1951, a terse circular reminded Independents that the CNIP was just an administrative body 'the titular secretary general of which has no power to lay down the policy of the Républicains Indépendants'.[4]

The Independents are hard to place. Unlike the Radicals, they did not belong to a clearly defined pre-war tradition; unlike the Rassemblement du Peuple Français (RPF), they did not have a single recognized leader; unlike

[1] Philip Williams, *Crisis and compromise: politics in the Fourth Republic* (London, 1972), p. 150, suggests that the Peasants joined the CNIP in early 1951.
[2] Duchet explained his departure from the Radical Party as follows: 'The old party was without leaders, without doctrine; I foresaw that soon it would be without militants.' Roger Duchet, *La république épinglée* (Paris, 1975), p. 11. Duchet's statement is rather odd in view of the fact that he went on to found a group that prided itself on lacking leaders, doctrine and militants.
[3] Archives Nationales (AN), 74 AP 33, Liautey to Reynaud dated 21 December 1951.
[4] AN, 74 AP 33, circular of 13 March 1951.

234

the Mouvement Républicain Populaire (MRP) and the Parti Républicain de la Liberté (PRL), they did not purport to have a coherent doctrine or effective party discipline. Indeed, the Independents were at pains to deny that they were members of a party at all. A leader in *la France Indépendante*, the CNI's official journal, described the group in purely negative terms: 'they are men who oppose the omnipotence of committees and parties, who do not accept orders or recommendations from anyone, who are only accountable for their votes to their constituents and their voters. The Independents do not form and will not form a party. They do not and will not have leaders. They do not have a rigid programme.'[5]

Parliamentary groups of Républicains Indépendants (RI) were formed in both houses of parliament at the beginning of the Fourth Republic. In the *conseil de la république* the group was presided over by Sérot while Duchet acted as its secretary.[6] Roclore and Bourgain fufilled the same functions in the chamber of deputies before being replaced by Coty and Triboulet.[7] In July 1948 Duchet set up the CNI that brought together the RI grouping with the PRL. The organization of the Independents was initiated from the top and the executive of the CNI was, at first, exclusively made up of members of parliament. In addition, an informal group of five prominent parliamentary conservatives (Pinay, Laurens, Duchet, Rogier and Riond) met weekly.[8] Duchet was keen to extend the role played by non-parliamentarians (not least because his most powerful rivals in the party derived their power from parliament). To this end he wrote to 1,000 local politicians throughout France inviting them to join the movement and to form departmental centres. This appeal had some success. But the CNI did not attempt to become a disciplined party. Local centres remained free to act as they wished, and Philip Williams estimated that the group only had the support of around 20,000 militants during elections and around 1,000 militants at other times.[9]

The RI group in parliament never managed to encompass or discipline all right-wingers who referred to themselves as 'independent'. *Chanoine* Kir, the irrepressible mayor of Dijon, even contested the 1951 election as an 'independent Independent'. At least four independent groups existed in the Fourth Republic and these parties had confused relations with each other and with the CNI. The first of these independent groups was the Union Démocratique des Indépendants (UDI) which was made up largely of men who had deserted from the MRP. Roger Duchet wrote contemptuously of this party as a 'groupuscule', although it had fourteen deputies in parlia-

---

[5] *La France Indépendante*, 22 April 1950.   [6] Duchet, *La république épinglée*, p. 11.
[7] R. Triboulet, *Un gaulliste de la IVème* (Paris, 1985), pp. 142 and 144.
[8] Georges Riond, *Chroniques d'un autre monde* (Paris, 1979), p. 227.
[9] Williams, *Crisis and compromise*, p. 151.

ment,[10] a respectable size by the standards of French conservative groups. It had been attached to the Rassemblement des Gauches Républicaines (RGR),[11] but in 1951 Duchet negotiated the entry of UDI deputies into the CNIP.[12]

The Union des Nationaux et Indépendants Républicains (UNIR) was set up by Pétain's defence counsel Jacques Isorni to contest the 1951 election. Isorni was helped by journalists like Jean Mazé and Roger de Saivre, who became the group's secretary, subsidized by André Boutemy and Eugène Schueller, and discreetly advised by several prominent politicians including the prime minister.[13] UNIR's request to join the CNIP was turned down, largely at the behest of Reynaud and Antier, but Duchet delegated a member of the CNIP to figure on the UNIR list in Paris. The five UNIR deputies who were successful in the 1951 election[14] became 'administratively attached' to the Peasant group in the National Assembly.[15]

A third independent group, the Rassemblement des Groupes Républicaines et Indépendants Français (RGRIF), was also established to contest the 1951 elections. The RGRIF was led by Chambaretaud (a dissident from the Radical party in Lyons). Chambaretaud had incurred the wrath of Herriot, the powerful Radical mayor of Lyons, because he supported Daladier as leader of the RGR and because he looked favourably on the RPF (though not, apparently, favourably enough to join it). The RGRIF brought together a disparate collection of renegades from other parties, including members of the Unions Démocratiques des Français Indépendants (UDFI) (see below), a dissident from the RPF and Paul Faure of the Parti Socialiste Démocratique (PSD). In addition it put forward a number of token candidatures in order to achieve the thirty electoral lists that were necessary to benefit from the *apparentement* system: one RGRIF leader put his chauffeur, plumber and secretary up for election.[16] After the election, the RGRIF claimed to have won seven seats and to have helped another

---

[10] Among these representatives were Bentous (Alger), Bosquier (Gard), Courant (Seine Inférieure), Chevallier (Alger), Guillant (Eure), Lécrivan-Servoz (Rhône), R. Marcellin (Morbihan), De Recy (Pas-de-Calais), Serre (Oran), Viard (Alger). It is not clear which of these deputies remained in the UNI when it joined the CNIP. According to Williams, Serre and Lécrivan-Servoz both became 'fellow travelling progressives' by 1951. Williams, *Crisis and compromise*, p. 399.

[11] Rassemblement des Gauches Républicaines, *Qu'est-ce le RGR?* (Paris, 1949).

[12] Duchet, *La république épinglée*, p. 14.

[13] Jacques Isorni, *Mémoires*. II: *1946–1958* (Paris, 1986), pp. 209–212.

[14] The five successful candidates were Isorni (in Paris), Loustaunau-Lacau (in the Pyrenees), Estèbe (in Bordeaux), Le Roi Ladurie (in Calvados) and de Saivre (Oran). Loustaunau Lacau and Le Roi Ladurie fought on joint lists with other parties.

[15] Jacques Isorni, *Ainsi passent les républiques* (Paris, 1959), p. 18.

[16] AN, 457 AP 175, Maroselli to Grimaud dated 16 July 1951.

thirty-six candidates[17] to obtain election through *apparentement* deals.[18] Some RGRIF deputies joined the Independents or Peasants after the election, but at least one became attached to the Socialist group.[19]

The most long-lasting of the minor independent groups was initiated by André Liautey. Liautey, a former Radical minister who had voted full powers to Marshal Pétain in 1940, edited a paper *l'Indépendant Français*,[20] which expounded standard conservative themes; it attacked *dirigisme*, high taxation and the ineligibility laws. In 1946, Liautey founded the UDFI.[21] It started out on good terms with other independent groupings. Liautey kept Reynaud informed of his activities; Bovin Chapereux, leader of the RI grouping in the *conseil de la république*, became president of the UDFI, and Arnold Lanote of the UDFI was commissioned to write articles for the official journal of the RI. The UDFI formed a national committee of Independents, and representatives of the UDFI attended the Journée des Indépendants in 1949, but in 1950 Duchet refused them permission to attend again and members of the RI were ordered to resign from positions in UDFI bodies.[22] Duchet suggested that Lanote, who was apparently considered too right-wing, was the reason for this exclusion,[23] though the fact that the UDFI supported Duchet's rival Reynaud may also have been relevant.[24]

---

[17] Of these fifteen were members of the RGR, eight of the Section Française de l'Internationale Ouvrière (SFIO), four were members of the CNIP and four were members of the RPF. AN, 457 AP 175, Chambaretaud to president, eighth bureau of national assembly, dated 28 July 1951.

[18] On the RGRIF see various correspondence in AN, 457 AP 175, and in particular Chambaretaud to eighth bureau of national assembly dated 28 July 1951. See also Philip Williams, *Politics in post-war France: parties and the constitution in the Fourth Republic* (2nd edition, London, 1958), pp. 150, 322 and 323. According to Williams the RGRIF gained only six seats in parliament.

[19] Conte stood for the Pyrénées Orientales on an RGRIF ticket before becoming attached to the SFIO group in parliament. *Recueil des textes authentiques des programmes et engagements électoraux des députés proclamés élus à la suite des élections générales du 17 juin 1951*, commonly known as *Barodet* (Paris, 1952), p. 610.

[20] The paper changed its name in 1951 to *l'Evénement*.

[21] In 1950, Liautey claimed to have founded the UDFI in 1946 (letter to André dated 21 December 1950, in AN, 74 AP 33). However, the UDFI's formation was not publicly announced until December 1948, 'En marge des vieux partis périmés', *l'Indépendant Français*, 11 December 1948. Curiously, the list of party officials given in the same paper on 18 December 1948 did not include Liautey.

[22] On the history of the UDFI see AN, 74 AP 33, Liautey to André, dated 21 December 1950.

[23] Ibid. The UDFI was associated with Pétainist groups, and the delegate that the party sent to negotiate with the CNIP was the Vichy apologist Louis Rougier. This may have been tactless at a time when Duchet himself was trying to defend his war record against Reynaud's attacks.

[24] On the UDFI's support for Reynaud see *l'Indépendant Français*, unsigned article of 25 November 1950.

The UDFI reveals some of the complexities and absurdities of organization among the Independents. The party was supported by a heterogeneous coalition of professional and business groups, and its leaders made no attempt to impose any coherent general programme on the interests that they represented. *L'Indépendant Français* became the official representative of the Alliance Economique Française and the Confédération Générale des Contribuables de France. Particular pages were devoted to the defence of particular interests so that, at times, *l'Indépendant Français* looked like the circulars of several different associations stapled together rather than a single paper.[25] Liautey himself was secretary general of the vociferous Association des Bouilleurs de Cru and president of the Confédération Générale des Contribuables.[26] When he presented himself for election in 1951 he did not even bother to find other candidates for his electoral list, but merely asked the Confédération Générale de l'Agriculture (CGA) to provide appropriate names from among its members. His manifesto declared his agricultural policy to be that of the CGA and his business policy to be that of the Front Economique.[27]

The UDFI had confusing relations with other independent groups. After its attempts to join the CNIP failed, Liautey contested the 1951 election on an RGRIF slate and was sufficiently associated with the RGRIF to make well informed observers believe that he was its leader[28] (though he did not relinquish the leadership of the UDFI); another UDFI member stood as a UNIR candidate while a third stood on a *liste des mécontents*.[29] After the election Liautey became 'administratively attached' to the Independent group in parliament though he had run against a CNIP candidate in the election.[30] In 1953, the UDFI merged with the Independent Radicals to form a Union des Indépendants.[31]

Even after the 1951 election, the Independents and Peasants were divided by faction struggles, and these sometimes led to the formation of completely separate parliamentary groups. The frequency with which Roger Duchet announced the 'successful unification' of parliamentary Independents reflected a repeated failure to bring this about.[32] Not surprisingly the press often had difficulty following these complicated developments and failed to distinguish between the various conservative groups.[33] In the

[25] See, for example, *l'Indépendant Français*, 24 June 1948 and 8 July 1948.
[26] *Barodet*, 1951, pp. 650–651.   [27] Ibid.
[28] AN, 447 AP 175, Maroselli to Grimaud dated 16 July 1951.
[29] On the various tickets of UDFI candidates in the 1951 election see *l'Evénement*, 23 June 1951.   [30] Williams, *Crisis and compromise*, p. 152.
[31] H. Coston, *Dictionnaire de la politique française* (Paris, 1967), p. 1,036.
[32] See, for example, Duchet's article on the unification of four separate independent groups in *la France Indépendante*, in 'Un grand événement politique', 24 June 1956.
[33] An Independent circular (dated 30 March 1949 in AN, 74 AP 33) complained that the press failed to distinguish between the various conservative groups.

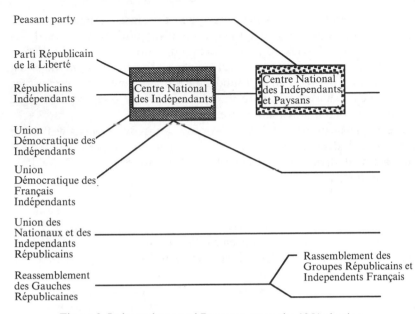

Figure 2 Independents and Peasants up to the 1951 election

absence of party discipline or doctrine, the identity of the Independents was defined largely in terms of personality. Emphasis was laid on local leaders around whom the movement could group. The electoral declarations of the Independents laid an even greater stress than those of their rivals on the particular services that candidates and their allies had rendered to constituencies. The centre piece of *la France Indépendante* was a profile of some prominent individual (businessman, lawyer or academic) whose career was held up for admiration. The men profiled in these articles were usually important in their field, but not famous on the national stage. This fitted in with the Independents' image as a party of modest men noted for professional competence rather than charisma.

One Independent leader, Antoine Pinay, achieved paradoxical status as a man who became celebrated for being very ordinary. He became, for a time, the most popular politician in France and the myth that grew up around him reveals a good deal about the more general appeal of the Independents. Pinay could have stepped straight from the pages of a conservative propaganda brochure. He owned a small family business (a tannery) in a small provincial town (Saint-Chamond in the Loire). When a collection of interviews with Pinay was published, it was entitled *Un français comme les autres*.[34] Pinay always suggested that he found it surprising, and perhaps

[34] A. Pinay, *Un français comme les autres. Entretiens avec Antoine Veil* (Paris, 1984).

rather distasteful, that he should be asked to join governments: it was claimed that he was summoned to take a ministry after he had already set off for his journey back to Saint-Chamond. Anti-Gaullists, like Fabre-Luce, played an especially active part in propagating the Pinay myth, and it was clear that many of them found him attractive precisely because he offered such a sharp contrast to the general: 'France prefered the honest management of a family man to pseudo-grandeur.'[35]

The emphasis on personality could prove a disadvantage as well as an asset for the Independents. The group was vulnerable to personal quarrels and factional divisions. Particular problems were presented by Paul Reynaud. Reynaud was the most eminent Independent: he had been prime minister before the war, he was minister of finance in 1948, he was respected by most conservatives for his economic liberalism and for his role in the crushing of strikes in 1938. He had an important personal following. Laniel was a loyal supporter and had been said to be 'unwilling to raise his little finger without Reynaud's permission' even before joining the Independents.[36] De Saivre, editor of an anti-Communist newspaper *Volonté*, wrote that Reynaud was recognized as 'the real leader of the liberals and anti-*dirigistes*'.[37] However, Reynaud was also a man of great personal awkwardness who took, and caused, offence easily.

Duchet was also an aggressive and awkward man who seems to have valued his position in the CNIP more than he valued the CNIP's position in national politics. He often undermined his own colleagues[38] and he annoyed even his ally Pinay.[39] The most savage of the numerous quarrels that Duchet and Reynaud initiated was their quarrel with each other. In 1950 Duchet sought to prevent Reynaud from speaking at the Journée des Indépendants in December 1950.[40] Reynaud responded by seeking to have Duchet removed from his post as party secretary. When an anonymous publication was circulated in Dunkirk that described Reynaud as having been 'vomited up by the country', Reynaud immediately suspected that Duchet was the author.[41] In May 1951, Duchet used his influence with

---

[35] P. Estèbe in *La France Réelle*, 33 (27 June 1952). See also Sapiens (pseudonym for Alfred Fabre-Luce), *Mendès ou Pinay* (Paris, 1953), p. 149: 'Last year General de Gaulle chose Antoine Pinay as the man to destroy. The average Frenchman has concluded from this that he is the man to choose.'

[36] On Laniel's respect for Reynaud see his interview with a representative of the FR on 25 October 1945 in AN, 317 AP 84.

[37] AN, 74 AP 33. Unsigned note quoting de Saivre, dated 10 June 1951.

[38] Georges Riond believed that Duchet had prevented him from becoming president of the assembly of the French union. Riond, *Chroniques d'un autre monde*, p. 227. Duchet's personality also caused problems when attempts were made to negotiate the adhesion of the AD to the Independents. See Bibliothèque Nationale, Alliance Démocratique Archives (AD), 4, Flandin's speech to meeting of AD on 28 May 1952.   [39] Ibid.

[40] AN, 74 AP 33, Duchet to Reynaud, 4 October 1950.

[41] AN, 74 AP 33, sub-prefect of Dunkirk to Reynaud, dated 20 November 1950 and Duchet to Reynaud, 25 November 1950.

Wolf, the wealthy proprietor of a newspaper, to insist that a violent attack on Reynaud was printed.[42]

The dispute between the two men tied in with broader conflicts in the CNIP. Reynaud had quarrelled before the war with Flandin, who was the patron of a certain faction of French conservatism. Laniel, Triboulet and most of those who joined the Independents from the PRL rallied to Reynaud. Antoine Pinay was associated with Duchet, as was Camille Laurens of the Peasant party. Duchet boasted in his memoirs that he launched 'brutal attacks' on Joseph Laniel and that he had prevented Laniel from becoming president of the Republic in 1954.[43] Pinay and Laniel formed governments (in 1952 and 1954 respectively), but of the eight Independents who obtained posts in these governments, only one served in both. The Reynaud/Duchet conflict spilled over into the provincial organization of the Independents. In December 1950 a committee of Independents in the Isère wrote to Reynaud: 'our affection for you does not seem to please the National Centre'.[44] Duchet responded to the Reynaud supporters in the Isère by setting up a rival Independent group in the same area at the beginning of 1951.[45]

If the Independents were often on bad terms with their colleagues, they were often on good terms with their supposed rivals from other political formations, and the loose structure of the CNIP permitted considerable inter-party co-operation. Relations were particularly close with the RGR. Many Independents had belonged to parties that went on to form part of the RGR. Furthermore, the two movements had many similarities. Both supported amnesty and rehabilitation for Pétainists, both were liberal in economic matters, and both disapproved of tight party discipline. The possibility of an alliance between the two formations was frequently discussed by leaders of both sides, and by outside commentators.[46] As early as December 1949, various Independent leaders thought it worthwhile to produce a comparative table showing the motions passed at the recent study days of the Radicals and the Independents. The text accompanying the table suggested that the two formations differed only with regard to the question of free schools (the Independents were in favour, the Radicals against) and the power of the parliament (the Radicals were more favourable than the Independents to a powerful legislature).[47]

Unlike the Independents, the Peasant party did belong to a clearly identifiable tradition. A Peasant party had been founded in France before

---

[42] AN, 74 AP 33, de Saivre to Giron, 15 May 1951 and unsigned note dated 10 June 1951.
[43] Duchet, *La république épinglée*, p. 16.
[44] AN, 4 AP 33, Eugène Condette to Reynaud, dated 14 December 1950.
[45] AN, 74 AP 33, Eugène Condette to Reynaud, dated 14 February 1951.
[46] *La France Indépendante* printed an article on 3 February 1951 entitled 'Les Radicaux et nous'.   [47] AN, 74 AP 33, circular dated 19 December 1949.

the Second World War, but it had never attained the success of similar groups in other European countries. On 11 July 1945 a new Peasant party was founded by Paul Antier. Its deputies were initially drawn from the backward and impoverished agricultural area of the Massif Central. The party's view of its own function was rather confused. Its manifesto stated an intention not to be a party of opposition or class struggle but to co-operate with parties of goodwill.[48] However, in practice the Peasant party was more intransigent in its attitude to governments than the Independents. Furthermore, the party's founder seemed, initially at least, to disdain contact with power. In private he proclaimed himself content to lead a small party that would not have to 'take any responsibility' even in parliamentary commissions, let alone governments.[49]

The Peasant party's official paper was full of savage attacks on *tripartisme* and the political system in general. Oddly, the Peasant group's apparent disdain for participating in government increased its power. The parliamentary Peasant party came to offer a right-wing version of what the Socialists called a *cure d'opposition*. Those, numerous, conservative deputies who had quarrelled with their own colleagues or rebelled against the discipline of their own group found a refuge in the Peasant party. The result of this was that the Peasant party, which had had seven parliamentary representatives after the legislative elections of 1946 had twenty-two just before the legislative elections of 1951.

The Peasant party liked to present itself as the extension of pressure group activity into the political sphere. However, the professional bodies that represented peasants never accepted that their political relations should be confined exclusively to Antier's party. The leading figure behind the CGA was Tanguy-Prigent, a Socialist,[50] and the Peasant party's leaders made it clear that they regarded the CGA as a nest of left-wing subversion.[51] The syndical branch of the CGA, the Fédération Nationale des Syndicats d'Exploitants Agricoles (FNSEA), was dominated by men of more conservative views, notably René Blondelle, and in 1947 the FNSEA managed to acquire a high degree of autonomy.[52] However, even it did not

---

[48] Manifesto of 11 July 1945. Philip Williams claims that the Peasants were allied with the MRP. Barrillon suggests that the Peasant party manifesto of 11 July 1945 expressed a willingness to ally with the Communist party. R. Barrillon,'Les modérés. Paysans et Indépendants Paysans', in J. Fauvet and H. Mendras (eds.), *Les paysans et la politique dans la France contemporaine* (Paris, 1958), pp. 131–148. In fact the party manifesto (published in *Unité Paysanne* of 6 October 1945) gives no such impression and the party's leaders launched vigorous attacks on the Communists: Benoit-Rambaud, 'La France a voté', *Unité Paysanne*, 3 November 1945.

[49] AN, 317 AP, 84, note of meeting between unnamed representative of FR and Antier on 15 October 1945.

[50] On Tanguy-Prigent see G. Wright, *Rural revolution in France* (Stanford, 1968), p. 101.

[51] Benoit-Rambaud, 'CGA et CGT', *Unité Paysanne*, 10 November 1945.

[52] Wright, *Rural revolution in France*, p. 108.

give exclusive support to the Peasant party. In the 1951 election, the FNSEA formed a 'civic action front' that backed candidates from a variety of conservative parties.[53] In addition to this, peasant representatives from the CGA or the FNSEA sometimes stood as parliamentary candidates without party affiliation. Members of Antier's party often found that they were standing against rival 'peasant lists' and the Peasant candidate in Indre et Loire querulously reminded his voters that 'he alone had been invested by the Centre National des Indépendants et Paysans'.[54]

The Peasant party's presentation of itself as a simple and non-political representative of small farmers also looked increasingly odd in the light of those who represented the party in parliament. Many of those drawn to the party were not peasants by any stretch of the imagination. A large number of them were professional lawyers. Many were not resident in agricultural areas, and some were not even resident in mainland France at all. André Petsch, the son of a wealthy electricity magnate and a member of the elite *cour des comptes*, became attached (*apparenté*) to the Peasant group, as did Francis Quilici (deputy for the Algerian town of Oran). Support from overseas France became so important that a publication – *Unité Paysanne d'Outre Mer* – was established to defend the '70 million peasants in France overseas'.[55] All this was particularly bizarre in view of the fact that very few European inhabitants of the French empire were small-scale farmers.

Some of the Peasant party's recruits after 1951 were even less close to the soil. Jacques Isorni, a deputy for western Paris, joined the Peasant group, as did Jacques Le Roy Ladurie, former Vichy minister of agriculture, wealthy Normandy landowner and father of the historian. André Boutemy, the paymaster of big business, became a Peasant senator. By 1951 the Peasant group was a parliamentary leper colony inhabited mainly by men whose extreme political opinions or personal awkwardness made it difficult for them to exist in any other formation. The party's choice of allies was equally incongruous. The Peasants' reputation for aggressive opposition to tripartism and *dirigisme* often drew admiration from parties on the extreme right. Links were particularly close with Réconciliation Française (RF) and the PRL (indeed the leader of the PRL ultimately joined the Peasant parliamentary group). But, in terms of the social basis of their support, the PRL and RF could not have been more remote from the Peasants. The PRL drew its support mainly from industrialized areas, while the RF was strongest in Paris and contained almost no farmers at all.

Two leaders were prominent in the Peasant party: Paul Antier and Camille Laurens. The two men were engaged in a constant struggle which resembled that in the Independents between Duchet and Reynaud. Antier

[53] Ibid., p. 117.   [54] *Barodet*, p. 330.
[55] *Unité Paysanne d'Outre Mer*, March 1953.

was hesitant about alliance with the Independents. Laurens supported the alliance with the Independents because he thought that it would weaken his rival's position.[56] After the 1951 election the two factions of the Peasant party split and reunited twice. The split was rooted in a variety of social and political differences, although it is notable that the Peasant party organization in the country seems to have been little affected by the divisions among its parliamentary leaders. Maresca pointed out that struggles between peasant groups were often in reality 'struggles between leaders who are much more mobilized by this competition than the group of farmers whose representation they seek to control'.[57]

The rise of the CNIP is often linked to the rehabilitation of those who had supported the Vichy regime. Antoine Pinay had been a member of Pétain's *conseil national* and had been declared ineligible after the war. The CNIP campaigned vigorously against the ineligibility laws and denounced the first amnesty given to Pétainists as an 'inadequate parody of a law'.[58] However, the CNIP was not a simple representative of Pétainism. There were men who opposed Vichy in both the Independents and the Peasants, and the factional struggles in both groups were linked to the legacy of Vichy. Antier had been a supporter of the Resistance while Laurens had been a Vichy official. Laniel and Reynaud had both been opponents of Vichy and they blamed Duchet and Pinay for having supported Pétain.[59] It should also be noted that overtures made by explicitly Pétainist bodies were often rejected even by the wing of the CNIP that had been most closely linked to Vichy.[60]

The Independents and Peasants never ceased to insist that they were 'apolitical', and that the categories of 'right' and 'left' had no meaning for them. This emphasis on 'apoliticism' was characteristic of all French conservative parties: Alain, the philopher of radicalism in the Third Republic, had said that 'when a man denies that he is either right or left, I know that he is not of of the left'. However, beneath the apparently solid and reassuring tradition of apoliticism lurked two different interpretations of what this concept meant, and the conflict between the two was to add to the divisions that plagued the CNIP. Some regarded all governments, and perhaps all parliaments, of the Fourth Republic with distaste. They condemned what Jean Mazé called *le système* or Desgranges called the *résistantialisme* that they believed to characterize all politics since the war,

---

[56] Duchet, *La république épinglée*, p. 14.
[57] S. Maresca, *Les dirigeants paysans* (Paris, 1983), p. 165.
[58] Jean Deshors, 'La parodie d'une loi', *la France Indépendante*, 25 November 1951.
[59] AN, 74 AP 33, Duchet to Reynaud (responding to allegations that Reynaud had made about Duchet's war record), dated 18 December 1951.
[60] For example Duchet rebuffed the approaches made by the extreme right paper *Paroles Françaises*. Circular from CNIP dated 16 December 1950, in AN, 74 AP 33.

and they defined themselves as the *opposition nationale*. Their attitude was summed up by Liautey's claim that it was better for the Independents to have thirty committed and resolute representatives in parliament than '300 molluscs who are vulnerable to every influence'.[61]

On the other hand, there were those Independents who might be described as pragmatically 'apolitical'. The pragmatists did not rule out office holding or political activity. Indeed, as one of his party colleagues pointed out, Pinay's reputation as 'a man who had never been involved in politics' sat oddly with the fact that Pinay had been involved in national and local politics for forty years.[62] What men like Pinay disdained was abstract ideological politics. They stressed that their aim was simply to 'get things done', and to look after their constituents. In practice this meant adopting an attitude close to that of the Radical party. Practical power was more important than abstract principle. Independents liked to hold ministerial office, particularly those offices that were, as Duchet put it, 'technical rather than political'.[63] Independents were particularly keen to hold the ministries – such as those of posts, public works, agriculture and ex-servicemen – that were perceived to give their holders great powers of patronage. Coty and Triboulet were both proud of their efforts to devolve public works to private sector contractors; both would have known that the small entrepreneurs in the building trade were an important part of the conservative constituency.[64] Even those Independents who were unable or unwilling to obtain ministerial office, often supported governments on the grounds that such support would give their constituents access to favours. *Abbé* Kir put this point succinctly when instructing the man who was delegated to cast his vote in the National Assembly: 'Only Dijon interests me and in the interests of my town I need to be on good terms with the government; my only request is vote for [the government].'[65]

The *opposition nationale* fitted in with their pragmatic colleagues in the Independent and Peasant parties during the period of tripartism when all conservatives were bound to be in opposition. However, once the prospect of ministerial office opened up for the CNIP then problems were bound to arise. In part these problems were reflected in further factional splits and in the eviction of a number of *opposition nationale* extremists, notably Dides, from the group in 1954.[66] However, there was also a sense in which the conflict engendered by the two varieties of apoliticism operated within individuals as well as between them. Even the most 'governmentalist'

[61] Speech made by Liautey on 14 June 1951 reprinted in *l'Evénement* for 23 June 1951.
[62] Triboulet, *Un gaulliste de la IVème*, p. 151.   [63] Duchet, *La république épinglée*, p. 16.
[64] Coty was minister of reconstruction, Triboulet was a member of the parliamentary commission on public works. F. de Baecque, *René Coty, tel qu'en lui-même*, p. 112. Triboulet, *Un gaulliste de la IVème*, p. 149 .
[65] Triboulet, *Un gaulliste de la IVème*, p. 145.
[66] Duchet, *La république épinglée*, p. 28.

conservative was influenced to some extent by the rhetoric of principled opposition to the system, and this rhetoric tended to inflame the struggles over posts and preferment that existed in the CNIP: all Independents were members of the *opposition nationale* when they were refused ministerial office.[67]

There was also an economic dimension to the 'apoliticism' of the Independents. Independent leaders liked to stress that their economic policy was not linked to an ideology, but that it simply represented a detached view of how the economy should be managed. Pinay argued: 'the remedies are neither right nor left. They have no parliamentary affiliation, they are technical measures to be taken in a climate of political truce.'[68] However, the very vigour with which the Independents repeated their attacks on high taxation and *dirigisme* showed that their economic policies stood no chance of being accepted as 'apolitical' or technical measures. This marked a new development in French economic thinking. Before 1940, there had been a wide consensus about how the economy should be managed. The liberal orthodoxy expounded by economists like Charles Rist was taught in universities and the *école libre des sciences politiques* and practised by the powerful civil servants of the finance ministry. Almost all politicians, even those of the Socialist party, accepted that the capitalist system could only be managed within the limits laid down by this orthodoxy. After 1945 all this changed. Civil servants regarded extensive intervention as necessary, and even desirable. The rise of planning was the most visible sign of changing attitudes. Finance ministry officials like Louis Franck and Bloch-Lainé regarded the liberalism of Antoine Pinay with open hostility, and Pinay found that his policies were sometimes impeded by men in his own department.[69] In short, the fact that certain orthodoxies were no longer defended outside the political sphere, meant that the CNIP was obliged to use political means to try to restore an 'apolitical consensus'.

The nature of the CNIP's dilemma was illustrated by the importance that Jacques Rueff assumed. Rueff was a classic representative of the civil service elite that had defended a certain financial orthodoxy before 1940: he was a graduate of the *école polytechnique* and an *inspecteur des finances*. In his writings Rueff defended austere free market economics; he attacked Keynesianism and social policies that distorted the operation of the labour market.[70] After the war as more interventionist civil servants came to power, Rueff was marginalized.[71] As his administrative star waned, Rueff's

---

[67] Ibid., p. 16.   [68] Cited in Christine Rimbaud, *Pinay* (Paris, 1990), p. 120.

[69] Ibid., p. 65.

[70] On Rueff's economic views and career see F. Bourricaud and P. Salin, *Présence de Jacques Rueff* (Paris, 1989).

[71] F. Bourricaud, 'Le libéralisme de Jacques Rueff', in F. Bourricaud and P. Salin (eds.), *Présence de Jacques Rueff*, p. 38. Rueff's marginalization was reflected in his appointment as minister of state in Monaco.

political star waxed. He became a hero of the CNIP[72] and in December 1950 he was asked to address the banquet of the Independents' Journées Nationales. His address, which was published and widely reported, made much of the need for restraint on public spending. However, this former member of the administrative elite recognized that public spending was high precisely because of the power exercised by an unaccountable administration, and his main proposed remedy was an increase in the powers of parliament.[73]

Resistance from civil service elites was not the only problem to dog Independent economic policy; even within the policies professed by the Independent leaders themselves, important contradictions existed. Rueff's views had developed in the library and the lecture room. He believed that 'society's economic problems only spring from confused thought', and he was impatient with the political instability that undermined the application of radical economic reforms.[74] Political instability had particularly damaging effects on the Independents. The Radicals and the MRP were able to maintain control of the ministries that mattered the most to them (interior and foreign affairs respectively) through endless changes of government. The CNIP was never able to exercise a similar control over the finance ministry. Petsche's tenure was too short for his plans to take effect and Reynaud's spell at the ministry was, in Bloch-Lainé's memorable phrase, 'just long enough to ruin our summer and dash our hopes'.[75]

There was a contrast between the academic liberalism advocated by Rueff and the policies practised by men like Pinay. Independent ministers understood that the application of Rueff's economic realism was politically unrealistic at a time when economic suffering might swell support for the Communists or the RPF. In the finance ministry and later as prime minister Pinay displayed what one commentator described as 'not a liberalism of the pure, but rather a modest pragmatism'.[76] Pinay's resort to extensive borrowing and his toleration of measures such as the introduction of a minimum wage aroused Rueff's disapproval. Furthermore, Pinay's economic policies hinged not around clear financial goals but around the psychological goal of creating confidence (a goal that mystified Rueff as much as it did the earnest young officials of the finance ministry).[77]

Independents called for low taxation, balanced budgets and a defence of

---

[72] *La France Indépendante*, 27 May 1950. Curiously, neither Rueff nor his biographers made any retrospective mention of the role that he had played in the CNIP.

[73] J. Rueff, *Discours aux Indépendants* (Paris, 1951), p. 27: 'Parliament has almost abandoned control of the budget. Though this is its primary *raison d'être*.'

[74] Bourricaud, 'Le libéralisme de Jacques Rueff', p. 44.

[75] F. Bloch-Lainé, *Profession fonctionnaire. Entretiens avec Françoise Carrière* (Paris, 1976), pp. 96–97.   [76] Rimbaud, *Pinay*, p. 68.

[77] On Bloch-Lainé's bemusement at Pinay's policies see Bloch-Lainé, *Profession fonctionnaire*, p. 125.

the franc. In practice these aims were often mutually exclusive. Low taxation meant that the chances of paying off debt and stabilizing the franc were reduced. The extent of ambiguity about the 'liberalism' of the CNIP was exposed by the Mayer plan of 1948. The Mayer plan involved loosening economic controls and balancing the budget (measures of which the Independents approved), but the plan also involved raising taxation for the peasants and small shopkeepers who made up such a large part of the CNIP electorate.[78] Reaction to the Mayer plan among the leaders of the CNIP reflected this contradiction. Rueff, the economic guru of the Independents, condemned the plan on a variety of technical grounds, Reynaud claimed to support the plan but covertly sought to undermine it,[79] and Pinay admitted that he supported the plan, though he disapproved of the manner in which it had been presented.[80]

Economic interests and policies represented by the CNIP often clashed with their policies on defence. The CNIP advocated cuts in taxation and government spending, but one of the most important drains on government resources was high armaments spending to defend western Europe against Soviet Russia and to maintain the French Union (both causes vigorously supported by the CNIP). The Peasants' leader Camille Laurens revealed the full extent of confusion that was induced by this contradiction when he abstained during a parliamentary vote on the 1951 budget saying that he accepted arms spending but not the means to provide for this.[81]

The clash between economic and defence policy also emerged over the European policy of the CNIP. An article in *la France Indépendante* stressed that 'the effective force for federation ... is the sense that we have a civilization to defend ... against all totalitarianism'.[82] However, European integration was also seen to threaten the economic interests of many of the small businessmen who were seen as being so important to the CNIP. It is significant that *la France Indépendante* carried admiring profiles of both Edmond Giscard d'Estaing[83] (an international businessman and the most vigorous supporter of European integration), and Léon Gingembre (the small business leader and fervent opponent of European integration).[84]

The contradictions in the economic policy of the CNIP reflected the contradictions in the social basis of their support. The most obvious of

---

[78] On the attitudes of the Peasant party to Mayer see *Unité Paysanne*, 27 December 1947.
[79] AN, 457 AP 175, unsigned political report made on night of 7 to 8 January 1948: 'Reynaud guette Mayer dans l'ombre'.
[80] Pinay, *Un français comme les autres*, pp. 38–39. Mayer himself was aware that Pinay supported the broad aims of his plan; see his account in Denise Mayer (ed.), *René Mayer. Etudes, témoignages, documents* (Paris, 1983), p. 171.
[81] AN, 350 AP 93, MRP *fichiers politiques*, 6 (the date of the vote was 6 January 1951).
[82] Jacques de Maupeau, 'Faire l'Europe, c'est faire la paix', *la France Indépendante*, 22 April 1950.   [83] Ibid.   [84] Ibid., 10 June 1950.

these contradictions was that between the Independent and the Peasant groupings. Two-thirds of those elected under CNIP patronage south of the Loire chose to join the Peasant group, while three-quarters of those elected in constituencies north of the Loire joined the Independents. The most economically advanced departments of France returned eighteen Independents and three Peasants while the least advanced departments returned two Independents and fifteen Peasants.[85] The interests of the peasantry and the bourgeoisie were often mutually exclusive. The Peasant party sometimes exhibited a primitive anti-capitalism, and their support for measures such as the nationalization of the banks irritated their future allies in the Independent grouping.[86] Both called for lower taxation, but a significant reason for the high taxes imposed on urban businessmen, represented by the Independents, was that small farmers, represented by the Peasant party, paid so few taxes and received so many state subsidies.

Even within each of the two groups there were substantial divisions of interest. The Peasant party was affected by conflicts between different kinds of farmers. It was widely accepted that there were 'two agricultures' in France. Large-scale modern producers had different interests from small-scale farmers with little machinery. Furthermore, beet and wheat producers, who were mostly large and modern operators in northern France, gained from state regulation of their markets as did, to a lesser extent, wine producers. The gulf between the two agricultures grew in the Fourth Republic both because of the modernization of some rural areas and because state spending on agriculture, particularly that channelled by the Monnet plan, tended to go to the most modern farmers.[87]

Divisions in the Peasant party were exacerbated by the fact that increasing numbers of its leaders were more linked to urban industrial areas than agricultural ones. This division partly underlay the split between Antier and Laurens. Barrillon wrote: 'The friends of M. Antier are more peasants than conservatives ... The friends of M. Duchet and M. Laurens ... are less interested in the FNSEA [the agricultural association] than the CNPF [the big business association] ... They are in some ways more conservatives than peasants.'[88] Williams described this division in terms of a clash between Antier's peasant/Peasants and Laurens' lawyer/Peasants, but even within these factions, there were divisions: Antier's supporters included several men with tenuous links to agriculture (and Antier himself was a lawyer).[89]

---

[85] Williams, *Politics in post-war France*, p. 114.
[86] François Gagnaire, 'Le Parti Paysan et nous', *la République*, 11 (20 April 1946). *La République* was an official organ of the PRL which later merged with the Independents.
[87] Wright, *Rural revolution in France*, p. 120.   [88] Barrillon, 'Les modérés', p. 132.
[89] At least one of Antier's associates, André Mutter, was also a lawyer.

Equally deep divisions were to be found inside the Independents. The fact that the Independents made so much of their function as professional representatives only served to exacerbate these differences. The Independents liked to imply that professional associations were models of common sense and consensus compared to the world of squabbling political parties. However, the truth was that conflicts between different sectors and rivalries within sectors made the business world at least as divided as the political one. The fact that the Independents lacked a disciplined party structure or any explicit ideology beyond 'economic pragmatism' to bind their supporters together meant that economic conflicts impinged directly on the life of the party.

One of these divisions was that between those representing large and small business. The Independents had links with small business leaders, and derived much of their electoral support from this group, but they also drew financial support from large-scale business which often favoured quite different policies. Conflicts between these two sectors was one element underlying the disagreement on European policy (described above) between the small business leader Gingembre and the international financier Giscard d'Estaing. Economic conflicts can be seen as one of the elements underlying the struggle between the Reynaud/Laniel faction and the Duchet/Pinay faction. Reynaud and Laniel both came from industrialized areas: Reynaud had been a friend of large-scale industry since his role in re-armament and the *revanche des patrons* of the 1930s;[90] Laniel was himself a large-scale textile manufacturer. Duchet and Pinay, on the other hand, came from relatively backward areas; Pinay presided over a business of modest size and was closely associated with Léon Gingembre's Confédération Générale des Petites et Moyennes Entreprises. In fact all four leaders of the Independents were closely linked to big business interests, but Duchet and Pinay were certainly perceived as being more representative of small business than their rivals.

Even within the sectors represented by different factions of the Independents there were contradictions. Large-scale industry was divided between relatively backward industries, such as textile manufacture, that depended on imperial markets and more dynamic industries, such as those making electrical goods, that looked to European markets. Conflict over this issue was to arise in the Independents during the 1950s. André Boutemy (who was a Peasant senator as well as a distributor of business funds) began to push for an end to France's expensive empire,[91] while Eugène Motte (a textile manufacturer and Independent deputy) became a leader of the

---

[90] On Reynaud's perceived links with large-scale industry see V. Auriol, *Journal du septennat* (7 vols, Paris 1970–80), I, p. 230, entry for 20 October 1947, 'The large industries of the North that support Reynaud'.   [91] Duchet, *La république épinglée*, p. 29.

campaign to defend Algérie Française. Small business was also divided between businesses employing up to fifty people and artisanal enterprises with no employees at all (which often gained from special legal privileges), and between producers and retailers. Men like Gingembre who claimed to represent small business lived precarious lives as they strove to reconcile the competing claims of various elements of their constituencies.

In some respects the CNIP was the largest single beneficiary of the 1951 election. It gained fewer seats than the MRP or the RPF, but its advance on the position that it had held a few years earlier was greater than that of any other party. The CNIP's success was reflected in Pinay's appointment as prime minister and in the election of another Independent, Coty, as president in 1953. However, the CNIP's success backfired. As the group approached power, the contradictions within it became increasingly apparent: it was a coalition of negatives able to agree only on what it opposed.

14 The Groupement de Défense des Contribuables

> In a general sense we saw an awakening on the part of certain sectors and a search for electoral outlets by the professions. Such phenomena, which were not confined to the Jura, were omens of wider movements, which would take the form of Poujadism. No doubt they deserved to receive more attention.[1]

The remark quoted above was made by Edgar Faure with reference to the general election of 1951, and particularly with reference to the role of the Groupement de Défense des Contribuables (GDC) in those elections. The GDC has received almost no attention from historians: the most comprehensive work on the parties of the Fourth Republic devotes precisely one paragraph to it,[2] and the official biography of the party's most prominent organizer – Léon Gingembre – discusses the episode in less than three pages.[3] This neglect is not surprising in view of the apparent electoral failure of the GDC, which put only one deputy in parliament and obtained more than 5 per cent of the vote in a mere five constituencies.

The historian's verdict on the GDC is, in some respects, a reflection of the party's own propaganda as well as its apparent electoral failure. The GDC's leaders presented their movement as one of simple 'little men' who were indignant at the machinations of professional politicians: 'The games of politics are incomprehensible to us. Alliances that form and break up at the whim of mysterious influences or obscure cabals, of which we can understand neither the importance nor the aims, confuse us and arouse our suspicions.'[4] The GDC's leaders were especially vigorous in their denunciation of the complicated alliance and *apparentement* system which flourished under the electoral law of 1951: 'In the half anonymous electoral lists, in the

---

[1] E. Faure, *Mémoires. I: Avoir toujours raison ... c'est un grand tort* (Paris, 1982), p. 308.

[2] Philip Williams, *Politics in post-war France: parties and the constitution in the Fourth Republic* (2nd edition, London, 1958), p. 149.

[3] Sylvie Guillaume, *La Confédération Générale des Petites et Moyennes Entreprises. Son histoire, son combat, un autre syndicalisme patronal 1944–1978* (Paris, 1987), pp. 42–45.

[4] Unsigned article headed 'A number of our friends, among the FRONT ECONOMIQUE have created this group because they are disgusted by the games of politics ... [and] contradictions.' In *La Volonté du Commerce et de l'Industrie*, 45 (June 1951).

doubly anonymous *apparentements*, in the uncertainty of votes that go to the party rather than the man, what contact can be established?'[5]

If we accept that the GDC was an attempt to challenge the political system of the Fourth Republic then we must recognize that it failed and deserves the obscurity into which historians have consigned it. However, this chapter will argue that, far from being a naive attack on the political system, the GDC was a sophisticated use of that system; it was in short an example of the 'mysterious influences' that it purported to attack. This interpretation hinges on two facts. First, the party was not, as has generally been assumed, the representative of an isolated and powerless group of small businessmen. It was funded, and to some extent controlled, by the influential large-scale industrialists who held power in the Conseil National du Patronat Français (CNPF); indeed, the archives of the CNPF relating to the GDC campaign provide the clearest available evidence of its direct involvement in politics. Secondly, the party's founders and leaders intended it to be primarily a means of pressuring and helping candidates from other parties, rather than a means of winning elections in its own right; to achieve this end it manipulated the alliance and *apparentement* system with considerable skill. In this context the GDC emerges not as a failed party but as a successful supra-party organization of the kind that played an important role in the reconstruction of French conservatism after 1945.[6]

The GDC originated with the Front Economique, a grouping of employers' and professional organizations set up in 1949 to oppose the financial policies of Georges Bidault.[7] In June 1950 the Front decided to intervene in the forthcoming general elections and, to this end, ordered the formation of committees in each department of France. In order to avoid compromising the Front Economique in an openly political campaign the GDC was established to co-ordinate electoral activities.[8]

Who the Front Economique and the GDC represented was not entirely clear. Both organizations sought support from a broad alliance of 'professionals'. The directing committee of the GDC contained representatives of peasants, artisans, small businessmen and the liberal professions. The leading personalities behind the GDC were Guy Desforges, representing small business, Boulland, representing the artisans, and Pierre Lefaurichon, representing the liberal professions.[9] The most publicly visible of the

[5] Pierre Lefaurichon, 'Voter pour des hommes', in ibid.
[6] René Rémond, *Les droites en France* (Paris, 1982), p. 394.
[7] On the foundation of the Front Economique see Michel Margairaz, *L'état, les finances et l'économie. Histoire d'une conversion 1932–1952* (2 vols, Paris, 1991), II, p. 1,116.
[8] Gingembre's speech to the *assises de l'économie privée* justified the establishment of the GDC on the grounds that 'It is inappropriate to use the Front Economique – which may be needed in the future for other services of defence of the private sector.' Archives Nationales (AN), 72 AS 118.   [9] *La Volonté du Commerce et de l'Industrie*, 45 (June 1951).

organizations behind the GDC/Front Economique campaign was the Confédération Générale des Petites et Moyennes Entreprises (CGPME). The president of the CGPME, Léon Gingembre, was also president of the Front Economique, and Guy Desforges, who became president of the GDC, was also treasurer of the CGPME. Most observers assumed that the CGPME was the 'moving force'[10] behind the GDC.

However, those who occupied the most prominent public positions in the GDC/Front Economique did not provide the cash that allowed them to function. Most small business and professional organizations found it notoriously hard to persuade their own members to pay their dues and certainly did not have surplus money for funding other bodies. In fact the bulk of money for the Front Economique came from large-scale industry. This was revealed in a letter that the secretary of the CNPF, Fabre, wrote to Gingembre in which he agreed to pay 500,000 francs towards the expenses of the Front Economique. In itself this was not a large amount of money, but the CNPF contribution was by far the largest made by any professional organization to the Front Economique which could only hope to extract 100,000 francs from its agricultural supporters and a 'symbolic'[11] 10,000 francs from the artisans and liberal professions.

Oddly, Fabre's letter of July 1952 argued, perhaps because of the *patronat*'s habitual discretion with regard to political subsidy, that the CNPF could not be held responsible for the expenses incurred by the electoral activities of the Front Economique. In reality the CNPF had been perfectly aware of the electoral use to which the Front Economique had put its funds the previous year,[12] and Fabre himself had admitted that the CNPF's apparent absence from the list of agencies behind the GDC was simply a matter of public relations: 'During the electoral period, action was conducted by a "Groupement National de Défense des Libertés Profession-nelles et des Contribuables" in which it was agreed that for psychological reasons the CNPF would not be represented.'[13]

The policies advocated by the GDC, or at least by those people who controlled the GDC at national level, were more surprising for what they did not include than for what they did. The party focused on the specific grievances liable to afflict the small businessmen to whom it addressed its message; special emphasis was laid on taxation. Broad political issues and in particular the issue of constitutional reform were not tackled by the party at national level,[14] though candidates were left free to adopt positions on

---

[10] Jacques Fauvet, 'En marge des partis', *le Monde*, 15 June 1951.

[11] AN, 72 AS 118, Fabre to Gingembre, 9 July 1952.

[12] AN, 72 AS 118, see, for example, the letter from Fabre of the CNPF to Segaud of the Front Economique calling on the latter to make his orgnization's manifesto more precise.

[13] AN, 72 AS 118, Fabre to Battut, dated 9 July 1951.

[14] Ibid. At a meeting of the *assises de l'économie privée* on 16 January 1951, Seches said that he believed constitutional reform to be necessary but hoped that the issue would be avoided during the forthcoming electoral campaign.

such issues within their own constituencies.[15] The reasons for this restraint were simple. The leaders of the Front Economique knew that the group that they were trying to bind together had a wide and diverse range of interests and opinions: attempting to uphold positions on broad political issues could only cause division.[16]

The absence of one issue in particular from the national statements of the Front Economique was conspicuous. Anti-Communism was the single most important motive behind business intervention in the Fourth Republic, and the electoral alliances, as opposed to the rhetoric, of the GDC were certainly directed against the Communist party. But the Front Economique never made any public statement hostile to the Communist party. Its own position on most issues was remarkably close to that of Communist backed organizations; indeed, the parliamentary Communist party expressed its support for the programme of the GDC.[17] Furthermore, the GDC's generally anti-*étatiste* position meant that it attacked many policies that had originated in the anti-Communist climate of the late 1940s. For example the GDC demanded to have the fiscal burden lightened through cuts in public expenditure though, as the group's leaders knew perfectly well, Cold War defence programmes accounted for much of that spending.[18] It complained about the delegation of parliament's powers to civil servants, though such delegation was, in part, designed to circumvent Communists in parliament. Most of all the GDC complained about the expenditure and controls involved in economic planning without mentioning the fact that the plan was, in part at least, designed to assuage grievances that might swell the support of the Communist party, and was financed largely from American Marshall aid.

The absence of open anti-Communism in the manifestos of the GDC was less incongruous than it might seem. The Communist party had made serious efforts after 1945 to win support outside the proletariat, and especially among small businessmen and artisans.[19] The leaders of the business organizations feared that these efforts had met with some success,[20] and seem to have recognized that the best way to win back the votes of a potentially Communist *petite bourgeoisie* was to offer it a manifesto resembling that of the Communist party.

Relations between the GDC and other non-Communist parties were confusing. Initially, the GDC sought to work within the existing parties by

[15] Ibid.

[16] AN, 72 AS 118, Marteau to meeting of *assises de l'économie privée* on 16 January 1951.

[17] AN, 72 AS 118, Duclos to Gingembre dated 13 November 1951.

[18] Account of history of GDC given to meeting of the Front Economique, 16 June 1951, in which Gingembre reported that deputies had been unwilling to cut taxation because of the need to sustain defence spending.

[19] Steven Zdatny, *The politics of survival: artisans in twentieth century France* (Oxford, 1990), p. 165.

[20] AN, 72 AS 74, at the meeting of the *conseil* of the CNPF on 7 January 1947.

applying pressure to deputies. This tactic was adopted largely because the leaders of the GDC knew that it would be impossible to unite their business backers in support of any single party: 'to proceed otherwise and favour one or other party would risk breaking up our organizations'.[21]

Even after it decided to present candidates on its own ticket, the primary aim of the GDC was never to get a large number of its men in parliament. Running candidates against other parties was only to be undertaken when all other options had failed and doing so was a sign of weakness rather than a sign of strength; the areas where the GDC presented candidates in opposition to other parties were almost invariably those areas where its organization was least well established.[22] Before resorting to this expedient the party would try to ensure that other parties put up candidates who would be sympathetic to its cause: 'figures who are well placed to represent us and who accept the responsibility of implementing our programme'.[23]

The manifestos of candidates give tantalizing glimpses of the influence that the GDC had exercised over party lists. In Calvados, the Union des Nationaux et Indépendants Républicains admitted that the choice of candidates owed much to the intervention of professional organizations: 'It was understandable that, faced with the poor behaviour of the outgoing assembly, men who are known and respected in their profession, [and] who have played an important role in Calvados for years, ceded to the requests of their respective organizations to present themselves to the voters.'[24] In the Ain the Independents subtitled their electoral declaration: 'Pour la défense des libertés professionnelles et des contribuables'.[25] One group of candidates referred to themselves as the Union des Indépendants, Paysans et Républicains Nationaux et pour la Défense des Libertés Profession-nelles.[26] Occasionally candidates were explicit about their relations with the GDC; the Independents in the Manche said of their economic policy: 'In

---

[21] AN, 72 AS 118, Marteau to meeting of *assises de l'économie privée* on 16 January 1951. At the same meeting Seches responded to Gingembre's expression of hope that the Front Economique would have representatives in parliament by saying 'It is questionable whether we are sufficiently confident of the discipline of professional men to adopt such a project.'

[22] AN, 72 AS 118. On 10 May 1951, Gingembre told the *assises de l'économie privée* that committees to prepare electoral tactics had been set up in twenty-nine departments which he listed. In only one of these departments, Loir et Cher, did the GDC present a candidate who was not linked to other parties through either alliances or *apparentement* agreements. It follows from this that in the remaining ten constituencies where the GDC presented isolated lists they had prepared their candidacies in weeks rather than months.

[23] AN 72 AS 118, Gingembre speaking to *assises de l'économie privée* on 10 May 1951.

[24] *Recueil des textes authentiques des programmes et engagements électoraux des députés proclamés élus à la suite des élections générales du 17 juin 1951* (commonly known as *Barodet*) (Paris, 1952), p. 113. UNIR was a Pétainist party lead by Jacques Isorni.

[25] Ibid., p. 7.

[26] Ibid., p. 67.

this area, our policy, is that of the Groupement de Défense des Libertés Professionnelles et des Contribuables.'[27]

The effects of the GDC campaign were widely felt: in June 1951 its leaders provided a list of over 314 candidates who had approved the programme of the Front Economique and agreed to join a parliamentary 'Group for the defence of the private sector' if elected.[28] It would be wrong to make too much of such a list. The fact that candidates had expressed approval of the GDC did not mean that the GDC approved of them – still less that it had influenced their selection. Furthermore the list of 314 included some politicians, such as Mendès-France, who were not noted for being easily swayed by business or professional pressure groups.

The GDC did not confine its attentions to any one party. Candidates from all the half dozen non-Communist parties received support, with varying degrees of openness, from the GDC.[29] The group did not spread its support over several parties because it was indiscriminate, but rather because it paid great attention to local circumstances and emphasized that the decision about which party to support could only be taken in this context: 'It is impossible to give general rules, there are almost as many cases as there are constituencies.'[30] There was no point in backing a party in an area where it stood no chance of winning or where all potential candidates were irredeemably hostile to business interests.

The local approach of the GDC fitted in with a desire to concentrate on individual candidates rather than the national parties that they ostensibly represented. The GDC regarded strong and disciplined parties with active disfavour; Gingembre explained the inadequacies of the current parliament thus: 'It simply shows, in a striking manner, the consequences of the monolithism of parties.'[31] One of the GDC's main aims was to restore the independence of deputies with regard to their party leaders, thereby freeing

---

[27] Ibid., p. 452.

[28] *La Volonté du Commerce et de l'Industrie*, 45 (June 1951). It should be stressed that this list, drawn up in the tumultuous and confused period before the election, was far from definitive. For example in Aveyron the GDC reported in June that they supported only the Radical candidate, but when the parliamentary inter-group was formed the following month it was the Independent deputy for the Aveyron who attended.

[29] It is of course impossible to know precisely how the GDC divided its support among the parties because its activities in many areas left no trace. We do know that all the major non-Communist parties benefited from either alliances or *apparentement* agreements with the GDC. In terms of direct alliances five successful candidates from the RGR had benefited from such arrangements as against two Independents, and one supporter of the RPF (three supporters of the RPF recorded in their electoral declarations that they had received the blessing of the GDC without, apparently, being in formal alliance). In terms of *apparentements* the major beneficiaries were the candidates of the SFIO, of whom seven benefited from arrangements with the GDC, as against six supporters of the MRP, five supporters of the Independents, one supporter of the RGR and one of the RPF.

[30] AN, 72 AS 118, Etienne addressing meeting of *assises de l'économie privée* on 16 January 1951.   [31] AN, 72 AS 118, meeting of 16 January 1951.

them to obey the dictates of their extra parliamentary sponsors: 'It is a question of supporting men who give us precise guarantees on precise questions, while freeing them as far as possible from the domination of their parties and making them answerable for their votes *vis-à-vis* their voters from our professions who supported them.'[32] It was no accident that the one GDC candidate who succeeded in entering parliament was a renegade from the Mouvement Républicain Populaire (MRP) who railed against the *caporalisme des partis*.[33]

The leaders of the GDC disliked excessive discipline within parties, but they were in favour of concerted action between parties. The bourgeois parties in France were divided by a large number of issues – religion, the constitution, debate over the legacy of Vichy and Gaullism – that had no direct bearing on business interests. Business could not hope to make these issues disappear but it could try to persuade candidates to form electoral alliances between parties that would prevent the Communists benefiting from these divisions. The GDC could apply pressure to candidates by threatening to put up its own candidates if alliances were not formed: 'It would perhaps be possible to oblige numerous lists likely to obtain the votes of our various professional categories, to agree with each other to present a single list, without which we would find ourselves obliged to establish our own list while recommending the boycott of all those who did not want to yield to reason.'[34]

Threats were not the only technique at the disposal of the GDC. It could also hold out positive advantages to candidates willing to co-operate. The most important of these advantages came in the form of electoral alliances. If parties behaved as business leaders wanted them to, then they might be allowed to ally with the GDC. Such an alliance would give candidates both the financial advantages that came from the GDC's funds and the moral advantages that could be derived from the prestige of the Front Economique. Sometimes GDC leaders would have themselves placed low on the list of a candidate of whom they approved so that they might attract votes for their *co-listiers* while not having any serious chance of winning a seat themselves.[35]

The GDC's strategy was made a great deal easier by the *apparentement* system that was introduced for the 1951 elections. *Apparentements* allowed votes to be tranferred from an unsuccessful list to another previously nominated one. The main purpose of the *apparentement* system was to

[32] Gingembre speaking to *assises de l'économie privée* of 10 May 1951.
[33] *Barodet*, 1951, p. 421.
[34] Gingembre speaking to *assises de l'économie privée* of 19 May 1951.
[35] 'One of our friends, M. Jacques, features, at his own request, quite low down on the Independent lists, the success of which he regards as necessary.' *La Volonté du Commerce et de l'Industrie*, 45 (June 1951).

prevent the anti-Communist vote from being split. The GDC was helped by the *apparentement* system in two ways. First, *apparentements* made it far easier to form alliances between bourgeois parties. Second, the *apparentements* made it easier for the GDC to help other parties by allowing votes cast for GDC candidates, who often stood no hope of winning in their own right, to be passed on to other parties.

The GDC was never intended to be the only means by which business influenced the 1951 elections. When the organization was established its founders recognized that their action would have to operate alongside that of other agencies – notably the rue de Penthièvre, Arbitrage Paysanne, the Union des Intérêts Economiques and the Comité Républicain du Commerce et de l'Industrie.[36] Sometimes the GDC put up candidates in opposition to politicians, such as François Mitterrand, who were known to have close links with business.[37] Sometimes the GDC itself used the complicated possibilities opened up by formal and informal alliances to work through several rival lists in a single constituency. In the Basses Pyrénées, for example, the GDC concluded a formal alliance with the MRP and the Independents as well as an *apparentement* deal with the Rassemblement des Groupes Républicaines et Indépendants Français (RGRIF),[38] but the Radical candidate, who stood in opposition to both these lists, also had informal links to the GDC.[39] Most strikingly of all, in the Cher the GDC ran a list against Raymond Boisdé, who was not only a prominent supporter of business interests but also a leading member of the Front Economique.[40]

There may be good reasons for such apparent conflicts. If more than one candidate from the bourgeois parties seemed bound to win then it made sense for the GDC to cultivate good relations with them all. Furthermore, there may have been circumstances in which an isolated GDC list, using radical language, may have helped all the non-Communist candidates by

---

[36] AN, 72 AS 118, *assises de l'économie privée*, 10 May 1951, report of commission of ways and means.

[37] The alliance of parties backing Mitterrand in the Nièvre was challenged by an alliance of the RPF and the GDC. In fact both Mitterrand and his GDC backed opponent were successful, so it may be that in this case business was simply trying to ensure that it had links with the maximum possible range of deputies. Mitterrand's links with the perfume manufacturer Eugène Schueller, who later replaced Boutemy as head of the Centre d'Etudes Economiques, were well known. See Roger Duchet, *La république épinglée* (Paris, 1975), p. 239. Mitterrand was supported in the 1951 by the PRL, which also had a reputation as a recipient of business funding.   [38] See appendix.

[39] This informal link was revealed by the fact that the Radical candidate turned up at the constitutive meeting of the Groupe de Défense de l'Economie Privée organized by the Front Economique; see *Les Informations Confédérales. Bulletin hebdomadaire de la Confédération Générale des Petites et Moyennes Entreprises*, 27 July 1951.

[40] AN, 72 AS 118, letter to H. Segaud dated 8 May 1951 listing representatives of commerce on the permanent committee of the Front Economique.

drawing votes of discontented artisans or small businessmen that would otherwise have gone to the Communist party. However, it would be wrong to see logic in everything that the GDC did. The businessmen behind the organization were themselves often divided on political matters, and the fact that the GDC had to devise its tactics in such a short space of time did not make it easier to achieve consistency.

An understanding of the electoral tactics of the GDC requires a new assessment of its achievements. Since the party only put up candidates in seats where it had failed to exercise influence by more subtle means, it can hardly be judged in terms of the number of seats or votes obtained. What needs to be examined is the influence that it was able to exercise in other parties. In some cases GDC connections with other parties are relatively easy to trace. We know that a total of ten successful candidates in the 1951 election had stood in alliance with the GDC; the Independents, Rassemblement des Gauches Républicaines (RGR) and Rassemblement du Peuple Français (RPF) each accounted for three of these while the MRP provided the tenth. We also know that twenty-four successful candidates in the 1951 election – eight from the Section Française de l'Internationale Ouvrière (SFIO), five from the MRP, five from the RGR, five from the Independents and one from the RPF – benefited from *apparentement* deals with the GDC (see appendix).

Most important of all was the influence that the GDC was able to exercise in areas where it never presented candidates. Since this influence was by definition subtle and discreet, it is hard to trace. What is known for sure is that the GDC had established an organization in at least twenty-six departments by May 1951, and that it presented candidates in only five of these. It seems reasonable to assume that the leaders of the GDC were content with the candidates presented by other parties in the remaining twenty-one departments. As has been pointed out, a professional journal listed over 300 candidates who had approved the programme of the Front Economique. After the election the Front Economique formed an inter-party group of sympathetic deputies in the National Assembly. The group was joined by some 317 deputies from all the major parties,[41] including four Socialists, and was headed by a committee that included three representatives from the RGR, the Independents and Peasants, the MRP and the RPF. Historians who believe that the GDC was meant to be a serious challenge to other political parties assume that the formation of the inter-

[41] The figure of 317 deputies is given by Sylvie Guillaume (*La Confédération Générale*, p. 45). Williams (*Politics in post-war France*, p. 332) suggests that the inter-group only had around 100 members. The CNPF claimed that 200 deputies had joined the intergroup. AN, 72 AS 118, Fabre to Battut, 9 July 1951. The July issue of *la Volonté du Commerce et de l'Industrie* listed seventy-two deputies who had actually attended the first meeting of the inter-group.

group marked a change of tactic on the part of the forces behind the Front Economique,[42] but if it is assumed that the primary aim of the GDC was always to exercise influence through other parties then the inter-group looks like a continuation of its pre-election strategy; the fact that so many deputies joined that inter-group suggests that the strategy had achieved considerable success.

What is known about the GDC calls into question conventional views in two areas. The first of these concerns the aims of business intervention in the politics of the Fourth Republic. There have been two views of this. One presents business as the all powerful *deus ex machina* manipulating bourgeois parties. The other, presented by bourgeois politicians themselves, is one of business scattering its largesse in a random manner and earning nothing in return.

The workings of the GDC suggest that neither of these views is right; business did have a strategy, but it was a subtle one that had to cope with a wide variety of limitations. The aim of this strategy was to unite the bourgeoisie around certain minimum aims, on which agreement could be obtained. The first of these aims was the exclusion of the Communist party from power. Though the GDC did not make explicit attacks on the Communist party, the effect of its intervention was invariably anti-Communist: the pressure that the GDC put on bourgeois parties to form alliances served to make it very difficult for the Communist party to gain seats. In a more complicated way *apparentements* also worked against the Gaullist RPF; Gaullists who refused to sign *apparentement* agreements reduced their chances of winning, while those who did enter into such agreements accepted the very political game that their leader affected to despise.[43]

Beyond the initial aim of excluding Communists and non-pragmatic Gaullists from power, the tactics of the GDC became more complicated. This complexity of strategy was rooted in a complexity of organizations: the CNPF operated through the Front Economique which operated through the GDC which, usually, operated through existing political parties. The big businessmen behind the CNPF, who were not always united among themselves, may have paid the piper during these operations but this did not give them an unlimited capacity to call the tune. Politics required cash but it also required the expertise and prestige that was provided by the peasant, small business and artisanal leaders of the Front Economique and by party politicians. Both politicians and leaders of

---

[42] Williams, *Politics in post-war France*, p. 332.
[43] Georgette Elgey, *La république des illusions 1945–1951 ou la vie secrète de la IVème république* (Paris, 1965), p. 515.

professional organizations had interests and ambitions of their own that prevented them from acting as simple tools of large-scale business.[44]

The extent to which business had been forced to make compromises during the 1951 campaign was reflected in the composition the parliamentary inter-group formed under the aegis of the Front Economique. This group was made up of men who had enjoyed some degree of support from the GDC during the elections and who had accepted the ground rules of the bourgeois system – i.e. not Communists or radical Gaullists. The leaders of the Front Economique seem to have been able to exercise some influence over those who had been elected under its aegis. In particular, Gingembre appears to have played a role in persuading some RPF deputies to desert their own leader and support the investiture of Antoine Pinay. However, parliament was not composed of business puppets. This was most obvious in the case of the four SFIO deputies who joined the group. Less obviously, but perhaps more importantly, the GDC's relations with Peasant party candidates reflected the limits of business power. The Peasants had been one of the main beneficiaries of GDC support; indeed, the only candidate to be elected on a purely GDC list subsequently joined the Peasant group in the assembly. Peasants could be relied on to defend the general interests of private property, but they could not be relied on to support specific economic policies favourable to industry. On the contrary, Peasant deputies were mainly concerned to extract tax concessions for agriculture. Since such concessions were inevitably paid for by industry, one result of the GDC campaign, which laid such emphasis on fiscal grievances, was to ensure that its main paymasters paid higher taxes for the next five years.[45]

The GDC has a more general significance. The Fourth Republic is usually seen through the eyes of the leaders of individual political parties. The fact that the party system of the Fourth Republic became increasingly fragmented and party discipline weaker, is therefore interpreted as a sign that the Fourth Republic as a whole failed. The GDC shows that this is not necessarily so. Weak party discipline was actively desired by some, and even the most apparently senseless aspects of the Fourth Republic, such as the *apparentement* laws, suited the GDC's aims. Most importantly, the GDC understood the success of a particular political programme did not have to be linked to the success of a particular political party. In this context it might be argued that the smallest conservative party of the Fourth Republic pursued the broadest and most ambitious strategy.

[44] Léon Gingembre, for example, had resigned from the CNPF in the late 1940s in protest against the activities of large-scale business. See Guillaume, *La Confédération Générale*, p. 27.

[45] The position after the elections was summed up by the president of the CNPF on 19 June 1951. He expressed general satisfaction with the election results but added that tax increases were likely: 'The question of the distribution of fiscal charges will be posed then. It must be noted on this subject that the proportion of representatives of agriculture is increased in the new assembly.'

Appendix. Candidacies, alliances and *apparentements* of the Groupement de Défense des Contribuables

Constituencies where the GDC stood in isolation

Constituency	Number of votes obtained
Ardèche	3,739
Belfort	308
Cher	1,447
Eure	1,338
Eure et Loir	1,342
Garonne	2,553
Indre	750
Jura	2,283
Loir et Cher	1,402
Meuse	1,103
Yonne	753

Direct alliances with the GDC

Constituencies	Parties involved	Votes obtained	Candidates elected
Aude	CNIP	3,126	
Cantal	UDSR	5,697	
Isère	CNIP	33,760	1
Haute Marne	CNIP	3,321	
Loire Inférieure	RGR, CNIP	46,204	1 (Radical-Socialiste)
Oise	RPF	65,314	3
Orne	CNIP	12,172	1
Pas-de-Calais (2nd)	UDSR	11,511	
Puy de Dôme	RGR	29,197	1
Pyrénées basses	MRP, CNIP		(1 CNIP, 1 MRP)
Seine	RGR	27,671	1

Apparentements

Constituencies	Parties involved	Candidates elected
Aisne	RGRIF, MRP	1 MRP, 1 CNIP
Cantal	CNIP, Radical-Socialiste, MRP	3 CNIP
Creuse	SFIO, RGR, MRP, RGRIF, UDSR	
Gard	[MRP, CNIP] UDSR, Radical-Socialiste, SFIO	2 SFIO, 1 MRP
Haute Marne	MRP, RGR	2 Radical-Socialiste
Lot	SFIO, MRP, RGR	1 RGR, 1 SFIO, 1 GDC
Marne	[RGR, CNIP] MRP, SFIO	2 MRP, 1 SFIO
Nièvre	RPF	1 RPF
Pas-de-Calais (2nd)	SFIO, MRP	3 SFIO, 1 MRP
Pyrénées basses	RGRIF	1 CNIP
Pyrénées (orient.)	RPF	
Seine et Marne	RGRIF, Radical-Socialiste, SFIO, CNIP, MRF	1 Radical-Socialiste, 1 SFIO

Sources

This appendix has been compiled using two sources: *Barodet* and the electoral results printed in *le Monde* on 19–21 June 1951. Neither of these sources is entirely satisfactory. *Barodet* only provides evidence relating to candidates who were successful, or who were allied to successful candidates; it therefore provides no information on areas where the GDC put up isolated lists. *Le Monde*'s electoral coverage claimed to be comprehensive, but there were frequent omissions, especially where the GDC was allied with other parties. Indeed, according to *le Monde*, the GDC would not have fielded the thirty departmental lists that were necessary to benefit from the electoral law on *apparentements*. I have used *le Monde* only in cases where *Barodet* provides no information. However, I would be surprised if the details given above are correct in every particular. A third source, the official election results published by the ministry of the interior, provides details of only nineteen GDC candidacies. A number of candidates elected on RGRIF tickets subsequently sat as members of the CNIP.

15   Conclusion

The history of France between 1945 and 1951 presents a paradox. On the one hand this is widely seen as a period of rapid social, economic and administrative change when the 'Malthusianism' of the 'stalemate society' that had characterized the Third Republic gave way to the dynamism of the *trente glorieuses*. On the other hand, in political terms, 1951 seemed to mark the return not just of the political right but of a kind of right that was particularly backward looking and archaic. Some broad interpretations of French history look odd when examined in the light of Fourth Republic politics. Charles Maier writes: 'After 1945 it would no longer be necessary or even comforting for conservatives to imagine the restoration of a bourgeois society as the endpoint of their efforts';[1] but can the election of Antoine Pinay as prime minister in 1952 be interpreted as anything other than a bid to restore bourgeois society? Stanley Hoffmann argues that the 'republican synthesis' that had united peasants, small shopkeepers and industrialists broke down after 1945, but what institution could have encapsulated the republican synthesis better than the Centre National des Indépendants et Paysans (CNIP)? The remainder of this chapter will attempt to place the detailed political history of the Fourth Republic in the context of broader social and economic changes.

The extent of change in post-war France can be made clear by a brief look at the historical context. Many bourgeois leaders had wanted to introduce radical change in France before 1940. Some industrialists, who wished to invest heavily and concentrate production, had chafed at the restraints on competition and on the continuous need to defer to the interests of small producers. Politicians like Tardieu and intellectuals like Auguste Detoeuf had discussed ambitious schemes of public investment or *dirigiste* economics. However, all these schemes had come to little. The barrier to rapid change in the Third Republic sprang partly, as Stanley Hoffmann has argued, from the continuous need to appease small producers and traders who were economically backward but politically useful as a means of

---

[1] C. S. Maier, *Recasting bourgeois Europe: stabilization in France, Germany and Italy in the decade after World War 1* (Princeton, 1975), p. 14.

checking the threat posed by the working classes. However, there was a more general problem than this. Resistance to change was to be found even among groups who might have been expected to benefit from it. Associations of large-scale industrialists, for example, were often incapable of producing long-term plans or of agreeing on broad political strategies. Radical change of any kind requires a sacrifice of short-term interests for long-term gain and the co-operation of people who might normally be divided by conflicting interests, economic competition or simply personal rivalry. France was a fragmented society in which groups and individuals were preoccupied with their own immediate interests. The kind of institutions that imposed discipline on conflicting and short-term interests in other countries were all weak in the Third Republic. The French state was reluctant to experiment with economic management; bourgeois political parties were loose groupings of notables mainly concerned with the provision of ministerial office for their deputies and local parish-pump benefits for their electorate; professional associations were rarely able to collect membership dues effectively, let alone co-ordinate strategy; banks were notoriously underdeveloped and such industrial investment as took place tended to come from retained profits.

After the Second World War, this changed. The state's power increased and some members of the bourgeoisie came to accept state intervention in the economy. Bourgeois political parties seemed, for a time at least, capable of exercising a new degree of discipline over their members, as did professional associations such as the Conseil National du Patronat Français (CNPF). Nationalization of banks and the need of industrialists to seek outside funds to replace plant after the war meant that decisions about investment were less likely to be taken within individual companies.

The bourgeois leaders of the early Fourth Republic had several advantages that their predecessors lacked. The first of these was the very awkwardness of their position *vis-à-vis* the political left. The large right-wing majority in the *bleu horizon* parliament of 1919 had encouraged complacency. The left-wing presence in the parliaments of the post-war period and the tripartite governments of 1946 and 1947 made even the most stubborn members of the French bourgeois aware that changes would have to be made. In particular, the desire to combat the threat of Communism made many willing to delegate power to the leaders of bourgeois parties, professional organizations and the state, on a scale that would have been almost unthinkable before 1940.

The second advantage that some bourgeois leaders of the Fourth Republic enjoyed was American aid. The Marshall plan provided ambitious projects with a degree of security that could never have been achieved in the atmosphere of financial crisis that prevailed in the Third

Republic. Aid was provided directly to support the modernization of French industry. This gave the men who dispensed that aid a high degree of autonomy: they did not have to ask parliament for subsidy or risk the taxpayer protests that so often erupted in France. The prospect of obtaining access to American aid encouraged French industrialists to co-operate with each other and exchange information on an unprecedented scale. American influence was based on more than just money. The Americans were seen as protectors of France against the external threat of Communism, and of the French bourgeoisie against the internal threats of redistributive economics and political purges. Many members of the bourgeoisie were willing to accept measures that they believed were willed by the Americans, or by those Frenchmen who were seen to be associated with America.

Thirdly, and most importantly, the prestige conferred on certain sections of the bourgeoisie by their careers in the Resistance strengthened their position. Studies of the Resistance legacy in post-war France often hinge on the assumption that it was confined to the left of the political spectrum. In fact, the influence that Resistance veterans acquired on the left was limited by the fact that they were so numerous. The Section Française de l'Internationale Ouvrière (SFIO) and the Parti Communiste Français (PCF) benefited as parties because of their associations with the Resistance, but very few individual Socialist or Communist leaders drew much advantage from such associations because their colleagues and rivals were able to boast similar records. Indeed, Resistance records could become a liability for Communist leaders because they were seen to be associated with excessively independent behaviour.[2]

In right-wing political parties and in business or civil service circles, by contrast, Resistance records were valuable precisely because they were rare. Many official positions were reserved for those who had not been compromised by the Vichy regime, and evidence of Resistance activity was often an advantage in gaining access to such positions. Furthermore, at a time of purges and economic restructuring, many members of the bourgeoisie felt that they needed representatives who were in positions of influence. Thus, for example, Aimé Lepercq, former industrialist, leader of the coal industry, Resistance hero and post-war minister of finance, was contacted by many employers who wished to defend their wartime records.[3] The result of all this was that the comparatively small group of bourgeois politicians, civil servants and business leaders who had been active in the Resistance acquired great power *vis-à-vis* their class as a whole.

It was such a Resistance background that accounts for the authority that

---

[2] It is significant that a party which was full of Resistance heroes should have finished up with a leader who had spent the war working in the Messerschmitt factory.

[3] R. Vinen, *The politics of French business 1936–1945* (Cambridge, 1991), p. 200.

Georges Villiers exercised in the CNPF, or that Bloch-Lainé exercised in the ministry of finance or that Mutter, Laniel, Bidault and Reynaud exercised in their respective political parties and in the political system generally. It would be wrong to suggest that all those advocating reform of bourgeois institutions were Resistance veterans. Some Resistance veterans, like Henri Queuille, were keen to restore the political balances of the Third Republic. Some bourgeois leaders, such as Robert Schuman, who did advocate reform had not been members of the Resistance, though they certainly gained from their association with Resistance leaders.

The bourgeois leaders who acquired power as a result of the peculiar circumstances of the Liberation were united by their belief that France needed long-term strategies for radical change, but they did not agree about what kind of strategy should be pursued; indeed, the various strategies pursued were often mutually exclusive. In the immediate aftermath of the Liberation it seemed that France was to be reformed by 'technocratic' ministers working outside conventional parties under the aegis of General de Gaulle. However, this strategy had begun to run into trouble even before the Liberation and was finally rendered irrelevant by de Gaulle's resignation. Thereafter many bourgeois politicians put their faith in strong parties; such parties were seen to mark a break with the Third Republic and a move towards an Anglo-Saxon pattern of politics. Parties would be made up of disciplined militants rather than powerful notables, and they would be means of implementing policy rather than responding to myriad local grievances. The most conspicuous example of such a strong party was the Mouvement Républicain Populaire (MRP), although the Union Démocratique et Socialiste de la Résistance (UDSR) and the PRL (Parti Républicain de la Liberté) had similar ambitions for a time. The Rassemblement du Peuple Français (RPF) also attempted to create a strong movement based on dedicated militants, though it denounced the very idea of political parties and sought to invest authority in a single individual rather than a parliamentary group or party secretariat.

However, the era of the strong party proved to be short lived. The return of Pétainists to office, the increasing leverage exercised by notables, and the damage to party discipline done by competition between groups that demanded unqualified loyalty all served to weaken the parties formed at the Liberation and to pave the way for the return of loose groups such as the Rassemblement des Gauches Républicaines (RGR) and the CNIP.

Alongside those who put their faith in strong parties were those who were indifferent to party politics and believed that the future lay in action by the state administration. Even among those who supported a strengthened state, there were important differences. Jean Monnet, the best-known member of this group, believed in intervention that would occur largely through informal pressure rather than direct control and exercised through agencies outside the normal structures of the civil service. Others wished to bring state interventions in the economy under control of the most established parts of the civil service, and to exercise control through mechanisms such as government control of credit, nationalized industries and the coercive possibilities of *exceptionalisme*.[4]

It is sometimes assumed that *dirigisme* and modernization are almost synonymous in modern France. Historians associate *dirigisme* with industrial concentration and organization, European integration and rapid growth; they equate liberalism with the defence of defunct orthodoxies or narrow vested interests. The reality was more complicated: the 'stalemate society' had been characterized not by absence of government intervention but by an incoherent structure of subsidies, controls and tariffs. Certain varieties of liberalism represented as much of a challenge to this order as the *dirigiste* projects of technocratic civil servants. Many liberals wanted an opening up of competition and balanced budgets that would mean an end to the fiscal privileges of certain groups. Both liberals and *dirigistes* wanted French production to be based on concentrated modern industries rather than small-scale traditional producers. Sometimes liberals and *dirigistes* recognized that their efforts were associated. Those who wanted the government to direct investment towards modern sectors of the economy also needed it to reduce subsidies to backward sectors and to counter the inflation that would otherwise have been generated by government spending. Jean Monnet appreciated that Mayer's liberal financial plan was a necessary pre-condition to his own interventionist industrial plan.[5]

Relations between liberals and *dirigistes* were not always characterized by mutual respect: Charles Rist, Jacques Rueff and Edmond Giscard d'Estaing vigorously denounced the Monnet plan and the increased government spending of the post-war period. However, the careers of these very individuals show that their vision of France was as innovative as that of Monnet. Edmond Giscard d'Estaing, for example, had a background in large-scale industry, supported European integration and was willing to countenance changes in the French empire.[6] Jacques Rueff's position in

---

[4] *Exceptionalisme* was the name given to the technique of civil servants who imposed deliberately unworkable regulations on industrialists and then demanded concessions in return for the granting of special authorizations to break these regulations.

[5] J. Monnet, *Mémoires* (Paris, 1976), pp. 310–311. On relations between Monnet and Mayer see also L. Franck, *697 ministres. Souvenirs d'un directeur général des prix 1947–1962* (Paris, 1990), p. 24.

[6] On the difficulty of interpreting Giscard d'Estaing's position (though with reference to a rather earlier period and to the empire rather than the metropole) see Jacques Marseille, *Empire colonial et capitalisme français. Histoire d'un divorce* (Paris, 1984), p. 224.

the 'modernization' debate was equally ambiguous. Most historians suggest that Rueff had failed to move with the times and that his liberalism condemned him to marginalization in the Fourth Republic, but the very same economic doctrines brought Rueff back to centre stage in 1958 when he presided over the plan that began the Fifth Republic and took France into the European Economic Community. Even the pure liberals like Rueff and Giscard d'Estaing had something in common with modernizing *dirigistes*. Both wanted a strong state: the *dirigistes* wanted a state strong enough to intervene in the economy to effect change, but the liberals looked to a state that would be strong enough to resist calls to prevent changes that threatened politically powerful groups.

Finally there were those who wanted to change bourgeois society through institutions that were neither explicitly political nor part of the state. The most obvious of such institutions were the various employers' associations and in particular the CNPF. Not everyone would accept that employers' associations were means of bringing about radical change. Mancur Olson has argued that interest groups which represent only a limited part of the population are an impediment to economic modernization and that the post-war continental economy gained from the fact that war and dictatorship had destroyed many interest groups.[7] Olson's arguments have been criticized on the grounds that they fail to allow for the fact that 'cogent'[8] or 'centralized' interest groups may make certain kinds of change easier. The history of French employers' associations would support these criticisms. Employers' associations were means of representing businessmen, but they were also means of co-ordinating, and sometimes imposing, long-term strategies. It has been suggested above that the circumstances that allowed the state and political parties to increase their power at the Liberation also allowed the leaders of business associations to increase their power *vis-à-vis* their members. Business leaders had two strategies open to them: they could work through political parties or they could adopt what Maier has described as a corporatist approach by maintaining direct relations with trade unions and/or the administration. It should be stressed that business leaders were always conscious of conflicts of interest with all bourgeois politicians and civil servants as well as with working class trade unionists. The question was not which of these groups was a business ally, but which of them was seen as a viable interlocutor. The corporatist strategy was evident in the CGT/CNPF

[7] M. Olson, *The rise and decline of nations: economic growth, stagflation and social rigidities* (New Haven and London, 1982), and *The logic of collective action: public goods and the theory of groups* (Cambridge, Mass., 1971).

[8] C. S. Maier, 'The two post-war eras and conditions for stability in twentieth century western Europe', *American Historical Review* 81, 1 (1981), 327–352.

accords of 1946 that were seen by one well placed civil servant as an outright attempt to circumvent parliament.[9] The political strategy was evident in business attempts to build the PRL into a single strong party that would represent business interests. Later business associations began to take their grievances directly to the government, though they were usually obliged to do so on terms laid down by the state. At this stage political parties became rivals of business associations rather than potential partners: business funding was no longer used to create a single strong business party, but rather distributed over a range of political parties, which were thus kept too weak and divided to threaten business interests.

When it is appreciated that there were several different bourgeois strategies in the early Fourth Republic, then the state of France in 1951 can be seen in a different light. French political life was not separate from its administrative and economic life; rather politics, administration and business were all spheres in which parallel, and often competing, strategies to reform bourgeois France were launched. The strategy based around strong political parties had failed by 1951 while those based on some degree of economic *dirigisme* and private sector corporatism had largely succeeded. Furthermore, the reasons for the failure of political reform were often connected to the reasons for the success of other forms of reform. American aid strengthened the *dirigiste* state and and helped private business associations enforce discipline on their members, but the perception that the Americans were favourable to the old parties of the Third Republic weakened the disciplined parties that had emerged at the Liberation. The strength of private business associations also weakened the disciplined parties as business leaders came increasingly to regard such parties as dangerous. Even anti-Communism, which had initially underlain so much bourgeois reform, came ultimately to work against disciplined parties as loose alliances, which were institutionalized by the *apparentement* law of 1951, replaced strong parties and attempts to enforce discipline came to be seen as a threat to 'split the anti-Communist vote'.

The division and incoherence of French party politics, which were apparent in the 1951 election, became even more obvious after this date. This was illustrated by the struggle over the European army, which was said to divide the political nation as much as the Dreyfus case had done,[10] by the revival of the clerical issue,[11] and by faction struggles in almost all

[9] Franck, *697 ministres*, p. 14. On the way in which the nature of the French labour movement undermined corporatist initiatives in France, see chapter 3.

[10] R. Aron and D. Lerner (eds.), *La querelle de la CED* (Paris, 1956).

[11] On the way in which the re-emergence of the clerical issue disturbed political order even at local level see Pierre Clément and Nelly Xydias, *Vienne sur le Rhône. La ville et les habitants, situations et attitudes. Sociologie d'une cité française* (Paris, 1955), p. 132. In Bordeaux it seems that even priests came to see that the clerical issue was undermining bourgeois unity

bourgeois parties.[12] In some ways the bourgeois elites that had been produced by the circumstances of the post-Liberation period had become victims of their own success. Once the threat presented by the Communist party had been contained and the ineligibility laws that excluded Pétainists repealed, then the bourgeoisie no longer needed Resistance veterans to represent it. Numerous politicians from the Third Republic returned to public life and the influence that any bourgeois leader was able to exercise over his constituents was much reduced.

The bourgeois political parties were also shaken by two new movements in the 1950s. The first of these was a tax rebellion of small shopkeepers and artisans that began under the leadership of Pierre Poujade in 1953. The movement applied considerable pressure to members of parliament in bourgeois parties and ultimately put up its own candidates in the 1956 election with unexpected success and forced important concessions from the government.[13] The second movement to shake France was the agitation of settlers, army officers and sympathetic figures on the mainland to preserve Algérie Française: an agitation that ultimately helped to bring down the Fourth Republic in 1958. Poujadism and Algérie Française were complicated phenomena that deserve to be examined in a degree of detail that is not possible here. However, certain broad points can be made about the links that both movements had with the general breakdown of the bourgeois system that had been established in the period leading up to 1951.

The first point to be made is that both the Poujadist and the Algérie Française campaigns were linked to economic backwardness. Poujadism originated in underdeveloped southern provinces; Algeria was comparatively underdeveloped, and those in mainland France who supported a French presence in Algeria were often linked to industries, such as textiles, that needed an imperial outlet for exports[14] or to the desire of 'military Poujadists' to preserve a traditional army that would not be revolutionized by the technologies of the nuclear age. In this sense both movements represented a rebellion by groups that had been marginalized by the modernization of France during the early years of the Fourth Republic.

The second point is that the enormous prestige that Resistance leaders had acquired among the French bourgeois, and which allowed some of those bourgeois Resistance leaders to impose reform on their class, counted

on more important issues. Jacques Lagroye quotes one priest as saying that free schools were 'a constant problem that ended up stalling initiatives in other domains'. J. Lagroye, *Société et politique. J. Chaban-Delmas à Bordeaux* (Paris, 1973), p. 177.

[12] Factional disputes occurred between the Laniel/Reynaud wing and the Pinay/Duchet wing of the Independents. Faction struggles eventually led to formal splits in the RPF, the Radicals and the Peasant parties.

[13] There are two general books on Poujadism. S. Hoffmann, *Le mouvement Poujade* (Paris, 1956) and D. Borne, *Petits-bourgeois en révolte? Le mouvement Poujade* (Paris, 1977).

[14] Marseille, *Empire colonial et capitalisme français*.

for far less in the social and geographical milieu from which the Poujadist and Algérie Française campaigners were recruited. The Resistance/Pétainist split meant little to inhabitants of Algeria because French North Africa had never been occupied by German troops. In Algeria it had been far easier to argue that loyalty to the Vichy government was linked to preparation for military revenge against the Germans and consequently that there was no sharp division between loyalty to Pétain and loyalty to the Resistance.[15] The Poujadists had been saved from compromising associations during the war by the fact that most of them were too young, and too plebeian, to have held office under Vichy. Poujade argued in his memoirs that Pétainist sympathies were perfectly compatible with anti-German action: it was possible to be 'pour le Maréchal; contre les Nazis'.[16] Neither the Poujadists nor the *pieds noirs* felt as compromised as the Pétainist *haute bourgeoisie* and notables of mainland France, and consequently neither of them saw any reason to accept the power exercised by the bourgeois Resistance elites.

The third, and most important, characteristic that distinguished Poujadism and the Algérie Française agitation from the movements of bourgeois France was their attitude to anti-Communism. As has been stressed, anti-Communism was a key element in bourgeois reconstruction after 1945. It united various sections of the bourgeoisie and it underlay much of their enthusiasm for atlanticism, economic planning and European integration. Poujadism was notable for its indifference to anti-Communism. The Poujadists and the Communists actually collaborated in some campaigns and Maurice Bardèche, a sympathetic right-wing commentator on Poujadism, recognized that Poujade did not subscribe to 'the anti-Communist feeling, that is so common among the French bourgeoisie'.[17]

The reasons for Poujadism's indifference to anti-Communism were rooted in the social structure of France. Anti-Communism was strongest in the northern industrial regions of France. It was these areas that felt the military threat of the red army most deeply. More importantly, the social threat of Communism was strongest in the industrial regions. It was in the industrial cities that the bourgeoisie confronted a large anonymous proletariat, trade unions, strikes and the visible threat of revolution. In the small market towns of southern France, where Poujadism flourished, social structures were very different.[18] These were areas of artisans and shop-

---

[15] This is the argument made by René Richard and Alain de Sérigny in *La bissectrice de la guerre: Alger 8 novembre 1942* (Algiers, 1946).
[16] This is the title of chapter 3 of Poujade's second autobiography: *A l'heure de la colère* (Paris, 1977).
[17] Maurice Bardèche, *Le poujadisme* (Paris, 1956), p. 18.
[18] The point that inhabitants of small towns defined themselves as 'bourgeois' in contrast to peasants rather than proletarians is made in L. Bernot and R. Blancard, *Nouville. Un village français* (Paris, 1953).

keepers where the bourgeoisie still defined themselves by contrast to the peasantry rather than in opposition to proletarians. In this context, Communists were more likely to be bloody-minded artisans, like Poujade's associate Frégeac, than threatening revolutionary proletarians.

The absence of anti-Communism was less explicit and conscious among the ranks of Algérie Française campaigners and many of them continued to insist that resistance to Arab nationalism was an integral part of the campaign to defend France against the expansion of Soviet rule. However, in reality Algeria contained even less of a revolutionary proletariat than the south of France and the threat to the French presence in Algeria came from Arab nationalists not Soviet influence. Desire to defend French Algeria led many to push for an army that was designed for fighting in the Third World rather than defending Europe. Furthermore, the eventual willingness of the most extreme partisans of Algérie Française to seek allies on even the extreme left of the political spectrum against de Gaulle, whom they regarded as their principal betrayer, reflected the irrelevance of the Communist/anti-Communist split to the Algerian issue.[19]

The instability induced by Poujadism and Algeria ultimately helped to bring the Fourth Republic down and brought about the creation of a new form of stability after de Gaulle's return to power in 1958. It would be possible to interpret this development as marking the final failure of bourgeois politics in the period 1945–51. Such an interpretation would present the Fourth Republic as a series of ruptures, occurring in 1945, 1951 and 1958: the bourgeois reformers of the post-war period tried to lead their political parties and organizations away from the habits of the Third Republic, but this attempt was shown to have failed by developments after 1951 and reform could only proceed after the total abandonment of the Fourth Republic constitution. This interpretation is one that many bourgeois reformers brought on themselves: men with dramatic ambitions usually seem like spectacular failures. However, there are three reasons why the legacy of the period 1945 to 1951 should not be dismissed. Firstly, not all the new men of 1945 were evicted from power by the return of old elites after 1951, some, such as Chaban-Delmas, Faure and Mitterrand, were sufficiently far sighted and subtle to build up links with the old elites. They survived well during the 1950s and beyond.

---

[19] On the hostility that some veterans of Algérie Française showed to de Gaulle, and their willingness to seek allies on the left, see W. B. Cohen, 'The legacy of empire: the Algerian connection', *Journal of Contemporary History*, 15 (1980); D. Tucker, 'The new look of the French extreme right', *Western Political Quarterly*, 21 (1968); T. A. Smith, 'Algeria and the French *modérés*: the politics of immoderation?', *Western Political Quarterly*, 18 (1965), 86–116; François Duprat, *Les mouvements de l'extrême droite en France depuis 1944* (Paris, 1972); Francis Bergeron and Philippe Vilgier, *De le Pen à le Pen. Une histoire des nationaux et des nationalistes sous la Vème République* (Paris, 1989).

Secondly, failed strategies may often be successful as tactics. None of the projects for reforming France that were floated in the late 1940s had the kind of dramatic and long-term impact that its authors hoped for, but each of these projects did play a more short-term role in heading off particular threats: Communism was contained, anti-Pétainist purges were restrained, the economy remained broadly capitalist. In this context the continuous change of the Fourth Republic might be seen not as a sign of failure but rather of a bourgeoisie that was innovative and willing to adjust to meet new problems.

Thirdly, the bourgeois reformers of the post-war period fell victim to their own success. This was partly, as has been suggested above, because the containment of Communism and the return of Pétainists to public life meant that the mechanisms that had brought these developments about were no longer necessary. There was also a more general sense in which the bourgeois reformers of 1945 to 1951 became victims of their own success. All of these reformers wished to see strong economic growth and some of them played a role in bringing such growth about after 1950. However, there was a difference between proponents of economic growth in France and those elsewhere. In most countries economic growth was seen as a means of escaping from the 'zero sum game' of political debate about the distribution of resources.[20] French politicians however, had been brought up in a society where expectations of growth were very low, especially after 1929. Consequently everyone, including those who thought of themselves as turning away from the legacy of the Third Republic, continued to think in terms of the zero sum game. Modernization was seen to be something that could only be brought about by abandoning the interests of traditional sections of the economy. The rhetoric of the most self-consciously modernizing elements of French society was full of words like discipline, sacrifice and choice.[21] However, in fact, economic growth during the 1950s provided politicians with the resources to buy off the traditional sectors of the economy.[22] The only problem too expensive to be solved with the benefits of economic success was that presented by the Algerian war. The

[20] Expectations of growth in countries other than France were influenced by economic experience before 1939. Countries such as America and Britain had begun to recover from the depression by 1939, while fascist leaders explicitly advocated growth as an alternative to arguments over distribution. C. S. Maier, 'The economics of Fascism and Nazism', in *In search of stability: explorations in historical political economy* (Cambridge, 1987), pp. 70–120.

[21] See Henry Ehrmann's remarks about the CNPF: 'It was quite typical that long before certain sections of French industry had improved productivity ... debates were already under way as to who was to benefit from the, as yet unknown, advantages.' H. W. Ehrmann, *Organized business in France* (Princeton, 1957).

[22] For an examination of the ways in which economic growth allowed France to avoid disturbing social change see, W. J. Adams, *Restructuring the French economy: government and the rise of market capitalism since World War II* (Washington, 1989).

success of the Fifth Republic was based on withdrawal from Algeria, but few other decisions were made that hurt significant parts of the population. De Gaulle continued to subsidize traditional sectors alongside modern ones, though he shifted some of the burden for agricultural subsidies from the French to the European tax-payer.[23] In this context, France did not have to choose between 'Mendésisme and Poujadisme':[24] it could afford to invest in new industries and to provide tax breaks for peasants and shopkeepers. The lesson of the Fourth Republic is that to govern is to avoid choice.

[23] On the continued subsidy to backward sectors during the Fifth Republic see S. Berger and M. J. Piore, *Dualism and discontinuity in industrial societies* (Cambridge, 1980).
[24] 'Mendésisme or Poujadisme' is the title of a chapter in J.-P. Rioux's *The Fourth Republic 1944–1958* (Cambridge, 1987).

Appendix   The electoral law of 1951 and *apparentements*

Fourth Republic elections were held under a system of proportional representation with multi-member constituencies. However, when confronted with the particular threats of Communism and Gaullism, the parties of the majority introduced complicated arrangements for the 1951 election. The eight constituencies in the Paris region (i.e. Seine and Seine et Oise) were the areas of greatest strength for Communism and Gaullism. Consequently, the electoral law laid down that these constituencies should be fought under a system of proportional representation by the largest remainder (this system favoured small parties). In the rest of the country, *apparentements* were permitted. This system allowed 'national parties' (defined as parties that fielded candidates in at least thirty constituencies) to sign agreements with each other before the election. If any single party or group of parties united by an *apparentement* agreement gained more than 50 per cent of the vote in a constituency they then took all the seats. If such a result was achieved by a group of parties in an *apparentement* agreement, the seats were then divided among them in proportion to the votes that each had obtained. If no party or group of parties gained more than 50 per cent of the vote the *apparentement* agreement could still prove beneficial. Any party within an *apparentement* agreement that failed to gain enough votes to elect a deputy, would then see all its votes transferred to its allies.

The net result of this system was twofold. Firstly, it encouraged small parties such as the Union Démocratique et Socialiste de la Résistance to field token candidates, who might only gain one or two votes, to allow them to enjoy the status of a national party. More importantly, the system benefited the centre parties. These parties had a tradition of negotiation and alliance (indeed many centre formations were alliances of several different parties). The Communists were excluded from *apparentement* agreements throughout the country. The Rassemblement du Peuple Français (RPF) concluded such deals in only thirteen constituencies. No *apparentement* deals were signed in twelve constituencies (outside Paris), two separate alliances were signed in seven constituencies and each of the remaining seventy-six constituencies contained one alliance. Overall, the centre parties obtained 62.5 per cent of seats with 51 per cent of the vote. It was reckoned that the law had deprived the Communists of seventy-one seats and the RPF of twenty-six seats. On average it took only 25,000 votes to elect each Radical deputy, and 51,000 to elect each Communist. For further details see Peter Cambell, *French electoral systems and elections since 1789* (London, 1958).

Bibliography

ARCHIVES

PARIS, ARCHIVES NATIONALES

Syndicat Professionnel des Fabricants de Matières Plastiques
56 AS 2
56 AS 50
56 AS 47

Papers of Jacques Warnier
57 AS 12
57 AS 22

Conseil National du Patronat Français
72 AS 74
72 AS 118
72 AS 128

Papers of Paul Reynaud
74 AP 32
74 AP 33

Papers of Louis Marin
317 AP 73
317 AP 81
317 AP 82
317 AP 84

Papers of the Mouvement Républicain Populaire
350 AP 55
350 AP 56
350 AP 73
350 AP 74
350 AP 76
350 AP 93
350 AP 94
350 AP 95

Papers of the Union Démocratique et Socialiste de la Résistance
412 AP 1
412 AP 4
412 AP 13
412 AP 16
412 AP 45

Papers of Joseph Paul-Boncour
424 AP 40
424 AP 41

Papers of Jean-Louis Anteriou
373 AP 7

Papers of Jacques Kayser
465 AP 7

Papers of Jean Locquin
310 AP 18
310 AP 71
310 AP 93

Papers of Edouard Daladier
496 AP 51

Papers of Georges Bidault
457 AP 135
457 AP 175

PARIS, BIBLIOTHÈQUE NATIONALE

Archives of the Alliance Démocratique
4
77

PARIS, CHAMBER OF COMMERCE ARCHIVES

4 AJ 29

NEUVIC D'USSEL, ARCHIVES OF HENRI QUEUILLE

C 19
D 1
D 5

PUBLICATIONS

Abélès, M., *Quiet days in Burgundy*, Cambridge, 1991.

Adams, W. J., *Restructuring the French economy: government and the rise of market capitalism since World War II*, Washington, 1989.

Agulhon, M. and Barrat, F., *CRS à Marseille. 'La police au service du peuple' 1944–47*, Paris, 1971.

Agulhon, M., Girard, L., Robert, J. L. and Serman, W. (eds.), *Les maires en France du consulat à nos jours*, Paris, 1986.

Algazy, J., *La tentation néo fasciste en France 1944–1965*, Paris, 1984.

Anderson, Malcolm, *Conservative politics in France*, London, 1974.

Andrieu, C., 'Paul Ramadier, un exemple de résistance légale 1940–1944'. In S. Bernstein (ed.), *Paul Ramadier, la république et le socialisme*, Paris, 1992.

Ariès, Philippe, *Un historien de dimanche*, Paris, 1980.

Arnal, Oscar L., *Priests in working class blue: the history of the worker priests (1943–1954)*, Mahwah, N.J., 1986.

Aron, R., 'Electeurs, partis et élus'. *Revue Française de Science Politique*, April–June 1955.

Aron, R. and Lerner, D. (eds.), *La querelle de la CED*, Paris, 1956.

Arzalier, F., *Les perdants. La dérive fasciste des mouvements autonomistes et indépendantistes au XXème siècle,* Paris, 1990.

Assemblée Nationale, *Recueil des textes authentiques et engagements électoraux des députés proclamés élus à la suite des élections générales du 17 juin 1951* (commonly known as *Barodet*), Paris, 1952.

Assouline, P., *Jean Jardin 1904–1976. Une éminence grise*, Paris, 1986.

Astoux, A., *L'oubli de Gaulle 1946–1958*, Paris, 1974.

Auriol, Vincent, *Journal du septennat (1947–53)*, 7 vols, Paris, 1970–80.

Baechler, C., *Le Parti Catholique Alsacien 1890–1939*, Paris, 1983.

Baecque, F. de, *René Coty, tel qu'en lui-même*, Paris, 1991.

Bankwitz, P. C. F., *Alsatian autonomist leaders 1919–1947*, Kansas, 1978.

Bar, Catherine de, 'Sur une témoignage Américaine'. *Questions Actuelles*, 10 (February 1946).

Bardèche, M., *Lettre à François Mauriac*, Paris, 1947.
   Le Poujadisme, Paris, 1956.

Barnett, C., *The audit of war*, London, 1986.

Barral, P., 'Pour qui votent les femmes à Vienne?'. In François Goguel (ed.), *Nouvelles études de sociologie électorale*, Paris, 1954, pp. 185–193.

Barrillon, R., 'Les modérés. Paysans et Indépendants Paysans'. In J. Fauvet and H. Mendras (eds.), *Les paysans et la politique dans la France contemporaine*, Paris, 1958.

Baudhuin, F., 'L'article de John Gillingham Phd sur la politique de production de l'industrie belge durant l'occupation nazie. Une réplique'. *Revue Belge d'Histoire Contemporaine*, 5, 1–2 (1974), 265–267.

Beau de Loménie, E., *L'Algérie trahie par l'argent. Réponse à M. Raymond Aron,* Paris, 1957.
   Les responsabilités des dynasties bourgeoises, 5 vols, Paris, 1977.

Beaumont, François de, 'Piteuse défense'. *La République*, 24 February 1946.

Bell, D. S. and Criddle, B., *The French Socialist party: the emergence of a party of government*, 2nd edition, Oxford, 1988.

Benoit-Rambaud, 'La France a voté'. *Unité Paysanne*, 3 November 1945.

'CGA et CGT', *Unité Paysanne*. 10 November 1945.

Berger, S. and Piore, M. J., *Dualism and discontinuity in industrial societies*, Cambridge, 1980.

Berl, Emmanuel, *La fin de la IIIème république. 10 juillet 1940*, Paris, 1968.

Bergeron, Francis, and Vilgier, Philippe, *De le Pen à le Pen. Une histoire des nationaux et des nationalistes sous la Vème République*, Paris, 1989.

Berghahn, V., *The Americanization of West German industry, 1945–1973*, Leamington Spa, 1986.

Bernard, Philippe, *Economie et sociologie de la Seine-et-Marne 1850–1950*, Paris, 1953.

Bernot, L. and Blancard, R., *Nouville. Un village français*, Paris, 1953.

Bernoux, P., *Les nouveaux patrons. Le centre des jeunes dirigeants d'entreprise*, Paris, 1974.

Béthouart, Bruno, *Le MRP dans le Nord–Pas-de-Calais 1944–1967*, Paris, 1984.

Bettelheim, Charles and Frère, Suzanne, *Une ville française moyenne. Auxerre en 1950. Etude de structure sociale et urbaine*, Paris, 1950.

Bichet, R., *La décentralisation, commune, région, départment? Faut-il supprimer le conseil général?*, Paris, 1977.

La démocratie chrétienne en France. Le Mouvement Républicain Populaire, Besançon, 1980.

Bidault, Georges, *Resistance: the political autobiography of Georges Bidault*, London, 1967.

Bidault, Suzanne, *Souvenirs*, Paris, 1987.

Billotte, P., *Le passé au futur*, Paris, 1979.

Birnbaum, Pierre, *Les sommets de l'état. Essai sur l'élite du pouvoir en France*, Paris, 1977.

La classe dirigeante française, Paris, 1978.

Biton, L., *La démocratie chrétienne dans la politique française. Sa grandeur, ses servitudes* (Angers, 1955).

Blackbourn, D., *Class, religion and local politics in Wilhelmine Germany*, New Haven and London, 1980.

Bloch-Lainé, F., *Profession fonctionnaire. Entretiens avec Françoise Carrière*, Paris, 1976.

Bloch-Lainé F. and Bouvier, Jean, *La France restaurée. Dialogue sur le choix d'une modernisation*, Paris, 1986.

Block, F., 'The ruling class does not rule: notes on the Marxist theory of the state'. *Socialist Revolution*, 33 (1977), 6–28.

Boisseau, A. de, *Pour servir le général 1946–1970*, Paris, 1982.

Boltanski, L., *The making of a class: cadres in French society*, Cambridge, 1987.

Bonafé, F., *Edmond Giscard d'Estaing. Un humaniste, homme d'action*, Paris, 1982.

Bonnefous, E., *Avant l'oubli. II: La vie de 1940 à 1970*, Paris, 1987.

Bonnet, G., *De Washington au Quai d'Orsay*, Geneva, 1945.

Borne, D., *Petits-bourgeois en révolte? Le mouvement Poujade*, Paris, 1977.

Bossuat, G., *La France, l'aide américaine et la construction européenne 1944–1954*, 2 vols, Paris, 1992.

Bosworth, R., *Catholicism and crisis in modern France: French Catholic groups at the threshold of the Fifth Republic*, Princeton, 1962.

Bouchardeau, Huguette, *Pas d'histoire, les femmes*, Paris, 1977.

Bourdet, C., *L'aventure incertaine de la résistance à la restauration*, Paris, 1975.

Bourricaud, F., 'Sociologie du chef d'entreprise: le "Jeune Patron"'. *Revue Economique*, 6 (1958), 896–911.

'Malaise patronal'. *Sociologie du Travail*, 111 (1961), 221–225.

'Le libéralisme de Jacques Rueff'. In F. Bourricaud and P. Salin (eds.), *Présence de Jacques Rueff*, Paris, 1989.

F. Bourricaud and P. Salin (eds.), *Présence de Jacques Rueff*, Paris, 1989.

Bourque, S. L. and Grosshultz, J., 'Politics an unnatural practice: political science looks at female participation'. *Politics and Society*, 4, 2 (1974), 225–266.

Brigneau, F., *Mon après guerre*, Paris, 1985.

Buron, Robert, *Le plus beau des métiers*, Paris, 1963.

La Mayenne et moi ou la démocratie chrétienne au socialisme, Paris, 1978.

Callot, E. F., *Le Mouvement Républicain Populaire. Un parti politique de la démocratie chrétienne en France. Origine, structure, doctrine, programme et action politique*, Paris, 1978.

L'action et l'oeuvre politique du Mouvement Républicain Populaire, Paris, 1986.

Cambell, Peter, *French electoral systems and elections since 1789*, London, 1958.

Capelle, Robert, *Dix-huit ans auprès du roi Léopold*, Paris, 1970.

Caulier-Mathy, N., 'Les dirigeants de l'industrie houillère belge de 1935 à 1955. Essai d'étude des comportements'. *Revue Belge d'Histoire Contemporaine*, 19, 1–2 (1988), 35–54.

CNPF, *CNPF. Structure et mission*, Paris, 1989.

Chaban-Delmas, J., *L'ardeur*, Paris, 1975.

Charbonnel, J., *Edmond Michelet*, Paris, 1987.

Charlot, J., 'Les élites politiques en France de la IIIème à la Vème république'. *Archives Européennes de Sociologie*, 14 (1973), 78–92.

Le gaullisme d'opposition 1946–1958, Paris, 1983.

Chassériaud, Jean-Paul, *Le Parti Démocrate Chrétien en Italie*, Paris, 1965.

Chovaux, Olivier, 'La dynastie des Farjon à Boulogne-sur-Mer. De la politique des affaires aux affaires politiques (1850–1979)'. *Revue du Nord*, 72, 228 (1990), 875–890.

Chubb, J., *Patronage and poverty in southern Italy: a tale of two cities*, Cambridge, 1982.

Claude, H., *Gaullisme et grand capital*, Paris, 1960.

Clément, Pierre and Xydias, Nelly, *Vienne sur le Rhône. La ville et les habitants, situations et attitudes. Sociologie d'une cité française*, Paris, 1955.

Closon, Françis, *Commissaire de la république du général de Gaulle. Lille septembre 1944–mars 1946*, Paris, 1980.

Cohen, W. B., 'The legacy of empire: the Algerian connection'. *Journal of Contemporary History*, 15 (1980), 97–124.

Collovald, Annie, 'Les Poujadistes, ou l'échec en politique'. *Revue d'Histoire Moderne et Contemporaine*, 36 (1989), 113–133.

Corbin, Alain, 'Les aristocrates et la communauté villageoise. Les maires d'Essay (1791–1986)'. In Agulhon et al. (eds.), *Les maires en France du consulat à nos jours*, Paris, 1980.

Cordier, D., *Jean Moulin. L'inconnu du Panthéon. II: Le choix d'un destin. Juin 1936–novembre 1940*, Paris, 1989.

Coston, Henry, *Dictionnaire de la politique française*, Paris, 1967.

Courtin, R., 'L'expérience monétaire belge'. *Les Cahiers Politiques*, 7 (1945), 47–58.

Crozier, M., *Petits fonctionnaires au travail*, Paris, 1956.

The bureaucratic phenomenon, London, 1964.

Le monde des employés de bureau, Paris, 1965.

Dacier, Michel, 'Les leçons de la Roche Tarpéienne'. *Questions Actuelles*, 10 (February 1946).

'Choisir'. *Bulletin Intérieur*, March 1946.

'Le résistantialisme'. *Ecrits de Paris*, 1 January 1947.

Darlan, Alain, 'L'amiral Darlan et la "Résistance"'. *Ecrits de Paris*, January 1953.

Debès, J., *Naissance de l'Action Catholique Ouvrière*, Paris, 1982.

Debré, M., 'Trois caractéristiques du système parlementaire français'. *Revue Française de Science Politique*, 5, 1 (1955), 21 48.

Trois républiques pour une France. Mémoires. II: *1946–1958. Agir*, Paris, 1988.

Démosier, Marion, *Rapport de recherche pour le musée du vin de Bourgogne à Beaune*. 'Les saints protecteurs de la vigne en Côte d'Or. Analyse anthropologique d'un culte. Nouvelles fonctions, nouvelles formes', 1991.

Descamps, Henri, *La démocratie chrétienne et le MRP de 1944 à 1959*, Paris, 1981.

Desgranges, J., *Les crimes masqués du résistantialisme*, Paris, 1949.

Deshors, Jean, 'La parodie d'une loi'. *La France Indépendante*, 25 November 1951.

Detoeuf, Auguste, 'Notre politique comerciale'. *Nouveaux Cahiers*, 14 (15 November 1937).

Documentation Française, *Les éléctions legislatives de 1951*, Paris, 1952.

Dogan, M. and Narbonne J., *Les françaises face à la politique. Comportement politique et condition sociale*, Paris, 1955.

Dreyfus, F.-G., *La vie politique en Alsace 1919–1936*, Paris, 1969.

Duchet, Roger, *La république épinglée*, Paris, 1975.

Dulphy, A., 'La politique de la France à l'égard de l'Espagne Franquiste 1945–49'. *Revue d'Histoire Moderne et Contemporaine*, 35 (1988), 123–140.

Dumaine, Jacques, *Quai d'Orsay, 1945–1951*, Paris, 1956.

Duprat, F., *Les mouvements de l'extrême-droite en France depuis 1944*, Paris, 1972.

Dupriez, Léon, *Monetary restoration in Belgium*, New York, 1947.

Duroy, L. and Moles, S., *Paroles de patrons*, Paris, 1980.

Dutroncy, J.D.M., *L'abbé Desgranges. Conférencier et député 1874–1958*, Paris, 1962.

Duverger, M., *The political role of women*, Paris, 1955.

Duverger, M. (ed.), *Partis politiques et classes sociales*, Paris, 1955.

Ecole national d'administration, *Rapport du directeur à son conseil d'administration 1945–1952*, Paris, 1952.

Ehrmann, Henry W., *Organized business in France*, Princeton, 1957.

Einaudi, Mario and Goguel, François, *Christian democracy in France and Italy*, Notre Dame, 1952.

Elgey, Georgette, *La république des illusions 1945–1951 ou la vie secrète de la IVème république*, Paris, 1965.

Estèbe, P., *La France Réelle*, 33 (27 June 1952).

Fabre-Luce, Alfred, *Au nom des silencieux*, Bruges, 1945.

En pleine liberté, no place of publication, 1945.

Journal de la France (1939–1944), Geneva, 1945.

Le mystère du maréchal. Le procès Pétain, Geneva, 1945.

Vingt-cinq années de la liberté. II: *L'épreuve 1939–1946* (Paris, 1963).

Le couronnement du prince, Paris, 1964.

(See also under pseudonym Sapiens)

Faligot, Roger and Kauffer, Rémi, *Les résistants. De la guerre de l'ombre aux allées de pouvoir 1944–1989*, Paris, 1989.

Faure, E., *Mémoires*. I: *Avoir toujours raison . . . c'est un grand tort*, Paris, 1982; II: *Si tel doit être mon destin ce soir*, Paris, 1984.

Faure, P., 'Régime pourri'. *La République Libre*, 26 November 1948.

Fauvet, Jacques, 'En marge des partis'. *Le Monde*, 15 June 1951.

La IVème république, Paris, 1959.

Febvre, Lucien, preface to Charles Bettelheim and Suzanne Frère, *Une ville française moyenne. Auxerre en 1950. Etude de structure sociale et urbaine*, Paris, 1950.

Fleckinger, R., 'Henri Queuille et les vétérinaires'. *Bulletin de l'Académie Vétérinaire de France*, 1985.

Fogarty, Michael P., *Christian democracy in western Europe 1820–1953*, London, 1957.

Fontaine, Pierre, 'Sur une pétition en faveur de Georges Bidault'. *Le Soleil*, 8 (September 1966).

Franck, L., *697 ministres. Souvenirs d'un directeur général des prix 1947–1962*, Paris, 1990.

Frenay, H., *Voilà la Résistance*, Paris, 1945.

La nuit finira, Paris, 1973.

Méthodes d'un parti alerte aux démocrates, Paris, n.d.

Gagnaire, François, 'Le redressement nécessaire'. *La République*, 3 (24 February 1946).

'Le Parti Paysan et nous'. *La République*, 11 (20 April 1946).

Gay, Francisque, *Dans les flammes et dans le sang. Les crimes contre les églises et les prêtres en Espagne*, Paris, 1936.

Les démocrates d'inspiration chrétienne à l'épreuve du pouvoir. Mémoire confidentiel, Paris, 1951.

Geiswiller, Marcel, 'Sauver le franc'. *Ecrits de Paris*, March 1947.

Gellner, E., 'Patrons and clients'. In E. Gellner and J. Waterbury (eds.), *Patrons and clients in Mediterranean societies*, London, 1977, pp. 1–6.

Germain, A., *La bourgeoisie qui brûle. Propos d'un témoin 1890–1940*, Paris, 1951.

Giesbert, F.-O., *François Mitterrand ou la tentation de l'histoire*, Paris, 1977.

Gillingham, J., *Belgian business in the Nazi new order*, Brussels, 1977.

Ginsborg, Paul, *A history of contemporary Italy: society and politics 1943–1988*, London, 1990.

Girard, Alain, Laugier, Henri, Weinburg, D., Charretier (sic) and Lévy-Leboyer, Claude, *La réussite sociale en France. Ses caractères, ses lois, ses effets*, Paris, 1961.

Girardet, R. with Boujou, M. and Thomas, J. P., *La crise militaire française 1945–1962. Aspects sociologiques et idéologiques*, Paris, 1964.

Godin, H. and Daniel, Y., *La France pays de mission*, Paris, 1950.

Goguel, François, *Géographie des élections françaises sous la troisième et la quatrième république*, Paris, 1970.

Goguel, François and Dupeux, Georges, *Sociologie électorale. Esquisse d'un bilan. Guide des recherches*, Paris, 1951.

Goodfellow, Samuel H., *Fascism in Alsace, 1918–1945*, PhD, Indiana University, 1992.

Graham, B.D., *French socialists and tripartisme*, London, 1965.

Grémion, Pierre, *Le pouvoir périphérique. Bureaucrates et notables dans le système politique français*, Paris, 1976.

Guichard, O., *Un chemin tranquille*, Paris, 1975.

Mon général, Paris, 1980.

Guillaume, Sylvie, *Antoine Pinay ou la confiance en politique*, Paris, 1984.

La Confédération Générale des Petites et Moyennes Entreprises. Son histoire, son combat, un autre syndicalisme patronal 1944–1978, Paris, 1987.

'Léon Gingembre défenseur des PME'. *Vingtième siècle. Revue d'Histoire*, 15 (1987), 69–81.

Guiol, P., *L'impasse sociale du gaullisme. Le RPF et l'Action Ouvrière*, Paris, 1985.

Halévy, D., *La fin des notables*, Paris, 1930.

Hall, P. A., *Governing the economy: the politics of state intervention in Britain and France*, Cambridge, 1986.

Handler, E. and Mulkern, J., *Business in politics: the campaign strategies of corporate political action committees*, Lexington, Mass., 1982.

Helmreich, J. E., 'United States policy and the Belgian royal question (March–October 1945)'. *Revue Belge d'Histoire Contemporaine*, 9, 1–2 (1978), 1–15.

'American strategic services planning for Belgium, 1943'. *Revue Belge d'Histoire Contemporaine*, 21, 1–2 (1990), 211–224.

Hoffmann, S., *Le mouvement Poujade*, Paris, 1956.

Hudelle, L., 'Faut-il rester Républicain?' *La République Libre*, 10 December 1948.

Isorni, Jacques, *Ainsi passent les républiques*, Paris, 1959.

Mémoires. II: 1946–1958, Paris, 1986.

Jacquin, F., *Les cadres de l'industrie et du commerce en France*, Paris, 1955.

James, Harold, *The German slump: politics and economics 1924–1936*, Oxford, 1987.

Jeanneney, J.-N. 'Un patronat au piquet, septembre 1944–janvier 1946'. *L'argent caché. Milieux d'affaires et pouvoirs politiques dans la France du XXème siècle*, Paris, 1984, pp. 242–264.

Jeanneney, J.-N. and Julliard, J., *'Le Monde' de Beuve-Méry ou le métier d'Alceste*, Paris, 1979.

Jenson, Jane, 'The Liberation and new rights for French women'. In M. Randolph Higonnet, Jane Jenson, S. Michel and M. Collins-Weitz (eds.), *Behind the lines: gender and the two world wars*, New Haven, 1987, pp. 272–284.

Jones, H., 'New tricks for an old dog? The Conservatives and social policy 1951–5'. In A. Gorst, L. Johnman and W. Scott Lucas (eds.), *Contemporary British history 1931–61: politics and the limits of policy*, London, 1991, pp. 33–43.

Judt, Tony, *Marxism and the French left: studies in labour and politics in France*, Oxford, 1986.

Kedward, H. R., *Resistance in Vichy France: a study of ideas and motivation*, Oxford, 1978.

Kelly, G., *Lost soldiers: the French army and empire in crisis 1947–62*, Boston, 1965.

Kérillis, H. de, *De Gaulle dictateur. Une grande mystification de l'histoire*, Montreal, 1945.

Kuisel, R. F., 'Auguste Detoeuf, conscience of French industry, 1926–1947'. *International Review of Social History*, 20, 2 (1975) 149–174.

Capitalism and the state in modern France: renovation and economic management in the twentieth century, Cambridge, 1983.

Lacouture, Jean, *De Gaulle*, 3 vols, Paris, 1984.

Lacroix-Riz, A., 'Les grandes banques françaises de la collaboration à l'épuration, 1940–1950. I: La collaboration bancaire'. *Revue de l'Histoire de la Deuxième Guerre Mondiale*, 141 (1986), 3–44.

'Les grandes banques françaises de la collaboration à l'épuration. II: La non épuration bancaire 1944–1950'. *Revue de l'Histoire de la Deuxième Guerre Mondiale*, 142 (1986), 81–101.

Lagroye, Jacques, *Société et politique. J. Chaban-Delmas à Bordeaux*, Paris, 1973.

Lalumière, P., *L'inspection des finances*, Paris, 1959.

Laniel, J., *Jours de gloire et jours cruels 1908–1958*, Paris, 1971.

Larkin, M., *France since the Popular Front: government and people 1936–1986*, Oxford, 1988.

Lebon, Pierre, *Le gaullisme au pouvoir*, Paris, no date.

Le Bras, G., 'Géographie électorale et géographie religieuse'. In C. Morazé (ed.), *Etudes de sociologie électorale*, Paris, 1947.

Leconte, Daniel, *Les pieds noirs. Histoire et portrait d'une communauté*, Paris, 1980.

Lefaurichon, Pierre, 'Voter pour des hommes'. *La Volonté du Commerce et de l'Industrie*, 45 (June 1951).

Lefranc, P., *Avec qui vous savez. Vingt-cinq ans avec de Gaulle*, Paris, 1979.

Leites, N., *On the game of politics in France*, Stanford, 1959.

Leites, N. and Melnik, C., *The house without windows: France selects a president*, White Plains, 1958.

Lemire, Laurent, *Georges Albertini 1911–1983*, Paris, 1990.

Lestier, F., 'Pas de politique'. *La République*, 24 February 1946.

Long, R., *Les élections législatives en Côte d'Or depuis 1870*, Paris, 1958.

Luthy, Herbert, *The state of France*, London, 1955.

MacRae, D., *Parliament, parties and society in France 1946–1958*, New York, 1967.

Magraw, R., *A history of the French working class. I: The age of artisan revolution 1815–1871*, London, 1992.

Maier, C. S., *Recasting bourgeois Europe: stabilization in France, Germany and Italy in the decade after World War 1*, Princeton, 1975.

'The post-war eras and conditions for stability in twentieth century Western Europe'. *American Historical Review* 81, 1 (1981), 327–352.

In search of stability: explorations in historical political economy, Cambridge, 1987.

Mair, Peter, 'The electoral universe of small parties in post-war Western Europe'. In G. Pridham and F. Muller-Rommel (eds.), *Small parties in western Europe*, London, 1991.

Malraux, André, *Les chênes qu'on abat*, Paris, 1971.

Manceron, C. and Pingaud, B., *Mitterrand l'homme, les idées, le programme*, Paris, 1982.

Marchand, Marie-Hélène, *Les conseillers généraux en France depuis 1945*, Paris, 1970.

Marès, A., *Un siècle à travers trois républiques. Georges et Edouard Bonnefous 1880–1980*, Paris, 1980.

Maresca, S., *Les dirigeants paysans*, Paris, 1983.

Margairaz, Michel, *L'état, les finances et l'économie. Histoire d'une conversion 1932–1952*, 2 vols, Paris, 1991.

Mariani, Maria Grovia, *Il Mouvement Républicain Populaire. Partito della IV Repubblica*, Rome, 1983.

Marin, Bernard, *De Gaulle de ma jeunesse 1944–1970*, Paris, 1984.

Marquand, D., *The unprincipled society*, London, 1988.

Marseille, Jacques, *Empire colonial et capitalisme français. Histoire d'un divorce*, Paris, 1984.

Martin, R., *Patron de droit divin*, Paris, 1984.

Matthews, R., *The death of the Fourth Republic*, London, 1954.

Maupeau, Jacques de, 'Faire l'Europe, c'est faire la paix'. *La France Indépendante*, 22 April 1950.

Mauriac, C., *The other de Gaulle: diaries, 1944–1954*, London, 1973.

Mayer, Denise (ed.), *René Mayer. Etudes, témoignages, documents*, Paris, 1983.

Mazé, Jean, *Le système*, Paris, 1951.

Mengin, R., *No laurels for de Gaulle*, London, 1967.

Michelet, Claude, *Mon père Edmond Michelet d'après ses notes intimes*, Paris, 1971.

Michelet, Edmond, *Le gaullisme, passionnante aventure*, Paris, 1962.

  La querelle de la fidélité. Peut-on être gaulliste aujourd'hui?, Paris, 1981.

Moch, Jules, *Une si longue vie*, Paris, 1976.

Monnet, J., *Mémoires*, Paris, 1976.

Montel, Pierre, 'Propos sur la liberté'. *La République* 4 (3 March 1946).

Morice, J., *La demande d'automobiles en France. Théorie, histoire, répartition géographique*, Paris, 1957.

Mottin, J., *Histoire politique de la presse*, Paris, 1949.

Moulin de Labarthète, H. du, *Le temps des illusions. Souvenirs juillet 1940–avril 1942*, Geneva, 1946.

Muselier, E., *De Gaulle contre le gaullisme*, Paris, 1946.

  Ma position devant le Parti Radical et le Rassemblement des Gauches Républicaines et l'Union des Gauches, Paris, n.d.

Mutter, A., 'Raisons d'un vote'. *Paroles Françaises*, 3 (1 December 1945).

  'Réconciliation par l'amnestie'. *Paroles Françaises*, 56 (6 December 1946).

Newton, S., 'The Keynesian revolution debate: time for a new approach?' In A. Gorst, L. Johnman and W. Lewis (eds.), *Contemporary British history 1931–1961: politics and the limits of policy*, London, 1991, pp. 75–79.

Nocher, J., *Le pamphlet atomique. Messieurs les grands, un petit vous dit merde,* Paris, 1947.

Noel, L., *La traversée du désert*, Paris, 1973.

Noiriel, Gerard, *Workers in French society in the 19th and the 20th centuries*, New York, 1990.

Nora, Pierre (ed.), *Essais d'ego-histoire*, Paris, 1987.

Nord, Philip, *Paris shopkeepers and the politics of resentment*, Princeton, 1986.

Novick, Peter, *The Resistance versus Vichy*, London, 1968.

Offe, C., 'Structural problems of the capitalist state: class rule and the political system. On the selectivity of political institutions'. *German Political Studies* (1974), 33–57.

Olson, M., *The logic of collective action: public goods and the theory of groups* Cambridge, Mass., 1971.

  The rise and decline of nations: economic growth, stagflation and social rigidities, New Haven and London, 1982.

Ott, Barthélemy, *Georges Bidault. L'indomptable*, Annonay, 1975.

Il était une fois le conseil de la république 1946–1948, Annonay, 1976.

Vie et mort du MRP. La démocratie chrétienne est-elle possible en France?, Annonay, 1978.

Paira, René, *Affaires d'Alsace*, Paris, 1990.

Parti Radical-Socialiste, *Le Parti Radical-Socialiste pendant la Résistance*, Paris, no date.

Parti Républicain de la Liberté, *Notes d'orientation à l'intention des orateurs du parti*, 1 (15 January 1946); 2 (5 February 1946); 3 (20 March 1946).

Pataut, J., *Sociologie électorale de la Nièvre au XXème siècle (1902–1951)*, 2 vols, Paris, 1956.

Paxton, Robert, *Vichy France: old guard and new order, 1940–1944*, New York, 1982.

Pépy, D., 'Note sur le Mouvement Républicain Populaire'. In M. Duverger (ed.), *Partis politiques et classes sociales*, Paris, 1955.

Perrot, M., *Le mode de vie des familles bourgeoises 1873–1953*, Paris, 1961.

Peyrefitte, R., *Les ambassades*, Paris, 1951.

Propos secrets, Paris, 1977.

Pinay, Antoine, *Un français comme les autres. Entretiens avec Antoine Veil*, Paris, 1984.

Pirenne, J., *Mémoires et notes politiques*, Verviers, 1973.

Planchais, J., *Une histoire politique de l'armée. II: 1940–1967, de de Gaulle à de Gaulle*, Paris, 1967.

Plantade, R., 'Le MRP'. In J. Fauvet and H. Mendras (eds.), *Les paysans et la politique dans la France contemporaine*, Paris, 1958, pp. 119–130.

Popot, Jean, *J'étais aumônier à Fresnes*, Paris, 1962.

Poujade, P., *A l'heure de la colère*, Paris, 1977.

Poulat, Emile, *Eglise contre bourgeoisie*, Paris, 1977.

Prost, A., *Les anciens combattants et la société française 1914–1939*, Paris, 1977.

Purtschet, C., *Le Rassemblement du Peuple Français 1947–1953* (Paris, 1965).

Ramsden, J., 'A party for owners or a party for earners? How far did the British Conservative party really change after 1945?'. *Transactions of the Royal Historical Society*, 37 (1987), 49–63.

Rassemblement des Gauches Républicaines, *Que veut le RGR?*, Paris, 1949.

Qu'est-ce le RGR?, Paris, 1949.

Rassimier, Paul, *Le parlement aux mains des banques*, Paris, 1956.

Rémond, René, 'Droite et gauche dans le catholicisme français contemporain'. *Revue Française de Science Politique*, 3 (September 1958), 529–542.

'Conclusion', in Réné Rémond, A. Coutrot and I. Broussard (eds.), *Quarante ans de cabinets ministériels. De Léon Blum à G. Pompidou*, Paris, 1982, pp. 232–242.

Les droites en France, Paris, 1982.

'Le contemporain du contemporain'. In P. Nora (cd.), *Essais d'ego-histoire*, Paris, 1987, pp. 293–350.

Rémy (pseudonym for Gilbert Renaud), *Mes grands hommes et quelques autres*, Paris, 1982.

Rendel, Margherita, *The administrative functions of the French conseil d'état*, London, 1970.

Richard, René and Sérigny, Alain de, *La bissectrice de la guerre: Alger 8 novembre 1942*, Algiers, 1946.

Rimbaud, Christine, *Pinay*, Paris, 1990.

Riond, Georges, *Chroniques d'un autre monde*, Paris, 1979.

Rioux, J.-P., *The Fourth Republic 1944–1958*, Cambridge, 1987.

Rivet, J.-A., 'Les maires d'Yssingeaux: 1814–1983. Une histoire de familles'. In M. Agulhon, L. Giraud, J. L. Robert and W. Serman (eds.), *Les maires en France du consulat à nos jours*, Paris, 1985.

Rollat, Félix, 'A propos d'une lettre'. *La République*, 3 March 1946.

'Pour un socialisme libéral et humain'. *La République*, 23 November 1946.

Rosanvallon, P., *L'état en France de 1789 à nos jours*, Paris, 1990.

Ross, G., Hoffmann S. and Malzacher, S., *The Mitterrand experience*, Oxford, 1987.

Rougier, L., *Mission secrète à Londres*, Geneva, 1946.

De Gaulle contre de Gaulle, Paris, 1948.

Rousso, Henry, *Le syndrome de Vichy (1944–198 ...)*, Paris, 1987.

Ruby, Edmond, 'L'épuration dans l'armée'. *Défense de l'Occident*, 39 (1957), 99–105.

Rueff, J. *Discours aux Indépendants*, Paris, 1951.

Saint-Charnot, H., 'Alfred Fabre-Luce, pyschoanalyste de la résistance'. *Questions Actuelles*, December 1946.

Sapiens (pseudonym for Alfred Fabre-Luce), *Mendès ou Pinay*, Paris, 1953.

Serre, R., *Croisade à coups de poings*, Givors, 1954.

Shennan, Andrew, *Rethinking France: plans for renewal 1940–1946*, Oxford, 1989.

Siegfried, André, *Tableau politique de la France de l'ouest sous la IIIème république*, Paris, 1912.

De la IIIème à la IVème république, Paris, 1957.

Silverman, S., 'Patronage as myth'. In E. Gellner and J. Waterbury (eds.), *Patrons and clients in Mediterranean societies*, London, 1977, pp. 7–19.

Skinner, Q., 'Some problems in the analysis of political thought and action'. In J. Tully (ed.), *Meaning and content: Quentin Skinner and his critics*, Cambridge, 1988.

Smith, T. A., 'Algeria and the French *modérés*: the politics of immoderation?' *Western Political Quarterly*, 18 (1965), 116–134.

Spaak, Paul-Henri, *Combats inachevés. De l'espoir aux déceptions*, Paris, 1969.

Suleiman, E. N., *Elites in French society: the politics of survival*, Princeton, 1978.

Sweets, J. F., *The politics of resistance in France 1940–1944: a history of the Mouvements Unis de la Résistance*, Dekalb, Ill., 1976.

Tarr, Francis de, *The French Radical party from Herriot to Mendès-France*, Oxford, 1961.

Tarrow, S., *Between centre and periphery: grassroot politicians in France and Italy*, New Haven, 1977.

Terrenoire, L., *De Gaulle 1947–1954. Pourquoi l'échec. Du RPF à la traversée du désert*, Paris, 1981.

Thoenig, J.-C., *L'ère des technocrates. Le cas des ponts et chaussées*, Paris, 1973.

Thompson, D., *Democracy in France: the Third and Fourth Republics*, Oxford, 1952.

Tixier-Vignancour, J., *La France trahie. Plaidoirie de Me Tixier-Vignancour dans l'affaire des fuites*, Paris, 1956.

J'ai choisi la défense, Paris, 1964.

Todd, E., *The making of modern France: politics, ideology and culture*, Oxford, 1991.

Tomlinson, J., 'Mr Attlee's supply side socialism'. *Economic History Review*, 46, 1 (1993), 1–22.

Touchard, Jean, 'Bibliographie et chronologie du Poujadisme'. *Revue Française de Science Politique*, 1956, 18–42.

Triboulet, R., *Un gaulliste de la IVème*, Paris, 1985.

Tucker, D., 'The new look of the extreme right in France'. *Western Political Quarterly*, 21 (1968), 86–97.

Vallon, L., *Le dilemme français*, Paris, 1951.

Vedel, Georges (ed.), *La dépolitisation. Mythe ou réalité?*, Paris, 1962.

Vendroux, J., *Souvenirs de famille et journal politique.* I: *Cette grande chance que j'ai eue: 1920–1957*, Paris, 1974.

Viannay, P., *Du bon usage de la France*, Paris, 1988.

Villiers, Georges, *Témoignages*, Paris, 1978.

Vinen, R., *The politics of French business 1936–1945*, Cambridge, 1991.

Vinen, R., 'Business intervention in the 1951 general election: the Groupement de Défense des Contribuables'. *Modern and Contemporary France*, 1 (1993), 3–16.

Vulpain, A. de, 'Physionomie agraire et orientation politique dans le departement des Côtes du Nord 1928–1946'. *Revue Française de Science Polititique*, 1 and 11 (1957), 110–132.

Wall, I., *L'influence américaine sur la politique française, 1945–1954*, Paris, 1989.
  The United States and the making of post-war France 1945–1954, Cambridge, 1991.

Walston, J., *The Mafia and clientelism: roads to Rome in post-war Calabria*, London, 1988.

Ward, M., *France pagan? The mission of abbé Godin*, London, 1949.

Weber H., *Le parti des patrons. Le CNPF (1946–1986)*, Paris, 1986.

Weil, S., 'Ne recommençons pas la guerre de Troie'. *Nouveaux Cahiers*, 2 (April 1937).

Werth, Alexander, *France, 1940–1955*, London, 1956.

Williams, Philip, *Politics in post-war France: parties and the constitution in the Fourth Republic*, 2nd edition, London, 1958.
  Crisis and compromise: politics in the Fourth Republic, London, 1972.

Wilson, G. K., *Business and politics*, London, 1985.

Wilson, Steven, 'The *Action Française* in French intellectual life'. *Historical Journal*, 12 (1969), 328–359.

Wright, G., *The reshaping of French democracy*, New York, 1948.
  Rural revolution in France, Stanford, 1968.

Young, J., *France, the Cold War and the western alliance 1944–1949*, Leicester, 1990.

Zdatny, Steven, *The politics of survival: artisans in twentieth century France*, Oxford, 1990.

Zeitlin, J., 'Shop floor bargaining and the state: a contradictory relationship'. In S. Tolliday and J. Zeitlin (eds.), *Shop floor bargaining and the state*, Cambridge, 1985.

Zeldin, T., *France 1848–1945: ambition and love*, Oxford, 1979.

REVIEWS

Bulletin Intérieur
Défense de l'Occident
Ecrits de Paris
Le Flambeau de la Réconciliation Française
La France Indépendante
L'Indépendant Français
La Liberté Républicaine
Le Monde
Paroles Françaises
La République
La République Libre
L'Unité Française
Unité Paysanne

Index

COLLECTED ECONOMIC ESSAYS

Volume 6

FURTHER ESSAYS ON APPLIED ECONOMICS

COLLECTED ECONOMIC ESSAYS
by Nicholas Kaldor

FURTHER
ESSAYS ON APPLIED
ECONOMICS

NICHOLAS KALDOR

HOLMES & MEIER PUBLISHERS, INC.
New York

First published in the United States of America 1978 by
HOLMES & MEIER PUBLISHERS, INC.
30 Irving Place, New York, N.Y. 10003

Library of Congress Cataloging in Publication Data
Kaldor, Nicholas, 1908–
    Further essays on applied economics
    (His Collected economic essays; v. 6)
    Includes index.
    1. Economic—Addresses, essays, lectures.
I. Title. II. Series.
HB171.K27 1978   330   78–15546
ISBN 0–8419–0295–X

Printed in Great Britain

CONTENTS

INTRODUCTION

THE present volume contains a selection of essays on applied economics written subsequent to those included in the two volumes of my *Essays on Economic Policy*, published in 1964. The distinction between "theoretical" and "applied" papers is bound to be an arbitrary one: all papers on economics, however abstract, contain policy implications; if they did not, it would not be worth writing them. But some of the papers are more consciously directed to specific issues of economic policy and/or make more extensive use of empirical material (whether of a statistical or a general historical kind) and these are best kept apart from those which reflect one's general outlook on the "laws of motion" of economic systems.

I have grouped the papers selected for the present volume under three heads. The first part, *Money and International Equilibrium*, contains one paper devoted to the views of Milton Friedman and the issues raised by "monetarism", followed by six papers relating to the international monetary system (or the international aspects of the monetary system) which were written over a period of 13 years, the earliest dating from 1964 and the latest written in 1977.

The paper "The New Monetarism"—originally prepared for a public lecture in 1970—stands apart from the others in that it is devoted to a critique of a particular creed, invented by Professor Milton Friedman[1] and assiduously propagated by a growing band of devoted disciples, according to which inflation is responsible for most, if not all, evils, and inflation is caused by excessive increases in the "money supply" and nothing else. Since my paper was published, Friedman has gained further influential adherents —politicians of the Right, ranging from General Pinochet in Chile to Sir Keith Joseph in England, numerous important stockbrokers, financial journalists and distinguished editors like Mr. Rees-Mogg

---

[1] This is true, even though Friedman himself would claim to be a lineal descendant of David Hume and other distinguished adherents of the quantity theory of money.

of *The Times* and, last but not least, the five economists of the Nobel Prize Committee of the Swedish Academy of Science, who awarded last year's Economic Nobel Prize to Friedman. This last event evoked much the same reaction among the majority of the world's professional economists who have not been converted to the new creed (or not yet), as would have occurred among biologists if Lysenko had been given the Nobel Prize in Physiology and Medicine.[1]

Despite the voluminous new writings on "monetarism" which have appeared since my paper was published in the July 1970 issue of *Lloyds Bank Review*, I would not modify the paper if I were writing it afresh, except perhaps that I would give more emphasis to the points relegated to a long footnote on pp. 11–12, and to the proposition that in a world where money consists of financial claims which come into existence as part of the process of bank lending, changes in the "money supply" (however defined) and changes in the "velocity of circulation" are to a large extent substitutes for one another (and depend also on how widely or narrowly the "money supply" is defined).[2]

For the convenience of readers I attached in an Appendix (with the publisher's permission) Friedman's "Comment" on my paper and my "Reply", which appeared in the subsequent issue of *Lloyds Bank Review*. I agree with Friedman that the central point of my criticism is that in a bank-money (or credit-money) economy "changes in the money supply must be regarded as the result, not the cause, of changes in economic activity" (to which he should have added "and/or of exogenous changes in the cost of labour or of raw material costs"). I was glad to see his confirmation that once this point is established, the "case against the monetar-

---

[1] See, for example, Myrdal, "The Nobel Prize in Economic Science", in *Challenge*, March-April 1977, where it is argued that in the "hard" sciences, such as physics and chemistry (in contrast to the social sciences, which are "soft"), such politically motivated awards would not be possible.

[2] This paper is a polemical piece, written as a criticism of Friedman and the Friedmanites, and should not be looked upon as a self-contained exposition of my views on the role of money in the economy. To set this piece in a proper context the reader is advised to read it in conjunction with my submission to the Radcliffe Committee, "Monetary Policy, Economic Stability and Growth", reprinted in Volume 3 of this series (pp. 128–53), together with my critique of the Radcliffe Report which is also reprinted in that volume (pp. 159–65). Reference should also be made to the paper on Latin American inflations (no. 8 of the present volume), and to my analysis of the causes of the recent "stagflation" in Volume 5.

ists is firm".[1] He failed, however, to make any reference to two
damaging pieces of evidence in this connection which I cited
against him in the paper: first, that, contrary to his emphatic
assertions in his Presidential address to the American Economic
Association, the Federal Reserve *expanded* the money base considerably in the years 1929–32, and did not *contract* it—which
latter assertion was his main evidence for suggesting that the
Great Depression of 1929–33 was the result of the "highly deflationary policies" pursued by the U.S. monetary authorities.
The other point on which Friedman remained silent was the
contrasting experience of the U.S. and Canada in the same
period: in the latter country the "money supply" fell by much less
(because in contrast to the U.S. there were very few bank failures)
but the velocity of circulation fell by much more, so that the
percentage fall in the money G.N.P. was much the same in both
countries.

Since that time Friedman himself has changed tack and in
contrast to other converts to monetarism has, in fact, abandoned
the emphasis on the behaviour of the monetary authorities as the
prime cause of inflation. Instead, in his later papers he blames governments for not being willing to face up to the full consequences
of their spending policies and preferring "printing money" to
taxation; and later still, he turned the focus of his attention to
the labour market with the new concept of the vertically-shaped
"expectations-augmented" Phillips curve, according to which
there is a single level of unemployment at which the labour
market is in both static and dynamic equilibrium, and at which
alone any particular rate of inflation—including the zero rate—
is capable of maintaining itself without an inherent tendency to
acceleration or deceleration. Hence every attempt to push unemployment below this "natural rate" necessarily results in an
acceleration of inflation, whilst a process of inflation, once begun,
can never be brought to an end without maintaining unemployment *above* the "natural level" for a certain length of time.

As Mr. T. F. Cripps emphasised in a recent paper[2] this new
theory of Friedman's is explicitly based on an atomistic model of

[1] See p. 23 below.
[2] "Money Supply, Wages and Inflation", *Cambridge Journal of Economics*, Vol. 1,
No. 1, March 1977.

competition in the labour market, where any excess demand for labour leads to a rise in *expected* real wages (thereby causing money wages to rise by more than "expected inflation") through the bidding-up of wages by employers in search of workers, and any excess supply to a fall in *expected* real wages through the bidding-down of wages by employees. Involuntary unemployment cannot exist because it is excluded by the assumptions; the labour market operates in the same way as the Chicago wheat market (or the perfect markets on Walrasian theory) where prices are always and continuously market-clearing. It is the dream world of neo-classical theory *in extremis*. And it implies an inverse relationship between actual (or ex-post) real wages and the level of employment; in other words the postulate of diminishing marginal productivity of labour in the short period (which implies that productivity is *negatively* correlated with the level of employment), a hypothesis which has been contradicted by numerous empirical investigations, in a number of industrial countries.

This was Friedman up to 1975. A year later, however (in his Nobel Memorial lecture),[1] this theory has already been overtaken by a new one, according to which the "Phillips curve" is not vertical, but has a *positive* slope—i.e., so far from there being a trade-off between unemployment and inflation, there is a negative trade-off: unemployment will be the greater the higher the rate of inflation. Friedman says he was driven to this conclusion by the postwar record of seven countries, but like other empirical generalisations of Friedman it is consistent with diametrically opposite interpretations. The one chosen by him relies on a model that places primary emphasis on a factor which is beyond the reach of empirical verification: the prevailing state of expectations of employers and workers concerning the future rate of inflation, which is essentially unobservable, and which he now says is also a most unstable factor, capable of unpredictable shifts.

The difficulty created by a positive association between inflation and unemployment arises from the basic assumption of monetarist theories, according to which *all* inflation is "demand-induced", i.e. it must be caused by an excess demand for goods and services.

---

[1] *Inflation and Unemployment: The New Dimension of Politics*, Institute of Economic Affairs Occasional Paper, London, 1977.

Once one allows for cost-induced inflations (whether from the side of raw materials or of labour) the difficulty disappears. In his latest paper Friedman acknowledges the rôle of the oil cartel in the recent inflation, which is a clear departure from the pure milk of the monetarist doctrine—but he does so only after his original prediction, according to which the oil cartel would collapse in a few months and the oil price would revert to "normal", has been proved completely wrong.[1]

The problem of creating a satisfactory international payments system that would reform or replace the system created at Bretton Woods occupied the minds of innumerable economists, government officials and international bankers for the best part of twenty years. That this system, despite the great advantages it brought in terms of greatly increased freedom of trading under conditions of world-wide prosperity, was bound to break down sooner or later—owing to the increasing imbalances between the fast growing and trade-gaining surplus countries (like Germany and Japan) and the slow growing and trade-losing deficit countries (the U.S. and the U.K.)—was clearly foreseeable in the early 1960s, as shown by my paper "The Problem of International Liquidity" written in 1964 (particularly the passages on pp. 36 ff.). The additional strains in the second half of the 1960s due to the enlarged U.S. balance of payments deficits (doubtless a consequence of the Vietnam war) accelerated the process and finally brought matters to a head in Nixon's dramatic move of August 1971.

Britain was of course in a much weaker position during the whole of this period than America, and her residual reserve currency rôle greatly accentuated the difficulty of seeking redress through an adjustment of the exchange rate in the way France did in 1957 and 1958. I myself was strongly in favour of devaluation from around 1957 onwards and argued for it on numerous occasions (mostly in letters to *The Times*) at a time when this whole subject was regarded as too delicate to be aired in public. When

---

[1] Writing in *Newsweek* on 4 March 1974, Friedman predicted that "in order to keep prices up, the Arabs would have to curtail their output by ever larger amounts. But even if they cut their output to zero, they would not for long keep the world price of crude at $10 a barrel. Well before that point the cartel would collapse."

the Labour Party was returned to power in October 1964 (albeit with a very small majority) the three senior members of the new Cabinet decided, within the first twenty-four hours, that they would maintain the parity of sterling, a decision which was regarded by most of the economic advisers brought in by the new Government as a catastrophic error which would have to be reversed sooner or later, but which in the meantime would frustrate the execution of the Government's major economic objectives.[1] However, the decision was maintained despite a succession of exchange crises (and the abandonment of the commitment to growth and full employment in the summer of 1966) until in the late autumn of 1967 devaluation became virtually unavoidable. And then the move was made to a new fixed parity that made the pound 14·3 per cent. cheaper in terms of foreign currencies (on account of the simultaneous abolition of export rebates and a small employment subsidy to manufacturing industry, the genuine extent of the devaluation was only 11·5 per cent.), which many regarded as insufficient to reverse the adverse trends in Britain's export trade for more than a brief period.

The paper on "The Relative Merits of Fixed and Floating Rates" is an abridged version of a memorandum written in my official capacity as an economic adviser to the Chancellor in the summer of 1965,[2] which sets out the arguments for and against two forms of devaluation: the change to a new fixed rate (as in 1949) or to a floating rate (as in 1931). My purpose was to show that the adoption of a floating rate, though it may have difficulties of its own, is far more likely to achieve the long-run objectives of securing sufficient exports for full employment and a satisfactory growth rate than the change to a new fixed rate.

However, the Government opted for a new fixed rate—largely I believe because the adoption of a floating rate was so much against the "ground rules" of the I.M.F., and also because it represented a threat to the dollar by creating the expectation that one day the U.S. might adopt the same course—which meant that

[1] For a description of these events, see M. J. Stewart, *The Jekyll and Hyde Years: Politics and Economic Policy since 1964*, London, 1977, pp. 27–30.

[2] It is reproduced here—after due excisions of confidential material—with official permission.

in the twelve months following the act of devaluation the main preoccupation of the Government was to avoid being forced off the new parity. This required a succession of drastic steps involving new conditional aid from the I.M.F., fresh international support through the Basle Agreement, as well as drastic increases in taxation. The policy paid off handsomely in terms of huge balance of payments surpluses in 1970 and 1971, but at the cost of a wholly unexpected and fast-developing rise in unemployment, which caused the new Conservative Government to put Mr. Jenkins' fiscal policy sharply into reverse, thereby initiating both an import boom and renewed runs on sterling. The response on this latter occasion (in June, 1972) was to float sterling rather than to devalue.

At first—in the first three years, in fact—the adoption of the floating rate appeared to have justified its protagonists, in that the move put an end to speculative attacks on sterling. The expectation of a further fall in the rate, which caused so much difficulty after the 1967 devaluation, seems to have disappeared when, with a floating rate, the rate was free to rise as well as to fall. In practice, the monetary authorities followed the policy of selling sterling in the market only in order to prevent (or to moderate) a rise, and not to bring about a fall, in the exchange rate.

In March 1976, however, following upon repeated large-scale interventions to prevent a rise in sterling, the rumour got around that the Government was determined to bring the rate down in order to improve the competitiveness of industry; and this started a run on sterling which the authorities found very difficult to control. The events of the spring and summer of 1976 have demonstrated that the internal inflationary effects of a sudden depreciation of the exchange rate, and their general effects on confidence (both internal and external), make it impossible to allow the rate to float freely, even when a downward float is fully in accordance with the Government's economic strategy.

The strategy advocated in my 1965 paper "The Relative Merits of Fixed and Floating Rates" thus proved in practice futile. In circumstances in which the rate of exchange *was* floating, and in which the Government's proclaimed policy of "export-led" growth clearly required that the rate should be allowed, or even encouraged, to fall further, the Government felt nevertheless

compelled to use every device for preventing the rate from falling, in order to "restore confidence" in sterling—in much the same manner as governments did under the fixed rate régime of Bretton Woods, both before and after the 1967 devaluation.[1]

The main reason for the Government's anxiety to protect the pound was that the price rise which further devaluation entailed would have put the "social contract" in jeopardy, causing a renewal of wage-inflation and following that, further depreciation and inflation, in an accelerating spiral. The extent of the depreciation of the currency had already breached the permissible limit by causing an *absolute* cut in real wages; any further depreciation therefore carried the danger of being offset by compensating increases in money wages, thus resulting in more rapid inflation without any marked improvement in competitiveness.

So the policy which I advocated in the 1960s and developed at greater length in my 1970 Presidential Address to the British Association,[2] of reconciling full employment growth with equilibrium in the balance of payments through adjusting the relationship between import and export propensities by a policy of continuous manipulation of the exchange rate, proved in the event a chimera. The main reason for this was that (in company with most other economists) I greatly overestimated the effectiveness of the price mechanism in changing the relationship of exports to imports at any given level of income. The doctrine that exports and imports are kept in balance through induced changes in their relative prices is as old and deeply ingrained as almost any proposition in economics. In Ricardo's theory the change in relative prices was assumed to be the automatic consequence of

---

[1] The full story of the events of 1976 and their causes still remains to be written. In 1974 and 1975 ,when the balance of payments was very heavily in deficit, there was no lack of confidence in the pound: in fact, the Bank managed to attract funds in excess of balance of payments needs through the maintenance of relatively high interest rates. But from March 1976 onwards (when the balance of payments prospects looked far more favourable) there was a "confidence crisis" in sterling and a rapid withdrawal of funds—mainly funds of the oil-producing countries—which went on despite attempts to stem it through large-scale international borrowing, high interest rates, etc. However, after the application to the I.M.F. and the acceptance of conditions which it entailed, there was a sea-change in international sentiment, and the Bank accumulated dollars even faster than it had lost them in the previous nine months.

[2] "Conflicts in Economic Objectives", reprinted in *Further Essays on Economic Theory*, pp. 155–75.

the self-correcting mechanism implied by the movement of gold across national frontiers, which was assumed to occur whenever exports and imports were out of balance, which caused prices (and wages!) to fall in a country with a balance of payments deficit, and *vice versa*, and thereby altered relative trade flows in an equilibrating direction. This doctrine was replaced, towards the end of the nineteenth century, by another version (the so-called "neoclassical" theory) according to which it is not so much the gold flows themselves (which were very small) but the changes of relative interest rates (imposed by central banks in order to protect their gold reserves) which brought about the required changes in relative prices.

This mechanism too looked increasingly improbable in twentieth-century conditions. A plausible solution to the problem was first provided by Harrod in 1933[1] when he argued that the balance of payments of an industrial country like Britain, under the gold standard, or under any system of fixed exchange rates, is automatically maintained through the operation of a "multiplier" process which adjusts the level of imports to the prevailing level of exports through induced variations of the level of domestic output and employment. Like the General Theory of Keynes, this theory assumes that the economy is *not* resource-constrained; the amount of labour effectively employed, and the amount of capital accumulated, is the resultant of past developments and of the current size of the market for a country's products.

In other words, what the Harrod theory asserts is that trade is kept in balance by variations of production and incomes rather than by price variations: a proposition which implies that the income elasticity of demand of a country's inhabitants for imports and those of foreigners for its exports are far more important explanatory variables than the corresponding price elasticities. If the Harrod theory provides the realistic explanation of the underlying forces which maintain the trade flows of an industrial exporter in balance (subject, of course, to the exceptions to this

---

[1] *International Economics*, Cambridge Economic Handbooks, Cambridge, 1st edition, 1933. Cf. also P. Barratt Whale, "The Working of the Pre-War Gold Standard", *Economica*, 1938, pp. 18–32, for an analysis of the reasons for preferring the Harrod mechanism as an explanation of how equilibrium in the balance of payments was maintained under the gold standard.

rule in the shape of long-term surplus and deficit countries, which must also be capable of being explained within the same framework)[1] this also carries the implication that the relationship of import propensities to exports will be relatively insensitive to such variations of relative prices as can be accomplished by monetary or exchange rate policies.[2]

This latter implication (though discussed in the 1930s) seems to have got lost when the debate on fixed versus flexible exchange rates flared up again in the 1960s. This explains perhaps the exaggerated hopes placed on variations in exchange rates as an instrument of the "adjustment process" in international trade and payments and, for Britain in particular, on a system of "managed

---

[1] If the level of savings of a particular country exceeds its domestic investment, the "leakage" through savings will prevent domestic incomes from expanding far enough (or fast enough) to increase imports to a level at which they are equal to the country's exports. There will therefore be a surplus on current account which implies overseas lending in some form (of an equivalent amount, if the accumulation of liquid claims on foreigners is also regarded as a form of lending) which, if it persists long enough, will cause interest rates to fall (through higher liquidity) in the surplus country relative to others, thereby inducing a flow of long-term lending. On this account the persistence of surpluses on current account, caused by excess domestic savings, induces, via the capital market, a flow of overseas lending. This is in contrast to the traditional view according to which the act of (long-term) foreign lending is the primary factor, and the emergence of a surplus on current account a consequence of the increased exports which result from foreign lending (on account of the additional expenditure of the borrowing countries). As far as nineteenth-century Britain is concerned, it is possible that both mechanisms played a rôle: the chronic current account surplus led to high liquidity and hence to the flotation of overseas bonds of all kinds in the London capital market; the proceeds of these flotations (for building the Indian or the Argentine railways, for example) undoubtedly caused, directly or indirectly, an increase in British exports.

Under post-World War II conditions however (where the U.S. and the U.K. were responsible for the great bulk of private overseas investment, and such investment mainly took the form of direct investment in overseas branches and subsidiaries of large corporations) it is very doubtful how far either of the two mechanisms played a decisive rôle. On account of their "reserve currency" rôle, both America and Britain were able to invest abroad far in excess of their current account of surplus; and it is possible to argue that the net effect of such foreign direct investment caused a deterioration, rather than an improvement, on current account. On the other hand, some exporting countries which invested very little abroad (as, for example, Germany and Japan until the last few years) had large and growing export surpluses, as a counterpart of which they accumulated huge dollar balances. Under postwar conditions the pattern of balances on current account (among the industrialised countries at any rate) had very little to do with the proclivities of different countries for foreign lending or investment.

[2] On the constraints operating on the relation of industrial to agricultural prices, cf. *Further Essays on Economic Theory*, pp. 207–10 and pp. 218–20, and also pp. 161–2 below. It is important to bear in mind that the Harrod theory of the foreign trade multiplier (just as Keynes' theory of the investment multiplier) presupposes that it is the demand for *manufactured goods* which is changed through a change of exports (or investment), that manufactured goods are *not* traded in perfect markets, and their prices are *not* "market-clearing" in the theoretical sense; indeed they are habitually in "excess supply", in that the level of production is demand-constrained and not resource-

floating" as a means of securing higher and more stable growth rates.[1]

The three papers dealing with the dollar crisis and the problems and prospects of international monetary reform were written in the aftermath of President Nixon's move in August 1971, and the widespread discussions which followed it—at both official (inter-governmental) level and at non-official levels, in numerous international meetings of economists—on how to create a new international system to replace the Bretton Woods system which was shattered by the American move.

On re-reading the three articles entitled "The Dollar Crisis", written for *The Times* in early September 1971, I am impressed by the confidence with which I predicted that the Nixon move "marks the beginning of a new era of floating exchange rates which will be of fairly long duration" since "if perchance fixed parities were restored . . . such an arrangement . . . would [not] have any permanence";[2] but I am less impressed with my confidence in the importance I then attached to under-valued or over-valued exchange rates as a factor in accelerating or retarding (as the case may be) the economic growth of different countries. I was convinced that once exchange rates are freed from the rigidities imposed by Bretton Woods, the forces of cumulative causation which made some countries grow fast and others slowly will no longer operate, or not in the same manner. That belief was badly shaken by the experience of subsequent years for reasons explained in my most recent paper on the subject, which is discussed below.

There is one important matter, however, on which subsequent experience served to strengthen my views, and not to weaken

constrained. The theory is not applicable therefore to countries whose main export consists of primary products, the prices of which are determined world-wide in highly organised markets. But its applicability to industrial exporters is not confined to situations of cyclical recession or unemployment, since the manufacturing sector is always able to respond to an increase in demand by the increase in supply (given time for adjustment) both through induced increases in physical capacity (which it itself creates) and the recruitment of labour from low-earnings sectors or from less developed areas.

[1] This was just as true of most of the economists who opposed devaluation before 1967 and of those who were in favour of it (in one form or another). The opponents of devaluation – with the honourable exception of Lord Balogh—opposed it because they held even more optimistic views about the sensitiveness of the price mechanism, and believed that the necessary correction to the balance of payments could be achieved without altering the exchange rate, merely by running the economy at a somewhat lower pressure of demand.

[2] See p. 67 below.

them. This concerns the need for a new international monetary medium which would replace gold, and would re-create a system in which individual countries would no longer be in a position to increase the supply of reserve assets by incurring deficits in their balance of payments. At the same time I was convinced that no artificial paper asset, such as Keynes' "bancor", or the S.D.R.s of the I.M.F., could function satisfactorily unless it had a "commodity backing"—i.e., unless it were issued in exchange for, and were convertible into, a selection of storable basic commodities, in the same way as in the old days national currencies were convertible into gold at given ratios. In the original version of this proposal (put forward jointly with A. G. Hart and J. Tinbergen) it was envisaged that the new reserve asset should have a "composite" commodity backing, i.e. that it should be convertible into a *bundle* of some 30 primary commodities (the composition of the bundle being decided and periodically revised according to rules laid down in advance).[1] It appeared that such a system would have all the advantages, in terms of automatic stabilising forces, which the gold standard was supposed to possess under the "idealised" conditions described by Ricardo, where gold is produced under conditions of constant cost (i.e. with an infinite elasticity of supply), and where the size of the annual gold production would be large (at least by implication) in relation to the total stock in existence. However, a more thorough consideration of the enormous difficulties involved in operating a *composite* commodity reserve convinced me later that the most that one could hope for would be to stabilise the world prices of the most important basic commodities individually in terms of the international reserve currency unit, by means of open market interventions of international commodity corporations set up for the purpose, whose purchases and sales would thus automatically regulate the outstanding amount of the reserve currency as a counterpart of the net purchases or sales of commodities by the corporations.

The two papers written in 1973, "Problems and Prospects of International Monetary Reform" and "International Monetary

[1] See "The Case for an International Commodity Reserve Currency", reprinted in *Essays on Economic Policy*, pp. 131–78.

Reform: The Need for a New Approach" (the latter being the text of a lecture given at the invitation of the Bank of Italy), review the nature of the problem, the state of the international discussions then reached (in the so-called "Committee of Twenty") concerning the new monetary agreement, as well as describing the *modus operandi* and the various advantages which a commodity-based "primary reserve asset" would bring in its train, as against a unit defined only in terms of a cocktail of currencies which was then under discussion. Events since 1973—with its vast increases in commodity prices, the world-wide inflation which they generated, and the uncontrolled increase in international liquidity which accompanied them[1]—have strongly confirmed me in the view that it is the stabilisation of commodity prices, more than the prevention of excessive wage increases in industrial countries, which is the prime condition for the re-establishment of international monetary stability. Under the stress of events of the last four years the ambitious plans for international monetary reform (like other ambitious international plans) have fallen by the wayside. But if the analysis of my recent paper on the causes of world inflation[2] is broadly correct, the creation of international buffer stocks for stabilising the prices of the most important commodities is an indispensable beginning, and I was glad to learn that this now appears to be recognised by the new American administration.[3]

The concluding paper of Part I, "The Effect of Devaluation on Trade in Manufactures", was written in the summer of 1977 and is published here for the first time.[4] It is intended as an

---

[1] Between December 1969 and December 1976, total international reserves rose from $79 bn. to $258 bn., or by $179 bn., of which only $15·3 bn. was "controlled" (on the I.M.F. definition); of the rest, no less than $68 bn. was represented by the growth of "official" deposits in the Euro-currency market (cf. O.E.C.D. *Economic Outlook*, July 1977, Table 30). On account of the growing practice of financing current official liabilities by borrowing from private sources, the gross reserves of monetary institutions have no longer the same significance as an indicator of "liquidity" (or of a country's ability to finance current liabilities).

[2] "Inflation and Recession in the World Economy", reprinted in *Further Essays in Economic Theory*, pp. 214–30.

[3] Statement of C. Fred Bergsten (the U.S. Assistant Secretary to the Treasury) before the Subcommittee on Economic Stabilisation of the House Committee on Banking, Finance and Urban Affairs, 8 June 1977, and his *Progress Report* on U.S. Commodity Policy before a New York Conference on Future Problems in Minerals and Energy Policy, 3 October 1977.

[4] Some of the statistical research for the paper was prepared earlier (in 1975–6) as supporting material for policy papers written while I was working as the Chancellor's adviser in the Treasury; these appear here in a revised and updated form.

appraisal of the effects of the widespread and frequent adjustment of effective exchange rates between the highly industrialised countries which was initiated by the dollar devaluation of 1971 (or perhaps earlier, with the devaluation of the pound in 1967 and the revaluation of the mark in 1969) and which became generalised after the breakdown of the so-called "Smithsonian agreement" in February 1973. The conclusion of the paper is that, contrary to everyone's expectations, exchange rate variations—on a scale that greatly exceeded what was thought necessary at the beginning—proved remarkably ineffective in changing the relative international trade performance of different countries.[1] Britain's performance continued to deteriorate, despite a very large reduction (of the order of 40 per cent. since 1972) in its effective exchange rate[2] in relation to other industrial countries; the deterioration is not adequately measured by the reduction in her share of world exports of manufactures, since her loss of share in the British home market was considerably greater.[3] In the case of Britain, however, much the greater part of the fall in the exchange rate was offset by differential inflation; the gain in "competitiveness" as measured by relative labour costs per unit of output was relatively modest—perhaps of the order of 10–15 per cent.[4] This was not so in the case of the United States, whose internal inflation was much *less* than that of most other industrial countries, so that a 15 per cent. fall in the effective exchange rate since 1970 corresponded to a 31 per cent. gain in terms of cost-competitiveness. However, despite all this her share of world trade continued

---

[1] In the light of subsequent events, the widespread fears of numerous industrial countries (such as France, Italy or Japan, to mention only a few) of the effects on their trading position of even 10 per cent devaluation of the dollar relative to their own currencies (which caused them to resist the very idea of any such appreciation) appear rather comic.

[2] The term "effective exchange rate" means the rate of exchange in terms of a (trade-weighted) average of other currencies.

[3] The rise in the share of imports in the total domestic absorption of *manufactures* was from 17 per cent to 23 per cent. between 1970 and 1976 (see *Economic Trends*, August 1977, p. 88). Even this is not an adequate measure, since the British economy, mainly as a consequence of increasing import penetration and falling net exports, is now in a state of considerable recession (*more* than other industrial countries), with unemployment nearly a million above the 1970 level. Under full employment, the share of imports in total expenditure would be very much greater.

[4] This was further extenuated by the net loss of protection to U.K. manufacturing industry, due to the removal of tariff barriers with E.E.C. countries and the reduction of protection in relation to the others resulting from the adoption of the common external tariff of the Common Market.

to fall, if the so-called "special category" exports (mainly military aid) are excluded, and is now lower than ever. At the same time import penetration (mainly from Japan) continues to increase in a dramatic fashion; the adverse balance of visible trade, on an f.o.b.-c.i.f. basis, promises to be some $37 bn. in the current year, or nearly 2 per cent. of G.N.P. Both in Britain and America employment and output would be considerably lower but for the stimulus to the economy imparted in the form of large budgetary deficits. On the other side the trade surpluses of both Germany and Japan continue at record levels.[1]

Unless the next few years bring some large and dramatic changes, the experiment of securing a more balanced relationship in the trade between industrial countries through exchange rate variations must be adjudged a failure. This will have far-reaching consequences. For the re-establishment of the Bretton Woods system of fixed exchange rates would not improve matters; if anything it would make the divergencies in economic trends due to "cumulative causation" worse.

The final section of the paper suggests that some instrument for planning or regulating the trade flows between the developed countries may have to be introduced if the interests of the working populations of individual countries are to be safeguarded. Full employment may become increasingly incompatible with Free Trade; growth may give way to stagnation (as it already appears to have done in Britain—though her situation may be temporarily obscured by the large balance of payments gain from North Sea oil); stagnation may turn into chronic decline, with a falling G.D.P., a falling employment capacity of the economy and possibly also a falling productivity of those remaining in employment. In the absence of some such instrument as suggested in the paper we are likely to be faced with a mushroom growth of protectionist measures taken by different countries individually on a temporary *ad hoc* basis: this would reduce the volume of trade in all directions, but without the assurance that the difficulties caused by the disproportionalities between import propensities and

---

[1] Both these countries claim that their current account surpluses are much smaller, on account of a net adverse balance on "invisibles". However, from the point of view of the level of employment and the potential for economic growth, the balance on visible trade is a far more important factor than the net balance on invisible account.

the full employment export/output ratios of certain industrial countries are thereby eliminated.

Part II of this volume consists of three papers concerned with different aspects of the problem of industrialisation and economic development. The first of these essays, "The Role of Industrialisation in Latin American Inflations", prepared for a conference on the economic problems of Latin America, was intended as an exposition of the so-called "structural theory" of the long-persisting inflations of certain Latin American countries, by setting out the precise historical conditions which made the emergence of a self-sustaining inflationary spiral inevitable in some cases and not in others. Where it occurred it was the product of mushroom industrialisation brought about by severe import restrictions—which was not due to any deliberate economic plan but was forced upon those countries as a result of the collapse of export earnings during the Great Depression. Imports were restricted in order to "ration" scarce foreign exchange, but the scarcities created thereby were the equivalent of indiscriminate protection of a rather violent kind, which raised the domestic prices of industrial goods (like motor-cars) by several hundred per cent. or more in terms of agricultural products. This led to considerable investment in industrial capacity, to increased urbanisation and increased industrial employment which in turn increased the demand for food and industrial materials, but contributed nothing to increased export earnings (which would have made it possible to satisfy this demand by imports). Hence the inflation generated was a consequence of a demand-induced rise in food prices and the cost-induced rise in industrial prices—the latter brought about by the pressure to compensate wage-earners for the rise in the cost of living. The countries which escaped the violent inflation were those (like Venezuela and Peru) which, for one reason or another, managed to generate sufficient exports, or those (like Mexico) who were able to increase their food production at an adequate rate.

This peculiar feature of inflationary processes—of a demand-induced rise in the prices of foodstuffs and other basic commodities combined with a cost-induced rise in the prices of manufactured

goods—is not confined to Latin American inflations; as readers of my paper on "Inflation and Recession in the World Economy"[1] will remember, it is a vital aspect in the explanation of the world-wide inflation of the 1970s (though *not* of the "mild inflations" of the industrial countries in the 1950s and 1960s). In fact these two papers, read in conjunction with the paper "The New Monetarism", provide a fairly full account of my own views on the subject of inflation and of my reasons for rejecting the now fashionable "monetarist" explanations.

The paper "Advanced Technology in a Strategy of Development", originally written in 1969, and revised for a special I.L.O. Conference in 1971, reflected the optimistic view concerning the future of humanity held by most economists of my generation (perhaps under the influence of Keynes) who saw no basic reason why the over-two-thirds of mankind who still live in abject poverty should not undergo the same process of rapid economic growth through industrialisation which caused such dramatic improvement, in the span of a generation or two, in the standard of living of the populations of the present "developed" countries. On that view it is all a question of providing the right kind of framework of public institutions (particularly education) and of following the right kind of "strategies" of development— an essential ingredient of which is to foster industrialisation by an economic plan which involves the protection of home industries, but does so in a judicious and discriminating fashion, and with due regard to an early development of an industrial export capacity: the "outward strategy" of industrialisation which paid off so handsomely in a varied number of countries, such as Germany, Switzerland, Sweden or Japan.

If I were writing today I would be more hesitant in saying that the route to future development lies in increasing the agricultural surplus through the use of modern technology in agriculture and in absorbing the labour surplus thereby created by building up a modern industrial sector whose expansion will itself generate the savings and the capital accumulation required for employing the available workers in manufacturing industry with high productivity technologies. This view pays insufficient atten-

[1] Reprinted in *Further Essays on Economic Theory*, pp. 214–30.

tion to the constraint on the growth of primary products (minerals and fuel as well as the products of agriculture) set by the limitations on man's power to exploit nature—a power which has improved at an extraordinary pace throughout the past two centuries, yet not at a pace fast enough to permit any large rise in living standards above subsistence levels for more than a modest proportion of the world's population. The sheer dimensions of the problem are terrifying. The part of the world's population which is in a state of open or thinly disguised unemployment must amount to many hundreds of millions. There must be further hundreds of millions who are effectively contributing to production at present but who would be released from agriculture as part of its modernisation and mechanisation. To find effective employment for such numbers in newly developed industrial and associated tertiary sectors could well mean that the basic material and energy requirements of world industry would be many times the present level. One does not need to be a believer in the early exhaustion of the world's mineral reserves to doubt whether the available supplies of primary products could be stepped up at a rate that would permit the absorption, through increased production, of the world's unemployed—the numbers of which appear to be still rising at a frightening rate, both absolutely and relative to the growth of world population. (The only qualification I feel one needs to add to this is that equally pessimistic predictions concerning the outlook for humanity could have been made, and actually were made, in almost every decade of the past two centuries, and the outcome, so far at any rate, has invariably been better than what was predicted.)

The third essay in this group, written in 1972, examines the role of industrialisation in economic development in the light of Britain's experience. It accords a major role in the causation of the Industrial Revolution to the introduction of the factory system which in turn was the result of a combination of factors, of which the emergence of a landless proletariat following upon the agricultural enclosures was one, and the existence of a powerful class of merchant-capitalists engaged in overseas trade was another. The importance of the factory system[1] lay partly in securing

---

[1] This is also emphasised in a paper by Stephen Marglin (written about the same time, but which came to my notice subsequently), "What Do The Bosses Do?",

improved production through work being performed under close supervision (and at minimal wages) and in permitting the use of power-driven machinery (first water power and later steam power) which was possible only when the scale of production was much in excess of that which the labour of a family unit could provide. But from a long-run point of view its main importance was that it converted the merchant-adventurer from being a trader to being a manufacturer. This meant that greater profits were sought, not just by finding cheaper markets to buy from and dearer markets to sell in, but through the introduction of new technological processes and of new products, and through the exploitation of economies of scale made possible by high profits and the fast accumulation of capital.

In Britain all this feverish expansion was at first largely concentrated on the cotton industry (this is not brought out in the paper) and was based, on the one hand, on fast growing sources of supply through the development of the American cotton plantations, and on the other hand on the rapid acquisition of new markets, secured through naval power, the expansion of colonies and the opening of the Continent after the Napoleonic wars. It is the prime example of rapid economic growth being conditioned by the fast growth of markets, i.e., of *demand*. Yet it is this aspect which—apart from Adam Smith's early chapters—was curiously neglected by the classical economists, who emphasised the rôle of the accumulation of *resources* (capital) but whose intellectual framework did not permit them to accord an independent role to the growth of demand—to the acquisition of new "Absatzmärkte". Indeed, the meaning of the word "Absatzmarkt" (which is critical to an understanding of how a capitalist economy works) has never been given a proper expression in the English language.

The last part of the paper analyses Britain's decline from around 1870 onward mainly as a consequence of the industrialisation of other countries, which caused the growth of Britain's exports to falter, and her exporters to be chased from country to country

---

published in the *Review of Radical Political Economics*, Vol. 6, No. 2, New York, 1974. Professor Marglin lays greater stress on the "disciplinary aspect" and less perhaps on the creation of technological dynamism which followed from the introduction of the factory system than I would.

and continent to continent, by competing industries in other countries which grew to become in time efficient competitors of Britain not only in foreign markets but also in Britain's home market.[1] The result was that for fifty years Britain's G.D.P. grew very slowly relative to the more successful of the newer industrialised countries, who overtook her, one after another, in the volume of manufacturing production and in exports and finally in real income per head.

These adverse long-term trends were briefly interrupted by the two world wars and the protectionist policies adopted between the two world wars and in the first ten years after World War II. Since then, despite the successful pursuit of Keynesian policies of economic management leading to full employment and higher levels of industrial investment, the adverse long term trends re-asserted themselves and operated with accelerated force during the last ten years.

The final section of this volume, Part III, reproduces papers written in the course of the "Great Debate" on the question of British membership of the Common Market in 1970 and 1971, and includes as a postscript a lecture on Free Trade written in 1977.

As this debate came to an end when Britain entered the market, a decision which was later confirmed in popular referendum with a 2:1 majority, the reproduction of these papers may strike the reader as otiose and serving little purpose other than the somewhat ignoble one of self-vindication in the eyes of future historians. However, if the long-run effects of our membership turn out to be as disastrous as I feared they would be in 1971—and nothing that has happened since has caused me to change my views—I think

---

[1] All these other countries protected their home industries by tariffs and subsidies, while the British market remained open to foreign competition, due to the continued dominance of free trade ideology. As Friedrich List so eloquently described in his *National System of Political Economy* (1841–4; English translation Longmans Green & Co., London, 1885) the establishment of Britain's early industrial predominance was due to the application of severe mercantilist policies, and she endorsed the philosophy of Free Trade only when it served the purpose of opening new markets to British manufactures. (See List, op. cit., Book I, Ch. IV). Where the British succeeded in gaining free entry for the goods, as through the Methuen treaty with Portugal (1703) and after 1815 in Prussia, France, and other countries on the Continent, it had disastrous effects on local manufactures and employment. List, up to about 30 years ago, was held in much the same reverence in Germany as Adam Smith was held in this country, but the present generation of German economists and politicians, not surprisingly, are all firm adherents of the "cosmopolitical" school of the classical English political economy.

it is of the utmost importance that the true arguments against membership should be accessible to successive generations of students, the more so since the political debate continues to be dominated by issues (such as the effects of membership on the cost of food, on our agriculture, or the net budgetary cost of membership) which I regard as secondary and which could be brushed aside if the long-run effects of membership on Britain's manufacturing industry and on our capacity to provide employment were favourable.

In the particular historical situation in which Britain found herself in the latter half of the twentieth century, it seemed to me inherently probable that the long-run "dynamic" effects of membership would turn out to be sharply negative and not positive. For in industrial competition, it is the more advanced, faster growing and better equipped industrial areas which are likely to benefit from free access to markets; the disadvantaged areas are likely to lose from it. Britain for the last 100 years or so was the more sedate, more slowly growing country with more outdated equipment, who was steadily losing her market share— except for brief periods when she benefited from newly introduced protection in the home market, or from the temporary incapacity of her competitors in foreign markets, as in the six years preceding and in the six years following the Second World War.

As I argued in the essay "The Dynamic Effects of the Common Market", unless we succeeded in entering the Market "on the right foot" and managed to gain more in exports than we lost in increased imports *from the start*, our industrial production and employment would diminish, both on account of the deterioration of the trade balance, and on account of the restrictive monetary and fiscal policies we would be forced to follow as a result of this, and "this would be aggravated by an increased capital outflow as domestic investment became unprofitable owing to the fall in domestic demand.... In those circumstances the U.K. would become the 'Northern Ireland' (or Sicily) of Europe—an increasingly depressed industrial area with mass emigration the only escape."[1]

At that time nobody took these gloomy predictions seriously and it is doubtful how far they are taken seriously now, despite

[1] p. 201 below.

our disastrous industrial record in the intervening years. Our industrial output is very little higher now (in the second quarter of 1977) than in 1971, whereas the other members of the E.E.C., including Italy, have increased their industrial output by 20 per cent., despite the prevailing recession.[1] The most vocal and fashionable group of our opinion-makers are wedded to the idea that the route to salvation lies in more competition and less intervention. No doubt this suits the interests of the 30-odd huge multi-national concerns whose profits are now increasingly derived from overseas sources and who are largely shielded from the ill-effects of Britain's economic decay by the freedom with which they can switch production from one country to another and concentrate new facilities in areas which promise the highest profits on investment. What is more, this indifference to the economic future of Britain and to the prosperity and full employment of her working classes appears increasingly prevalent also in the Conservative Party, traditionally the party of national greatness and patriotism. Some of its greatest leaders, such as Disraeli and Joseph Chamberlain, had been the champions of the interests of the working man, in contrast to their present-day leaders who have embraced the traditions of *laisser-faire* liberalism, with their calculated indifference to the fate of any victims of the operation of the free market.

The contrast between these two schools of thought is brought out in the last essay of this volume, "The Nemesis of Free Trade", which recounts the arguments in the great debate on Free Trade and Protection conducted at the beginning of the century between Herbert Asquith and Joseph Chamberlain. The points made on both sides seem to have lost none of their freshness or relevance in the intervening 70 years. What has changed is our freedom to act. In 1905 we were free to decide whether to continue with the

[1] Between 1970 and 1976 our share of manufactures in the market of the Six declined fractionally despite the increasing preferences we enjoyed in this market since 1973. On the other hand the Six's share in the U.K. market increased from 28 to 48 per cent. in the same period. Furthermore, our share of the Danish and Irish markets has declined much more rapidly since the enlargement of the E.E.C. The difference between the success of other Common Market countries in the penetration of the U.K. market and the absence of any increase in our penetration of the market of the others is the main explanation why our industrial performance relative to other E.E.C. countries was so much worse in the 1970s than in earlier periods; and it is in sharp contrast to the predictions of all those who advocated entry into the E.E.C. as a means of *improving* our industrial performance.

policy of free imports or to protect our industries. In 1977 the choice is no longer open to us, except at a political cost of withdrawing from the Common Market, an act which few people would contemplate seriously so soon after accession.

In putting together the papers for this volume I became conscious of the problem of overlapping and repetition of theorems and propositions which is in some degree unavoidable in a collection of papers written at different times for different occasions. In order to minimise this I excluded papers whose purpose and content is largely covered by others and kept only those which appeared to me to add something—or sometimes take away something—from what I published in this and the other volumes. Inevitably certain basic ideas—such as the consequences of increasing returns and the "Verdoorn Law" on international trade, or of the implications of the absence of a "resource-constrained" equilibrium on the behaviour of economic systems—keep re-appearing in application to different issues.

I could have avoided that only if I had devoted my energies to the writing of a treatise in which my ideas were put together in a systematic and comprehensive way within a single conceptual framework in the manner of the great economists of the nineteenth century. I have not done this because I have never felt that one's understanding of economic processes has reached a stage where it is no longer liable to radical revision and development in the light of new experience.

I am grateful to friends and colleagues too numerous to mention for stimulus and help in the original preparation of these papers, and to Mrs. Sheila Woodward for checking the proofs. Three of the papers printed here have not been published previously (one of which appeared in Italian only) and for the rest I am indebted to the editors or publishers for permission to reprint them.

King's College   NICHOLAS KALDOR
Cambridge
October 1977

Part I

MONEY AND INTERNATIONAL EQUILIBRIUM

MONEY AND INTERNATIONAL EQUILIBRIUM

1

THE NEW MONETARISM[1]

THE Keynesian Revolution of the late 1930s has completely displaced earlier ways of thinking and provided an entirely new conceptual framework for economic management. As a result, we think of day-to-day problems—of inflationary or deflationary tendencies, unemployment, the balance of payments or growth—on different lines from those of economists of earlier generations. We think of the pressure of demand as determined by autonomous and induced expenditures, and we seek to regulate the economy by interfering at various points with the process of income generation: by offsetting net inflationary or deflationary trends emanating from the private sector or the overseas sector by opposite changes in the net income generating effect of the public sector. Previously, economists had thought of the level of demand—the volume of spending—as being directly determined by the supply of money and the velocity of circulation, and thought of regulating the level of expenditure mainly by monetary controls.

For the last twenty or thirty years we have felt we have much better insight into the workings of the market mechanism than our predecessors, and felt much superior to them. However, we now have a "monetary" counter-revolution whose message is that during this time we have been wrong and our forbears largely, if not perhaps *entirely*, right; anyhow, on the right track, whereas we have been shunted on to the wrong track. This new doctrine is assiduously propagated from across the Atlantic by a growing band of enthusiasts, combining the fervour of early Christians with the suavity and selling power of a Madison Avenue executive. And it is very largely the product of one economist with exceptional powers of persuasion and propagation: Professor Milton

[1] A public lecture given at University College, London on 12 March, 1970 and originally published in the *Lloyds Bank Review*, July 1970.

B

Friedman of Chicago. The "new monetarism" is a "Friedman Revolution" more truly than Keynes was the sole fount of the "Keynesian Revolution". Keynes's *General Theory* was the culmination of a great deal of earlier work by large numbers of people: chiefly Wicksell and his followers, Myrdal and Lindahl in Sweden, Kalecki in Poland, not to speak of Keynes's colleagues in Cambridge and of many others.

The new school, the Friedmanites (I do not use this term in any pejorative sense, the more respectful expression "Friedmanians" sounds worse) can record very considerable success, both in terms of the numbers of distinguished converts and of some rather glittering evidence in terms of "scientific proofs", obtained through empirical investigations summarised in time-series regression equations. Indeed, the characteristic feature of the new school is "positivism" and "scientism"; some would say "pseudo-scientism", using science as a selling appeal. They certainly use time-series regressions as if they provided the same kind of "proofs"as controlled experiments in the natural sciences. And one hears of new stories of conversions almost every day, one old bastion of old-fashioned Keynesian orthodoxy being captured after another: first, the Federal Reserve Bank of St. Louis, then another Federal Reserve Bank, then the research staff of the I.M.F., or at least the majority of them, are "secret", if not open, Friedmanites. Even the "Fed" in Washington is said to be tottering, not to speak of the spread of the new doctrines in many universities in the United States. In this country, also, there are some distinguished and lively protagonists, like Professor Harry Johnson and Professor Walters, though, in comparison to America, they write in muted tones and make more modest claims, which makes it more difficult to discover just what it is they believe in, just where the new doctrine ceases to be a matter of semantics and becomes a revelation with operational significance.

ELEMENTS OF NEW DOCTRINE

What are the essential propositions of the new doctrine? For this, it is no good turning to the "moderates", who do not really say anything, or to the "extremists"—like Messrs. Andersen,

Jordan and Keran of St. Louis—who both vulgarise and discredit the new creed by the blatant simplicity of their beliefs and the extravagance of their claims. One must turn to the archpriest, Friedman himself, and such of his close disciples, like Meiselman, Anna Schwartz and Philip Cagan, who can be relied on to follow the master closely and interpret him correctly.

The essential elements of the creed can, I think, be summarised in the following four propositions:

(1) Money alone matters in determining *"money things"*, such as the *money* G.N.P., the level and the rate of changes of *money* prices, and the level and the rate of change of *money* wages. *Per contra,* other things—such as fiscal policies, taxation, trade union behaviour, etc.—do not (or do not really) matter.

(2) Money cannot change *"real"* things, except temporarily, and in the manner of throwing a spanner into the works—a "monkey-wrench into the machine", to use Friedman's more homely expression[1]—at the cost of painful adjustments afterwards. There is a unique real equilibrium rate of real interest, a unique real equilibrium real wage, an equilibrium level of real unemployment. By monkeying around with money, these things can temporarily be made to change—interest reduced, unemployment cut, the real wage cut (or raised, I am not sure which)—only by making, in each case, reverse changes (abnormally high interest rates, abnormal unemployment, etc.) the inevitable sequel.

All this part of the Friedman doctrine is closely reminiscent of the Austrian school of the twenties and the early thirties—the theories of von Mises and von Hayek—a fact which so far (to my knowledge) has received no acknowledgment in Friedmanite literature. (Very few people these days know the works of the Mises–Hayek school; unfortunately, I am old enough to have been an early follower of Professor von Hayek, and even translated one of his books, and there is nothing like having to translate a book, particularly from the German language, to force you to come to grips with an argument.) Friedman differs from von Mises and von Hayek in being more liberally spiced with the new empiricism. On the other hand, he misses some of the subtleties of the Hayekian

---

[1] "The Role of Monetary Policy", *American Economic Review*, March 1968, p. 12.

transmission mechanism, and of the money-induced distortions in the "structure of production".

(3) While the money supply alone determines money expenditures, incomes and prices, it does so with a time lag which is, unhappily, not a stable one. It can vary, for reasons yet unknown, between two quarters and eight quarters. This is what the regression equations show.

(4) Hence, while control of the money supply is the only powerful instrument of control, it is hopeless for central banks to pursue a positive stabilisation policy by varying the money supply in a contra-cyclical manner. Indeed, their attempts to do so may have been the very cause of the cyclical instabilities in the economy which they aimed to prevent. Hence, the best thing for stability is to maintain a steady expansion of the money supply of 4–5 per cent. (in the latest version, the ideal has come down to 2 per cent.) and, sooner or later, everything will fall into line. There will be steady growth without inflation.

All this is argued not, like the Keynesian theory, in terms of a structural model which specifies the manner of operation of various factors. The results are based on direct and conclusive historical evidence; on statistical associations which appear—to the authors —so strong and clear as to rule out other interpretations. The actual mechanism by which exogenous changes in the supply of money influence the level of spending—how the money gets into circulation, whom it is received by, whether the recipients treat it as an addition to their spendable income or to their wealth, or whether it comes into existence in exchange for other assets without augmenting either wealth or income—is hardly considered by the orthodox Friedman school. It is significant perhaps that when Friedman in his latest essay does attempt a graphic description of how an increase in the money supply leads to a rise in prices and incomes, the money is scattered to the population from the air by a helicopter.[1]

The basis of all this is the "stable demand function for money", derived from empirical observations over longer and shorter periods; with varying definitions of money, and varying time lags between changes of money and income, where the choice of the

---

[1] Cf. Friedman, *The Optimum Quantity of Money*, London, Macmillan, 1969, pp. 4 ff.

time lag, and the choice of the definition of what is "money", are both determined by the criterion of the best statistical "fit" (in terms of R^2 and "t" values) of the regression equation. It is sometimes expressed in terms of a "money supply multiplier" which is clearly implied by the "stable demand function", though the empirical values of the "multiplier" are not consistent with a unity elasticity in the demand for money (*i.e.*, an equi-proportional relationship between the change in money and that of money income) which the quantity theory postulates; sometimes in terms of a relationship between changes in the money supply and changes in consumption expenditure, together with the demonstration that the money multiplier invariably "outperforms" the Keynesian multiplier. (This latter contention, for what it is worth, has been shown to be dependent on arbitrary and inappropriate definitions of "autonomous" expenditures in a Keynesian model.[1])

Friedman interprets his empirical findings in a strict Walrasian (or Marshallian) manner, as an indication that "people" wish to keep a constant proportion of their real income (or their permanent real income) in the form of money, a proportion which is not (very) sensitive to interest rates. But who are "the people" in this connection? Are they the wage- and salary-earners, who, between them, account for 70 per cent. of the national income, but hold, at any one time, a much lesser proportion, perhaps 10 to 20 per cent., of the total money supply? Or are they the "rentiers", whose "portfolio selection" and "portfolio shifts" are much influenced at any time by short-term expectations, as well as by the relative yields of various types of financial assets? Or are they businesses, for which holding money is just one of a number of ways of securing liquidity—unexploited borrowing power, unused overdraft limits and so on being other ways—and for which the state of liquidity is only one of a number of factors that influence current expenditure decisions?

RELATION OF MONEY TO G.N.P.

Before we consider these contentions further, one might pause

---

[1] Cf. Ando and Modigliani, "Velocity and the Investment Multiplier"; De Prano and Mayer, "Autonomous Expenditures and Money"; together with Replies and Rejoinders, *American Economic Review*, September 1965.

to ask whether there is anything surprising in a "stable money" function.

Clearly, in a broad sense the "money supply", however defined, correlates with the money G.N.P.—so does everything else: consumption, investment, wealth, the wage-bill, etc. All these things move over time, normally upwards, and in any time series the movement of any one item is bound to be highly correlated with the others. Thus Richard Stone demonstrated years ago that for the U.S. economy in the inter-war years *all* principal items of income and expenditure (eighteen of them) were closely correlated with three independent factors, which he identified as the G.N.P., the change in the G.N.P. and a time trend.[1]

The important questions to ask are:

First, does a high correlation indicate a causal relationship either way? Does it imply that the supply of money determines the level of income, or the other way round? Or are both determined simultaneously by a third factor (or factors)?

Second, does the existence of a strong statistical association imply that by controlling one of the variables, say the money supply, one can induce a predictable variation in the other? In other words, would the "money multiplier" survive if it were subjected to serious pressure?

In the U.K., the best correlation is undoubtedly found, not between the so-called "money supply" and the G.N.P., or that and consumers' expenditure, but between the quarterly variation in the amount of *cash* (that is notes and coins) in the hands of the public, and corresponding variations in personal consumption at market prices.[2] This, of course, was broadly known long before multiple regressions were invented (or computers to calculate them with ease). Every schoolboy knows that cash in the hands of the public regularly shoots up at Christmas, goes down in January and shoots up again around the summer bank holiday.

[1] R. Stone, "On the Interdependence of Blocks of Transactions", *Journal of the Royal Statistical Society, Supplement*, 1947.

[2] Thus, for 83 observations in the period 1948–69, the R^2 is ·884, the "cash multiplier" 2·3, the "t" value 3·7, *after* allowing for seasonality. The "cash multiplier" is 6·1, the "t" value 9, the R^2 is ·494, without correction for seasonality. Even better sounding results can be attained by relating the change in expenditure to both current and lagged changes in the cash supply, lagged for each of the four quarters, which yield positive and negative multipliers in regular sequence—which only goes to show what "t" values and R^2s are worth. (For equations, see Appendix on p. 22.)

Nobody would suggest (not even Professor Friedman, I believe) that the increase in note circulation in December is the cause of the Christmas buying spree. But there is the question that is more relevant to the Friedman thesis: Could the "authorities" prevent the buying spree by refusing to supply additional notes and coins in the Christmas season?

Of course, most people would say that it would be quite impossible to prevent the rise in the note circulation without disastrous consequences: widespread bank failures, or a general closure of the banks as a precautionary measure. If I were asked to advise, I would say that it could be done by less dramatic means: by instructing the banks, for example, not to cash more than £5 at any one time for each customer; by keeping down the number of cashiers, so as to maintain reasonably long queues in front of each bank window. If a man needed to queue up ten times a day, half an hour a time, to get £50 in notes, this would impose a pretty effective constraint on the cash supply.

But would it stop Christmas buying? There would be chaos for a few days, but soon all kinds of money substitutes would spring up: credit cards, promissory notes, etc., issued by firms or financial institutions which would circulate in the same way as bank notes. Any business with a high reputation—a well-known firm which is universally trusted—could issue such paper, and any one who could individually be "trusted" would get things on "credit". People who can be "trusted" are, of course, the same as those who have "credit"—the original meaning of "credit" was simply "trust". There would be a rush to join the Diners Club, and everyone who could be "trusted" to be given a card would still be able to buy as much as he desired.

The trust-worthy or credit-worthy part of the population—the people who can be trusted *not* to spend in excess of what they can afford to spend—would thus live on credit cards. The rest of the population—the mass of weekly wage-earners, for example, who have no "credit", not being men of substance—would get paid in chits which would be issued in lieu of cash by, say, the top five hundred businesses in the country (who would also, for a consideration, provide such chits to other employers). And these five hundred firms would soon find it convenient to set up a clearing system

of their own, by investing in some giant computer which would at regular intervals net out all mutual claims and liabilities. It would also be necessary for the member firms of this clearing system to accord mutual "swops" or credit facilities to each other, to take care of net credit or debit balances after each clearing. When this is also agreed on, a complete surrogate money-system and payments-system would be established, which would exist side by side with "official money".

CHARACTERISTICS OF MONEY

What, at any time, is regarded as "money" are those forms of financial claims which are commonly used as means of clearing debts. But any shortage of commonly-used types is bound to lead to the emergence of new types; indeed, this is how, historically, first bank notes and then chequing accounts emerged. To the extent that no such new forms have emerged recently—in fact, they are emerging, though not as yet in a spectacular way—this is only because the existing system is so managed as to make it unnecessary, with the "authorities" providing enough money of the accustomed kind to discourage the growth of new kinds. They thereby also condition our minds into thinking that money is some distinct substance, a real entity, whose "quantity" is managed and controlled quite independently by the monetary authority.

Of course, within limits, the ultimate monetary authority can and does exercise control over the volume of borrowing, because it can control interest rates, particularly at the short end, through open market operations, far more powerfully than other operators, and because, within limits, it can control the volume and direction of lending by the clearing banks, which have such a powerful role in the system as suppliers of credit. But, as the Radcliffe Committee has shown, when credit control is operated as an independent instrument—as a substitute for fiscal policy, and not as a complement to it—any forceful initiative by the monetary authorities weakens their hold over the market by diverting business from the clearing banks to other financial institutions. The post-war experiments in monetary policy caused a lot of disorganisation—"a diffused difficulty of borrowing", in the words of Radcliffe, with

firms having to borrow money from unaccustomed sources, or else to delay paying bills so as to achieve a better synchronisation between receipts and outlays—but with little discernible effect on spending. When the central bank succeeds in controlling the quantity of "conventional money", lending and borrowing is diverted to other sources, and the "velocity of circulation", in terms oɪ conventional money, is automatically speeded up.

VELOCITY OF CIRCULATION

Friedman's main contention is that the velocity of circulation, in terms of conventional money,[1] has been relatively stable. That may well be, but only because, in the historical periods observed, the supply of money was unstable. In other words, in one way or another, an increased demand for money evoked an increase in supply. The money supply "accommodated itself" to the needs of trade: rising in response to an expansion, and vice versa. In technical terms, this may have been the result of the objective of "financial stabilisation", of maintaining the structure of interest rates at some desired level, or the so-called "even keel policy", of ensuring an orderly market for government debt.[2]

[1] The precise meaning of "conventional money" differs from author to author (and from country to country); in the U.K. context it is usually defined as cash plus clearing bank deposits (both current and deposit accounts) in the hands of the public.

[2] A great deal of the current discussion on the importance of "money" is devoted to the issue of the "interest elasticity" of money balances—i.e. to the question of how the ratio between the "money supply" (as conventionally defined) and the national income can be expected to vary with changes in interest rates. Evidence of a low-interest elasticity is supposed to support the "monetarist school", while a high-interest elasticity is supposed to lend support to the "Keynesian" view. In fact, it does neither the one nor the other. The interest-elasticity of the demand for money really concerns a different issue: the power of the monetary authorities to vary the money supply in an exogenous manner. The *less* prepared the public is to absorb more cash in response to a reduction in interest rates, or to release cash in response to a rise, the *less* possible it is for the monetary authorities to expand the "money supply" relative to demand, or to prevent it from rising in response to a rise in the public's demand. This is because the authorities' sole policy instrument for changing the "money supply" is the buying and selling of financial assets in exchange for money; this presupposes that such sales or purchases can be effected in reasonable amounts without creating violent instabilities in the financial markets. Hence, the more Friedman and his followers succeed in demonstrating the insensitiveness of the demand for money to interest rates, the more they denigrate the role of money as an autonomous influence on the economy. The "stable money function" is evidence, not of the "importance of money", but only of the impotence of the authorities in controlling it. If it required a 50 per cent. fall in Consols to effect a 5 per cent. reduction (or to prevent a 5 per cent. rise) in the amount of money held by the public (i.e., assuming an interest elasticity of 0·1), any *autonomous* regulation of the "money supply" would in practice be rendered impossible by the exigencies of the financial and banking system. Those who hold that an "excess supply"

More fundamentally (and semi-consciously rather than in full awareness) it may have sprung from the realisation of the monetary authorities, be it the Federal Reserve or the Bank of England, that they are in the position of a constitutional monarch: with very wide reserve powers on paper, the maintenance and continuance of which are greatly dependent on the degree of restraint and moderation shown in their exercise. The Bank of England, by virtue of successive Acts of Parliament, has a monopoly of the note issue, at least in England and Wales. But the real power conferred by these Acts depended, and still depends, on maintaining the central role of the note issue in the general monetary and credit system; and this, in turn, was not a matter of legal powers, but of the avoidance of policies which would have led to the erosion of this role.

The explanation, in other words, for all the empirical findings on the "stable money function" is that the "money supply" is "endogenous", not "exogenous".

This, of course, is the crux of the issue, and it is vehemently denied by the monetarist school. They base their case on two kinds of evidence:

---

of money under these circumstances would *directly* increase spending forget that, barring helicopters, etc., the "excess supply" could never materialise.

One of the main contentions of the Friedman school is that, whenever the central bank changes the money supply by open market operations, say, by selling bonds in exchange for cash, it does not follow that the individuals who buy the bonds which the central bank sells will reduce their holding of money correspondingly—they may continue to hold the same amount of money, and economise instead on the buying of "goods". In this way, it is contended, a reduction in the money supply will have a "direct effect" on the demand for goods, and not only an "indirect effect", via the rate of interest. But there is a confusion here between "stocks" and "flows". The amount of money held by an individual is part of his *stock* of wealth; if he buys additional bonds, and this purchase represents an addition to his total stock of wealth, and not merely a substitution between one form of holding wealth and another (i.e. he continues to hold the same amount of money, *plus* a larger amount of bonds) this is only another way of saying that the individual bought the additional bonds out of income (i.e. out of foregone consumption), which in plain language means that he was induced to save more as a result of the opportunity of buying bonds on more attractive terms. No one has ever denied that monetary policy operating through changes in interest rates (or through direct controls over the volume of bank lending) could have an effect on the propensity to save as well as on the inducement to invest. But, unless the monetarists assume a high-interest elasticity in the propensity to save, and attribute the major influence of monetary action to this factor (in which case this should be made explicit), they *cannot* be saying anything different from Keynes—i.e. that the effects of "monetary action" on the level of demand depend on the effects of the consequential changes of interest rates (or, what comes to the same thing, of credit rationing by the banks) on the level of investment.

(1) The first is the time lag. Peaks and troughs in the money supply (in the U.S., at any rate) have regularly preceded peaks and troughs in G.N.P., though with a variable lag of two to six quarters, and one that tended to shorten in the post-war era to one quarter or less.[1] If the money supply changes first, and the level of income (or business activity) afterwards, it is contended that the one that came first must have been the *cause* of the other.

(2) The second is the contention that in the U.S., at any rate, banks are always "loaned up", more or less. Hence, the "money supply" (which includes bank deposits, as well as notes and coins held by the public) is fairly closely related to "high-powered money"—to the so-called "monetary base", which is under the sole control of the Federal Reserve, and who exercise their power, wisely or foolishly, but quite autonomously.

In my opinion, neither of these arguments *proves* that money plays—in the U.S., let alone in the U.K.—the causal role: that the "money supply" governs the level and the rate of growth of money incomes or expenditures.

THE TIME LAG

With regard to the time lag, it is now fairly generally admitted that it does not prove anything about the nature of the causal relationships. If one assumed a purely Keynesian model where expenditure decisions govern incomes, and if one assumed a purely passive monetary system—with reserves being supplied freely, at constant interest rates—it would still be true that the turn-round in the money supply would precede the turn-round in the G.N.P., for much the same reasons for which the Keynesian multiplier invariably involves a time lag.

Suppose the initiating change is a decision of some firms to increase their inventories, financed by borrowing. The first impact is to cause some other firms whose sales have increased unexpectedly to incur some involuntary disinvestment. It is only when that is made good by increased orders that productive activity is expanded; any such expansion will cause higher wage outlays,

[1] Richard G. Davis, "The Role of the Money Supply in Business Cycles", *Monthly Review of the Federal Reserve Bank of New York*, April 1968, p. 71.

which in turn may involve further borrowing. The ultimate effects on income involve further increases in productive activity arising from the expenditure generated by additional incomes. There is every reason for supposing, therefore, that the rise in the "money supply" should precede the rise in income—irrespective of whether the money-increase was a cause or an effect.

There may be other explanations which would need to be investigated, such as the contra-cyclical behaviour in the fiscal balance which, particularly in the U.S., has been a very important feature of the scene, especially in the post-war years. I am referring to the so-called "built-in fiscal stabiliser", which means that the fiscal deficit automatically rises in times of declining activity and automatically falls in times of rising activity. Owing to lags in tax collection, particularly in taxes on corporate profits, this operates so that the maximum swings occur sometimes after the turning point in economic activity.

Now, it is well known that changes in the government's net borrowing requirement are the most important cause of changes in the money supply. This is only partly due to the fact that the government's own balances are excluded from the "money supply", so that any depletion of such balances automatically augments the money supply. Partly it is due to the fact that the government is the one borrower with unlimited borrowing power: an increase in government borrowing, whether due to a decline in tax receipts, a rise in expenditure, or both, involves an increase in the money supply as an automatic result of a "passive" monetary policy, which supplies reserves as part of a policy of stabilising interest rates or simply to ensure orderly conditions in the bond market.[1] Moreover, since, in the U.S. at any rate, the government's borrowing requirement is largest when the economy is depressed, it occurs at a time when the Federal Reserve system is least inclined to follow a "tough" credit policy; whilst in times when it wishes to

[1] As Hawtrey has repeatedly emphasised, in the case of private borrowing the maintenance of orderly conditions in the bond market invariably involved some policy of "credit-rationing" or rather "issue rationing" by the issuing houses, who made sure that the volume of issues for public subscription at any one time was no greater than what the market could absorb. This is his explanation for the long-term rate of interest being largely a "conventional phenomenon". (Cf., e.g., *A Century of Bank Rate*, London, 1938, pp. 177 ff.) But there is nothing equivalent to this in the case of *government* borrowing.

restrain the expansion of credit, the government itself is likely to be in surplus. Hence, the large observed fluctuations in the money supply, preceding in time the business cycle, may merely be a reflection of the operation of the built-in fiscal stabiliser.

An interesting bit of evidence for this view is the abnormal behaviour of the money supply following the Korean War, when the money supply peaked about a year after, not in the year preceding, the peak of the post-Korean boom. A possible explanation is that the rise in government expenditure (and the deficit) followed on this occasion the sharp rise in activity, which was induced, no doubt, by the large rise in military procurement but which had been reflected in a sharp increase in federal expenditure only some time later on, when the bills came to be paid.

CHANGES IN MONEY SUPPLY: U.S. EXPERIENCE

This brings me to Friedman's second contention and the one on which he would himself lay the most emphasis: that in the United States, at any rate, changes in the money supply have been "exogenous" and were largely determined by autonomous policy decisions of the Federal Reserve Board. Since Friedman and Anna Schwartz have written a book of eight hundred pages to prove this point,[1] it is not easy to deal with their massive evidence in a few sentences. None the less, I shall try but will confine myself to some key issues and to some general observations.

In the first place, while the correlation between the "monetary base" (defined above) and the "money supply" was good in general, it was not sufficiently good to be able to regard changes in the one as being the equivalent of changes in the other. In particular, it appears that on occasions when the Federal Reserve went out of its way to increase reserves (as in the 1929–39 period), the reaction on the total money supply was small. Moreover, the effects of changes in the "monetary base" on the "monetary multiplier" were consistently negative in all periods.[2]

[1] *A Monetary History of the United States*, 1867–1960, National Bureau of Economic Research, Princeton University Press, 1963.
[2] Cf. Keran, "Monetary and Fiscal Influences on Economic Activity—The Historical Evidence", *Review of the Federal Reserve Bank of St. Louis*, November 1969, Tables VII and VIII.

More important than this, the variations in the "monetary base" are themselves explained by factors—such as the desire to stabilise interest rates, or to ensure government debt financing (the so-called "even keel" objective[1])—which makes the "monetary base" automatically responsive to changes in the demand for money. In other words, if variations in the money supply were closely related to changes in the "monetary base", this is mainly because the latter has also been "endogenous", as well as the former.

Friedman himself regards the monetary history of the Great Contraction, 1929–33, as the ultimate test of his basic contention. It is worth quoting the critical passage in his Presidential Address to the American Economic Association[2] at some length:

"The revival of belief in the potency of monetary policy was fostered also by a re-evaluation of the role money played from 1929 to 1933. Keynes and most other economists of the time believed that the Great Contraction in the United States occurred despite aggressive expansionary policies by the monetary authorities—that they did their best, but their best was not good enough. Recent studies have demonstrated that the *facts* are precisely the reverse: the U.S. monetary authorities followed highly *deflationary* policies. The quantity of money in the United States fell by one-third in the course of the contraction. And it fell not because there were no willing borrowers—not because the horse would not drink. It fell because the Federal Reserve System *forced or permitted* a sharp reduction in *the monetary base*, because it failed to exercise the responsibilities assigned to it in the Federal Reserve Act to provide liquidity to the banking system. The Great Contraction is tragic testimony to the power of monetary policy—not, as Keynes and so many of his contemporaries believed, evidence of its impotence."

I cannot understand the reference to the "sharp reduction in *the monetary base*" in the above passage, which is absolutely critical to the argument. According to Friedman's own figures,[3] the

---

[1] Keran, *op. cit.* Table VI.
[2] "The Role of Monetary Policy", *American Economic Review*, March 1968, p. 3. (My italics.)
[3] Friedman and Schwartz, *op. cit.*, Table B–3, pp. 803–4.

amount of "high-powered money", which is Friedman's own synonym for the "monetary base" (i.e. currency held by the public plus member bank reserves with the Federal Reserve) in the U.S. increased, not decreased, throughout the Great Contraction: in July, 1932, it was more than 10 per cent. higher than in July, 1929, whereas it was held constant in the three previous years (1926-9). The Great Contraction of the money supply (by one-third) occurred *despite* this rise in the monetary base. This was partly because the ratio of currency held by the public to bank deposits rose substantially. This is attributed by Friedman to a confidence crisis: the public's diminished confidence in the banks. But it is important to observe that this dramatic rise in the ratio of currency held by the public to bank deposits was never reversed subsequently. In July, 1960, it was still at approximately the same level as in July, 1932, which in turn was nearly twice as high as in July, 1929. If it was a matter of confidence in the banks, why was it not reversed in the subsequent thirty years? The fact that the currency–deposit ratio was at its highest during the war years, 1944-5 (when it stood 45 per cent. *above* the July, 1932, level), suggests rather that the main explanation may lie elsewhere—in the change in the pattern of expenditure between goods (or assets) normally paid for in cash and those normally paid for by cheque, which was due partly to the fall in the volume of financial transactions in relation to income transactions (this would explain why the deposit–currency ratio rose so much during the years of the Wall Street boom[1]) and partly also to the rise in the share of wages and fall in the share of property incomes during the slump.

The other reason was the fall in the ratio of bank deposits to bank reserves—in other words, a rise in commercial bank liquidity by some 27 per cent. between July, 1929, and July, 1932—which *may* have reflected prudential motives by the banks, but may also have been the consequence of an insufficient demand for loans—

---

[1] The demand for money is usually considered as a function of income and wealth; this is legitimate on the assumption that the volume of money transactions is itself uniquely related to income and wealth. However, in times when people make frequent "switches" in their portfolios, and the volume of financial transactions is large relative to the total value of assets, it is inevitable that the amount of money held by speculators as a group should also relatively be large, even if no one individual intends to hold such balances for more than a short period.

of the horse *refusing* to drink (particularly the fall in the demand for loans for speculative purposes). There is nothing in these figures, in my view, to support the far-reaching contentions which I have just quoted and, in a complex issue of this kind, I would put far more trust in the "feel" and judgment of contemporary observers, like Keynes or Henry Simons, than in some dubious (and tendentious) statistics produced thirty years later.

I have also perused the one hundred and twenty pages devoted to the Great Contraction in the book on the monetary history of the U.S. and, while I would agree that he makes out a good case for saying that the policy of the Federal Reserve, particularly after Britain's departure from the gold standard, was foolish and un-imaginative, and that the succession of bank failures in the course of 1932 might have been avoided if the Federal Reserve had followed more closely the classic prescription for a financial panic of Mr. Harman of the Bank of England in 1825 (quoted by Bagehot)[1]—of lending like mad on the security of every scrap of respectable looking paper—I do not believe that it would have made all that difference. In particular, I do not believe that the Great Depression (with all its tragic consequences, Hitler and the Second World War) would not have occurred but for Governor Benjamin Strong's untimely retirement and death in 1928. Indeed, I am not sure whether Governor Strong's policies in the years prior to 1928 might not have contributed to the financial crisis following the crash in 1929. For he kept the volume of reserves—the supply of "high-powered money"—rigidly stable in the years 1925-9. This occurred at a time when the U.S. economy and the national income was expanding, with the result that the banking system became increasingly precarious: the ratio of bank deposits to bank reserves, and the ratio of deposits to currency in the hands of the public, rose well above the customary levels established prior to the First World War, and to very much higher levels than these ratios have ever attained subsequently.[2]

Indeed, the best answer to Friedman's main contention is provided by Friedman himself, in comparing U.S. and Canadian

---

[1] Bagehot, *Lombard Street*, London, 1873, pp. 51-2; quoted in Friedman and Schwartz, *op. cit.*, p. 395.

[2] Friedman and Schwartz, *op. cit.*, Table B-3, pp. 800-8.

experience during the Great Contraction.[1] In Canada, there were no bank failures at all; the contraction in the money supply was much smaller than in the U.S.—only two-fifths of that in the U.S., or 13 against 33 per cent.—yet the proportionate contraction in money G.N.P. was nearly the same. The difference in the proportional change in the money supply was largely offset by differences in the decline in the velocity of circulation: in the U.S. it fell by 29 per cent., in Canada by 41 per cent. This clearly suggests that the relative stability in the demand for money is a reflection of the instability in its supply; if the supply of money had been kept more stable, the velocity of circulation would have been more *un*stable.

This last statement may appear to be in contradiction to Friedman's empirical generalisation according to which the movement in the velocity of circulation in the U.S. has historically been positively correlated with movements in the money supply— the velocity of circulation was at its most stable when the money supply was most stable. But the two propositions are not inconsistent, which shows how easy it is to draw misleading conclusions from statistical associations. If one postulates that it is the fluctuation in the economy that causes the fluctuations in the money supply (and not the other way round), but that the elasticity in the supply of money (in response to changes in demand) is less than infinite, then, the greater the change in demand, the more *both* the supply of money and the "velocity" will rise in consequence. If the supply of money had responded less, the change in velocity would have been greater; if the supply of money had responded fully, no change in velocity would have occurred (under this hypothesis).

WHAT ABOUT BRITAIN?

In this country, at least since the Second World War, it is even less plausible to argue that the "money supply" is under the direct control of the monetary authorities, regulated through the rate of creation of bank reserves. Clearly, it is not controlled through the 8 per cent. minimum cash ratio, for there is an agreement between the Bank and the clearing banks to supply sufficient reserves to

[1] *Ibid.*, p. 352.

validate this ratio week by week without any window-dressing. Nor can it be said that the "money supply" is controlled by the agreement of the clearing banks to observe the 28 per cent. prudential liquidity ratio, since there are numerous ways open to the banks to maintain this latter ratio which do not involve recourse to central bank credit.

What, then, governs, at least in the U.K., the changes in "money supply"? In my view, it is largely a reflection of the rate of change in money incomes and, therefore, is dependent on, and varies with, all the forces, or factors, which determine this magnitude: the change in the pressure of demand, domestic investment, exports and fiscal policy, on the one hand, and the rate of wage-inflation (which may also be partly influenced by the pressure of demand), on the other hand. This basic relationship between the money supply and G.N.P. is modified, however, in the short period by the behaviour of the income-expenditure relation (or, as I would prefer to call it, the receipt-outlay relation) of those particular sectors whose receipt-outlay relation is particularly unstable—in other words, whose net dependence on "outside finance" is both large and liable to large variations, *for reasons which are endogenous, not exogenous, to the sector*. This is true, of course, to a certain extent of the business sector, though business investment in fixed capital and stocks has not been nearly as unstable in the last twenty years as it was expected to be in pre-war days. But it is chiefly true of the public sector, whose "net borrowing requirement" has been subject to very large fluctuations year by year. I am convinced that the short-run variations in the "money supply"—in other words, the variation relative to trend—are very largely explained by the variation in the public sector's borrowing requirement.[1]

Over the last five years we have witnessed a dramatic change in the rate of increase in the money supply: it fell from 9·8 per cent. in 1967 to 6⅔ per cent. in 1968 and to only 2·9 per cent. in 1969. The last of these years has also witnessed a dramatic turn-round

---

[1] In fact, a simple regression equation of the annual change of the money supply on the public sector borrowing requirement for the years 1954–68 shows that the money supply increased almost exactly £ for £ with every £1 increase in the public sector deficit, with "t" $= 6·1$, $R^2 = ·740$, or, in fashionable language, 74 per cent. of the variation in the money supply is explained by the deficit of the public sector *alone*. (See Appendix.)

in the balance of payments. This is regarded as a "feather in the cap" for the monetarists, who point with pride to the effectiveness of monetary policy—not in stopping wage and price inflation, for this unfortunately has not happened—but at least in restoring a healthy balance of payments. They forget that the same period witnessed an even more dramatic turn-round in the net borrowing requirement of the public sector—from over £2,000 million in 1967–8 to *minus* £600 million in 1969–70. The recent "credit squeeze" is not really a "credit squeeze" but a "liquidity squeeze". It is a direct consequence of a big fall in the receipt-expenditure relationship of the business sector which, in turn, was a reflection of the big improvement in the receipt–expenditure relationship of the public sector, only partially offset by the (more recent) improvement in the outlay–receipt relationship of the overseas sector.

What, if anything, follows from all this? I have certainly no objection to Friedman's prescription that the best thing to do is to secure a steady expansion of x per cent. a year in the money supply. But I doubt if this objective is attainable by the instruments of monetary policy in the U.S., let alone in the U.K. If it is ever attained, it will be because, contrary to past experience, we shall succeed in avoiding stop-go cycles emanating from abroad, or from the private business sector, or, what is more likely, from the very changes in fiscal policy which aim to compensate for other instabilities; and if, by some combination of incomes policy and magic (but more by magic), we shall also succeed in keeping the rate of increase in money wages in both a stable and a reasonable relationship to the rate of growth of productivity.

SOME REGRESSION EQUATIONS

I   *Regression Equations relating Changes in Consumers' Expenditure in the U.K. to Changes in Currency in Circulation held by the Public.*

    Data: Quarterly changes in £ millions; 1948 II—III to 1969 II—III

    Notation: $\triangle$ C = Change in Consumers' Expenditure

              $\triangle$ N = Change in average currency in circulation with the public;

$$
\left.\begin{matrix} d_1 \\ d_2 \\ d_3 \\ d_4 \end{matrix}\right\}
\begin{matrix} \text{Dummy variables} = \text{1 for quarter} \\ \text{to quarter changes} \end{matrix}
\left\{\begin{matrix} I—II \\ II—III \\ III—IV \\ IV—I \end{matrix}\right\}, \text{0 otherwise.}
$$

Standard deviation in brackets; R^2 unadjusted; s = standard error (adjusted for degrees of freedom).

Lags in quarters denoted by negative subscripts.

Results:

$$\triangle C = -65{\cdot}99 + 6{\cdot}127\,\triangle N \qquad\qquad R^2 = 0{\cdot}494$$
$$(24{\cdot}23)\ \ (0{\cdot}681) \qquad\qquad\qquad s\ = 183{\cdot}8$$

$$\triangle C = 170{\cdot}35 - 166{\cdot}77\,d_2 + 3{\cdot}71\,d_3 - 476{\cdot}48\,d_4 +$$
$$(38{\cdot}78)\quad\ (29{\cdot}74)\quad\ (40{\cdot}57)\quad\ \ (49{\cdot}83)$$
$$2{\cdot}350\,\triangle N \qquad\qquad\qquad\qquad\qquad\qquad R^2 = 0{\cdot}884$$
$$(0{\cdot}636) \qquad\qquad\qquad\qquad\qquad\qquad\ \ s\ = 89{\cdot}5$$

$$\triangle C = 5{\cdot}77 + 3{\cdot}855\,\triangle N - 2{\cdot}565\,\triangle N_{-1} + 2{\cdot}725\,\triangle N_{-2} -$$
$$(23{\cdot}52)\ \ (0{\cdot}639)\qquad\ \ (0{\cdot}411)\qquad\qquad(0{\cdot}417)$$
$$5{\cdot}640\,\triangle N_{-3} + 4{\cdot}220\,\triangle N_{-4} \qquad\qquad\qquad R^2 = 0{\cdot}878$$
$$(0{\cdot}417)\qquad\quad\ (0{\cdot}644)\qquad\qquad\qquad\qquad\ \ s\ \ = 94{\cdot}62$$

$$\triangle C = 96{\cdot}84 - 31{\cdot}51 d_2 + 37{\cdot}54 d_3 - 310{\cdot}88 d_4 + 2{\cdot}624\,\triangle N -$$
$$(49{\cdot}17)\ \ (63{\cdot}52)\quad\ \ (69{\cdot}18)\quad\ \ (68{\cdot}15)\quad\ \ (0{\cdot}672)$$
$$2{\cdot}062\,\triangle N_{-1} + 1{\cdot}528\,\triangle N_{-2} - 2{\cdot}205\,\triangle N_{-3} + 1{\cdot}947\,\triangle N_{-4}$$
$$(0{\cdot}706)\qquad\quad (0{\cdot}699)\qquad\quad (0{\cdot}702)\qquad\quad (0{\cdot}665)$$
$$R^2 = 0{\cdot}920$$
$$s\ \ = 78{\cdot}33$$

II *Regression Equations showing the Relationship of Changes in the Money Supply in the U.K. to the Public Sector Borrowing Requirement.*

Data: Annual figures in £ millions, relating to calendar years.

Notation: $\triangle M$ = increase in money supply.

P = Net acquisition of financial assets by the public sector.

Standard deviation in brackets.

Results:

(1) Period 1954–68

$$\triangle M = -\ 299 \cdot 1 - 1 \cdot 035 P \qquad R^2 = 0 \cdot 740$$
$$(0 \cdot 170) \qquad\qquad s\ \ = 210 \cdot 2$$

(2) Period 1960–68

$$\triangle M = -\ 246 \cdot 3 - 0 \cdot 979 P \qquad R^2 = 0 \cdot 714$$
$$(0 \cdot 231) \qquad\qquad s\ \ = 212 \cdot 1$$

APPENDIX II

A REPLY BY MILTON FRIEDMAN AND A REJOINDER[1]

IN the article he contributed to the July issue of this *Review*, Professor Kaldor makes one central point: that changes in the money supply must be regarded as the result, not the cause, of changes in economic activity. He states this point in different ways, embellishing it with assorted illustrations, each time as if it were a profound idea that had never occurred to the well-meaning but benighted monetarists he is attacking. Strip this point from his discussion and there remains mostly rhetoric—some of it clever, some of it accurate, much of it neither. Establish this point, and his case against the monetarists is firm; pins move with the cycle; money moves with the cycle; this is evidence of neither a pin theory of the cycle nor a monetary theory of the cycle but of the pervasive influence of cyclical fluctuations.

As it happens, Professor Kaldor is a Johnny-come-lately with this point. The monetarists themselves recognised its importance

[1] Originally published in the *Lloyds Bank Review*, October 1970.

from the outset, and, if they had not, their U.S. critics have for the past decade repeatedly flourished it—just as Kaldor does, with all the air of Little Jack Horner extracting a plum from his Christmas pie.

As a result, this issue has been explored intensively. The outcome is about as decisive as the answer to any such question can ever be: clearly, there are influences running from income to the quantity of money, as Professor Kaldor asserts but, equally clearly, there are strong influences running from the quantity of money to income. The latter do not and should not exclude the former.

I have summarised the evidence for the influence of money in an article reprinted in a book to which Professor Kaldor refers, but which he apparently has not read.[1] I began the summary as follows:

> "The specific issue I propose to consider is . . . whether the cyclical behavior of money is to be regarded as a major factor explaining business fluctuations or as simply a reflection of business fluctuations produced by other forces . . .
>
> ". . . The alternatives contrasted are not mutually exclusive. Undoubtedly there can be and are influences running both ways . . .
>
> "[Moreover], there can be and almost certainly are factors other than money that contribute to the cycle, whatever may be the role of money. The question at issue, is therefore, whether money exerts an important independent influence, not whether it is the only source of business fluctuations and itself wholly independent of them.
>
> "What kind of evidence can be cited on this issue?"

I then cited five kinds of evidence:

(a) Qualitative historical circumstances, which I termed "perhaps the most directly relevant kind of evidence"; (b) the behaviour of the determinants of the money stock; (c) consistency of timing on positive and inverted basis, in the course of which I emphasised that "regular and sizable leads of the money series

---

[1] "The Monetary Studies of the National Bureau" (1964), reprinted in *The Optimum Quantity of Money and Other Essays*, Chicago, Aldine, 1969, pp. 266–84.

are themselves suggestive of an influence running from money to business but they are by no means decisive", and cited three reasons why the timing evidence could be misleading; (d) serial correlation of amplitude of cycle phases; (e) evidence from foreign countries.

After summarising the evidence under these five headings, I concluded:

"In a scientific problem, the final verdict is never in. Any conclusion must always be subject to revision in the light of new evidence. Yet I believe that the available evidence of the five kinds listed justifies considerable confidence in the conclusion that the money series is dominated by positive conformity, which reflects in some measure an independent influence of money on business. The feedback effect of business on money, which undoubtedly also exists, may contribute to the positive conformity and may also introduce a measure of inverted conformity."

The reader can judge the weight of the casual empirical evidence for Britain since the Second World War that Professor Kaldor offers in rebuttal by asking himself how Professor Kaldor would explain the existence of essentially the same relation between money and income for the U.K. after the Second World War as before the First World War, for the U.K. as for the U.S., Yugoslavia, Greece, Israel, India, Japan, Korea, Chile and Brazil? If the relation between money and income is a supply response, as Professor Kaldor asserts that it is for the U.K. since the Second World War, how is it that major differences among countries and periods in monetary institutions and other factors affecting the supply of money do not produce widely different relations between money and income?

A REJOINDER

PROFESSOR FRIEDMAN makes no attempt to refute any of my contentions; instead, he refers to his 1964 paper to show (a) that he has known all along that none of his findings rule out an inter-

pretation of causal relationships diametrically opposed to his own;[1] (b) that he himself believes that there are influences running in both directions; (c) that it was the result of "intensive exploration" and careful sifting of five different kinds of evidence which led him to believe that the important influence is from money to business, and not the other way round.

Since Friedman and I are agreed that it is the exogenous or endogenous character of the observed changes in the money supply on which the whole issue turns, and since Friedman rests his case, not on a fully specified model of how the economy works, but on five different kinds of "empirical evidence", he must not take it amiss if his critics have to keep on making the same point "in different ways" in various contexts. This is forced on them by the Friedman technique of "defence in depth"—i.e., of the falling back on some other kind of "evidence" whenever he is forced to yield on a major assertion.

Thus, at one time all the emphasis was placed on Exhibit (c)— the time lag. By 1964, this was relegated to the status of evidence which is "suggestive but by no means decisive". In his latest publication he is ready to "expunge that section from the summary" without altering in any way "the confidence attached to our conclusions"; he also asserts that his long-standing interest in time lags was pursued only to elucidate the mode of operation of monetary changes "*given that money exerts an independent influence on income*" (italics in the original), and not as a means of establishing that conclusion.[2]

On Exhibit (a), which he regards as the "most directly relevant kind of evidence", it was Friedman (not myself) who chose, both in his book on monetary history and his presidential address, the Great Contraction 1929–33 as the test case. Here, I have shown

---

[1] Since Professor Friedman calls me "a Johnny-come-lately" on this point, perhaps I ought to point out that virtually all the points I made in my paper in criticism of the "Chicago School" were put forward by me in a succession of meetings at the Merrill Center in Southampton, Long Island, in 1958. These views are also implicit (without any reference to the Chicago School) in both my written and oral evidence to the Radcliffe Committee in 1958. It is a tribute to Friedman's growing influence (in the U.K., as well as the U.S.) that I thought it worth while to publish a paper solely devoted to a criticism of his views in 1970 which I did not think worth while twelve years earlier.

[2] Cf. *Quarterly Journal of Economics*, May 1970, pp. 321–2. This was a *Comment* on J. Tobin, "Money and Income: Post Hoc Ergo Propter Hoc?", published in the same issue.

that the "evidence" falls to pieces as soon as one examines it and in his present reply he says nothing to contradict my findings on this.

Equally, he says nothing to refute my contentions concerning Exhibit (b) which I thought were pretty conclusive.[1]

This leaves (d) and (e). I admit I have not dealt with (d)— mainly because I did not understand it; but if Friedman so wishes, I shall take a wet towel and look at it again to see whether it stands up any better than the rest of his contentions.[2]

On (e), however, I did say quite a bit in my paper (at least, in relation to the U.K. and Canada), and I said much more in my evidence to the Radcliffe Committee which Friedman apparently has not read.[3] It is nonsensical to suggest that the relation between money and income is "essentially the same" for different countries. In fact, international comparisons throw the strongest possible doubt on the Friedman postulate of a "stable demand function" for money. And if, by "essentially the same relation", Friedman merely means that in all countries the time-series on money and money income are correlated (and *not* that the ratio between money and income is the same) this should be "expunged from the evidence" for the same reasons as for the U.S.[4]

---

[1] For a more extensive and carefully-reasoned analysis of why central banks in a credit-money economy *cannot* behave in the manner Friedman and his followers assert that they do (or at least *should*), the reader is referred to Dr. A. B. Cramp's paper, "*Does* Money Matter?", (in *Lloyds Bank Review*, October 1970). This analysis has been developed in "Monetary Policy: Strong or Weak" a lecture by Dr. A. B. Cramp to the Durham meeting of the British Association in *Conflicts in Policy Objectives*, Blackwell, Oxford 1971.

[2] The "evidence" is found on pp. 271–5 of *The Optimum Quantity of Money* (Macmillan, 1969) and I gladly invite interested readers to participate in the effort.

[3] *Memoranda of Evidence*, Vol. 3, p. 146; reprinted in my *Essays on Economic Policy*, Vol. I (Duckworth, 1964), p. 128; also *Minutes of Evidence*, pp. 712 ff.

[4] He also raises the question of how it is that "the relation was the same" in pre-First World War U.K. as in post-Second World War U.K. I can only refer him to A. G. Ford's paper on "British Economic Fluctuations, 1870–1914" (*Manchester School*, June 1969) for evidence to show that money was no more important as a *cause* of pre-First World War fluctuations in the U.K. economy than of post-Second World War fluctuations. (See also Professor F. W. Paish, "Business Cycles in Britain", published in *Lloyds Bank Review*, October 1940.)

2

THE PROBLEM OF INTERNATIONAL LIQUIDITY[1]

THE decade of the nineteen fifties was a period of remarkable growth in the volume of world trade, particularly in the world trade in manufactured products. Between 1948 and 1960 the quantum of world exports increased at a compound rate of 6·6 per cent. a year, that of manufactures at 8·1 per cent. per year and primary products other than fuels at 4·6 per cent. per year.[2] One needs to go back to the latter half of the nineteenth century to find a ten-year period with a comparable record of growth. Part of the explanation for this lies in the remarkable growth of productivity and the national income in the developed countries, particularly in the countries of Western Europe and Japan; part is due to the relaxation of trade restrictions in the trade between the developed countries, as shown in the gradual abandonment of quantitative import restrictions and the reduction in the weight of protective tariffs. As a result of this, the proportion of imports in the total supplies of manufactured goods of the developed industrialised countries has attained a figure which is well above the pre-war relationship and which approximates to the ratio attained in the late nineteen twenties, before the introduction of the various protectionist and trade-repressing measures which followed the onset of the Great Depression.

During this whole period the rise in international reserves of the central banks of the countries outside the communist bloc lagged considerably behind the rise in the volume of trade. While the value of world imports more than doubled between 1950 and 1962 (from $58·7 to $131·5 billion) the value of the "gross reserves"

[1] Originally published in the *Bulletin of the Oxford University Institute of Economics and Statistics*, Vol. 26, No. 3, 1964.

[2] *Source:* United Nations *Statistical Yearbook, 1962,* calculated from data in Table 154. Manufactures include metals. The data exclude the centrally planned economies.

held by the central banks increased by only 33 per cent. (from $50·1 to $65·5 billion)[1] and only one third of the increase consisted of gold, the remainder represented balances in "reserve" currencies, mostly U.S. dollars, or in increased drawing rights with the International Monetary Fund.[2] The ratio of (gross) currency reserves to the annual imports of the different trading countries had thus fallen from 85 per cent. at the end of 1950 to 50 per cent. at the end of 1962.

Such overall comparisons of the relative movements in trade and in currency reserves may be misleading, however, since they conceal the very important changes that have taken place in the distribution of reserves over the period. The countries of continental Western Europe had persistent surpluses in their overall balances of payments; and they steadily gained reserves in consequence, which more than kept pace with the very rapid growth in their external trade: indeed, it was this rapid growth in reserves which played an important role in their dismantlement of numerous trade and exchange barriers erected both before and after the war. The reserves of the rest of the world (apart from Canada and Japan) remained practically unchanged.[3] The counterpart of Western Europe's (and also Japan's and Canada's) gain in reserves was the persistent reduction in the net reserve position of the United States, whose overall balance of payments (i.e. on both current and capital account) showed a cumulative deficit of $25·9 billion in the thirteen years 1950–62 (or $20·6 billion if recorded short-term capital outflow of $5·3 billion is excluded) which was settled as to $8·1 billion through sales of gold, $11·2 billion

---

[1] In addition there has been an increase of around $6 billion in the I.M.F.'s holdings of convertible currencies. The source of these and the following figures (except where otherwise indicated) is I.M.F. *International Financial Statistics*, Supplement to 1963–4 issues.

[2] The volume of sterling reserves decreased slightly over this period, and the amounts held in other currencies (French francs and German marks) is relatively small.

[3] Between the beginning of 1950 and the end of 1962 the ratio of gold and foreign exchange reserves to annual imports improved from 25 to 51 per cent. in the case of the six countries of the E.E.C. and from 34·4 to 50·5 per cent. in the case of all countries of continental Europe. In the case of most other countries the ratio of reserves to imports declined over the period, even when (as in the case of Canada and Japan) there was an appreciable improvement in the total *size* of the reserves. Excluding continental Europe, the United States and the United Kingdom, the world ratio of reserves to annual imports declined from 69·8 to 38 per cent. (The latter figure is of course an average concealing considerable variations. Thus the ratio of reserves to imports for all countries of Latin America was only 22·5 per cent. in 1962; for all countries of the overseas sterling area it was 45·2 per cent.)

through the increase in U.S. liabilities to foreign monetary authorities (including the I.M.F.) and $6·6 billion through the increase
of other short-term liabilities.[1] As a result of this the net reserve
position of the United States (gold assets less *net* short-term
liabilities) declined from $20·5 billion at the beginning of 1950 to
$0·36 billion at the end of 1962.[2]

One important consequence of the persistent deficit in the overall balance of payments of the United States has been that the use
of the so-called "gold exchange standard" spread much wider,
and assumed far greater importance, than was envisaged at the
time when the new monetary arrangements were made at Bretton
Woods. Previously, both the pound sterling and the dollar (and
to a smaller extent also the French franc) acted as the reserve
currencies to a group of countries which for reasons of their intimate economic ties and the advantages derived from using a
single major currency for international clearing, chose to keep
their currency reserves, as a matter of formal and permanent
arrangement, in the form of balances in "key" currencies rather
than in the form of gold. But in the course of the nineteen fifties,
the central banks of Western Europe, Canada and Japan also
came to hold a rising proportion of their total assets in the form of
"dollar balances", but without accepting the formal arrangements
of the so-called "gold-exchange standard" (which would have
implied that the members of the system renounced the claim to an
independent gold reserve, and cleared all their international transactions through a single financial centre).[3] For many of the central

[1] It should be noted that for the whole of this period, the trading surplus on commercial transactions (including re-invested foreign earnings of U.S. subsidiaries)
amounted to $84·5 billion, net U.S. Government expenditure abroad (in the form of
military expenditures, aid and capital) amounted to some $69 billion, which means
that after allowing for private remittances abroad, there was a net current surplus of
$9 billion available for private foreign investment. The net international investment
position of the United States (excluding all Government investment, and after allowing for the reduction in the gold stock and the net increase in short-term liabilities)
improved throughout the period as net private foreign invesment exceeded the
cumulative "deficit", as officially reckoned. (See Table I of the Appendix.)

[2] The above estimates include the rise in both the official and unofficial short-term
liabilities, and *deduct* short-term assets held by U.S. banks. If the net position is defined
as the gold stocks less *official* liabilities, the decline in the net reserve position of the
U.S. is from $23·2 billion at the beginning of 1950 to $3·9 billion at the end of 1962.
("Official liabilities" include dollar balances held by the I.M.F.)

[3] The willingness of the European central bankers to absorb and hold increasing
amounts in dollar balances was undoubtedly reinforced by the knowledge that a part
at least of their accession of reserves had their origin in "hot money flows", and the

banks which hold increasing dollar balances, such balances are regarded as temporary media for holding reserves rather than as a permanent fixture, to be liquidated as and when the United States balance of payments swings the other way.

The evolution of this system during the last few years has given rise to increasing misgivings both in official circles and among academic economists. The situation in which the rate of increase of international reserves is dependent on the size, and the continuance of, an overall deficit in the balance of payments of the country whose currency is used as an international reserve is clearly unsatisfactory. If the present U.S. balance of payments deficit was brought to an end, the currency reserves of the world would cease to grow; if it is not brought to an end, the continued deterioration in the *net* international liquidity position of the United States is bound to undermine, sooner or later, the acceptability of the dollar as a reserve currency. The basic shortcoming of a "key-currency" system lies precisely in the fact that it only provides international liquidity when the key currencies are "weak", whereas the whole system presupposes that the currencies which serve as the reserve for others should be exceptionally "strong".

As a result of the increasing recognition of these shortcomings, and the dangers inherent in the present system, a whole crop of suggestions and plans emerged for the reform of the existing international monetary arrangements and institutions—partly on the initiative of individual experts and partly of Governments—and this problem formed the principal subject of discussion in the recent annual meeting of the International Monetary Fund. As a result of that meeting two important study groups were initiated which are to report their findings to the next annual meeting of the Fund.

Before we can discuss the merits of the various plans and suggestions, it is necessary to consider in more detail the nature of the "liquidity" problem with which the world is confronted at the present time. As most of the speakers in the I.M.F. meeting emphasised, it is important to separate the question of the growth and

---

alternative might have been the imposition of exchange restrictions on free capital movements by the United States (or possibly the devaluation of the dollar) which was clearly not in their interest.

the adequacy of the world's monetary reserves, and the risks inherent in the current payments system, from the question of the balance of payments problems of the United States. Whatever steps may be taken to improve the former, does not in itself solve the problems connected with the latter. As Mr. Dillon stated at the last meeting of the International Monetary Fund, "the United States does not view possible improvements in the method of supplying international liquidity as relieving it of the compelling and immediate task of reducing its own payments deficit". He also said that "without effective adjustments by both deficit and surplus countries, no amount of liquidity will enable us to achieve the mutual benefits of a closely integrated economy within a framework of steady growth accompanied by monetary stability".

THE PROBLEM OF BALANCES OF PAYMENTS OF THE UNITED STATES AND THE EUROPEAN COUNTRIES

It is important to bear in mind that the imbalances that have given rise to the present anxieties in regard to the international payments system concern the imbalances in the international transactions of the developed, industrial nations of the world *in relation to each other*, and not the imbalances arising from the trade between developed and under-developed areas. Both the United States and the states of continental Western Europe had, and continue to have, large surpluses in their *trading* accounts with the outside world; in a more fundamental sense therefore a real balance of payments problem arises only in relation to the trade between developed and under-developed nations, rather than in the trade between different industrial or individual developed countries. Since the under-developed countries possess only scanty reserves, and are only able to finance an excess of imports over exports through loans or grants received from the developed countries (either directly or through international agencies), the total of trading surpluses earned by the developed countries are ultimately governed by the scale on which loans or grants are made from the developed countries to the under-developed nations. The precariousness of the present world liquidity position is simply a reflection of the fact that the U.S. has consistently made

grants or long-term loans to the outside world in excess of its own share in the total trading surplus, whilst the countries of continental Europe were unable, or unwilling, to make long-term loans or grants to the outside world on a scale corresponding to their own trading surpluses. This in turn arose, partly at least, from the fact that the share of the European countries in world exports rose rapidly throughout the past decade (which made it difficult for their international lending policies to keep pace with it) while the United States exports failed to increase as rapidly as her own international commitments and lending policies would have made necessary. In a sense therefore the United States has played the same role as a banker who, by acting as an intermediary between the ultimate lender and the ultimate borrower, is willing to assume such risks associated with the investment of savings which the ultimate savers are not ready to assume directly. By accepting deposits repayable on demand a banker provides the "savers" with the liquid assets which they desire; placing such funds on long-term and relatively illiquid investments enlarges the supply of finance for productive investments—which in turn is a necessary condition for the continued accumulation of "savings" by the ultimate lenders.

The above picture, like all analogies, is only accurate up to a point. Not *all* foreign lending by the United States qualifies for the description that it "enlarges the supply of finance for productive investment". While this is certainly true of the greater part of foreign private investment as well as of the government loans and grants made for capital purposes, another part (which has played an increasing role in recent years) represented the transfer of funds to Western Europe, either in the form of short-term loans to the so-called Euro-dollar market, or of portfolio investments in publicly quoted secutities. These have been prompted partly by the maintenance of relatively high interest rates in the Western European financial centres and partly by the relatively high yields and earnings prospects of ordinary shares in the European capital markets. Foreign investment of this latter type (which may have accounted for as much as one-half of the overall U.S. balance of payments deficit in the last few years) does not really serve to enhance the rate of growth of the world economy, since the rate of

economic expansion in the countries of Western Europe is not really limited by any shortage of funds, or any shortage in the supply of risk capital, but by the inflationary pressures resulting from the prevalence of labour shortages.

From the point of view of the world economy and particularly of the under-developed countries, it is, of course, a matter of great importance that the steps that are to be taken to rectify the present imbalance between the United States and the other industrialised countries should not be of a character that exerts an unfavourable effect on either the development of international trade or the flow of funds to the under-developed countries. Since world trading relations constitute a highly complex inter-locking pattern, any policy of adjustment which operates through a contraction of the volume of purchases from the outside world, or by reducing the net flow of international aid to under-developed countries, is bound to have a detrimental effect on the economies of third countries. The United States Government has shown a most commendable awareness of this, and has avoided taking any major step (apart from tightening up various provisions concerning expenditures under aid programmes) that would have prejudiced the interests of under-developed countries. Recently, however, she felt compelled to take steps to discourage foreign lending through the proposal (which has not yet passed the legislature) to introduce a tax of 15 per cent. on new foreign issues in the U.S. capital markets, which may serve to discourage productive investment in certain countries (e.g. Japan) even though the tax is not intended to apply to investment in under-developed areas. From the point of view of the growth and the stability of the world economy it might have been preferable if the United States had introduced some forms of selective control on the outflow of private capital which would have served to discourage capital transfers of a "perverse" or unproductive kind (such as "hot money" flows) without limiting foreign investment of a productive nature. Such provisions are in force in the United Kingdom as regards capital transfers by domestic residents, and through the control of new issues by the Capital Issues Committee. The Articles of Association of the International Monetary Fund envisaged from the beginning the maintenance of controls on capital

transfers by domestic residents, and they recognise that such controls need not interfere with the general convertibility of the currency to foreign holders, or its use as a reserve currency to other countries.

It is equally important that the measures taken to rectify the imbalance between the U.S. and other developed industrial countries should comprise effective remedial measures taken by the surplus countries and not only by the deficit countries. In particular it is an essential requirement of international economic stability that the countries which have absorbed (and are still absorbing) gold and foreign exchange in excess of reasonable needs should accelerate their long-term foreign lending programmes to under-developed countries (or to the United States)[1] or else take constructive steps for the elimination of their current account surpluses through an expansion of imports. While it is appreciated that the interest of domestic economic stability makes it difficult for the countries of Western Europe to follow the traditional method of expanding domestic incomes *pari passu* with the rise in their reserves (since this would aggravate domestic inflationary tendencies) there is no such conflict between domestic stability and balance and stability in the world economy in a policy of import promotion achieved by the reduction or elimination of existing barriers to imports. Indeed the import restrictions that are still in force on imports of manufactures from low-wage countries (both through differential tariffs and quotas) are far more extensive in the countries of the European Economic Community than in the United States or in the United Kingdom. This is eloquently shown by the fact that the proportion of imports of all manufactures (excluding non-ferrous metals) coming from *all* under-developed countries (excluding Japan) amounted in 1962 to only 3·8 per cent. in the case of Germany, 3·2 per cent. in the case of

---

[1] If the basic difficulty was really found to reside in the inability or unwillingness of the countries of Western Europe to assume the risk involved in direct long-term investment to the under-developed countries, they might find it preferable to lend on long-term to the United States (through the flotation of U.S. bonds, for example, in the European capital markets) the proceeds of the loans being used to finance that part of the U.S. foreign aid and lending programme which is in excess of the net surplus of the U.S. on current account (and possibly also for funding some of the outstanding short-term liabilities). In this manner, the United States would be able to continue its present role as a world banker without assuming increasing risks on account of a continued deterioration in her net reserve position.

C

France and 1·3 per cent. in the other countries of the E.E.C., as against 11·3 per cent. in the United States and 12·3 per cent. in the United Kingdom.[1] In addition, the importation of tropical products is hampered both by high internal revenue duties and high protective duties in the interests of Common Market agriculture.

An analysis of the current pattern of trade flows and of payment balances is bound to suggest the conclusion that one of the most important contributions that the developed, high-income countries could make to the acceleration of growth of the world economy and to the improvement of the balance of world trade is the lowering of existing barriers on imports coming from the underdeveloped areas.

THE PROBLEM OF THE FUTURE GROWTH OF INTERNATIONAL RESERVES

Since the U.S. balance of payments deficit which has been the major source of increased reserves to other countries in the last twelve years is bound to be eliminated sooner or later, the question arises how the future expansion of international reserves is to be assured, and if it is not assured, how far will the expansion of world trade be hampered by a shortage of international liquidity?

Despite the formal abandonment of the international gold standard in the nineteen thirties, gold remained the preferred medium of international reserve for currencies—buttressed no doubt by the universal belief that its use for this purpose cannot be dispensed with, and for that very reason no country will refuse to accept gold at its official value in final settlement of its financial claims on other countries. However, the value of annual gold production (excluding the U.S.S.R.) amounted in the period 1950–62 to $13·2 billion or around $1 billion a year (in recent years it averaged $1·2 billion which was 1·8 per cent. of the monetary reserves of the world in 1962)[2] and an increasing proportion of this was absorbed by private hoards. The total increase in the "visible" gold stock in the hands of monetary authorities amounted to only

---

[1] *Trade in Manufactures and Semi-Manufactures*, U.N. document (mimeograph) E/Conf. 46/6, February 1964, Table 8.
[2] Source: Annual Report of the B.I.S.

$6·4 billion in the period 1950–62 and in the last few years the increase in private hoards absorbed almost the whole addition from current output. Unless gold is supplemented by other reserve media (or unless there is a revaluation of gold itself) the total volume of reserves is not likely to increase by significant amounts once the deficits of the present "key-currency" countries are eliminated.

It would be wrong to suggest that the expansion of world trade necessarily "requires" a corresponding expansion of reserve media, or that there is some necessary or "optimal" relationship between the size of reserves and the value of trade. Reserves are needed to finance trade deficits, not trade flows; the existence of reserves does not obviate the need to correct disequilibria in the balances of payments; it allows more time for adjustments. This means that when the deficit of a particular country turns out to have been only temporary in character (there can never be any assurance about this beforehand) the existence of an adequate reserve enables the country to tide over the period without having to take measures that have a disturbing effect either on its own economy or on that of other countries. Such measures would be particularly inappropriate when the "deficit" in the balance of payments is the result of financial transactions (such as hot money flows from one financial centre to another) and not, or only to a minor extent, the reflection of some more basic imbalance in the trading pattern.

When on the other hand the basic cause of the deficit resides in factors which govern the current account balance (as for example, when it is a reflection of an inappropriate relationship of exchange rates in relation to the money costs of production of commodities in the various exporting countries) the existence of a large reserve, by postponing necessary adjustments, may aggravate the problem of adjustment instead of alleviating it.

Since the beginning of the nineteen fifties, the major industrial nations of the world followed a policy of fixed exchange rates; exchange rate adjustments (devaluation or revaluation) have only been resorted to on a few occasions, as e.g. by France in 1957 and 1958, and by Germany and Holland in 1961. The monetary agreement of Bretton Woods prescribed that member countries

should maintain fixed rates of exchange, as the system most conducive to the development of freer trading relations and freer international capital movements, though it also envisaged that countries should adjust their exchange rate in cases of "fundamental disequilibrium". These provisions have no doubt been animated by the classical view according to which, with relatively free trading conditions, forces are steadily at work tending to equalise the level of money costs between the various trading areas and thereby to eliminate such imbalances as may initially prevail at any given relationship of exchange rates. On this view, the very fact that the currency of any particular trading nation is under-valued initially will cause its money wages level to increase faster than that of countries whose currencies are initially overvalued; and these differences in the relative movements of money wages will gradually eliminate the disequilibrium.

The record of the nineteen fifties does indeed show that, in general, the rate of money wages tended to increase faster in those industrial countries which showed a fast rate of growth of industrial output and exports, and which steadily gained reserves, than in countries whose share of trade was declining and whose reserve position was deteriorating. However, such differences were more than counter-balanced by the fact that the productivity of labour has also increased much faster in the fast expanding areas than in the slow growing countries. As a result, in the period 1953–60, the differences in unit costs of production in the manufacturing industries have become steadily wider between the United States and the United Kingdom on the one hand, and the other main manufacturing exporters (Germany, France, Italy, Japan and Belgium) on the other hand: the balance of forces thus operated so as to enlarge differences in the export costs and export prices, and not to reduce them.[1] There is evidence that since 1961 the

---

[1] The level of export prices of the U.S. and the U.K. had risen by 20 per cent. between 1953 and 1960 relatively to the other five main industrial exporters, and their share in the total exports of manufactures of this group of seven countries declined from 56 per cent. to 43 per cent. (See Tables 2 and 3 in the Appendix for a comparison of export prices, export volumes, wage movement and productivity movements between these two groups of exporters. A comparison of column (3) in Table 2 with column (7) of Table 3—which have been derived from independent statistical sources —and of both with column (6) in Table 2 lends strong support to the view that the relative movement of efficiency wages was the major factor in the differing export performances of the various countries.)

differences in costs have narrowed again—partly owing to the re-valuation of the German mark in 1961 and partly to the exceptionally fast increases in money wages in continental Europe in the last few years—but so far this has not manifested itself in any noticeable change in relative export trends.

Thus in the light of the experience of the major industrial countries in the last decade it is a matter of doubt whether the maintenance of an equilibrium of steady expansion in international trade is really compatible with a system of fixed exchange rates or not. There is no assurance that under fixed exchange rates differences in the relationship of "efficiency wages" will call forth forces of adjustment tending to eliminate them; it is quite possible that the underlying forces at work would operate, for prolonged periods if not permanently, in a contrary direction. In that case a fixed set of relations between exchange rates becomes steadily more inappropriate with the passage of time, with serious consequences to individual trading countries and to the world economy as a whole. It is certainly arguable that if the progressive under-valuation of the German mark and of other Western European currencies had been effectively reversed earlier, the present international "liquidity crisis" might not have arisen, and the rate of growth of world trade, both of manufactures and primary products, would not have slowed down in the latter half of the nine-teen fifties.[1]

These factors must be borne in mind when the various plans for reforming the present international monetary system are considered. The present situation in which the increase in world currency reserves is largely dependent on the continued increase in short-term indebtedness of the two major "key-currency" countries is clearly unsatisfactory, for the reasons already analysed. At the same time care must be taken to ensure that if it is to be extended or replaced by more formal arrangements, it is replaced by something better and not by something worse. Some of the proposals advanced which aim at generalising the present "key-currency" system by providing that each country should keep

[1] For a reasoned argument supporting this conclusion, cf. Jaroslav Vanek, "Over-valuation of the Dollar; Causes, Effects and Remedies", in *Factors Affecting the United States Balance of Payments*, Joint Committee Print, United States Congress, United States Government Printing Office, Washington, D.C., 1962.

part of its reserves in the form of balances with the other members of the group (the so-called "multiple currency standard") would necessarily entail tying these currencies, and the monetary and credit policies pursued by the individual members of the group, more firmly to each other.[1] It presupposes a large measure of confidence, and hence of co-ordination in the credit and fiscal policies of individual members, which may well create a bias in favour of more conservative and less expansionist economic policies. For similar and obvious reasons it would make the use of exchange rate adjustments in cases of "fundamental disequilibrium" even more difficult than it has been hitherto.[2]

The advantage of gold as a universal reserve medium lies precisely in the fact that it enables individual countries to possess an international reserve that in no way limits their independence in matters of monetary and credit policy, or in following a policy of fixed or flexible exchange rates. So long as they are confident that gold remains a universally accepted medium of international payments, they are free to meet a deficit by using the reserve, or by altering the exchange rates as they think fit. At the same time, reliance on gold as the universal reserve medium is subject to serious drawbacks, owing to the very rigidity of its supply. The value of monetary gold stocks at present amounts to less than one third of the value of world imports, and most of it is held by the ten leading countries which account for some 60 per cent. of world

---

[1] This criticism would thus not apply (or not to the same extent) to less formal arrangements of co-operation among central banks, according mutual borrowing facilities to each other. But for the same reason, such arrangements, though highly valuable as a safeguard against "speculative runs" on individual currencies, are not really substitutes for an increase in freely spendable reserves.

[2] The same kind of objection applies with even greater force to more ambitious plans which aim at the creation of a world central bank with the same kind of credit-creating powers as national central banks possess at present. The power over credit is intimately bound up with political sovereignty. The proper exercise of that power by a World Bank is inconsistent with the retention of the existing credit-creating powers of the national central banks. If the world were to adopt, to all intents and purposes, a single currency, there would of course no longer be any balance of payments problems between individual countries—any more than they exist between the individual federal reserve districts of the United States—but that is because the individual country would be *deprived* of its power to create credit, not because the World Bank would be obliged to foot its bill. So long as countries think of themselves as separate entities, they will necessarily regard money issued (in exchange for bonds, or as an over-draft) to country A, which is used to settle claims against B, as a *loan* made by B to A but a loan granted at the discretion of the international authority, and not that of the lender. (For this reason even the plans for a common currency of the E.E.C. countries have run into serious difficulties.)

trade. If world trade continues to expand at the rate of 6 per cent. a year in the next decade, and if the private hoarding of gold continues at the rate at which it proceeded in recent years, the ratio of the monetary gold stock to world imports will fall to 20 per cent. or less by 1970—a state of affairs which most countries would find so unsatisfactory as to make either a large-scale revaluation of gold, or its replacement by other reserve media, inevitable.

For this reason there are many advocates of a revaluation of gold as a simple remedy to the present or prospective monetary problems. However, there are a number of serious objections that can be raised against such a solution, and which justify the attitude of the major currency authorities of the world in not having recourse to this expedient as a method of ridding themselves of their difficulties. For one thing, in order to effect a lasting cure, the necessary revaluation would have to be very large—of the order of 100 or even 200 per cent.—partly because any more moderate adjustment would give a powerful encouragement to private hoarding (by giving rise to the expectation of further increases) and partly because a lasting solution requires not only a rise in the value of the existing gold stock (in terms of commodities) but a rise in annual gold production in relation to the existing stock, that is sufficient to generate an adequate rate of growth in monetary reserves. Such a large increase in the value of gold in terms of commodities would be highly undesirable partly because it would bring a large uncovenanted gain to private hoarders (the *increase* in private gold hoards since the Second World War has been estimated at $9 billion; the total size of these hoards is unknown but may be twice this amount); partly because it would benefit only the limited number of countries which own the great bulk of monetary gold reserves; and partly also because it would greatly increase the cost to the world community of maintaining the status of gold as a monetary reserve. Since the commodity value of gold is in any case artificial—it is determined by its official price, and not by its intrinsic value—any large increase in the commodity value of current gold production would be hard to justify the more so since it would concentrate the benefit on the few countries which produce the great bulk of the world's gold output.

The current discussions concerning international monetary reform (largely conducted within the confines of the "Paris Club") may eventuate in the creation of some kind of international currency unit which will consolidate some of the outstanding dollar and sterling balances which will then cease to be convertible into gold, and be distributed among the members of the group in (more or less) even proportions. This will remove the present threat of large scale devaluations (in terms of gold) occurring as a result of a sudden collapse of the "key-currency" system. But it will mainly represent a consolidation of *existing* short-term liabilities, and not a mechanism for the creation of *additional* reserves; indeed a reform of this kind may make it more difficult for the present key-currency countries to finance their "excess-lending" in future through an increase in their short-term liabilities. The basic problem of ensuring a continued increase in reserves *pari passu* with the expansion of world trade will not be solved thereby—unless the new currency authority is also endowed with credit-creating powers (on an adequate scale) which is most unlikely. It will also leave unsolved the question of how relative exchange rates are to be adjusted among members of the group in cases of "fundamental disequilibrium".

These considerations suggest that the world may ultimately find that the best solution to the problem lies not along the lines of a further extension of the "key-currency" system, or in the creation of a world currency backed by other currencies, or in a large-scale re-valuation of gold, but in the monetisation of assets other than gold—i.e. in the creation of an international commodity reserve currency. The role of gold as the sole commodity which serves as a reserve is purely historical in origin and it lost its real justification when gold ceased to be a universal medium of exchange. On the national level it has now been everywhere replaced by a managed paper currency. On the international level, however, there is continuing need for a "real" standard, because so long as the world is divided into a number of separate sovereign entities, the creation and management of a world paper currency raises insoluble problems. It was for this reason that the abandonment of the international gold standard made no real difference to the status of gold as the ultimate reserve medium of currencies. However

"artificial" the value of gold may be, it cannot be dispensed with except by other assets of intrinsic value. So long as the world is divided into a number of separate areas of jurisdiction, it cannot be effectively replaced by "paper" titles such as I.M.F. deposits or "currency bundles"—partly because the value of these as *assets* is a matter of legal rights and obligations, the preservation of which is subject to the *fiat* of independent jurisdictions; and partly also because the supply of a "paper" reserve currency cannot be regulated by automatic rules, and individual countries are not prepared to endow an international authority with large discretionary powers.

An international commodity reserve currency—i.e. a system under which national currency reserves consisted of certificates issued by the I.M.F. which are fully backed by stocks of all the main commodities entering into international trade—would avoid many of the problems associated with an international "managed" currency, and would be far more responsive to the needs of an expanding world economy than a system based on gold. Precisely because the value of the stock carried as a monetary reserve (of all principal storable commodities which could be included in the "bundle") would be *small* in relation to annual production and consumption, its operation would exert a far more powerful stabilising effect on the world economy without affecting significantly the value of commodities taken individually. It would automatically cure any shortage of liquidity or excess of liquidity by increasing or decreasing the rate of absorption of commodity stocks; and it would also ensure that as additional reserves come into existence they directly enter into the stream of world income.[1] Proposals for the creation of a multi-commodity reserve currency on the "symmetallic principle" have been repeatedly put forward in the past—on the last occasion by a group of experts of the United Nations reporting in 1953[2]—and the present concern with a reform of the international monetary system suggests that they might

[1] This latter advantage also resides with gold but in the case of a multi-commodity standard, the benefits would be far more widely and evenly spread.

[2] *Commodity Trade and Economic Development*, report of a group of experts appointed by the Secretary-General, United Nations, New York, 1953. The first advocate of a multi-commodity currency was W. S. Jevons (*Money and the Mechanism of Exchange*, 1875); its most prominent recent advocate Benjamin Graham (*World Commodities and World Currency*, New York, 1944).

be given renewed consideration. The most important drawback of such a system is the high annual storage cost of the commodities (which might amount to 2–3 per cent. of the stocks carried) but it must be remembered that a large part (perhaps two thirds) of the stocks that would be required for the initial reserve are already carried by various governments, as part of domestic price stabilisation programmes, or for strategic purposes. Another, practically important drawback, is the highly complex character of the negotiations that would be involved, even when the main principles of the scheme are agreed upon. These must be set against the great boon which the operation of such a system would confer on the world in the long run, in terms of greater economic stability and enhanced growth.

APPENDIX

Table 1

U.S. PRIVATE FOREIGN INVESTMENT 1950–62 AND SOURCES OF FINANCE
(CUMULATIVE TOTALS)

		$ billion
Long-term investment		24·4
of which		
Direct Investment	16·0	
Portfolio Investment	8·4	
Undistributed earnings of U.S. subsidiaries directly invested abroad		12·7
Net short-term investment by banks and other private holders		5·6
Total of above		42·7
Less long-term investment by foreigners in the U.S.		−5·5
Net private foreign investment		37·2
Financed by:		
Current account surplus available for net private investment		9·2
Reduction in monetary gold stock[1]		8·1
Increase in short-term liabilities for foreign monetary authorities[2]		11·2
Increase in short-term liabilities to other than foreign monetary authorities[3]		6·6
Errors and omissions		2·1
Net private foreign investment		37·2

Source: Survey of Current Business, Balance of Payments Supplement, 1961, and August 1963.

[1] Includes as from March 1961 changes in holdings of foreign convertible currencies by U.S. monetary authorities.
[2] Includes change in liquid liabilities to the I.M.F.
[3] Includes foreign private holders, banks, and international organisations excluding the I.M.F.

Table 2

RELATIONSHIP BETWEEN EXPORT UNIT VALUES AND EXPORT VOLUMES IN MANUFACTURING FOR THE U.S. AND THE U.K. AND FOR FIVE OTHER MAJOR INDUSTRIAL EXPORTERS,[1]

1953–62

Year	(1) U.S., U.K. Combined Export Unit Value	(2) Average Export Unit Value Index for Other Industrial Countries	(3) Ratio (1) ÷ (2)	(4) U.S., U.K. Combined Export Volume Index	(5) Average Export Volume Index for Other Industrial Countries	(6) Ratio (4) ÷ (5)
1953	100	100	100	100	100	100
1954	99	97	102	105	118	89
1955	101	96	105	114	142	80
1956	106	99	107	124	160	78
1957	110	101	109	131	178	74
1958	112	99	113	118	186	63
1959	113	95	119	119	219	54
1960	116	97	120	130	257	51
1961	118	99	119	131	271	48
1962	119	99	120	134	296	45

[1] Germany, France, Italy, Belgium–Luxembourg and Japan.

Source: B. Balassa, *Recent Developments in the Competitiveness of American Industry and Prospects for the Future.* Yale University, Economic Growth Center, 1963.

Weighted averages based on 1953 weights. "Export unit values" expressed in U.S. dollars.

Table 3

MOVEMENT OF PRODUCTIVITY, AVERAGE HOURLY EARNINGS AND LABOUR COSTS PER UNIT OF OUTPUT IN MANUFACTURING FOR THE U.S. AND THE U.K. AND FOR FIVE OTHER MAJOR INDUSTRIAL EXPORTERS,[1] 1953–62

| | U.S. and U.K. | | | OTHER INDUSTRIAL COUNTRIES[1] | | | |
| | (1) | (2) | (3) | (4) | (5) | (6) | (7) |
	Output per man hour	Hourly Earnings	Unit Labour Costs (2) ÷ (1)	Output per man hour	Hourly Earnings	Unit Labour Costs (5) ÷ (4)	Relative movement of labour costs (3) ÷ (6)
1953	100	100	100	100	100	100	100
1954	101	104	103	107	104	97	106
1955	107	111	104	114	110	96	108
1956	107	117	109	119	121	102	107
1957	108	125	116	127	129	102	114
1958	110	128	116	133	133	100	116
1959	117	133	114	142	134	94	121
1960	121	141	117	152	145	95	123
1961	123	147	120	160	160	100	120
1962	126	152	121	165	176	107	113
1961	123	147	120	160	160	100	120
1962	126	152	121	165	176	107	113

[1]Germany, France, Italy, Belgium-Luxembourg and Japan.
Source: U.N. Monthly Bulletin of Statistics, International Labour Review. Weighted averages of output and earnings based on 1963 weights. Unit labour costs are $\dfrac{\text{Earnings}}{\text{Output per man}} \times 100$.

THE RELATIVE MERITS OF FIXED
AND FLOATING RATES[1]

THE decision to devalue a country's currency can be accomplished in various ways. This paper examines the different ways in which this can be done, and discusses the advantages and disadvantages of each method. The considerations advanced here apply generally to any major currency, and the argument is illustrated with reference to the experience of the pound, the franc, and the deutschmark.

In practice, in view of existing international commitments, a Government is faced with the choice between two courses. It may announce, with or without prior agreement of the other leading members of the I.M.F., a new parity immediately; or else it may declare that the attainment of a new parity is the ultimate objective but that, because it is impossible to know beforehand what the appropriate rate should be, the currency will, for an interval, be traded in a free market so that it can find its equilibrium level (subject to *ad hoc* official intervention). In other words, it adopts a "floating rate" for a period. There may be other possibilities, such as allowing a floating rate for an indefinite period, or adopting a fixed rate with wider margins. But it is assumed for the purposes of this paper that these others can be ruled out by prevailing international commitments and will not therefore be considered further.

THE ADVANTAGES AND DISADVANTAGES OF
ADOPTING A NEW PARITY

The main advantage of a simple change of the parity rate is that it creates the least disturbance to the existing monetary order.

[1] An unpublished paper written in 1965.

Fixed rates have been enshrined in the Bretton Woods Agreement, and apart from Canada no important country has had a floating rate since the war for any prolonged period. If the Bretton Woods Agreement is followed literally, the devaluing country is obliged to have prior consultations with the I.M.F. as to the proper rate, so as to do no more than is necessary to correct the "fundamental disequilibrium". But even without such consultation, an exchange rate adjustment that is not unduly large might be acceptable to the non-devaluing countries as giving no undue competitive advantage to the devaluing country, provided that no other country followed suit.

As against this one major advantage of adopting a new fixed parity, there are a number of disadvantages. First, the devaluation of a major reserve currency is bound to create a major disturbance, and its ultimate consequences cannot be forecast or taken into account. For example, a devaluation of sterling could tempt a number of other countries suffering from balance of payments problems, such as Japan or Italy, to take advantage of the "umbrella" provided by sterling to adjust their exchange rates for reasons of their own. If that were to happen, the dollar would be bound to be exposed to speculative pressure, which could easily reach a pitch that the American gold reserves could not stand. If this in turn were to lead to a devaluation of the dollar, the whole matter would pass beyond the range of the mere adjustment of relativities between the major currencies, and would call into the question the gold parity of currencies in general. Such a process could well end up with a large scale revaluation of gold.

Second, the purpose of a devaluation is to enable the devaluing country to regain competitive power sufficiently to bring about an adequate rate of growth of exports in the long run. For this, it is not the change in gold parity, but the change in the exchange rate in relation to other major currencies, which is alone relevant. Since it is impossible to take consequential adjustments of other currencies into account in fixing the new parity, the danger is that the advantage of the initial devaluation could be lost, unless it were followed by further acts of devaluation.

Third, the likelihood of consequential exchange rate adjustments by other countries will be smaller, the smaller is the extent

of the initial devaluation; but so is the advantage to be gained from it. When an exchange rate has been over-valued for a number of years, even a relatively large adjustment may prove insufficient to secure the desired results. The French franc was increasingly over-valued in the years 1954–7. In November 1957 there was a devaluation of 20 per cent., but it was only when this was followed by a further devaluation by General de Gaulle of 17.5 per cent. in December 1958 that France got into a position that enabled her to regain her previous share in world exports. French exports increased in volume by 50 per cent. in the following two years.

Fourth, the correct amount of devaluation depends on the objectives to be aimed at. It is frequently argued that the U.K. share of world manufacturing trade is too low: even if the U.K. were to succeed in future in keeping in step with the *growth* in world trade, so that exports expanded at 8–10 per cent. per year (assuming that the growth of world trade continues at the trend rate of the last 15 years), the maintenance of the payments balance would remain precarious, and could necessitate import restrictions of one sort or another to keep the growth of imports within the limits set by the growth of exports. It must be remembered that a high rate of growth of exports is bound to enhance the rate of growth of G.N.P. generally, and hence be associated with a higher rate of growth of imports. It would be preferable to raise Britain's share of world trade sufficiently to avoid the necessity for import restrictions (including protective tariffs), since this would have the optimum effect on economic efficiency and growth—it should be noted that the "successful" economies of Western Europe (France, Germany, and Italy) all had a high rate of growth of exports in the last decade or so. This could require a "target" for the U.K. share in world exports somewhere between the present level and the 1951 level—say 16·5 per cent. instead of 13 per cent. This presupposes a bigger recovery than France attained after the 1957–8 devaluations (from 8 per cent. in 1956 of world manufactured exports to 9·7 per cent. in 1960), and one that could be attained only over a series of years.

It also presupposes strongly deflationary internal policies while the process of structural adjustment is going on, as well as a succession of downward adjustments in the exchange rate, and

not a single, once-for-all adjustment. The reason for this is that both the acquisition of new markets and the adaptation of the internal production structure in favour of "international goods" takes time, and the exchange rate that may ultimately be necessary to attain the "target", whether this is stated in terms of a share in world trade, or in terms of a strong balance of payments position sustained without import restrictions, would represent an "excessive adjustment" if adopted initially—excessive, in that the economy could not respond to the change in relative prices, which would, consequently, be largely nullified by inflation. This last consideration is one of the most potent arguments in favour of a floating rate which is maintained over a series of years.

Fifth, the appropriate amount of devaluation (in the short-term) is dependent also on the consequential change in the internal wage and cost level, relative to those of other countries. If a devaluation occurs at a time of low unemployment, these consequential effects are likely to be greater, and whilst they could broadly be taken into account, they would have the effect of making the devaluation appear larger initially (in terms of competitive advantage *vis-à-vis* other countries) than it would prove to be in fact. This is an additional reason why the minimum adjustment necessary from the point of view of the balance of payments is likely to be greater than the maximum which other countries would accept without further repercussions.

Finally, a *moderate* degree of devaluation has its own dangers, in that it may prove just as difficult to sustain as the initial rate. Whilst in the short-term even a moderate degree of devaluation is likely to be followed by an inflow of speculative funds, these may quickly be reversed if international opinion (guided by the movement of the trade figures) forms the view that the move was inadequate to restore the fundamental position: the German revaluation of 1961 was followed by a large influx (not *e*fflux) of speculative funds into Germany, when the continuance of her favourable trade position led to the expectation that a further revaluation might prove necessary.

THE MODUS OPERANDI OF A FLOATING RATE

If a floating rate is adopted, the day-to-day movement of the rate is likely to be subject to official intervention just as was the case in Britain in the period after 1931. Contrary to a widespread view I would argue that such a policy ought always to be governed by long-term strategy and not by the desire to secure a maximum inflow of speculative funds in the short-term or to punish speculators. For this reason I would argue strongly against the philosophy behind the British devaluation of 1949 which presupposed a *large* initial devaluation, to be followed by a series of upward revisions later (which was never actually carried out). A *large* initial devaluation can have most undesirable repercussions both internally and internationally. Internally, it would create a large disturbance to the cost of living and the wage level without any compensating advantages in terms of the current balance, because in the short-run the devaluing country is not in a position either to increase its exports very substantially or to achieve a substantial import substitution. These considerations, together with those advanced above, dictate a strategy which allows for a gradual downward drift in the rate over a longer period, interrupted by brief, sharp, and irregularly timed, recoveries. Although it is not possible to be certain, it is likely that such a policy is quite consistent with substantial gains in foreign exchange to the reserves. And even if it could be shown that the gain in reserves would not be as great as with a policy of a gradual upward drift, this should 'not weigh heavily against the very great long-run gains of this policy. A gradual upward drift presupposes a *large* initial devaluation, and this would be almost certain to cause the vital long-run objectives of the move to be frittered away. To reverse a declining trend in competitive power in the world's markets would require an intense effort of salesmanship, a large scale adaptation of technology and of the industrial structure, and this could be pursued only in a favourable environment. Devaluation, by making exports more profitable relative to home sales, does provide such an environment, provided the stimulus is kept up and provided that it is not too large at any one time in relation to the opportunities which the prevailing economic structure

(including both the prevailing productive capacity and the irrepressible internal claims on it) permits.

It does not follow, of course, that the long-term policy of a gradual "downward drift" would reduce the size of the speculative gains accruing to the reserves. Indeed, as the post-1931 British experience showed, a floating rate combined with a reasonable amount of expertise in the day-to-day management of the exchange rate has strong strategic advantages in the game of beating private speculators, both because official resources are large, and, still more, because those managing the account are alone in having inside knowledge of the overall position. In essence, the strategy consists of allowing the rate to fall whenever this can be done through small interventions or without intervention (as a result of moderate excess of market supply over demand) and of being prepared for occasional large-scale interventions in favour of the currency in order to cause a recovery of the rate when a further fall has come to be accepted: the intervention being reversed when there is large-scale speculation in favour of the currency. Provided that the rate is kept, on balance, slightly undervalued (i.e. slightly below the average rate that would be established in the absence of intervention) there is nothing inconsistent in the central bank acquiring large foreign currency reserves over a period in which the trend in the exchange rate has been downwards. In brief, success in the management of a floating rate depends on the authorities being in a position to counteract whatever happens to be the dominant expectation at the time: to prevent any sharp recovery in the rate through official purchases of foreign exchange whenever the general expectation is that the rate is too low, and to cause a recovery of the rate, whenever a strong expectation develops that the rate is likely to fall further.

It must be understood, of course, that the success of such a long-term strategy depends on the success of the monetary authorities in keeping the world "guessing" both as to the country's true position and to its intentions, and in turn on the country's success in keeping its long-term intentions completely in the dark.

RESERVE CURRENCIES AND A FLOATING RATE

One of the most frequent objections to the adoption of a floating rate is that it is inconsistent with a currency's role as a reserve currency. Certainly this objection has frequently been raised in connection with sterling. Given that this is an inherited status, and that little can be done to change the position, it is important to examine how far reserve currency status prevents a country from pursuing a course of action that would otherwise be in its interest.

The adoption of a floating rate in 1931 did not imply the end of the role of sterling as a reserve currency: on the contrary, it could be argued that it was as a result of this move that the sterling area, as it is now known, came into existence. It could also be argued, however, that this may have been due to peculiar circumstances which are no longer valid. In the world economic depression of the 1930s, there were a large number of countries, both inside and outside the Commonwealth, who were anxious to tie their parity to sterling in preference to gold. It is less likely that nowadays all the countries of the outer sterling area would wish to follow sterling, although there must be many who, given the present low level of raw material prices, would be under a strong temptation to do so, and thereby obtain a competitive advantage *vis-à-vis* other raw material producers. Indeed much the same group of countries which followed sterling in 1931 might do so again in any subsequent sterling devaluation. But if they would not do so, the question at issue would become whether they would wish to continue to hold their reserves in sterling.

The answer to this would depend, in large part, on the terms that were offered to official holders of sterling. Irrespective of whether devaluation took place immediately to a fixed rate, or whether a floating rate were adopted, it is arguable that it would be very much to the advantage of Britain to give some compensation to official holders of sterling in order to induce them to continue to hold their balances in sterling rather than in some other reserve currency. This offer ought ideally to take the form of a guarantee to "write up" the value of the official balances held on the eve of devaluation day by a percentage corresponding

to the change in the rate between sterling and the other reserve currencies, *as and when the new parity is fixed.* This offer should relate to the lower of two amounts, the first being the official balances held before devaluation day, and the second being the balances held on the day on which the new parity is fixed. In this way any net balances acquired after devaluation day would be excluded from the scheme for compensation, and so would any net withdrawals between devaluation day and the date of the new parity. This would have the effect of telling official creditors that while it is not possible to say in advance what the ultimate parity will be, or when it will be established, nevertheless they will not fare worse than if they had held their balances in some other reserve currency. This kind of guarantee would be perfectly acceptable so long as the interval between devaluation day and parity day were not unduly long. If it is prolonged, however, and the arguments advanced above suggest that it should be, the above scheme does present a problem to those sterling creditors who have to run their sterling balances down for perfectly legitimate reasons in the intervening period (e. g. a trade deficit *vis-à-vis* other reserve currencies) and would thereby lose the advantage that they would have had if they had been able to maintain their balances unimpaired. However this problem is capable of a solution. For example, it could be met by special arrangements for periodic adjustments with the individual central banks concerned. Thus it might be agreed with those countries which expect to make substantial drawings for current purposes that such drawings, up to a pre-arranged limit for any one year, or any one six-month period, would be "added-back" to the balances held at the date of the establishment of the new parity, when the compensation is finally arranged.

If devaluation took place to a fixed rate, it could be argued that compensation payments would not be necessary: holders of sterling must always be aware, in the light of past experience, that a risk of devaluation exists; if they nevertheless choose to hold sterling, it must be because in their own judgment the advantages of holding sterling in terms of higher interest rates etc. outweigh the risks. It can further be argued that they would not *expect* to be compensated, since no such compensation has been offered in

similar circumstances in the past. All this may be true; yet it would arguably be foolish nowadays to refuse compensation since the risks that would be run by not doing so would far outweigh the cost. If some countries were induced or compelled by their own public opinion to withdraw their reserves from London, others might follow, and this could face the U.K. with an impossible financial problem. Hence, since it would be required in either circumstance, the need to compensate official holders is not relevant to the choice between a fixed and a floating rate.

The above considerations do not justify the extension of a compensation scheme to non-official holders (which in any case would be impracticable, since it would be difficult to define such holders, and to draw a firm line between private holders of "sterling balances" and other creditors). Guarantees at low cost are already granted to all holders who care to take them through the forward market, a facility which, it seems, has not been extended to official holders.

DISADVANTAGES OF THE FLOATING RATE SYSTEM

There are three other disadvantages that a floating rate might be said to involve. The first is that it might lead to a period of competitive exchange devaluations which would be branded as international currency chaos and thus be condemned. The danger of competitive devaluations cannot be ruled out even in the case of a devaluation to a fixed rate (as has been discussed), although with a floating rate, the danger of this occurring at some stage or other might well be greater. But such a "war" over exchange rates could not last for very long and would probably be ended within a brief period by some informal arrangements between the major central banks on the lines of the Tripartite Agreement of 1935. The country which should be least afraid of such a war is that whose exchange position is *weakest*, for the country with the weakest currency is bound to be on the winning side and not on the losing side. The reason for this is that if the monetary authorities of several countries intervene in the market in order to frustrate one another's policies, the country which is in the worst position to do so is the one that is least ready to

accumulate the currencies of the others; the country which is in the best position to do so is the one which is most ready to accumulate the currencies of its rivals. Manoeuvering will come to a stale-mate only when a "bargaining balance" is reached; the latter implies that the monetary authorities of the main countries are *equally* ready to accumulate each other's currencies, and that presupposes in turn that all of them possess equally "strong" currencies. But the main point is that, without a floating rate system, a particular country may never be able to get itself into a state of "bargaining balance" *vis-à-vis* other countries.

The second possible disadvantage of a floating rate system is that the policy could be frustrated by the devaluing country being forced to re-peg, long before its objectives had been achieved. But even under such circumstances, it is not clear that the country would actually lose by adopting a floating rate policy: it would simply fail to reap its full advantages. For an offer to give up a floating rate is a strong bargaining counter. In exchange for it it ought to reap advantages both in assurances about relative exchange rates and possibly in the form of converting or funding all or some part of short-term liabilities. The possibility that the rate might have to be pegged sooner than is desirable is not therefore an argument against adopting a floating rate in the first place—except in the event of a return to a fixed rate in a *very short* period, which would clearly be, and be seen to be, an enforced abandonment of the original intention, and which could involve a certain loss of prestige.

The third possible disadvantage of a floating rate is the risk of a "cumulative descent" engendered by adverse speculation. If that were to happen, the level of the reserves required to counter it would be high—some would argue that the resources needed to operate a floating rate in a satisfactory manner are even greater than those needed for a fixed rate. But in my opinion the risk of any such thing happening is a mirage which does not merit serious consideration. Speculation can be "price-destabilising" only *within* a certain range of price variation. There is always a certain maximum and minimum price outside which speculative forces act in a *stabilising* direction. Whenever it is contended that in a particular market a fall in price *induces* the expectation

of a further fall (or *vice versa*) and thereby causes the price to fall (or rise) further, purely as a result of speculation, what is really meant is that speculators have no firm view of what the "normal" or the "equilibrium" price is, except in terms of a "zone", and they do not therefore regard as abnormal a situation where price moves upward or downward *within* that zone. Sooner or later any speculative trend reverses itself: prices do not fall to zero, or rise to infinity. The important question is, how wide the "destabilising zone" is likely to be.

In this respect different commodity and security markets show great divergencies of behaviour, depending on the firmness of the expectation of a "normal" price. The latter is greatly influenced by past experience as well as by the elasticities of the non-speculative demand and supply in the market. At the one end of the scale, the long-term gilt-edged market in the U.K. is one where the "destabilising zone" had been a very narrow one; as Hawtrey has once shown, "in the half-century up to 1914 there was only one occasion when the yield of Consols diverged by as much as ¼ per cent. from the seven years' moving average.[1] At the other end of the scale, the market for some agricultural commodities, such as cotton or wheat, is a highly unstable one: the annual range of price-variation in one year amounted to as much as 67 per cent. of that of the average price of the previous ten years.[2] The reason for this is that the price elasticities of the non-speculative demand and supply, i.e. of production and consumption, are both low, so that a *large* change in price can occur in the short period without creating any marked change in the balance of production and consumption. In markets of this kind, prices can deviate from the "normal" (or the past average of prices) without setting up speculative forces to reverse the trend, simply because speculators do not expect the price to revert to "normality" at all quickly; their short-period expectations concerning prices may run counter to their long-period judgment.

Fortunately, the market for foreign exchange is one where the "destabilising zone" is likely to be a very narrow one, precisely

1 *Capital and Employment*, p. 114.
2 Keynes, *Economic Journal*, September 1938, p. 451. See also L. St. Clair Grondona, *National Reserves for Safety and Stabilisation*, 1939; *Utilising World Abundance*, 1958.

because foreign exchange is a "multi-commodity" market, where the elasticities of the non-speculative factors are likely to be large. For example, when someone purchases sterling, he buys an entitlement not just to one commodity, but to any number of commodities—to all exportable commodities made by British labour. The elasticity of world demand for all products made in Britain is likely to be very much greater than the elasticity of demand for any *one* commodity, or any one *group* of commodities. Hence, given the purchasing power of sterling in terms of British commodities, speculators can form a pretty firm idea of what the *range* for a reasonable exchange rate should be, and they would base their future expectations concerning price movements, not on the price movements of the previous day, but on their judgment as to whether sterling were too dear or too cheap by the test of relative costs and prices. This is not to deny that there is always a range within which judgments are infirm and where therefore speculation can be price-destabilising, but it is most unlikely that this range should exceed 5 per cent. on either side from the theoretical "equilibrium price". Since the policy of the monetary authorities would aim at keeping the floating currency slightly under-valued most of the time—say 5 per cent. below the "equilibrium price" that would equate the (non-speculative) demand and supply—it is most unlikely that speculative forces could persistently act in a perverse direction. This certainly appears to have been borne out by the U.K. experience with the Exchange Equalisation Account in the post-1931 period.

There is only one qualification to be made to the above argument—it presupposes that the level of internal prices and costs are stable, or if not completely stable, that the rate of domestic price inflation is not appreciably larger than is the case with other industrial countries. If the fall in the exchange rate itself induces an acceleration in the rate of increase of money wages, this will react on the purchasing-power-parity rate, and may in time cause speculators to expect a falling trend rate. For this reason the successful pursuit of a policy of a floating rate requires reasonable stability of internal wages and prices, which constitutes a further argument for the well-known proposition that a successful ex-

change rate adjustment *of any kind* presupposes that the home economy should not be fully stretched.

CONCLUSION

The adoption of a floating rate requires a great deal of skill, a clear strategy, and the courage to stick to the policy in the face of opposition. By comparison the adoption of a devaluation to a new fixed rate is an easy option. But it offers no certain solution to fundamental problems caused by uncompetitiveness, and could cause endless difficulties.

4

THE DOLLAR CRISIS[1]

I. THE ERA OF THE WORLD DOLLAR STANDARD

FOR reasons largely unsuspected by its creators, the Bretton Woods agreement ushered in a period of unprecedented economic growth and prosperity in the world. This was not due to the role played by the two institutions created at Bretton Woods (the Fund and the Bank) which turned out to have been far less central in shaping events than Keynes and other progenitors envisaged. Nor was it due to the new international rule-book agreed on at Bretton Woods—multilateralism, general convertibility, a system of fixed exchange rates, the abolition of quantitative restrictions and discriminations—which latter, together with Gatt, served as the indispensable background to post-war economic expansion.

These rules would not have been important if they had not been observed; the fact that they have, at least for two decades, been so generally observed was not the result of the formal obligations assumed in international treaties but of the creation of an international climate which enabled the major capitalist powers (with some conspicuous exceptions) to observe the rules without damage to their interests.

But for the creation of this climate neither the institutions nor the rules were primarily responsible, but a relatively minor technical feature of the arrangements which passed almost unnoticed at the time—a by-product of Bretton Woods, which was not even made explicit in the treaty. This was the rule which made the United States dollar the universal "intervention currency" of I.M.F. members. Under these rules no country was obliged to do either more or less than to maintain in its own financial market the parity of its own currency in terms of the United States dollar

[1] Originally published in *The Times* on 6, 7 and 8 September 1971.

(within a ¾ per cent. limit on either side of parity). The United States alone was obliged to buy gold in unlimited amounts and to tender gold at a fixed price on request from "official" creditors.

At first these provisions did not mean much. The world suffered from a tremendous scarcity of dollars as well as of gold, which the resources of the I.M.F. could do little to alleviate. But after the dramatic currency realignments of 1949—largely inspired and strongly supported by the U.S. Government—and the rapid restoration of pre-war productivity levels both in Continental Europe and in Japan (again largely induced by United States economic aid) the world economic situation underwent a sea-change, which none of the world's economists then living was able to foresee, or indeed to appreciate for a fair number of years after its occurrence. The only economist who *could* have claimed to have anticipated the possibility was Keynes himself, who died five years earlier. This sea-change consisted in the fact that the dollar, which had been a "scarce currency" more or less continuously since 1914— that is, for the previous 35 years—became increasingly "unscarce" or "plentiful" on account of the persistent deficit which developed in the United States balance of payments on basic transactions around 1951. Since over most of the period, the United States economy was far from fully employed, this deficit reflected the overvaluation of the dollar in relation to other currencies, and not an "inflationary" fiscal or monetary policy by the United States.

This situation had two consequences. The dollar increasingly replaced gold (and other "key" currencies, mainly sterling) as the basic international medium of exchange and of international reserves. And the continued excess of dollar outlays over receipts provided the rest of the world with a steady increase in international purchasing power which in turn enabled other countries (with one or two conspicuous exceptions!) to reap the benefit of continued and accelerating export-led growth. As a result world production, and particularly world industrial production, grew at a pace and with a continuity never before experienced in human history. If it had not been for the growth of world income generated by the continued rise in *net* dollar outlays by the United States, Germany, Japan, Italy and dozens of smaller countries could

never have experienced the fast growth of production, employment and real income which the (much faster) rates of growth of their exports made possible.

Nor could the developed capitalist world have indulged in the luxury of increasing freedom of international trade, achieved both through the Kennedy Rounds and the creation of free trade areas.

The important aspect of the establishment of a world-wide "dollar standard" in place of the pre-1914 gold standard was not (as most people believe) that it increased the volume of international reserves and thereby enabled countries to feel "more secure" in the adoption of liberal trade policies. The important aspect was that it ensured a steady increase in world effective demand for goods and services and thereby, through a succession of "multiplier" and "accelerator" effects, induced a faster growth of productive capacity and living standards in most, if not all, market economies.

The difference between these two aspects, vital to an understanding of the international monetary problem, can best be shown by contrasting the effects of a large-scale revaluation of gold (in terms of national currencies) with that of a similar increase in the value of the monetary gold stock attained through a succession of new gold discoveries. If the price of gold were doubled tomorrow (in terms of currencies in general) there would no doubt be some, once-and-for-all, effect on world demand. But since most of the gold is held by a few rich countries, the effect would be no different from that on a millionaire who finds that his shares have doubled in price and he is now worth 20 million and not 10 million.

If, on the other hand, the value of gold reserves is increased through an increase in gold production, the value of world investment goes up *pari passu*. It means increasing the output of a commodity the price of which can never fall, however much production exceeds consumption. This latter change will cause an addition to world incomes that is many times the value of the increase of the gold stock, and not just a fraction of it. The persistent large deficits in the United States balance of payments—given the universal role of the dollar as the medium for settling inter-country

debts—acted in the same way as a corresponding annual addition to gold output, not as an annual revaluation of a given gold stock of an equivalent extent.

What went wrong? So long as countries preferred the benefits of fast growth and increasing competitiveness to the cost of part-financing the United States deficit (or what comes to the same thing, preferred selling more goods even if they received nothing more than bits of paper in return), and so long as a reasonable level of prosperity in the United States (in terms of employment levels and increases of real income) could be made consistent with the increasing uncompetitiveness of United States goods in relation to European or Japanese goods, there was no reason why any major participant should wish to disturb these arrangements. But with the passage of time these preconditions became increasingly tenuous. At least one major beneficiary of the great world export boom, Germany, found that exports can be too much of a good thing. It preferred to reduce its own competitiveness through revaluations and upward floating to further increases in inflation-ary pressures in circumstances in which it had a net excess demand for nearly a million workers, in spite of the importation of two million foreign workers.

Note the contrasting attitudes of Germany and Japan on this issue. Japan, whose labour reserves are far from exhausted, greatly prefers an undervalued yen and the accumulation of further billions of unwanted dollars to a slow-down in its growth rate. Germany, whose real rate of growth is constrained by the scarcity of labour, prefers an easing of inflationary pressures, even if it means a less competitive position, lower profits, lower business investments and, in the long run, lower growth.

On the other side, keeping the American economy prosperous required measures of steadily increasing unorthodoxy, equally repugnant to Congress, the American public at large, and the world outside. Under the rules of the game of the world-dollar-standard it is, of course, the responsibility of the "key currency" country to keep its *own* economy prosperous by generating enough internal purchasing power to maintain the level and the rate of growth of effective demand. Unlike all other countries, it is able to do so without having to worry about its balance of payments.

Nevertheless, as the products of American industry are increasingly displaced by others, both in American and foreign markets, maintaining prosperity requires ever-rising budgetary and balance of payments deficits, which makes it steadily less attractive as a method of economic management.

If continued long enough it would involve transforming a nation of creative producers into a community of *rentiers* increasingly living on others, seeking gratification in ever more useless consumption, with all the debilitating effects of the bread and circuses of Imperial Rome. In addition, the objectives on which successive American governments spent their freely-printed money appeared either so useless or morally repellent—lunar flights or Vietnam wars—as to arouse increasingly universal hostility against the System, both inside and outside the United States.

Sooner or later it had to break down; in the event, the unwillingness of some countries to absorb further dollars coincided more or less in time with the urgent need of President Nixon to do something to kick America back into prosperity.

II. THE NEW ERA OF FLOATING EXCHANGE RATES

There was a time within living memory when America regarded "competitive exchange devaluation" as a major calamity to humanity, comparable to wars or pestilence, which must be guarded against by the strongest possible system of defences. One of the main functions of the Bretton Woods pact, from the United States point of view, was to erect such defences. In fact there was no real evidence that "competitive exchange devaluation" has ever been extensively or deliberately employed as a weapon of trade warfare, or that it had the calamitous effects which some economists attributed to it. The main historical instance, President Roosevelt's misguided attempt in 1933 to devalue the dollar in the face of an exceptional dollar scarcity, was not really motivated by the desire to boost the sales of United States goods abroad, but only by the naive belief that raising the gold price is some magic that re-creates domestic prosperity automatically through raising the general price level.

However, it is not difficult to see why, in 1945, the prospect of

"competitive exchange devaluation" was regarded with such distaste by the Americans. It is a game in which the ordinary roles of
the strong and the weak are reversed: in which the poor man has
an inherent advantage over the rich man. This is so simply because
the central bank of a *weak* currency is naturally far keener on
accumulating balances of a *strong* currency than the other way
round. What the Americans were afraid of was that unless exchange rate adjustments are made a matter of international
surveillance and regulation, they would be increasingly exposed
to the danger of being priced out of the market by the attempt of
weaker countries to undervalue their currencies relative to the
United States dollar, which America would not be able to counter
except by putting more dollars at the disposal of these countries.
In this way they would be blackmailed into giving more dollar
aid than they wished to give.

The danger that such developments might prevent America from
exploiting its economic potential fully—because the "weak" countries will increase their employment levels at the expense of
American employment—was thus clearly foreseen. But the safeguards and remedies adopted were better designed, as events have
shown, to maximise the likelihood of its occurrence than to
prevent it. Indeed, there could be few clearer instances in history
of a country being hoist with its own petard than America's
attempt to prevent the dollar from becoming overvalued through
the introduction of the Bretton Woods rules.

Part of the reason for this has been that when a country really
wanted to devalue in order to improve its competitiveness—like
France in 1957, 1958 or 1969, or Britain in 1967, not to speak of
numerous instances of lesser importance—the Bretton Woods
rules were quite inadequate to prevent this. I.M.F. approval of
such changes became a piece of ritual.

A more important reason, entirely unforeseen in 1945, has been
that the currencies of "successful" countries became increasingly
undervalued, not on account of deliberate acts of exchange devaluation, but simply because of the "Verdoorn Law" which
makes productivity growth a function of production growth, production growth a function of export growth, and the latter in turn
a function of productivity growth.

The prospects of the American economy were beclouded by the increasing undervaluation of the mark and the yen; this was the result, not of Germany or Japan indulging in "competitive exchange devaluation"—in fact, Germany has repeatedly done the very opposite—but of America's total inability to employ that very weapon in order to counter its own increasing uncompetitiveness.

In retrospect there can be little doubt that a system of floating exchange rates would have protected the interests of countries which for structural reasons were bound to be at the losing end of the competitive game—such as the United States and even more, the United Kingdom—far better than the Bretton Woods system. The role of the "banker"—the ability to borrow automatically through creating money—though a much envied privilege contained their freedom of action and forced both the United States and the United Kingdom to accept lower growth rates than they would have attained if they had been free to adjust their exchange rates vis-à-vis their industrial rivals whenever their export performance lagged markedly behind their own growth potential as well as the performance of rival exporters.

The efforts and gestures of the United States in the field of foreign economic policy during the last few years make sense only as part of a grand design to get the world away from Bretton Woods, and towards a system in which the "strong" currencies of surplus countries can be forced to appreciate in terms of the "weak" currencies of the deficit countries—the very opposite of America's original intention. The more America succeeds in discouraging other countries from adding to their dollar holdings, the more currencies are induced to float, the stronger the world economic position of the United States is likely to become in the long run. It is an effort to demonetise, not just gold, but also the dollar.

For psychological more than for economic reasons, the very announcement of the formal suspension of the dollar's gold convertibility (de facto it was virtually inconvertible for some years) has forced a number of trading countries to go "floating", at least formally, almost immediately that is, to renounce any obligation to maintain the parity of their currencies in terms of the dollar. Others, like Japan, held out against it but were forced to follow

suit in a week or so. Though all this appears at this moment as a temporary "currency upheaval", soon to be followed by a new settlement, there is in fact a very strong probability that it marks the beginning of a new era of floating exchange rates which will be of fairly long duration.

Though economic prophecies are notoriously hazardous, I cannot at present see how the Group of Ten or the I.M.F. at the end of September could reach an agreement on a new set of fixed parities that would satisfy both the United States and the other main trading countries, or that such an arrangement would have any permanence if perchance fixed parities were restored.

Any major country that formally announces that it will maintain its exchange rate within fixed limits faces the risk of vast speculative inflows or outflows. It is only the uncertainty of a floating rate that can rise or fall within *unknown* limits which keeps speculation at bay by creating risks in both directions. (The best proof of this is the effect of the withdrawal of support by the gold pool in the free gold market in March 1968. So long as the rate was pegged it required vast quantities of gold, in some weeks well over $100m a day, to satisfy the speculative demand. As soon as the peg was removed, a moderate rise in price by a few dollars an ounce was sufficient to elimate this demand and to reduce the volume of trading to modest proportions.)

If the above prediction on the improbability of a settlement on a new set of parities is correct, the imposition of the 10 per cent. surcharge by the United States was an unfortunate move—a gamble that will not come off. As an inducement to countries to allow their currencies to float up freely, it will have a perverse effect, since no single country will wish to carry the risk of a double penalty if it appreciated its currency and yet the surcharge was not removed; nor could any definite *quid pro quo* be given in return for removing the surcharge so long as exchange rates remain formally floating.

The sole value of the surcharge as a bargaining weapon depends on the assumption that it is possible to get all countries to agree to a return to a fixed parity at a new set of rates satisfactory to the United States. But if this will not happen in any event, the United States (as well as the rest of the world) may well lose rather than

D

gain on balance by having imposed it. In any event central banks will continue to intervene at their discretion (and possibly *with* the utmost discretion) to prevent undue appreciation or sometimes depreciation. And *faute de mieux* the dollar will continue to function as the general "intervention currency". And since it is unlikely that the major European countries or Japan will allow a sufficient appreciation of their currencies to make any dramatic change to the United States balance of payments (which in the best circumstances would take some years) the "phasing out" of the dollar standard is bound to be a long drawn out process.

Yet a true system of floating rates which would prevent some countries from being pushed out of the world's markets through over-valuation and others from gaining at their expense through under-valuation, is only conceivable when the dollar is fully "de-monetised" internationally—i.e., when it ceases to be a reserve asset. This could happen only if the existing dollar balances were transformed into some new international monetary unit divorced from the domestic currency of the United States—for example into units of I.M.F. "bancor"—which would make it possible for the United States to vary the dollar in terms of it in the same way as other countries. For evident reasons, such a move would be most unwelcome to America's industrial rivals. But the United States has pretty strong cards in its hands and recent events have shown that, when driven to extremes, it does not hesitate to use them. If America's creditors would not agree to transform dollar balances into "bancor", America might threaten, for example to block all such balances and make them useless and unnegotiable.

So the next stage in the monetary evolution of the world, probably still some time ahead, will be the creation of an I.M.F. reserve currency that is independent of the dollar. The vital question is how it would—or could—operate.

III. THE BASIC REQUIREMENTS OF AN INTERNATIONAL RESERVE CURRENCY

Assuming that the main industrial countries will agree, willy-nilly, to a transformation of dollar balances (and presumably, one hopes, also of sterling balances) into "bancor units" of the Inter-

national Monetary Fund—which are not pegged to the dollar—immediately a number of basic questions arise. What will ensure the general acceptability of the new money? And how will its supply be regulated?

In the voluminous international discussions, both official and unofficial, which have been proceeding for a large number of years on the future of the monetary system (and which finally led to the agreement to create special drawing rights, a kind of embryo I.M.F. currency) it was increasingly taken for granted that the creation of "paper gold" would not give rise to any special problems on account of its "paper" character—i.e., the fact that it will have no backing in terms of "real" assets.

And it was also taken for granted that the problem of regulating its supply will not (or need not) give rise to any very difficult problems: it is just a matter of deciding how much to distribute every year and to whom. On the latter question the simplest solution—and the one actually adopted in connexion with the S.D.R. scheme—was to distribute the new money among I.M.F. members in proportion to their existing quotas.

Much of this discussion on "paper gold", conducted with a great deal of expertise on technical detail, revealed a surprising *naïveté* among experts on fundamental issues. The limited experience with S.D.R.s offers very little guidance to the problems that would arise if such "drawing rights" were not only a small adjunct to existing reserves (rigidly linked to the dollar) but are to form the main international payments medium that has no permanent link with any national currency, and which is expressed as "the equivalent of" so many ounces or grains of gold, but without being actually convertible into gold (or without gold being convertible into it). The main requirement of an international "fiat money" is that its supply should be fully controlled by the institution which issues it (i.e., by the governments which are behind the institution). But if such "fiat money" is not permanently tied to any major currency, what is there to ensure its continued acceptability in the face of changes in its conversion ratios into national currencies? In the case of a national currency the general acceptability of "fiat money" is ultimately linked to political sovereignty. Everyone in Britain accepts payments in pounds in the confident

knowledge that the Government accept pounds in payment of taxes and the courts will support any debtor who tenders payment in pounds to a creditor. But in a conclave of sovereign states, there can be no such enforceability: the willingness of any one country to hold assets in paper "bancor" depends entirely on its confidence that it will continue to be fully acceptable to all other countries.

Any change in the commodity value of "bancor" resulting from changes in prices or in individual currency rates might create doubt about its continued acceptability; and once such doubt arises, there is nothing to stop it from becoming wholly unacceptable. Once a major country imposes some kind of restriction on its acceptability—for example, by demanding part payment in gold or in national currencies; this might arise as part of a dispute on relative exchange values between, say, the dollar and the yen—such "bancor" units would become rapidly worthless. Just because the new money is to be an *international* medium of exchange, and not a *national* one, it seems essential therefore that it should be backed by real assets into which the units are convertible at the option of the individual holder, and which give some guarantee of compensation to holders in case of liquidation. If it is to be independent of individual currencies, it must have a direct commodity-value, and not just an indirect one, through its assumed convertibility into national currencies.

There is also the problem, in the case of such "fiat money", of how to regulate its supply over time. It is all very well to say that "the world economy is best served by increasing 'bancor' at the rate of X per cent. a year; if X turns out to be the wrong figure, it could always be changed subsequently", but the right value of X will depend on to *whom* the new money is issued, and on *what* happens to it. If it is brought into existence by some automatic formula, like the one applied to S.D.Rs, most of it will be just so much added to reserves, and for reasons explained on page 62, it will be quite ineffective in performing the vital function of ensuring that the effective demand for goods and services in international trade should go on rising, and that hence the world economy should go on expanding.

If on the other hand the new money is brought into existence so as to generate expenditure or income directly—as, for example,

if it were linked to investment in developing countries, or to finance the current account balance of "deserving" deficit countries—it is very difficult to see how a group of sovereign nations would be ready to delegate such powers to a Mr. McNamara or a M. Schweitzer, or alternatively how they could be made to agree directly on its distribution year by year.

One solution to all these problems, favoured by central bankers and French intellectuals, is to restore the international Gold Standard—or rather a streamlined version of it, consistent with individual countries having flexible or floating exchange rates. This would be a "bancor" that is fully backed by gold—fully convertible into gold, and freely issued in exchange for gold.

Let us be clear that this would be a perfectly feasible solution that would solve all above-mentioned problems, provided the value of gold (in terms of currencies and commodities) is initially made high enough to ensure that the yearly addition to the gold stock *through new production* is large enough, and increases at an adequate rate annually, to ensure a fast rate of growth of effective demand, i.e., to ensure that the growth potential of the world economy is reasonably fully exploited. To play the same role which the United States deficit performed in the past 10–20 years, this would require an annual value of gold output of perhaps $10,000 m. a year, rising by 10 to 15 per cent. annually. No doubt there is some particular gold value—it may be $100 to $150 an ounce, at the present level of world prices—that would ensure these results.

But as a solution it would have a number of disadvantages that make it politically unattractive. One of these is that it would transfer the role and the privileges of being "the international money-maker" from the United States to the two main gold producers, South Africa and the Soviet Union. The prospect of Russia being forced into a position in which unwittingly it becomes one of the two main sources of the growth of demand which ensures the prosperity and survival of the capitalist system has undoubtedly a certain intellectual appeal. (This may be one of the subtle reasons why so many highly intelligent and sophisticated Frenchmen are attracted to it.) On the other hand the prospect of rewarding South Africa for its racial policies by making it so much

richer and more powerful will be even less appealing to world opinion than when America used its moneymaking power to make war in Vietnam.

The alternative and far superior solution is to leave the price of gold alone (there is no point whatever in a *small* rise in the official dollar price, except as a kind of moral punishment for the United States) but make gold just one of many commodities which provide the backing for "bancor". A detailed plan for an I.M.F. "bancor" as a commodity reserve currency, being convertible into "bundles" containing 30 basic commodities which satisfy certain basic criteria of eligibility—and including wheat, butter, sugar, tropical products, fibres, natural rubber and metals —was put before the United Nations Conference on Trade and Development in 1964 by three economists, A. G. Hart, J. Tinbergen and myself. It received very little attention.

I have not in any way changed my views on this since 1964, except that I now believe a project of this kind could be made a great deal simpler—that is, by making "bancor" separately convertible into a series of individual commodities, instead of only into a *bundle* of commodities. The latter variant would need additional provisions for the periodic revision of relative bancor prices of individual commodities, based on past movements of stock/turnover ratios, but this should not pose insoluble problems. It would amount to the same as if worldwide buffer stock schemes were introduced for all the major commodities and financed through the issue of "bancor".

The major attraction of a scheme of this kind, for which it is difficult to find a substitute, is that it spreads the sources of "money-making power" far and wide—among all the commodity producers of the world—and would thereby tend to generate the maximum attainable rate of growth in the world economy, and under conditions of stable prices, at least for basic materials. By ensuring that any increase in the output of basic commodities will generate a corresponding increase in purchasing power in terms of international money, it will also ensure, through adequate "multiplier" and "accelerator" effects, that the growth of commodity absorption will proceed fast enough to match the rate of growth of commodity production. In other words, it would ensure

that it is the supply of food and basic materials which sets the limit to the rate of growth of world industrial production and not, as now, the rate of growth of effective demand, emanating in the advanced countries, which governs the growth of demand and production of primary commodities.

Its possible disadvantage for advanced capitalist countries is that it would make the "rich" countries, not poorer, but less influential and powerful—since it would ensure a steady growth of income to the primary producing countries, and make them far less dependent on aid.

A minor advantage of the scheme which in current circumstances is worth a mention is that it would make it far more attractive for Britain to enter the Common Market. For when the I.M.F. itself will ensure that there is an unlimited market at fixed prices for wheat, butter, sugar, &c., there will obviously be no scope for the Brussels Agricultural Fund to do the same—and financing it out of taxation, not by money creation—and the Common Agricultural Policy would have to be liquidated.

However, all this is Stage III, a likely development in the more distant future, perhaps in 10 or 20 years' time. Before it is seriously considered for adoption the world would first have to go through Stage II—replacement of the present dollar reserves by "paper gold"—which must be given the chance to be shown to be unworkable.

5

PROBLEMS AND PROSPECTS OF
INTERNATIONAL MONETARY REFORM[1]

THE formal occasion for the breakdown of the Bretton Woods system was the suspension of the gold convertibility of the dollar on August 15, 1971—something which had existed only on paper for some years previously, at any rate after the Washington agreements of March, 1968. The real cause of the breakdown, as everyone realises, lay much deeper—in the continued and accelerating accumulation of unwanted dollars by some of the central banks (notably in Germany) who felt that the system made it impossible for them to have any effective control over domestic inflation, and in the inability of the United States to restore its balance of payments by a downward adjustment of its own exchange rate in relation to its industrial competitors. It was therefore both in the surplus countries' interest to be rid of the obligation of having to buy up all dollars offered in the market at a fixed rate and also in America's interest that her creditors should refrain from honouring that obligation. So the "formal" suspension of gold convertibility was really a lucky stroke which provided the occasion for bringing about a change that was desired on both sides.

After that, the world went through a series of experiments and failures of experiments, together with endless discussion at both official and unofficial levels. There was an initial period of reluctant floating—with some countries such as Japan holding out against any currency re-adjustment until the last possible moment, and others being accused of indulging in "dirty floating" which was the odd description given by the Americans to the reluctance of other central banks to refrain from buying dollars altogether. This phase ended with the Smithsonian agreement—hailed at the

[1] Originally published in *The Banker*, September 1973.

time by President Nixon as "the most significant monetary agreement in the history of the world"—which restored fixed parities with rather broader margins, and restored also the dollar as the universal intervention currency, but without direct convertibility of dollars into gold or anything else. Though the pound was formally floated six months later—being forced, after a few days of violent speculation, to withdraw from the special E.E.C. currency agreements—the Smithsonian "system" survived for rather more than a year. Then, with the continued failure of the U.S. balance of payments to show the expected improvement, a new wave of anti-dollar speculation arose with terrifying suddenness. This brought about a desperate attempt by the leading countries, in the course of a dramatic weekend, to save the Smithsonian "system" by a further devaluation of the dollar of 10 per cent. in terms of other currencies.

But though everybody was agreed that at this new set of parities the dollar could not be regarded by any stretch of imagination as an over-valued currency (or the mark and the franc as still under-valued) this new Smithsonian settlement was swept away by a renewed hurricane of speculation in a matter of a few days.

Since then there have been no formal rules or obligations. Some of the European countries have maintained a joint float though it is too early to say whether this system will survive in its present form. Others (including Japan and the United Kingdom) have remained effectively pegged to, or are in fairly stable relationships with, the dollar. But as between the dollar-group and the European mark-group speculation has driven exchange ratios to quite unreasonable and highly unstable relationships in recent months—with only a slight improvement as a result of the latest Basle agreement which revived arrangements for active central bank co-operation. There is universal agreement among governments and experts that a new and more stable system is urgently needed. But what should it be?

LEARNING SOME LESSONS

Three important and highly disturbing conclusions emerge from the experience of recent years.

(1) The first of these is that a system of convertible currencies with *firmly fixed* exchange rates cannot work, at least over longer periods, because this system cannot reconcile the maintenance of international payments equilibrium with the successful pursuit of full employment and economic growth policies in each of the industrialised countries. Whatever may have been true in the nineteenth century when the international and inter-regional flows of precious metals in themselves brought into train (or at least were supposed to) an "adjustment process" in the balance of payments through the consequential variation in local wages and prices, this mechanism is clearly not applicable to a world where wages are not flexible, upwards or downwards, in response to small variations in demand for labour; and where, moreover, there are built-in tendencies to disequilibrium in international trade and payments as a result of self-reinforcing divergences in the trends of industrial productivity and of competitiveness.

Certainly none of the authors of the Bretton Woods agreement could have foreseen that currencies like the dollar or the pound sterling would become progressively more over-valued, and the mark and the yen more under-valued, as a result not of differential rates of inflation between these countries, nor of acts of competitive exchange devaluations which were so much feared as a weapon of trade warfare (Germany, so far from devaluing, has repeatedly up-valued her currency in the course of the last twelve years in order to *reduce* the demand for her exports) but as a result of the cumulative trading advantages of countries which have been gaining an increasing share of world trade in manufactures, and the cumulative handicap of those whose market shares were curtailed in consequence. This follows from the principle of "circular and cumulative causation" (Myrdal) due to static and dynamic economies of scale, which bring it about that countries which have some initial advantage in terms of competitiveness and thereby succeed in improving their share of trade in relation to others, tend to enhance that advantage on account of the faster rate of growth of their exports. It is well known that all industrialised countries with a fast rate of growth in the G.D.P. had an even faster rate of growth in their manufacturing output, and this was associated with a rate of growth of exports of manufactures which

in turn was considerably in excess of their rates of growth of total manufacturing output.[1]

EXPORT-LED GROWTH

The theoretical explanation of these tendencies (which lie outside the basic tenets of traditional economics) is twofold. In the first place the rate of productivity growth in most (though not necessarily all) sectors of manufacturing industry, as well as in manufacturing activities as a whole, obeys the so-called "Verdoorn Law": i.e. the rate of productivity growth is closely related to the rate of growth of total output with a coefficient of around 0·6 (which means that a 1 per cent. addition to the rate of growth of total output is associated with a 0·6 per cent. addition to the growth of productivity). In the second place the relative rate of increase in wages tends to follow the rate of productivity growth of the fast-growing industries but in a "diminutive" fashion—the difference in the rise in wages between industries tends to be considerably less than the difference in the growth of productivity in those industries. Hence, despite the fact that a faster rate of growth of output and productivity induces a faster rate of increase in wages, unit-costs and prices in the fast-growing industries tend to fall relatively to the others—and by more than is the case in countries where the rhythm of expansion as between different industries is more uniform. "Export-led" growth enables the country's fast-growing industries to sustain much higher rates of growth of total output than they could have if they were mainly dependent on the growth of domestic demands (which requires the expansion of different industries to keep far more in step with one another).

In a typical country with export-led growth (such as Germany) the volume of exports rises 15–20 per cent. a year when total manufacturing output rises by 8 per cent. a year and G.D.P. as a whole by 5 per cent. a year. This makes the rate of growth of out-

[1] Not all countries in this category had increasing *shares* in world trade in manufactures. Owing to the fact that the total world trade in manufactures had grown at a very fast rate (greatly in excess of the rate of growth of world manufacturing output), for most countries even the maintenance of a constant share in the world trade of manufactures meant a rate of growth of exports that was greatly in excess of the growth of their total manufactured output.

put in the export industries much higher than the general rate of growth of the economy; it also forces, via the wage-mechanism, relatively inefficient sectors to contract and thereby release their labour to the fast-growing sectors. It is well known that all countries whose manufactured exports have risen much faster than their total manufacturing output, have also had a rate of growth of manufactured imports that has been greatly in excess of the growth of their output. Hence, while the rate of output growth and of productivity growth in the "favoured" industries was faster than the average, these industries have also accounted for a rising fraction of total employment as well as output.

By contrast, in countries such as the United Kingdom or the United States which follow "full employment" fiscal policies and whose economic growth has been "consumer-led", the rate of growth of exports is generally in line with the growth of industrial capacity and output. The increase in output capacity induced by an increase in domestic demand tends to increase exports as well since it encourages firms to sell abroad (at lower prices) a certain fraction of the output produced by the new capacity.

But in these countries firms rely on home sales, not on exports, to cover their overheads and the bulk of their profits; industrial development is home-oriented, and the stimulus of the spearhead of fast-growing industries—the penetration of foreign markets—is absent.

It was as a result of these factors that international competitiveness increasingly diverged as between the countries whose growth has been "export-led" and the countries whose growth was "consumer-led". In the course of these developments the "export-led" group of countries experienced a consistent balance of payment surplus and the "consumption-led" countries growing deficits. But it is important to understand that these payments imbalances were reflections of more basic trends—and not even unfavourable reflections. Surpluses earned by the first group were reflections of the deficits of the second group. If the United States (and Britain) had pursued economic policies sufficiently deflationary as to have avoided balance of payments deficits, the surpluses in the balance of payments of other countries would not have materialised either. But the basic handicap from which the former countries suffered as a result of growing uncompetitiveness would have been aggra-

vated and not alleviated—the growth of productivity in the United States and the United Kingdom would have been even smaller. Given the existence of cumulative trends towards increasing competitiveness or uncompetitiveness, the emergence or non-emergence of payments imbalances is a relatively slight matter.

The basic issue, which the United States has recognised only very belatedly, resides in the fact that it is only by adjustments of the exchange rates (or, if necessary, by a succession of such adjustments) that the trade-losing countries can counter the cumulative disadvantages resulting from increasing inroads by the trade-earning countries both in their own markets and in third markets. Reserve currency countries encounter special problems in bringing about downward adjustments in their exchange rates. This has been true of countries with "secondary" reserve currencies such as Britain, but of course it has been very much more true of the primary reserve currency country, the United States. If the United States had devalued the dollar in terms of gold at any time after 1950 (while maintaining convertibility), other countries would have responded immediately by an identical devaluation in terms of gold: maintaining the value of their currency in terms of gold would have brought them no advantages whatever. (This is contrary to traditional economic theory, according to which a *re*valuation of the currency of a trading country is always advantageous if it merely serves to eliminate unrequired exports.) The fact that in practice countries with under-valued currencies are found so reluctant to allow their currencies to appreciate proves that they recognise that exports have far more significance to their economies than being just a means of paying for imports. As shown by their attitude and actions they recognise the vital role of exports in the growth of industrial productivity and in the rate of economic growth generally.[1]

However, as a result of the events of the past two years it is now

[1] Nor can their attitude be explained by some mercantilist preference for a surplus in their balance of payments, or for the potential of large and growing reserves as such, by which some economists attempt to explain their seemingly irrational behaviour. In fact, both Germany and Japan have been successful in spite of the growth of their reserves, which made internal monetary controls far more difficult to operate. Nor do they require a current account surplus as a "prop" to sustain effective demand. If these countries were at first so reluctant to float or otherwise revalue, this was *in spite of* the embarrassment caused by the rapid growth in their reserves: it could certainly not be explained by the hypothesis that they had an insatiable appetite for reserves.

generally accepted that a system of convertible currencies with fixed exchange rates cannot work satisfactorily unless the set of exchange rate relativities are periodically adjusted so as to offset these divergent trends in competitiveness. Such periodic adjustments, preferably agreed on in concert between the parties, should form an integral part of the "adjustment process".[1] That is the first lesson.

(2) The second disturbing conclusion, which as yet is less generally recognised, is that the alternative of a system of "fixed but adjustable" parities (envisaging fairly prompt and frequent adjustments in *pegged* rates) is not, in practice, workable either because it offers the maximum scope for anticipatory speculation, the force of which is likely to be the greater the more easily and the more frequently the official rates are changed. This is best shown by the history of the various up-valuations of the German mark in recent years, the timing of which was forced on the German monetary authorities—whatever their justification may have been on long-term considerations—by the sudden onrush of speculative funds; but which, as the most recent example has shown, can just as easily lead to a further aggravation, than to the stemming or reversal of the movement of such funds. It is a *naïveté* to think that anticipatory speculative movements can be countered by the authorities themselves "anticipating" them. Just as in a game of musical chairs the players can never beat the band, so the monetary authorities collectively cannot beat the speculators. So long as parity adjustments are guided by objective criteria— such as the trends in the balance of payments, or the movement in reserves, reflecting "long-term" or non-speculative factors—a system of "fixed or adjustable" parities could only work satisfactorily if nobody ever "anticipated" anything, or else nobody had much ready money (or borrowing power) to turn their anticipations into a speculative gain.

(3) The third conclusion which gained rapidly growing acceptance in the light of even more recent experience is that a universal

---

[1] This recognition of the need for such periodic general adjustments in the structure of parities is of course a different and more far-reaching idea than the principle embodied in the Bretton Woods agreement of giving individual countries the right to adjust their parities in cases of "fundamental disequilibrium". This latter was presumably intended to cover situations that are peculiar to an individual country rather than situations of a general imbalance in trading relationships.

system of *freely* floating exchange rates does not provide a viable solution either. This is because (a) the day-to-day movements of individual exchange rates tend to be dominated by speculative influences; (b) contrary to the views of those who hold that speculation must exert a price stabilising influence (since otherwise speculators as a class would make losses) the de-stabilising effects of speculation tend to predominate over the stabilising effects over a range of price-oscillation which is far too wide to be consistent with stable and orderly developments in trade. Nobody doubts that in a perfectly "free" market for, say, German marks, with the mark rising day by day on account of the expectation that it will rise even further—a sentiment which is partly nourished by its prolonged previous rise, and partly by the strength of the trade figures which reflect past, and not current, price and cost relationships—the day must nevertheless come when the mark will have risen so high—that is to say, so much above the level which could conceivably be justified by the underlying factors which govern long-term trends—that the "bears" will get the upper hand: speculation will go into reverse, causing the price to fall and go on falling—possibly much below the level required for long-term balance. However, there is no reason to suppose that in the complete absence of official intervention, price fluctuations in the foreign exchange market would be much inferior to those experienced in unregulated commodity markets—where annual price variations of 40 per cent. or more between "high" and "low" points are not uncommon. Such fluctuations would have serious destabilising effects not only on international trade but also on internal cost and price levels.

It was for this reason that within a few months of Britain abandoning gold convertibility in September, 1931, the government found it necessary to set up a new instrument—the Exchange Equalisation Account—for regular official interventions in the foreign exchange market so as to stabilise prices; while a large number of smaller countries found it convenient to "peg" their rates either on sterling or on the dollar.

Britain's experience with a system of "managed floating" in the years 1932–1935 was by no means an unfavourable one. But it was much criticised by other countries, and in 1935 Britain agreed in

the so-called Tripartite Agreement to peg the sterling/dollar exchange rate and also its relation to the "gold block", within fairly narrow limits.[1]

While each of the alternatives mentioned above—a system of firmly fixed rates, a system of "fixed but adjustable" parities, or a system of "freely floating" rates—could thus be shown to be unworkable, there is nothing impossible about a system of "managed floating rates". This would be likely to consist of a limited number (perhaps three or four) of currency groups—such as the dollar, sterling and the yen, the European group and maybe one or two others—each of which would be the "host" or the "reserve currency" to a number of smaller countries. Indeed in the absence of any major agreement on a new Bretton Woods, this is the system that is likely to evolve automatically as a result of the mutual interest of the major central banks in maintaining orderly conditions in the world's foreign exchange markets.[2]

It does *not* require the creation of a new international reserve unit, since each of the main central banks could hold its reserves in the form of balances (or swap facilities) with the other central banks and intervene in the market by buying or selling its own currency against any or all of these other "key currencies".[3] Provided that the main central banks can agree as to what the "reasonable" exchange rate relationships should be—and it would not be too difficult to agree on a set of criteria to serve as the test of such "reasonableness", the system would not involve the kind of "currency war" which was the great bogey of the Bretton Woods conference.[4]

---

[1] It would be intriguing to know just what the considerations were which induced the British Conservative Government in 1935 to sacrifice the proved advantages of the system of "managed floating" for the sake of the Tripartite Agreement. The difference between that system and the post-war Bretton Woods system was only that the former was a much less formal arrangement, renewable annually and which could be abrogated at six months' notice.

[2] Some people might argue that as soon as you introduce an element of management into a float, you immediately bring back the problem of "one'way option" open to speculators. However, there is a major difference between informal (and unannounced) "guidelines" agreed on between central banks and formal and explicit obligations; experience of the 1930s (when the system was operated by Britain for some years) does not provide any justification for such fears.

[3] So long as these currencies are freely convertible into each other, private arbritrage arrangements could be relied on to ensure consistency of cross rates.

[4] The most suitable criterion for industrialised countries would be the trend of exports of manufactures relative to their own requirements and the growth of world trade.

Nevertheless, the very operation of the system would tend to generate a continuous creation of international reserves which would be difficult to control quantitatively, and which could undoubtedly impart an "inflationary bias" to the world economy. The individual "key currency" countries would be more anxious to prevent their currencies from appreciating, and thereby impairing their competitiveness, than to avoid an undue absorption of other currencies; they would also be more ready to extend swap facilities to other central banks to enable them to deal with adverse speculative movements against their currencies rather than to allow these other countries' exchange rates to fall. Hence with the passage of time each of the main central banks would acquire more ample reserves in the form of balances and swap facilities of other currencies; this would make it (politically) more difficult to deal with domestic inflationary pressures arising from insufficient taxation and the expansion of credit.

It was no doubt the fear of accelerating world inflation which made some governments (particularly that of France) so anxious to restore "convertibility" as soon as possible—that is to say, to impose a universal obligation on central banks to settle their balances with each other in some "international reserve asset" of which there is only a fixed total quantity, and which can only be augmented annually by a limited amount agreed in advance.

Everyone has been in agreement (since the current negotiations on monetary reform started) that this international reserve asset cannot be a trading currency such as the dollar, but must be something in terms of which all currencies (including the dollar) can be varied in value. Most governments are also agreed that the problem could not be solved by restoring gold to the role of the primary reserve asset. Apart from other considerations, such a move to restore gold to its historic role would require a very large revaluation of gold in terms of commodities; this would present an enormous unrequited gain to the central banks of the few rich countries which hold most of the monetary gold, as well as to private gold hoarders; it would also bring a large redistribution of world income in favour of the main gold producers, South Africa and the U.S.S.R.

Hence the new reserve asset must be a new creation—some

form of a credit balance with the International Monetary Fund, such as Special Drawing Rights at present, which, once created, cannot disappear; even if some of it were issued in connection with the making of a loan, it would not be cancelled through the re-payment of that loan. This primary reserve asset would be more akin therefore to the "bancor" of the original Keynes plan for an international currency union which envisaged that each member country be given an initial quantity of it; any reduction of which for any single country (through an excess of payments over receipts) would automatically swell the balances of other member countries.

In the meetings of the Committee of Twenty the main discussion has tended to circumvent the issue of how this asset should be defined (what, if any, real assets should be behind it) and how its supply should be regulated. The main discussion has concerned itself with the safeguards which the United States would require before it could reassume the obligation of convertibility, and the obligations which the creditor countries would accept in return for this. At first the Americans insisted on an automatic obligation by the surplus countries to revalue their currencies whenever their total stock of "primary" assets exceeded certain critical levels. This was quite unacceptable to the Europeans, especially since the rise in these assets may largely reflect speculative factors which are only indirectly influenced, and by no means strictly related, to surpluses earned on current transactions. Indeed the Europeans were strongly opposed to any automatic obligation to alter their par values under certain conditions; and it is not at all obvious why the aim of maintaining general equilibrium in international payments could not be just as well secured by unilateral changes in the par values of deficit countries without simultaneous adjustment of an opposite sign in the par values of surplus countries. However, at the last meeting of the Committee of Twenty in Washington both sides adopted more conciliatory positions. The French—who were the main opponents of the American approach—were ready to concede that persistent "surplus" countries should be subject to penalties (in the form of negative interest on excess holdings of primary assets, non-participation in new allocations of such assets, and even the automatic inconvertibility of reserves

in foreign currencies in case of excess holdings), while the Americans appeared less insistent on the multilateral adjustment of parities (as against unilateral adjustment) in cases of payments disequilibrium. Hence this last meeting ended in a highly optimistic mood since agreement appeared to be in sight *on the major issues so far discussed*.

However, this optimism may simply have been due to the fact that the really critical issues have not yet come up for discussion. The first of these concerns the nature and distribution of the new "primary reserve asset". The idea originally canvassed was that existing official holdings of various currencies should be converted into S.D.R.s, which would be backed by corresponding long-term obligations of the (debtor) reserve currency countries. This procedure, however, would not provide the United States with an initial stock of such primary assets, and could not therefore achieve the major objective of restoring the convertibility of the dollar. The original U.S. view seems to have envisaged that the restoration of dollar convertibility would come into effect only after a period in which the United States (thanks to the recent currency realignments) would be in continual surplus in its balance of payments and thereby accumulate an adequate stock of the primary assets. This, however, would mean putting off the introduction of the new system to an uncertain date in the future, particularly as rising U.S. expenditures on oil imports and other commodities may for a long time offset the benefits of increased exports.

The alternative course, of making a special issue of S.D.R.s to the United States (and possibly also to Britain) of a sufficient size to enable it to operate convertibility in advance of any dramatic improvement in its balance of payments, would not be easy to justify politically. It is also difficult to see just what could be achieved by it. For it would mean the continuation of the existing system under another guise—the surplus countries, instead of accumulating dollars, would be accumulating "chits" issued to the United States to serve as a substitute for dollars. So long as the stock of "chits" lasted, the situation would be no different from what it is now. If and when the stock of "chits" were exhausted, there would be nothing to prevent a future U.S. President from suspending chit-convertibility, in the same way as President

Nixon suspended gold-convertibility (indeed, if chits, being less prestigious objects than gold, go on being used in settlement of debts until their stock is *literally* exhausted, the future U.S. President could suspend convertibility with a better conscience and even less hesitation).

PAPER GOLD MINES

But in whatever way the initial issue of the new assets is distributed (and it is increasingly recognised that there is little need or justification for converting the existing dollar balances, as distinct from newly accruing balances, into primary assets) this does not settle the question of how *additional* supplies are to be brought into existence. Under the old gold standard countries *acquired* additional gold, not as a gift, but through surpluses of exports over imports. In other words the gold-absorbing countries paid for it in goods and services of equivalent value which ultimately constituted the incomes earned in the form of wages, profits, royalties etc., of the gold producers. The equivalent under the new dispensation would be to endow the poorest countries of the world (there is obviously no justification to make such gifts to the rich countries) with imaginary gold mines—with "paper gold" mines—and to pay them the equivalent of so much gold per year, on condition that they use the money for employing people on the same sort of scale as if they were producing gold, but on socially more useful projects, such as making ditches, canals, irrigation works, dams, etc. This proposal, known as the "link", has met with a great deal of opposition by the rich countries (particularly America and Germany) on the ground that it would constitute a vast automatic charity operation which, unlike real gold production—which requires a lot of toil and sweat—might have a thoroughly demoralising effect on the recipients. And, needless to say, its annual distribution amongst the poor—how much "imaginary gold" each country is deemed to have produced—would give rise to endless quarrels and wrangles.

Another possibility—which is too radical to have yet been given any serious attention—is to issue the new money, not against imaginary goods, but in payment for real goods—in other words

to use it to finance world-wide "intervention boards" for maintaining the world prices of basic commodities—such as wheat, rice, sugar, cotton, wool, copper, tin, etc., etc.—at stable minimum levels in terms of primary reserve assets.[1] This would have several important advantages. First, the additional international money would come into existence as additional income of the world's primary producers—irrespective of whether they are situated in rich or poor countries (though the benefit of the primary producers of the rich countries will of course be smaller if they already obtain higher-than-world-prices on account of price support schemes, like the Common Agricultural Policy). Secondly, it would come into existence only to the extent necessary to prevent world prices from falling—it would therefore not "finance" inflation, since in times of rising world prices (such as the present) no additional money would be issued. Thirdly, the additional income of the primary producers would generate additional demand for industrial goods, thereby stepping up the rate of growth of world industrial production to the maximum extent consistent with the growth of supplies of primary products at stable prices. Since the labour and capital required for industrial production in the world is almost indefinitely expandable, this aspect again would not be inflationary, since it would serve to increase production, not prices.

Finally, it would ensure that industrialised countries devalued their currencies in terms of the international unit only to the extent that the benefits gained thereby through higher exports more than offset the deterioration of the terms of trade of the manufactured goods which they export in terms of the primary products, food and raw materials, which are directly or indirectly embodied in their exports. At the present time the "real" cost of devaluation may be very different in case of a large country than a small one, and much of the prevailing hostility to devaluations (or floating rates) as an instrument of balance of payments adjustments stems from the feeling that the very use of this instrument discriminates in favour of the powerful country with large markets and to the detriment of the smaller countries. When the pound went off gold

[1] A rather more ambitious proposal for an I.M.F. composite-commodity reserve currency was put before the 1964 U.N.C.T.A.D. Conference by A. G. Hart, J. Tinbergen and myself but failed to attract attention in official discussions. The present article puts forward a modified version which (I hope) will appear more feasible.

in 1931, all important suppliers of the United Kingdom devalued alongside—with the result that Britain gained a competitive edge over the industrial countries which remained under the gold standard without paying any price for it in terms of a deterioration in its terms of trade. In the same way, the recent spectacular fall in the dollar in terms of the European currencies means very little to the United States in terms of a deterioration of the terms of trade, since the great bulk of its suppliers of the "inputs" of industry, domestic or foreign, remain tied to the dollar. In the case of a smaller industrial country (including the United Kingdom in present circumstances) any deterioration of the exchange rate automatically raises the cost of the food and the raw materials consumed in the process of producing the manufactured goods which are exported. But when the international reserve asset has a stable value in terms of basic commodities—irrespective of its conversion ratios into individual currencies—devaluation invariably involves the *same* real cost, whether the devaluing country is large or small; and any temptation to indulge in "competitive devaluation" for the sake of gaining undue trading advantages is very greatly lessened.

ANOTHER INTRACTABLE PROBLEM

But whichever method of creating a new international reserve asset is adopted, a new system of convertible currencies with fixed par values—which are adjustable only in cases of basic disequilibrium as shown by agreed indicators—faces a seemingly intractable problem which did not exist on any previous occasion when a new international monetary arrangement was brought into being. This stems from the vast amount of non-official liquid funds, held in the form of bank balances or short-term financial assets, which have accumulated with the growth of the giant international companies and of the unspendable surpluses of the oil-producing countries of the Middle East, and which are still growing at an alarming rate. A recent U.S. estimate puts the liquid assets of all large international conglomerates, American and foreign, at around $250 billion, half of which is in cash or short-term paper like treasury bills, and half of it in inventories, debts receivable,

etc., against which money can be borrowed. The Eurocurrency market consisting of non-resident currency holdings of all kinds amounts to $130 billion; the extent of the overlap between these two magnitudes is unknown, but either of these magnitudes taken singly is very large in relation to the total *gross* currency reserves of I.M.F. members (of $176 billion at March 1973). Their shiftability across frontiers in response to anticipations of exchange rate adjustment has been amply proved by recent experience. Nothing of this sort existed in the 1920s when the gold standard was restored, in 1935 when the Tripartite Agreement was introduced, or in 1946 when Bretton Woods was conceived. The only analogy to such a vast accumulation of unofficial liquidity was the post-war situation in Germany prior to the currency reform of 1948: the legacy of the war left a huge overhang of spending power which had to be eliminated (by cancelling-nine tenths of all existing financial assets) before a free market economy could be restored.

It is possible that the ultimate solution of the world monetary problem will require a similar once-and-for all surgical operation. But just because the excess money is world-wide, and takes the form of both resident and non-resident balances in a whole host of currencies and not just in dollars, it boggles the imagination even to conceive of the kind of international action that would be required to deal with it.

6

INTERNATIONAL MONETARY REFORM:
THE NEED FOR A NEW APPROACH[1]

UNTIL it was overshadowed by the more acute crisis caused by the threat to oil supplies, the Western world lived in the shadow of a continuing crisis in its international monetary system. And there was general agreement that we urgently needed a new world monetary order, prescribing new rules that will be universally followed and which will provide a remedy to the shortcomings of the system of Bretton Woods.

The three main aspects of the currency problem which were successively felt as endangering the growth and stability of the world economy were the following:

(1) Chronic payments inbalances;
(2) The difficulties in the so-called "adjustment process", particularly felt by the U.S.;
(3) Steadily accelerating inflation in terms of all Western currencies, accompanied by an explosive increase in central bank reserves in the form of reserve currency holdings.

In my view, the current official discussions in the so-called Committee of Twenty and the results of which were reflected in the first *Outline of Reform* have not been on the right lines and they are unlikely to provide a fundamental solution to any of the three problems mentioned above. Indeed, they are likely to get bogged down in the endless complexity of provisions which the proposed structure generates.

The proposals aim at re-establishing a universal obligation of convertibility in terms of a "primary reserve asset" which is in-

[1] A lecture delivered in the Banca d'Italia, Rome, 12 December 1973, and published (in Italian) in *Bancaria*, March 1974.

tended to be a purely artificial creation. The unit is to be defined in terms of an average of either a comprehensive list of currencies or of a selected number of such currencies, but without being convertible into any of them by the issuing authority.

The basic conception is to establish S.D.R.s as the main, if not the sole, reserve asset, which would replace both gold and reserve currency holdings as instruments of international liquidity. It is generally understood that in order to attain its objective, there must be effective provision for a global limitation on the amount of S.D.R.s in existence and on the rate of creation of new S.D.R.s over time; equally, there must be some provision which would prevent central banks from settling their balances with one another in terms of other media—as, for example, in terms of reserve currency balances—and there by circumventing the discipline of settling in a medium the outstanding quantity of which is strictly limited.

It is clear from the Committee's published *Outline* that the Committee has not yet faced up to the main issues involved in its own general conception: the question of how global liquidity in all its forms is to be regulated; how countries will be compelled to hold their reserves in S.D.R.s in preference to other reserve assets, or at least, to hold a certain minimum proportion of their total reserves in S.D.R.s (which would come to much the same thing); how the original issue of S.D.R.s is to be settled and how subsequent issues are to be regulated. It is evident that the Committee has so far mainly concerned itself with the rules and regulations concerning the automatic indicators to be employed for changing the exchange rate, downwards or upwards; when and how to float; when and how to deflate the internal economy so as to avoid either devaluation or floating; how these rules can be made symmetrical to both surplus and deficit countries; and how the "currency basket" of which the S.D.R. is to be a nominal equivalent is to be defined.

Such elaborate rules would never work in practice, except perhaps in relation to weak or to small countries. And here lies the basic injustice involved in any artificial paper system. Take the case, for example, of what would have happened if the new system had already been in operation now, and the western countries

were suddenly asked to pay three times as much, or four times as much, for oil. Clearly, they would not be able to meet the requirements of settling their balances in S.D.R.s. Hence they would be tempted to suspend S.D.R. convertibility—in much the same way as America suspended gold convertibility on 15 August, 1971. If this happened, the whole laboriously built system would collapse. In order to avert this danger no doubt large emergency issues of S.D.R.s would have been made to make it possible to settle the accounts with the Arab countries in terms of the accepted international unit. But if a small country found itself in the same kind of emergency situation—for example, on account of the failure of its main export crop, or for some other reason peculiar to that country—it might face severe penalties if it attempted to break the rules; it certainly could not expect the whole system to accommodate itself to it, as would be the case when large and powerful countries were involved. In my view, it is inevitable with any such system, whatever the built-in safeguards to ensure symmetry and impartiality, that the powerful countries would, *de facto*, receive a different and more favourable treatment than the small countries.

Moreover, whilst the purpose of the new system is to impose more severe disciplines on *individual* countries, there is really nothing in the system to avoid a perpetual and growing inflation—not of any individual country, but of the group of leading countries as a whole. For when the major countries tolerate inflation, it is almost inevitable that the others will "toe the line": if for no other reason, in order to preserve their own efficiency and competitiveness.

What we need is a system under which each country is perfectly free to take whatever measures it deems desirable to adjust its own balance of payments—in other words, to be free to deflate or devalue, or to do so by an adjustment to a new pegged rate, or through floating—provided that it is ready to bear the cost of the adjustment, and does not throw that cost on to other countries. This is precisely what is not likely to happen under an S.D.R. system. For under that system the true cost of any such adjustment is necessarily dependent on the nature and extent of similar adjustments made by other countries. For example, let us suppose that

the United States, having an adverse balance of payments, devalues its own currency in terms of the S.D.R. This increases the
competitiveness of U.S. goods if other countries stay put. But if
other countries followed suit—so that, in the end they all devalued
in terms of S.D.R.s—the net effect would be zero. Hence, to
make the system work, one needs an elaborate set of rules to
decide in what circumstances one country should be free to,
or else should be made to, adjust its exchange rate, and how
and when other countries should be allowed, or not allowed,
to react to this by making exchange rate changes of their
own.

It must be remembered that as between industrialised countries
—and the question of using variations of the exchange rate as an
instrument of adjustment is really only important in relation to
such countries—the effects and the costs of devaluation as between
major or minor countries may be very different. In this connection, one should recall the experience of the United Kingdom
when it devalued in 1931. Most of her suppliers of food and raw
materials kept their exchange rates unchanged in terms of sterling.
Hence by devaluing she lowered the price of her exports in relation
to her industrial competitors, but not in relation to the prices of
food and raw materials which she was importing.

In these circumstances, devaluation gives a costless benefit to
the devaluing country. It *gains* in relation to its competitors without having to incur a *cost* by making its goods cheaper in terms of
the things which it buys. But if a small industrial country did the
same thing, its position would be different. It would have to purchase its advantage of higher competitiveness at the cost of lowering the prices of its own products in terms of the goods for which
they are exchanged.

ADVANTAGES OF A COMMODITY STANDARD
VERSUS A PAPER STANDARD

Most of the problems sketched out above would not arise if a
new international currency were created which is directly convertible into basic commodities, in much the same way in which under
a gold standard, or under a bi-metallic standard, paper currency

was convertible into precious metals. A commodity S.D.R. could not, of course, be made as rigid as the gold standard had been in the past, or the old bi-metallic standard. The unit could not be *defined* in terms of ounces (or tons) of specified grades of various commodities without making the system unnecessarily rigid and complicated. But it would be possible to make the issue of S.D.R.s and the variation of the total amount of S.D.R.s outstanding as part of a world-wide operation of stabilising the prices of the main primary products.

This would be the case if an International Commodity Corporation were set up which would be entrusted with the task of stabilising the prices of the main basic products—foodstuffs, metals, fibres, etc.—by holding (either directly or through subsidiaries) buffer stocks of all the major commodities suitable for storage and which are both essential either for personal consumption or as inputs in industrial processes, and also are produced competitively in a number of different regions of the globe. The Corporation would be under the control of an international monetary authority, such as the I.M.F., and would have fixed buying and selling prices with a margin of say 5 per cent. between them in terms of S.D.R.s. The Corporation would pay for net purchases in S.D.R.s and would demand S.D.R.s in payment of its net sales of commodities. In this way the whole of the outstanding issue of international currency would be "backed" by stocks of commodities, and the net purchases by the Corporation would cause an equivalent increase in the amount of S.D.R.s in circulation, whilst the net sale of commodities would cause a corresponding decrease. Thus world liquidity would increase whenever the current rate of world production of primary products exceeded their consumption; it would decrease when consumption exceeded production. But in contrast to the existing system which "allocates" S.D.R.s to individual central banks according to certain quotas, the international money would directly generate additional income as it came into existence: in the same way as under the old gold standard, any addition to the stock of monetary gold out of new production generated income of a corresponding value to the gold producers (in the form of wages, profits, etc.) the spending of which caused the current account receipts of the recipient coun-

tries to exceed their current outlays; thus adding to the level of effective demand of the countries whose gold reserves had been increased thereby.

It is not envisaged—nor is it necessary for the satisfactory operation of the scheme—that the buying and selling prices of individual commodities should not be capable of adjustment relative to each other. While the Commodity Corporation would be instructed to keep the price level of the group of commodities under its control as stable as possible, this need not exclude provisions for the downward adjustment of both the buying and selling price of any particular commodity whose stock/turnover ratio had shown, over some minimum period, a faster rate of growth than the average, or of an upward adjustment whenever the stock/turnover ratio decreased relative to the average for more than a certain length of time.

A system of this kind would have three important advantages:

(1) Since exchange rate adjustment as a means of improving competitiveness in exports is mainly relevant in relation to the industrialised countries who export manufactured goods, a commodity standard would ensure that any industrial exporter who devalues its currency in terms of the international standard bears the same real cost irrespective of whether it is a large or small country: for in each case the price of the "value added" by manufacture is lowered in the same manner in relation to the prices of industrial inputs or of food (which is the basic wage-good of industrial workers). It can, therefore, be expected that countries will only devalue their currencies in terms of the international unit to the extent that the benefits gained thereby through higher exports more than offset the costs in the form of a deterioration of their terms of trade.

(2) The advantages of stabilising the prices of raw materials are well known. In competitive markets these prices tend to fluctuate by very large amounts: as many studies have shown, the average annual fluctuation may be in the range of 50 per cent. or more. The experience of producing countries which stabilise internal prices by means of Marketing Boards (which buy up supplies at a fixed price) has been that the very stabilisation of the price has generally been followed by considerable increase in production on

account of the reduction in risks involved. This is particularly so in the case of agricultural products. But, in the present inflationary world, there is also an important parallel advantage of possessing an international liquid asset—a reserve unit which serves as a store of value as well as a medium of settlement between central banks—which is itself *stable* in terms of commodities. Countries whose domestic price levels rise as a result of inflation would have to devalue their currencies in terms of the international unit. But there would be enormous benefits from the mere existence of a unit which is stable in real terms, irrespective of the degree of inflation and the generality of the inflation of individual countries. (By contrast under the proposed S.D.R. system, if all countries inflated, the value of the S.D.R. unit in terms of goods would fall in much the same way as the value of any national currency in terms of goods. There would be no currency unit which is proof against inflation.)

(3) The third and perhaps most important advantage is that a system under which all the important commodities can be sold at fixed prices to an international commodity reserve corporation, would ensure that world industrialisation, and therefore world economic development, proceeds to the maximum extent which is sustainable in view of the increase in the availabilities of primary products.

In the last analysis, this would be the most important benefit derived from an international commodity reserve currency, but also one that is the most difficult to explain. Taking the world economy as a whole, economic growth can only proceed if there is a certain harmony between the expansion of food and raw material production and the expansion of the industrial or processing activities which absorb the raw materials and food produced by the primary sectors of the world economy and convert them into finished goods.

This harmony is threatened whenever (1) industrial expansion runs ahead of the raw material base: that is to say if the demand for raw materials and goods increases faster than their production, which can lead to a crisis situation, attended by sharp increases in the price of food and raw materials. (There are some signs that the world has reached such a stage in the last two years, quite

apart from artificial scarcities as in the case of oil.) (2) in the opposite case, when the raw material base "runs ahead" of the growth of industrial absorption of raw materials, which would cause a collapse in raw material prices which in the past has normally tended to bring industrial stagnation in its wake (as for example, during the great Depression after 1929).

The important thing to bear in mind is that over a longer period world industrial production cannot be constrained either by the shortage of labour or of capital, because both the amount of labour employed in industry and the capital invested in industry can be increased almost indefinitely in response to the incentive of increasing demand. Few would quarrel with the proposition that the world supply of labour is almost unlimited. It is only a question of activating it, either by moving labour to areas of labour shortage, or by moving capital to areas of labour surpluses. When countries like Germany or Switzerland "outgrow" their own labour supplies, a situation is created in which there are more places of employment in industry than men available, the remedy is found (to a greater or lesser extent depending only on political hesitations) in the consequential inflow of foreign labour drawn from labour surplus areas. In other cases the consequence of labour shortages is a transfer of industrial activity to areas where large labour reserves exist and wages are low. (This happened recently on a large scale in the Far East: in countries like Hong Kong, Taiwan, Korea, Singapore etc., all of which had rapid increases in industrial employment due to foreign firms opening up branches to produce parts and components in commodities which were then exported for assembly into finished goods in the industrial countries in which the parent firms are situated.) But whether the movement is that of labour or capital, it is clear that under-utilised labour exists in sufficiently large quantities to rule out the possibility that world industrial production can be constrained by the quantity of labour.

Equally, in the case of capital, it must be emphasised that industrial capital is largely financed out of business profits and capital accumulation proceeds *in response* to investment opportunities: the growth of demand for industrial output is normally followed by increased investment and a faster rate of growth of

capital. It is not possible to say therefore that capital accumulation is confined by an exogenous savings constraint, any more than the growth of employment can be said to be confined by the available world population.

In this situation, if the world were rationally organised, the only true constraint on the growth of world industrial production would be the availability of basic materials and food. But with the present system of the organisation of markets where the world prices of basic products tend to move violently up and down in response to relatively small variations of the volume of stocks carried in relation to turnover (resulting from discrepancies—sometimes only minor discrepancies—between the flow of production and consumption) the growth in the output in primary products itself tends to be checked by the fluctuation in demand emanating from the industrial regions and of unfavourable changes in the terms of trade. If one could establish a system which gives the primary producers a steadily growing income in terms of international currency, and one that is proportionate to the physical growth of production, so that the primary producers' purchasing power for industrial goods increases proportionately to the increase in the output of primary products, then the growth of demand for industrial goods emanating from the primary sectors of the world economy would set up multiplier and accelerator effects which would ensure that the (technologically determined) maximum growth of primary production determines the rate of growth of industrialisation, and not the other way round.

Whether in the long run it is a good thing or a bad thing for mankind that world economic growth should be accelerated to the maximum feasible extent is a question that is perhaps open to debate. But given the objectives of maximum economic prosperity there can be little doubt that a commodity reserve standard as an international reserve currency would be an ideal instrument for promoting that end.

7

THE EFFECT OF DEVALUATIONS ON TRADE IN MANUFACTURES[1]

IN the course of the 1960s there was a growing conviction in a number of countries that the international monetary system of general convertibility and fixed exchange rates laid down at Bretton Woods did not provide a satisfactory mechanism for securing a continuing equilibrium in the balance of international payments. Some countries—notably Germany—were in a chronic state of surplus on current account which was not offset by long-term capital investment abroad and led instead to an accumulation of liquid reserves, mainly in the form of dollar balances. The United States, after a long period during which she was in a chronic surplus position leading to the "world dollar shortage" which many economists regarded as a permanent feature of the capitalist world,[2] settled into a deficit position on "basic transactions" after 1951 (with its current account surplus more than offset by its net outflow on account of aid and foreign investment) and later, in the course of the 1960s, she was gradually brought into a deficit on current account as well. Britain was also in a deficit on "basic transactions" with her net foreign investment (mainly in the form of direct investment) largely financed by the accumulation of sterling balances or other forms of short-term borrowing; in addition, in years of relatively fast expansion, her current account was usually also in deficit.

These trends had their counterpart, or origin, in the differing experiences of the leading industrial countries in their export trade in manufactures. As a result of trade liberalisation and successive

[1] Written in 1977 and not previously published. I am indebted to Mr. John Rhodes, of the Department of Applied Economics, Cambridge, and Mr. I. F. Edwards, of the Treasury, for their assistance in the preparation of the tables.

[2] Cf. e.g. G. D. H. MacDougall, *The World Dollar Problem*, London, 1957.

E

reductions in tariffs under the G.A.T.T. world trade in manufactures began to expand (from the mid-1950s onwards) at a faster rate than world manufacturing output. The share of world industrial output moving across national frontiers thus began to rise, in contrast to the forty years preceding World War II which was marked by increasing "self-sufficiency" (or autarchy) among the industrial countries.

However, the rate of growth of exports of the different countries was very uneven. There were some countries (of which Germany and Japan, and up to the mid-1960s Italy, were the most conspicuous) whose exports of manufactures rose a great deal faster than their manufacturing production, and whose share in a fast-expanding world trade was continually rising.[1] This process was accompanied by a growing uncompetitiveness of the U.S. and the U.K. in relation to other industrial countries as measured by the relative movement of "efficiency wages" (or unit labour costs) in terms of dollars, as well as by the relative movement of export prices (or rather export unit values).[2] There was a widely accepted view that Britain and America, as the two reserve currency countries, were not subject to the same balance of payments "disciplines" as the others, and this caused them (or enabled them) to follow more "inflationary" policies.

However, on any non-tautological definition of the term "inflation" this was not correct. The level of prices in the United States (as measured by the index of consumer prices) showed a smaller rate of increase in the post-Korean period than in any of the other countries; in the case of the United Kingdom, the rate of inflation of consumer prices was somewhat higher than in the case of the U.S. or of Germany, but a great deal lower than in some of the fast expanding countries like Japan, Italy or France. What is more relevant, the rate of increase of money wages was also lower in the U.S. and the U.K. than in the countries with a fast rate of growth of exports.[3] The reason why the two reserve

---

[1] Between 1956 and 1976 the share of world trade of manufactures of Germany, Japan and Italy rose from 26 to 42 per cent and the share of the U.S. and U.K. fell from 44 to 26 per cent, while the share of the remaining industrial exporters increased slightly from 30 to 32 per cent.

[2] For the period 1953–62, see the tables printed on pp. 45–46 above. For later periods see Tables 1–2 below.

[3] As shown by a comparison of columns (2) and (5) in Table 3, p. 46 above.

currency countries became increasingly uncompetitive (as measured by the movement of relative unit costs and export prices) is that their *productivity* per man-hour grew so much more slowly than that of the fast growing countries—a difference which in the case of the U.K., Germany, Italy and Japan at any rate may itself have been caused by, or at least reinforced by, their comparative success or failure in export performance.[1]

Hence from the early 1960s there were numerous advocates of a more prompt and more frequent use of exchange rate adjustment as a means of ensuring harmonious development of the production and trade of the different industrial countries. The protagonists of more frequent adjustments in relative exchange rates were reinforced by the success of the two devaluations of the French franc in 1957 and 1958 which ushered in a period of a more rapid and stable progress in France. However, the two countries which chiefly benefited from increasing competitiveness and fast growing exports were not unnaturally disinclined to put these advantages at risk by upward revision of their exchange rates,[2] and the two countries with over-valued currencies felt inhibited from devaluing on account of their reserve currency role.[3] There was also the difficulty (in the case of the United States) that a change in the par value of the dollar in terms of gold would not in practice have achieved the object of cheapening the dollar in terms of other currencies since all other countries were anxious to follow the dollar in any increase in the official price of gold. This latter difficulty was only overcome by President Nixon in 1971 through

---

[1] As I wrote in a paper published in 1964: "in the light of the experience of . . . the last decade it is a matter of doubt whether the maintenance of . . . steady expansion in international trade is really compatible with a system of fixed exchange rates or not. There is no assurance that under fixed exchange rates differences in the relationship of 'efficiency wages' will call forth forces of adjustment tending to eliminate them; it is quite possible that the underlying forces at work would operate, for prolonged periods if not permanently, in a contrary direction." (See p. 39, above.)

[2] Germany, after a great deal of pressure, did undertake a modest revaluation (together with Holland) of 5 per cent. in 1961, but resisted any further move—despite a vast inflow of speculative funds which (rightly or wrongly) greatly worried the German monetary authorities—until 1969.

[3] The U.K. did devalue in 1949 (by 30 per cent) without any great ill-effects on the reserve role of sterling, but also without any visible benefits on exports: the rate of growth of exports in the years 1951 to 1959 was only 1½ per cent. per annum, as against 15 per cent. in the years 1946–50. The explanation must be sought in the over-loading of the U.K. economy (particularly the engineering industry) following upon the vast re-armament programme after the outbreak of the Korean war and the increased priority given to personal consumption (as against investment and exports) after the return of the Conservative Government in 1951.

the suspension of the gold convertibility of the dollar accompanied by the imposition of a 10 per cent. surcharge on all manufactured imports as a bargaining counter for a general adjustment of relative exchange rates.

Inhibitions of both Conservative and Labour Governments in Britain (together with U.S. pressures) postponed the devaluation of the pound until 1967, and then only to a new fixed rate which was 14·3 per cent. lower.[1] A general readjustment of the official par values was only reached in the Smithsonian agreement in December 1971 and this was short-lived since, with the renewed pressures caused by vast speculative flows of hot money, the Smithsonian parities were abandoned in early 1973, since when most currencies have followed a régime of "managed" floating rates, i.e. the rates being free to move up or down in the market without any pre-announced limits, but subject to discretionary official intervention (at varying degrees in different times and in different countries).

These events brought about vast changes in the exchange rates of the currencies of major industrial countries in relation to each other—not just nominally, but also in "real terms", i.e. after allowing for differences in the changes in labour costs per unit of output in terms of local currencies. But contrary to the general expectation they failed to bring about any large change in the relative position of "surplus" and "deficit" countries. At first this was attributed to time lags, but the periods that have elapsed since large changes in international cost-relationships occurred (particularly in the relation between the U.S. and other industrial countries) have now become too long for this to remain a plausible explanation.

The relative movements of exchange rates, relative labour costs and export performance as between selected years in the period 1956–76 are shown in Table 1. The table shows, over the period as a whole, a "perverse" relationship between changes in "competitiveness" as measured by the relative change in labour costs per unit of output and changes in export performance.[2] This

---

[1] Allowing for the simultaneous withdrawal of subsidies on wages and rebates for various indirect taxes, the effective nominal devaluation (i.e. without taking into account consequential effects on wages, productivity etc.) was only 11.3 per cent.

[2] As measured by the change in a country's share in world exports of manufactures.

appears to be true for the period as a whole, and is more pronounced for the period 1970–76 despite widespread changes in
relative exchange rates in an "equilibrating" direction. As the
table shows, the two countries, the U.S. and the U.K., which
suffered a steady decline in their share of world trade had become
more competitive as measured by changes in relative labour costs

Table 1

INDEX NUMBERS OF TRADE-WEIGHTED EXCHANGE RATES AND OF
UNIT LABOUR COSTS IN DOLLAR TERMS AND PERCENTAGE EXPORT
SHARES OF MANUFACTURES (SELECTED YEARS 1956–76).

	1956	1960	1965	1970	1975	1976
United Kingdom						
Exchange Rate[1] (1956=100)	100	106	105	89	68	59
Relative Costs[2] (1956=100)	100	110	109	101	101	94
Export Share of manufactured						
goods[3]	18·7	15·9	13·5	10·8	9·3	8·7
United States						
Exchange Rate	100	106	105	108	87	94
Relative Costs	100	104	85	80	51	55
Export Share	25·5	21·7	20·5	18·5	17·7	17·3
West Germany						
Exchange Rate	100	106	113	128	178	185
Relative Costs	100	116	135	146	165	163
Export Share	16·5	19·7	19·2	19·8	20·3	20·6
Japan						
Exchange Rate	100	105	104	106	111	119
Relative Costs	100	87	87	105	132	136
Export Share	5·7	6·9	9·4	11·7	13·6	14·6
France						
Exchange Rate	100	71	70	62	69	66
Relative Costs	100	79	75	67	80	79
Export Share	7·9	9·7	8·8	8·7	10·2	9·8
Italy						
Exchange Rate	100	105	104	106	85	69
Relative Costs	100	94	107	104	119	108
Export Share	3·6	5·2	6·8	7·2	7·5	7·1

[1] For each country an index of average exchange rates was divided by a trade
weighted index of the average annual exchange rates of the other five countries,
weighted by 1970 export shares.

[2] For each country unit labour costs in dollars (manufacturing earnings divided by
indices of trends in productivity) are divided by the weighted average of the unit
labour costs of the other five countries—the weights in each case being determined by
the export shares of each country in 1970.

[3] Each country's share of the value of manufactured exports of major developed
market economies, in U.S. dollars. "Special category" exports are excluded in the
case of the U.S.

Source: O.E.C.D. data on earnings and productivity, U.N. data on export shares and
I.M.F. data on exchange rates.

per unit of output[1] while the countries (West Germany, Japan and Italy) which increased their share substantially had rising relative labour costs (which were highest in the case of West Germany but pretty substantial also in the case of Japan from 1970 onwards).[2]

On these figures there thus appears to be a negative correlation between changes in export shares and in competitiveness. The reason for such a negative correlation can only be that the true causal relationship is the other way round: the changes in exchange rates and in "competitiveness" as conventionally measured were not the cause, but the consequence of differing *trends* in the market shares of different industrial countries, and the "trends" themselves must then be due to factors not susceptible to measurement.

This view finds further confirmation in Table 2 which presents an inter-country comparison of the longer-term relationship between the proportionate percentage changes in relative unit labour costs and of the relative prices of exports (or rather of export unit values) in manufacturing on the one hand and of the proportionate percentage changes in the value of exports of manufactures as measured in dollar terms. (By taking a relatively long period, the impact of time lags should be minimised. The twelve years 1963–75 was found to be the longest series for which all three sets of figures are available.)

The theoretical expectation is that the figures in the first two columns should be of the same sign while those in the third column should be of the opposite sign—i.e. that an improvement in competitiveness should manifest itself in a reduction in relative

---

[1] As the table shows, the U.K. made only a modest gain of 15 per cent between 1965 and 1976 in relative unit labour costs at the cost of a very large reduction of 46 per cent. in its trade-weighted exchange rate, whereas in the case of the U.S. a relatively modest fall in the (trade-weighted) exchange rate of 11 per cent. over the same period was accompanied by a 35 per cent. improvement in its (trade-weighted) relative labour costs. The explanation is that the U.S. had a lower rate of inflation than other countries, and owing to its high degree of self-sufficiency, the feed-back of any given depreciation of the exchange rate on domestic costs and prices was relatively small.

[2] It is also interesting to observe that the joint loss of the two trade-losing countries was roughly equal to the gain of the three trade-gaining countries for the period as a whole, and also for the periods of 1956–60 and 1960–65. However, in the period of 1965–70 the loss of shares of the U.K. and the U.S. exceeded the gain of the three gaining countries, while in 1970–76 it was the other way round. To that extent the currency realignments seem to have had *some* effect in slowing down the loss of market shares of the losers and moderating the gain in share of the gainers.

unit labour costs as well as in export prices,[1] and this should be associated with an improvement in export performance (by the test of the share of exports in world trade), and *vice versa* in the case of a fall in competitiveness. Of the eleven countries shown,

Table 2

LONG-RUN RELATIONSHIP OF CHANGES IN COMPETIVENESS AND CHANGES IN TRADE PERFORMANCE IN MANUFACTURES 1963–1975

Percentage Changes in

Country	Relative Labour Costs per unit of output	Relative Export Prices	Export Shares
United Kingdom	−21·4	−12·4	−37·9
United States	−43·7	−14·1	−17·8
France	− 8·6	+ 4·9	+17·8
West Germany	+42·9	+10·1	+ 3·0
Italy	+24·1	− 9·3	+18·3
Netherlands	−10·5	− 0·5	+19·0
Belgium–Luxemburg	+ 7·2	− 1·8	+ 1·7
Sweden	−10·4	+22·0	+ 8·8
Switzerland	+33·3	+31·7	−11·8
Canada	−22·3	−13·3	+ 2·3
Japan	+27·1	+ 4·5	+72·0

Note: Export prices are obtained by taking official estimates of changes in export unit values of manufactured goods of each country translated into U.S. dollars at current rates of exchange. Equally labour costs per unit of output and export shares are expressed in terms of U.S. dollars. The figures indicate in each column the proportionate percentage changes in the relevant item between the beginning and the end of the period.
Source: As in Table 1.

only three satisfy this criterion: the Netherlands, Switzerland and Canada (the latter only marginally) and it is perhaps more than just a coincidence that these are the countries one would normally regard as "sound" capitalist market economies.[2]

But the others all exhibit perverse behaviour in varying degrees, the U.K. and the U.S. combine falling costs and prices with a loss

---

[1] As is shown by the table, the changes in export prices (with one exception) are numerically always smaller than the changes in labour costs per unit of output, largely because, owing to the nature of competition, it does not pay exporters to reduce prices fully in line with costs (or conversely). In the case of Sweden, which forms the exception to this rule the rise in export prices reflected (in part) changes in the quality of goods exported.

[2] Of the two, the Netherlands shows a big gain in market share over the period, associated with an appreciable fall in unit labour costs, whereas Switzerland shows a big rise in both labour costs and export prices associated with a deteriorating market performance. (Both countries' currencies appreciated relative to the S.D.R.s, but the appreciation of the Swiss franc was nearly twice as great.)

in market shares; with Germany and Japan it is the other way round. Italy combined—apparently—a large rise in unit labour costs with falling export prices to achieve a big rise in her export share, while Sweden achieved a more modest rise in her export share by a combination of falling labour costs and rising export prices.

What these figures reveal is that the customary statistical measures of "competitiveness", whether they be unit labour costs or export prices, are arbitrary and not an adequate indicator of a country's true competitive position. For "export prices" are no more than "export unit values" obtained by dividing the value of exports with the weight of commodities exported in *particular* categories; a rise in export unit values may therefore signify no more than that a country is trading "up-market", i.e. selling machinery of higher quality, while the countries with falling export unit values are trading "down-market" selling machinery of the more primitive kind. There is a great deal of casual evidence that countries like Switzerland, Sweden and West Germany have concentrated on machine tools and precision machinery of the more advanced kind, whereas in the case of Britain, at any rate, exports became more concentrated on machinery of the more simple kinds.

The estimates concerning the movement of relative labour costs of different countries also require to be interpreted with a great deal of caution. The figures are based on official estimates in each country concerning the change in productivity in manufacturing *as a whole*. But in countries with fast rising exports the rate of productivity growth in the export industries is likely to be far ahead of the rate of productivity growth generally—for all the reasons for which the successful fast growing industries are likely to show much greater productivity gains than the average of industries. In countries of relatively slow export growth on the other hand (such as Britain), the estimates of the average rate of productivity growth are more likely to be typical of the export industries as well as of others.

Be that as it may, the fact remains that the instrument of exchange rate adjustment, even when it is successful in reducing the devaluing country's wage level relative to its competitors, can

only serve to improve its *average* efficiency wages in the economy as a whole. The effect of a reduction in the exchange rate by 10 per cent. with a *given* level of money wages is exactly the same as the effect of a general cut in wages by 10 per cent, at a *given* exchange rate. The associated change in real wages after allowing for the consequential change in the level of consumer prices— upwards in one case, downwards in another—should be the same in both cases; and in both cases the reduction of real wages will be greater than that caused by the unfavourable change in the terms of trade—the increase in the price of primary products relative to wages, or in terms of the products of industrial labour —on account of the fact that with either method there will be a rise in the share of profits and a fall in the share of wages in the "value added" by manufacturing. Hence there are limits to the extent to which a policy of improving competitiveness through devaluation can be carried; the limits are given by the extent to which wage-earners are prepared to accept a reduction in the rate of change of real wages. This is clearly more likely to be attainable when the necessary reduction in (relative) real wages[1] involves only a slow-down in the rate of improvement in living standards rather than an absolute cut.

The extent to which the repeated currency realignments of the last ten years have failed to bring about any change in the favourable or unfavourable trends of different countries is best shown by analysing the changes in the bilateral trading relationships of the two main devaluing countries, the U.K. and the U.S., with other industrialised countries, as shown in Tables 3 and 4. In the pre-devaluation years 1963–67 Britain had an appreciable deficit in net trade in manufactures with Germany only; she had a net surplus with Italy, Japan and France and was virtually in balance with the United States. On the latest available figures (1977 first quarter) we were in deficit with all five countries and the biggest deterioration in net trade occurred with the two countries, Germany and Japan, in relation to which the improvement in our competitiveness was among the highest. On the other hand, with the one country in relation to which our competitive-

---

[1] This depends of course also on how fast the real wages of a country's competitors are rising.

ness has suffered a net deterioration of 15 per cent., the
United States, our net balance was no worse in 1976 than in
1963–67.[1]

The most striking evidence of the deterioration of Britain's
position during the last decade resides in the fact that whereas in
1963–67 we were in virtual balance in our trade in manufactured
goods with the five most important industrial competitors—our
exports were £890 million and our imports £918 million—in 1976
we had an import surplus in manufactures of £2,003 million (with
exports £5,756 million and imports £7,759 million) or 35 per cent.
of our exports, despite the fact that in 1963–67 we had virtual full
employment for most of the period, with real G.N.P. rising at the
rate of 2·8 per cent. a year, whereas in 1976 the British economy
was in deep recession with 1¼ million unemployed, and a near
stagnant output, whilst the five competitors were in a strong
recovery phase, with (the weighted average) real G.N.P. rising by
5·9 per cent. in the year.

It has frequently been argued by economists of the orthodox
neo-classical school that Britain suffers from all kinds of restrictions
on market forces which cause her economy to be sluggish in
responding to price or profit incentives. This however is never said
about the United States, and the figures relating to the trading
relationship of the U.S. shown in Table 4, which exhibit very
much the same picture, are therefore of special significance. They
show that in relation to Japan the "real" devaluation as measured
by the index of relative manpower costs was greater in her case
than in the case of the U.K.—a reduction of 48·8 per cent. as
against 26·1 per cent. between 1970 and 1976—yet the deterioration of the net trade balance by 124 per cent. of exports
(i.e. from –187 per cent. to –311 per cent.), while less than that
of the U.K. (which was 178 per cent. over the same period), involved the U.S. in a uniquely unfavourable net trading position.
In relation to Germany also the U.S. shows a greater "real"
devaluation (30·9 per cent. as against 18·4 per cent.) between
1970 and 1976 coupled with an insignificant improvement in net exports (from –70 to –60 per cent.) as against

---

[1] On this see also p. 111 below

Movements of net exports and competitiveness £m. and Index numbers.

	Average 1963–67	1970	1971	1972	1973	1974	1975	1976	First Quarter 1977
USA									
UK Exports	385·2	747·9	876·5	1011·2	1282·9	1474·6	1394·0	2045·6	547·2
UK Imports	419·5	866·2	775·0	828·9	1169·1	1656·2	1700·0	2230·1	694·5
Net UK exports of manufactures (%)	−8·9	15·8	11·6	18·0	8·9	−12·3	−22·0	−9·0	−26·9
Index of unit manpower costs:									
UK/US ratio ($) (*)	109·1 (**)	100·0	109·1	116·1	114·8	125·2	140·5	125·5	n.a.
Germany									
UK Exports	184·5	404·0	426·1	469·4	628·4	798·9	1000·3	1424·9	431·7
UK Imports	248·6	499·5	593·7	776·2	1253·2	1699·7	1744·9	2457·1	782·1
Net UK exports of manufactures (%)	−34·7	23·6	−39·3	−65·4	−99·4	−112·7	−74·3	−72·4	−81·2
Index of unit manpower costs:									
UK/German ratio ($) (*)	113·0 (**)	100·0	97·5	95·3	79·0	82·5	90·1	86·1	n.a.
Italy									
UK Exports	111·5	193·0	336·0	224·8	308·7	416·9	441·0	636·3	209·6
UK Imports	87·3	168·9	203·1	261·0	378·8	527·4	631·0	832·7	282·2
Net UK exports of manufactures (%)	21·7	12·5	39·6	−16·1	−22·7	−26·5	−43·1	−30·9	−34·6
Index of unit manpower costs:									
UK/Italian ratio ($) (*)	121·9 (**)	100·0	99·5	107·8	96·1	88·8	85·5	68·9	n.a.
Japan									
UK Exports	52·5	125·8	134·8	143·0	216·7	263·0	249·0	285·6	95·7
UK Imports	45·3	106·4	167·1	282·8	412·3	531·0	627·0	750·6	234·5
Net UK exports of manufactures (%)	13·7	15·4	−24·0	−97·8	−90·2	−101·9	−151·8	−162·8	−145·0
Index of unit manpower costs:									
UK/Japanese ratio ($) (*)	107·0 (**)	100·0	95·3	86·2	74·9	71·1	71·5	67·9	n.a.
France									
UK Exports	156·6	287·3	336·0	421·2	542·7	757·5	933·6	1363·6	407·3
UK Imports	117·7	229·2	291·1	419·8	632·9	867·3	1058·9	1488·6	449·5
Net UK exports of manufactures (%)	24·8	20·0	13·4	0·3	−16·6	−14·5	−13·4	−9·2	−10·4
Index of unit manpower costs:									
UK/French ratio ($) (*)	96·0 (**)	100·0	103·0	99·5	84·6	91·2	79·7	78·5	n.a.
Index of unit manpower costs:									
UK weighted 1970 competitors ratio ($) (*)	109·0 (**)	100·0	101·0	100·3	88·4	90·4	93·1	86·1	n.a.

(*) 1970=100   (**) Average for 1966   n.a.—not available.

Source: Overseas Trade Statistics of the United Kingdom, S.I.T.C. 5–8. O.E.C.D. estimates of earnings and productivity and I.M.F. data on exchange rates.

Table 4

MOVEMENTS OF NET EXPORTS OF MANUFACTURES AND COMPETITIVENESS IN THE TRADE BETWEEN THE U.S.A. AND THREE MAJOR TRADING PARTNERS

£m. and Index numbers

Year	1967	1968	1969	1970	1971	1972	1973	1974	1975	1976	1977*
U.S.A. and Germany											
Exports	914	1028	1299	1737	1705	1775	2129	2618	2838	3149	864
Imports	1803	2536	2438	2950	3450	4029	4979	5908	4983	5169	1447
Net Exports as percentage of exports	−97%	−146%	−88%	−75%	−102%	−127%	−133%	−126%	−75%	−64%	−67%
Index of unit manpower costs in dollars											
U.S.A./German ratio	100·0	106·9	104·2	91·6	82·6	75·1	63·0	60·4	58·7	63·3	n.a.
U.S.A. and Japan											
Exports	1098	1170	1537	1951	1905	2188	3130	3979	3209	3652	977
Imports	2798	3807	4648	5592	6945	8659	9182	11895	11025	15042	4039
Net Exports as percentage of exports	−154%	−225%	−202%	−187%	−265%	−295%	−193%	−199%	−244%	−311%	−313%
Index of unit manpower costs in dollars											
U.S.A./Japan ratio	100·0	100·1	100·8	97·1	84·8	72·0	63·3	55·1	49·8	51·7	n.a.
U.S.A. and the U.K.											
Exports	1159	1294	1435	1802	1630	1859	2529	3404	3354	3503	940
Imports	1308	1563	1663	1689	1918	2446	2993	3202	3039	3426	861
Net Exports as percentage of exports	−13%	−21%	−16%	+6%	−18%	−31%	−18%	+6%	+9%	+2%	+8%
Index of unit manpower costs in dollars											
U.S.A./U.K. ratio	100·0	117·1	114·8	106·4	97·5	91·7	92·7	85·0	75·7	83·9	n.a.

* First quarter

Source: US Commerce Department, S.I.T.C. 5–8, O.E.C.D. estimates of earnings and productivity, and I.M.F. data on exchange rates.

a deterioration in the case of the U.K. of 49 per cent.[1]

Even more puzzling is the record in regard to the trade between the U.S. and the U.K. as shown both on the basis of British figures in Table 3 and American figures in Table 4.[2] Though the Americans achieved a very considerable improvement in cost competitiveness (of over 21 per cent. between 1970 and 1976 and far more for the period 1968–75) they did not succeed in achieving anything but a very moderate improvement in their merchandise trade balance with the U.K. This is the more remarkable since the kind of explanation adduced in the U.K. and the U.S. for the failure to make headway against the increasing penetration of Germany and Japan—the "non-price" advantages of the latter countries in the form of exceptional productivity growth and technological lead in the export industries: early deliveries, punctuality in deliveries etc.—would hardly serve to explain why the U.S. failed to gain trade at the expense of the U.K. in spite of the latter's great apparent loss of competitiveness. Both the U.K. and the U.S. showed a lack of response to incentives in relation to the fast-growing countries like Germany and Japan, but they seem to be showing the same lack of incentives in the trade with each other. At least it would be difficult to maintain that it was some kind of technological lead which kept British exports growing at the rate they did despite increasing cost disadvantages.

The general picture which emerges from a study of the trade record of the last five or six years is that the comparative export performance of the main industrialised countries remained remarkably impervious to very large changes in effective exchange

[1] It would be tempting to conclude that in the U.S. case the 31 per cent. devaluation was "just large enough" to offset an adverse trend, were it not for the fact that in the ten years previous to 1970 the net trading position of the U.S. in relation to Germany was not much different from that of the period 1970–76; in both periods net exports fluctuated around − 100 per cent. with a range of variations between − 60 and − 150 per cent. depending on the state of the U.S. economy. In the case of the trade with Japan, on the other hand, where net exports have shown a deteriorating trend throughout the 1960s, the trend continued to be adverse in the 1970s. (Expressed as a percentage of G.N.P., imports of manufactures from Japan rose from 0·6 to 0·9 per cent. between 1970 and 1976, and *net* imports—in excess of exports—from 0·4 to 0·7 per cent.).

[2] The two sets of figures are not identical, partly because of differences in estimation and partly because the U.K. figures show American goods on a c.i.f. basis and British goods on an f.o.b. basis; with the American figures it is the other way round. However the general trend shown by the two sets of figures is pretty much the same.

rates. The surplus countries tended to remain in surplus and the deficit countries to remain in deficit in much the same way as in the 1960s, when the complications caused by the fivefold increase in oil prices and their different impact on different countries are allowed for. The important thing is that Britain and America, who seemed to be losing out to the new industrial giants, Germany and Japan, continued to do so after the real exchange rates between them underwent drastic alterations.

The main result of these currency changes was thus not so much in export performance but in the differing movement of the terms of trade of the manufacturing sectors in relation to primary commodities. Currency devaluations invariably worsened the terms of trade of the industrial sectors, the extent of the deterioration being much greater in the case of Britain, whose imports of food and raw materials are relatively large, than in the case of the U.S., whose imports of primary products are much smaller in relation to their total consumption. On the other hand, Germany, and to a lesser extent perhaps Japan, were able to compensate for the effect of rising food, industrial materials and oil prices by the appreciation of their exchange rates, so that their terms of trade did not suffer so much deterioration. Even more important were the effects of revaluations and devaluations on domestic inflation. The revaluing countries, like Germany and Switzerland, managed either to get rid of their inflation altogether or reduce it to very low levels, while inflation in both Britain and America has undoubtedly been much aggravated by the additional rise in commodity prices in terms of local currencies. The benefits derived by the revaluers from lower commodity prices and the parallel burden imposed on the devaluers through higher commodity prices may go far to explain why the former were able to compensate for the very large increase in their "efficiency wages" in relation to the latter and they may have reaped other advantages in the form of smoother running of the economy as a result of avoiding, or minimising, their rates of inflation.

The quantitative importance of these factors still remains to be investigated. At the moment we do not really know the reason why the currency realignments failed to produce the results that

were expected of them,[1] but if it turns out that the main effect of currency realignment is to redistribute the gains from international trade by giving an extra reward to the more successful and an extra penalty to the less successful, this will have far-reaching long-run implications on policies concerning international trade and payments.

So long as the world continues to be divided amongst sovereign states, each of which regards the interest of its own citizens as its first priority, universal free trade may not be compatible with that objective in the long run any more than in the short run—whether the world is under a régime of fixed rates or under a régime of floating rates. At the same time a general retreat into protectionism of the sort that existed before 1914 or during the period between the two wars would not produce a satisfactory solution either, since this would be bound to rebound to the disadvantages of smaller countries who may find that a great deal of beneficial trade gets suppressed as well as trade which threatens their industrial existence.

What is needed is some system which prevents the industrially dominating "go-ahead" countries—like Germany and Japan at the present time—from growing *at the expense* of other industrial countries through maintaining chronic and growing surpluses in

---

[1] At the same time it would be wrong to suggest that currency devaluations have been invariably unsuccessful. We noted already the success of the two French devaluations in the late 1950s and figures indicate that France's later devaluation of 1969 was almost equally successful in increasing her share of world trade in manufactures in subsequent years. Similarly the U.K. devaluation of 1967 certainly improved our trade performance, as the following table shows:

United Kingdom:
PERCENTAGE ANNUAL INCREASES IN EXPORTS AND IMPORTS OF MANUFACTURES, AT CONSTANT PRICES

	1963–67	1967–71	1971–76
Exports	2·9	8·2	4·9
Imports	10·2	9·1	8·5
Rate of Growth of G.D.P.	2·9	2·4	1·7
Percentage of unemployment (end of period)	2·3	3·4	5·4

In the four years of 1967–71 the volume of exports grew nearly as fast as the volume of imports in contrast to the four years 1963–67 or the five years 1971–76. It should be noted however that the rate of growth of the economy was appreciably higher, and the pressure of demand, as measured by unemployment, much greater in the first period than in the second, so that the improved ratio of export growth to import growth cannot entirely be attributed to devaluation, while in the third period the export/import growth relationship was much worse, despite low pressure of demand (after 1973) and low G.D.P. growth.

their manufacturing trade with other manufacturing exporters which may make it impossible for the latter countries to exploit their own growth potential and to pursue policies of full employment.[1,2] To ensure that this does not happen, it is necessary that in the trade of manufactured goods between the highly industrialised countries, the exports of any one country to other members of the group should be fully balanced by the imports of manufactures of a corresponding value from the countries taken as a group. For example, if Japan's exports of manufactures to the U.S., the U.K., Germany, France and Italy were balanced by corresponding imports from these five countries taken together, and the same were true of each of the other countries' exports, then each country would be assured that its own industrial growth would not be inhibited by the predatory behaviour of the others. In this way international specialisation through trade would be carried to an optimal point and no further—i.e., it would be carried to the point where each country derived the maximum benefit from trade subject to the condition that the other countries also maximised such benefits.

There are several ways of securing such a trading system with a minimum of detailed control or regulation, for example the

---

[1] It was a major premise of both classical and neo-classical theory that while the actual division of the gains from international trade might be uneven, *every* country must be better off as a result of trade, and therefore anything which promotes trade must promote welfare. These conclusions, however, were wholly dependent on two assumptions: (a) that there is always full employment; (b) that constant returns to scale—in terms of common or transferable factors—prevail in every single industry. (These two assumptions are themselves closely related to one another—as I showed in another paper reprinted in *Further Essays on Economic Theory*, p. 209 n—in that under conditions (b) each country can always obtain any desired "product-mix" and hence there is no scope for the "overproduction" which results from an ill-assortment of output.) If these assumptions are not fulfilled (and particularly if increasing returns to scale prevail) it is perfectly possible that unrestricted imports from an industrially more developed country cause a net loss of welfare to the importing country by reducing its domestic employment and/or its labour productivity, thereby diminishing its total income and output. (Much the same analysis may apply to individual regions of countries who may suffer decline and impoverishment as a result of the competition of more developed regions. Cf. also the paper on *The Case for Regional Policies*, reprinted in *Further Essays on Economic Theory*, pp. 139–154.)

[2] The extent to which the competition from such "surplus" countries exerts a harmful effect on the others cannot be measured by their actual surpluses in trade, since these are themselves diminished by the reduced incomes and employment of the countries which are in a deficit position. It should be measured by the *potential* export surpluses of countries like Japan and Germany, which would accrue if their chief markets—say, the U.S., the U.K. and France—were operating under conditions of full employment.

imports of manufactures (on a broad definition) from the selected group of countries which participate in this arrangement could be made subject to a general licence; such licences should be issued for each month or each quarter up to a total value which is equal to a coefficient (either a fraction or a multiple) times the country's exports of manufactures to other members of the group in the previous month (or quarter). When the trade between the countries is mainly in manufactures, the coefficient would normally be unity—i.e., each participating country should limit its total imports from the group to the value of its exports to the group. But where the country is a net importer of primary produces (food, fuel and raw materials) from the others the coefficient could be less than unity, to enable the country to have an export surplus in manufactures which would balance its net imports of primary products; by the same token in the reverse case the coefficient should be greater than unity. If the demand for licences exceeded the supply, they should be auctioned off; the price paid at the auction per £1 of licence would represent the equivalent of a uniform *ad valorem* duty on manufactured imports; to get optimal results, this should be balanced by a corresponding subsidy on the exports of manufactures. This means that the best way of administering such a scheme would be to issue the import licences directly to exporters as the goods pass out of customs, the exporters would then be free to sell the licences to the importers; and a market for such licences would soon develop, the price of which would indicate the duty/subsidy required to attain the target ratios of exports to imports.

The danger of individual countries being forced to follow deflationary policies through the export surpluses of other countries figured prominently in pre-war discussions and was no doubt responsible for the incorporation of the "scarce-currency clause" in the Bretton Woods Agreement. This clause remained a dead letter, however, and it was naivety to suppose that it could ever be made effective, since the countries which maintain chronic surpluses in their trade balances will achieve much the same objective of enhancing their economic growth and employment at the expense of others even when they ensure that by some form of lending (or better still, through purchase of property in foreign

countries) they put sufficient currency at the disposal of their debtors to finance their trade deficit. The elimination of a persistent creditor position in the I.M.F., through the G.A.B. or other forms of foreign lending or investment, does not itself ensure that international trade is *mutually* beneficial.

Part II

ECONOMICS OF DEVELOPMENT

THE ROLE OF INDUSTRIALISATION IN
LATIN AMERICAN INFLATIONS[1]

I. INTRODUCTION: THE PROBLEM TO BE EXPLAINED

MOST Latin American economies have been characterised by a proliferation of policies designed to promote industrialisation, and by persistent rapid inflation. The extent to which there is causal connection between these two phenomena is, however, a controversial subject. The views held by many of the professors of economics in the United States and in Europe are not shared by many distinguished economists in Latin America, and neither are they shared by what was once called the "underworld" of economics—people of heterodox views who are not well represented among those holding academic appointments. In order to examine the basis of the controversy, it is necessary to examine the fundamental issues concerning not only industrialisation, but also the broader issues concerning economic development and trade.

It is best to start with the peculiarities of Latin American inflations. It is generally agreed that Latin America is "peculiar" in its inflations in that they are not like other countries' inflations, or have not been considered to be such until recently. In recent years the difference has undoubtedly become less pronounced. The rate of inflation in the United States and in the countries of Western Europe has accelerated although it has not yet reached Latin American dimensions. In Latin America the countries which have suffered from these inflations have maintained very high rates of price increases, of the order of 25 to 50 per cent. per year on the average, over periods as long as thirteen or fifteen

---

[1] Paper read at the Latin American Conference in Gainsville, Florida, February 1971 and published in David T. Geithman (ed.), *Fiscal Policy for Industrialization and Developments in Latin America* (University of Florida Press, 1974).

years. And their further peculiarity has been that such high rates of price increases have been maintained over long periods without exploding into what are termed "hyperinflations". Hyperinflations occur once the annual rate of price increases exceeds a kind of "sound barrier" of 400 per cent. a year. Past experience has tended to show that once a rate of price increase of 400 per cent. a year is attained, inflation becomes a "galloping" phenomenon, with a strong built-in acceleration, leading to a situation where prices are doubled weekly or even daily. This is what happened in Germany after the First World War and in a number of other countries (such as Hungary and Greece) after the Second World War; and it invariably ends with a complete collapse of the currency and its replacement by an entirely new monetary system.

But nothing like this ever happened in Latin America. One reason is that the rates of inflation, although they were high, were never very steady, and this is their second important characteristic. If one looks at the figures the rates of inflation fluctuated; they reached and sometimes exceeded 100 per cent. for one or two years, but then they slowed down again to under 50 per cent. or even to 20 per cent., and afterwards they tended to start up again. So, the course of these inflations has never been *certain* for the near future—the movement of prices is unpredictable in the short term even though, on past showing, one may be confident of the continuance of rising prices in the long term. All the inflationary countries exhibited these queer fluctuations—periods of high inflations followed by years of relative quiescence; in some cases, violent inflations flaring up after quite a long period of price stability, and in other cases inflations apparently dying out altogether, although no one can ever be certain that they would not start up again without any major visible cause (such as a major war or a revolution).

The third characteristic is that although all Latin American countries show important similarities in their political and social framework, in the matter of inflationary experience they are by no means all alike. The high inflations were confined to a particular group of countries, notably Chile, Brazil, Bolivia, Argentina, Paraguay and, more recently, Uruguay. Other Latin American countries may have had inflations in the past but, looking at

the post-war period, they escaped it altogether or almost entirely; in the latter category I would put Mexico, Peru, Venezuela, and many, but not all, of the Central American republics.

On the face of it, there is nothing very much to distinguish one of the two groups of countries from the other: we have some more-developed and some less-developed countries, some un-developing countries (as someone called it) and some rapidly growing countries both in the inflationary group and in the non-inflationary group.

The questions which need to be answered are why these inflations occurred, and why they had the peculiar characteristics described.

II. ALTERNATIVE EXPLANATIONS

The possible explanations are of three different types, which I should like to call the "monetary", the "terms of trade", and the "structural", respectively. Not all of these are mutually exclusive; and, except for the naïve version of the "monetary" explanation, none of them can be dismissed as necessarily wrong.

The "naive version" of the monetary explanation attributes inflations to an increase in the "money supply" *per se*. The most distinguished proponent of this view is Professor Milton Friedman in Chicago, whose views could be paraphrased in a sentence or two: "Show me a country which had a major inflation *without* an increase in the money supply. Until such an example is found, and until somebody shows that the money supply *cannot* be controlled by the monetary authority, the change in the money supply must be the 'main and only necessary cause' (to use a famous classical expression) of the rise in prices." In other words, provided a good correlation is found between the G.N.P. and the money supply in *all* cases, and especially when the change in the money supply *leads* the G.N.P., there is no need to go beyond that relationship and to look for a "mechanism" or a "model". This is the message of the so-called "positive economics" *à la* Chicago.

The more sophisticated adherents of the "monetary explanation" do find the intellectual need for something more, and look for the causes of inflation either in excessive private investment financed

out of bank cred.; or in excessive government borrowing, i.e., in a lax fiscal policy by the government. In other words, the ultimate cause of inflation according to this view must be looked for either in the government's ability to cover its needs by printing money combined with its inability, or disinclination, to raise enough in taxation to avoid having recourse to the printing press; or else in the greed of the banks and other financial intermediaries to expand their business and increase their profits through excess lending, which is insufficiently kept in check by the central bank.

These are possible hypotheses—the question is, do they receive enough empirical support to be preferred to other explanations? Excessive lending to private business should manifest itself in an "excessive" proportion of the G.N.P. being devoted to private investment, either in the form of fixed investment or of addition to stocks. Lax fiscal policy leading to excessive borrowing (or "resort to the printing press", which comes to the same thing) should show itself in relatively large fiscal deficits as a percentage of the G.N.P.

I do not think that either of these hypotheses can be adequately supported by the available evidence. The countries which experienced large inflations do not show that private investment (as a proportion of G.N.P.) was large relative to that in the non-inflationary countries. If anything, the statistics point the other way. If one looks at the budgetary deficits, it is true that, taking the inflationary group as a whole, deficits as a percentage of the G.N.P. tended to be somewhat larger; but, there is not very much in it. The important exception is the Argentine, where the fiscal deficit reached 4–5 per cent. of G.N.P. for a number of years. (On the other hand, Venezuela, a non-inflationary country, had even larger budgetary deficits.)

My feeling is that, insofar as the budget deficits of inflationary countries have been larger in percentage terms than those of the non-inflationary countries, this was a symptom (or consequence), and not the cause, of the inflationary process. It is well known from European studies that inflation causes budgetary deficits simply on account of the lag in tax collections; so even when a country's level of taxation is adequate, the process of inflation can cause the rise in tax receipts to lag behind the rise in expenditure. But this would not in itself add to the inflationary fuel: the larger

fiscal deficit may have its offset in enlarged "tax reserves" of the private sector. Hence, the existence of a budget deficit does not necessarily indicate the presence of a demand inflation emanating in the public sector.

Of course, the true Friedmanite would say that it does not matter what *causes* inflations: if the central bank resolutely refused to countenance any increase in the money supply, there would be no inflation; in that sense, inflation is always the fault of the central bank! On this view, if Venezuela and Mexico avoided inflations, it was because their central bankers were clever and/or virtuous; if Chile and Brazil did not, it was because they were wicked and/or stupid. There is nothing to explain why some countries should be so much luckier in their choice of central bankers than others.

A more reasonable view (in my opinion) is that central bankers are much the same kind of people everywhere; what differs is the pressure to which they are subject. They always, I presume, wish to do the right thing, but they cannot resist certain pressures; they are not the "powerful people" they are made out to be. This is only another way of saying that the "money supply" is not *really* under their control: the supply of money (in each country) responds to the demand; and this, in my view, is the basic explanation of the correlations found between the money supply and the changes in the money-G.N.P., both in Latin America and elsewhere.

One important feature that distinguishes the inflationary group of countries from the non-inflationary group in Latin America is the existence of import restrictions. No country experienced inflation for any length of time which did not restrict the import of consumer goods—i.e., which did not have quantitative import controls of some kind—either through direct import licensing or the licensing of foreign exchange. If this is accepted as an empirically valid generalisation (and I have no doubt that it must be), then the question is whether the "balance of payments constraint" which caused the adoption of quantitative import restrictions is itself an effect, or a symptom, of the inflationary process or whether it may have a causal role in creating inflation. The answer to this clearly depends on an analysis of the causes of the "shortage" of

foreign exchange. If it is a consequence of inflationary excess spending in the domestic economy due to budgetary deficits, this would show itself in an "abnormal" rise in the volume of imports resulting from the fact that home demand exceeded the capacity to produce.

But the need for import restrictions *could* arise from other causes as well, which are not associated with excessive demand and are not "monetary" or "fiscal" in origin. One such cause is a sharp deterioration in the terms of trade—a fall in the prices of a country's exports relative to the prices of imports—an extreme example of which was the collapse of export earnings during the Great Depression of the 1930s. It could also occur as a result of crop failure, or of a fall in world demand for the particular product which provides the major source of exports to a particular country. In all these cases a country may be compelled to restrict imports; if as a result, the domestic price of some basic consumer goods rises, there will be pressures to find compensation for the fall in urban living standards (manifesting itself in a rise in the cost of living) through compensating increases in money wages and salaries. In these cases the consequential inflation is really a reflection of the inability of the country to distribute an inevitable reduction in its real income in a manner that is acceptable to its inhabitants.

Finally, one can conceive of situations in which there is a disproportion between the structure of production and the structure of final demand which, for special reasons that need to be explained, cannot be eliminated through international trade; and which leads to a disproportion between the import requirements and the export capacity associated with the production structure of a particular country.

It is true, of course, of any region or country which is not wholly self-contained that the proportion in which it produces different things is not the same as the proportions in which they are required for consumption or investment. This difference between the "product-mix" and the "consumption-mix" or "final-demand-mix" should, in normal cases, be eliminated through international trade—any particular region or country exports the things which it produces in excess of domestic needs and obtains in return, through imports, the goods in which it is deficient. Under ideal

conditions the world market is an enormous mart in which any particular "mix" of goods can be changed into any other "mix" at given conversion ratios, i.e., at the given system of world prices.

"Structural bottlenecks" arise when this harmonisation of the "product-mix" with the "final-demand-mix" cannot take place in the normal manner through international trade; and the explanation *why* it cannot lies at the heart of the problem of "structural inflations".

III. INDUSTRIALISATION AND STRUCTURAL INFLATIONS

That the basic cause of Latin American inflations is "structural" and not "monetary" has been repeatedly asserted in the past, mainly by Latin American economists, and if their views have failed to carry conviction among the more sophisticated academic economists of the U.S. or Western Europe, this was perhaps because they failed to show the "necessary and sufficient" conditions for the occurrence of such "structural bottlenecks". Why should these bottlenecks have occurred in Latin American countries (or rather in *some* Latin American countries) and not elsewhere?

My contention is that the changes in the production structures of Latin American countries, which caused the prevalence of "strong" inflations as a long-continuing process, had their origin in the circumstances and manner in which industrialisation and the associated urbanisation proceeded in these countries following upon the collapse of export earnings during the Great Depression of the 1930s and the further stimulus to industrialisation afforded by the Second World War.

To understand this it is necessary to begin by drawing attention to the basic connection between industrialisation and economic development, and to the pre-conditions of industrial development.

It is perhaps not sufficiently understood that the kind of economic growth that involves the use of modern technology and eventuates in high real income per head is inconceivable without the development of modern manufacturing industry. The reason for this is not only (or even mainly) because, as real income rises, only a diminishing proportion of income is spent on food and a rising proportion on industrial products and services. The main

reason is that when primary production is efficiently conducted, high productivity agriculture (or mining) cannot absorb more than a fraction of the labour force on the exploitation of the available land and mineral resources. Hence, a country that specialised entirely in primary products and obtained all its industrial goods from abroad could never be a country with a high real income per head. The best proof of this is that even those "advanced" high-income countries which "specialised" in the exportation of agricultural goods, forest products, or minerals (such as Australia, New Zealand or Denmark until recently, or Sweden in the earlier part of this century) have nevertheless had only a low proportion of their labour force in agriculture and mining, not only absolutely but relative to the labour force in industry. Wherever the proportion of the labour force in agriculture is large (as it still is in the countries of Latin America), this is a symptom of poverty and under-development, and of the existence of "disguised unemployment" on a large scale.

In a self-contained economic region (the world was divided into such non-trading regions, particularly in land-locked areas, before the great transport revolution of the 19th and 20th centuries), the rate of growth of manufacturing or "processing" activities was conditioned by the rate growth of land-productivity (in yields per acre, rather than per man) that made it possible for a surplus to emerge over the consumption needs of the agricultural producers. This "agricultural surplus" generated a market demand for industrial goods; it also provided the supply of "wage-goods" for non-agricultural employment. Under favourable conditions, the expansion of each of these two sectors had a stimulating effect on one another. While the growth of marketable food supplies increased the demand for industrial goods, the increased availability of industrial goods led to further technological improvements in agriculture. Before the advent of the industrial revolution, however, the pace of this "chain reaction" was normally too slow to be perceived as a continuing process by contemporary observers.

With the transport revolution of the last two centuries vast areas of the world became accessible to trade, and regions previously self-contained were increasingly drawn into the network of the world economy. Historically, this had two consequences. First, the

cheap products of the manufacturing industries of the developed capitalist countries increasingly displaced the local manufactures of primitive small-scale industry. Second, with the growth of industries in the "advanced" countries of Europe, markets were created for temperate foodstuffs, tropical products and minerals. Frequently this meant the establishment of foreign owned mines and plantations, the products of which were mainly destined for export. As a result of both of these factors industrial development became increasingly polarised in certain "industrialised" countries, whilst the others (such as the countries of Latin America) became "specialised" in the production of raw materials and foodstuffs for the use of the industrial countries. The countries of Latin America, up to the 1930s, enjoyed rising export earnings from the sale of foodstuffs, minerals and plantation products, which they spent on industrial goods produced in Western Europe or the U.S. While their export earnings were growing, and there was a prosperous landowning class in all these countries, the standard of living of the population remained low. This was true partly because wages were low, but mainly because only a fraction of the population was in regular employment.

In order to raise real income per head, the Latin American countries should have pursued from an early stage the same policies of fostering domestic industries by judiciously chosen methods of "import substitution"—the replacement of imports of manufactures by domestic production—which were so successfully pursued by the countries of Western Europe, North America, Japan and other "developed" countries in the late 19th century and the present century. Apart from the case of Britain, which initiated the industrial revolution and for a time had a near-monopoly of the world market in factory-made goods, all the other present "developed" or "industrialised" countries established their industries through "import substitution" by means of protective tariffs and/or differential subsidies. As the German economist Friedrich List first emphasised in the middle of the last century, in manufacturing industry productivity is very low to start with; hence, without special measures of protection such industries cannot be established as they cannot compete with the products of the industrial centres at higher stages of development. However, owing

to the existence of increasing returns to scale and learning-by-doing, productivity rises rapidly as these industries develop under the umbrella of protection; and assuming that wages remain low in comparison to those in the more advanced industrial centres, the industrialising country will pass from the stage of "import substitution" to become an exporter of manufactures on an increasing scale. For such a policy to be successful, the protective measures must be both moderate and discriminating: they must not be such as to encourage the mushroom-growth of high-cost enterprises; the protection itself should be reduced with the growth of domestic output—as the industries pass beyond their "infancy" —so as to put them in a position to develop an export potential. Moreover, the policy needs to be selectively applied: the "light industries" (such as textiles), which require less industrial know-how and smaller scale for efficient production, should be established first; the "heavy industries" (such as chemicals, steel and engineering) at a later stage, when the "light industries" have already passed into the stage in which they export an important share of their output.

The Latin American countries did not follow this pattern. The initial impetus to industrialisation did not come from suitably designed policies for industrial promotion. It came as a by-product of widespread and severe import restrictions imposed on account of a sudden collapse of export earnings. The prime motive was the necessity to save foreign exchange. The stimulus to the establishment of local industries came from the rise of internal prices brought about by the shortages of goods previously imported. These import restrictions were, thus, the equivalent of an indiscriminate protection of a rather violent kind—raising the prices of industrial goods sometimes by several hundred per cent in terms of agricultural products. Thus, it was made profitable to produce goods for the home market even when the cost, in terms of primary products, was many times as high as the external price (or the world price) of such products.

This led to a considerable investment in industrial capacity, in increased urbanisation, and an increase in total employment. In the earlier phases of this process, the gross domestic product grew quite rapidly (even in terms of world prices, not only domestic

prices) because the newly-established industries meant a net addition to resources, both capital and labour. The newly-created capacity was the fruit of additional savings generated by the rise in profits, and the increase in industrial employment meant a net addition to employment—it did not cause any offsetting reductions in the effective utilisation of labour in the rest of the economy.

However, while the additional output went largely to replace goods previously imported, the additional incomes which the new productive activity generated led to an increase in demand for consumption goods, primarily food, which was greater than could be satisfied by the available supplies. At the same time, the industrial activity did nothing to alleviate the balance of payments constraint. Though many goods previously imported were replaced by domestic production, the process itself generated an additional demand for imports—partly because the investment needed to establish productive capacity had a very high import content; partly because some of the current inputs of raw materials and components had to be imported; and, partly also because industrialisation meant additional incomes—additional profits, salaries and wages—which generated additional consumption, and some part of that consumption, however severe the restrictions, was inevitably spent on imported goods or services. At the same time, owing to the circumstances of their creation, very few of the new industries were efficient enough to develop a capacity to export. Thus, the pressure for imports in excess of current earnings became greater, not less; the balance of payments constraint was not alleviated by industrialisation, but was aggravated by it.

Even this constellation of circumstances would not have necessarily caused prolonged inflations if it had not been combined with a third factor: the failure of agriculture to respond to increased urban demand by increasing marketable food supplies in an adequate manner. This lack of response on the side of agriculture had partly institutional and partly economic causes. It may have been due to vestiges of feudalism, ancient forms of land tenure, and absentee ownership, or it may have been due to an adverse change in the terms of trade (despite the shortage of agricultural products). The relative importance of these two factors

varied in different countries. In the Argentine, where agriculture was more "commercialised", the unfavourable change in the terms of trade (particularly in the years of the Peron regime) was the important factor. In Chile, on the other hand, it was more a matter of absentee ownership and lack of incentives in the absence of land reform.

It was the combination of an increase in both the volume of employment and output per head in non-agricultural employment and the absence of a corresponding increase in food supplies that made continued inflation inevitable. It caused a persistent upward pressure in the prices of food paid by the urban consumer, and it was the rise in food prices which caused the persistent rise in urban wages and salaries (in order to maintain real wages), which in turn raised the general level of industrial costs and prices. The inflation, therefore, was "demand-induced" as far as food prices were concerned, and "cost-induced" as far as the rise in the prices of non-agricultural goods and services are concerned. Or, putting it in different words, the basic cause of the inflation was the disproportionality in the growth of production in different sectors of the economy, particularly as between "wage goods" and "non-wage goods". Given this fact, inflation could only have been prevented if (a) production and employment in the non-agricultural sectors had been cut so as to eliminate the excess purchasing power for foodstuffs; (b) non-agricultural employees had been ready to put up with a cut in real earnings without demanding (and obtaining) compensating increases in money wages. As it was (in some of the countries at any rate), real wages tended to remain constant and the share of wages in the national income fell. It must also be borne in mind that when real wages are low enough for the cost of food to take up a high proportion of the wage-earner's budget (as is the case in most Latin American countries) it is not in the interest of a capitalist employer to allow the purchasing power of his employees to fall, since any such reduction might cause a rise in costs through reduced work performance (owing to lower food intake) that is greater than the increase in cost involved in paying higher wages. In other words, there is a certain real wage that minimises the cost of labour per unit of output, and it is in the interests of the employer to ensure that

wages do not fall below that level. The periodic upward adjustment
in money wages to compensate for the rise in living costs (which
alone made the inflation a *continuing* process) was, therefore,
not just a matter of "trade union pressure"; it might have
occurred in much the same way even if such pressure had not
existed.

In a paper on Chile written in 1956,[1] I predicted that "no lasting cure of the inflationary tendencies of Chile can be found either
in stricter monetary and credit policies or even in administrative
reform which secured more effective taxation"; it can "only be
found through a more rapid increase in the productivity of agriculture (which in turn hinges upon the reform of land tenure) or a
more liberal policy of importing foodstuffs from abroad".[2] Events
in the subsequent fifteen years have certainly not contradicted
this prediction. Despite repeated attempts to secure "stabilisation"
by far-reaching monetary and fiscal reform (some under the aegis
of the I.M.F.), inflation could not be slowed down, let alone
halted, for more than brief periods.

The orthodox instruments of credit control cannot prevent the
increase in bank credit required in consequence of the rise of the
money value of the "normal" working capital, which is a consequence of the rise in money wages. The banking system could
withstand this pressure only at the cost of serious interference with
the normal processes of production and circulation of goods, or by
causing a general breakdown of contracts. It would be idle, for
example, to charge the banks with the responsibility of *preventing*
increases of money wages through a refusal of credit if the employers themselves regard the adjustment of money wages as fair and
reasonable in the light of the rise in the cost of living. It would be
equally idle to expect the banks to force businesses to reduce their
scale of operations by enforcing a reduction in working capital

---

[1] "Economic Problems of Chile", a study prepared for the Economic Commission of
Latin America, printed in *Essays on Economic Policy*, vol. 2 (London, Duckworth, 1964),
pp. 233–77.

[2] *Ibid.*, p. 277. As was noted in that paper, the deficiency in domestic food production was increasingly supplemented by food imports; but owing to the ever-present
shortage of foreign exchange, these imports were not on the scale required to satisfy
the growth in demand resulting from the rise in employment and incomes. In another
(unpublished) paper on the Argentine, it was also argued that the acceleration of its
inflationary trends in the post-Peron period in the 1950s could be traced to the restriction of food availabilities for domestic use owing to the need to restore (or prevent a
further erosion of) the volume of agricultural exports.

F

tied up in "goods in process" in order to compensate for a rise in demand that originates from another quarter—e.g., from increased government spending. The responsibility of the banking system cannot be extended beyond ensuring that an inflationary process is not aggravated by abnormal speculative demands arising out of the process of inflation itself; and there is no evidence, in the case of Latin American inflations, that such "speculative demands" (fed by easy credit) played an important role in the process. Moreover, if monetary measures *could* be made effective, they would remedy the disproportionality by cutting output and employment in the non-agricultural sectors; this is clearly not a solution that would recommend itself on welfare criteria.

Equally, it is idle to expect that the basic disproportionalities can be eliminated by devaluation. For countries whose main exports are primary products (like coffee or copper), the prices of which are determined by world markets, devaluation is unavailing in increasing the export proceeds in terms of such products. To develop industrial exports, on the other hand, the necessary devaluation would have to be pretty severe—partly because industrial costs and prices in these countries, when measured in terms of primary products, are so much higher than world prices, and partly also because there are high initial marketing and selling costs connected with such exports. And devaluations of this order, by raising the domestic prices of traditional exports as well as of imports, cause a further bout of inflation that cancels the effects of devaluation in a fairly short period.

Devaluation may be an appropriate remedy for balance of payments disequilibria of industrialised countries which export manufactured goods and which become uncompetitive (or insufficiently competitive) in relation to other industrial exporters because their "efficiency wages" (money wages divided by productivity) are excessive at the prevailing exchange rates. But, in the case of "developing" countries whose major exports are primary products, the trouble is not with the general level of costs or prices. The trouble is with the price *structure* rather than the price *level*— the cost of industrial products is too high not just in terms of international currency, but in terms of food and primary products— and this defect cannot be remedied by an over-all change in the

exchange rate, for much the same reasons that a rise in the cost of living is unavailing in securing a lasting reduction in real wages.

The countries of Latin America that have succeeded in avoiding inflations, or in gradually eliminating the inflationary process, were those that succeeded in avoiding or getting out of the impasse of a chronic balance-of-payments constraint, one way or another. One country, Venezuela, escaped inflation largely because her foreign exchange earnings, on account of oil, were large enough to permit liberal importation of foodstuffs as well as of investment goods and goods serving luxury consumption. The lag in agricultural production in relation to the growth of urban food requirements was no different, as far as I can see, than in Chile; but unlike Chile, Venezuela was able to import all basic foods that were needed to prevent shortages and rising prices in the domestic markets. Then there were countries which from the start paid more attention to the development of an export potential. This is true of Peru, which developed a large export in fishmeal and various other products, and thanks to rising export earnings could allow a far more liberal import policy. A third type of country is one that, thanks to land reform or to a revolution which gave the land to a new lot of owners, managed to make agriculture more "dynamic" or "responsive" and thus to keep the growth of marketable food supplies in line with the growth of urban demand. This, I think, is the explanation for the comparative absence of inflation in Mexico. And finally, there is a group of countries which did not attempt to industrialise (or not on any scale), and therefore were not subject to the pressures arising from an industrialisation policy, and which were able to take the reduction of their export earnings in the 1930s in their stride without the need to impose severe import restrictions. I am thinking here of many Central American republics (many of which escaped the need for such severe import controls partly I suppose because, in the critical period, they were still the colonies of European powers).

IV. REMEDIES

If the above analysis is correct, the remedies to Latin American inflations will not be found in monetary or fiscal reforms—though

this is not to say that these, particularly fiscal reform, may not be necessary, and important as accompanying measures. The remedies must be "structural" and this means changing the framework of institutions and of basic policies, which takes some time to become effective. The two basic remedies are first stimulating domestic food production, which requires far-reaching land reform in most countries, as well as public investment and promotional policies, e.g., in irrigation schemes, etc., and second, appropriate policies for industrial rationalisation and the promotion of exports of manufactures.

Industrial rationalisation is necessary because as a result of excessive protection production is scattered over too wide a field and in too many separate plants, each of which is operating on an uneconomic scale. There is also (in relation to developed countries) too much surplus operating capacity. This, as I said, was the unintended consequence of quantitative import restrictions (the original purpose of which was to cut "luxury" consumption—like motor cars—not to stimulate the domestic production of such "luxuries"). The remedy lies, in the first place, in replacing import quotas by protective duties which, I gather, has already taken place to a considerable extent; and in the second place, in cutting the "peaks" and levelling up the "troughs" in the *ad valorem* equivalent of import duties so as to withdraw protection from those activities or enterprises which are exceptionally inefficient. One needs to make a sharp distinction between the *average level* of import duties—which may have to remain pretty high if industrial activity and employment in the aggregate are not to contract—and the degree of unevenness in the incidence of the duties as between different goods. Of course, it is desirable that the average level of protection should also be reduced as rapidly as possible, provided this is consistent with the continued growth in the scale of industrial activities. But whatever the average level of protective duty that is found necessary for that purpose, the policy of levelling out the height of the tariff as between one industrial product and another allows the law of comparative costs to operate within the industrial sector; less efficient firms and industries will be eliminated and the more efficient will expand and thereby achieve further gains due to increasing returns. It is in this way that a

situation could be created in which the Latin American countries secured an increasing share of world trade in manufactures.

The other aspect—deliberate export promotion—is best undertaken by a system of "dual exchange rates", a suggestion which I developed in a paper in the E.C.L.A. *Bulletin* several years ago.[1] Because protection involves a change in the internal price-structure (between industrial goods and primary products) in relation to the structure of world prices, no *single* exchange rate is appropriate for promoting industrial exports without an undue domestic rise in the prices and incomes of primary producers. The ideal way of promoting industrialisation, as several economists pointed out, is not by tariffs at all but by straightforward subsidies paid to industry by the government, the money being raised by taxes collected on the incomes of primary producers. In that way the *internal* cost relationship is adjusted to the *external* price structure and not the internal price structure to the internal cost structure. But this involves large budgetary transfers: the raising of large sums in taxation from the agricultural sector which most countries (not only those of Latin America) find very difficult.[2] However, much the same result could be attained without the need for large budgetary transfers if the protective import duty on industrial goods were "matched", so to speak, by equivalent export subsidies. This means if the level of import duties is 50 per cent. there should be a 33 per cent. subsidy on industrial exports, and so on. Assuming the duties on industrial goods are uniform and the export subsidies are uniform, this means that the industries which remain profitable at the chosen rate of tariffs and subsidies can compete with the goods produced by other countries on the same terms in their own internal market as in the world market. The industries that will prosper under this system will be those in which the comparative efficiency of any particular country is greatest. Each country will go on developing its industrial activities, but these developments will be consistent with the maximum benefit of international specialisation. Such a policy, if universally

---

[1] "Dual Exchange Rates and Economic Development", *Economic Bulletin for Latin America*, September 1964, reprinted in *Essays on Economic Policy*, vol. 2, pp. 178–99.

[2] The countries which have succeeded in doing this—such as Japan through the land tax after the Meiji restoration—and were thereby able to establish industries through subsidies without the need for high protective tariffs, reaped their reward in an early development of industrial exports.

pursued, would combine the advantages of free trade with the elimination of the handicap to economic development of the less developed areas arising from the very existence of more highly developed countries. No amount of research and planning could predict beforehand which particular industry any particular country is best fitted to develop. (Who could have predicted, for example, that Hong Kong in a matter of a few years would develop an export trade of $150 million in wigs?)

The simplest and most effective way of giving effect to such a policy is through a system of dual exchange rates—with one particular rate applicable to "traditional" exports (of primary products) and basic imports (of foodstuffs and industrial materials) and another exchange rate applicable to both the exports and imports of manufactured goods, the difference between the two rates being the greater the less developed a country's industry is. The present international rules regarding money and trade (Bretton Woods and G.A.T.T.) rule out both dual exchange rates and export subsidies. These rules were invented for the benefit of the developed countries (who are, however, as recent events have shown, also ready to break them whenever it suits their interests), and clearly in a sensible world they would not be applied to developing countries. There would be different rules for the one group and for the other. Indeed, the developed countries have already acknowledged the case for giving preferential treatment to imports from the developing countries and have taken effective steps to this end, albeit on a rather meagre scale. Much the best way to give effect to the principle of helping the developing countries through the adaptation of the "ground rules" in their favour would be to abolish quantitative restrictions on imports from the developing countries (which many of the developed countries now maintain, under the escape clauses of G.A.T.T., to protect themselves from "trade disruption") and to permit them to operate dual exchange rates (or a linked system of import duties and export subsidies), provided they agree to eliminate in stages their own quantitative import controls and also their protective duties other than those involved in the operation of the dual exchange rate or its equivalent. This would be a far better way of developing the world economy than the creation of discriminating blocks

(common markets or free trade areas), either amongst the developed or amongst the developing countries, and in the particular matter of inflation, would be the best way to get Latin America out of the wood.

9

ADVANCED TECHNOLOGY IN A STRATEGY OF DEVELOPMENT[1]

THERE has been a great deal of discussion in economic literature in recent years as to the most appropriate technology that underdeveloped countries should adopt in order to secure the best means of economic development—that is, in order to attain the fastest sustainable increase in real income per head. This problem has become particularly acute in the light of recent advances in the field of automation, electronic data processing and control, and so on.

Two main aspects of this discussion can be distinguished: a wider one, and a narrower one.

The first aspect relates to the strategy of economic development. Given the limitation of available resources, how should they be applied between the different economic sectors? Should they be concentrated on developing technological standards in the traditional economic activities (which means improving the efficiency of agriculture) or on developing new activities, that is to say, on establishing modern industries?

The second aspect relates to the question: What are the most appropriate techniques for adoption in any one industry? Should the underdeveloped countries copy the latest electronically controlled technologies of the advanced countries, or import something a little older, or should they develop new technologies, appropriate to their circumstances? Should they aim at creating the maximum increase in new employment opportunities, or should they aim at higher productivity per worker, even if this involves a slower increase in the volume of employment?

[1] An early version of this paper was presented to the Conference on Technological Change and Human Development, Jerusalem , 1969. First published in the present version in *Automation and Developing Countries*, International Labour Office, Geneva, 1972.

Neither question permits a simple, general answer; the most that one can expect from economic analysis is for it to set out the relevant factors and establish certain general criteria for judgement. The present paper aims at presenting a brief survey of both aspects.

THE STRATEGY OF DEVELOPMENT

The post-war development plans of many underdeveloped countries have frequently been criticised on the grounds that they concentrated on industrial development on a broad front, to the neglect of agricultural development, and that they concentrated on developing substitutes for imports, even when this involved a very wasteful use of resources, to the neglect of developing exports. These inward-looking strategies of development meant that, despite very large investments of capital (financed by external aid or through varying forms of taxation of the agricultural sector), they brought a very meagre social return, either in terms of additional employment or in terms of improvement of living standards.

As a criticism of the post-war economic policies of many underdeveloped countries this is no doubt well founded. No one who examines the disappointing record of a number of underdeveloped countries in Latin America or in south-east Asia could fail to be impressed by the fact that the pursuit of indiscriminate import substitution, without regard to cost, led to perpetual balance-of-payments problems, inflation, low rates of growth, and meagre results in terms of additional employment or higher consumption per head of population. Yet it is a criticism concerning methods, rather than aims; of tactics, rather than of long-run strategy.

For there can be little doubt that the kind of economic growth which involves the spread of modern technology, and which eventuates in high real income per head, is inconceivable without industrialisation. In that broad sense there are no alternative roads to economic development. It is no accident that all advanced countries with relatively high incomes per head have a large manufacturing industry and, in most cases, are also large exporters of manufactured goods.

The reason for this is not only that, as real income rises, a diminishing proportion of income is spent on food and a growing proportion is spent on industrial goods and services. One could, in theory, conceive of a country specialising entirely in agriculture and obtaining all its industrial requirements from abroad. But it could never become a high-income country simply because technologically developed agriculture could never absorb more than a fraction of the working population on the available land. Though in all underdeveloped countries the greater part of the working population is "occupied" in agriculture, most of this represents disguised unemployment; a rural community maintains all its members and expects everyone to share in the work. Much the greater part of this labour could be withdrawn from agriculture without any adverse effect (and probably with a beneficial effect) on total agricultural output, if alternative employment opportunities were available; for the relief of the pressure of labour on the land is itself a most potent factor in inducing improvements in technology which raise yields per acre, as well as the yield per man. These improvements would normally require an increase in the capital employed on the land; but the savings necessary for the increase in capital are themselves a by-product of reduced population pressure. The reduction in the agricultural population and the increased use of capital in agriculture are thus different aspects of the same process. As there are fewer mouths to feed, the "agricultural surplus" rises (the excess of agricultural production over the self-consumption of the farming population). The rise in the surplus enables the farmers to plough back a higher proportion of their output (in the form of better tools, improved seeds, fertilisers, etc.), and such improvements tend to be both "labour saving" and "land saving": they diminish the labour requirements at the same time as they increase the yield of the land.

Hence a technological revolution in agriculture leading to a faster growth in output is generally associated with a steady reduction, not an increase, in the agricultural labour force. The best proof of this is to be found in the fact that those advanced high-income countries which have specialised in exporting agricultural products and importing manufactured goods (and which export the greater part of their agricultural output), such as Australia,

Denmark and New Zealand, have nevertheless only a low proportion of their labour force in agriculture—of the order of 10 to 20
per cent., as against the 70 to 80 per cent. in low-income countries
which barely produce enough to feed their populations on a very
low standard. And it is one of the best-established generalisations
of economic history that with improvements in technology, and a
rise in real income per head, there is a continued reduction in the
proportion of the labour force employed in agriculture.

The advance in agricultural technology thus depends on, and is
conditioned by, the growth of the agricultural surplus. At the same
time, the growth of this surplus is the main factor determining the
growth of employment opportunities in the non-agricultural
sectors of the economy. This has two aspects.

In the first place, the growth of the non-agricultural employment potential depends on the rate of growth of marketed (as
against self-consumed) food supplies. Food is the "wage good" par
excellence, and any attempt to increase urban employment at a
faster rate than the agricultural surplus permits, is bound, sooner
or later, to be vitiated through violent inflation. In the second place,
the growth of the agricultural surplus is an essential condition for
providing the growth of purchasing power necessary for sustaining the growth of demand for industrial products. The growth of
industrial activities is generally regarded as being conditioned by
the rate of capital accumulation in industry. No doubt the accumulation of capital is an essential part of this process; in capitalistic
economies, however, the process of industrial capital accumulation
is itself conditioned by the growth of profits associated with the
process of expansion, and with the growth of profitable investment
opportunities provided by the increase of effective demand for
industrial products.

Although the expansion of industrial production itself provides
an element of this growth of demand, since part of the incomes
generated by industrial activities is spent on goods produced by
the industrial sector, this self-generated component of demand
cannot alone be sufficient to make an increase in production
profitable. The growth in demand, which has a determining
influence on the pace of expansion—both of the growth of production and employment and of the growth of productive capa-

city—must be external to the industrial sector: it reflects the increase in the supply of other goods (mainly food and raw materials) for which the products of industry are exchanged. In an advanced economy, with a highly developed manufacturing sector, the most important exogenous factor in the growth of demand is the increase of world demand for its exports. But for a country in the earlier stages of industrialisation which is unable to break into the export markets, the exogenous component of demand is the surplus of its own agricultural sector.

Hence in any sustained process of economic growth, the expansion of the agricultural surplus provides the source of demand for the growth of industry; the growth of industry, with its manifold associated tertiary activities, provides the source for the growth of urban employment; and the latter provides the resources, and the incentives, for technological improvements in agriculture, which in turn, by raising the agricultural surplus, ensure the continued growth of demand for industrial goods. Thus industrialisation and the growth of agricultural productivity go hand in hand, and are complementary to one another. Any improvement in either one of these sectors facilitates the growth of the other, in the manner of a chain reaction.

This has undoubtedly been true of all the present developed countries which have attained their privileged position (with levels of real income per head that are 20 to 30 times as high as in the underdeveloped countries) only as a result of a long-sustained process of rapid technological improvement in both manufacturing and agriculture. In the countries which failed to participate in this process of long-sustained growth, some constraint must have inhibited the chain reaction process: for one reason or another, the environment was not favourable, or not sufficiently favourable, for this process really to start, or if it did start, to be long sustained.

I should like to distinguish between four different factors which could provide the cause of such constraints; this list is not intended to be exhaustive, and in any particular historical case there may have been other (largely political or educational) factors at work.

1. The first of these is the lack of responsiveness in agriculture to outside stimuli on account of economic or social factors. In

countries in which agricultural overpopulation has reached very high levels and where, in consequence, the rural community is very poor, the response to better market opportunities may be well-nigh non-existent. Harvests may vary with weather conditions, but a good harvest simply means less starvation: it does not generate a higher cash income, nor provide the opportunities for improving the land through more investment. Even when the physical conditions are more favourable and the population pressure is not so great, ancient forms of land tenure, the survival of feudal institutions, or absentee landlords, for instance may make it impossible for the actual cultivators of the soil to exploit the opportunities for improvement in the arts of cultivation. It is no accident that institutional reforms in the system of land ownership played such a critical role in the process of industrialisation in Europe. In England, as elsewhere in Western Europe, the so-called "agricultural revolution" historically preceded the Industrial Revolution. In some countries, as in England, this was brought about by the landlords expropriating the hereditary tenants; in others, as in France, by the hereditary tenants expropriating the landlords. Land reform, with the consequent agricultural revolution, also played a vital role in the development of Japan after the Meiji Restoration. By contrast, in countries where this agricultural revolution failed to occur (as in many countries of Latin America, the Middle East and south-east Asia), industrial development was stifled despite State support; economic development failed to reach the stage at which it became self-sustaining through rising levels of real income.

2. A second factor, equally important, is the failure to develop exports *pari passu* with the growth of the economy. For the early industrialisers who were able to supply the world with the products of advanced technology, the rate of industrialisation was export-led from the start. For the late developers this presented a far more difficult problem, since they were trading the advantages of low wages against the superior technology of the older industrial countries; but those which succeeded in passing through the critical phases to become high-income countries were invariably the countries which managed to sustain a buoyant growth of their exports.

For many of the countries outside Europe the initial stimulus to development came from the growth of exports from plantation agriculture and mining. With the growth of industry in Europe, markets were created for temperate foodstuffs, tropical products and minerals. The exploitation of these opportunities proceeded sometimes on the initiative of native producers, but more frequently through European capital and enterprise. It is often contended that the growing foreign-controlled mines and plantations were foreign enclaves which contributed little to the economic growth of the countries in which these developments occurred. This is broadly but not wholly accurate. They brought with them the educational stimulus of foreign contacts; and what is more important, they were a source of export earnings which could be channelled, in a suitable political environment, to provide opportunities for developing local industries. By contrast, the countries which did not have resources for the development of exports of primary products (because of an unfavourable climate or a lack of minerals in their territory) were under the greatest handicap to get economic development started.

3. Export earnings through agriculture or mining do not, however, in themselves suffice to launch the process of industrialisation without State support in the form of subsidies to industry or the adoption of protective tariffs. In the absence of these, the high initial costs (in terms of agricultural products) of home-produced manufactures imposes too severe a handicap on any latecomer to industrialisation to make manufacturing activities commercially profitable. The advantage of any underdeveloped country in the industrial field resides in low wages. In the initial stages of industrialisation this advantage is more than offset by low productivity. Hence under conditions of free trade, when the domestic price of manufacturers in terms of primary products is determined by world prices, the process of industrialisation may never begin.

4. However, whilst the competition of more advanced countries may prevent the domestic establishment of industries in the absence of *some* measure of protection, such policies are likely to succeed only if they are applied sensibly and with moderation. Excessive or indiscriminate protection may itself inhibit continued development for a number of reasons. In the first place, any

degree of protection involves a levy on agricultural producers, who are forced to sell their produce on less favourable terms in relation to the industrial goods for which they are exchanged; if the protection is excessive, the terms of trade will deteriorate so much as to deprive the farming community of the advantage of a growing real income, which is indispensable for the adoption of more advanced technologies. Hence it makes for agricultural stagnation, which will sooner or later bring industrial expansion to a standstill.

Import duties are efficacious in promoting industrialisation so long as there is scope for creating an internal demand for home-produced manufactured goods through the replacement of the pre-existing imports of such goods. But once the limits of "easy" import substitution have been reached, the momentum for further industrialisation is virtually exhausted—particularly where this development was only brought about by slowing down the growth of agricultural production. For as soon as import substitution is accomplished, the further growth of domestic industry becomes dependent either on the development of industrial exports or on the growth of production in the complementary sector of the economy, that is, in agriculture.

However, industrialisation fostered through high tariffs itself militates against the development of exports. Where the support to industry takes the form of a protective tariff and not of a direct subsidy, the internal price structure is adaped to the internal cost structure—not the internal cost structure to the external price structure. Industries are developed on the basis of a price relationship between manufactured goods and primary products which is divorced from the prevailing world price relationship; and the higher the protection, the greater the deviation between the system of internal prices and world prices will tend to be.

The theory of protective tariffs as a means of industrial development was originally presented as an "infant industry" argument: once the industries are well established, the protection should gradually be withdrawn, or else the industries will fail to become competitive in export markets. But this assumes that the initial degree of protection is none too high, and the degree of protection

fairly uniform between different industrial products. This has definitively not been the case in those countries which followed an inward strategy of economic development, that is to say, in those which attempted comprehensive industrialisation on a broad scale, with each separate industry obtaining the differential subsidy required for domestic manufacture, regardless of comparative cost. This meant that the cost of industrialisation was too high, for it involved an excessive burden on the agricultural sector; and since the growth of total employment is always limited by the growth of the non-agricultural employment potential, the growth of industrial activities as a whole was held down. Furthermore, the hoped-for improvements in productivity failed to materialise (or did so only to a moderate extent). With so many industries established more or less simultaneously, none of them could reach a sufficient size to become efficient: the economies of specialisation and large-scale production tended to get lost.

The dangers of such inward strategies are well illustrated by the history of many Latin American countries. For example, Argentina, Brazil and Chile each passed through a phase of relatively rapid growth, following the establishment of highly protective tariffs or import prohibitions during the Great Depression. But in each case this phase was followed by a prolonged period of very slow growth or stagnation, combined with prolonged and violent inflation, as the growth of urban employment tended to rise faster than the growth of marketed food supplies. The conditions under which the initial phase of rapid growth were attained made subsequent stagnation inevitable.

By contrast, the history of many of the smaller European countries which have been comparative latecomers in industrialisation, such as Switzerland or the Scandinavian countries, shows the advantages of an outward strategy. In each case tariffs were kept low and reasonably uniform; this made specialisation in industrial development possible from the start; some industries were developed to the stage of becoming internationally competitive before starting with the establishment of others; the range of domestic production of manufactured goods was broadened only gradually. In this manner the growth of exports kept pace with the growth of production; this provided the means for a steady growth in the

employment potential of the industrial sector, and thus made it possible for the disguised unemployment in agriculture to be gradually liquidated.

THE CHOICE OF TECHNOLOGY

I should now like to turn to the second of the two aspects mentioned at the beginning of this paper, which has also been the subject of a great deal of controversy. What kind of technologies should the underdeveloped countries adopt in order to secure the fastest rates of growth?

There has been much criticism of the policies of underdeveloped countries wishing to imitate the advanced technologies of the Western countries without inquiring whether these are appropriate to their circumstances. The advanced countries employ techniques which require a very large amount of capital per worker; since the underdeveloped countries have plenty of labour and very little capital, they should, according to this view, develop intermediate technologies which have a lower capital requirement and a higher labour requirement per unit of output.

Allied to this point of view is the suggestion that, since the great majority of their populations live in rural areas, they should avoid the high economic and social cost of large urban conglomerations and, instead, bring industrialisation to the villages. The development of cottage industries was at one stage an important feature of Indian economic planning; some years later, the idea of creating small-scale metal smelting and engineering works in the villages was the main feature of the "great leap forward" phase of the People's Republic of China. Both of these proved costly failures.

The fact that in all known historical cases the development of manufacturing industries was closely associated with urbanisation must have deep-seated causes which are unlikely to be rendered inoperative by the invention of some new technology. The regional concentration of industries has very important advantages which go well beyond the economies of large-scale operations. They are to be found in the availability of specalised skills, know-how and easy access to markets which make it profitable for firms using similar or related processes to be located close to each other. The concentra-

tion of particular phases of cotton textile production in particular cities (and sometimes in special regions of cities) in Lancashire was not the result of any deliberate planning: it emerged spontaneously, as a result of market forces. The same is true of the concentration of the engineering industry in Birmingham and of the jewellery industry in the little town of Pferzheim in Germany (which at one time had 20,000 jewellery workers); one could mention innumerable other examples. In none of these cases could the geographical concentration be explained by the technical need for particularly large-scale plant. The advantages of geographical concentration lay in the opportunities for a higher degree of specialisation between different enterprises and the consequent subdivision of industrial processes; in the availability of labour with many specialised skills; of a wide range of engineering and marketing knowledge, and so on. Though the cheapness of transport and the increasing use of electricity as a source of power made the location of industries far less dependent on their proximity to sources of raw materials and fuel, none of these factors lessened the advantages of a close concentration of industrial activities in large urban centres. Rural industries are unlikely to show the same continued tendency to technological change and improvement which comes from easy communication and shared experience.

In the same way, the idea that underdeveloped countries would stand to gain from the use of special labour-intensive technologies is of doubtful validity. It is of course obvious that countries which are short of capital should use techniques which make the best use of capital, that is, which have a low investment requirement per unit of output. It is a mistake to believe, however, that more primitive or less mechanised techniques which require less capital per worker are also more economical in capital per unit of output. A lower capital/labour ratio does not necessarily imply a lower capital/output ratio—indeed, the reverse is often the case. The countries with the most highly mechanised industries, such as the United States, do not require a higher ratio of capital to output. The capital/output ratio in the United States has been falling over the past 50 years whilst the capital/labour ratio has been steadily rising; and it is lower in the United States today than in the manufacturing industries of many underdeveloped countries. Techno-

logical progress in the present century led to a vast increase in the productivity of labour, but this was not accompanied by any associated reduction in the productivity of capital investment.

One reason for this is that the greater speed of "through-put" with modern technical processes led to economies in the amount of working capital required per unit of output. It was found in India, for example, that non-mechanical processes like hand-spinning or weaving are more costly in capital than modern machine processes, despite the fact that the cost of a hand-spinning wheel or a hand-loom per worker is only a small fraction of the cost of power-driven machinery per worker. The reason for this was found to be the very much greater requirement for working capital in the case of hand-made processes. Just because processing takes so much longer with non-mechanical methods, the working capital locked up per unit of raw material input, or per unit of final output, is much greater.

Nor is it correct to suggest that, just because there is a large amount of surplus labour, labour ought to be regarded as a "free good". However great the level of open or disguised unemployment, employed labour still has to be paid wages. A higher level of employment means a high wage bill, and a correspondingly higher demand for consumption goods, particularly for food. This is not only because at a low standard of living workers prefer to consume any additional income. Employment requires a greater expenditure of physical energy than idleness; a man can perform a full day's work only if he has a much higher calorie consumption than is necessary to sustain life in the absence of work. For this reason it is often profitable for employers to pay higher wages than the minimum at which they can hire workers: when earnings are low, calorie consumption becomes insufficient for efficient work performance—hence, beyond a point, a lower-wage worker involves a higher wage outlay per unit of output. This, I believe, is the main reason why even in the least developed countries with the largest ratio of surplus labour, the wages of factory workers are so much higher than the "opportunity cost" of labour, that is, the level of earnings per head in the rural sector. Indeed, the difference between industrial wages and agricultural earnings tends to vary in inverse proportion to the degree of development of an economy.

This is not to suggest that the need to maintain efficient work

performance is the only, or even the main, reason for the wide and growing earnings differentials between the organised industrial sector and the other sectors of developed countries. Indeed, the need to ensure a certain calorie consumption can hardly explain why in many underdeveloped countries real wages in industry are continuously rising, not only in terms of the goods which the workers produce, but also in terms of the goods which they consume, i.e. in terms of food. This phenomenon has not in my view been satisfactorily explained: it may have something to do with the existence of union bargaining, with legislative controls, and also with the monopolistic character of the manufacturing industries of underdeveloped countries, as a result of which a reduction in costs is not normally passed on in prices, so that, with rising productivity, only rising money wages can ensure that the workers share in the benefits of greater productivity.

But whatever the reason may be, there can be no doubt that the fast rate of increase in wages in the manufacturing sectors of underdeveloped countries (both in money and in real terms, and in relation to the rate of growth of earnings in the economy as a whole) represents a serious handicap to their industrial development and to the growth of employment in the organised sectors. The main reason for this is that, on account of this mechanism, the growth of productivity is prevented from having its normal effect in lowering the prices of industrial goods in terms of agricultural products: it does not therefore lead to any increase in the purchasing power of the rest of the community for industrial goods; nor does it involve any adaptation of the internal cost structure to the world price structure which, as I emphasised, is a precondition for the development of exports.

This process of continuously rising wages may also involve the adoption of a more capital-intensive technology (and therefore a smaller volume of employment for any given output) than would be socially desirable. For reasons mentioned earlier, however, this particular factor may not be of such importance as it is often thought to be in theoretical literature, precisely because technologies involving a lower capital/labour ratio do not necessarily imply a more economic use of capital per unit of output.

All this does not mean that the use of the most highly mechanised

technologies, yielding the highest output per worker, is necessarily the best means to be chosen. Nor is it correct to suppose that the best technology for underdeveloped countries is that which yields the highest output per unit of investment (irrespective of labour requirements) as would be the case if labour could really be treated as a "free good". The best general rule, as several economists have pointed out, is to choose the techniques which, at the prevailing and expected level of wages, yield the highest rate of profit per unit of investment: for, as a general rule, the techniques which yield the highest rate of profit serve to maximise the ratio of output to the additional consumption generated in producing that output: the greater the additional output available for reinvestment, the higher the rate of capital accumulation which the economy can sustain.

The most profitable technology for a capitalist employer may thus be no different from the theoretical "optimal technique" in a planned socialist economy. The question which needs further examination is whether this "most profitable" technique is necessarily different, in underdeveloped countries with relatively low wages per head, from the optimal techniques in the advanced countries with high wages per worker.

If the above characterisation of technological progress is correct, and the latest technologies normally yield the highest output per worker without any greater outlay of capital per unit of output, then the latest techniques must be superior to all others, irrespective of the level of wages, and irrespective of the amount of capital required per worker. However, this may not be true of all cases or of all industries. A highly capital-intensive technology (in the sense of one requiring a large investment per worker) may have a relatively lower labour productivity in a less developed country than in an advanced country, as against less advanced techniques. Owing to the greater difficulty of operating complex machines, which are liable to mechanical breakdowns, these may be relatively more costly to use in underdeveloped countries than simpler technologies requiring less skill. A bulldozer, for example, may be the cheapest way of moving earth for road-building or dam-building, in terms of both capital and labour, in a technically advanced country; yet it may be more expensive to operate than simpler instruments in a

less advanced country if, in the latter, it is idle half the time owing to mechanical breakdowns, or requires a large force of mechanics to keep it in good repair.

On the other hand, it is also true that in many cases the use of the most advanced technologies saves skilled labour, which is particularly scarce in underdeveloped countries; it may also be contended that in many cases the alternative to the use of such techniques is a more complex human organisation requiring skills of organisation and management which are even more difficult to obtain than capital. Therefore the question whether the most advanced technologies are more or less suitable for underdeveloped countries than for developed countries is one of considerable complexity, the answer to which might well differ in particular cases.

Apart from this, there are two main reasons why the latest machinery may not be the most suitable for use in underdeveloped countries.

The first derives from the opportunity to buy, at a relatively low cost, second-hand machinery which, though physically perfectly fit for use, is no longer profitable to operate in the advanced countries, owing to the competition of more recent and technologically more advanced plant and machinery. It is well known that equipment in advanced industrial countries is withdrawn from use long before it is physically worn out, owing to the continued rise in wages in relation to product prices which causes rapid obsolescence. This gradually eliminates the profit on their operation long before the physical efficiency of the equipment is impaired through wear and tear. Such obsolescent equipment can be acquired at low prices; and in countries where wages are low relative to product prices, it may thus be more profitable to install than the latest new equipment, which is more costly. There is a considerable international trade in such second-hand equipment: and given the opportunity to buy such machinery at low prices relative to their original cost of production, underdeveloped countries may well benefit from adopting, not the latest technologies of the advanced countries, but the technologies that were the most advanced 10 or 15 years ago.

The second reason is that the most advanced technologies require too large an output for their optimal utilisation. Technologi-

cal advance is biased in favour of large-scale production: the most efficient generating station, the most efficient steel mill, the most efficient tanker, and so on, require a much larger rate of throughput than was the case a generation ago. In 1950 the optimal output of an integrated steel plant was around 2 million tons a year. At present it is around 6 million tons, and in another 10 to 20 years it is likely to be twice as much again. This is partly because there are always inherent economies in large-scale operations; and technical advance consists in overcoming the constructional problems of making things to an ever larger size (for example, the largest tanker that can be built is necessarily the cheapest, since the carrying capacity of a larger tanker increases at a higher rate than the labour and materials cost of its construction, or the labour and fuel cost of its operation). It is partly also because much of the research and development expenditure in advanced countries is undertaken by giant firms whose economic interest is to develop techniques which give a differential advantage to the large-scale producer. The underdeveloped countries whose market for industrial goods is limited have neither the resources nor the market opportunities for the installation of plant with a very large capacity. Perhaps the most important respect in which they require technologies different from those of the advanced countries, and for the sake of which they would be justified in incurring heavy research and development expenditures of their own, is in the development of ways in which modern technological processes in the steel and chemical industries, for instance, could be adapted to efficient operation on a smaller scale.

Finally, one cannot emphasise too strongly that the efficiency and speed with which modern technology can be introduced in underdeveloped countries is very much a matter of the quality and character of the system of education. In many underdeveloped countries too much is spent in providing high-level education of a theoretical kind, and too little in creating a cadre of qualified managers, engineers and technicians. Together with the creation of efficient transport and communication systems, this is the most important aspect in which the development of a social infrastructure promotes economic development.

10

CAPITALISM AND INDUSTRIAL DEVELOPMENT: SOME LESSONS FROM BRITAIN'S EXPERIENCE[1]

UNTIL fairly recently economic theory of the orthodox kind had very little to contribute to an understanding of the most important questions which occupy the minds of historians and politicians: why some countries or regions of the world grow relatively fast whilst the others stagnate or grow only slowly. The division of the world into rich and poor areas is now known to be the cumulative result of differences in the compound rates of economic growth which only emerged with modern industrial capitalism—the so-called Industrial Revolution which started in England in the late eighteenth century. Up to that time—as far as one can tell—the rate of economic growth was very slow everywhere and the differences in the living standards of the inhabitants of the different areas were comparatively small. The differences in the endowment of natural resources of different parts of the globe were largely balanced by differences in the density of population of those areas —the innate advantages of the areas of high fertility tended to be offset by comparatively high population density—with the exception of the newly colonised areas of the Western Hemisphere or Oceania where the settlers brought with them a superior technology capable of providing far more food than was required for their own numbers.

But with the Industrial Revolution, particular regions began to grow at exceptionally high rates by past standards, whilst others were left behind. Fast economic growth was largely, if not exclusively, the result of the establishment of large-scale enterprises in manufacturing industry. The countries which have succeeded

[1] Written in 1972 and first published (in Spanish) in *Política Económica en Centro y Periferia (Ensayos en Honor a Felipe Pazos)*, eds. Diaz Alejandro, Teitel and Tokman, Fondo di Cultura, Mexico.

in becoming large centres of industry have become richly endowed with capital—both in terms of plant, machinery etc. and of human skills, resulting from education. But while capital is the most important condition or prerequisite of high efficiency production, one cannot *explain* differences in the wealth of nations in terms of differences in "capital endowment" of the different countries, in the same manner as one *can* explain differences in population density by reference to differing endowments of natural resources, such as climate, rainfall, geology, etc. For in contrast to natural resources which exist independently of human activities, "capital endowment" is necessarily the *result* of such activities. It is impossible therefore to separate cause and effect: it is just as sensible —indeed more enlightening—to say that capital accumulation has resulted from industrial development than that it was the cause of such development. For taking manufacturing activities as a whole, the growth of output and the accumulation of capital are merely different aspects of a single process. Capitalistic production is "production of commodities by commodities"; individual industrial activities make use of goods produced by other industrial processes as their inputs, and provide outputs which (in the great majority of cases) serve as the inputs of further processes. If all the various commodities were "non-durable"—i.e., if they were consumed, or rather transformed into other products, in a relatively short period—the gross output of industry per unit period could be looked upon both as the capital stock which serves as an aid to labour in production and as the product of that labour. The fact that some goods are durable does not create any basic difference: capital and output would still grow together at much the same rate so long as in the course of growth, the product-mix between durable and non-durable goods remained roughly the same.

A. CAUSES OF THE RISE OF MODERN CAPITALISM

To explain why certain countries have become industrialised and in the course of it have become richly endowed with capital, and gradually developed relatively high standards of living, we must enquire why modern industrial capitalism developed *when* it

did—and why it developed in England and not in some other country, say in France for example, which at that time was a much larger entity and just as advanced, or even more advanced, in culture and economic prosperity. And we must further explain why and how it spread to a limited number of other countries in the following two centuries.

This is a standard question which economic historians of every generation attempt to answer afresh in the light of the prevailing doctrines of economics and sociology. (It is a commonplace that each generation of economic historians rewrites history in the light of the latest prevailing theory.) Thus a generation ago it was fashionable, under the influence of Weber and Tawney, to emphasise the role of Protestant ethic in the development of modern capitalism. Protestantism generated a favourable attitude to trade and money-making, whereas in Catholic countries the acquisitive instinct was suppressed and the bourgeois tradesmen had a much lower social status than the bourgeois professional, such as a lawyer.

An even earlier view regarded the industrial revolution as the result of a number of important technological inventions in the eighteenth century which, by accident rather than any more basic cause, happened to have been first invented in England. The most important of these were Watt's steam engine; the invention by Abraham Darby of coke (and gas) from the heating of coal which made it possible to smelt iron without the use of charcoal (by this invention, at one stroke, Western civilisation was freed from the menace of economic decline through deforestation and the exhaustion of timber supplies); and finally, there were the vast improvements in labour productivity in the textile industry through the invention of a fast spinning machine (the so-called "spinning jenny") and a fast weaving machine (the "flying shuttle").

No doubt these inventions played a very important role. So did the triumph of the reformation—not so much on account of changes in psychological attitudes, or in the social status of commercial activities, but through the development of laws and institutions, which were favourable to the establishment of freedom of trading, both in goods and in property, and thus of competition and market-orientated enterprise.

B. THE FACTORY SYSTEM

But in themselves none of these developments would have transformed the productive powers of society and its rhythm of change as dramatically as they did had it not been for another change, which was a great social innovation which could by no stretch of the meaning of words be regarded as a "discovery" or "invention" in the sense of being the product of the progress of physical or engineering knowledge—I am referring to the introduction of the "factory system". It is worth pausing to inquire how this came about, and what were its principal consequences.

Though there is no settled view on these things, there were two important factors which in my view led to the introduction of this system in England in the closing stages of the eighteenth century: first, the rise of a powerful class of merchant-capitalists resulting from the development of overseas trade, following on the establishment of the American colonies, and also from the "glorious revolution" of 1689 which secured in England the political and institutional framework for the development of competitive market enterprise.

The second important factor was the agrarian revolution of the eighteenth century—also connected with important technical discoveries, in the form of new crops, new methods of ploughing and planting, and new methods of breeding animals—which was peculiar in that it meant the expropriation, not of feudal "absentee" landlords, but of the peasantry. It was therefore the very opposite of what happened in France during the Great Revolution when the peasants freed themselves of feudal dues and took effective possession of the land which they cultivated. In England, through many hundreds of special Acts of Parliament, the landowners took effective possession by depriving the peasantry of their traditional grazing land, and the opportunity to raise crops in open fields. The newly "enclosed" land was thus cultivated in much larger units, and by new techniques, mostly by commercially minded tenant farmers who rented the land from the landlords. This had two important consequences. First, it led to a dramatic increase in the "agricultural surplus": the proportion of output which was in excess of agriculture's own needs for food,

seed and feeding stuffs, and which was then produced for sale in the markets. (The existence of such a surplus is an essential prerequisite of urbanisation.) Second, it led to large numbers of peasants losing their traditional means of support on the land and being forced to seek employment away from their native surroundings—by "selling their labour", as Marx put it.

Until about 1780, the capitalist merchant-manufacturer made his profit mainly by buying raw materials—wool from domestic agriculture and cotton from overseas—and getting the spinner, the weaver, the dyer, etc. to process these materials in their own homes and with the aid of their own equipment much as a small dressmaker who would make a dress out of materials supplied by her customers in her own home, on her own sewing machine, and at her own pace. The capitalist entrepreneur owned the circulating capital through all stages of processing and occasionally made advance payments to the cottage artisans on their work contracts. But the latter owned the *tools* of their trade—the spinning wheel or the shuttle—and controlled the speed and the regularity with which the work was performed.

Even without the invention of new and more costly instruments —assisted first by water power and later by steam power—it was obvious that, given the emergence of a fast-growing urban proletariat without independent means of livelihood, the cost of processing materials into finished goods could be greatly reduced by erecting large buildings—"factories"— and fitting them up with enough equipment to occupy a large number of workers, who were hired to work for a fixed number of hours a day under close supervision: the workers would then be paid by the *hour*, or by the *day*, and not by the *piece*. This "factory system" had enormous advantages for the capitalist entrepreneur even without the possibility of using large and more complex machinery than the individual artisan could obtain or use with advantage. For it made the close supervision of work performance much easier and far more economical and thus got the maximum out of any given labour force. But it became *practicable* only when there were large numbers of workers thrown off the land seeking to be hired.

The long-term consequences of the introduction of this factory system were even more revolutionary, for they led to a tremendous

acceleration in the rate of technical progress. For once the merchant-capitalists cottoned on to the idea of "manufacturing" by building factories, equipping them with plant and machinery and with workers to man them, a process of cumulative technological change had begun—a permanent technological revolution the end of which is still not in sight. For the very system of "factory production" gave a continued and powerful incentive to the invention and installation of "bigger and better machines" which were increasingly labour-saving and able to produce goods on an ever-increasing scale. It also gave a continuous incentive for the invention of new products, of new processes, and for increasing specialisation in the making of parts and components.

Before the factory system was invented profit-seeking or "profit-maximising" enterprise was largely confined to trade: in other words, to buying things from the producers and transporting them to places where they could be sold to the best advantage. The merchant-capitalist of the Renaissance was "dynamic" enough in the continued search for new sources of supply and of new markets (hence the voyages of discovery and the emergence of the great trading companies of India, the Far East and of the West Indies) but he did not become directly responsible for the production of raw materials or their processing into finished products which remained in the hands of peasants, handicraftsmen or skilled artisans: in other words, traditionally minded producers, working largely with their own tools and their own labour, resistant by nature to change or innovation.

But with the introduction of the factory system, the thought of making fortunes by making goods cheaper—by introducing new methods and producing on a large scale with the aid of power-driven machinery—opened up a new dynamic phase in which the individual enterprise continually enlarged its scale of operations by accumulating capital and hiring more and more workers; and where the profits available for plough-back into the business set the limit to the rate of growth of the individual enterprise. Since increasing returns (the economies of large-scale production) appeared virtually inexhaustible, each entrepreneur strove to accumulate capital as fast as possible in order to keep ahead of, or at least to keep pace with, his rivals.

C. THE ROLE OF DEMAND

In the view of some of the keenest contemporary observers—such as Ricardo, John Stuart Mill or even Marx (at some stage)—the pace of this feverish expansion "fed on itself". So long as labour was available—and an unlimited supply of wage labour appeared to be ensured, partly through the destruction of independent small-scale enterprise which attended this development and partly by the rapid increase in population attributed, in a Malthusian manner, to the very fact that the demand for labourers was increasing—it was taken for granted that an increase in production itself generated the increase in purchasing power to ensure that the market for the commodities produced by capitalist enterprise increased *pari passu* with the scale of production. Since in the market, commodities are exchanged against commodities, money is just a circulating medium—"supply creates its own demand" and "there is no amount of capital which may not be employed in a country, because demand is only limited by production".[1] The point has been made even more forcibly by John Stuart Mill: "All sellers are inevitably and *ex vi termini* buyers. Could we suddenly double the productive powers of the country, we should double the supply of commodities in every market; but we should, by the same stroke, double the purchasing power." Hence "there is no over-production; production is not excessive, but merely ill-assorted".[2]

However if the "capitalist sector" of the economy does not embrace economic activity of *all kinds* (and in *all areas*) but is mainly confined to "manufactures"—i.e. the processing of crude materials through the aid of wage-labour—the purchasing power generated by the additional production of the capitalist sector will not in itself be sufficient to match the increase in supply: for only a proportion of the incomes earned in the capitalist sector (whether in the form of wages, profits or rents) will be spent on goods produced within that sector; the rest will generate demand for the products of other sectors, mainly agriculture.

Now it is in this context that the Say–Mill method of reasoning leads one astray. Mill would have said that if production in the

---

[1] Ricardo, *Principles* (Sraffa, ed.), pp. 290–2.
[2] John Stuart Mill, *Principles*, Book III, ch. xiv.

industrial sector expands too fast relative to the agricultural sector, production becomes "ill-assorted": but the movement of prices that would accompany that event, together with the free mobility of labour and capital, would bring its own remedy. Agricultural prices would rise in terms of industrial prices; this would cause capital (and labour) to flow from industry to agriculture until the returns on investment were again equalised: when that happened, the necessary balance between the sectors would have been re-established, and the demand for each commodity (and hence the demand for *all* commodities) would again be in balance with the supply. This result moreover would not have been regarded as being dependent on agriculture responding to an increase in demand for its products by increasing the supply of agricultural commodities. Even if—on account of the Law of Diminishing Returns—the supply of agricultural goods were inelastic, the operation of competitive markets would still ensure that equilibrium between market demand and supply in individual *sectors* is restored through the movement in prices. If agricultural goods are scarce, relative to industrial goods, agricultural prices will rise in terms of industrial prices: this will mean a transfer of "real" purchasing power from industry to agriculture; and this process will go on until the producers in the agricultural sector are able (and willing) to buy all the goods which industry is capable of producing in excess of industry's *own* requirements for industrial goods, whether for purposes of consumption, or capital investment.

Now it has long been perceived, though somewhat dimly, that there is something basically wrong with this account of how a capitalist market economy works. But few economists have been able to show convincingly just what is wrong with it: *which* is the critical point in the argument where the reasoning goes astray. In my view it is at the stage where the argument presupposes that the terms of trade "will go on improving" in favour of agriculture (i.e. agricultural prices will *go on* rising in terms of industrial prices) until the "excess supply" of industrial goods is eliminated.

This cannot happen (or is unlikely to happen) simply because "industry" is not an independent form of activity: it consists of the *processing* of goods produced on the land—either directly, as when

raw wool or raw cotton is made into finished textiles; or indirectly, when the food produced in agriculture serves as the means of employing labour in industry.

Since industrial wages in terms of food cannot fall below a certain minimum, the "value added" by manufacturing activities cannot fall in terms of agricultural products below a certain minimum either (at any given productivity of labour in terms of industrial goods) and this sets a limit to the extent to which agricultural prices can rise in terms of industrial prices. (If agricultural prices rise in money terms, this will invariably carry with it, as the experience of many Latin American countries has shown, a corresponding rise in money wages in industry, so that a rise in agricultural prices induced by excess demand may result in a general rise in prices, even though in the relevant sense, there is an excess supply, not an excess demand, for industrial products.)

Given this fact—i.e. that the supply of goods produced by the capitalist industrial sector is highly elastic at a particular price in terms of agricultural goods (meaning that at given terms of trade between industry and agriculture the quantity supplied is highly responsive to the quantity demanded) it follows that both the level and the rate of growth of output of the capitalist sector is dependent on the level, or rate of growth, of the effective demand for its products coming from *outside* the capitalist sector. The pace at which both output and employment can grow and at which industrial capital will accumulate will thus be dependent on the growth of exogenous demand. The capitalist sector, beyond a certain stage, cannot grow on its own, lifting itself by its own bootstraps.

This means however that "Say's Law" will not apply when one considers the economic relationships between the "capitalist" and the "non-capitalist" sectors of the world economy, or, what comes to the same thing in broad approximation, the relationship between "industry" and "agriculture". Since in most areas of the world the population density of rural areas is adapted to, and varies with, the "productive powers" of the soil, it is these "productive powers" and not the available supply of labour, which will determine how much will be produced at any given time in any given area. Labour is an essential factor in all agricultural production,

but it will not (normally) be a "scarce" factor—there will be "disguised unemployment" which will ordinarily be large relative to the population of working age. Hence the withdrawal of labour from rural areas will not cause any reduction in the amount of output derived from the soil; indeed any sizeable reduction in the population will normally be associated with an increase in land, as well as labour productivity, owing to the consequential changes in the organisation of farms and in technology.

Hence the "opportunity cost" of labour to industry, in terms of agricultural products foregone, will be zero or negative, but its actual cost will always be positive—the worker cannot survive, let alone perform work, below a certain real wage in terms of food.

It is this factor which makes the supply of industrial products elastic in terms of agricultural goods (in the sense defined above), irrespective of whether there is "full employment" or not. And it is the basic reason why Say's Law does not apply to the processing part of economic activities looked at in isolation; why Ricardo's statement that "there is no amount of capital which may not be employed in a country because demand is only limited by production" is basically untrue, if the term "country" is taken to apply to any actual country, such as Britain. This is because the demand generated by incomes earned in production *in* Britain can never be sufficient to match the production that gave rise to those incomes, since part of the demand thus generated is for goods produced in other countries, i.e. for imports. On the other hand, part of the demand for goods produced in Britain comes from abroad, and this part can be taken to be given more or less independently of incomes generated by production in Britain. For a country which imports food and raw materials and exports manufactures the Ricardian mechanism showing the equalisation of price levels and of payments balances through changes in the international distribution of precious metals (or, what comes to the same thing under modern conditions, through changes in the exchange rate) may be unavailing in securing "full employment equilibrium" through a lowering of the price of exports in terms of imports, precisely because, owing to the downward rigidity of the level of wages in terms of imported goods, the *price* of exports (given

G

the productivity of labour) may not be reduced, or not lastingly reduced, beyond a certain level.

This is the basis of the doctrine of "foreign trade multiplier" according to which the production of a country will be determined by the *external* demand for its products and will tend to be that multiple of that demand which is represented by the reciprocal of the proportion of *internal* incomes spent on imports. This doctrine asserts the very opposite of Say's Law: the level of production will not be confined by the availability of capital and labour; on the contrary, the amount of capital accumulated, and the amount of labour effectively employed at any one time, will be the resultant of the growth of external demand over a long series of past periods which permitted the capital accumulation to take place that was required for enabling the amount of labour to be employed and the level of output to be reached which was (or could be) attained in the current period.

Keynes, writing in the middle of the Great Depression of the 1930s, focussed his attention on the consequences of the failure to *invest* (due to unfavourable business expectations) in limiting industrial employment *below* industry's attained capacity to provide such employment; and he attributed this failure to excessive saving (or an insufficient propensity to consume) relative to the opportunities for profitable investment. Hence his concentration on liquidity preference and the rate of interest, as the basic cause for the failure of Say's Law to operate under conditions of low investment opportunities and/or excessive savings; and the importance he attached to the savings/investment multiplier as a short-period determinant of the level of production and employment.

In retrospect I believe it to have been unfortunate that the very success of Keynes's ideas in connection with the savings/investment multiplier diverted attention from the "foreign trade multiplier" which, over longer periods, is a far more important and basic factor in explaining the growth and rhythm of industrial development. For over longer periods Ricardo's presumption that capitalists only save in order to invest, and hence the *proportion* of profits saved would adapt to changes in the profitability of investment, seems to me more relevant; the limitation of effective

demand due to over-saving is a short-run (or cyclical) phenomenon, whereas the rate of growth of "external" demand is a more basic, long run determinant of both the rate of accumulation and the growth of output and employment in the "capitalist" or "industrial" sectors of the world economy.

From the point of view of any particular centre of industry (I use this term advisedly—in preference to "country") the growth of such "outside" demand is partly the result of increased "market penetration" (which means gains in trade achieved at the expense of producers in other industrial centres or of small-scale "precapitalist" enterprise) and partly it reflects the increased purchasing power of the agricultural sector due to a rise in agricultural productivity and the consequent rise in the marketable surplus. The rate of industrial growth will thus be dependent on the growth of "exports"—using that term in the specific sense of sales *outside* the particular industrial centre, as against sales *within* it.

Contrary to the traditional view which attributed the rate of industrial development in England to the rate of saving and capital accumulation and to the rate of technical progress due to invention and innovation, more recent evidence tends to suggest that Britain's industrial growth was "export-led" from a very early date. This is clearly shown by the timing of fluctuations in industrial output and investment which, both in the eighteenth century and since the early railway boom at any rate, were regularly preceded by fluctuations in the volume of exports.

Britain, being the first country to manufacture goods in factories on a large scale, was able to increase her exports at a fast rate, partly at the expense of other exporting countries (such as France) but largely by competing successfully with small local producers in other countries. The growth of exports of British-made cotton goods to India and China in the nineteenth century meant a severe shrinkage of local small-scale enterprise—the virtual disappearance of locally made handwoven cloth—without any compensation in the form of alternative employment opportunities for the people displaced. With the transport revolution, vast areas became accessible to trade, and regions previously self-contained were increasingly drawn into the network of the world economy. But while the growth of industries in Britain (followed by

other countries of Western Europe) created new markets for temperate foodstuffs, tropical products and minerals, it also meant the increasing displacement of local small-scale industries, with the attendant increase in disguised unemployment and poverty.

D. CAUSES OF BRITAIN'S DECLINE

The third quarter of the nineteenth century—more precisely, the years 1846–73—saw the zenith of Britain's predominance in industrial production. This was the period in which Britain's share of world trade in manufactured goods was at its highest, and British exports showed the fastest growth.

From then on, Britain experienced a continuing loss of foreign markets caused by the industrialisation of other countries. A succession of countries—Germany, then France, then the United States, then the smaller countries of Western Europe, and finally Japan—went through the same succession of stages of industrial development, fostered in every case by protective tariffs and other forms of Government support. The first stage was the substitution of home production for imports in the so-called "light industries" (consumer goods) and then the development of an export potential in such goods; then the development of the so-called "heavy industries", or the capital goods industries—such as steel, engineering and shipbuilding—again, first to provide substitutes for imports in these categories and then to develop an export potential. Each of these countries provided at some stage a major market for British goods; indeed a large increase in the demand for British made plant and machinery accompanied the early stages of industrialisation in most countries—including that of the United States or Japan. But in each case this was a *transitional* phenomenon: as industrial development proceeded, each of these countries became not just self-sufficient but an important supplier of such goods in the world market, and thus an important competitor to Britain in third markets. So the destination of British exports was constantly shifting: the British machinery sold to Germany in the 1880s and to America in the 1890s went to Japan in the 1900s and to India, Australia and South Africa after the First World War. This meant that the rate of growth of British

exports to the outside world became slow and uncertain: for a period of about sixty to seventy years, Britain succeeded in making up for the loss of exports in a succession of markets by the development of new markets in other places, supported by heavy British investment, as in the railways of India or Latin America. But the net outcome was not only that Britain's share in world trade kept on declining, but the rate of growth of her manufactured exports, and that of her manufactured production as a whole, remained considerably lower than that of the countries the industrialisation of which was of more recent origin.

Thus the very fact of being the country which gave birth to modern industry—the "arch-capitalist" country—which gave Britain such a strong competitive advantage over other countries in the first seventy-five years of the last century, actually turned into a serious handicap in the subsequent seventy-five years. This is because of two basic features of capitalism which are rarely emphasised or properly understood. The first of these is that in an unregulated market economy the *growth* of industrial production is strongly dependent on the growth of the market, which means demand originating from outsiders—the latter may come from the growth of her own agriculture or through exports to other countries. The second is the so-called "Verdoorn Law"—the strong correlation between the growth of output per worker and the growth of *total* output, which in turn is a reflection of "increasing returns" or the economies of large-scale production. As a result of the latter, the faster the "effective demand" for a country's industry is growing, the faster the rate of growth of productivity and of real income per head.

As the experience of the last hundred years has shown, the *successful* latecomers to industrialisation were able to attain much faster rates of growth both of "outside" sales and of total production than Britain achieved in the heyday of her industrial supremacy, and for that reason were able to overtake her, one after another, in a relatively short space of time. This is because, given the size and the rate of growth of the world market at any one time (including in that notion any particular country's "own" or "protected" market) the *successful* challenger who is able to increase its share in the world market is bound to have a faster rate of

growth than that of the market as a whole and, *a fortiori*, of the country whose share in the world market is reduced in consequence.

There can be little doubt that throughout the nineteenth century and also in the present century, right up to the Second World War, Great Britain's economic growth was closely dependent on the growth of her exports. Given the fact that her share of the world market was bound to decline continually as a result of the industrialisation of other countries, whereas the share of the later industrialisers—at least of the "successful" industrialisers (on this more below)—was bound to increase over sustained periods, it was quite inevitable that both the growth of production and the accumulation of capital should be much lower in Britain than in the countries that were subsequently industrialised and became major competitors of Britain as exporters of manufactured goods. As the world was "catching up" with Britain in the development of modern capitalism, her opportunities for continued economic growth were continually threatened and became increasingly precarious.

Many economic historians have attributed the major cause of Britain's relative decline from the last quarter of the nineteenth century onwards to poor industrial management,[1] to the failure to keep up with the growth of modern technology in comparison to countries such as Germany and the United States which had a more advanced network of educational institutions in industrial technology. No doubt such factors played a role in the speed with which Britain lost markets to her more "dynamic" competitors. But so long as other countries were able to expand their industries under the umbrella of protective tariffs and thereby reduce the market for British goods through the process of "import-substitution" and through exports to third markets, Britain was bound to operate under a strong handicap, as the growth of both her industrial investment and her labour productivity lagged increasingly behind the others, steadily weakening her competitive strength, and for these basic disadvantages the exploitation of the international advantages and know-how of the London capital market, and the development of protected overseas markets under

---

[1] See, e.g., D. H. Aldcroft: "The Entrepreneur and the British Economy, 1870–1914", *Economic History Review* (2nd series), August 1964, pp. 113–34.

Imperial preference could offer but temporary and limited compensation.

The last twenty-five years have had a number of unique and unexpected features. There was an unprecedented boom in the world economy, sustained over several decades and interrupted only by short and minor setbacks. Due to the successive reductions in obstacles to trade—through the G.A.T.T. treaties, the creation of the Common Market and of E.F.T.A. and other preferential areas—there was an increasing interchange of industrial goods *between* the highly industrialised countries; both their exports and imports of manufactured goods increased at a faster rate than the total domestic production or consumption of such goods. This was in sharp contrast to the period 1880–1940, which was characterised by increased economic nationalism and industrial autarky: international trade in manufactures grew *less fast* than world industrial production. The post-First World War policies were more successful in exploiting economies of specialisation and large-scale production, and were attended by much faster rates of growth of the productivity of labour.

All fast-growing industrial countries had an even faster rate of growth of output in their manufacturing sector and this was associated with a rate of growth of *exports* of manufactures which in turn was considerably higher than the rates of growth of their *total* output of manufactured goods. This was true of nine of the eleven industrialised countries which account for 85–90 per cent. of total world trade in manufactures—the two exceptions being the U.S. and the U.K., whose joint share of world trade diminished from 40 per cent. to 20 per cent. in the last twenty years. (By contrast the share in world trade of the three trade-gaining countries— Germany, Italy and Japan—rose from 20 to 40 per cent., while the remaining countries maintained a more or less stable share of world trade in manufactures, the overall volume of which showed an almost uninterrupted accelerating trend.)

Thus the growth of all fast-growing countries appears to have been "export-led". The two conspicuous exceptions were Britain and the U.S., whose rates of economic growth, however, were also

highly satisfactory by their own historical standards—though their growth was appreciably lower than that of the other advanced industrial countries of the post-war period.

In the case of Britain the adoption of Keynesian policies of economic management after 1945 meant that the growth of demand for industrial production, and therefore the level of industrial investment, was no longer *dependent* on the growth of export demand. The pursuit of "full employment policies" involved the substitution of "consumption-led" growth for "export-led" growth.[1] This meant that instead of having a chronic insufficiency of effective demand, manifesting itself in low investment and heavy unemployment, there was a chronic tendency for the growth of imports to outpace the growth of exports, leading to periodic balance of payments crises and consequent sharp reversals of domestic policies—the so-called "stop-go". Despite these periodic interruptions, the quarter of the century following the Second World War recorded a higher rate of growth in G.N.P., in output per head, and even in exports than any previous twenty-five-year period in British history. It appears paradoxical, but in the light of our analysis by no means surprising, that during the very period when Britain was consistently at the bottom of the "League tables" in terms of the rate of economic growth in relation to other advanced countries, she was at the top in terms of her *own* historical record. This was because despite its obvious limitations (particularly under a regime of fixed exchange rates) a deliberate policy of demand management through fiscal measures *did* ensure a certain rate of growth of industrial capacity and this in turn induced, as a by-product, a steady growth in the capacity to export which might not have occurred otherwise.[2]

In the case of the United States also, Keynesian policies of demand management, combined with a large increase in the scale of public expenditure in relation to the G.N.P., ensured a rate of growth of effective demand independently of exports which

[1] This distinction, and the consequential effects of the two kinds of growth on productivity etc. are set out at some length in my paper "Conflicts in National Economic Objectives", *Economic Journal*, March 1971, pp. 10–16, and reprinted in *Further Essays on Economic Theory*, pp. 155–75.

[2] The proportion of the G.N.P. devoted to industrial investment was more than twice as great as in the inter-war period. See R. C. O. Matthews, *Economic Journal*, September 1968, p. 559.

in the latter parts of the period was attended by a chronic and growing deficit in the balance of payments: though unlike Britain, the U.S., by virtue of the international position of the dollar, was never forced into the position of having to contract demand internally for the sake of the balance of payments.

It is an open question how far the growing payments deficit of the U.S.—which was largely a reflection of her own fiscal policies —was not itself a major contributory factor to the sustained expansionary climate of the world economy. Clearly this rapid progress would not have occurred without a rapid growth in the overall world demand for industrial goods—which involved in turn a rapid growth in the supply of food and basic materials absorbed by the industrial sectors. The rapid and sustained growth of agricultural yields was the most important and perhaps the least expected feature of this period. So far, despite growing forebodings of the shape of things to come, the growth, both of agricultural productivity and of raw material extraction—fuels, fibres and minerals—kept pace, or more than kept pace, with the demands of the industrial centres.[1]

This post-war period was conspicuous however for its failures as well as its successes; and the really intriguing question is why industrial capitalism failed to "take off" in so many countries when it succeeded in others.

In the pre-First World War period (and to a large extent also in the pre-Second World War period) a considerable part of the underdeveloped world had a colonial status—their development policies were governed by the colonial powers that ruled over them and whose interest dictated that they should develop as raw material producers and provide markets for the industrial goods which they themselves produced.

But with the disappearance of colonies there was no reason why the process of industrial development should not "take off" in these countries in much the same way as it did in say, Germany of the 1880s or in Japan of the 1920s.

Yet in a large number of countries industrialisation has not succeeded in raising productivity, employment and living stan-

---

[1] This was true at the time of writing. Since then the situation has changed as described in my 1976 paper. See *Further Essays on Economic Theory*, pp. 214-30.

dards in the dramatic manner of the "successful" developers of Western Europe or Japan. In a number of Latin American countries the tempo of economic growth originating in the industrialisation which began in the 1930s and was much stimulated during the Second World War, tended to peter out subsequently. In others, such as India and Pakistan, a succession of comprehensive development plans failed to bring about any significant improvement in living standards.

The single common characteristic of all these countries is that they failed to develop a significant volume of exports in manufactured goods. The stimulus to industrial production came from high tariffs or severe quantitative restrictions on imports. This made it profitable to develop home industries in substitution for imports, but since the exogenous component of demand for the products of industry was confined to the purchasing power of the agricultural sector, which was limited, and improved only slowly, the basis for a sustained growth of industrial production was lacking, once the opportunities for "easy" import substitution were exhausted.

Their failure to follow up the import-substitution stage with the export stage no doubt reflected the fact that the productivity of labour in industry, given the level of real wages in terms of foodstuffs and raw materials, had not risen to the point at which the costs of "value-added by fabrication" became low enough, in terms of unprocessed materials, to enable them to compete in the world market.

This is not just a matter of the *size* of the market in the individual country, but of the degree of concentration and dispersion in industrial development. There have been a number of small countries—from Switzerland to Hong Kong—who succeeded in becoming major exporters of industrial products by concentrating their industrial effort over a narrow field—i.e. by developing *certain* industries to the stage at which they have become major exporters before extending import-substitution to others. The secret of "successful" industrialisation thus appears to be an "outward strategy"—to develop the ability to compete in export markets in selected fields at a relatively early stage of development, and to keep the growth of export capacity in line with the growth of industrial activities.

Part III

THE COMMON MARKET

11

EUROPE'S AGRICULTURAL DISARRAY[1]

THE fundamental objectives and the basic justification of the Common Agricultural Policy of the European Economic Community are rarely if ever questioned in authoritative quarters. For the bulk of articulate public opinion, the opinion of parliaments, political parties, or officials, the C.A.P. is still regarded as the cornerstone of the whole concept underlying the Common Market. As an important French official told me a few years ago in conversation, without a Common Agricultural Policy the Common Market is nothing. It is the Common Agricultural Policy which gives it flesh and blood. This is still widely believed.

My purpose today is to question these premises. I will first state my views, and then try to justify them. I think the whole Common Agricultural Policy is fundamentally misconceived—in terms of the objectives which European integration is intended to serve. It hinders, and does not promote, the growth of welfare to the peoples of Europe. It hinders, and does not promote, the welfare and development of the rest of the world. It is a stumbling block to the attainment of the best allocation of resources within the Common Market. Finally, it hinders the rationalisation and development of agriculture itself. It hinders Europe's exports, and thus her economic growth, both through its adverse effects on the growth of demand for industrial products by overseas countries and through its adverse effects on the competitiveness (or potential competitiveness) of European industry as against other industrial producers, who obtained their food more cheaply in terms of industrial goods. It is Europe's good fortune that its most important industrial competitors—the U.S. or Japan—have so far succumbed to the same temptations of taxing their industrial

[1] An abbreviated version of a lecture originally delivered to the International Press Institute in Paris, 13 January 1970, and published in the *New Statesman*, 3 April 1970.

workers for the benefit of their farmers. This latter impediment is not therefore as important now as it could be in the future. Finally, and I put this point last deliberately, it raises serious and wholly avoidable obstacles to the adhesion of other countries, particularly of Britain, which Europeans *qua* Europeans may regard as inherently desirable—something which is in the interest of Europe, and not just in the interest of the United Kingdom.

I should now like to argue these contentions. I should like to start by asking what are the objectives of the Common Agricultural Policy? How far are these objectives legitimate in the first place? Second, assuming that the objectives are legitimate, how far are the *means* adopted appropriate to realising the objectives?

THE QUEST FOR UNIFORMITY

It is not easy to answer these questions because one cannot just turn to the Rome Treaty to find an authoritative statement on the objectives of the C.A.P. The Rome Treaty does refer to the need for stable prices for agricultural products, for stable and rising incomes for agricultural producers, but goes no further. There are other known objectives which may or may not have been explicitly formulated. There is the objective of making the Common Market self-sufficient in food, and possibly also to go beyond that and make the Common Market a large agricultural surplus area. Without the desire of making it a surplus area, it is difficult to see the justification for the very elaborate provisions for subsidising agricultural exports.

A second objective (self-sufficiency apart) is to ensure uniform prices. This was basic to the whole conception of Jean Monnet (who really invented the idea of a Common Market from the beginning). But, of course, what is meant by "uniform prices" is not always the same. One can ensure "uniform prices" merely by removing barriers to trade so that price differences between consuming areas are no greater than can be accounted for by differences in transport costs. One can also ensure that there are uniform "prices" and uniform "terms of competition" at the same time—which is a far more difficult notion; going beyond the mere removal of trade barriers. The latter involves the removal of all

differential advantages to the different trading areas—such as differential subsidies or subventions; railway tariffs, and numerous other questions of that kind.

In the case of the agricultural policy, one important purpose was to ensure that European workers *pay* the same prices for food, because food is an essential element in the cost of labour. If some countries' industrial workers pay higher food prices in terms of industrial goods than those of other countries, then that industrial centre is put at a disadvantage in relation to the others. There was also the idea that *producers* should get the same prices—which is based on yet another conception of "fairness". Thus, the basic purposes of the C.A.P. are more fuzzy and muddled than those governing industrial integration. There is the question of uniform prices to consumers, as well as to producers—where transport costs and distributive margins differ, the former is not really ensured by the latter.

On the other hand, uniform prices to consumers do *not* require uniform prices for the producers—the mere removal of trade barriers would ensure uniform prices in the former sense. But the objective of uniform prices to producers is to secure fair competition, I suppose, between the different agricultural countries, and to integrate agriculture into a single market as a counterpart of industrial integration; thereby giving the same opportunities for specialisation and the division of labour that comes from the removal of industrial tariffs.

But here the analogy with industry breaks down. As the post-war experience has shown (long before the Common Market) the reduction and stabilisation of tariffs and the removal of quantatitive restrictions which resulted from G.A.T.T. and the O.E.E.C. arrangements has increased the scope for international interchange of industrial goods enormously—in components even more than in finished goods. There has been a tremendous growth in trade between Britain, Germany, France, Italy, Sweden and others in industrial goods—although they are all large industrial producers and exporters. The reason for that is the importance of economies of scale in industrial production, which has been greatly underestimated in the past. As soon as restrictions were removed and tariffs made moderate—I would regard a 10 per cent. tariff as

moderate in this context—it paid automobile makers in the various countries, say, Britain and France, to buy some components—say, some parts of a carburettor—from a German manufacturer, and it paid German and other motor-car makers to buy some other component manufactured, say, in Britain. So the European motor-car industry became far more "integrated" than appeared on the surface, because an increasing proportion of what goes into a car in all these countries is made by one or a few manufacturers in one or other of the producer countries. The larger the total market, the further this kind of specialisation and differentiation will be carried. There is thus a large scope for increasing productivity by making the market larger—by removing impediments to trade.

INDUSTRY AND AGRICULTURE

But there is nothing comparable to this kind of advantage in agriculture. Agricultural productivity of a farmer in north-western France, in Germany or Belgium, is not in the least affected by the enlargement of the market. It is affected by investment, by improvements in technology, by changes in the system of land tenure —these are far more important than the size of the market, or greater opportunities for specialisation. Modern methods of agriculture are incompatible, as the Mansholt Report so convincingly argues, with the kind of peasant farming in which many of the farms are of the size of 1 hectare or less, or between 1–10 hectares. Efficiency requires large-scale units of at least 80 to 100 hectares. But whether production is organised in a 100-hectare farm or in 1-hectare farms, the size of the market—whether it is for 200 million consumers or 50 million or 3 million consumers— makes no difference to efficiency. In the case of carburettor components, electronics, and many other things, it makes a great deal of difference. Hence the advantages of integration, very real in industry, are illusory in agriculture.

Moreover, there is no reason to suppose that in agriculture (as distinct from manufacturing) common prices in money terms (in dollar terms, at ruling rates of exchange) serve the interest of the best allocation of resources, either within a country, or between

the member countries. This is because the true "opportunity costs" of agricultural production, in terms of industrial goods, may be very different, and are not properly measured in terms of money costs. Thus, high money costs of agriculture in Germany—despite relatively high efficiency in terms of yields per hectare, or yield per man—may be an indication of *high* opportunity costs; which in turn is reflected in the fact that the German farmer's earnings are more closely related to industrial earnings. High prices are needed to keep people on farms who could easily be absorbed in industry, where their contribution to the G.N.P. would be much greater. In a country like Germany, which suffers from labour shortage (as shown by the introduction of nearly 2 million foreign workers in the last few years) a highly protectionist agricultural policy seems contrary to the national interest. In the case of Italy, on the other hand, where money costs of agriculture are also high—not because earnings are high, but because agriculture, particularly in the South, is highly inefficient—the "opportunity cost" of protecting agriculture is very low—almost zero in fact. For if, on account of low prices, the farmers were squeezed out of existence, there would be no increase in alternative lines of production, there would simply be more unemployment, and nothing to offset the fall in agricultural production. In France, on the other hand, high prices mean that the less efficient farms are kept in existence, the transfer of labour to industrial occupations is slowed down, and despite high prices the earnings-differential between rural and urban workers remains large.

PRICE LEVEL AND PRICE STRUCTURE

In a situation like this—with countries in differing stages of development, and with differing degrees of disguised unemployment—a common system of producers' prices is hardly conducive to the best allocation of resources. The same price which *stimulates* efficiency in country A is an *impediment* to higher efficiency in country B. Therefore no *uniform* price could meet the real needs of the different countries. Indeed, the "uniform" Common Market prices, arrived at after a good deal of haggling and bargaining, necessarily reflect a compromise which, unlike a true compromise,

is not an expression of the "highest common factor" of mutual interest—is not the "best" for each, in the light of what is "best" for the others—but a compromise which is not in the interest of any one of the parties.

Take the wheat price, for example. This was arrived at after a great deal of bargaining between France and Germany; and it is, of course, somewhere in between the price which the Germans wanted and the price which the French wanted. But it is not a satisfactory price for either country. It is too high for France, since it hinders the progress of French agriculture by enabling high-cost production to be maintained. And it is not satisfactory to Germany, since it requires Germany to supplement the incomes of her farmers by budgetary measures, given her objectives—be they good or bad— of protecting the standard of living of her farmers. The plain fact is that in all these cases, the interest of each of the member countries, and the best allocation of resources would be served by *different* prices, not by *common* prices.

Apart from the level of prices, there is also the question of the price structure. Most experts on agriculture agree that for high productivity, a high standard of living economy, the type of agriculture required is one that concentrates on high quality foods, such as meat and dairy products. This is the principle on which Danish agriculture, and to some extent also British agriculture— is based—on the import of cheap feeding stuffs, which are then used for conversion into high-quality foods, like meat, poultry, eggs, milk, etc. But it requires *low* cereal prices in relation to meat prices. The Common Market price structure is the very opposite.

To conclude, there are no great economies of scale in agriculture and no great potentialities resulting from a common market in agricultural products as such. I would also add that there is no great virtue in agricultural self-sufficiency. In the past, there may have been military and strategic reasons for countries to be self-sufficient in food. Such arguments are less plausible today. It is not conceivable that western Europe should be cut off from overseas food supplies in a future conflict.

A great disadvantage of this policy of self-sufficiency is that it deprives the less developed primary producing countries of markets. This limits the growth of their purchasing power, and thus their demand for the industrial products of Europe, with adverse effects on Europe's industrial growth. Moreover, when protection takes the old-fashioned form of import levies, rather than direct subsidies, it has the added disadvantage of raising food prices for the consumer, relatively to industrial prices. If there is anything in the argument that industrial competitiveness depends on food prices through the wage factor, as I mentioned before, the policy of high food prices militates against competitiveness. It also changes the distribution of real incomes in a regressive manner. It has been well known for a century—the so-called Engel's Law—that the poorer a man is the higher the proportion of his income which he spends on food. So, the higher food prices are in relation to the prices of other things, the poorer are the people with low incomes in relation to people with high incomes.

This of course would not be true if the system of agricultural support followed the lines of the U.K., of subsidising farmers by means of guaranteed prices whilst allowing free imports. I would not like to defend fully the U.K. system, which also suffers from giving excessive protection to agriculture. But in relation to the C.A.P. it is a better system—more efficient and more humane, and from a long-run point of view it is better for agriculture also. Under the U.K. system, the cost of subsidising agriculture is borne by the general taxpayer and not by the consumer of food.

The argument usually put forward by Common Market economists and politicians is that countries like France and Germany could not adopt anything like the British system because it would impose an intolerable budgetary burden. But I do not think there is anything in this argument. For one thing, half the total cost of supporting agriculture is already on the budget—only one-half is financed through high food prices; for another thing, the countries of the Common Market have now adopted a new tax: the value-added tax, the great virtue of which is that it is a tax on *all* consumption and, as such, a perfect substitute for

special taxes on food. So, if the countries of the E.E.C. replaced the import levies with direct subsidies to the farmers, in the British manner, and financed them by an appropriate *addition* to the value-added tax, there would be no burden on the community, since the consequential rise in the prices of things *other than food* would be balanced, in terms of the retail price level, by the fall in food prices. There would be no change in the cost of living. But the real cost of living would be reduced to the poorer members of the Community, and it would be somewhat higher to the richer members, whose expenditure "basket" contains less food.

With the value-added tax you have an instrument in Europe which is just as efficient in raising money as import levies are in raising the price of food. Nobody could therefore argue that, owing to limited taxable capacity, agriculture cannot be supported through direct subsidies, and must therefore be supported through import levies. Import levies are also a tax on food—in Britain they have always been regarded as such—so once there is an overall tax on personal consumption which is just as efficient as a money raiser, it is meaningless to say that it is easier to finance agriculture in one way than another. Abolishing the import levy and financing agricultural support through the V.A.T. would have the added advantage of abolishing the distortions and the limitations on international trade which the present system involves.

The system adopted by the Common Market in the third quarter of the twentieth century is in fact identical with the system adopted by Britain after Waterloo, the so-called Corn Laws. This was abandoned by Britain after a tremendous amount of intellectual agitation—an agitation such as has never been seen before or since—in 1846. Nobody, as far as I know, has since advocated the re-introduction of the Corn Laws. Indeed, not many people now know what the Corn Laws were. But, as the history books explain, they were very much the same as a system of variable import levies introduced under the Rome Treaty. The system was somewhat more primitive in that it prohibited the import of wheat entirely if the price of wheat fell below a certain level, restricted imports if the price was above it, and freed it entirely if the price rose to a yet further level. So it stabilised the

internal price by means of variable restrictions, the extent of which depended on the price.

In a sense, the whole of modern economics was a by-product of British anti-Corn Law propaganda. Ricardo's *Principles*, which is generally regarded as the basis of modern economics, was origin- ally conceived as an instrument for convincing his countrymen that agricultural protection is bad for the country—because it necessarily reduced the accumulation of capital, and thereby the rate of economic growth; it thus reduces both the prosperity of Britain and the prosperity of others. This was such an intellectually difficult argument that, after putting the basic ideas in an essay on the "Influence of a Low Price of Corn on the Profits of Stock", he was encouraged to develop it more systematically in a basic treatise.

RICARDO AND LIST

Ricardo's argument, rephrased in modern terms, could be put in this way. For a developed industrial country, exporting manu- factured goods, there is no justification whatsoever for protecting its agriculture, and indeed every reason against it. By protecting its agriculture, it absorbs unnecessary labour on the land; it reduces the profitability of industry by raising the real cost of labour to manufacturers; it reduces its export potential, as well as its growth potential. This proposition has never been contradicted by subsequent theories.

British free trade theory has suffered intellectual defeats since Ricardo's day—first and foremost perhaps by the German econo- mist, Friedrich List, in the middle of the nineteenth century, who has demonstrated in his *National System of Political Economy* that, whilst the idea of free trade is very suitable for a developed country exporting manufactures, it is less appropriate for an underdeveloped country, wishing to develop and industrialise. But the List argument (which has since become the universal creed of the underdeveloped countries of the world) relates to the question of protecting *industrial* production in a less developed country against the competition of manufacture produced in *more* developed countries. It provides no justification whatever for

highly developed countries like the countries of Europe, North America or Japan, to protect their *agriculture* against the competition of *less* developed countries.

The solution, in the interest of Europe, as well as of Britain and the other countries wishing to join the Common Market, is to dismantle the Common Agricultural Policy as at present conceived. It obviously could not be dismantled overnight. But it could be done in a series of steps—and the step-wise liquidation of pre-existing arrangements should be familiar enough to members of the Common Market, since all its present attainments have been brought about by this method. In an analogous way, the C.A.P. should be gradually dismantled over a period—say five to ten years. By "dismantle" I mean that the internal prices for agricultural products should be progressively reduced, until the import levy serves mainly the purpose of price stabilisation and not of protection. Clearly, guaranteed prices to farmers are preferable to fluctuating prices. There is much to be said in favour of guaranteed prices, in the interests of efficiency, but these are consistent with *low* prices and not just with high prices. Low prices are essential for modernising European agriculture—it could simply not be accomplished without it. That is why the Mansholt Report, an admirable document though it is, strikes one like *Hamlet* without the Prince of Denmark. The Mansholt Report mentions every possible aspect of the agricultural problem—how to educate farmers, how to compensate them, how to induce farmers to retire, to move, to do this, that or the other, but it avoids mentioning the market environment in which these changes are to take place. To expect all the radical changes in European agriculture without a reduction in prices is like expecting water to flow uphill. It could never be accomplished.

Each country should be encouraged to assist its farmers to modernise, to consolidate the land into large holdings; compensate farmers who are willing to give up farming, by early retirement or by retraining for some other occupation—exactly as the Mansholt Report recommended. Each country should, over a transitional period, also be allowed (or even encouraged) to protect the standard of living of the farming community through subsidies of some kind—possibly through acreage subsidies, or guaranteed

prices, provided only that it is part of a plan of transition extending over, say, a decade, in order to bring about the modernisation of agriculture, which still makes it possible to have a prosperous farming community in Europe, without the protection of high prices.

I also think that it is equitable and reasonable that the burden of carrying out a Mansholt-type programme should not be left to each member country, but should be shared among all members of the Community, on the basis of some reasonable criterion of need. It is *reasonable* that each member country should make a contribution depending on its G.N.P., possibly weighted in some way by real income per head; and that these funds should be channelled to countries, according to the amount they need to spend (in relation to the G.N.P.) in order to carry out the programme, and not according to the irrelevant (and rather ludicrous) principle of how much they produce in excess of what can be absorbed within the Community at the agreed prices.

On any reasonable criterion of need, Italy should be the largest net recipient—it has 25 per cent. of its labour force in agriculture, and therefore the size of the problem of absorbing surplus labour is very much greater in her case than in the case of the other countries; also it has the lowest real income per head. But under the present Community system, Italy hardly breaks even; France and Holland are the net gainers—the two countries with the highest real income per head, and with an agricultural surplus labour force that is proportionately much smaller (in the case of Holland, very much smaller) than that of Italy.

But quite apart from the question of the allocation of Community funds between member States, an even more important issue is that the contributions are paid for the *wrong* purpose; they are paid according to each country's surplus production—in other words, they are paid to ossify agriculture in its present pattern, not to modernise it and to transform it.

Britain, with the smallest agricultural labour force, and with a high real income per head, ought clearly to be a large net contributor to this Fund—perhaps the largest. I am sure the British people would be ready to pay this price for the sake of a common future—if only they knew that they are asked to pay it for a good

purpose and not a bad one; if they could be assured that it is in the nature of an investment that will pay dividends in the form of lower prices, freer world trade, higher real income for the peoples of all the member states; and is not in the nature of a growing annual subsidy to entrench inefficiency—an ever-increasing membership fee in order to enable other members to pursue a nonsensical agricultural policy. They will be the more ready to pay it if they are not asked at the same time to break their intimate historical ties with the overseas members of the British family of nations, such as New Zealand and Australia, so as to divert their trade artificially from its traditional pattern, and to substitute high cost imports for the sake of preserving and perpetuating surplus labour in European agriculture.

12

THE DYNAMIC EFFECTS OF THE COMMON MARKET[1]

IT is generally agreed that the initial effects of joining the Common Market are likely to be unfavourable to Britain, mainly owing to the heavy cost of assuming the obligations of the Common Agricultural Policy. It is argued however that these unfavourable impact effects are likely to be more than offset by the long-term advantages—the so-called "dynamic effects" of membership. Last year's White Paper on *Britain and the European Communities*[2] described the nature of these advantages in the following terms:

"For industry and trade, the main consequences of United Kingdom membership of an enlarged community would be that we should form part of a Customs Union of up to 300 million people stretching from Scotland to Sicily and from the Irish Republic to the borders of Eastern Europe. Within this vast area, industrial products would move freely—without tariff or quota restrictions—as soon as any transitional period had been completed. And over the years ahead it would be the intention to convert this Customs Union into a full economic union by the progressive alignment and harmonisation of commercial policy, i.e., trading relations with third countries; of economic and fiscal policy; of company and patent law; of standards for industrial products . . . etc.

"The creation of such an enlarged and integrated European market would provide in effect a much larger and a much faster growing 'home market' for British industry. It would provide the stimuli of much greater opportunities—and competition—

---

[1] First published in the *New Statesman*, 12 March 1971, and later in the volume *Destiny or Delusion? Britain and the Common Market*, London 1971.
[2] Cmnd. 4289, February 1970.

than exists at present or would otherwise exist in future. There
would be substantial advantage for British industry from membership of this new Common Market, stemming primarily from
the opportunities for greater economies of scale, increased
specialisation, a sharper competitive climate and faster growth.
These may be described as the 'dynamic effects' of membership
on British industry and trade. It has not been found possible to
measure the likely response of British industry to these new
opportunities nor, therefore, the effects on our economic
growth and balance of payments."[1]

In the concluding section the White Paper strikes an even more
confident note about the "dynamic effects" resulting from membership of a "much larger and faster growing market":

"This would open up to our industrial producers substantial
opportunities for increasing export sales, while at the same time
exposing them more fully to the competition of European industries. No way has been found of quantifying these dynamic
effects but, if British industry responded vigorously to these
stimuli, they would be considerable and highly advantageous.
*The acceleration in the rate of growth of industrial exports could then
outpace any increase in the rate of growth of imports* with corresponding
benefits to the balance of payments. Moreover, with such a
response, the growth of industrial productivity would be accelerated as a result of increased competition and the advantages
derived from specialisation and larger scale production. This
faster rate of growth of productivity would, in turn, accelerate
the rate of growth of national production and real income."[2]

The same argument has been repeated in other documents[3] but
without adding anything of substance to the case as presented in
these quotations. There are frequent references to the fact that the
countries of the E.E.C. have experienced much higher growth
rates than the U.K. since the war, with the implication that if

---

[1] Cmnd. 4289, paras 52–3.
[2] Para. 77. Italics not in the original.
[3] See for example, Confederation of British Industry, *Britain in Europe: A second industrial appraisal*, January 1970.

Britain formed part of the Community, her own growth rate would be assimilated to that of the other members. Since the rate of economic growth of the U.K. has been so much lower than that of the countries of the Common Market—around 3 per cent. a year, in the period 1958–69, as against 5·4 per cent. for the Six— this in itself would establish a strong presumption in favour of joining the Community.

But whether any such tendency can be presumed to exist or not is a matter that requires closer analysis of the causes of high and low growth rates, and of the effects of increased competition on growth. It cannot be taken for granted as a self-evident matter that the intensification of competition between different industrial regions brought about by a Customs Union will automatically en- hance the rate of growth of *each* of the participating regions taken separately.[1] Indeed, as the italicised passage of the White Paper indicates, the favourable effects on our growth rate depend on the hypothesis that opportunities created by the Common Market will lead to an acceleration in the rate of growth of industrial exports which will "outpace any increase in the rate of growth of imports". But what if the response were the other way round, with an acceleration in the rate of growth of imports that "outpaced" any increase in our exports? It could not then be maintained that the rate of growth of national production and real income would be higher as a result; on the contrary, the effect would be to make our rate of economic growth lower than it would be otherwise, or even to make it negative. The question in other words, is not only one of "quantifying" the magnitude of these "dynamic effects" but of discovering, in the first place, whether they should be entered on the credit side or the debit side.

The White Paper is certainly correct in suggesting that the

---

[1] There is certainly no evidence to show that the creation of the Common Market enhanced the rate of economic growth of *each* of the participating countries taken separately, or even of the area as a whole. The rate of economic growth of the Six countries taken together was lower in 1958–69 than in 1950–58, while the rates of growth of other O.E.C.D. countries (both inside and outside Europe) were higher in the latter period than in the former. The formation of the Customs Union seems to have clearly benefited Italy (which increased its share of total trade in manufactured goods, both inside and outside the Community) and probably also Belgium, but there is no clear evidence in the case of the others. Cf. R. L. Major and associates, *Another Look at the Common Market*, National Institute Economic Review, November 1970, pp. 29–43. For reasons adduced below, the experience of the Six countries is not necessarily relevant from the point of view of the effects of entry on the U.K.

"dynamic effects" on our growth rate are likely to be far more important over a run of years than the "impact effects", however large the latter may be. An increase in our growth rate, by one per cent.—that is, from say 3 per cent. to 4 per cent. a year—is likely to compensate for the initial cost of entry in three years even if the latter is as much as 3 per cent. of our national income, or £1,200 million a year. Conversely, a 1 per cent. diminution in our growth rate is likely to double the annual cost of membership in three years, treble it in six years, and so on.

The basic question therefore is whether entry into the E.E.C. is likely to have a favourable effect on our growth rate or an adverse one. This question cannot be answered without considering the more fundamental question of what makes the rate of growth of productivity relatively fast in some countries and relatively slow in others.

The argument that follows is wholly in accord with the White Paper's own intellectual approach to the problem—the question is only whether the White Paper's optimistic conclusions concerning our growth rate follow from their premises.

CAUSES OF HIGH AND LOW GROWTH RATES

There is a substantial amount of evidence in favour of the view that causes of high and low rates of productivity growth of various countries or regions are closely bound up with the rates of growth of manufacturing production. There are two main reasons for this. The first is that economies of large-scale production, due to ever-increasing differentiation and subdivision of processes, are peculiar to manufacturing ("processing activities") as distinct from either primary production (agriculture or mining) or tertiary production (transport, distribution and miscellaneous services). The second is that in the sectors other than manufacturing (chiefly in agriculture but also in services) there is in most countries a considerable surplus of labour (some kind of "disguised unemployment") so that when the manufacturing sector expands and draws more labour from other sectors, these other sectors are not forced to curtail their output; on the contrary their output will also tend to increase if they provided goods or services that are complementary (or

ancillary) to manufacturing activities. Hence the faster manufacturing output expands, the faster productivity will rise, both in the manufacturing sector and in the non-manufacturing sectors.[1]

Added to these is the fact that in "capitalist" economies at any rate the increase in industrial capital necessary for an expansion of output is largely self-generated: the more production expands, the greater is the inducement to invest in the expansion of capacity, and the higher are the profits which provide the finance for such investment.

Under these conditions the economic growth of particular industrial regions will largely be determined by the growth of demand for the products of those regions which emanates from *outside* the region—i.e., the growth of its exports. A faster rate of growth of exports will induce a faster rate of growth of production, an acceleration in industrial investment, and both of these will lead to a faster growth of consumption.

If the world consisted of a single industrial area which sold its products to an outside world of primary producers in exchange for food and basic materials, the growth of demand for its exports would itself be governed by the purchasing power it provided to the outside world either through its purchases of food and raw materials or through foreign investment.[2] In a world however where there are a number of competing industrial regions, the growth of demand for the products of *any one* of these regions will depend, not just on the growth of total demand, but on whether it is gaining or losing in competitiveness—i.e., whether it manages to enlarge its share in the total market, or whether it has to put up with a diminishing share.

---

[1] Empirical evidence derived from the comparative experience of a number of advanced industrial countries suggests that a 1 per cent. increase in the rate of growth of manufacturing production requires an addition of about 0·5 per cent. to the rate of growth of employment in manufacturing and will be associated with a 0·5 per cent. addition to the rate of growth of non-manufacturing output. (See my paper, "Causes of the Slow Rate of Growth of the United Kingdom", Cambridge University Press, 1966, reprinted in *Further Essays in Economic Theory*.)

[2] This was largely the situation of Britain in the middle of the nineteenth century when she had a near monopoly as an exporter of manufactures, and also provided the main world market for food and basic materials. The pace of industrial expansion in Britain rose and fell with exports, which in turn depended on rising or falling primary product prices (which governed the purchasing power of the producers of primary products) and the latter in turn on whether the growth of supplies of primary products ran ahead or fell behind the growth of world demand.

Owing to the existence of economies of scale both comparative success and comparative failure tend to have self-reinforcing effects. Industrial areas tend to become more "competitive" when their growth of productivity is faster than average; but a higher rate of productivity growth is itself the reflection of the faster rate of growth production made possible by the gain in "competitiveness".

Myrdal coined the phrase of "circular and cumulative causation"[1] to explain why the pace of economic development of the various areas of the world does not tend to a state of even balance, but on the contrary, tends to crystallise in a limited number of fast-growing areas whose success has an inhibiting effect on the development of the others. This tendency could not operate if changes in money wages were always such as to offset differences in the rates of productivity increase. This, however, is not the case; for reasons that are not perhaps fully understood, the dispersion in the growth of money wages as between different industrial areas tends always to be considerably smaller than the dispersion in productivity movements.[2] It is for this reason that within a common currency area, or under a system of convertible currencies with fixed exchange rates, relatively fast-growing areas tend to acquire a cumulative competitive advantage over relatively slow growing areas. "Efficiency wages" (money wages divided by productivity) will, in the natural course of events, tend to fall in the former, relatively to the latter—even when they tend to rise in both areas in absolute terms. Just because the differences in wage increases are not sufficient to offset the differences in productivity increases, the comparative costs of production in fast-growing areas tend to fall in time relatively to those in slow-growing areas and thus enhance their competitive advantage over the latter.

---

[1] *Economic Theory and Underdeveloped Regions*, London, 1957.

[2] The differences in the rates of increase in money wages between industrial countries in the post-war period tended to be small relative to differences in rates of productivity growth. In the last year or two the rate of increase in money wages accelerated very considerably in all major industrial countries, but without creating large differences in the rates of increase of wages between countries. Cf. O.E.C.D. study *Inflation: The Present Problem*. December 1970, Table 8. For further evidence on the relation of changes in competitiveness to differences of productivity growths, see also O.E.C.D. study of An Empirical Analysis of Competition in Export and Domestic Markets in O.E.C.D. *Economic Outlook, Occasional Studies*, December 1970.

Thus Britain's rate of productivity growth has been relatively slow in relation to other "developed" countries mainly because the rate of growth of her manufacturing output was low; the latter was low because the rate of growth of her exports was low; and the latter in turn was low because owing to her relatively slow productivity growth, she was steadily losing ground to her competitors.

If we take the ten years prior to the 1967 devaluation the volume of world trade in manufactures grew at a compound rate of 8·5 per cent. a year. Over the same period U.K. exports of manufactures increased only by 2·5 per cent. a year; her share of world exports fell from 18·2 per cent. in 1957 to 11·9 per cent. in 1967. Over the same period Japan's share of world exports rose from 5·9 to 9·8 per cent.; Italy's from 3·8 per cent. to 7 per cent. and Germany's from 17·5 per cent. to 19·7 per cent. The combined gain in the market shares of these three countries was two-thirds at the expense of the U.K., and one-third at the expense of the U.S. (whose share of world exports also fell from 25·4 to 20·5 in the ten year period).

In a detailed analysis of international competition of engineering products in both domestic and external markets recently published by the O.E.C.D.[1] it is shown that in the five years 1962–3 to 1967–8 the U.K. lost $2,814 million worth of sales of engineering goods (the equivalent of 13 per cent of her total output in 1962–5) to foreign competitors.[2] Of this total $1,077 million was lost in the domestic market of the U.K.—largely to goods produced in the U.S. and Canada ($545 million) and in the E.E.C. countries ($369 million)—and $1, 737 millions of sales in foreign markets; of these much the greater part, $1,400 million, was in the more distant markets of the Far East, Oceania, Central and South Africa (where Japanese competition was particularly strong). Only $216 million was lost in the domestic markets of the E.E.C. countries. She lost in market share vis-à-vis every other producing country; of the total loss of $2,184 million in all,

[1] Cf. O.E.C.D. *Economic Outlook*: Occasional Studies, December 1970, 'Analysis of Competition in Export and Domestic Markets', by Raoul Gross and Michael Keating.
[2] "Loss" is defined by the difference between the actual increase in sales and the increase in sales which would have been achieved if the market share had remained constant in each market, including the domestic market.

$838 million was lost to U.S. producers, $583 to Japanese producers and $1,179 to producers in the E.E.C. countries; most of the latter was lost however, not in E.E.C. markets themselves, but in the U.K.'s domestic market and in third markets.

These competitive losses were the equivalent of 6·7 per cent. of 1962–3 sales of U.K. products in the U.K. domestic market, 21·4 per cent. of such sales in the E.E.C. markets, 17·3 per cent. of sales in E.F.T.A. markets and 37·9 per cent. of sales in all other foreign markets. The remarkable feature of these figures is that our losses in E.E.C. markets (where we faced growing tariff discrimination in relation to E.E.C. producers) were only slightly larger than in E.F.T.A. markets (where the discrimination was increasingly in our favour) and in both cases were much smaller than in other foreign markets.

The rapid fall in our market shares shown by these figures was not unavoidable. It could have been largely, if not entirely, prevented if we had taken more prompt and more frequent steps to offset the effects of our growing loss of competitiveness by devaluation. This is best shown by our trading experience in the two years following devaluation. The volume of our exports between 1967 and 1969 grew at an annual rate of 12·7 per cent. (as against the 2·5 per cent. in the ten years up to 1967) so that we managed to maintain our share of world trade almost intact over these two years, despite the fact that world trade grew at an unprecedented rate of 13·5 per cent. a year, or at a 60 per cent. higher rate than during the previous ten years. By 1970, the gain in competitiveness resulting from the 1967 devaluation was at least partially spent; the volume of exports in 1970 is likely to show a rise of only 6 per cent. over 1969 (and most of the increase occurred in the first half of the year) while the volume of world trade as a whole continued to rise at the same rate as in the previous two years.

There can be little doubt, in the light of this experience, that if we had adjusted our exchange rate much earlier, and at more frequent intervals—say a devaluation of 5 per cent. in 1957, repeated in both 1962 and 1967—we should have secured a much better and steadier export performance—say, a compound rate of 6 per cent. a year over the whole period instead of 2·5 per cent. in the decade 1957–67—and this would have meant that industrial productivity

and real income per head would have attained a considerably higher level. For reasons of our economic maturity (the absence of large labour reserves in agriculture and in low-earnings sectors) we could not have equalled the growth rate of countries such as Germany, Italy and Japan (Germany's own growth rate had to slow down quite considerably in the 1960s owing to the appearance of labour shortages) but we *could* have maintained, with a rate of growth of exports of 6 per cent. a year, a rate of growth of G.D.P. of around 4 per cent a year (instead of the 2·7 per cent. actually attained) which would have meant that real income per head (taking into account the adverse effects of devaluations on the terms of trade) would now be at least 10 per cent. higher.

In addition to that our future economic prospects would be more secure. For trade which is once lost is difficult to regain. If we had fought harder, by not allowing ourselves to be "priced out of the market" by the newer and more dynamic competitors (or not so easily) the task of maintaining our position in the future would be less difficult.

The question could legitimately be asked: if a higher rate of productivity growth is so much dependent on the rate of growth of exports, why was there no greater acceleration in the U.K. productivity growth in the years following devaluation, when exports rose three to four times their previous rate? The answer lies mainly in the circumstances surrounding the 1967 devaluation: the need to convert a large deficit into a large surplus in the balance of payments over a short period (owing to the lack of reserves and the pressing need to repay short-term debts) which could not have been achieved except by a severe cut in home demand (through higher taxation, public expenditure cuts and a more stringent credit policy) and this largely balanced the increase in foreign demand. The benefits to be gained from "export-led" growth are long-term: they require an adaptation of the economic structure to a higher growth rate of demand for manufactured goods; a change in both the volume and the structure of capital investment which would come about gradually, as a result of a steady and sustained stimulus. They require in other words, small and frequent adjustments in the exchange rate (such as could be secured by a free market rate subject to market intervention by the central

H

bank); it would be hopeless to expect that the long-term "dynamic benefits" of greater competitiveness could be brought about permanently by a single act of devaluation, however large.

EFFECTS OF THE COMMON MARKET ON COMPETITIVENESS

But can they be brought about by joining the E.E.C.? In the light of our large losses of trade in overseas markets in the post-war period, the idea of a "secure home market of 300 million people" sounds very tempting at first sight as a long-term solution to our problems. But a closer analysis of the likely magnitude of both the costs and the benefits, and the restraints on our freedom of action which would follow from membership of the Community, do not sustain the favourable first impression.

As the issue is a complex one, it is best to tackle its various aspects one by one.

(1) First, what are the benefits of a "larger home market" and what precisely does a "home market" mean in this context? The only tangible gain is free access to the markets of the other members of the Community, in exchange for giving free access to Community producers in the U.K. market. The meaning of "free access" in this connection is the abolition of import duties on U.K. goods which, under the Community's new Common External Tariff, amount to only 7–7½ per cent. *ad valorem*, and the abolition of U.K. customs duties on manufactured imports from the Community, the level of which is estimated at 10–11 per cent. *ad valorem*. Since the E.E.C. market now takes about 25 per cent. of our exports, the benefit gained is the same as a 7½ per cent. reduction of U.K. prices on one-quarter of our exports, in return for a 10–11 per cent reduction in the U.K. prices of rather more than one-quarter of our imports of manufactures. So long as the Community's tariff remains a moderate one, the creation of a customs union cannot in itself make a great deal of difference. We shall derive benefit from a fast-growing Community whether we are inside the Common Market or not—as indeed is shown by the fact that our exports to E.E.C. countries have increased much faster (despite the tariff discrimination) than our exports to other areas. Furthermore the extraordinary new evidence which emerges

from the recent O.E.C.D. study shows that in competition with individual E.E.C. exporters (Belgium, Luxembourg, France, Germany, Italy and the Netherlands) we fared better, in relation to each of the E.E.C. producers, in the "internal" market of the E.E.C. than in "neutral" markets.[1] While the mutual abolition of tariffs is bound to increase the share of each trading partner in the market of the other, in the longer term the growth of our exports to the Community would be subject to much the same competitive influences (both from inside and outside competitors) as if we remained outside. And if the experience of other E.E.C. countries is any guide, we could not hope for more than a modest increase in our share of the E.E.C. market, as a result of being part of the Customs Union.[2]

(2) On the other hand, by joining the Market we should lose the benefit of the existing preferences in favour of U.K. goods in the Commonwealth Markets, in E.F.T.A. and in the Irish Republic.[3] Since these markets account for a much larger share of our total exports than the E.E.C., the net effect of our exports will be adverse: the White Paper estimates that there will be a net loss of exports of £75–£175 million in consequence. At the same time the net effect on our imports of manufactures are also likely to be adverse, since the abolition of duties on E.E.C. goods will have a greater impact on our imports than the abolition of preferential treatment to Commonwealth goods and to goods imported from those E.F.T.A. members who remain outside. The White Paper estimates the net increase in imports of industrial goods as £50–£100 millions, so that the net demand for U.K. manufactures will be adversely affected to the tune of £125–£275 millions.

(3) This is without taking into account the adverse effects on

[1] Cf. the O.E.C.D. publication referred to, Appendix II, "The Measurement of Possible Trade Discrimination Resulting from Customs Unions", Table II.1. For the purposes of this analysis each E.E.C. country's own domestic market has been excluded from the definition of "E.E.C." markets. For the average of the Six countries the percentage reduction in sales of U.K. goods between 1962–3 and 1967–8 attributable to a reduction of market shares vis-à-vis individual E.E.C. producers was 41 per cent. in E.E.C. markets and 63 per cent. in "neutral" markets.
[2] For evidence of the effects of the E.E.C. on the market shares of member countries in each other's markets see Appendix below.
[3] In the case of those E.F.T.A members who also join the Common Market, we shall retain the benefit of duty-free entry, and lose only the benefit of the existing tariff discrimination in relation to E.E.C. producers. But in the case of the Commonwealth and those E.F.T.A. members (like Switzerland or Sweden) who are not likely to join E.E.C. we shall lose the benefit of the present preferential treatment altogether.

H*

real income and on the balance of payments of assuming the obligations of the Community's Common Agricultural Policy. The E.E.C. is a relatively low-tariff area for manufactures but a highly protected area for agriculture. While the tariff on industrial goods is (as a result of the Kennedy round) only 7–7½ per cent., the average level of effective protection accorded to agriculture—the excess of Common Market prices over world prices—is 45 per cent.[1] By joining the Common Market we therefore face a large adverse change in the relationship of the prices of industrial goods to agricultural goods. There will be a loss on our external "terms of trade" of at least £400 million a year—i.e., our food imports will cost that much more, in terms of our industrial exports[2]— and there will be an equal shift in our "internal" terms of trade, in that the prices paid to our own farmers will cost about £400 million more for the same output as now.[3] The real income generated by the industrial sector at any given level of physical productivity will be reduced on both counts: each unit of manufactured goods produced in the U.K. will buy 20–30 per cent. *less* in foodstuffs than now.

(4) In addition to the loss due to the unfavourable change in price relationships, we shall face the further loss on account of the net contribution to the Community's Agricultural Fund in excess of the receipts from the agricultural levy (which have already been included in the above calculation). This will come to a further £230–£470 million, depending on the scale of Community expenditure on the support of European agriculture[4] but whether the Mansholt Plan is adopted or not it is unlikely that the contribution

---

[1] See Table 9 of the report by an expert group, *A Future for European Agriculture*, published by the Atlantic Institute, (The Atlantic Papers, No. 4, Paris, 1970).

[2] This is made up of two components: (i) the higher food prices on goods imported from the Community, estimated around £200 m.; (ii) the levy imposed on food imports from the rest of the world, also around £200 m. the proceeds of which has to be paid over to the Community, and therefore comes to the same as if we paid higher prices on those imports.

[3] The present level of E.E.C. agricultural prices is around 27 per cent. higher than the U.K. *guaranteed* prices.

[4] Under the Community's new financial arrangements we shall have to pay over to the Community—after the end of the transitional period which might be 1978 or 1981 —in addition to the 90 per cent. of the receipts from import levies, 90 per cent. of the receipts from Customs duties (estimated at £240 m.) and up to 1 per cent. of the value added tax (estimated at £230 m.) or up to £670 million altogether. The return flow from this outlay (in the form of payments by the Community to U.K. agriculture) is estimated at only £50–£100 million.

we shall be called upon to make will be much below the maximum that we shall be committed to pay (see Appendix II on the Community's Budget).

(5) This means that in terms of balance of payments cost on current account, we shall start off (apart from the change in the export-import balance of industrial goods referred to above) with a debit of between £530–£820 million[1] (£400 million on account of the additional cost of imported food; £230–£470 million in further contributions to the Agricultural Fund, *less* £50–£100, million in receipts from the Agricultural Fund) which will have to be covered by additional exports if a deterioration in the balance of payments on current account is to be avoided. To obtain these additional exports, inside or outside the Common Market, we should have to lower our export prices in relation to our competitors (depending on the size of the cost) by 5–10 per cent. This would require an additional devaluation (at the present relationship of our productivity and of our industrial wages to the industrial productivity and wages of our competitors) of 10–15 per cent., which, in terms of the further resources that we would have to transfer from domestic consumption to the balance of payments, means an additional burden of at least £205–£340 million.[1] Hence in terms of total resource cost, the balance of payments cost of £650–£1,125 million is the equivalent of £1,000–£1,500 million.

(6) However this takes no account of the deterioration in our competitiveness on account of the rise in money wages that is bound to result from the rise in the cost of living. The counterpart to the deterioration in the terms of trade is a rise in food prices of 18–26 per cent. (on the White Paper's estimates) which would cause a cut in real wages of 4–5 per cent. for the higher paid workers, and 6–8 per cent. for the lower paid.[2,3] If past (and present) experience is any guide, the rise in food prices will cause

---

[1] It was a deplorable omission of the White Paper that it failed to take any account of the additional resource cost of the adjustment process in the balance of payments. The requirement for the balance of payments adjustment is the equivalent of £735–£1,160 million. This estimate also allows for the resource cost of making good the initial reduction in net exports of manufactures (see Appendix III "The Resource Cost of Entry").

[2] The range of variation between 18 and 26 per cent. mainly reflects differences of assumptions concerning distributive and retail margins. The higher figure assumes that the percentage addition to first-hand prices on account of wholesale and retail distribution remains unchanged, the lower estimate presumably assumes that the

a compensating rise in wages which will call for *more* devaluation if adverse effects on our exports are to be avoided.

(7) But once we are inside the Common Market, it will be far more difficult to regain competitiveness through adjustments in the exchange rate. One reason for this is that under the Community rules, the prices paid for both imported and home produced food are fixed in terms of "international units" so that whenever the exchange rate is altered, domestic food prices will be raised by the full extent of the adjustment. This increases the real resource cost of achieving any given improvement in the balance of payments; and it means that the rise in the cost of living resulting from devaluation is greater than it would be now. On both these grounds it will be harder to regain competitiveness by devaluation. The second and more fundamental reason is that the possibility of offsetting adverse trends in competitiveness through exchange rate adjustments will itself become impossible as the Community proceeds with its current plans for full economic and monetary union.[1]

The long-term benefits to the U.K. of joining the Common Market depend entirely on attaining a higher rate of growth of productivity. But we could only hope to achieve this if the rate of growth of our industrial production is accelerated, which in turn presupposes, as the White Paper recognises, a faster rate of growth of exports—both absolutely and in relation to industrial imports. For all the reasons listed, this would require a large *initial* cut in the level of our real wages—and salaries—of the order of 10 per

[1] This is discussed on pp. 202–7 below.

---

amount charged by wholesalers and retailers per unit product remains unchanged—i.e. that distributive margins will be reduced *pari passu* with the rise in prices. The latter is not a reasonable assumption in the absence of price controls.

[3] Since the White Paper was published last February there has been some rise in world agricultural prices in relation to E.E.C. prices so that at present the excess of E.E.C. prices is more like 40 than 45 per cent. Also the new Government announced its intention to replace the existing system of deficiency payments by import levies; this will raise first-hand food prices by some £250–300 m., and will cause a rise in retail food prices of 5–7 per cent., quite independently of entry into the Common Market. On this basis it has been argued that the addition to the cost of living due to entry into the C.A.P. will only be 2¼–3¼ per cent., not 4–5 per cent. However, it is too early to say that the improvement in relationship of E.E.C. food prices to world prices is more than temporary (it may well be reversed on the basis of recent forecasts of world production trends); and as to the replacement of the system of deficiency payments by import levies, it is not really relevant to the issue discussed in this paper—i.e., by how much real wages will need to be reduced in order to preserve our competitiveness.

cent. or more, if both the adverse change in the terms of trade, the adjustment in the tax structure, and the need to cover the cost of our net contribution to the Community Fund by additional exports is taken into account—and this in turn is unlikely to be achieved—in any industrial community, not just Britain—by a straightforward reduction in money wages: it will require a succession of downward adjustments in the exchange rate.[1] But owing to the Common Market Agricultural Policy, any act of devaluation will have a greater resource cost in terms of real income and both generates greater inflationary consequences internally and makes the necessary reduction in real wages that much greater; and as the Community proceeds towards a full monetary union, the possibility of devaluation will be ruled out altogether.

If we failed to reduce real wages initially (or failed to reduce them to the extent required)[2] the "dynamic effects" of membership would not be favourable but increasingly adverse. Industrial production and employment would fall, both on account of the deterioration of the trade balance, and on account of the restrictive policies we would be forced to adopt in order to restore the balance of payments and to finance our contribution to the Community. This would be aggravated by an increased capital outflow as domestic industrial investment became unprofitable owing to the fall in domestic demand, and full transferability of capital funds were introduced under E.E.C. rules; and this would necessitate further restrictive fiscal and monetary measures to avoid a balance of payments crisis. In those circumstances the U.K. would become the "Northern Ireland" (or the Sicily) of Europe—an increasingly depressed industrial area, with mass emigration the only escape.

[1] The last occasion in which an attempt was made to achieve a straight reduction of money wages of the order of 10 per cent. was in the coal-mining industry in 1926, which led to the General Strike.

[2] This "initial" reduction need not of course be attained overnight—it may be spread over five years or more, so that it could be argued that it need not cause an actual *fall* in real wages, but merely a slowing down in the "normal" rate of increase in real wages. But this argument ignores that during the transitional phase our production is likely to be held back by the need to generate a growing surplus in the balance of payments in which case the rate of productivity growth will also be lower; so that one cannot reckon on the "normal" annual rise in real wages due to the growth of production.

The critical assumptions which lead to this gloomy prognosis are: (a) that we can enter the Community only by assuming the obligations of the Common Agricultural Policy and the relation of E.E.C. agricultural prices to world prices remains much the same as now;[1] (b) that we shall not be able to offset the adverse initial effects on our *industrial* export-import balance by devaluation.

If we could enter the E.E.C. on the same terms as we entered E.F.T.A., and also made sure—by devaluation or by a general cut in money wages—that our industry benefited from entry from the beginning, we might gain considerably through greater industrial specialisation as well as through a higher rate of growth of total output. For the labour-releasing effects of sharper competition (due to the abolition of U.K. import duties on E.E.C. products) would then serve to enhance the growth of our more efficient industries, and the growth of these industries would more than compensate for the decline of the others. On the vital issues of long-term "dynamic benefits" it all depends on whether one starts off on the right foot or the wrong one.

The overwhelming probability is however that just because of the heavy initial cost of entry we shall start off on the wrong foot, and the "impact effects" will then be aggravated by adverse "dynamic effects", not offset by beneficial ones. In that event, entry into the Common Market, if it were really irreversible, would be a national disaster. In reality, this will never happen. Nations do not commit hara-kiri for the sake of international treaties, however solemnly and sincerely entered into. But in addition to incurring the odium of default, we would be blamed for the break-up of Community arrangements, even though this would have happened anyway.

THE CONSEQUENCES OF A FULL ECONOMIC
AND MONETARY UNION

The events of the last few years—necessitating a revaluation

---

[1] It is possible that the present high level of agricultural prices would be gradually reoded by inflation if E.E.C. prices remained constant in dollar terms while world garicultural prices rose. The latter does not appear probable at the moment as the current forecasts indicate rising world surpluses in agricultural products. But the continued rise in industrial prices will itself alleviate the adverse effects on our terms of trade if E.E.C. agricultural prices remained constant.

of the German mark and a devaluation of the French franc—have demonstrated that the Community is not viable with its present degree of economic integration. The system presupposes full currency convertibility and fixed exchange rates among the members, whilst leaving monetary and fiscal policy to the discretion of the individual member countries. Under this system, as events have shown, some countries will tend to acquire increasing (and unwanted) surpluses in their trade with other members, whilst others face increasing deficits. This has two unwelcome effects. It transmits inflationary pressures emanating from some members to other members; and it causes the surplus countries to provide automatic finance on an increasing scale to the deficit countries.

Since exchange-rate adjustments or "floating rates" between members are held to be incompatible with the basic aim of economic integration (and are incompatible also with the present system of common agricultural prices fixed in international units) the governments of the Six, at their Summit meeting in The Hague in December 1969, agreed in principle to the creation of a full economic and monetary union, and appointed a high-level committee (the so-called "Werner Committee") to work out a concrete programme of action.

The Werner Committee's recommendations have not yet been adopted in detail, though its principal objectives have been confirmed by the Community's Council of Ministers.

The realisation of economic and monetary union, as recommended in the Werner Report, involves three kinds of measures, each introduced in stages: monetary union, tax harmonisation, and central community control over national budgets. It envisages a three-stage programme, with each stage lasting about three years, so that the whole plan is designed to be brought into operation by 1978–80.

In the monetary field in the first stage the interest and credit policy of each central bank is increasingly brought under common Community surveillance and permitted margins of variations between exchange rates are reduced or eliminated. In the second stage exchange rates are made immutable and "autonomous parity adjustments" are totally excluded. In the third stage the individual central banks are abolished altogether, or reduced to

the status of the old colonial "Currency Boards" without any credit-creating power.[1]

In the field of tax harmonisation it is envisaged that each country's system should be increasingly aligned to that of other countries, and that there should be "fiscal standardisation" to permit the complete abolition of fiscal frontiers, which means not only identical *forms* but also identical *rates* of taxation, particularly in regard to the value added tax and excise duties.

In the field of budgetary control the Werner Report says "the essential elements of the whole of the public budgets, and in particular variations in their volume, the size of balances and the methods of financing or utilising them, will be decided at the Community level".

What is *not* envisaged is that the main responsibility for public expenditure and taxation should be transferred from the national Governments to the Community. Each member country will continue to be responsible for raising the revenue for its own expenditure (apart from the special taxes which are paid to finance the Community's own budget but which will remain a relatively small proportion of total public expenditure and mainly serve the purposes of the Agricultural Fund and other development aid).

And herein lies the basic contradiction in the whole plan. For the Community also envisages that the scale of provision of public services (such as the social services) should be "harmonised"—i.e., that each country should provide such benefits on the same scale as the others and be responsible for financing them by taxation raised from its own citizens. This clearly cannot be done with *equal* rates of taxation unless all Community members are equally prosperous, and increase their rate of prosperity at the same rate as other members. Otherwise the taxation of the less prosperous and/or the slower-growing countries is bound to be higher (or rise faster) than that of the more prosperous (or faster-growing) areas.[2]

[1] Different currencies (marks, francs, etc.) might be nominally retained so long as each currency has always a 100 per cent. backing in terms of the Community's reserve currency.
[2] A further reason for differences in the burden of taxation necessary to provide a given level of service lies in differences in demographic structure—e.g. some countries have a larger proportion of pensioners or schoolchildren than others.

The Community will control each member country's fiscal balance—i.e. it will ensure that each country will raise enough in taxation to prevent it from getting into imbalance with other members on account of its fiscal deficit. To ensure this the taxes in the slow growing areas are bound to be increased faster; this in itself will generate a vicious circle, since with rising taxation they become less competitive and fall behind even more, thereby necessitating higher social expenditures (on unemployment benefits, etc.) and more restrictive fiscal policies.[1] A system on these lines would create rapidly growing inequalities between the different countries, and is bound to break down in a relatively short time.[2]

This is only another way of saying that the objective of a full monetary and economic union is unattainable without a political union; and the latter pre-supposes fiscal *integration*, and not just fiscal *harmonisation*. It requires the creation of a Community Government and Parliament which takes over the responsibility for at least the major part of the expenditure now provided by national governments and finances it by taxes raised at uniform rates throughout the Community. With an integrated system of this kind, the prosperous areas automatically subsidise the poorer areas; and the areas whose exports are declining obtain automatic relief by paying in less, and receiving more, from the central Exchequer. The cumulative tendencies to progress and decline are thus held in check by a "built-in" fiscal stabiliser which makes the "surplus" areas provide automatic fiscal aid to the "deficit" areas.

Even so, there is need for special regional policies—such as the U.K. differential grants and subsidies to the development areas—to alleviate the problems of growing regional inequalities. The need for the latter is recognised (in a vague way) in the Werner Report, which mentioned "community measures which should

[1] It is for this reason that in most countries it been found necessary to transfer a rising proportion of social expenditure (on poor relief, education, roads etc.) from local authorities to the Central Government, and to supplement an increasing proportion of local tax revenues by grants from the Centre (such as the rate-equalisation grants in the U.K.).

[2] To imagine the consequences one should ask what would happen if the inhabitants of each county in the U.K. were required to finance all their social expenditure by local taxes. Living in Cumberland would be enormously penalised; living in Surrey would be a tax haven.

primarily concern regional policy and employment policy" and whose "realization would be facilitated by an increase in financial intervention at the Community level". What the Report fails to recognise is that the very existence of a central system of taxation and expenditure is a far more powerful instrument for dispensing "regional aid" than anything that special "financial intervention" to development areas is capable of providing.

The Community's present plan on the other hand is like the house which "divided against itself cannot stand". Monetary union and Community control over budgets will prevent a member country from pursuing full employment policies on its own— from taking steps to offset any sharp decline in the level of its production and employment, but without the benefit of a strong Community government which would shield its inhabitants from its worst consequences.

Some day the nations of Europe may be ready to merge their national identities and create a new European nation—the United States of Europe. If and when they do, a European Government will take over all the functions which the Federal government now provides in the U.S., or in Canada or Australia. This will *involve* the creation of a "full economic and monetary union". But it is a dangerous error to believe that monetary and economic union can *precede* a political union or that it will act (in the words of the Werner Report) "as a leaven for the evolvement of a political union which in the long run it will in any case be unable to do without". For if the creation of a monetary union and Community control over national budgets generates pressures which lead to a breakdown of the whole system it will prevent the development of a political union, not promote it.

But it would also be dangerous to dismiss the Werner Report on the ground that it is not likely to be implemented, particularly if Britain is inside the Community and will have a voice in deciding what happens. For the problems that led to The Hague decisions and to the Werner Report are genuine enough: the framework of institutions and arrangements which make up the present European Community do not constitute a viable system. The Community must either go forward towards full integration (*via* a political union) or else relax the rigidity of its present

arrangements, particularly in regard to agriculture and exchange rates. And it would be hopeless for Britain to join the Community not knowing whether it wishes to move in the one direction or the other.

THE EFFECTS OF THE COMMON MARKET ON THE TRADE
BETWEEN MEMBER COUNTRIES

The recent O.E.C.D. study referred to in the text[1] makes it possible to examine the effects of the creation of the Common Market on the trade of member countries in relation to each other in much greater detail. This analysis refers to engineering goods only (metal manufacture, electrical and non-electrical machinery, transport equipment and precision instruments) which accounted for 58 per cent of total U.K. exports of manufactures in 1962–3; and it relates to the composition of each country's trade, both in its domestic market and in other E.E.C. markets in the years 1962–3 and 1965–8. It must be borne in mind that while the Common Market has been in existence throughout the whole of this period, the full removal of duties between members only came into effect at the end of the period. The results therefore may not show the full effects of the Customs Union on trade relationships.

The results of the analysis are summarised in the Table which shows for each of the two periods the share of each country's production (i) in its own domestic market; (ii) in other E.E.C. countries; (iii) in the E.E.C. as a whole (including the domestic market of each producing country). For comparison, the U.K.'s share of trade has also been included, both in the U.K. market and in E.E.C. markets.

The table shows that each of the E.E.C. countries managed to increase its share of trade in the *other* E.E.C. countries, though the change was a moderate one for all countries with the exception of Italy, and an insignificant one (in percentage terms) in the case of Germany (Germany already had a much greater share of this trade at the beginning of the period than the other countries). Belgium, Luxembourg and France show a loss in their share of

[1] Cf. footnote 1 p. 193 above.

MARKET SHARES IN ENGINEERING GOODS OF E.E.C. COUNTRIES AND THE UNITED KINGDOM IN THEIR DOMESTIC MARKETS AND IN E.E.C. MARKETS IN 1962-3 AND 1967-8

Producing Countries	I Domestic Output $ Billion	II Share in Total Consumption in Domestic Markets		III Market Share in Total Consumption in "other" E.E.C. Markets		IV Market Share in Total Consumption in total E.E.C. Market (including Domestic Markets)[1]	
	1962-3	1962-3	1967-8	1962-3	1967-8	1962-3	1967-8
Belgium-Luxembourg	3·0	61·0	52·6	1·3	1·7	5·4	5·1
France	15·0	87·6	84·3	2·2	2·8	26·8	26·8
W. Germany	28·0	90·4	89·2	8·8	9·8	45·5	45·6
Italy	6·4	73·7	75·5	1·3	2·1	10·5	11·6
Netherlands	2·8	50·9	57·2	1·1	1·3	4·4	5·2
Total: E.E.C.	55·2	82·9	80·9	..	..	92·7	93·7
U.K.	21·4	93·4	88·6	..	..	2·0	1·7

[1] Including the domestic markets of the six E.E.C. producers.

Source.—O.E.C.D. *Economic Outlook*: Occasional Studies, December 1970: "Analysis of Competition in Export and Domestic Markets", by Raoul Gross and Michael Keating.

.. = Not relevant.

trade, both in their domestic trade and in E.E.C. markets as a whole (including their domestic market), while Germany shows only a slight reduction in her domestic market and an unchanged share of trade in E.E.C. as a whole. Italy and the Netherlands on the other hand increased their share both in their own markets and in other E.E.C. markets; in the case of Italy, the increase was substantial in other E.E.C. markets and a moderate one in her own market, while the Netherlands, on the contrary, showed a substantial increase in her share in her domestic market and only a moderate gain in other E.E.C. markets.[1] The U.K. showed a reduction in her (initially small) share of 2 per cent. of trade to 1·7 per cent. but this loss was appreciably smaller than her loss in the rest of the world market in the same period (including all "domestic" markets other than the U.K.) which was from 2·7 to 2·1 per cent.[2] However, the U.K. producers' share in the total world consumption of engineering products (including the huge internal market of the U.S.) was in 1967–8 still 25 per cent. higher in the world outside E.E.C. than in E.E.C. markets.

Three main conclusions emerge from these figures. The first is that while the creation of the Common Market involved some diversion of E.E.C. consumption from non-E.E.C. producers to E.E.C. producers, the extent of this diversion was remarkably small. E.E.C. producers supplied 92·7 per cent. of total E.E.C. consumption in 1962–3 and 93·7 per cent. in 1967–8; a net diversion of 1 per cent. in favour of E.E.C. producers.[3]

The second conclusion is that anything like "economic integration" in the E.E.C. is still a very long way off. In a truly integrated economy—in a "single home market" which the White Paper holds out in prospect—one would expect that the share of each country's producers in the total consumption of its own area is not

---

[1] In relation to the three others, both Italy and the Netherlands were "developing" or "industrialising" countries—with the Netherlands more in the "import-substitution" phase (hence the higher rate of gain in her *domestic* market) and Italy in the "early exportive" phase.

[2] This latter figure, not shown in table, is derived from Tables 2 and 6 of the O.E.C.D. paper.

[3] This is in seeming contradiction to the results of Professor Truman's study (*The European Economic Community: Trade Creation and Trade Diversion*, Yale Economic Essays, Spring 1969) according to which there was no net diversion at all in favour of Community producers as a result of the Common Market. This study however makes a ten-year comparison, 1958–68, and relates to the trade in manufactures as a whole.

very different from its share in the markets of other producers—
apart from differences due to transport costs (which cannot, in
themselves, be very important) there is no reason why say, German
buyers should buy German-made products in any higher proportion than other E.E.C. buyers. Yet after ten years of E.E.C.'s
existence, each country's producers still had an enormously higher
share in their *own* domestic market than in the rest of the Community. In 1967–8 German producers supplied 89·9 per cent. of
the German market but only 9·8 per cent. of other E.E.C. markets;
French producers supplied 84·3 per cent. of the French market but
only 2·8 per cent. of other E.E.C. markets; Italian producers supplied 75·5 per cent. of the Italian market but only 2·1 per cent. of
other E.E.C. markets. The degree of Germany's "self-sufficiency"
in engineering goods at 89·2 per cent. was slightly higher than that
of the U.K. in the same year—despite the fact that Germany was
part of a Community which produced engineering products of
more than twice the value of German output. To appreciate the
significance of these figures they should be seen in the light of
analogous estimates concerning the inter-state trade of a truly
integrated economy, such as the United States. For the year 1963,
and for the same group of engineering products as are covered in
the O.E.C.D. study, producers in the state of Michigan accounted
for 42·3 per cent. of the total consumption of such goods in
Michigan and 24.3 per cent of other states of the U.S.A.; producers in the state of New York accounted for 20·1 per cent. of the
New York market and 9·7 per cent of other U.S. markets.[1]

The third conclusion is that though the U.K. performed relatively better inside the Common Market than outside (in the sense
that the loss in her share of trade was proportionately smaller) her
share in the E.E.C. market is very small—the same as that of
Belgium–Luxembourg, which only had one-seventh of U.K. output. This also means that the potentialities of the E.E.C. market
for the U.K. are very large *provided only that U.K. products are competitive with other Community producers*. The case against joining the
Common Market is that, when account is taken of *all* the consequences, it is likely to make the U.K. less, rather than more

---

[1] I am indebted for these estimates to Miss Karen Polenske of the Regional Economic
Research Project of Harvard University.

competitive than she is outside it. But if this were not so—if we could, by waving a magic wand, attain a large initial cut in our efficiency wages, or else obtain terms that make this unnecessary —there is plenty of scope for increased trade in the Common Market. This is best seen in a comparison with Germany which is a large producer of a comprehensive range of engineering pro ducts, just like the U.K. is, but with a total output which is 50 per cent higher in value terms. Germany supplied in 1967–8 9·8 per cent of the Community markets outside Germany whilst the U.K. supplied 2·4 per cent.[1] If this market were shared between the two countries in equal proportion to their respective outputs, the U.K. share would be 4·9 per cent. instead of 2·4 per cent., while Germany's share would be 7·3 instead of 9·8 per cent. There is a great deal to be gained therefore from increased competitiveness —though for reasons explained, this is unlikely to come about as a result of entering the Common Market on the terms that are likely to be offered to us.

APPENDIX II

THE COMMUNITY'S BUDGET

The Community's expenditure on the agricultural fund increased at an alarming rate from £205 million in 1966–7 to £950 million in 1968–9 and £1,085 million in the calendar year 1970, an annual rate of increase of £250 million a year. For 1971, the latest estimate of the Commission (as of 1 March 1971) envisages an expenditure of £1,450 million of which £350 million is in respect of past commitments and £1,100 million in respect of current liabilities.[2]

---

[1] This relates to E.E.C. markets excluding Germany. The figure of 1·7 per cent. referred to earlier and shown in table relates to the *total* E.E.C. market including Germany.

[2] The accumulated backlog in respect of past commitments (payable to member Governments) amounted to £980 million as of 1 January 1971 of which only £350 million is expected to be paid in the current year, the rest carried forward. These backlogs arose because the expenditure on market intervention and export restitution were undertaken by member governments, with the right of subsequent re-imbursement by the agricultural fund. Since 1970, however, a new system is in operation by which the Community makes direct re-imbursements to individual traders, so that it is hoped to avoid further accumulation of "backlogs" in the future.

Practically the whole of this increase represented expenditure out of the "guarantee fund"—on market intervention and export restitution—in other words, on maintaining prices in the face of growing surpluses, particularly of wheat, dairy products, fats and sugar, on which the bulk of expenditure was spent.[1] Six-sevenths of the total expenditure in recent years has been on price support and only the remaining one-seventh on the "guidance section", i.e., on reforming the structure of agriculture.

However, the Commission hoped that with the adoption of the Mansholt Plan this situation would be changed. Expenditure on structural reform (under the so-called "guidance section") was envisaged to rise from the level of £119 million a year in the years 1967–70 to £260 million in 1971 and £575 million in 1975.[2] At the same time the Commission envisaged that, as a result of structural improvements and other factors, expenditure under the "guarantee section" will be contained at the level of around £900–£1,000 million a year up to 1975 and afterwards reduced.

But whether the Mansholt Plan is adopted or not there is no mechanism to ensure that the expenditure on market intervention will be contained at any particular level, unless the common agricultural *prices* are progressively reduced. The Mansholt Plan, even though it envisages taking a certain amount of land out of cultivation, is bound to increase the efficiency of agriculture (by consolidating farms into larger units, etc.) and this would tend to raise surpluses further, not reduce them. So far too, expenditure under the "guarantee section", which is an open-ended commitment, has risen in almost every year faster than was envisaged: for 1968–9, for example, the liability incurred was £831 million as against a forecast of £572 million.[3]

The Community's expenditure has so far been financed by contributions from the budgets of member states according to a

[1] Table 1 of the report by the Atlantic Institute (referred to on p. 198) gives details of the cost of market support for the various commodities in different years.

[2] See Cmnd. 4289, Table C. This plan appears however to be shelved for the present and current authorisations only provide a constant £119 million expenditure under the "guidance section" for the three years 1971–3, the same as in previous years.

[3] Cf. Cmnd. 4289, para 16. The exception appears to be 1970 when market intervention on dairy products (chiefly butter) turned out to be lower than expected. It is too early to say however whether this signifies any change in trends.

certain key which was revised each year. As a result, each member government had to provide its agreed share of total outlay (which depended on the scale of market intervention). This was clearly not a tenable situation and was the main reason for the introduction of the new financial arrangements by which the Community provides for its "own resources" by obtaining the proceeds of certain taxes. This system is to be brought into operation in stages in the years 1971-5, with certain "correctives" (designed to prevent the share of any one country's contribution from rising too fast) up to 1978.

The new system sets both a certain minimum and maximum to the contribution raised in each country. Each country hands over the proceeds of its import levies and customs duties (less 10 per cent. to cover the costs of collection) in any case. In addition it is liable to hand over part of the proceeds of the value added tax (depending on financial requirement) up to a tax of 1 per cent. on value added. The White Paper estimates that in the late 1970s this would imply a U.K. contribution of £670 million at the maximum and £430 at the minimum. Since the U.K. would collect relatively more in agricultural import levies (and probably also in customs duties) than the other members of the Community its share in Community finance would be higher than its share in the national income, at present levels of G.N.P. the U.K. would account for less than 20 per cent. of the G.N.P. of the larger community, while its liability would be more like 27 per cent.[1] By the late 1970s, the U.K.'s share in the total G.N.P. might be 16–18 per cent., and its share of the Community yield of these taxes might be 22–5 per cent.

On the latter basis, the minimum U.K. liability implies a total Community revenue of around £1,600 million and its maximum liability a total revenue of £2,900 million. This revenue serves primarily to finance the Agricultural Fund, and other purposes only in so far as there is a surplus of revenue over expenditure by the Fund. It is not clear what is to happen if the Community expenditure comes to exceed the maximum revenue under the new

[1] The latter figure assumes a value added tax of comparable coverage in all countries and makes some allowance for the fact that the share of personal consumption in the G.N.P. is higher in Britain than in the Six. All figures relate to an enlarged Community including Britain but without taking into account the entry of other countries.

arrangements—presumably the 1 per cent. limit on the value-added tax would be raised.

Current expenditure plans do not extend beyond 1973, and envisage a budget of £1,170 million for that year (£70 million more than for 1971) without provision for increased expenditure for the Mansholt Plan. However this is no more than guesswork, since actual expenditure incurred will depend entirely on the size of the surpluses that will accrue. Since the Community is unable, for political reasons, to agree on any reduction in the prices of surplus commodities (if anything, prices are likely to be further increased) it would be prudent to reckon that expenditures under the "guarantee section" will continue to rise at least at half the rate of the previous four years. This means that by 1977 expenditure under the "guarantee section" might be around £2,000 million with total expenditure around £2,200–£2,600 million according to whether the Mansholt Plan is adopted or not. Britain, according to Mr Rippon's statement (*Hansard*, 16 December, 1970, col. 1,355), suggested to the Community that its budget for 1977 should be limited to £1,875 million. Whether the Community will be ready to accept the idea of such a ceiling or not, it would be reasonable to assume that by the time Britain makes its full contribution to the Community budget, expenditures will be at a level at which the contribution of member countries will be not far short of their present maximum commitments. (Excluding Britain's contribution, the current total of agricultural expenditures is already considerably in excess of the full yield from import levies and customs duties, which is around £930 million.)

How much benefit the U.K. will derive from that expenditure has not anywhere been analysed. The White Paper put it at £50–£100 million, but it did not specify whether these sums would arise under the "guarantee section" or the "guidance section". It is difficult to see how the U.K. could make claims on the Community Fund under the "guarantee section" until a situation is reached where its production of cereals, meat or butter exceeds its domestic consumption—which is very far from the case at present. Again, it is difficult to see on what grounds the U.K. could claim under the "guidance section" since the projected expenditure

under the Mansholt Plan on consolidation of farms into larger units and compensation to retired farmers or for retraining, etc. is of a kind which would not apply to the bulk of British agriculture. It would be inconsistent with the Community's system to bargain in terms of a certain "net contribution"—i.e., to make a certain minimum receipt a condition for a certain gross contribution. Indeed, as Mr. Rippon emphasised at the recent Brussels ministerial meeting on 2 February 1971, Britain fully accepts the existing Community arrangements concerning both the finance of the Fund and the purposes of expenditures out of the Fund, at the end of the transitional period.

The current negotiations therefore are only concerned with the length of the transitional period, the size of the initial contribution and the rate of build-up during the transitional period. The current British proposal is that the initial contribution should only be 3 per cent. of total expenditure, rising gradually to 13–15 per cent. by 1978 and attaining the full level of 22–25 per cent. only in 1981.

The French position (which is shared in a greater or lesser degree by the other members of the Community) is that the need for a transitional period for the adaptation of tariffs and the adjustment of agricultural prices does not in itself justify such a postponement of financial liability. The U.K.'s balance of payments is exceptionally strong at present by historical standards, and there is no reason why it should improve in the course of the adjustment period—indeed, the deterioration of the terms of trade and the adverse impact effect on our industrial exports and imports would suggest in the initial phases at any rate that the balance of payments is likely to deteriorate. Hence the very insistence on a postponement of the assumption of financial liabilities calls into question the sincerity of the Government's intentions of adhering to its obligations under the system at the end of the transitional period.

Such suspicion is probably unjustified, but there can be little doubt (in the light of Mr. Rippon's statement in the House of Commons during the Common Market debate)[1] that the Government hopes that by the early 1980s either the situation concerning

[1] *Hansard*, 20 January 1971, cols. 1082–3.

British agriculture will be different from what it is now or else the Community's current agricultural price policies could be so changed after 1973 (when Britain expects to enter as a full member and will have a voice in the decisions concerning agricultural prices etc.) so that the net benefit the U.K. will derive from the Community's expenditure will be very much larger in relation to her contribution than it would be now. How far such expectations are justified will depend *inter alia* on whether the Community's decisions on these matters will be taken under a majority rule or under a unanimity rule. Under a unanimity rule, the U.K. could prevent by its veto any further rise in E.E.C. agricultural prices but it would be unable to effect any reduction in the face of growing surpluses; under the majority rule, it is quite possible that the interests of a sufficient number of countries will operate in favour of a progressive reduction of prices and a gradual elimination of agricultural surpluses.

APPENDIX III

THE RESOURCE COST OF ENTRY

The cost of entry into the Common Market will be made up of a number of elements: (i) the net contribution to the Community budget; (ii) the higher cost of food imports from E.E.C. countries; (iii) the cost of financing the additional capital outflow; (iv) finally, the additional cost, in terms of domestic resources, of adjusting the balance of payments for the above factors, as well as for the deterioration in our balance of exports and imports of manufactured goods (resulting from tariffs and preference changes).

(i) With regard to the contribution to the Community's budget, it is best to show the position in the first year following upon the completion of transitional arrangements—which, depending on negotiation, might be any of the years between 1978 and 1981—since this alone shows the ultimate burden to which the transitional arrangements must lead. Britain has already conceded that it accepts in full the commitment under the new financial arrangements according to which each country

pays into the Community the proceeds of certain taxes, irrespective of what this represents as a share of the Community's total expenditure, and how it relates to the payments received by a particular country from the agricultural fund. The White Paper estimated that Britain's gross contribution under these arrangements will be between £430 million at the minimum and £670 million at the maximum, and its net contribution between £330 million and £620 million. We have already given reasons why the actual figure is likely to be nearer the upper, rather than the lower, limit of these estimates.

(ii) For the additional cost of food bought from E.E.C. farmers, the White Paper gives a wide range of different estimates: all the *low* estimates depend however on the assumption that the British consumer will react to higher food prices by a "tightening of belts"—i.e., by a relatively large reduction of food consumption. We regard this as *a priori* unlikely; on the basis of a smaller change of consumption, and a "middle production response" of British agriculture, £200 million appeared to be the best estimate to take for this item.

(iii) With regard to net capital outflow, the White Paper refrained from any quantitative estimate beyond saying that it "must be expected in a typical year to involve a sizeable cost to the United Kingdom balance of payments" (para. 94). It would indeed be pretty useless to make any estimate of its magnitude: its size may vary within very wide limits depending on the relative profitability of investment in Britain and in other E.E.C. countries, and on how far we shall succeed in matching long-term lending with short-term borrowing (as we have done in the past). It is also difficult to imagine any British government raising extra resources through taxation or by further deflation for the sake of providing finance for additional private investment on the Continent. We have therefore made *no* allowance for the cost of this item in our estimate, or for other charges of a capital nature as would arise, for example, if we were required to fund and amortise the sterling balances.

(iv) Finally, there is the additional cost in terms of resources, of adjusting the balance of payments—the cost of increasing our exports and/or reducing our imports sufficiently so as to pay for

the above items. The White Paper omitted this entirely from the calculation. The size of this additional resource cost will vary with the method chosen for adjusting the balance of payments— i.e., whether it is by deflation or devaluation. With deflation, the method relies largely on the reduction of imports achieved through a reduction of domestic incomes and employment; this would involve a loss of output that is likely to be many times as large as the required balance-of-payments adjustment. With devaluation, this extra resource-cost is very much smaller—just how great it is, depends on a large number of factors such as the response of exports to changes in prices and in profits, the saving in imports resulting from higher import prices, and the extent to which the prices of imports fail to rise by the full extent of de-valuation. In the latter respect we shall be in a worse position than at the time of the 1967 devaluation, since under E.E.C. rules food prices are bound to rise by the full extent of the exchange rate adjustment.

On the basis of a complex set of assumptions which can be largely justified by the experience of the 1967 devaluation but which it would be too tedious to set out in detail, this extra resource cost can be put at $33\frac{1}{3}$ per cent. of the balance-of-payments adjustment required on account of the budgetary contribution and the higher food prices paid on imports from E.E.C. countries, and something of the order of 16·5 per cent. of the deterioration in the export-import balance of manufactured goods (which does not in itself represent a "resource cost"). On this basis the net additional resource cost of the balance-of-payments adjustment can be put at £205–£340 million and the total resource cost £735–£1,160 million (without making allowance for capital movements).

But this is not the end of the story. As a result of adopting the Community's price system and of "harmonising" with the Community's tax system there will be a gain to farmers, to distributors and processors of food and to industrial profits. Farmers will gain £300 million (the market value of present farm output will rise by £450 million, but they will lose £150 million in subsidies); distributors will gain (in higher absolute margins on both imported and home produced food) £300; and as a result of the

adoption of V.A.T. at the rates prevailing in the Community, and the adjustment in insurance contributions, there will be an appreciable net shift in the burden of taxation in favour of higher incomes. The industrial wage-earner will thus be made to pay far more than his proper share of the total resource cost of adjustment. Whereas this total resource cost (at the higher figure) would amount to only 5 per cent. of the current total wage and salary bill, and to 3 per cent. of G.N.P., the reduction in industrial real wages would be more like 10 per cent: the rise in food prices alone would cause a cut of 5 per cent., and the introduction of V.A.T. and of higher social insurance contributions, after allowing for all compensating changes, a further 5 per cent.

THE DISTORTIONS OF THE 1971 WHITE PAPER[1]

THE Heath White Paper on the Common Market is a page shorter than the Wilson White Paper, but costs 25 per cent more. This annual rate of increase of 20 per cent accords ill with the government's declared intention to contain inflation. But against the higher price it contains only a small fraction, perhaps one-tenth, of the "facts and figures" of the former document. The rest is propaganda about our destiny. Moreover, such information as it does contain is most misleadingly presented. By comparison, last year's White Paper, itself a highly tendentious document, was a model of honesty and objective presentation. And for the select few who will take the trouble to study the paper with care, its crudities, disastrous logical contradictions, vaguenesses and deliberate omissions are bound to produce the opposite impression to that intended—that the case for going into Europe must be a very bad one indeed.

BRITAIN'S CONTRIBUTION

Let us begin with the question on which the White Paper is at its most misleading: the contribution to the Community budget (p. 12). In para. 42 we are told that this will rise in terms of "net" cost from £100 million in 1973 to £200 million in 1977 "if the structure of the budget were to remain unchanged". For the basis of these figures one must turn to para. 93. There it is explained that the figures given in para. 42 are no more than "possible" figures, based on the assumption (a) that the Community's budget will amount to £1,400 million in 1973, rising gradually to £1,600 million in 1977; and (b) that our receipts from that

[1] First published in the *New Statesman*, 16 July 1971.

budget will rise from £20 million to £100 million over the same period. No indication is given anywhere how these "assumptions" were arrived at.

Nowhere does the paper mention that expenditure from the Agricultural Fund is an open-ended commitment—the Commission spends whatever it is required to spend to "keep prices at intervention levels in all the producing areas". Over the past five years, with the exception of the last year, these expenditures were always considerably higher than initially estimated, and it looks as if the same will happen in the current year with a record grain crop in prospect. The annual rise in expenditure since 1966 was £250 million a year. Why assume a rise of only £65 million a year between 1971 and 1973, and £40 million a year between 1973–77? The experience of the past two years—when there was a coincidence of poor harvests in both the Southern and the Northern hemispheres—is more likely to be an aberration than a change of trend. The actual expenditure might thus turn out to be very much higher than £1,600 million. The fact that we shall have a "veto" after 1973 cannot prevent this from happening—we could veto price increases, but have no power to bring about price reductions. Nor could we prevent a bumper crop, or a jump of Community expenditure in consequence of it.

Moreover, as Annexe A explains, the new financial system comes fully into operation on 1 January 1975 and from then on the basic liability will consist of the yield of import levies and customs duties and, depending on financial requirements, up to a 1 per cent. tax on value added. In the case of Britain the transitional arrangements will put a ceiling figure to the contribution in terms of a gradually rising percentage of total expenditure, up to 1977. From then on the new system will be applicable subject to certain "correctives" for two more years. But it is clear from the White Paper's description (para. 94) that the liability under the new system will have to be computed for 1977 and every subsequent year. This new system sets a different kind of ceiling to our liability: irrespective of the needs of the C.A.P. we cannot be asked to pay more than the yield of the three taxes mentioned above, which means we shall no longer have an open-ended commitment once we pay in full.

It is therefore very important to know what that maximum liability is. Last year's White Paper put it at £670 million for 1977 and subsequent years, made up of £200 million for the import levy, £240 million customs duties and £230 million for a 1 per cent. V.A.T. But this year the White Paper refuses to give any figures on the ground that "it is not possible to make any valid estimates of our levy and duty receipts in the 1980s". But it is the changeover from the transitional arrangements to the permanent system in the years 1978–80 which is important, and for that we need to know the levy receipts for 1977 (see para. 94). It would be nonsensical to suggest that no "valid estimate" can be made of expected levy and duty receipts for 1977 (and note that the White Paper carefully refrains from saying this)—the more so since earlier, in para. 43, the White Paper *does* give a "firm" estimate of the additional cost of food imports at £50 million for that year and as every statistician knows, it is impossible to estimate the one item without estimating the other. Clearly there must exist an agreed estimate in Whitehall for the yield of the import levy for 1975 and subsequent years at least up to 1980. If these estimates have not been published it is because the government wished to suppress them, not because they were not available. The same must of course be true of the yield of customs duties under the C.E.T. and of the yield of V.A.T. In fact these things are far easier to forecast or estimate than the Community's expenditure in 1977 which the White Paper predicts with such confidence.

The fraudulent element in the presentation lies in bandying about the figure of £200 million, which is treated as though it were both a "firm" figure and a "final" figure—something which Mr. Rippon has negotiated and agreed with the Six and beyond which we could not be compelled to go. (Mr. Maudling called it the "exact cost" of our contribution on television last week.) In reality it is nothing of the kind. It is not a "projection", a "median" or a "best estimate" in the sense that statisticians use these terms. Rather, it is the "best-looking" estimate that could be put before the public with any shred of plausibility. And by virtue of being the only figure mentioned in the paper for the end of the transitional period it is designed to give the impression that it is, in some sense, a final figure. Who would pay much heed to £200

million in 1977 if it were admitted that the figure three years later could be twice as large or more?

The £50 million figure given for the extra cost of food imports is also highly suspicious. The estimates in the 1970 White Paper varied from –£85 million to +£255 million with the "best estimate", on the basis of the then prevailing price gap, of around £200 million. How this figure has been trimmed down to £50 million is not explained and is all the more mysterious since this particular item (as Table 8 of last year's White Paper shows) becomes *larger* not smaller), with a smaller difference in prices.

A presentation in keeping with the tradition of state papers would have set out the issue quite differently. It would have explained the principles which will govern the finance of Community expenditure before it explained the transitional arrangements designed to ease our position for the first seven years. It would have explained the nature of the open-ended commitment with regard to agriculture and the reasons why the rise of our commitment over that transitional period cannot be forecast with any accuracy. It would have given estimates for the first seven years both on the basis of what we would have been liable to pay under the new financial arrangements, and the corresponding figure under the terms agreed or in Brussels for the transitional period, for various hypothetical assumptions on the scale of Community expenditure and for receipts from the Community Fund.

FOOD PRICES

The same disingenuousness is shown in the treatment of food prices. Para. 43 says that this depends on the difference between Community and world prices which has "narrowed significantly in the last two or three years". If so, why not give the figures? As this is a matter relating to past, not future, events the government cannot plead ignorance, nor that disclosure would be prejudicial to national interests. However, on the basis of the figures given in the Mansholt Plan and in the recent report of the Atlantic Institute, it can be assumed that the excess of E.E.C. prices

averaged around 50 per cent. in 1967–68. Since then world prices have risen by 12 per cent., E.E.C. prices by around 4 per cent. On this basis the significant narrowing of the gap may have amounted to one-fifth. Yet in the very same paragraph it is asserted that assuming "the continuation of the present price gap" the rise in average retail food prices *during the transitional period* resulting from the adoption of the common agricultural policy will amount to about 2½p in the £ each year (italics added). This is only one-half, not four-fifths, of the 5 per cent. a year estimate given in last year's White Paper. The explanation no doubt is that the government takes credit here for the changeover to the levy system which will increase U.K. food prices whether we go into the Market or not, and thereby cuts the rise in prices *"resulting from the adoption"* of the C.A.P. By the same token the price-effect of the C.A.P. could be reduced to nil by the simple expedient of aligning U.K. farm prices to those of the E.E.C. independently of entry. The true increase in food prices, on the White Paper's own assumption, is therefore, more like 20–22 per cent., not 16 per cent.—quite apart from the effect of devaluation.

A FURTHER DEVALUATION?

Though the White Paper keeps silent on the subject, every economic expert in the country would agree on the present showing that if we entered the Market the pound will have to be devalued before January 1973 by something of the order of 15 per cent. (whether this is done by floating or changing the peg is another matter). This is partly because the "full-employment-balance-of-payments" is already in deficit; partly because our competitiveness, on past experience, diminishes by something of the order of 1 per cent. a year even if "efficiency wages" keep in step; partly because, as a result of entering the Market, imports will increase more than exports (again, on this issue the White Paper is silent—does the government reject the estimates of last year's White Paper?) and partly in order to secure the additional export surplus necessary for paying our contribution to the Community budget, to finance capital movements etc.

The first two reasons would operate in any case, the second two only if we entered the E.E.C. An ordinary devaluation, as post-1967 experience has shown, raises domestic food prices by less than one half of the rate of devaluation. But if we enter the E.E.C. the prices of both imported and home produced food will rise in strict proportion to the change in the exchange rate (allowing perhaps for a strictly temporary period of grace, as was the case with the French devaluation). Hence, assuming that the additional devaluation necessitated by entry is no greater than one half of the total, there will be a further increase in food prices in relation to wages of three quarters of 15 per cent., or say 11–12 per cent. which would not arise otherwise. The total rise in food prices "resulting from our adoption of C.A.P." should therefore be put at 31–4 per cent., not 15 per cent. (All this does *not* include future price increases or devaluations due to "inflation"—i.e. those which are offset by wage increases.)

Because it keeps silent on the subject of devaluation and exchange rates, the White Paper avoids having to deal with one of the most harmful long-term consequences of adopting the common agricultural policy; that it forces on us the necessity to cut real wages with every adjustment in the exchange rate. The purpose of any devaluation is to make our products more competitive by lowering the costs of our manufactured goods relative to other industrial exporters. The more we can do this without having to lower our prices in terms of food and raw materials at the same time, the smaller the real cost of the adjustment. In the good old days of the British Empire, when all our suppliers were pegged on sterling, we could use devaluation to make ourselves more competitive without any harmful effects on domestic costs and prices. As Keynes said in 1931, it was gold which went off sterling. Even in 1967, the fact that some agricultural suppliers devalued with us was enough to ensure that the rise in food prices, whether domestic or imported, lagged greatly behind devaluation. Under the C.A.P. this will no longer be possible.

The White Paper makes no attempt to estimate the total balance of payments cost, and makes no mention whatever (any more than its predecessor) of the "resource cost" of the whole operation. In other words, it refuses to answer the simple question:

by how much will real national income be reduced (at the level of full employment) *before* taking into account any beneficial effects of "joining Europe" or productivity? In my article in the *New Statesman* last March I made an attempt to calculate this, and have since learnt that I failed to take into account certain items—such as the additional resources absorbed in domestic agriculture as the result of import saving and the fact that we shall be paying New Zealand £60 million more for the same amount of butter—which would raise the figures by another £100 million to £150 million above the £700 million to £1,100 million range which I estimated. But why can't we have an official estimate? If the government persists in saying that no such estimation is possible, how can they say, in the same breath (para. 56), that "the government are confident that membership of the enlarged Community will lead to much improved efficiency and productivity in British industry, with a higher rate of investment and a faster growth of real wages"? If nothing can be estimated or "quantified", where does this confidence come from?

The answer is that it springs from mystical beliefs like the basic tenets of religion which are no more susceptible to logical scrutiny or empirical verification than the doctrine of the Holy Trinity. These are set out in paragraphs 44–5, 47–8, 49–54. The term "dynamic effects" is now dropped and there is no reference as in last year's White Paper to the growth of exports "outpacing" the growth of imports. The direct stimulus to exports is now only one of two "parallel . . . influences operating on industry"; the other, and far more important, one will be the "radical change in planning, investment, production and sales effort" due to taking advantage "by structural changes of the opportunities opened up by the creation of a permanent, assured and greatly enlarged market". As far as I can make out from a careful and repeated perusal of paragraphs 44–5 these two "parallel influences" are supposed to operate independently of each other.

But if so what is the link between the political act of joining the Market and all the "radical changes in industry" with "positive and substantial" productivity effects if they do not stem from a higher demand, and a faster growth of demand, for the products of the firms concerned? And why should industry invest more in

Britain just because we are "in the Market" unless at the same time existing capacity is more fully utilised, and profit prospects are higher as a consequence? And whether this *would* happen or the very opposite is the main question to be examined—it cannot be taken for granted any more than belonging to the "assured British market" ensures the prosperity of Scotland or Northern Ireland.

Another great mystique is the importance of huge international concerns and the suggestion that they require a home market of 290 million and could not prosper with a home market base of only 90 million (as we now have with E.F.T.A.). If 90 million are too few for advanced modern technology, how did Japan manage to get ahead of the U.S. in electronics and over a large field of steel engineering? And if increasing the size of the home market has such a miraculous effect in itself, why has this not shown itself in a more modest way through the creation of E.F.T.A.? This, after all, has nearly doubled the size of our "home market"; joining the E.E.C. now would treble it again. A baby is still a baby, even if only a little one. Yet our growth rate was no higher after 1968 (after E.F.T.A. became fully operational) than before, and no British industrialist would now argue that the creation of E.F.T.A. made for great "structural opportunities" generating a lot of planning, investment and sales effort.

This paean for joining the Six ends appropriately by recounting how much faster the Six have grown, how much greater their investments were and how much better their balance of payments have been. It does not occur to the authors of the White Paper that some E.F.T.A. countries (such as Sweden, Switzerland or Austria) have done even better than the Six, not to speak of Japan or Taiwan. The idea that comparative success or failure may have causes other than the size of the home market is a tenet of which the authors of the White Paper are wholly oblivious.

In a parliamentary democracy it seems almost unbelievable that Parliament should be asked to come to a decision of such unique importance on the basis of such a flimsy document. In America a proposal of this nature coming from the Administration would immediately be remitted to various committees of both Houses who would thoroughly examine every aspect, extract every ounce

of relevant information from officials and be served by a group of professional experts. Here we are offered 10 days of debate on the floor of the House. This gives plenty of opportunity for making speeches but it is hardly a suitable method for eliciting precise information or for probing a complex issue requiring exhaustive analysis. Perhaps the best thing that could happen would be to appoint a small select committee of Parliament to examine the proposal in depth and report on it before the final vote is taken.

TIIE COMMON MARKET — A FINAL ASSESSMENT[1]

1971 will mark an important watershed in British constitutional history. For the first time since 1689 the House of Commons will vote in favour of a major change in Britain's constitution to which the electorate is definitely opposed. It is also evident, though less clearly, that 1971 will mark an important watershed in the history of the European Economic Community—and for reasons unconnected with Britain's entry. It will be the year in which 10 years of seemingly uninterrupted progress towards European unity came to a standstill and in which, for the first time since the signing of the Treaty of Rome, the drive towards unification and integration was put into reverse.

It is important to be clear how all this happened. The members of the E.E.C. succeeded, in the course of the 1960s, in putting all their stated policy objectives into operation according to plan. Internal industrial tariffs were wholly abandoned, a common external tariff was agreed on and brought into operation. The Common Agricultural Policy, ensuring common prices, a common system of market intervention and complete freedom of movement of goods across frontiers was brought into being and extended to all major agricultural commodities. Finally, the Brussels Commission succeeded in establishing itself, and putting into effect numerous acts of "harmonisation", large and small, extending from the shape of milk bottles to the commitment to adopt a value added tax.

However, the currency re-alignments of 1969—the devaluation of the franc and the revaluation of the mark—brought home the incongruity of the existing monetary and economic arrangements. Freedom of trade in agricultural goods had to be temporarily suspended, as neither France nor Germany was prepared to adjust

[1] Published in the *New Statesman*, 22 October 1971.

its internal agricultural prices *pari passu* with the change in currency parities. What was shown was the impossibility of creating a truly "integrated" economic area if individual member countries pursue separate monetary and fiscal policies or separate wages policies. Given the freedom to vary exchange rates, the terms of competition between the different regions can be altered in the same way as if each member country remained free to levy flat-rate import duties or pay out flat-rate export subsidies on its frontiers, and to do so at a stroke.

After the experience of the exchange crises of the summer and autumn of 1969, a summit meeting was called in The Hague in December (on the initiative of the French President) which represented the high watermark in the drive for European integration. This meeting agreed that a full "economic and monetary union" should be created, with a single Community currency, and asked for a detailed plan to be worked out for its implementation by stages, according to a fixed timetable.

The resulting "Werner Report" brought the inherent conflict between Europeanism and national sovereignty into the open. Community control over national fiscal policies, *à la* Werner— without a central parliament, and a central taxing and spending authority—would mean the worst of both worlds. It would prevent the individual countries from pursuing policies of economic management, yet it would not put in their place a federal government to perform these functions.

The first *dénouement* came in February when decisions had to be taken on the Werner Report. Clearly the governments were not prepared to surrender control over national monetary or budgetary policies. They agreed to have further consultations, but without any commitment to proceed further with the plan. Then came the Schiller plan of "joint floating" of the Community currencies against the dollar, which the French decisively rejected, both in April and May, and after the Nixon crisis in August. The different countries of the E.E.C. now follow widely different currency policies, some floating together, others floating separately, yet others with dual exchange rates, all of which makes mockery of economic integration in general and of the Common Agricultural Policy in particular.

The Germans now raise border taxes on their imports from France (revised week by week) and the German Minister of Agriculture has already announced that Germany will not be prepared to abolish these even if currencies come to be re-pegged. This puts the whole conception of supporting agriculture by means of a Community fund into jeopardy. If each country's internal agricultural market is isolated from the others, what is the justification for the food-deficient countries paying vast sub-ventions to the food-surplus countries? Indeed, there are influential voices in Germany (including that of Dr. Dahrendorf, a member of the Brussels Commission) which call into question the need, or the justification, for having a Common Agricultural Policy at all. In other respects too, there are voices critical of the working of the E.E.C. institutions—the "harmonisation mania", as one of Dahrendorf's articles put it—which makes it increasingly probable that the "Second Europe" of the 1970s will develop very differently from the "First Europe" of the Rome Treaty, and will be something more akin to the present E.F.T.A. than to the present or projected E.E.C.

If the above analysis is correct—and Britain's accession will no doubt strengthen these tendencies, not weaken them—joining the Market will not make the great difference to Britain's economic prospects which either its opponents fear or its advocates hope for. There will be *no* European monetary or economic integration, or political federation: we shall *not* lose our sovereignty, or our freedom to introduce frequent mini-budgets without prior approval by Brussels.

Should one conclude therefore that this is largely a sham battle, the issue of which will not, in the end, make a great deal of difference? Unfortunately this is not so, largely on account of Mr. Heath, and the Tory philosophy he represents. If you believe that Britain's "decadence" in the present century is largely the result of feather-bedding, and our salvation lies in a return to the bracing atmosphere of the Victorian age—making the rewards of success so much greater and the penalties of failure so much more severe—there is no better way of bringing this about than by a system of high food prices, heavy indirect taxes on articles of mass consumption and reliance on universal employers' contributions

(the incidence of which falls *wholly* on wage and salary earners) for financing social expenditure. As war-time experience has shown, keeping the price of necessities low is a far more potent method for reducing economic inequalities than altering the distribution of incomes through direct taxation. Equally, there is no better way of changing the distribution of incomes in favour of the middle and upper classes than to raise the price of things like food or rents, on which the poor man necessarily spends a much greater proportion of his resources than the rich man.

Hence the determination in the Selsdon programme to introduce V.A.T. and to replace agricultural subsidies by import levies irrespective of entry into the Market. Hence also the drive to raise rents and to substitute means-tested for universal benefits. While all these things *could* be done without the Market, doing them as part of a process of going into Europe has obvious advantages, not least of which is that it would be difficult for a future Labour government to go back on them if this involved "de-harmonising" with Europe.

Moreover, by entering Europe, the change in distribution of *incomes* can be combined with a change in the distribution of *power*. The kind of situation which happened at Fords last winter when, after a prolonged strike, the company was forced to grant practically all the unions' demands, could not happen if Fords could equally well supply their U.K. distributors with German-made cars.

When the Labour Party adopted the slogan "no entry on Tory terms" they spoke better than they knew. With the trends now unfolding in Europe, the chances are that a Labour government could bring us into the Market without any great sacrifice either to our balance of payments or to the British way of life. But with a Tory government in power, there is little chance of this precisely because it is the reactionary aspects of the "harmonisation" process which provide for them one of the main attractions of entering Europe.

THE NEMESIS OF FREE TRADE[1]

LET me begin with a quotation:

"I was brought up, like most Englishmen, to respect Free Trade not only as an economic doctrine which a rational and instructed person could not doubt but almost as a part of the moral law. I regarded departures from it as being at the same time an imbecility and an outrage. I thought England's unshakeable Free Trade convictions, maintained for nearly a hundred years, to be both the explanation before man and the justification before heaven of her economic supremacy. As lately as 1923 I was writing that Free Trade was based on fundamental truths which, stated with their due qualifications, no one can dispute who is capable of understanding the meaning of words."

This was not said by John Stuart Mill, nor Alfred Marshall, nor even by a great Liberal statesman like Asquith. It forms the introductory paragraph to two articles written by J. M. Keynes entitled "National Self-Sufficiency" which appeared in the *New Statesman and Nation* in July, 1933—written, that is to say, nearly two years *after* Britain's departure from the gold standard. Keynes advocated a "revenue tariff" two years earlier as an *alternative* to going off the gold standard and as a way of re-expanding the economy in a state of depression. But in these two articles he looked at the issue of international trade from a more long-term point of view, and asked himself whether the advantages of the

[1] Originally a public lecture delivered at the University of Leeds, 21 March 1977. I am indebted to Mr. Robert Skidelsky for drawing my attention to the passages quoted in the speeches of Joseph Chamberlain and Herbert Asquith, which were taken from Charles W. Boyd (ed.), *Mr. Chamberlain's Speeches*, ii, 1914, pp. 120–372; *Speeches by the Earl of Oxford and Asquith*, 1927, pp. 45–81.

international division of labour or specialisation were as great in the twentieth as in the nineteenth century, and whether the case for greater self-sufficiency is not stronger if one takes into account the gains in terms of greater economic stability.

Yet these articles were curiously disappointing—Keynes searched for reasons why free trade failed to deliver the goods but at that point in time did not know how to find them. In particular he failed to come to grips with the two crucial issues of the free trade *versus* protection controversy: the question of the level of *employment* and the rate of economic *growth*. These questions figured prominently in the debate initiated by Joseph Chamberlain 30 years earlier—in the famous tariff reform campaign of 1903. The issues considered and the arguments displayed in that debate sound curiously familiar to those who listened to or participated in recent discussions on economic policy—with the difference only that the protagonists seem to have changed sides— what was then considered "right-wing" is now considered "left-wing" and *vice-versa*. Perhaps this is too simple, and it is wrong to attach political labels to economic arguments—Joe Chamberlain was after all a radical who became Conservative in later life. However that may be, many of the points made in Joe Chamberlain's speeches in 1903–5 (and their whole tone) would be more likely to be heard today from a member of the Tribune group than from a member of the Conservative Party, whilst the arguments of his great opponent, Mr. Asquith (as he then was), are much closer to those advanced by right-wing Conservatives such as Sir Keith Joseph or Mr. Brittan, or the present editor of *The Times*. It is worth therefore recalling some of the things that Chamberlain said, and the counter-arguments that were advanced against them.

(i) His main concern was "to secure *more employment* at fair wages for the working men of this country". He said in 1905 (that is, 30 years before Keynes!) that the "question of *employment* has now become the most important question of our time. Cheap goods, a higher standard of living, higher wages—all these things are contained in the word '*employment*'. If my policy gives you more *employment*, the others will be added unto you."

(ii) His second concern was to maintain a satisfactory rate of

growth—not just absolutely, but *relatively* to Britain's competitors.[1]

(iii) He explained that the effects of industrial decline are very different on the *manufacturer* and the *worker*. The manufacturer may save himself—he may invest his capital abroad, where profits are higher (because you can operate there on a protected home market). "Yes, the manufacturer may save himself [he could have added 'he might become a multinational']. But it is not for him that I am chiefly concerned. It is for you—the workers—I say to you the loss of employment means more than the loss of capital to any manufacturer. *You cannot live on your investments in a foreign country.* You live on the labour of your hands—and if that labour is taken from you, you have no recourse except perhaps to learn French or German." (This is just what the left-wing opponents of the Common Market have been saying in recent years.)

(iv) The counter-arguments, put forward by Asquith, all centred around the proposition that Britain's difficulties were due to inefficiency and this in turn is due to her stubborn industrial conservatism. Protection would *freeze* inefficiency instead of encouraging the necessary shift in resources. If a trade becomes unprofitable, this is only because *the resources engaged in making it must have more important uses elsewhere.* Chamberlain's reply to this is worth quoting in full:

"I believe that all this is part of the old fallacy about the transfer of employment. . . . It is your fault if you do not leave the industry which is failing and join the industry which is rising. Well, sir, it is an admirable theory: it satisfies everything but an empty stomach. Look how easy it is. Your once great trade in sugar refining is gone; all right, try jam. Your iron trade is going; never mind, you can make mousetraps. The cotton trade is threatened; well, what does that matter to you? Suppose you try doll's eyes. . . . But how long is this to go on? Why on earth are you to suppose that the same process which ruined the sugar refining will not in the course of time be applied to jam? And when jam is gone? Then you have to find something else. And believe me, that although the industries of this country are very various, you cannot go on for ever. You cannot go on watching

---

[1] He was convinced that a *relatively* slow rate of industrial growth constitutes a serious handicap in itself in competition with the industries of faster growing countries.

with indifference the disappearance of your principal industries."

(v) Asquith's next answer was—again it is one that we have encountered frequently in recent years—that Chamberlain made an unpardonable mistake in concentrating on "visible" trade— the trade in commodities, as if this were all that mattered, whereas Britain had a rapidly growing source of "invisible" earnings which paid for a growing share of imports. But Chamberlain replied *"by what kind of export is the import balanced? If we import something which is the equivalent to a pound of labour, a pound of wages*—do we export the equivalent of a pound of wages? Finance, and other invisibles, or earnings from abroad, do not give rise to *home* employment, or not in the same way. Workmen could starve in the midst of un-precedented abundance."

Yet the essence of the anti-free-trade case—which was not seen or understood *at all* by Asquith and other free traders—was only dimly perceived by Chamberlain, as is shown by the following passage:

"When **Mr.** Cohen preached his doctrine, he believed . . . that while foreign countries would supply us with our foodstuffs and raw materials, we should send them in exchange our manu-factures. But that is exactly what we have *not* done. On the contrary, in the period to which I have referred, we are sending less and less of our manufactures to them and they are sending more and more of their manufactures to us."

(This relates to the 1900s, not the 1970s!)

Why is the one kind of trade different from the other? The answer is that manufacturing activities are subject to *increasing returns to scale*—both of a static and dynamic kind—and under these conditions the presumption derived from Ricardo's doctrine of comparative costs—the presumption that free trade secures the best allocation of resources to each and every participant, and that there must be a net gain from trade all round—no longer holds. For under these conditions it can be demonstrated that free trade may lead to stunted growth, or even impoverishment of some regions (or countries) to the greater benefit of others.

This is a point which Adam Smith—who laid the strongest

emphasis on the benefits of "the division of labour" which depend "on the extent of the market"—certainly did not perceive, though he was well aware of the fact that increasing returns—the reduction in costs resulting from large-scale production—apply to manufacturing industry, and not to agriculture, where diminishing returns prevail.

Ricardo's pamphlet on the influence of the price of corn on the profits of stock—which was as influential in shaping the whole thinking of the nineteenth century as any other pamphlet of that century—was a strong argument *against* protecting *agriculture*. The question of protecting manufactures did not arise, since at that time Britain was pre-eminent in the world as a manufacturing country, and the question of her industries needing protection was not one that anyone considered. On the contrary, the free importation of corn by enlarging the income of foreign producers had a beneficial effect on our exports of manufactures. Hence in the context of Ricardo's theory, and Britain's historical situation, free trade could bring nothing but advantages: (1) lower food prices; (2) lower wages in terms of manufactured goods; (3) higher profits and faster capital accumulation in industry; (4) enlarged markets for British manufactured goods, on account of higher imports. For completion he should have added that free trade may not be *equally* advantageous to foreign countries who, whilst exporting more foodstuffs and raw materials to Britain, may suffer a loss of income through the shrinkage of their *own* manufacturing activities. Indeed, the arrival of cheap factory-made English goods *did* cause a loss of employment and output of small-scale industry (the artisanate) both in European countries (where it was later offset by large-scale industrialisation brought about by protection) and even more in India and China, where it was not so offset.

But while Ricardo's original pamphlet, and the policy arguments based on it, were perfectly sound, Ricardo's later formulations of the doctrine of "comparative costs" insinuated further assumptions into the argument with the unfortunate consequence that more was claimed for "free trade" than was in fact justified. For in demonstrating, or attempting to demonstrate, that all countries will benefit from trade, irrespective of whether they are high cost or low cost, rich or poor, Ricardo introduced (without

fully realising its importance or consequences) the main neo-classical assumption of "linearity"—the universal assumption of linear-homogeneous production functions or constant returns to scale, i.e. constant costs per unit of output irrespective of how much or how little is produced. It is only under these assumptions that the hypothesis that Portugal will necessarily be made richer by free trade, even though free trade causes Portugal to specialise on the production of wine (i.e. on agriculture, a diminishing returns industry) and England to specialise on the production of cloth, is valid; and under these assumptions there is indeed no case for interference with trade, either on employment grounds or on productivity grounds. Under these assumptions free trade must always be a Good Thing, whether it is one-sided or not.

This formal extension of the theory had highly unfortunate consequences from which we still suffer today. For whilst free trade suited Britain perfectly while it served to enhance the *share of U.K. manufactures in the world market*, and thereby enhanced the rate of growth of our manufacturing industry and of the G.D.P., the reverse was the case when other countries—Germany, France, the United States, Japan, to name only the most important—began to foster their manufacturing industries behind the shelter of protective tariffs. Our continued adherence to free trade meant that a lot of *new* industries—such as chemicals or industries based on electricity—could not be properly established here. As the traditional industries became increasingly unprofitable our savings were increasingly invested abroad. British exports were chased from pillar to post, as one market after another became closed—"whenever we begin to do a trade, the door is slammed in our faces with a whacking tariff" (Chamberlain).

After 25 prosperous years of fast growth ($3\frac{1}{2}$ per cent.), ending in 1873 we had 40 years of slow growth ($1\frac{1}{2}$ per cent.), the last 14 of which, falling in this century, having been the worst—with productivity declining, G.D.P. stagnant, home investment halved (down to 5 per cent of G.D.P. compared with 15 per cent. in Germany), capital exports reaching unprecedented levels. Net emigration from Great Britain alone (not counting Ireland) was nearly 6 million between 1880 and 1910.

The great Liberal victory of 1906, by reconfirming the

adherence to free trade, made the continuation of economic stagnation certain, from which Britain was relieved only by the First
World War. (It is arguable that without the world wars, the
present crisis would have been reached 50 years earlier.) After
that, things were never quite so bad again until the 1970s. For
World War I witnessed a fast re-industrialisation of Britain, forced
by the necessities of war and the boundless energy of Mr. Lloyd
George; and after that, some industries—the so-called "key
industries", like chemicals and optics, and others, such as the
motor industry—remained protected. Then, following one more
abortive attempt (by Stanley Baldwin, in 1923) the Tories finally
succeeded in introducing a general tariff of 20 per cent. *ad valorem*
on all manufactures (with 30 per cent. in steel and chemicals) in
1932. After that, for a time Britain became the fastest growing
country in the world. Over the twenty-three years 1932–55,
industrial production grew at a compound rate of 4 per cent. a
year—faster than ever before or since.

But since 1968 our *relative performance* has deteriorated more than
ever before, and the experience since 1972 has shown that even
with a succession of devaluations under a régime of a floating rate,
we have not been able to reverse the adverse trends facing us in
world trade. These have made for a continued shrinkage of
demand for British products. The nemesis of the belief in free
trade and in free markets, after a century of failures, haunts us
still. Certainly none of the great original advocates of free trade—
Cobden in particular—would have thought it possible that the
abolition of import restrictions could lead to a shrinkage of
industrial production and employment. Under the particular
conditions prevailing in the first half, or the first three-quarters, of
the nineteenth century they were undoubtedly right. But the
great ideological victory of the free traders meant that the
arguments continued to be used successfully, and are used still—
witness the agitation concerning the great "dynamic benefits" of
a home market of 250 millions which preceded our entry into
Europe—long after they have ceased to have validity. At the present
time, it is German industry, not the British, which derives great
benefits from the "home market of 250 million". British industry
is threatened with continued shrinkage and progressive decline.

Supposing we had not been ideologically wedded to free trade but had adopted a policy of fostering the growth of our manufacturing industries by much the same methods as those by which Germany, France, the United States and Japan fostered the growth of their industries—that is, mainly by a protective tariff and also by the planned development of basic industrial capacity —what would have happened?

We could not of course have maintained the industrial pre-eminence we enjoyed in the mid-nineteenth century. It was quite inevitable that the techniques of large-scale factory production and of mechanical power should have spread to the rest of Europe and to North America. It was inevitable moreover that the successful latecomers to industrialisation should in some ways have surpassed Britain just because they had the benefit of learning from our experience without the handicap of well-entrenched traditions such as "learning on the job" as against formal technical education.

But I have little doubt that with a protected home market we could have enjoyed much higher growth rates and as a result we would now have much higher living standards and more secure employment. Even a 1 per cent. addition to our annual growth rate in the century following 1873 would have meant that our living standards today would be nearly three times higher than they are.

If we had followed these policies, other industrial countries would not have been able to grow at our expense—or at least not nearly as much. This is particularly true of Germany in the period 1880–1914 and of Japan in the period 1950–75. This does not necessarily imply that total rate of growth of world industrial production would have been lower and not higher as a result of a protectionist policy by Britain.

However that may be, it is useless to speculate on what *might* have happened. Time is irreversible, and even if we made a fresh start tomorrow, the time lost could never be entirely regained.

INDEX TO AUTHORS

T